Exploring Premium Media Site

Improve your grade with hands-on tools and resources!

- Master *Key Terms* to expand your vocabulary.
- Prepare for exams by taking practice quizzes in the *Online Chapter Review*.
- Download *Student Data Files* for the applications projects in each chapter.

And for even more tools, you can access the following Premium Resources using your Access Code. Register now to get the most out of *Exploring!*

- *Hands-On Exercise Videos* accompany each Hands-On Exercise in the chapter. These videos demonstrate both how to accomplish individual skills as well as why they are important.*
- *Soft Skills Videos* are necessary to complete the Soft Skills Beyond the Classroom Exercise, and introduce students to important professional skills.*

*Access code required for these premium resources

Your Access Code is:

Note: If there is no silver foil covering the access code, it may already have been redeemed, and therefore may no longer be valid. In that case, you can purchase online access using a major credit card or PayPal account. To do so, go to **www.pearsonhighered.com/exploring**, select your book cover, click on "Buy Access" and follow the on-screen instructions.

To Register:

- To start you will need a valid email address and this access code.
- Go to **www.pearsonhighered.com/exploring** and scroll to find your text book.
- Once you've selected your text, on the Home Page, click the link to access the Student Premium Content.
- Click the Register button and follow the on-screen instructions.
- After you register, you can sign in any time via the log-in area on the same screen.

System Requirements

Windows 7 Ultimate Edition; IE 8
Windows Vista Ultimate Edition SP1; IE 8
Windows XP Professional SP3; IE 7
Windows XP Professional SP3; Firefox 3.6.4
Mac OS 10.5.7; Firefox 3.6.4
Mac OS 10.6; Safari 5

Technical Support

http://247pearsoned.custhelp.com

Photo credits: Goodluz/wrangler/Elena Elisseeva/Shutterstock

(ex·ploring)

SERIES

1. Investigating in a systematic way: examining. 2. Searching into or ranging over for the purpose of discovery.

Microsoft®

PowerPoint® 2013

COMPREHENSIVE

Series Editor **Mary Anne Poatsy**

Rutledge | Lawson

Series Created by Dr. Robert T. Grauer

PEARSON

Boston   Columbus   Indianapolis   New York   San Francisco   Upper Saddle River
Amsterdam   Cape Town   Dubai   London   Madrid   Milan   Munich   Paris   Montréal   Toronto
Delhi   Mexico City   São Paulo   Sydney   Hong Kong   Seoul   Singapore   Taipei   Tokyo

Editor in Chief: Michael Payne
Senior Editor: Samantha McAfee Lewis
Editorial Project Manager: Keri Rand
Product Development Manager: Laura Burgess
Development Editor: Linda Harrison
Editorial Assistant: Laura Karahalis
Director of Marketing: Maggie Moylan Leen
Marketing Manager: Brad Forrester
Marketing Coordinator: Susan Osterlitz
Marketing Assistant: Darshika Vyas
Managing Editor: Camille Trentacoste
Production Project Manager: Ilene Kahn
Senior Operations Specialist: Maura Zaldivar
Senior Art Director: Jonathan Boylan
Interior Design: Studio Montage
Cover Design: Studio Montage
Cover Photos: Supri Suharjoto/Shutterstock, wavebreakmedia/Shutterstock, Terry Chan/Shutterstock, Csaba Peterdi/Shutterstock
Associate Director of Design: Blair Brown
Digital Media Editor: Eric Hakanson
Director of Media Development: Taylor Ragan
Media Project Manager, Production: Renata Butera
Full Service Project Management: Andrea Stefanowicz/PreMediaGlobal
Composition: PreMediaGlobal

Credits and acknowledgments borrowed from other sources and reproduced, with permission, in this textbook appear on the appropriate page within text.

Microsoft and/or its respective suppliers make no representations about the suitability of the information contained in the documents and related graphics published as part of the services for any purpose. All such documents and related graphics are provided "as is" without warranty of any kind. Microsoft and/or its respective suppliers hereby disclaim all warranties and conditions with regard to this information, including all warranties and conditions of merchantability, whether express, implied or statutory, fitness for a particular purpose, title and non-infringement. In no event shall Microsoft and/or its respective suppliers be liable for any special, indirect or consequential damages or any damages whatsoever resulting from loss of use, data or profits, whether in an action of contract, negligence or other tortious action, arising out of or in connection with the use or performance of information available from the services.

The documents and related graphics contained herein could include technical inaccuracies or typographical errors. Changes are periodically added to the information herein. Microsoft and/or its respective suppliers may make improvements and/or changes in the product(s) and/or the program(s) described herein at any time. Partial screen shots may be viewed in full within the software version specified.

Microsoft® and Windows® are registered trademarks of the Microsoft Corporation in the U.S.A. and other countries. This book is not sponsored or endorsed by or affiliated with the Microsoft Corporation.

10 9 8 7 6 5 4 3

ISBN 10: 0-13-340644-X
ISBN 13: 978-0-13-340644-3

Dedications

For my husband, Ted, who unselfishly continues to take on more than his share to support me throughout the process; and for my children, Laura, Carolyn, and Teddy, whose encouragement and love have been inspiring.

Mary Anne Poatsy

To my husband Dan, whose encouragement, patience, and love helped make this endeavor possible. Thank you for taking on the many additional tasks at home so that I could focus on writing. To Michelle and Stephanie, thank you so much for your hard work and dedication on this project. The long hours we all spent together did not go unnoticed. I have very much enjoyed working with you and I wish you the best in your future careers. To all my family and friends for their love and support. I want to thank Jennifer, Keri, Sam, and the entire Pearson team for their help and guidance and for giving me this amazing opportunity. Also, a big thanks to Cynthia and her family for her photos and videos.

Amy Rutledge

This book is dedicated to my children and to my students to inspire them to never give up and to always keep reaching for their dreams.

Rebecca Lawson

About the Authors

Mary Anne Poatsy, Series Editor

Mary Anne is a senior faculty member at Montgomery County Community College, teaching various computer application and concepts courses in face-to-face and online environments. She holds a B.A. in Psychology and Education from Mount Holyoke College and an M.B.A. in Finance from Northwestern University's Kellogg Graduate School of Management.

Mary Anne has more than 12 years of educational experience. She is currently adjunct faculty at Gwynedd-Mercy College and Montgomery County Community College. She has also taught at Bucks County Community College and Muhlenberg College, as well as conducted personal training. Before teaching, she was Vice President at Shearson Lehman in the Municipal Bond Investment Banking Department.

Amy Rutledge, PowerPoint Author

Amy Rutledge is a Special Instructor of Management Information Systems at Oakland University in Rochester, Michigan. She coordinates academic programs in Microsoft Office applications and introductory management information systems courses for the School of Business Administration. Before joining Oakland University as an instructor, Amy spent several years working for a music distribution company and automotive manufacturer in various corporate roles including IT project management. She holds a B.S. in Business Administration specializing in Management Information Systems, and a B.A. in French Modern Language and Literature. She holds an M.B.A from Oakland University. She resides in Michigan with her husband, Dan.

Rebecca Lawson, Office Fundamentals and PowerPoint Author

Rebecca Lawson is a professor in the Computer Information Technologies program at Lansing Community College. She coordinates the curriculum, develops the instructional materials, and teaches for the E-Business curriculum. She also serves as the Online Faculty Coordinator at the Center for Teaching Excellence at LCC. In that role, she develops and facilitates online workshops for faculty learning to teach online. Her major areas of interest include online curriculum quality assurance, the review and development of printed and online instructional materials, the assessment of computer and Internet literacy skill levels to facilitate student retention, and the use of social networking tools to support learning in blended and online learning environments.

Dr. Robert T. Grauer, Creator of the Exploring Series

Bob Grauer is an Associate Professor in the Department of Computer Information Systems at the University of Miami, where he is a multiple winner of the Outstanding Teaching Award in the School of Business, most recently in 2009. He has written numerous COBOL texts and is the vision behind the Exploring Office series, with more than three million books in print. His work has been translated into three foreign languages and is used in all aspects of higher education at both national and international levels. Bob Grauer has consulted for several major corporations including IBM and American Express. He received his Ph.D. in Operations Research in 1972 from the Polytechnic Institute of Brooklyn.

Brief Contents

Contents

Microsoft Office 2013

■ CHAPTER ONE **Office Fundamentals and File Management:** Taking the First Step **1**

Microsoft Office PowerPoint 2013

■ CHAPTER ONE **Introduction to PowerPoint:** Creating a Basic Presentation **83**

■ **Application Capstone Exercises**

Acknowledgments

The Exploring team would like to acknowledge and thank all the reviewers who helped us throughout the years by providing us with their invaluable comments, suggestions, and constructive criticism.

We'd like to especially thank our Focus Group attendees and User Diary Reviewers for this edition:

Stephen Z. Jourdan
Auburn University at Montgomery

Ann Rovetto
Horry-Georgetown Technical
College

Jacqueline D. Lawson
Henry Ford Community College

Diane L. Smith
Henry Ford Community College

Sven Aelterman
Troy University

Suzanne M. Jeska
County College of Morris

Susan N. Dozier
Tidewater Community College

Robert G. Phipps Jr.
West Virginia University

Mike Michaelson
Palomar College

Mary Beth Tarver
Northwestern State University

Alexandre C. Probst
Colorado Christian University

Phil Nielson
Salt Lake Community College

Carolyn Barren
Macomb Community College

Sue A. McCrory
Missouri State University

Lucy Parakhovnik
California State University, Northridge

Jakie Brown Jr.
Stevenson University

Craig J. Peterson
American InterContinental University

Terry Ray Rigsby
Hill College

Biswadip Ghosh
Metropolitan State University of Denver

Cheryl Sypniewski
Macomb Community College

Lynn Keane
University of South Carolina

Sheila Gionfriddo
Luzerne College

Dick Hewer
Ferris State College

Carolyn Borne
Louisiana State University

Sumathy Chandrashekar
Salisbury University

Laura Marcoulides
Fullerton College

Don Riggs
SUNY Schenectady County Community
College

Gary McFall
Purdue University

James Powers
University of Southern Indiana

James Brown
Central Washington University

Brian Powell
West Virginia University

Sherry Lenhart
Terra Community College

Chen Zhang
Bryant University

Nikia Robinson
Indian River State University

Jill Young
Southeast Missouri State University

Debra Hoffman
Southeast Missouri State University

Tommy Lu
Delaware Technical Community College

Mimi Spain
Southern Maine Community College

We'd like to thank everyone who has been involved in reviewing and providing their feedback, including for our previous editions:

Adriana Lumpkin
Midland College

Alan S. Abrahams
Virginia Tech

Ali Berrached
University of Houston–Downtown

Allen Alexander
Delaware Technical & Community College

Andrea Marchese
Maritime College, State University of New York

Andrew Blitz
Broward College; Edison State College

Angel Norman
University of Tennessee, Knoxville

Angela Clark
University of South Alabama

Ann Rovetto
Horry-Georgetown Technical College

Astrid Todd
Guilford Technical Community College

Audrey Gillant
Maritime College, State University of New York

Barbara Stover
Marion Technical College

Barbara Tollinger
Sinclair Community College

Ben Brahim Taha
Auburn University

Beverly Amer
Northern Arizona University

Beverly Fite
Amarillo College

Bonita Volker
Tidewater Community College

Bonnie Homan
San Francisco State University

Brad West
Sinclair Community College

Brian Powell
West Virginia University

Carol Buser
Owens Community College

Carol Roberts
University of Maine

Carolyn Barren
Macomb Community College

Cathy Poyner
Truman State University

Charles Hodgson
Delgado Community College

Cheri Higgins
Illinois State University

Cheryl Hinds
Norfolk State University

Chris Robinson
Northwest State Community College

Cindy Herbert
Metropolitan Community College–Longview

Dana Hooper
University of Alabama

Dana Johnson
North Dakota State University

Daniela Marghitu
Auburn University

David Noel
University of Central Oklahoma

David Pulis
Maritime College, State University of New York

David Thornton
Jacksonville State University

Dawn Medlin
Appalachian State University

Debby Keen
University of Kentucky

Debra Chapman
University of South Alabama

Derrick Huang
Florida Atlantic University

Diana Baran
Henry Ford Community College

Diane Cassidy
The University of North Carolina at Charlotte

Diane Smith
Henry Ford Community College

Don Danner
San Francisco State University

Don Hoggan
Solano College

Doncho Petkov
Eastern Connecticut State University

Donna Ehrhart
State University of New York at Brockport

Elaine Crable
Xavier University

Elizabeth Duett
Delgado Community College

Erhan Uskup
Houston Community College–Northwest

Eric Martin
University of Tennessee

Erika Nadas
Wilbur Wright College

Floyd Winters
Manatee Community College

Frank Lucente
Westmoreland County Community College

G. Jan Wilms
Union University

Gail Cope
Sinclair Community College

Gary DeLorenzo
California University of Pennsylvania

Gary Garrison
Belmont University

George Cassidy
Sussex County Community College

Gerald Braun
Xavier University

Gerald Burgess
Western New Mexico University

Gladys Swindler
Fort Hays State University

Heith Hennel
Valencia Community College

Henry Rudzinski
Central Connecticut State University

Irene Joos
La Roche College

Iwona Rusin
Baker College; Davenport University

J. Roberto Guzman
San Diego Mesa College

Jan Wilms
Union University

Jane Stam
Onondaga Community College

Janet Bringhurst
Utah State University

Jeanette Dix
Ivy Tech Community College

Jennifer Day
Sinclair Community College

Jill Canine
Ivy Tech Community College

Jim Chaffee
The University of Iowa Tippie College of Business

Joanne Lazirko
University of Wisconsin–Milwaukee

Jodi Milliner
Kansas State University

John Hollenbeck
Blue Ridge Community College

John Seydel
Arkansas State University

Judith A. Scheeren
Westmoreland County Community College

Judith Brown
The University of Memphis

Juliana Cypert
Tarrant County College

Kamaljeet Sanghera
George Mason University

Karen Priestly
Northern Virginia Community College

Karen Ravan
Spartanburg Community College

Kathleen Brenan
Ashland University

Ken Busbee
Houston Community College

Kent Foster
Winthrop University

Kevin Anderson
Solano Community College

Kim Wright
The University of Alabama

Kristen Hockman
University of Missouri–Columbia

Kristi Smith
Allegany College of Maryland

Laura McManamon
University of Dayton

Leanne Chun
Leeward Community College

Lee McClain
Western Washington University

Linda D. Collins
Mesa Community College

Linda Johnsonius
Murray State University

Linda Lau
Longwood University

Linda Theus
Jackson State Community College

Linda Williams
Marion Technical College

Lisa Miller
University of Central Oklahoma

Lister Horn
Pensacola Junior College

Lixin Tao
Pace University

Loraine Miller
Cayuga Community College

Lori Kielty
Central Florida Community College

Lorna Wells
Salt Lake Community College

Lorraine Sauchin
Duquesne University

Lucy Parakhovnik (Parker)
California State University, Northridge

Lynn Mancini
Delaware Technical Community College

Mackinzee Escamilla
South Plains College

Marcia Welch
Highline Community College

Margaret McManus
Northwest Florida State College

Margaret Warrick
Allan Hancock College

Marilyn Hibbert
Salt Lake Community College

Mark Choman
Luzerne County Community College

Mary Duncan
University of Missouri–St. Louis

Melissa Nemeth
Indiana University-Purdue University Indianapolis

Melody Alexander
Ball State University

Michael Douglas
University of Arkansas at Little Rock

Michael Dunklebarger
Alamance Community College

Michael G. Skaff
College of the Sequoias

Michele Budnovitch
Pennsylvania College of Technology

Mike Jochen
East Stroudsburg University

Mike Scroggins
Missouri State University

Muhammed Badamas
Morgan State University

NaLisa Brown
University of the Ozarks

Nancy Grant
Community College of Allegheny County–South Campus

Nanette Lareau
University of Arkansas Community College–Morrilton

Pam Brune
Chattanooga State Community College

Pam Uhlenkamp
Iowa Central Community College

Patrick Smith
Marshall Community and Technical College

Paul Addison
Ivy Tech Community College

Paula Ruby
Arkansas State University

Peggy Burrus
Red Rocks Community College

Peter Ross
SUNY Albany

Philip H. Nielson
Salt Lake Community College

Ralph Hooper
University of Alabama

Ranette Halverson
Midwestern State University

Richard Blamer
John Carroll University

Richard Cacace
Pensacola Junior College

Richard Hewer
Ferris State University

Rob Murray
Ivy Tech Community College

Robert Dušek
Northern Virginia Community College

Robert Sindt
Johnson County Community College

Robert Warren
Delgado Community College

Rocky Belcher
Sinclair Community College

Roger Pick
University of Missouri at Kansas City

Ronnie Creel
Troy University

Rosalie Westerberg
Clover Park Technical College

Ruth Neal
Navarro College

Sandra Thomas
Troy University

Sheila Gionfriddo
Luzerne County Community College

Sherrie Geitgey
Northwest State Community College

Sophia Wilberscheid
Indian River State College

Sophie Lee
California State University, Long Beach

Stacy Johnson
Iowa Central Community College

Stephanie Kramer
Northwest State Community College

Stephen Jourdan
Auburn University Montgomery

Steven Schwarz
Raritan Valley Community College

Sue McCrory
Missouri State University

Susan Fuschetto
Cerritos College

Susan Medlin
UNC Charlotte

Suzan Spitzberg
Oakton Community College

Sven Aelterman
Troy University

Sylvia Brown
Midland College

Tanya Patrick
Clackamas Community College

Terri Holly
Indian River State College

Thomas Rienzo
Western Michigan University

Tina Johnson
Midwestern State University

Tommy Lu
Delaware Technical and Community College

Troy S. Cash
NorthWest Arkansas Community College

Vicki Robertson
Southwest Tennessee Community

Weifeng Chen
California University of Pennsylvania

Wes Anthony
Houston Community College

William Ayen
University of Colorado at Colorado Springs

Wilma Andrews
Virginia Commonwealth University

Yvonne Galusha
University of Iowa

Special thanks to our development and technical team:

Barbara Stover

Cheryl Slavick

Elizabeth Lockley

Heather Hetzler

Jennifer Lynn

Joyce Nielsen

Linda Pogue

Lisa Bucki

Lori Damanti

Mara Zebest

Susan Fry

Very special thanks to Sallie Dodson for her work kicking off the PowerPoint Comprehensive revision.

Preface

The Exploring Series and You

Exploring is Pearson's Office Application series that requires students like you to think "beyond the point and click." In this edition, we have worked to restructure the Exploring experience around the way you, today's modern student, actually use your resources.

The goal of Exploring is, as it has always been, to go further than teaching just the steps to accomplish a task—the series provides the theoretical foundation for you to understand when and why to apply a skill.

As a result, you achieve a deeper understanding of each application and can apply this critical thinking beyond Office and the classroom.

You are practical students, focused on what you need to do to be successful in this course and beyond, and want to be as efficient as possible. Exploring has evolved to meet you where you are and help you achieve success efficiently. Pearson has paid attention to the habits of students today, how you get information, how you are motivated to do well in class, and what your future goals look like. We asked you and your peers for acceptance of new tools we designed to address these points, and you responded with a resounding "YES!"

Here Is What We Learned About You

You are goal-oriented. You want a good grade in this course—so we rethought how Exploring works so that you can learn the how and why behind the skills in this course to be successful now. You also want to be successful in your future career—so we used motivating case studies to show relevance of these skills to your future careers and incorporated Soft Skills, Collaboration, and Analysis Cases in this edition to set you up for success in the future.

You read, prepare, and study differently than students used to. You use textbooks like a tool—you want to easily identify what you need to know and learn it efficiently. We have added key features such as Step Icons, Hands-On Exercise Videos, and tracked everything via page numbers that allow you to navigate the content efficiently, making the concepts accessible and creating a map to success for you to follow.

You go to college now with a different set of skills than students did five years ago. The new edition of Exploring moves you beyond the basics of the software at a faster pace, without sacrificing coverage of the fundamental skills that you need to know. This ensures that you will be engaged from page 1 to the end of the book.

You and your peers have diverse learning styles. With this in mind, we broadened our definition of "student resources" to include Compass, an online skill database; movable Student Reference cards; Hands-On Exercise videos to provide a secondary lecture-like option of review; Soft Skills exercises to illustrate important non-technical skills; and the most powerful online homework and assessment tool around with a direct 1:1 content match with the Exploring Series, MyITLab. Exploring will be accessible to all students, regardless of learning style.

Providing You with a Map to Success to Move Beyond the Point and Click

All of these changes and additions will provide you with an easy and efficient path to follow to be successful in this course, regardless of your learning style or any existing knowledge you have at the outset. Our goal is to keep you more engaged in both the hands-on and conceptual sides, helping you to achieve a higher level of understanding that will guarantee you success in this course and in your future career. In addition to the vision and experience of the series creator, Robert T. Grauer, we have assembled a tremendously talented team of Office Applications authors who have devoted themselves to teaching you the ins and outs of Microsoft Word, Excel, Access, and PowerPoint. Led in this edition by series editor Mary Anne Poatsy, the whole team is equally dedicated to providing you with a **map to success** to support the Exploring mission of **moving you beyond the point and click**.

Key Features

- **White Pages/Yellow Pages** clearly distinguish the theory (white pages) from the skills covered in the Hands-On Exercises (yellow pages) so students always know what they are supposed to be doing.

- **Enhanced Objective Mapping** enables students to follow a directed path through each chapter, from the objectives list at the chapter opener through the exercises in the end of chapter.
  - **Objectives List:** This provides a simple list of key objectives covered in the chapter. This includes page numbers so students can skip between objectives where they feel they need the most help.
  - **Step Icons:** These icons appear in the white pages and reference the step numbers in the Hands-On Exercises, providing a correlation between the two so students can easily find conceptual help when they are working hands-on and need a refresher.
  - **Quick Concepts Check:** A series of questions that appear briefly at the end of each white page section. These questions cover the most essential concepts in the white pages required for students to be successful in working the Hands-On Exercises. Page numbers are included for easy reference to help students locate the answers.
  - **Chapter Objectives Review:** Appears toward the end of the chapter and reviews all important concepts throughout the chapter. Newly designed in an easy-to-read bulleted format.

- **Key Terms Matching:** A new exercise that requires students to match key terms to their definitions. This requires students to work actively with this important vocabulary and prove conceptual understanding.

- **Case Study** presents a scenario for the chapter, creating a story that ties the Hands-On Exercises together.

Watch the Video for this Hands-On Exercise!

- **Hands-On Exercise Videos** are tied to each Hands-On Exercise and walk students through the steps of the exercise while weaving in conceptual information related to the Case Study and the objectives as a whole.

- **End-of-Chapter Exercises** offer instructors several options for assessment. Each chapter has approximately 12–15 exercises ranging from multiple choice questions to open-ended projects. Newly included in this is a Key Terms Matching exercise of approximately 20 questions, as well as a Collaboration Case and Soft Skills Case for every chapter.

- **Enhanced Mid-Level Exercises** include a **Creative Case** (for PowerPoint and Word), which allows students some flexibility and creativity, not being bound by a definitive solution, and an **Analysis Case** (for Excel and Access), which requires students to interpret the data they are using to answer an analytic question, as well as **Discover Steps**, which encourage students to use Help or to problem-solve to accomplish a task.

- **MyITLab** provides an auto-graded homework, tutorial, and assessment solution that is built to match the book content exactly. Every Hands-On Exercise is available as a simulation training. Every Capstone Exercise and most Mid-Level Exercises are available as live-in-the-application Grader projects. Icons are included throughout the text to denote which exercises are included.

Instructor Resources

The Instructor's Resource Center, available at www.pearsonhighered.com, includes the following:

- **Instructor Manual** provides an overview of all available resources as well as student data and solution files for every exercise.

- **Solution Files with Scorecards** assist with grading the Hands-On Exercises and end-of-chapter exercises.

- **Prepared Exams** allow instructors to assess all skills covered in a chapter with a single project.

- **Rubrics** for Mid-Level Creative Cases and Beyond the Classroom Cases in Microsoft® Word format enable instructors to customize the assignments for their classes.

- **PowerPoint® Presentations** with notes for each chapter are included for out-of-class study or review.

- **Lesson Plans** provide a detailed blueprint to achieve chapter learning objectives and outcomes.

- **Objectives Lists** map chapter objectives to Hands-On Exercises and end-of-chapter exercises.

- **Multiple Choice and Key Terms Matching Answer Keys**

- **Test Bank** provides objective-based questions for every chapter.

- **Grader Projects** textual versions of auto-graded assignments for Grader.

- **Additional Projects** provide more assignment options for instructors.

- **Syllabus Templates**

- **Scripted Lectures** offer an in-class lecture guide for instructors to mirror the Hands-On Exercises.

- **Assignment Sheet**

- **File Guide**

Student Resources

Companion Web Site

www.pearsonhighered.com/exploring offers expanded IT resources and self-student tools for students to use for each chapter, including:

- Online Chapter Review
- Glossary
- Chapter Objectives Review
- Web Resources
- Student Data Files

In addition, the Companion Web Site is now the site for Premium Media, including the videos for the Exploring Series:

- Hands-On Exercise Videos*
- Audio PPTs*

*Access code required for these premium resources.

Student Reference Cards

A two-sided card for each application provides students with a visual summary of information and tips specific to each application.

Office Fundamentals and File Management

Taking the First Step

Andresr/Shutterstock

OBJECTIVES AFTER YOU READ THIS CHAPTER, YOU WILL BE ABLE TO:

1. Log in with your Microsoft account p. 2
2. Identify the Start screen components p. 3
3. Interact with the Start screen p. 4
4. Access the desktop p. 4
5. Use File Explorer p. 10
6. Work with folders and files p. 13
7. Select, copy, and move multiple files and folders p. 15
8. Identify common interface components p. 22
9. Get Office Help p. 28
10. Open a file p. 36
11. Print a file p. 38
12. Close a file and application p. 39
13. Select and edit text p. 45
14. Use the Clipboard group commands p. 49
15. Use the Editing group commands p. 52
16. Insert objects p. 60
17. Review a file p. 62
18. Use the Page Setup dialog box p. 66

CASE STUDY | Spotted Begonia Art Gallery

You are an administrative assistant for Spotted Begonia, a local art gallery. The gallery deals in local artists' work, including fiber art, oil paintings, watercolors, prints, pottery, and metal sculptures. The gallery holds four seasonal showings throughout the year. Much of the art is on consignment, but there are a few permanent collections. Occasionally, the gallery exchanges these collections with other galleries across the country. The gallery does a lot of community outreach and tries to help local artists develop a network of clients and supporters. Local schools are invited to bring students to the gallery for enrichment programs. Considered a major contributor to the local economy, the gallery has received both public and private funding through federal and private grants.

As the administrative assistant for Spotted Begonia, you are responsible for overseeing the production of documents, spreadsheets, newspaper articles, and presentations that will be used to increase public awareness of the gallery. Other clerical assistants who are familiar with Microsoft Office will prepare the promotional materials, and you will proofread, make necessary corrections, adjust page layouts, save and print documents, and identify appropriate templates to simplify tasks. Your experience with Microsoft Office 2013 is limited, but you know that certain fundamental tasks that are common to Word, Excel, and PowerPoint will help you accomplish your oversight task. You are excited to get started with your work!

Windows 8.1.1 Startup

You use computers for many activities for work, school, or pleasure. You probably have never thought too much about what makes a computer function and allows you to do so many things with it. But all of those activities would not be possible without an operating system running on the computer. An *operating system* is software that directs computer activities such as checking all components, managing system resources, and communicating with application software. *Windows 8.1.1* is a Microsoft operating system released in April 2014 and is available on laptops, desktops, and tablet computers.

The *Start screen* is what you see after starting your computer and entering your username and password. It is where you start all of your computing activities. See Figure 1.1 to see a typical Start screen.

FIGURE 1.1 Typical Start Screen Components and Charms

In this section, you will explore the Start screen and its components in more detail. You will also learn how to log in with your Microsoft account and access the desktop.

Logging In with Your Microsoft Account

Although you can log in to Windows 8.1.1 as a local network user, you can also log in using a Microsoft account. When you have a Microsoft account, you can sign in to any Windows 8.1.1 computer and you will be able to access the saved settings associated with your Microsoft account. That means the computer will have the same familiar look that you are used to seeing. Your Microsoft account will allow you to be automatically signed in to all of the apps and services that use a Microsoft account as the authentication. You can also save your sign-in credentials for other Web sites that you frequently visit.

Logging in with your Microsoft account not only provides all of the benefits just listed, but also provides additional benefits such as being connected to all of Microsoft's resources on the Internet. These resources include a free Outlook account and access to cloud storage at OneDrive. *Cloud storage* is a technology used to store files and to work with programs that are stored in a central location on the Internet. *OneDrive* is an app used to store, access, and share files and folders. It is accessible using an installed desktop app or as cloud storage using a Web address. Files and folders in either location can be synced. For Office 2013 applications, OneDrive is the default location for saving files. Documents saved in OneDrive are accessible from any computer that has an Internet connection. As long as the document has been saved in OneDrive, the most recent version of the document will be accessible from any computer connected to the Internet. OneDrive allows you to collaborate with others. You can easily share your documents with others or add Reply Comments next to the text that you are discussing together. You can work with others on the same document simultaneously.

STEP 1 >> You can create a Microsoft account at any time by going to live.com. You simply work through the Sign-up form to set up your account by creating a username from your e-mail address and creating a password. After filling in the form, you will be automatically signed in to Outlook and sent to your Outlook Inbox. If you already have a Microsoft account, you can just go ahead and log in to Outlook. See Figure 1.2 to see the Sign-up page at live.com.

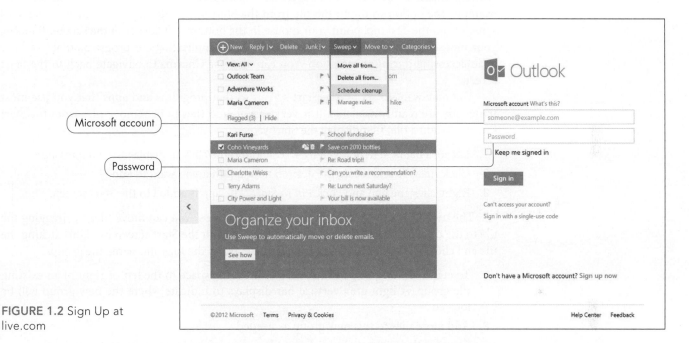

FIGURE 1.2 Sign Up at live.com

Identifying the Start Screen Components

The first thing you will notice when you turn on a computer running Windows 8.1.1 is that the Start screen has a new sleek, clean look and large readable type (refer to Figure 1.1). The user is identified in the top-right corner of the screen. You can click the user's name to access settings such as locking or signing out of the account. You can also change the picture associated with the account here.

You will notice that the Start screen is made up of several colorful block images called *tiles*. When you click a tile, you will be taken to a program, file, folder, or other *Windows 8.1.1 app*. Windows 8.1.1 apps are applications specifically designed to run in the Start screen interface of Windows 8.1.1. Some Windows 8.1.1 apps, such as desktop, Mail, and OneDrive, are already installed and ready to use. Others can be downloaded from the Windows Store. The default apps are brightly colored. Tiles for programs that run on the traditional Windows desktop are smaller and more transparent. The look of the tiles is customizable, but all tiles include the name of the app or program. Depending on the number of apps that you have installed, as you move your mouse to the bottom of the screen, you will see a horizontal scroll bar display. This can be used to access any app that does not display within the initial view of the Start screen.

STEP 2 >> The traditional Start button is not present in Windows 8.1.1. Instead, the *Charms* are available (refer to Figure 1.1). The Charms are made up of five icons that provide similar functionality to the Start button found in previous versions of Windows. The icons are Search, Share, Start, Devices, and Settings. Using the Charms, you can search for files and applications, share information with others within an application that is running, or return to the Start screen. You can also control devices that are connected to your computer or modify various settings depending on which application is running when accessing the Setting icon. To display the Charms, point to the top-right or bottom-right corners of the screen. Refer to Figure 1.1 to view the Start screen components and the Charms.

Interacting with the Start Screen

To interact with any tile on the Start screen (refer to Figure 1.1), simply click it. If you have signed in with your Microsoft account, you will automatically be able to access any of the Internet-enabled programs. For example, if you click Mail, you will go straight to your Outlook Inbox. If you right-click a tile, you will see several contextual options displayed. For example, the option to unpin the tile from the Start screen displays. To return to the Start screen from the desktop, point your mouse in the bottom-left corner of the screen. Pointing your mouse to the top-left corner reveals the open applications or programs that you have been accessing during this session. You can also use Charms to navigate back to the Start screen.

You may want to set up the Start screen so that programs and apps that you use most frequently are readily available. It is very easy to add tiles to or remove tiles from the Start screen. To add a tile, first display the Start screen.

1. Locate a blank area of the Start screen and right-click to display the *All apps* icon.
2. Click *All apps* and locate the desired new app that you want to add.
3. Right-click the app and click *Pin to Start*. The app is added to the Start screen.

The new app's tile is added at the end of your apps. You can move tiles by dragging the tile to the desired location. You can remove a tile from the Start screen by right-clicking the tile and clicking *Unpin from Start*. You can also group the tiles and name the groups:

1. To create a new group of tiles, drag a tile to the space to the left or right of an existing tile group. A light gray vertical bar displays to indicate where the new group will be located.
2. Add more tiles to this new group as needed.
3. To name the group, right-click any blank area of the Start screen and click Name groups. Type in the space provided to name a group. If a name is not entered for a group, the horizontal Name group bar disappears.

Accessing the Desktop

Although the Start screen is easy to use, you may want to access the more familiar desktop that you used in previous versions of Windows. The Desktop tile is available on the Start screen. Click the tile to bring up the desktop. Alternatively, you can be pushed to the desktop when you click other tiles such as Word. In Windows 8.1.1, the desktop is simplified to accommodate use on mobile devices where screen space is limited. However, on a laptop or desktop computer, you may want to have more features readily available. The familiar Notification area is displayed in the bottom-right corner. You will see the Windows Start screen, File Explorer, and Internet Explorer icons. See Figure 1.3 to locate these desktop components.

Taskbar

File Explorer

Internet Explorer

FIGURE 1.3 Desktop Components

 STEP 3

You can add more toolbars, such as the Address bar, to the taskbar by right-clicking the taskbar, pointing to Toolbars, and then selecting Address. The Address bar can be used to locate Web sites using the URL or to perform a keyword search to locate Web sites about a specific topic. You can also add programs such as the ***Snipping Tool***. The Snipping Tool is a Windows 8.1.1 accessory program that allows you to capture, or ***snip***, a screen display so that you can save, annotate, or share it. You can remove all of the icons displayed on the taskbar by right-clicking the icon you want to remove and selecting *Unpin this program from taskbar*.

TIP Using the Snipping Tool

The Snipping Tool can be used to take all sizes and shapes of snips of the displayed screen. Options include Free-form Snip, Rectangle Snip, Window Snip, and Full-screen Snip. You can save your snip in several formats, such as PNG, GIF, JPEG, or Single file HTML. In addition, you can use a pen or highlighter to mark up your snips. This option is available after taking a snip and is located under the Tools menu in the Snipping Tool dialog box.

You can return to the Start screen by clicking the Start screen icon on the taskbar.

Quick **Concepts** ✓

1. Logging in to Windows 8.1.1 with your Microsoft account provides access to Internet resources. What are some benefits of logging in this way? ***p. 2***

2. OneDrive allows you to collaborate with others. How might you use this service? ***p. 3***

3. What is the Start screen, and how is it different from the desktop? ***p. 3***

4. The desktop has been a feature of previous Windows operating systems. How is the Windows 8.1.1 desktop different from previous versions? ***p. 4***

Hands-On Exercises

Watch the Video for this Hands-On Exercise!

MyITLab®
HOE1 Training

1 Windows 8.1.1 Startup

The Spotted Begonia Art Gallery has just hired several new clerical assistants to help you develop promotional materials for the various activities coming up throughout the year. It will be necessary to have a central storage space where you can save the documents and presentations for retrieval from any location. You will also need to be able to collaborate with others on the documents by sharing them and adding comments. To begin, you will get a Microsoft account. Then you will access the desktop and pin a toolbar and a Windows 8.1.1 accessory program to the taskbar.

Skills covered: Log In with Your Microsoft Account • Identify the Start Screen Components and Interact with the Start Screen • Access the Desktop

STEP 1 ⟫ LOG IN WITH YOUR MICROSOFT ACCOUNT

You want to sign up for a Microsoft account so you can store documents and share them with others using the resources available with a Microsoft account, such as OneDrive. Refer to Figure 1.4 as you complete Step 1.

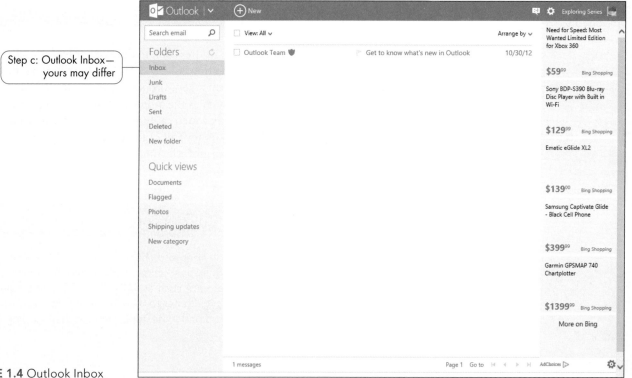

FIGURE 1.4 Outlook Inbox

a. Start your computer and enter your local username and password. On the Start screen, click the **Internet Explorer tile**. Click in the **Address bar** at the bottom of the screen. Type **live.com** and press **Enter**.

Internet Explorer displays, and you are taken to the Sign-up page for Outlook. This is where you can create a username and password for your Microsoft account.

> **TROUBLESHOOTING:** If you already have a Microsoft account, you can skip Step 1 and continue with Step 2. If someone else was already signed in at your computer, you can locate your username and click it to begin to log in.

b. Click the **Sign up now** link at the bottom of the screen. Fill in all text boxes and make all menu selections on the screen. Scroll down as needed. Type the **CAPTCHA code** carefully.

CAPTCHA is a scrambled code used with online forms to prevent mass sign-ups. It helps to ensure that a real person is requesting the account. You can choose not to accept e-mail with promotional offers by clicking the check box near the bottom of the screen to remove the check.

> **TROUBLESHOOTING:** You may want to write down your username and password so that you do not forget it the next time you want to log in with your Microsoft account. Keep this information in a safe and confidential location.

c. Click **I accept**. Your screen should display similarly to Figure 1.4.

Your Microsoft account is created, and you are taken to your Outlook Inbox.

d. Keep Internet Explorer open if you plan to continue using Outlook. Otherwise, sign out of Outlook and close Internet Explorer.

STEP 2 ≫ IDENTIFY THE START SCREEN COMPONENTS AND INTERACT WITH THE START SCREEN

You decide to explore the Start screen components. Then you use the Desktop tile on the Start screen to access the desktop. Refer to Figure 1.5 as you complete Step 2.

Step d: Display the Windows 8.1.1 desktop

FIGURE 1.5 Desktop

a. Point to the top-right corner to display the Charms. Click the **Start screen charm**.

Because you finished on the desktop after completing Step 1, clicking the Start screen charm takes you to the Start screen.

> **TROUBLESHOOTING:** If you skipped Step 1, log in to Windows with your username and password to display the Start screen.

b. Point to the bottom of the Start screen to display the horizontal scroll bar. Drag the scroll bar to the right to view all of the tiles available. Then drag the scrollbar back to the left to its original position.

Many components of the Start screen do not display until they are needed. This saves screen space on mobile devices. In this case, the horizontal scroll bar is hidden until needed.

c. Point to the bottom-right corner of the screen to display the Charms.

The Charms will display whenever you point to the top-right or bottom-right corners of the screen, regardless of the application you are using.

d. Locate and click the **Desktop tile**. See Figure 1.5.

STEP 3 ➤➤ ACCESS THE DESKTOP

You would like to add some components to make the desktop easier to use. You customize the desktop by adding the Address toolbar and the Snipping Tool to the taskbar. Refer to Figure 1.6 as you complete Step 3.

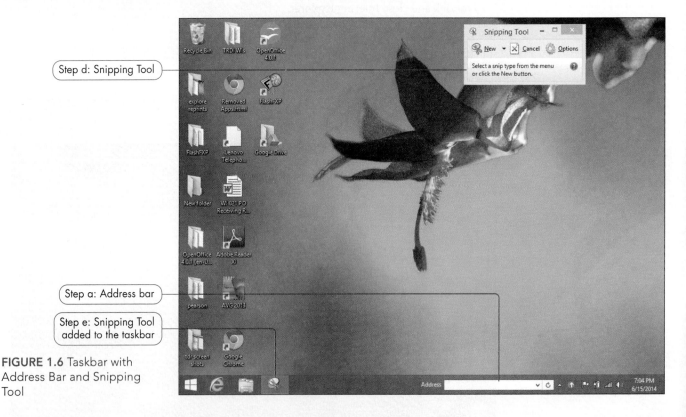

Step d: Snipping Tool

Step a: Address bar

Step e: Snipping Tool added to the taskbar

FIGURE 1.6 Taskbar with Address Bar and Snipping Tool

a. Locate and right-click the taskbar. Point to *Toolbars* and select **Address**.

The Address bar now displays on the right side of the taskbar.

b. Point to the top-right corner of the screen to display the Charms. Click the **Search charm**.

The Search pane displays on the right. The Search pane is organized into categories that you may want to search. For whatever category is selected, the relevant content is displayed.

TIP Viewing Dialog Box Components

In Windows 8.1.1, many dialog boxes have been changed to panes. This is in keeping with the sleek, clean look of Windows 8.1.1. Even though the look is different, the functionality remains the same.

c. Type **Sn** in the **Search box**. Below the search box the results listed display everything that begins with Sn.

d. Click the **Snipping Tool app** in the results list.

The Snipping Tool app displays on the desktop and the Snipping Tool icon displays on the taskbar.

e. Right-click the **Snipping Tool icon** on the taskbar. Click **Pin this program to taskbar**. See Figure 1.6.

The Snipping Tool and the Address bar will now be part of your taskbar.

> **TROUBLESHOOTING:** If you are in a lab and cannot keep these changes, you can remove the Snipping Tool icon from the taskbar. Right-click the icon and click *Unpin this program from taskbar*. You can remove the Address bar by right-clicking the taskbar, pointing to Toolbars, and then clicking Address to remove the check mark.

f. Click the **Snipping Tool icon**. Click the **New arrow** in the Snipping Tool on the desktop. Click **Full-screen Snip**.

A snip of your desktop displays in the Snipping Tool program.

g. Click **File** and click **Save As**. Navigate to the location where you are saving your student files. Name your file **f01h1Desktop_LastFirst** using your own last name and first name. Check to see that *Portable Network Graphic file (PNG)* displays in the *Save as type* box. Click **Save**.

You have created your first snip. Snips can be used to show what is on your screen. Notice the Snipping Tool app does not display in your snip. When you save files, use your last and first names. For example, as the Office Fundamentals author, I would name my document *f01h1Desktop_LawsonRebecca*.

> **TROUBLESHOOTING:** If PNG does not display in the *Save as type* box, click the arrow on the right side of the box and select *Portable Network Graphic file (PNG)*.

h. Close the Snipping Tool. Submit the file based on your instructor's directions.

i. Shut down your computer if you are ready to stop working. Point to the top-right corner to display the Charms. Click the **Settings charm**, click the **Power icon**, and then click **Shut down**. Otherwise, leave your computer turned on for the next Hands-On Exercise.

Files and Folders

Most activities that you perform using a computer produce some type of output. That output could be games, music, or the display of digital photographs. Perhaps you use a computer at work to produce reports, financial worksheets, or schedules. All of those items are considered computer *files*. Files include electronic data such as documents, databases, slide shows, and worksheets. Even digital photographs, music, videos, and Web pages are saved as files.

You use software to create and save files. For example, when you type a document on a computer, you first open a word processor such as Microsoft Word. In order to access files later, you must save them to a computer storage medium such as a hard drive or flash drive, or in the cloud at OneDrive. And just as you would probably organize a filing cabinet into a system of folders, you can organize storage media by *folders* that you name and into which you place data files. That way, you can easily retrieve the files later. Windows 8.1.1 provides tools that enable you to create folders and to save files in ways that make locating them simple.

In this section, you will learn to use File Explorer to manage folders and files.

Using File Explorer

File Explorer is an app that you can use to create and manage folders and files. The sole purpose of a computer folder is to provide a labeled storage location for related files so that you can easily organize and retrieve items. A folder structure can occur across several levels, so you can create folders within other folders—called *subfolders*—arranged according to purpose. Windows 8.1.1 uses the concept of libraries, which are folders that gather files from different locations and display the files as if they were all saved in a single folder, regardless of where they are physically stored. Using File Explorer, you can manage folders, work with libraries, and view favorites (areas or folders that are frequently accessed).

Understand and Customize the Interface

You can access File Explorer in any of the following ways:

- Click the File Explorer icon from the taskbar on the desktop.
- Click File Explorer from the Start screen.
- Display the Charms (refer to Figure 1.1) and click the Search charm. Type F in the Search box and in the results list on the left, click File Explorer.

Figure 1.7 shows the File Explorer interface containing several areas. Some of those areas are described in Table 1.1.

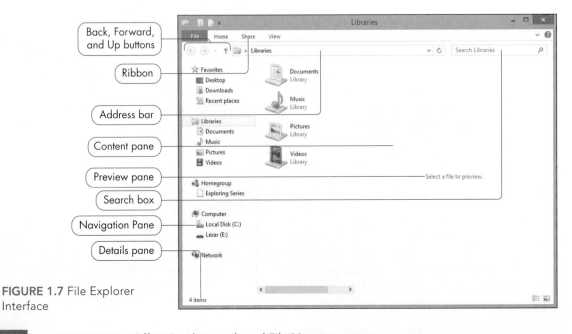

FIGURE 1.7 File Explorer Interface

TABLE 1.1 File Explorer Interface

Navigation Pane	The Navigation Pane contains five areas: Favorites, Libraries, Homegroup, Computer, and Network. Click an item in the Navigation Pane to display contents and to manage files that are housed within a selected folder.
Back, Forward, and Up Buttons	Use these buttons to visit previously opened folders or libraries. Use the Up button to open the parent folder for the current location.
Ribbon	The Ribbon includes tabs and commands that are relevant to the currently selected item. If you are working with a music file, the Ribbon commands might include one for burning to a CD, whereas if you have selected a document, the Ribbon would enable you to open or share the file.
Address bar	The Address bar enables you to navigate to other folders or libraries.
Content pane	The Content pane shows the contents of the currently selected folder or library.
Search box	Find files and folders by typing descriptive text in the Search box. Windows immediately begins a search after you type the first character, further narrowing results as you type.
Details pane	The Details pane shows properties that are associated with a selected file. Common properties include information such as the author name and the date the file was last modified. This pane does not display by default but can display after clicking the View tab.
Preview pane	The Preview pane provides a snapshot of a selected file's contents. You can see file contents before actually opening the file. The Preview pane does not show the contents of a selected folder. This pane does not display by default but can display after clicking the View tab.

File Explorer has a Ribbon like all the Office applications. As you work with File Explorer, you might want to customize the view. The file and folder icons might be too small for ease of identification, or you might want additional details about displayed files and folders. Modifying the view is easy. To make icons larger or to provide additional detail, click the View tab (refer to Figure 1.7) and select from the views provided in the Layout group. If you want additional detail, such as file type and size, click Details. You can also change the size of icons by selecting Small, Medium, Large, or Extra Large icons. The List view shows the file names without added detail, whereas Tiles and Content views are useful to show file thumbnails (small pictures describing file contents) and varying levels of detail regarding file locations. To show or hide File Explorer panes, click the View tab and select the pane to hide or show in the Panes group. You can widen or narrow panes by dragging a border when the mouse changes to a double-headed arrow.

Work with Groups on the Navigation Pane

The *Navigation Pane* provides ready access to computer resources, folders, files, and networked peripherals such as printers. It is divided into five areas: Favorites, Libraries, Homegroup, Computer, and Network. Each of those components provides a unique way to organize contents. In Figure 1.8, the currently selected area is Computer.

Earlier, we used the analogy of computer folders to folders in a filing cabinet. Just as you would title folders in a filing cabinet according to their contents, computer folders are also titled according to content. Folders are physically located on storage media such as a hard drive or flash drive. You can also organize folders into *libraries*, which are collections of files from different locations that are displayed as a single virtual folder. For example, the Pictures library includes files from the My Pictures folder and from the Public Pictures folder, both of which are physically housed on the hard drive. Although the library content comes from two separate folders, the contents are displayed as a single virtual folder.

Windows 8.1.1 includes several libraries that contain default folders or devices. For example, the Documents library includes the My Documents and Public Documents folders, but you can add subfolders if you wish so that they are also housed within the Documents library. To add a folder to a library, right-click the library, point to New, and then select Folder. You can name the folder at this point by typing the folder name. To remove a folder from the Documents library, open File Explorer, right-click the folder, and then select Delete.

The Computer area provides access to specific storage locations, such as a hard drive, CD/DVD drives, and removable media drives, including a flash drive. Files and folders housed on those storage media are accessible when you click Computer. For example, click drive C, shown under Computer in the Navigation Pane, to view its contents in the Content pane on the right. If you simply want to see the subfolders of the hard drive, click the arrow to the left of drive C to expand the view, showing all subfolders. The arrow is filled in and pointing down. Click the arrow again to collapse the view, removing subfolder detail. The arrow is open and pointing right. It is important to understand that clicking the arrow—as opposed to clicking the folder or area name—does not actually select an area or folder. It merely displays additional levels contained within the area. Clicking the folder or area, however, does select the item. Figure 1.8 illustrates the difference between clicking the folder or area name in the Navigation Pane and clicking the arrow to the left.

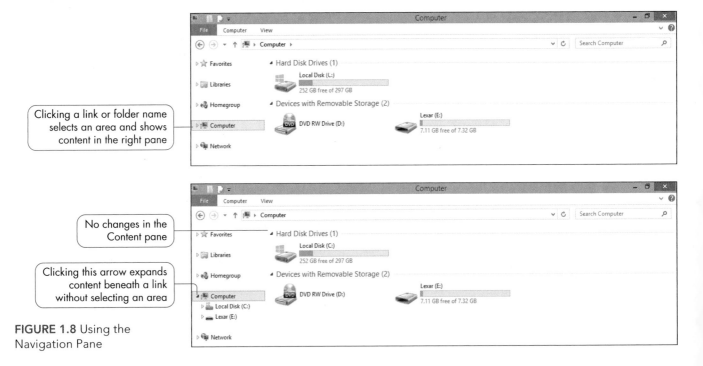

Clicking a link or folder name selects an area and shows content in the right pane

No changes in the Content pane

Clicking this arrow expands content beneath a link without selecting an area

FIGURE 1.8 Using the Navigation Pane

To locate a folder using File Explorer:

1. Click the correct drive in the Navigation Pane (or double-click the drive in the Content pane).
2. Continue navigating through the folder structure until you find the folder that you want.
3. Click the folder in the Navigation Pane (or double-click the folder in the Content pane) to view its contents.

The Favorites area contains frequently accessed folders and recent searches. You can drag a folder, saved search, library, or disk drive to the Favorites area. To remove a favorite, simply right-click the favorite and select Remove. You cannot add files or Web sites as favorites.

Homegroup is a Windows 8.1.1 feature that enables you to share resources on a home network. You can easily share music, pictures, videos, and libraries with other people in your home through a homegroup. It is password protected, so you do not have to worry about privacy.

Windows 8.1.1 makes creating a home network easy, sharing access to the Internet and peripheral devices such as printers and scanners. The Network area provides quick access to those devices, enabling you to see the contents of network computers.

Working with Folders and Files

As you work with software to create a file, such as when you type a report using Microsoft Word, your primary concern will be saving the file so that you can retrieve it later if necessary. If you have created an appropriate and well-named folder structure, you can save the file in a location that is easy to find later.

Create a Folder

You can create a folder a couple of different ways. You can use File Explorer to create a folder structure, providing appropriate names and placing the folders in a well-organized hierarchy. You can also create a folder from within a software application at the time that you need it. Although it would be wonderful to always plan ahead, most often you will find the need for a folder at the same time that you have created a file. The two methods of creating a folder are described next.

STEP 1 ≫ Suppose you are beginning a new college semester and are taking four classes. To organize your assignments, you plan to create four folders on a flash drive, one for each class. After connecting the flash drive and closing any subsequent dialog box (unless the dialog box is warning of a problem with the drive), open File Explorer. Click Computer in the Navigation Pane. Click the removable (flash) drive in the Navigation Pane or double-click it in the Content pane. You can also create a folder on the hard drive in the same manner, by clicking drive C instead of the removable drive. Click the Home tab on the Ribbon. Click *New folder* in the New group. Type the new folder name, such as Biology, and press Enter. Repeat the process to create additional folders.

Undoubtedly, you will occasionally find that you have just created a file but have no appropriate folder in which to save the file. You might have just finished the slide show for your speech class but have forgotten first to create a speech folder for your assignments. Now what do you do? As you save the file, a process that is discussed later in this chapter, you can click Browse to bring up the Save As dialog box. Navigate to the drive where you want to store your file. Click *New folder* (see Figure 1.9), type the new folder name, and then double-click to save the name and open the new folder. After indicating the file name, click Save.

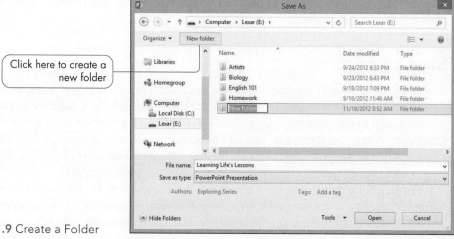

FIGURE 1.9 Create a Folder

OneDrive makes it easy to access your folders and files from any Internet-connected computer or mobile device. You can create new folders and organize existing folders just as you would when you use File Explorer. Other tasks that can be performed at OneDrive include opening, renaming, and deleting folders and files. To create a new folder at OneDrive, you can simply click the OneDrive tile on the Start screen. By default, you will see three items: Documents, Pictures, and Public Shared. You can right-click any of these three items to access icons for creating a new folder or to upload files. Once files and folders are added or created here, you can access them from any computer with Internet access at onedrive.live. com. Similarly, you can create folders or upload files and folders at OneDrive and then access them using the OneDrive tile on your Start screen.

Open, Rename, and Delete Folders and Files

You have learned that folders can be created in File Explorer but files are more commonly created in other ways, such as within a software package. File Explorer can create a new file, and you can use it to open, rename, and delete files just as you use it for folders.

Using the Navigation Pane, you can locate and select a folder containing a file that you want to open. For example, you might want to open the speech slide show so that you can practice before giving a presentation to the class. Open File Explorer and navigate to the speech folder. In your storage location, the file will display in the Content pane. Double-click the file. The program that is associated with the file will open the file. For example, if you have the PowerPoint program associated with that file type on your computer, then PowerPoint will open the file. To open a folder and display the contents, just click the folder in the Navigation Pane or double-click it in the Content pane.

STEP 3 At times, you may want to give a different name to a file or folder than the one that you originally gave it. Or perhaps you made a typographical mistake when you entered the name. In these situations, you should rename the file or folder. In File Explorer, move through the folder structure to find the folder or file. Right-click the name and select Rename. Type the new name and press Enter. You can also rename an item when you click the name twice—but much more slowly than a double-click. Type the new name and press Enter. Finally, you can click a file or folder once to select it, click the Home tab, and then select Rename in the Organize group. Type the new name and press Enter.

It is much easier to delete a folder or file than it is to recover it if you remove it by mistake. Therefore, be very careful when deleting items so that you are sure of your intentions before proceeding. When you delete a folder, all subfolders and all files within the folder are also removed. If you are certain you want to remove a folder or file, the process is simple. Right-click the item, click Delete, and then click Yes if asked to confirm removal to the Recycle Bin. Items are placed in the Recycle Bin only if you are deleting them from a hard drive. Files and folders deleted from a removable storage medium, such as a flash drive, are immediately and permanently deleted, with no easy method of retrieval. You can also delete an item (file or folder) when you click to select the item, click the Home tab, and then click Delete in the Organize group.

Save a File

STEP 2 As you create or modify a project such as a document, presentation, or worksheet, you will most likely want to continue the project at another time or keep it for later reference. You need to save it to a storage medium such as a hard drive, CD, flash drive, or in the cloud with OneDrive. When you save a file, you will be working within a software package. Therefore, you must follow the procedure dictated by that software to save the file. Office 2013 allows you to save your project to OneDrive or to a location on your computer.

The first time that you save a file, you must indicate where the file should be saved, and you must assign a file name. Of course, you will want to save the file in an appropriately named folder so that you can find it easily later. Thereafter, you can quickly save the file with the same settings, or you can change one or more of those settings, perhaps saving the file to a different storage device as a backup copy. Figure 1.10 shows a typical Save As pane for Office 2013 that enables you to select a location before saving the file.

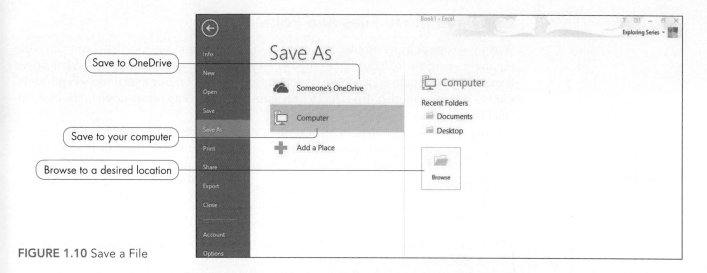

Save to OneDrive

Save to your computer

Browse to a desired location

FIGURE 1.10 Save a File

Selecting, Copying, and Moving Multiple Files and Folders

You will want to select folders and files when you need to rename, delete, copy, or paste them, or open files and folders so that you can view the contents. Click a file or folder to *select* it; double-click a file or folder (in the Content pane) to *open* it. To apply an operation to several files at once, such as deleting or moving them, you will want to select all of them.

Select Multiple Files and Folders

You can select several files and folders, regardless of whether they are adjacent to each other in the file list. Suppose that your digital pictures are contained in the Pictures folder. You might want to delete some of the pictures because you want to clear up some hard drive space. To select pictures in the Pictures folder, open File Explorer and click the Pictures library. Locate the desired pictures in the Content pane. To select the adjacent pictures, select the first picture, press and hold Shift, and then click the last picture. All consecutive picture files will be highlighted, indicating that they are selected. At that point, you can delete, copy, or move the selected pictures at the same time.

If the files or folders to be selected are not adjacent, click the first item. Press and hold Ctrl while you click all desired files or folders, releasing Ctrl only when you have finished selecting the files or folders.

To select all items in a folder or disk drive, use File Explorer to navigate to the desired folder. Open the folder, press and hold Ctrl, and then press A on the keyboard. You can also click the Home tab, and in the Select group, click *Select all* to select all items.

 TIP Using a Check Box to Select Items

In Windows 8.1.1, it is easy to make multiple selections, even if the items are not adjacent. Open File Explorer and select your drive or folder. Click the View tab and select Item check boxes in the Show/Hide group. As you move the mouse pointer along the left side of files and folders, a check box displays. Click in the check box to select the file. If you want to quickly select all items in the folder, click the check box that displays in the Name column heading.

Copy and Move Files and Folders

When you copy or move a folder, you move both the folder and any files that it contains. You can move or copy a folder or file to another location on the same drive or to another drive. If your purpose is to make a **backup**, or copy, of an important file or folder, you will probably want to copy it to another drive. It can be helpful to have backup copies saved in the cloud at OneDrive as well.

STEP 4 »

To move or copy an item in File Explorer, select the item. If you want to copy or move multiple items, follow the directions in the previous section to select them all at once. Right-click the item(s) and select either Cut or Copy on the shortcut menu. In the Navigation Pane, locate the destination drive or folder, right-click the destination drive or folder, and then click Paste.

Quick **Concepts**

1. The File Explorer interface has several panes. Name them and identify their characteristics. *p. 11*

2. After creating a file, such as a PowerPoint presentation, you want to save it. However, as you begin to save the file, you realize that you have not yet created a folder in which to place the file. Is it possible to create a folder as you are saving the file? If so, how? *p. 13*

3. What should you consider when deleting files or folders from a removable storage medium such as a flash drive? *p. 14*

4. Office 2013 enables you to save files to OneDrive or your computer. Why might it be helpful to save a file in both locations? *p. 14*

5. You want to delete several files, but the files are not consecutively listed in File Explorer. How would you select and delete them? *p. 15*

Hands-On Exercises

Watch the Video
for this Hands-
On Exercise!

MyITLab®
HOE2 Training

2 Files and Folders

You will soon begin to collect files from volunteers who are preparing promotional and record-keeping material for the Spotted Begonia Art Gallery. It is important that you save the files in appropriately named folders so that you can easily access them later. You can create folders on a hard drive, flash drive, or at OneDrive. You will select the drive on which you plan to save the various files. As you create a short document, you will save it in one of the folders. You will then make a backup copy of the folder structure, including all files, so that you do not run the risk of losing the material if the drive is damaged or misplaced.

Skills covered: Create Folders and Subfolders • Create and Save a File • Rename and Delete a Folder • Open and Copy a File

STEP 1 ≫ CREATE FOLDERS AND SUBFOLDERS

You decide to create a folder titled *Artists* and then subdivide it into subfolders that will help categorize the artists' artwork promotional files as well as for general record keeping for the art gallery. Refer to Figure 1.11 as you complete Step 1.

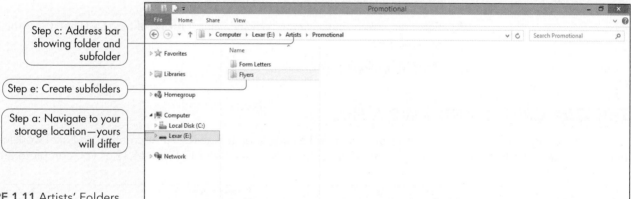

Step c: Address bar showing folder and subfolder

Step e: Create subfolders

Step a: Navigate to your storage location—yours will differ

FIGURE 1.11 Artists' Folders

a. Navigate to the location where you are storing your files. If storing on your computer or a flash drive, navigate to the desktop. Click **File Explorer** on the taskbar and maximize the window. Click the **VIEW tab** and click to display the **Preview pane**, if necessary.

A removable drive is shown in Figure 1.11 and is titled *Lexar (E:)*, describing the drive manufacturer and the drive letter. Your storage area will be designated in a different manner, perhaps also identified by manufacturer (or perhaps you are saving your files on OneDrive). The storage area identification is likely to be different because the configuration of disk drives on your computer is unique.

> **TROUBLESHOOTING:** If you do not have a flash drive, you can use the hard drive. In the next step, simply click drive C in the Navigation Pane instead of the removable drive. You can also create and save folders and files at OneDrive.

b. Click the removable drive in the Navigation Pane (or click **drive C** if you are using the hard drive). Click the **HOME tab**, click **New folder** in the New group, type **Artists**, and then press **Enter**.

You create a folder where you can organize subfolders and files for the artists and their promotional materials and general record-keeping files.

> **TROUBLESHOOTING:** If the folder you create is called *New folder* instead of *Artists*, you probably clicked away from the folder before typing the name, so that it received the default name. To rename it, right-click the folder, click Rename, type the correct name, and then press Enter.

c. Double-click the **Artists folder** in the Content pane. The Address bar at the top of the File Explorer window should show that it is the currently selected folder. Click the **HOME tab**, click **New folder** in the New group, type **Promotional**, and then press **Enter**.

You decide to create subfolders of the *Artists* folder to contain promotional material, presentations, and office records.

d. Check the Address bar to make sure *Artists* is still the current folder. Using the same technique, create a new folder named **Presentations** and create a new folder named **Office Records**.

You create two more subfolders, appropriately named.

e. Double-click the **Promotional folder** in the Navigation Pane. Right-click in a blank area, point to *New*, and then click **Folder**. Type **Form Letters** and press **Enter**. Using the same technique, create a new folder named **Flyers** and press **Enter**.

To subdivide the promotional material further, you create two subfolders, one to hold form letters and one to contain flyers (see Figure 1.11).

f. Take a full-screen snip of your screen and name it **f01h2Folders_LastFirst**. Close the Snipping Tool.

g. Close File Explorer.

STEP 2 ▶▶ CREATE AND SAVE A FILE

To keep everything organized, you assign volunteers to take care of certain tasks. After creating an Excel worksheet listing those responsibilities, you will save it in the Office Records folder. Refer to Figure 1.12 as you complete Step 2.

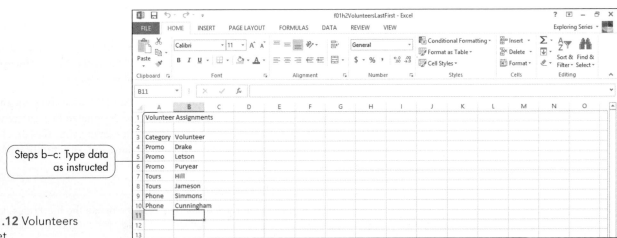

FIGURE 1.12 Volunteers Worksheet

a. Navigate to the Start screen. Scroll across the tiles and click **Excel 2013**. If necessary, use the Search charm to locate Excel.

You use Excel 2013 to create the Volunteers worksheet.

b. Click **Blank workbook** in the Excel 2013 window that displays. Type **Volunteer Assignments** in cell **A1**. Press **Enter** twice.

Cell A3 is the active cell, as indicated by a green box that surrounds the cell.

c. Type **Category**. Press **Tab** to make the next cell to the right the active cell and type **Volunteer**. Press **Enter**. Complete the remaining cells of the worksheet as shown in Figure 1.12.

> **TROUBLESHOOTING:** If you make a mistake, click in the cell and retype the entry.

   d. Click the **FILE tab** and click **Save**.

   The Save As pane displays. The Save As pane is where you determine the location where your file will be saved, either your Computer or OneDrive.

   e. Click **Browse** to display the Save As dialog box. Scroll down if necessary and click **Computer** or the location where you are saving your files in the Navigation Pane. In the Content pane, locate the Artists folder that you created in Step 1 and double-click to open the folder. Double-click **Office Records**. Click in the **File name box** and type **f01h2Volunteers_LastFirst**. Click **Save**. Refer to Figure 1.12.

   The file is now saved as *f01h2Volunteers_LastFirst*. The workbook is saved in the Office Records subfolder of the Artists folder. You can check the title bar of the workbook to confirm the file has been saved with the correct name.

   f. Click the **Close (X) button** in the top-right corner of the Excel window to close Excel.

STEP 3 ▶ RENAME AND DELETE A FOLDER

As often happens, you find that the folder structure you created is not exactly what you need. You will remove the Flyers folder and the Form Letters folder and will rename the Promotional folder to better describe the contents. Refer to Figure 1.13 as you complete Step 3.

Step d: Current folder structure

FIGURE 1.13 Artists Folder Structure

   a. Navigate to the desktop, if necessary. Click **File Explorer** on the taskbar. Click the location where you are saving your files. Double-click the **Artists folder** in the Content pane.

   b. Click the **Promotional folder** to select it.

> **TROUBLESHOOTING:** If you double-click the folder instead of using a single-click, the folder will open and you will see its title in the Address bar. To return to the correct view, click Artists in the Address bar.

   c. Click the **HOME tab**. In the Organize group, click **Rename**, type **Promotional Print**, and then press **Enter**.

   Because the folder will be used to organize all of the printed promotional material, you decide to rename the folder to better reflect the contents.

d. Double-click the **Promotional Print folder**. Click **Flyers**. Press and hold **Shift** and click **Form Letters**. Both folders should be selected (highlighted). Right-click either folder and click **Delete**. If asked to confirm the deletion, click **Yes**. Click **Artists** in the Address bar.

Your screen should appear as shown in Figure 1.13. You decide that dividing the promotional material into flyers and form letters is not necessary, so you deleted both folders.

e. Take a full-screen snip of your screen and name it **f01h2Artists_LastFirst**. Close the Snipping Tool.

f. Leave File Explorer open for the next step.

STEP 4 ≫ OPEN AND COPY A FILE

You hope to recruit more volunteers to work with the Spotted Begonia Art Gallery. The Volunteers worksheet will be a handy way to keep up with people and assignments, and as the list grows, knowing exactly where the file is saved will be important for easy access. You will modify the Volunteers worksheet and make a backup copy of the folder hierarchy. Refer to Figure 1.14 as you complete Step 4.

Step d: Save a copy of the Artists folder to the desktop

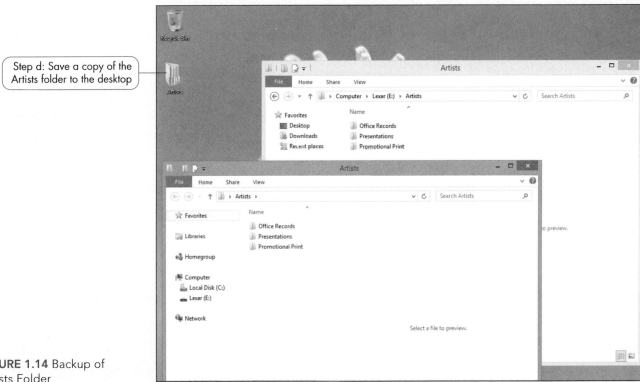

FIGURE 1.14 Backup of Artists Folder

a. Double-click the **Office Records folder**. Double-click *f01h2Volunteers_LastFirst*. Save the file with the new name **f01h2Stp4Volunteers_LastFirst** in the same location.

Because the file was created with Excel, that program opens, and the Volunteers worksheet is displayed.

b. Click **cell A11**, if necessary, and type **Office**. Press **Tab**, type **Adams**, and then press **Enter**. Click the **FILE tab** and click **Save**. The file is automatically saved in the same location with the same file name as before. Close Excel.

A neighbor, Sarah Adams, has volunteered to help in the office. You record that information on the worksheet and save the updated file in the Office Records folder.

c. Click the location where you save files in the Navigation pane in File Explorer so that the Artists folder displays in the Content pane. Right-click the **Artists folder** and click **Copy**.

d. Right-click **Desktop** in the Favorites group on the Navigation Pane and click **Paste**. Close File Explorer. If any other windows are open, close them also.

You made a copy of the Artists folder on the desktop.

e. Double-click the **Artists folder** on the desktop. Double-click the **Office Records folder**. Verify that the *f01h2Stp4Volunteers_LastFirst* worksheet displays in the folder. Take a full-screen snip of your screen and name it **f01h2Backup_LastFirst**. Close the Snipping Tool and close File Explorer.

f. Right-click the **Artists folder** on the desktop, select **Delete**, and then click **Yes** if asked to confirm the deletion.

You deleted the Artists folder from the desktop of the computer because you may be working in a computer lab and want to leave the computer as you found it. You may also want to empty the Recycle Bin.

g. Submit your files based on your instructor's directions.

Microsoft Office Software

Organizations around the world rely heavily on *Microsoft Office* software to produce documents, spreadsheets, presentations, and databases. Microsoft Office is a productivity software suite including a set of software applications, each one specializing in a particular type of output. You can use *Word* to produce all sorts of documents, including memos, newsletters, forms, tables, and brochures. *Excel* makes it easy to organize records, financial transactions, and business information in the form of worksheets. With *PowerPoint*, you can create dynamic presentations to inform groups and persuade audiences. *Access* is relational database software that enables you to record and link data, query databases, and create forms and reports.

You will sometimes find that you need to use two or more Office applications to produce your intended output. You might, for example, find that a Word document you are preparing for your investment club should also include a summary of stock performance. You can use Excel to prepare the summary and then incorporate the worksheet in the Word document. Similarly, you can integrate Word tables and Excel charts into a PowerPoint presentation. The choice of which software applications to use really depends on what type of output you are producing. Table 1.2 describes the major tasks of these four primary applications in Microsoft Office.

TABLE 1.2 Microsoft Office Software	
Office 2013 Product	**Application Characteristics**
Word 2013	Word processing software used with text to create, edit, and format documents such as letters, memos, reports, brochures, resumes, and flyers.
Excel 2013	Spreadsheet software used to store quantitative data and to perform accurate and rapid calculations with results ranging from simple budgets to financial analyses and statistical analyses.
PowerPoint 2013	Presentation graphics software used to create slide shows for presentation by a speaker, to be published as part of a Web site, or to run as a stand-alone application on a computer kiosk.
Access 2013	Relational database software used to store data and convert it into information. Database software is used primarily for decision making by businesses that compile data from multiple records stored in tables to produce informative reports.

As you become familiar with Microsoft Office, you will find that although each software application produces a specific type of output, all applications share common features. Such commonality gives a similar feel to each software application so that learning and working with Microsoft Office software products is easy. In this section, you will identify features common to Microsoft Office software, including such interface components as the Ribbon, the Backstage view, and the Quick Access Toolbar. You will also learn how to get help with an application.

Identifying Common Interface Components

As you work with Microsoft Office, you will find that each application shares a similar *user interface*. The user interface is the screen display through which you communicate with the software. Word, Excel, PowerPoint, and Access share common interface elements, as shown in Figure 1.15. One of the feature options includes the availability of templates as well as new and improved themes when each application is opened. A *template* is a predesigned file that incorporates formatting elements, such as a theme and layouts, and may include content that can be modified. A *theme* is a collection of design choices that includes colors, fonts, and special effects used to give a consistent look to a document, workbook, or presentation. As you can imagine, becoming familiar with one application's interface makes it that much easier to work with other Office software.

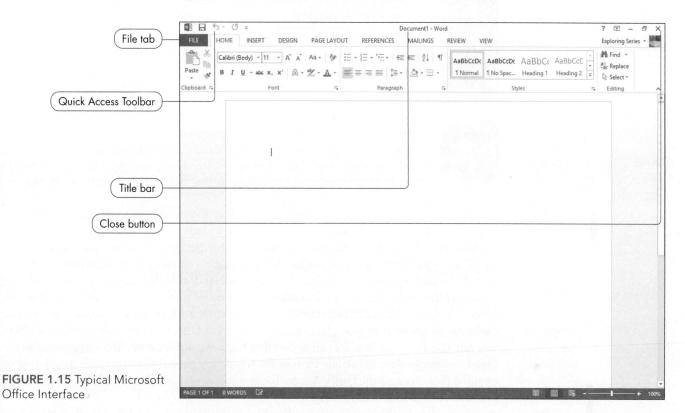

FIGURE 1.15 Typical Microsoft Office Interface

Use the Backstage View and the Quick Access Toolbar

The *Backstage view* is a component of Office 2013 that provides a concise collection of commands related to an open file. Using the Backstage view, you can find out information such as protection, permissions, versions, and properties. A file's properties include the author, file size, permissions, and date modified. You can create a new document or open, save, print, share, export, or close. The *Quick Access Toolbar*, located at the top-left corner of any Office application window, provides fast access to commonly executed tasks such as saving a file and undoing recent actions. The *title bar* identifies the current file name and the application in which you are working. It also includes control buttons that enable you to minimize, maximize, restore down, or close the application window (see Figure 1.15).

You access the Backstage view by clicking the File tab. When you click the File tab, you will see the Backstage view (see Figure 1.16). Primarily focusing on file activities such as opening, closing, saving, printing, and beginning new files, the Backstage view also includes options for customizing program settings, signing in to your Office account, and exiting the program. It displays a file's properties, providing important information on file permission and sharing options. When you click the File tab, the Backstage view will occupy the entire application window, hiding the file with which you might be working. For example, suppose that as you are typing a report you need to check the document's properties. Click the File tab to display a Backstage view similar to that shown in Figure 1.16. You can return to the application—in this case, Word—in a couple of ways. Either click the Back arrow in the top-left corner or press Esc on the keyboard.

Back arrow

Properties

FIGURE 1.16 The Backstage View

STEP 4

The Quick Access Toolbar provides one-click access to common activities, as shown in Figure 1.17. By default, the Quick Access Toolbar includes buttons for saving a file and for undoing or redoing recent actions. You will probably perform an action countless times in an Office application and then realize that you made a mistake. You can recover from the mistake by clicking Undo on the Quick Access Toolbar. If you click the arrow beside Undo—known as the Undo arrow—you can select from a list of previous actions in order of occurrence. The Undo list is not maintained when you close a file or exit the application, so you can erase an action that took place during the current Office session only. Similar to Undo, you can also Redo (or Replace) an action that you have just undone. You can customize the Quick Access Toolbar to include buttons for frequently used commands such as printing or opening files. Because the Quick Access Toolbar is onscreen at all times, the most commonly accessed tasks are just a click away.

To customize the Quick Access Toolbar, click Customize Quick Access Toolbar (see Figure 1.17) and select from a list of commands. You can also click More Commands near the bottom of the menu options. If a command that you want to include on the toolbar is not on the list, you can right-click the command on the Ribbon and click *Add to Quick Access Toolbar*. Similarly, remove a command from the Quick Access Toolbar by right-clicking the icon on the Quick Access Toolbar and clicking *Remove from Quick Access Toolbar*. If you want to display the Quick Access Toolbar beneath the Ribbon, click Customize Quick Access Toolbar (see Figure 1.17) and click *Show Below the Ribbon*.

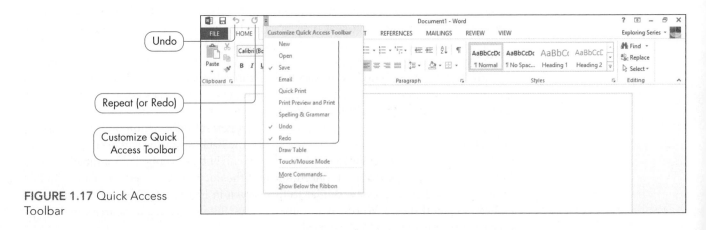

Undo

Repeat (or Redo)

Customize Quick Access Toolbar

FIGURE 1.17 Quick Access Toolbar

Familiarize Yourself with the Ribbon

The **Ribbon** is the command center of Office applications. It is the long bar located just beneath the title bar, containing tabs, groups, and commands. Each **tab** is designed to appear much like a tab on a file folder, with the active tab highlighted. The File tab is always a darker shade than the other tabs and a different color depending on the application. Remember that clicking the File tab opens the Backstage view. Other tabs on the Ribbon enable you to modify a file. The active tab in Figure 1.18 is the Home tab.

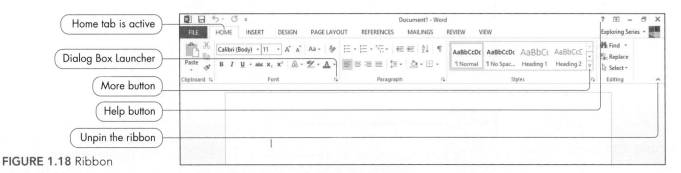

FIGURE 1.18 Ribbon

When you click a tab, the Ribbon displays several task-oriented **groups**, with each group containing related **commands**. A group is a subset of a tab that organizes similar tasks together. A command is a button or area within a group that you click to perform tasks. Microsoft Office is designed to provide the most functionality possible with the fewest clicks. For that reason, the Home tab, displayed when you first open an Office software application, contains groups and commands that are most commonly used. For example, because you will often want to change the way text is displayed, the Home tab in each Office application includes a Font group with activities related to modifying text. Similarly, other tabs contain groups of related actions, or commands, many of which are unique to the particular Office application.

Because Word, PowerPoint, Excel, and Access all share a similar Ribbon structure, you will be able to move at ease among those applications. Although the specific tabs, groups, and commands vary among the Office programs, the way in which you use the Ribbon and the descriptive nature of tab titles is the same regardless of which program you are working with. For example, if you want to insert a chart in Excel, a header in Word, or a shape in PowerPoint, you will click the Insert tab in any of those programs. The first thing that you should do as you begin to work with an Office application is to study the Ribbon. Take a look at all tabs and their contents. That way, you will have a good idea of where to find specific commands and how the Ribbon with which you are currently working differs from one that you might have used previously in another application.

If you are working with a large project, you might want to maximize your workspace by temporarily hiding the Ribbon. You can hide the Ribbon in several ways. Double-click the active tab to hide the Ribbon and double-click any tab to redisplay it. You can click *Unpin the ribbon* (see Figure 1.18), located at the right side of the Ribbon, and click any tab to redisplay the Ribbon.

The Ribbon provides quick access to common activities such as changing number or text formats or aligning data or text. Some actions, however, do not display on the Ribbon because they are not so common but are related to commands displayed on the Ribbon. For example, you might want to change the background of a PowerPoint slide to include a picture. In that case, you will need to work with a **dialog box** that provides access to more precise, but less frequently used, commands. Figure 1.19 shows the Font dialog box in Word, for example. Some commands display a dialog box when they are clicked. Other Ribbon groups include a **Dialog Box Launcher** that, when clicked, opens a corresponding dialog box (refer to Figure 1.18).

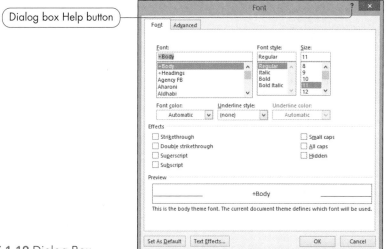

FIGURE 1.19 Dialog Box

The Ribbon contains many selections and commands, but some selections are too numerous to include in the Ribbon's limited space. For example, Word provides far more text styles than it can easily display at once, so additional styles are available in a ***gallery***. A gallery also provides a choice of Excel chart styles and PowerPoint transitions. Figure 1.20 shows an example of a PowerPoint Themes gallery. Most often, you can display a gallery of additional choices by clicking the More button (refer to Figure 1.18) that is found in some Ribbon selections.

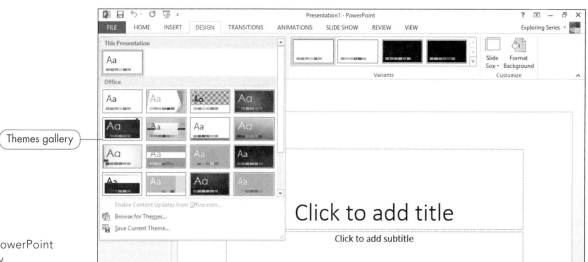

Themes gallery

FIGURE 1.20 PowerPoint Themes Gallery

STEP 3 »

When editing a document, worksheet, or presentation, it is helpful to see the results of formatting changes before you make final selections. The feature that displays a preview of the results of a selection is called ***Live Preview***. You might, for example, be considering changing the font color of a selection in a document or worksheet. As you place the mouse pointer over a color selection in a Ribbon gallery or group, the selected text will temporarily display the color to which you are pointing. Similarly, you can get a preview of how color designs would display on PowerPoint slides by pointing to specific themes in the PowerPoint Themes group and noting the effect on a displayed slide. When you click the item, such as the font color, the selection is applied. Live Preview is available in various Ribbon selections among the Office applications.

Office applications also make it easy for you to work with objects such as pictures, ***clip art***, shapes, charts, and tables. Clip art is an electronic illustration that can be inserted into an Office project. When you include such objects in a project, they are considered separate components that you can manage independently. To work with an object, you must click to select it. When you select an object, the Ribbon is modified to include one or more ***contextual tabs*** that contain groups of commands related to the selected object. Figure 1.21 shows a contextual tab related to a selected SmartArt object in a Word document. When you click outside the selected object, the contextual tab disappears.

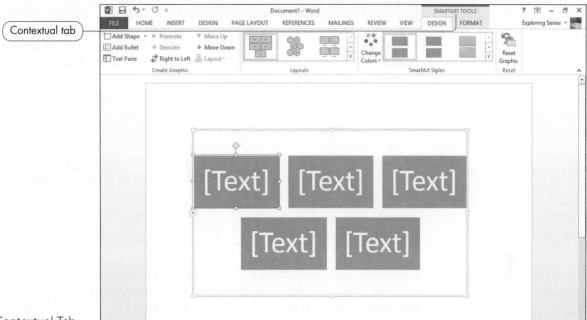

Contextual tab

FIGURE 1.21 Contextual Tab

TIP | **Using Keyboard Shortcuts**

You might find that you prefer to use keyboard shortcuts, which are keyboard equivalents for software commands, when they are available. Universal keyboard shortcuts include Ctrl+C (copy), Ctrl+X (cut), Ctrl+V (paste), and Ctrl+Z (undo). To move to the beginning of a Word document, to cell A1 in Excel, or to the first PowerPoint slide, press Ctrl+Home. To move to the end of those items, press Ctrl+End. Press Alt to display keyboard shortcuts, called a ***Key Tip***, for items on the Ribbon and Quick Access Toolbar. You can press the letter or number corresponding to Ribbon items to invoke the action from the keyboard. Press Alt again to remove the Key Tips.

Use the Status Bar

The ***status bar*** is located at the bottom of the program window and contains information relative to the open file. It also includes tools for changing the view of the file and for changing the zoom size of onscreen file contents. Contents of the status bar are unique to each specific application. When you work with Word, the status bar informs you of the number of pages and words in an open document. The Excel status bar displays summary information, such as average and sum, of selected cells. The PowerPoint status bar shows the slide number, total slides in the presentation, and the applied theme. It also provides access to notes and comments.

STEP 3

Regardless of the application in which you are working, the status bar includes view buttons and a Zoom slider. You can also use the View tab on the Ribbon to change the current view or zoom level of an open file. The status bar's view buttons (see Figure 1.22) enable you to change the ***view*** of the open file. When creating a document, you might find it helpful to change the view. You might, for example, view a PowerPoint slide presentation with multiple slides displayed (Slide Sorter view) or with only one slide in large size (Normal view). In Word, you could view a document in Print Layout view (showing margins, headers, and footers), Web Layout view, or Read Mode.

Zoom slider

View buttons

FIGURE 1.22 Word Status Bar

Additional views are available in the View tab. Word's Print Layout view is useful when you want to see both the document text and such features as margins and page breaks. Web Layout view is useful to see what the page would look like on the Internet. The Read Mode view provides a clean look that displays just the content without the Ribbon or margins. It is ideal for use on a tablet where the screen may be smaller than on a laptop or computer. PowerPoint, Excel, and Access also provide view options, although they are unique to the application. The most common view options are accessible from *View shortcuts* on the status bar of each application. As you learn more about Office applications, you will become aware of the views that are specific to each application.

STEP 1 ≫ The ***Zoom slider*** always displays at the far right side of the status bar. You can drag the tab along the slider in either direction to increase or decrease the magnification of the file. Be aware, however, that changing the size of text onscreen does not change the font size when the file is printed or saved.

Getting Office Help

One of the most frustrating things about learning new software is determining how to complete a task. Thankfully, Microsoft includes comprehensive help in Office so that you are less likely to feel such frustration. As you work with any Office application, you can access help online as well as within the current software installation. Help is available through a short description that displays when you rest the mouse pointer on a command. Additionally, you can get help related to a currently open dialog box by clicking the question mark in the top-right corner of the dialog box, or when you click Help in the top-right corner of the application.

Use Office Help

STEP 2 ≫ To access the comprehensive library of Office Help, click the Help button, displayed as a question mark on the far right side of the Ribbon (refer to Figure 1.18). The Help window provides assistance with the current application as well as a direct link to online resources and technical support. Figure 1.23 shows the Help window that displays when you click the Help button while in Excel. For general information on broad topics, click a link in the window. However, if you are having difficulty with a specific task, it might be easier to simply type the request in the Search online help box. Suppose you are seeking help with using the Goal Seek feature in Excel. Simply type *Goal Seek* or a phrase such as *find specific result by changing variables* in the Search box and press Enter (or click the magnifying glass on the right). Then select from displayed results for more information on the topic.

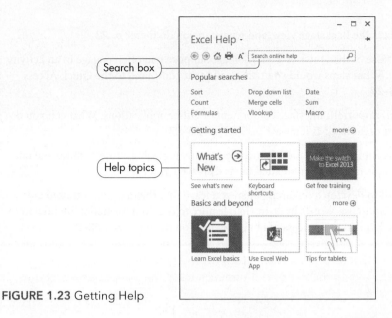

FIGURE 1.23 Getting Help

Use Enhanced ScreenTips

For quick summary information on the purpose of a command button, place the mouse pointer over the button. An *Enhanced ScreenTip* displays, giving the purpose of the command, short descriptive text, and a keyboard shortcut if applicable. Some ScreenTips include a suggestion for pressing F1 for additional help. The Enhanced ScreenTip in Figure 1.24 provides context-sensitive assistance.

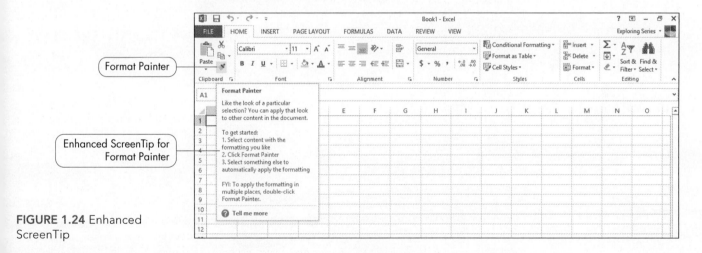

FIGURE 1.24 Enhanced ScreenTip

Get Help with Dialog Boxes

Getting help while you are working with a dialog box is easy. Simply click the Help button that displays as a question mark in the top-right corner of the dialog box (refer to Figure 1.19). The subsequent Help window will offer suggestions relevant to your task.

Quick Concepts ✓

1. How do you access the Backstage view, and what can you do there? *p. 23*

2. What is the purpose of the Quick Access Toolbar? Suppose you often engage in an activity such as printing. What steps would you take to add that command to the Quick Access Toolbar? *pp. 23–24*

3. The Ribbon is an important interface component of Office applications. What can you do with it? How is it organized? Is it always visible? *pp. 25–27*

4. Occasionally, the Ribbon is modified to include a contextual tab. Define a contextual tab and give an example of when a contextual tab is displayed. *p. 27*

5. After using Word to develop a research paper, you learn that the margins you used are incorrect. You plan to use Word's built-in Help feature to obtain information on how to change margins. Explain the process of obtaining help on the topic. *pp. 28–29*

Hands-On Exercises

Watch the Video for this Hands-On Exercise!

MyITLab®
HOE3 Training

3 Microsoft Office Software

As the administrative assistant for the Spotted Begonia Art Gallery, you need to get the staff started on a proposed schedule of gallery showings worksheet. Although you do not have access to information on all of the artists and their preferred media, you want to provide a suggested format for a worksheet to keep up with showings as they get booked. You will use Excel to begin design of the worksheet.

Skills covered: Open an Office Application, Get Enhanced ScreenTip Help, and Use the Zoom Slider • Get Help and Use the Backstage View • Change the View and Use Live Preview • Use the Quick Access Toolbar and Explore PowerPoint Views

---

STEP 1 ≫ OPEN AN OFFICE APPLICATION, GET ENHANCED SCREENTIP HELP, AND USE THE ZOOM SLIDER

Because you will use Excel to create the gallery showings worksheet, you will open the application. You will familiarize yourself with items on the Ribbon by getting Enhanced ScreenTip Help. For a better view of worksheet data, you will use the Zoom slider to magnify cell contents. Refer to Figure 1.25 as you complete Step 1.

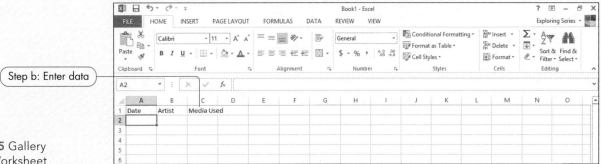

FIGURE 1.25 Gallery Showings Worksheet

a. Navigate to the Start screen. Scroll across the tiles, if necessary, and click **Excel 2013**. Click **Blank workbook** in the Excel 2013 window that displays.

   You have opened Microsoft Excel because it is the program in which the gallery showings worksheet will be created.

b. Type **Date** in **cell A1**. As you type, the text appears in the current worksheet cell. Press **Tab** and type **Artist**. Press **Tab** and type **Media Used**. Press **Enter**. See Figure 1.25.

   The worksheet that you create is only a beginning. Your staff will later suggest additional columns of data that can better summarize the upcoming gallery showings.

c. Hover the mouse pointer over any command on the Ribbon and note the Enhanced ScreenTip that displays, informing you of the purpose of the command. Explore other commands and identify their purpose.

d. Click the **PAGE LAYOUT tab**, click **Orientation** in the Page Setup group, and then select **Landscape**.

   The PAGE LAYOUT tab is also found in Word, enabling you to change margins, orientation, and other page settings. Although you will not see much difference in the Excel screen display after you change the orientation to landscape, the worksheet will be oriented so that it is wider than it is tall when printed.

e. Drag the tab on the Zoom slider, located at the far right side of the status bar, to 190% to temporarily magnify the text. Take a full-screen snip of your screen and name it **f01h3Showings_LastFirst**.

f. Click the **VIEW tab** and click **100%** in the Zoom group to return the view to its original size.

   When you change the zoom, you do not change the text size that will be printed or saved. The change merely magnifies or decreases the view while you work with the file.

   g. Keep the workbook open for the next step in this exercise. Submit the file based on your instructor's directions.

STEP 2 ≫ GET HELP AND USE THE BACKSTAGE VIEW

Because you are not an Excel expert, you occasionally rely on the Help feature to provide information on tasks. You need assistance with saving a worksheet, previewing it before printing, and printing the worksheet. From what you learn, you will find that the Backstage view enables you to accomplish all of those tasks. Refer to Figure 1.26 as you complete Step 2.

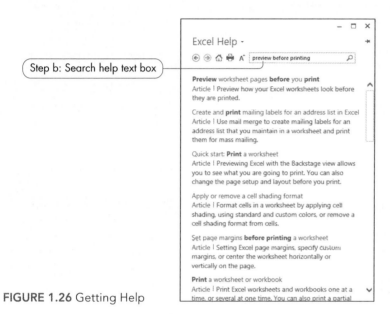

FIGURE 1.26 Getting Help

   a. Click **Help**, which is the question mark in the top-right corner of the Ribbon.

   The Help dialog box displays.

> ### TIP | Using Shortcuts to Access Help
>
> You can discover alternative ways to access Help. For example, the ScreenTip that displays as you point to the Help button suggests that you could press the F1 key.

   b. Click in the **Search online help text box** at the top of the Help dialog box. Type **preview before printing** and press **Enter** (see Figure 1.26). In the Excel Help window, click **Preview worksheet pages before you print**. Read about how to preview a worksheet before printing. From what you read, can you identify a keyboard shortcut for previewing worksheets? Click the **Close (X) button**.

   Before you print the worksheet, you would like to see how it will look when printed. You used Help to find information on previewing before printing.

   c. Click the **FILE tab** and click **Print**.

   Having used Office Help to learn how to preview before printing, you follow the directions to view the worksheet as it will look when printed. The preview of the worksheet displays on the right. To print the worksheet, you would click Print. However, you can first select any print options, such as the number of copies, from the Backstage view.

d. Click the **Back arrow** on the top left of the screen. Click **Help**. Excel Help presents several links related to the worksheet. Explore any that look interesting. Return to previous Help windows by clicking **Back** at the top-left side of the Help window. Close the Help dialog box.

e. Click the **HOME tab**. Point to *Bold* in the Font group.

You will find that, along with Excel, Word and PowerPoint also include formatting features in the Font group, such as Bold and Italic. When the Enhanced ScreenTip appears, identify the shortcut key combination that could be used to bold a selected text item. It is indicated as Ctrl plus the letter B.

f. Click the **Close (X) button** in the top-right corner of the Excel window to close both the workbook and the Excel program. When asked whether you want to save changes, click **Don't Save**.

You decide not to print or save the worksheet right now because you did not change anything during this step.

STEP 3 ≫ CHANGE THE VIEW AND USE LIVE PREVIEW

It is important that the documents you prepare or approve are error free and as attractive as possible. Before printing, you will change the view to get a better idea of how the document will look when printed. In addition, you will use Live Preview to experiment with font settings before actually applying them. Refer to Figure 1.27 as you complete Step 3.

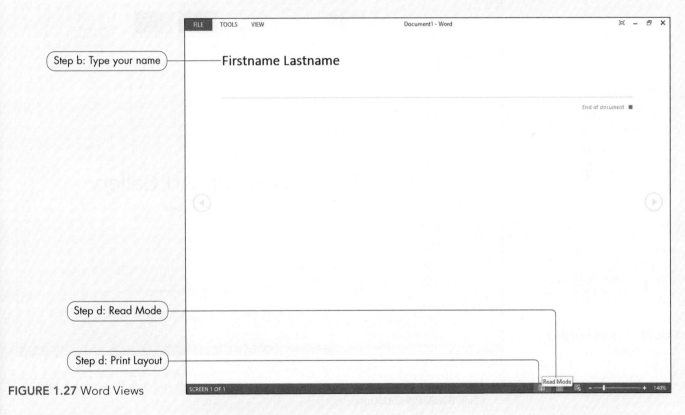

FIGURE 1.27 Word Views

a. Navigate to the Start screen. Scroll across the tiles, if necessary, and click **Word 2013**. Click **Blank document**.

You have opened a blank Word document. You plan to familiarize yourself with the program for later reference.

b. Type your first and last names and press **Enter**. Drag to select your name.

Your name should be highlighted, indicating that it is selected. You have selected your name because you want to experiment with using Word to change the way text looks.

c. Click the **Font Size arrow** in the Font group. If you need help locating Font Size, check for an Enhanced ScreenTip. Place the mouse pointer over any number in the list, but do not click. As you move to different font sizes, notice the size of your name changes. The feature you are using is called Live Preview. Click **16** in the list to change the font size of your name.

d. Click any white space to deselect your name. Click **Read Mode** in the *View shortcuts* group on the status bar to change the view (see Figure 1.27). Click **Print Layout** to return to the original view.

e. Save the file as **f01h3Read_LastFirst** and click the **Close (X) button** to close the Word program. Submit the file based on your instructor's directions.

STEP 4 ›› USE THE QUICK ACCESS TOOLBAR AND EXPLORE POWERPOINT VIEWS

In your position as administrative assistant, you will be asked to review documents, presentations, and worksheets. It is important that you explore each application to familiarize yourself with operations and commonalities. Specifically, you know that the Quick Access Toolbar is common to all applications and that you can place commonly used commands there to streamline processes. Also, learning to change views will enable you to see the project in different ways for various purposes. Refer to Figure 1.28 as you complete Step 4.

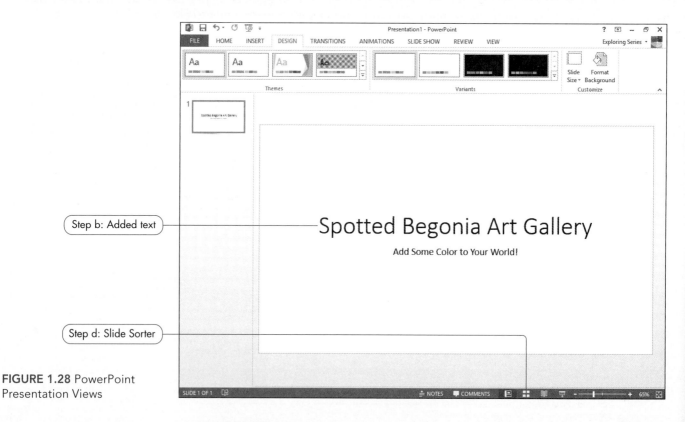

FIGURE 1.28 PowerPoint Presentation Views

a. Navigate to the Start screen. Scroll across the tiles, if necessary, and click **PowerPoint 2013**. Click **Blank Presentation**.

You have opened PowerPoint. A blank presentation displays.

b. Click **Click to add title** and type **Spotted Begonia Art Gallery**. Click in the bottom, subtitle box and type **Add Some Color to Your World!** Click the bottom-right corner of the slide to deselect the subtitle. Your PowerPoint presentation should look like that shown in Figure 1.28.

c. Click **Undo** two times on the Quick Access Toolbar.

The subtitle on the current slide is selected and removed because those are the most recent actions.

> **TROUBLESHOOTING:** If all of the subtitle text is not removed after two clicks, you should continue clicking until it is removed.

d. Click **Slide Sorter** in the *View shortcuts* group on the status bar.

The Slide Sorter view shows thumbnails of all slides in a presentation. Because this presentation has only one slide, you see a small version of one slide.

e. Move the mouse pointer to any button on the Quick Access Toolbar and hold it steady. See the tip giving the button name and the shortcut key combination, if any. Move to another button and see the description.

The Quick Access Toolbar has at least three buttons: Save, Undo, and Redo. In addition, a small arrow is included at the far-right side. If you hold the mouse pointer steady on the arrow, you will see the ScreenTip Customize Quick Access Toolbar.

f. Click **Customize Quick Access Toolbar** and select **New**. The New button is added to the toolbar. The New button enables you to quickly create a new presentation (also called a document).

g. Right-click **New** and click **Remove from Quick Access Toolbar**. The button is removed from the Quick Access Toolbar.

You can customize the Quick Access Toolbar by adding and removing items.

h. Click **Normal** in the *View shortcuts* group on the status bar.

The presentation returns to the original view in which the slide displays full size.

i. Click **Slide Show** in the *View shortcuts* group on the status bar.

The presentation is shown in Slide Show view, which is the way it will be presented to audiences.

j. Press **Esc** to end the presentation.

k. Save the presentation as **f01h3Views_LastFirst** and click the **Close (X) button** to close the PowerPoint program. Submit the presentation based on your instructor's directions.

The Backstage View Tasks

When you work with Microsoft Office files, you will often want to open previously saved files, create new ones, print items, and save and close files. You will also find it necessary to indicate options, or preferences, for settings. For example, you might want a spelling check to occur automatically, or you might prefer to initiate a spelling check only occasionally. Because those tasks are applicable to each software application within the Office 2013 suite, they are accomplished through a common area in the Office interface—the Backstage view. Open the Backstage view by clicking the File tab. Figure 1.29 shows the area that displays when you click the File tab in PowerPoint. The Backstage view also enables you to exit the application and to identify file information, such as the author or date created.

In this section, you will explore the Backstage view, learning to create, open, close, and print files.

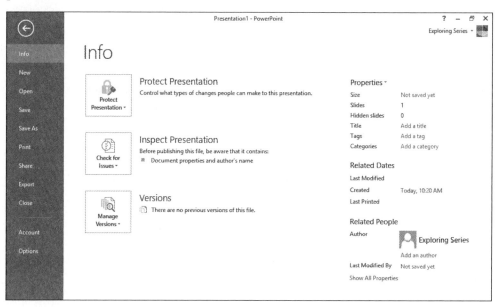

FIGURE 1.29 The Backstage View

Opening a File

When working with an Office application, you can begin by opening an existing file that has already been saved to a storage medium, or you can begin work on a new file. Both actions are available when you click the File tab. When you first open an application within the Office 2013 suite, you will need to decide which template you want to work with before you can begin working on a new file. You can also open a project that you previously saved to a disk.

Create a New File

After opening an Office application, such as Word, Excel, or PowerPoint, you will be presented with template choices. Click *Blank document* to start a new blank document. The word *document* is sometimes used generically to refer to any Office file, including a Word document, an Excel worksheet, or a PowerPoint presentation. Perhaps you are already working with a document in an Office application but want to create a new file. Simply click the File tab and click New. Click *Blank document* (or *Blank presentation* or *Blank workbook*, depending on the specific application).

Open a File Using the Open Dialog Box

STEP 1 ≫ You may choose to open a previously saved file, such as when you work with the data files for this book or when you want to access any previously created file. You will work with the Open dialog box, as shown in Figure 1.30. The Open dialog box displays after you click Open from the File tab. You will click Computer and the folder or drive where your document is stored.

If it is not listed under Recent Folders, you can browse for it. Using the Navigation Pane, you will make your way to the file to be opened. Double-click the file or click the file name once and click Open. Most likely, the file will be located within a folder that is appropriately named to make it easy to find related files. Obviously, if you are not well acquainted with the file's location and file name, the process of opening a file could become quite cumbersome. However, if you have created a well-designed system of folders, as you learned to do in the "Files and Folders" section of this chapter, you will know exactly where to find the file.

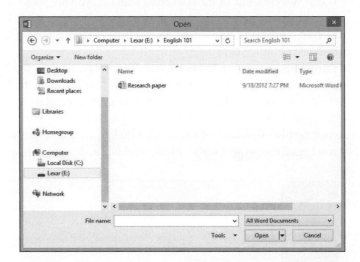

FIGURE 1.30 Open Dialog Box

Open a File Using the Recent Documents List

STEP 3 >>

You will often work with a file, save it, and then continue the project at a later time. Office simplifies the task of reopening the file by providing a Recent Documents list with links to your most recently opened files (see Figure 1.31). To access the list, click the File tab, click Open, and then select Recent Documents. Click any file listed in the Recent Documents list to open that document. The list constantly changes to reflect only the most recently opened files, so if it has been quite some time since you worked with a particular file, you might have to work with the Open dialog box instead of the Recent Documents list.

Pin this item to the list

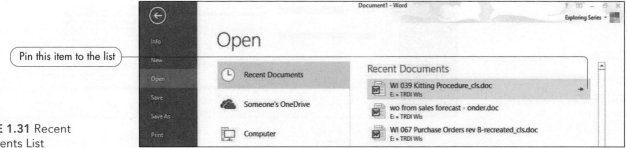

FIGURE 1.31 Recent Documents List

TIP | **Keeping Files on the Recent Documents List**

The Recent Documents list displays a limited list of only the most recently opened files. You might, however, want to keep a particular file in the list regardless of how recently it was opened. In Figure 1.31, note the *Pin this item to the list* icon displays to the right of each file. Click the icon to pin the file to the list. At that point, you will always have access to the file by clicking the File tab and selecting the file from the Recent Documents list. The pushpin of the "permanent" file will change direction so that it appears to be inserted, indicating that it is a pinned item. If later you want to remove the file from the list, click the inserted pushpin, changing its direction and allowing the file to be bumped off the list when other, more recently opened, files take its place.

Open a File from the Templates List

You do not need to create a new file if you can access a predesigned file that meets your needs or one that you can modify fairly quickly to complete your project. Office provides templates, making them available when you click the File tab and New (see Figure 1.32). The Templates list is comprised of template groups available within the current Office installation on your computer. The Search box can be used to locate other templates that are available from Office.com. When you click one of the Suggested searches, you are presented with additional choices.

For example, you might want to prepare a home budget. After opening a blank worksheet in Excel, click the File tab and click New. From the template categories, you could click Budget from the *Suggested searches* list, scroll down until you find the right template, such as Family Budget, and then click Create to display the associated worksheet (or simply double-click Family Budget). If a Help window displays along with the worksheet template, click to close it or explore Help to learn more about the template. If you know only a little bit about Excel, you could then make a few changes so that the worksheet would accurately represent your family's financial situation. The budget would be prepared much more quickly than if you began the project with a blank workbook, designing it yourself.

Templates available from Office.com

Templates available in a typical Office installation

FIGURE 1.32 Working with Templates

Printing a File

There will be occasions when you will want to print an Office project. Before printing, you should preview the file to get an idea of how it will look when printed. That way, if there are obvious problems with the page setup, you can correct them before wasting paper on something that is not correct. When you are ready to print, you can select from various print options, including the number of copies and the specific pages to print. If you know that the page setup is correct and that there are no unique print settings to select, you can simply print the project without adjusting any print settings.

STEP 2 ›› It is a good idea to take a look at how your document will appear before you print it. The Print Preview feature of Office enables you to do just that. In the Print pane, you will see all items, including any headers, footers, graphics, and special formatting. To view a project before printing, click the File tab and click Print. The subsequent Backstage view shows the file preview on the right, with print settings located in the center of the Backstage screen. Figure 1.33 shows a typical Backstage Print view.

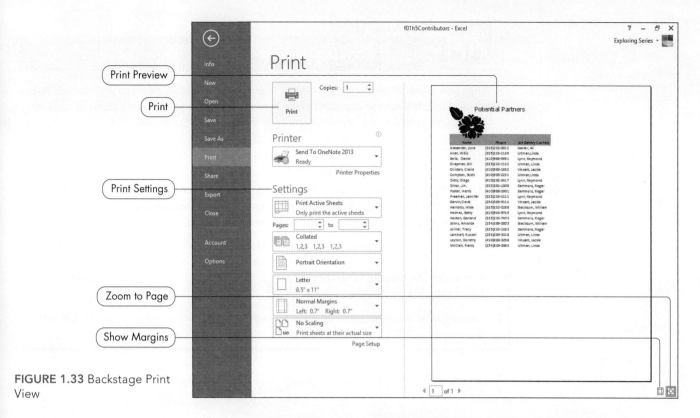

Print Preview

Print

Print Settings

Zoom to Page

Show Margins

FIGURE 1.33 Backstage Print View

To show the margins of the document, click Show Margins (see Figure 1.33). To increase the size of the file preview, click *Zoom to Page* (see Figure 1.33). Both are found on the bottom-right corner of the preview. Remember that increasing the font size by adjusting the zoom applies to the current display only; it does not actually increase the font size when the document is printed or saved. To return the preview to its original view, click *Zoom to Page* once more.

Other options in the Backstage Print view vary depending on the application in which you are working. Regardless of the Office application, you will be able to access Settings options from the Backstage view, including page orientation (landscape or portrait), margins, and paper size. You will find a more detailed explanation of those settings in the "Page Layout Tab Tasks" section later in this chapter. To print a file, click Print (see Figure 1.33).

The Backstage Print view shown in Figure 1.33 is very similar across all Office applications. However, you will find slight variations specific to each application. For example, PowerPoint's Backstage Print view includes options for printing slides and handouts in various configurations and colors, whereas Excel's focuses on worksheet selections and Word's includes document options. Regardless of software, the manner of working with the Backstage view print options remains consistent.

Closing a File and Application

Although you can have several documents open at one time, limiting the number of open files is a good idea. Office applications have no problem keeping up with multiple open files, but you can easily become overwhelmed with them. When you are done with an open project, you will need to close it.

You can easily close any files that you no longer need. With the desired file on the screen, click the FILE tab and click the Close (X) button. Respond to any prompt that might display suggesting that you save the file. The application remains open, but the selected file is closed. To close the application, click the Close (X) button in the top-right corner.

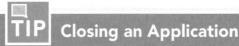
TIP Closing an Application

When you close an application, all open files within the application are also closed. You will be prompted to save any files before they are closed. A quick way to close an application is to click the X in the top-right corner of the application window.

Quick
Concepts

1. You want to continue to work with a PowerPoint presentation that you worked with yesterday, but cannot remember where you saved the presentation on your hard drive. How can you open a file that you recently worked with? ***p. 37***

2. As part of your job search, you plan to develop a resume. However, you find it difficult to determine the right style for your resume, and wish you could begin with a predesigned document that you could modify. Is that possible with Word? If so, what steps would you take to locate a predesigned resume? ***p. 38***

3. Closing a file is not the same as closing an application, such as closing Excel. What is the difference? ***p. 39***

Hands-On Exercises

4 The Backstage View Tasks

Projects related to the Spotted Begonia Art Gallery's functions have begun to come in for your review and approval. You have received an informational flyer to be distributed to schools and supporting organizations around the city. It contains a new logo along with descriptive text. Another task on your agenda is to keep the project moving according to schedule. You will identify a calendar template to print and distribute. You will explore printing options, and you will save the flyer and the calendar as directed by your instructor.

Skills covered: Open and Save a File • Preview and Print a File • Open a File from the Recent Documents List and Open a Template

STEP 1 ›› OPEN AND SAVE A FILE

You have asked your staff to develop a flyer that can be used to promote the Spotted Begonia Art Gallery. You will open a Word document that may be used for the flyer, and you will save the document to a disk drive. Refer to Figure 1.34 as you complete Step 1.

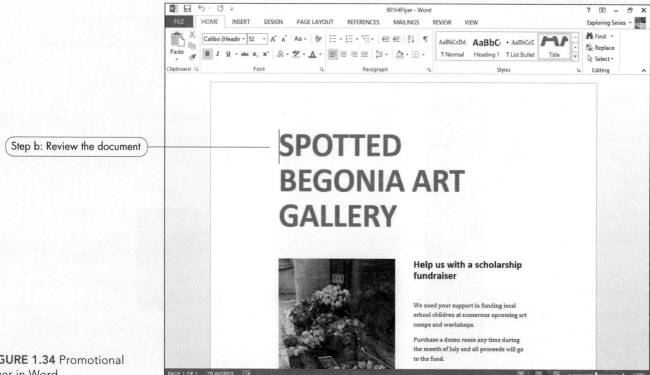

FIGURE 1.34 Promotional Flyer in Word

a. Navigate to the Start screen. Scroll across the tiles, if necessary, and click **Word 2013**. Click **Open Other Documents** at the bottom-left corner of the Word 2013 window.

You have opened Microsoft Word because it is the program in which the promotional flyer is saved.

b. Click **Computer** and click **Browse**. Navigate to the location of your student files. Double-click *f01h4Flyer* to open the file shown in Figure 1.34. Familiarize yourself with the document. Then, if necessary, click **Read Mode** in the *View shortcuts* group on the Status bar to change to that view. Read through the document.

The graphic and the flyer are submitted for your approval. A paragraph next to the graphic will serve as the launching point for an information blitz and the beginning of the fundraising drive.

Read Mode displays the document. If the document is large enough, multiple screens may display. You can use the arrows found on the middle edges of the document to navigate and view the entire document.

c. Click **Print Layout** on the Status bar to change to that view. Click the **FILE tab** and click **Save As**.

You choose the Save As command because you know that it enables you to indicate the location to which the file should be saved, as well as the file name.

d. Click **Browse**, navigate to the drive where you save your files, and then double-click the **Artists folder** you created earlier. Double-click **Office Records**, click in the **File name box**, type **f01h4Flyer_LastFirst**, and then click **Save**.

STEP 2 ≫ PREVIEW AND PRINT A FILE

You approve of the flyer, so you will print the document for future reference. You will first preview the document as it will appear when printed. Then you will print the document. Refer to Figure 1.35 as you complete Step 2.

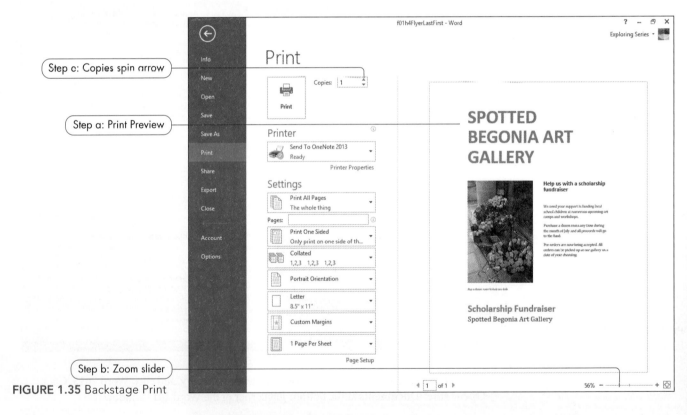

FIGURE 1.35 Backstage Print

a. Click the **FILE tab** and click **Print**.

Figure 1.35 shows the flyer preview. It is always a good idea to check the way a file will look when printed before actually printing it.

b. Drag the **Zoom slider** to increase the document view. Click **Zoom to Page** to return to the original size.

c. Click **Portrait Orientation** in the Print settings area in the center of the screen. Click **Landscape Orientation** to show the flyer in a wider and shorter view.

d. Click **Landscape Orientation** and click **Portrait Orientation** to return to the original view.

You decide that the flyer is more attractive in portrait orientation, so you return to that setting.

e. Click the **Copies spin arrow** repeatedly to increase the copies to **5**.

You will need to print five copies of the flyer to distribute to the office assistants for their review.

f. Click **Close** on the left side of the screen. When asked, click **Don't Save** so that changes to the file are not saved. Keep Word open for the next step.

STEP 3 ≫ OPEN A FILE FROM THE RECENT DOCUMENTS LIST AND OPEN A TEMPLATE

A large part of your responsibility is proofreading Spotted Begonia Art Gallery material. You will correct an error by adding a phone number in the promotional flyer. You must also keep the staff on task, so you will identify a calendar template on which to list tasks and deadlines. Refer to Figure 1.36 as you complete Step 3.

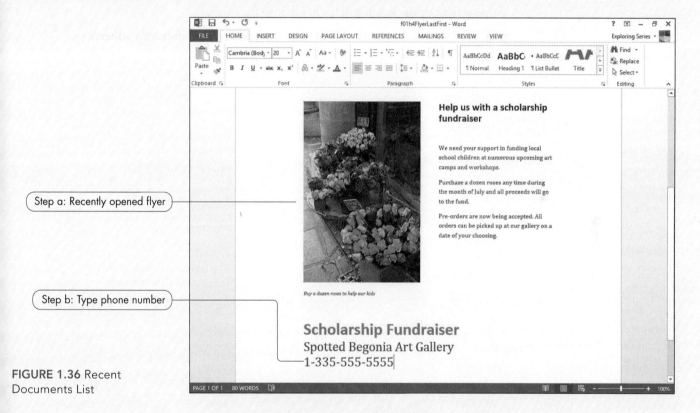

Step a: Recently opened flyer

Step b: Type phone number

FIGURE 1.36 Recent Documents List

a. Click the **FILE tab**, click **Recent Documents** if necessary, and then click **f01h4Flyer_LastFirst** in the **Recent Documents list**.

> **TROUBLESHOOTING:** If the file opens in Read Mode, use the status bar to change to the Print Layout view.

b. Press **Ctrl+End** to move the insertion point to the end of the document and press **Enter**. Type **1-335-555-5555**.

Figure 1.36 shows the phone number correction.

c. Click **Save** on the Quick Access Toolbar, click the **FILE tab**, and then click **Close**.

When you click Save on the Quick Access Toolbar, the document is saved in the same location with the same file name as was indicated in the previous save.

d. Click the **FILE tab** and click **New**. Click **Calendar** from the list of the *Suggested searches* category just beneath the *Search online templates* box.

Office.com provides a wide range of calendar choices. You will select one that is appealing and that will help you keep projects on track.

e. Click a calendar of your choice from the gallery and click **Create**. Respond to and close any windows that may open.

The calendar that you selected opens in Word.

> **TROUBLESHOOTING:** It is possible to select a template that is not certified by Microsoft. In that case, you might have to confirm your acceptance of settings before you click Download.

f. Click **Save** on the Quick Access Toolbar. If necessary, navigate to your Office Records subfolder (a subfolder of Artists) on the drive where you are saving your student files. Save the document as **f01h4Calendar_LastFirst**. Because this is the first time to save the calendar file, the Save button on the Quick Access Toolbar opens a dialog box in which you must indicate the location of the file and the file name.

g. Click **Save** and exit Word. Submit your files based on your instructor's directions.

Home Tab Tasks

You will find that you will repeat some tasks often, whether in Word, Excel, or PowerPoint. You will frequently want to change the format of numbers or words, selecting a different *font* or changing font size or color. A font is a complete set of characters, both upper- and lowercase letters, numbers, punctuation marks, and special symbols, with the same design including size, spacing, and shape. You might also need to change the alignment of text or worksheet cells. Undoubtedly, you will find a reason to copy or cut items and paste them elsewhere in the document, presentation, or worksheet. And you might want to modify file contents by finding and replacing text. All of those tasks, and more, are found on the Home tab of the Ribbon in Word, Excel, and PowerPoint. The Access interface is unique, sharing little with other Office applications, so this section will not address Access.

In this section, you will explore the Home tab, learning to format text, copy and paste items, and find and replace words or phrases. Figure 1.37 shows Home tab groups and tasks in the various applications. Note the differences and similarities between the groups.

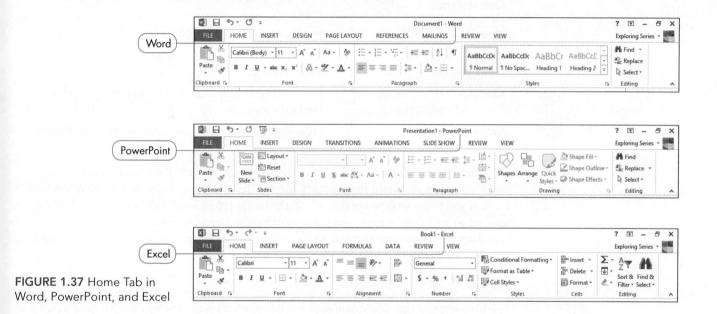

FIGURE 1.37 Home Tab in Word, PowerPoint, and Excel

Selecting and Editing Text

After creating a document, worksheet, or presentation, you will probably want to make some changes. You might prefer to center a title, or maybe you think that certain budget worksheet totals should be formatted as currency. You can change the font so that typed characters are larger or in a different style. You might even want to underline text to add emphasis. In all Office applications, the Home tab provides tools for selecting and editing text. You can also use the Mini toolbar for making quick changes to selected text.

Select Text to Edit

Before making any changes to existing text or numbers, you must first select the characters. A general rule that you should commit to memory is "Select, then do." A foolproof way to select text or numbers is to place the mouse pointer before the first character of the text you want to select, and then drag to highlight the intended selection. Before you drag, be sure that the mouse pointer takes on the shape of the letter *I*, called the *I-bar*. Although other methods for selecting exist, if you remember only one way, it should be the click-and-drag method. If your attempted selection falls short of highlighting the intended area, or perhaps highlights too much, simply click outside the selection and try again.

Sometimes it can be difficult to precisely select a small amount of text, such as a single character or a single word. Other times, the task can be overwhelming, such as when selecting an entire 550-page document. Shortcut methods for making selections in Word and PowerPoint are shown in Table 1.3. When working with Excel, you will more often need to select multiple cells. Simply drag the intended selection, usually when the mouse pointer displays as a large white plus sign. The shortcuts shown in Table 1.3 are primarily applicable to Word and PowerPoint.

TABLE 1.3 Shortcut Selection in Word and PowerPoint

Item Selected	Action
One word	Double-click the word.
One line of text	Place the mouse pointer at the left of the line, in the margin area. When the mouse changes to a right-pointing arrow, click to select the line.
One sentence	Press and hold Ctrl while you click in the sentence to select.
One paragraph	Triple-click in the paragraph.
One character to the left of the insertion point	Press and hold Shift while you press the left arrow on the keyboard.
One character to the right of the insertion point	Press and hold Shift while you press the right arrow on the keyboard.
Entire document	Press and hold Ctrl while you press A on the keyboard.

After having selected a string of characters, such as a number, word, sentence, or document, you can do more than simply format the selection. Suppose you have selected a word. If you begin to type another word, the newly typed word will immediately replace the selected word. With an item selected, you can press Delete to remove the selection. You will learn later in this chapter that you can also find, replace, copy, move, and paste selected text.

Use the Mini Toolbar

STEP 3 ≫

You have learned that you can always use commands on the Ribbon to change selected text within a document, worksheet, or presentation. All it takes is locating the desired command on the Home tab and clicking to select it. Although using the Home tab to perform commands is simple enough, an item called the *Mini toolbar* provides an even faster way to accomplish some of the same formatting changes. When you select any amount of text within a worksheet, document, or presentation, you can move the mouse pointer only slightly within the selection to display the Mini toolbar (see Figure 1.38). The Mini toolbar provides access to the most common formatting selections, such as adding bold or italic, or changing font type or color. Unlike the Quick Access Toolbar, the Mini toolbar is not customizable, which means that you cannot add or remove options from the toolbar.

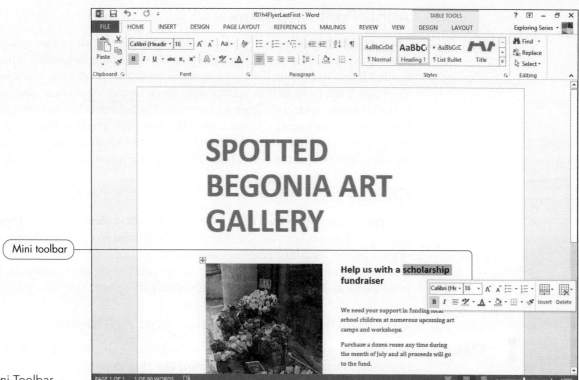

FIGURE 1.38 Mini Toolbar

The Mini toolbar will display only when text is selected. The closer the mouse pointer is to the Mini toolbar, the darker the toolbar becomes. As you move the mouse pointer away from the Mini toolbar, it becomes almost transparent. Make any selections from the Mini toolbar by clicking the corresponding button. To temporarily remove the Mini toolbar from view, press Esc.

If you want to permanently disable the Mini toolbar so that it does not display in any open file when text is selected, click the FILE tab and click Options. As shown in Figure 1.39, click General, if necessary. Deselect the *Show Mini Toolbar on selection* setting by clicking the check box to the left of the setting and clicking OK.

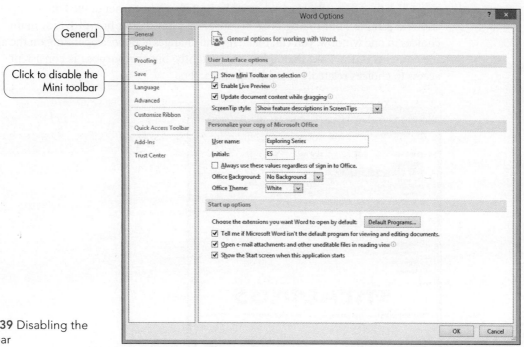

FIGURE 1.39 Disabling the Mini Toolbar

Apply Font Attributes

The way characters appear onscreen, including qualities such as size, spacing, and shape, is determined by the font. Each Office application has a default font, which is the font that will be in effect unless you change it. Other font attributes include boldfacing, italicizing, and font color, all of which can be applied to selected text. Some formatting changes, such as Bold and Italic, are called *toggle* commands. They act somewhat like light switches that you can turn on and off. For example, after having selected a word that you want to add bold to, click Bold in the Font group of the Home tab to turn the setting "on." If, at a later time, you want to remove bold from the word, select it again and click Bold. This time, the button turns "off" the bold formatting.

Change the Font

All applications within the Office suite provide a set of fonts from which you can choose. If you prefer a font other than the default, or if you want to apply a different font to a section of your project for added emphasis or interest, you can easily make the change by selecting a font from within the Font group on the Home tab. You can also change the font by selecting from the Mini toolbar, although that works only if you have first selected text.

Change the Font Size, Color, and Attributes

STEP 2 » At times, you will want to make the font size larger or smaller, change the font color, underline selected text, or apply other font attributes. For example, if you are creating a handout for a special event, you may want to apply a different font to emphasize key information such as dates and times. Because such changes are commonplace, Office places those formatting commands in many convenient places within each Office application.

You can find the most common formatting commands in the Font group on the Home tab. As noted earlier, Word, Excel, and PowerPoint all share very similar Font groups that provide access to tasks related to changing the character font (refer to Figure 1.37). Remember that you can place the mouse pointer over any command icon to view a summary of the icon's purpose, so although the icons might at first appear cryptic, you can use the mouse pointer to quickly determine the purpose and applicability to your desired text change. You can also find a subset of those commands plus a few additional choices on the Mini toolbar.

If the font change that you plan to make is not included as a choice on either the Home tab or the Mini toolbar, you can probably find what you are looking for in the Font dialog box. Click the Dialog Box Launcher in the bottom-right corner of the Font group. Figure 1.40 shows a sample Font dialog box. Because the Font dialog box provides many formatting choices in one window, you can make several changes at once. Depending on the application, the contents of the Font dialog box vary slightly, but the purpose is consistent—providing access to choices related to modifying characters.

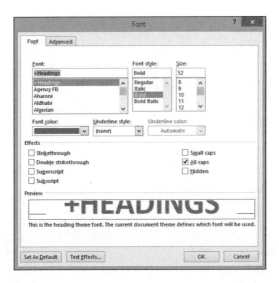

FIGURE 1.40 Font Dialog Box

Using the Clipboard Group Commands

On occasion, you will want to move or copy a selection from one area to another. Suppose that you have included text on a PowerPoint slide that you believe would be more appropriate on a different slide. Or perhaps an Excel formula should be copied from one cell to another because both cells should be totaled in the same manner. You can easily move the slide text or copy the Excel formula by using options found in the Clipboard group on the Home tab. The Office **Clipboard** is an area of memory reserved to temporarily hold selections that have been **cut** or **copied** and allows you to paste the selections. To cut means to remove a selection from the original location and place it in the Office Clipboard. To copy means to duplicate a selection from the original location and place a copy in the Office Clipboard. Although the Clipboard can hold up to 24 items at one time, the usual procedure is to **paste** the cut or copied selection to its final destination fairly quickly. To paste means to place a cut or copied selection into another location. When the computer is shut down or loses power, the contents of the Clipboard are erased, so it is important to finalize the paste procedure during the current session.

The Clipboard group enables you not only to copy and cut text and objects but also to copy formatting. Perhaps you have applied a font style to a major heading of a report and you realize that the same formatting should be applied to other headings. Especially if the heading includes multiple formatting features, you will save a great deal of time by copying the entire set of formatting options to the other headings. In so doing, you will ensure the consistency of formatting for all headings because they will appear exactly alike. Using the Clipboard group's **Format Painter**, you can quickly and easily copy all formatting from one area to another in Word, PowerPoint, and Excel.

In Office, you can usually accomplish the same task in several ways. Although the Ribbon provides ample access to formatting and Clipboard commands (such as Format Painter, Cut, Copy, and Paste), you might find it convenient to access the same commands on a **shortcut menu**. Right-click a selected item or text to open a shortcut menu such as the one shown in Figure 1.41. A shortcut menu is also called a *context menu* because the contents of the menu vary depending on the location at which you right-clicked.

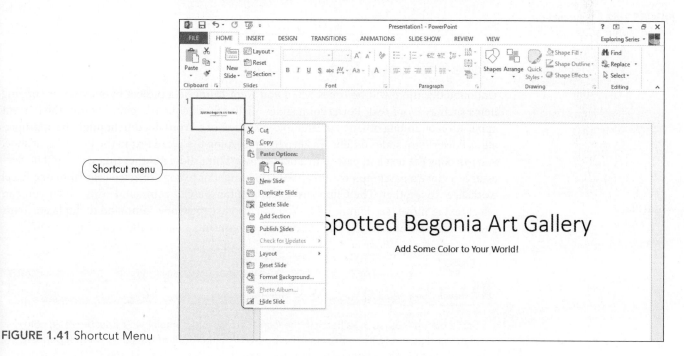

FIGURE 1.41 Shortcut Menu

Copy Formats with the Format Painter

STEP 3 As described earlier, the Format Painter makes it easy to copy formatting features from one selection to another. You will find the Format Painter command conveniently located in the Clipboard group of the Home tab (see Figure 1.42). To copy a format, you must first select the text containing the desired format. If you want to copy the format to only one other selection, *single-click* Format Painter. If, however, you plan to copy the same format to multiple areas, *double-click* Format Painter. As you move the mouse pointer, you will find that it has the appearance of a paintbrush with an attached I-bar. Select the area to which the copied format should be applied. If you single-clicked Format Painter to copy the format to one other selection, Format Painter turns off once the formatting has been applied. If you double-clicked Format Painter to copy the format to multiple locations, continue selecting text in various locations to apply the format. Then, to turn off Format Painter, click Format Painter again or press Esc.

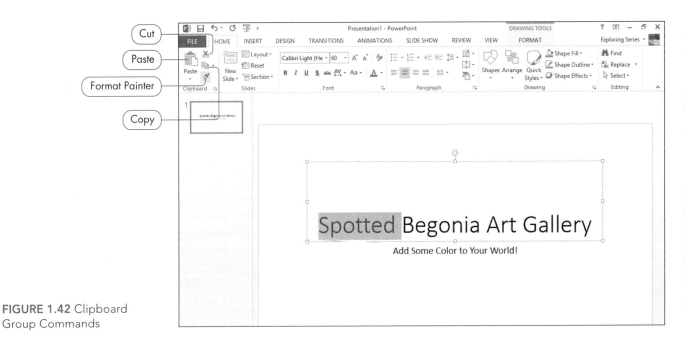

FIGURE 1.42 Clipboard Group Commands

Move and Copy Text

Undoubtedly, there will be times when you want to revise a project by moving or copying items such as Word text, PowerPoint slides, or Excel cell contents, either within the current application or among others. For example, a section of a Word document might be appropriate as PowerPoint slide content. To keep from retyping the Word text in the PowerPoint slide, you can copy the text and paste it in a blank PowerPoint slide. At other times, it might be necessary to move a paragraph within a Word document or to copy selected cells from one Excel worksheet to another. The Clipboard group contains a Cut command with which you can select text to move (see Figure 1.42). You can also use the Copy command to duplicate items and the Paste command to place cut or copied items in a final location (see Figure 1.42).

TIP | Using Ribbon Commands with Arrows

Some commands, such as Paste in the Clipboard group, contain two parts: the main command and an arrow. The arrow may be below or to the right of the command, depending on the command, window size, or screen resolution. Instructions in the *Exploring* series use the command name to instruct you to click the main command to perform the default action (e.g., Click Paste). Instructions include the word *arrow* when you need to select the arrow to access an additional option (e.g., Click the Paste arrow).

The first step in moving or copying text is to select the text. Then do the following:

1. Click the appropriate icon in the Clipboard group either to cut or copy the selection. Remember that cut or copied text is actually placed in the Clipboard, remaining there even after you paste it to another location. It is important to note that you can paste the same item multiple times, because it will remain in the Clipboard until you power down your computer or until the Clipboard exceeds 24 items.
2. Click the location where you want the cut or copied text to be placed. The location can be in the current file or in another open file within any Office application.
3. Click Paste in the Clipboard group on the HOME tab.

In addition to using the Clipboard group icons, you can also cut, copy, and paste in any of the ways listed in Table 1.4.

TABLE 1.4   Cut, Copy, and Paste Options

Command	Actions
Cut	• Click Cut in Clipboard group. • Right-click selection and select Cut. • Press Ctrl+X.
Copy	• Click Copy in Clipboard group. • Right-click selection and select Copy. • Press Ctrl+C.
Paste	• Click in destination location and select Paste in Clipboard group. • Right-click in destination location and select Paste. • Click in destination location and press Ctrl+V. • Click the Clipboard Dialog Box Launcher to open the Clipboard task pane. Click in destination location. With the Clipboard task pane open, click the arrow beside the intended selection and select Paste.

Use the Office Clipboard

When you cut or copy selections, they are placed in the Office Clipboard. Regardless of which Office application you are using, you can view the Clipboard by clicking the Clipboard Dialog Box Launcher, as shown in Figure 1.43.

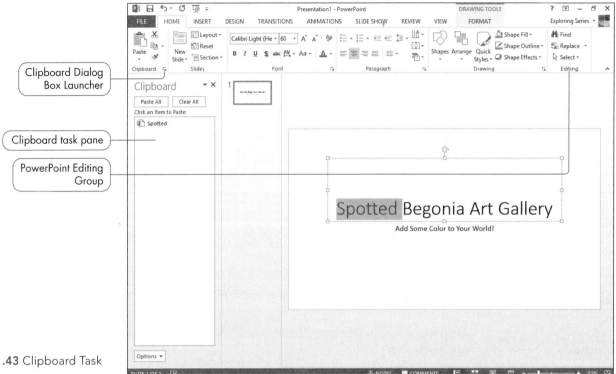

Clipboard Dialog Box Launcher

Clipboard task pane

PowerPoint Editing Group

FIGURE 1.43 Clipboard Task Pane

Unless you specify otherwise when beginning a paste operation, the most recently added Clipboard item is pasted. You can, however, select an item from the Clipboard task pane to paste. Similarly, you can delete items from the Clipboard by making a selection in the Clipboard task pane. You can remove all items from the Clipboard by clicking Clear All. The Options button in the Clipboard task pane enables you to control when and where the Clipboard is displayed. Close the Clipboard task pane by clicking the Close (X) button in the top-right corner of the task pane or by clicking the arrow in the title bar of the Clipboard task pane and selecting Close.

Using the Editing Group Commands

The process of finding and replacing text is easily accomplished through options in the Editing group of the Home tab. The Editing group also enables you to select all contents of a project document, all text with similar formatting, or specific objects, such as pictures or charts. The Editing group is found at the far-right side of the Home tab in Excel, Word, and PowerPoint.

The Excel Editing group is unique in that it also includes options for sorting, filtering, and clearing cell contents; filling cells; and summarizing numeric data. Because those commands are relevant only to Excel, this chapter will not address them specifically.

Find and Replace Text

STEP 4 » Especially if you are working with a lengthy project, manually seeking a specific word or phrase can be time-consuming. Office enables you not only to *find* each occurrence of a series of characters, but also to *replace* what it finds with another series. You will at times find it necessary to locate each occurrence of a text item so that you can replace it with another or so that you can delete, move, or copy it. If you have consistently misspelled a person's name throughout a document, you can find the misspelling and replace it with the correct spelling in a matter of a few seconds, no matter how many times the misspelling occurs in the document. To begin the process of finding and replacing a specific item:

1. Click Replace in the Editing group on the HOME tab of Word or PowerPoint.
2. Or click Find & Select in the Editing group on the HOME tab of Excel. Then click Replace. The dialog box that displays enables you to indicate the word or phrase to find and replace.

The Advanced Find feature is one that you will use often as you work with documents in Word. It is beneficial to find each occurrence of a word you are searching for. But it is also very helpful to see all the occurrences of the word at once. Click Reading Highlight in the *Find and Replace* dialog box and select Highlight All to display each word highlighted, as shown in Figure 1.44. Click Reading Highlight again and select Clear Highlighting to remove the illumination.

FIGURE 1.44 Highlight All

TIP Using a Shortcut to Find Items

Ctrl+F is a shortcut used to find items in a Word, Excel, or PowerPoint file. When you press Ctrl+F, the *Find and Replace* dialog box displays in Excel and PowerPoint. Pressing Ctrl+F in Word displays a feature—the Navigation Pane—at the left side of a Word document. When you type a search term in the Search Document area, Word finds and highlights all occurrences of the search term. The Navigation Pane also makes it easy to move to sections of a document based on levels of headings.

To find and replace selected text, type the text to locate in the *Find what* box and the replacement text in the *Replace with* box. You can narrow the search to require matching case or find whole words only. If you want to replace all occurrences of the text, click Replace All. If you want to replace only some occurrences, click Find Next repeatedly until you reach the occurrence that you want to replace. At that point, click Replace. When you are finished, click the Close button (or click Cancel).

Use Advanced Find and Replace Features

The *Find and Replace* feature enables you not only to find and replace text, but also to restrict and alter the format of the text at the same time. To establish the format criteria associated with either the *Find or Replace* portion of the operation:

1. Click the More button to expand the dialog box options. Click Format in the bottom-left corner of the dialog box.
2. Add formatting characteristics from the Font dialog box or Paragraph dialog box (as well as many other formatting features).

In addition to applying special formatting parameters on a *Find and Replace* operation, you can specify that you want to find or replace special characters. Click Special at the bottom of the *Find and Replace* dialog box to view the punctuation characters from which you can choose. For example, you might want to look for all instances in a document where an exclamation point is being used and replace it with a period.

An Excel worksheet can include more than 1,000,000 rows of data. A Word document's length is unlimited. Moving to a specific point in large files created in either of those applications can be a challenge. That task is simplified by the Go To option, found in the Editing group as an option of the Find command in Word (or under Find & Select in Excel). Click Go To and enter the page number (or other item, such as section, comment, bookmark, or footnote) in Word or the specific Excel cell. Click Go To in Word (or OK in Excel).

Quick Concepts

1. After selecting text in a presentation or document, you see a small transparent bar with formatting options displayed just above the selection. What is the bar called and what is its purpose? *p. 46*

2. What is the difference between using a single-click on the Format Painter and using a double-click? *p. 50*

3. What is the first step in cutting or copying text? How are cutting and copying related to the concept of the Clipboard? *p. 51*

4. What feature can you use to very quickly locate and replace text in a document? Provide an example of when you might want to find text but not replace it. *p. 52*

Hands-On Exercises

Watch the Video
for this Hands-
On Exercise!

MyITLab®
HOE5 Training

5 Home Tab Tasks

You have created a list of potential contributors to the Spotted Begonia Art Gallery. You have used Excel to record that list in worksheet format. Now you will review the worksheet and format its appearance to make it more attractive. You will also modify a promotional flyer. In working with those projects, you will put into practice the formatting, copying, moving, and editing information from the preceding section.

Skills covered: Move, Copy, and Paste Text • Select Text, Apply Font Attributes, and Use the Mini Toolbar • Use Format Painter and Work with the Mini Toolbar • Use the Font Dialog Box and Find and Replace Text

STEP 1 >> MOVE, COPY, AND PASTE TEXT

Each contributor to the Spotted Begonia Art Gallery is assigned a contact person. You manage the worksheet that keeps track of those assignments, but the assignments sometimes change. You will copy and paste some worksheet selections to keep from having to retype data. You will also reposition a clip art image to improve the worksheet's appearance. Refer to Figure 1.45 as you complete Step 1.

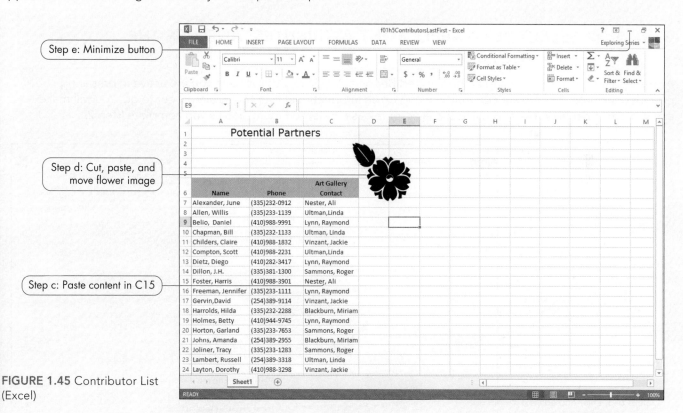

FIGURE 1.45 Contributor List (Excel)

a. Navigate to the Start screen. Scroll across the tiles, if necessary, and click **Excel 2013**. Click **Open Other Workbooks**.

    You have opened Microsoft Excel because it is the program in which the contributors list is saved.

b. Open the student data file *f01h5Contributors*. Save the file as **f01h5Contributors_LastFirst** in the Office Records folder (a subfolder of Artists) you created.

    The potential contributors list shown in Figure 1.45 is displayed.

c. Click **cell C7** to select the cell that contains *Nester, Ali*, and click **Copy** in the Clipboard group on the HOME tab. Click **cell C15** to select the cell that contains *Sammons, Roger*, click **Paste** in the Clipboard group, and then press **Esc** to remove the selection from *Nester, Ali*.

Ali Nester has been assigned as the Spotted Begonia Art Gallery contact for Harris Foster, replacing Roger Sammons. You make that replacement on the worksheet by copying and pasting Ali Nester's name in the appropriate worksheet cell.

d. Click the picture of the begonia. A box displays around the image, indicating that it is selected. Click **Cut** in the Clipboard group, click **cell D2**, and then click **Paste**. Drag the picture to resize and position it as needed (see Figure 1.45) so that it does not block any information in the list. Click anywhere outside the begonia picture to deselect it.

You decide that the picture of the begonia will look better if it is placed on the right side of the worksheet instead of the left. You move the picture by cutting and pasting the object.

> **TROUBLESHOOTING:** A Paste Options icon might display in the worksheet after you have moved the begonia picture. It offers additional options related to the paste procedure. You do not need to change any options, so ignore the button.

e. Click **Save** on the Quick Access Toolbar. Click **Minimize** to minimize the worksheet without closing it.

STEP 2 » SELECT TEXT, APPLY FONT ATTRIBUTES, AND USE THE MINI TOOLBAR

As the opening of a new showing at the Spotted Begonia Art Gallery draws near, you are active in preparing promotional materials. You are currently working on an informational flyer that is almost set to go. You will make a few improvements before approving the flyer for release. Refer to Figure 1.46 as you complete Step 2.

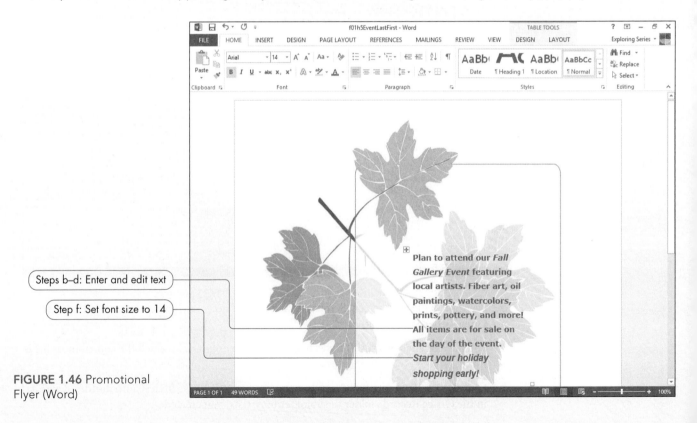

Steps b–d: Enter and edit text

Step f: Set font size to 14

FIGURE 1.46 Promotional Flyer (Word)

a. Navigate to the Start screen. Scroll across the tiles, if necessary, and click **Word 2013**. Click **Open Other Documents**. Open *f01h5Event* and save the document as **f01h5Event_LastFirst** in the Promotional Print folder (a subfolder of Artists) you created.

You plan to modify the promotional flyer slightly to include additional information about the Spotted Begonia Art Gallery.

> **TROUBLESHOOTING:** If you make any major mistakes in this exercise, you can close the file without saving it, open *f01h5Event* again, and then start this exercise over.

b. Click after the exclamation mark after the word *more* at the end of the first paragraph. Press **Enter** and type the following text. As you type, do not press Enter at the end of each line. Word will automatically wrap the lines of text.

All items are for sale on the day of the event. Start your holiday shopping early! You'll find gifts for everyone on your list.

> **TROUBLESHOOTING:** If you make any mistakes while typing, press Backspace and correct them.

c. Select the sentence beginning with *You'll find gifts*. Press **Delete**.

When you press Delete, selected text (or characters to the right of the insertion point) is removed. Deleted text is not placed in the Clipboard.

d. Select the words *Start your holiday shopping early!* Click **Italic** in the Font group on the HOME tab and click anywhere outside the selection to see the result.

e. Select both paragraphs but not the final italicized line. While still within the selection, move the mouse pointer slightly to display the Mini toolbar, click the **Font arrow** on the Mini toolbar, and then scroll to select **Verdana**.

> **TROUBLESHOOTING:** If you do not see the Mini toolbar, you might have moved too far away from the selection. In that case, click outside the selection and drag to select it once more. Without leaving the selection, move the mouse pointer slightly to display the Mini toolbar.

You have changed the font of the two paragraphs.

f. Click after the period following the word *event* before the last sentence in the second paragraph. Press **Enter** and press **Delete** to remove the extra space before the first letter, if necessary. Drag to select the new line, click **Font Size arrow** in the Font group, and then select **14**. Click anywhere outside the selected area. Your document should appear as shown in Figure 1.46.

You have increased font size to draw attention to the text.

g. Save the document and keep open for Step 3.

STEP 3 ⟩⟩ USE FORMAT PAINTER AND WORK WITH THE MINI TOOLBAR

You are on a short timeline for finalizing the promotional flyer, so you will use a few shortcuts to avoid retyping and reformatting more than is necessary. You know that you can easily copy formatting from one area to another using Format Painter. The Mini toolbar can also help you make changes quickly. Refer to Figure 1.47 as you complete Step 3.

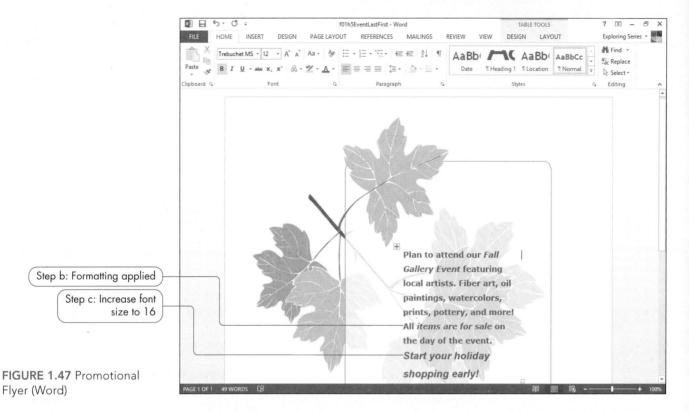

Step b: Formatting applied

Step c: Increase font size to 16

FIGURE 1.47 Promotional Flyer (Word)

a. Select the words *Fall Gallery Event* in the first paragraph and click **Format Painter** in the Clipboard group.

b. Select the words *items are for sale* in the sixth line. Click anywhere outside the selection to deselect the phrase.

The format of the area that you first selected (*Fall Gallery Event*) is applied to the line containing the phrase.

c. Select the text *Start your holiday shopping early!* in the Mini toolbar, click in the **Font Size box**, and then select **16** to increase the font size slightly. Click outside the selected area.

Figure 1.47 shows the final document as it should now appear.

d. Save the document as **f01h5Stp3Event_LastFirst** in the Promotional Print folder you created and close Word. Submit your file based on your instructor's directions.

The flyer will be saved with the same file name and in the same location as it was when you last saved the document in Step 2. As you close Word, the open document will also be closed.

STEP 4 ➤➤ USE THE FONT DIALOG BOX AND FIND AND REPLACE TEXT

The contributors worksheet is almost complete. However, you first want to make a few more formatting changes to improve the worksheet's appearance. You will also quickly change an incorrect area code by using Excel's *Find and Replace* feature. Refer to Figure 1.48 as you complete Step 4.

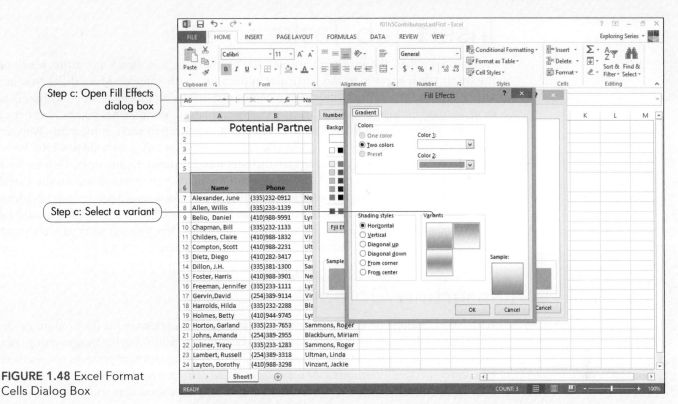

Step c: Open Fill Effects dialog box

Step c: Select a variant

FIGURE 1.48 Excel Format Cells Dialog Box

a. Click the **Excel icon** on the taskbar to redisplay the contributors worksheet that you minimized in Step 1.

The Excel potential contributors list displays.

> **TROUBLESHOOTING:** If you closed Excel, you can find the correct worksheet in your Recent Documents list.

b. Drag to select **cells A6** through **C6**.

> **TROUBLESHOOTING:** Make sure the mouse pointer looks like a large white plus sign before dragging. It is normal for the first cell in the selected area to be a different shade. If you click and drag when the mouse pointer does not resemble a white plus sign, text may be moved or duplicated. In that case, click Undo on the Quick Access Toolbar.

c. Click the **Dialog Box Launcher** in the Font group to display the Format Cells dialog box. Click the **Fill tab** and click **Fill Effects**, as shown in Figure 1.48. Click any style in the *Variants* section, click **OK**, and then click **OK** once more to close the Format Cells dialog box. Click outside the selected area to see the final result.

The headings of the worksheet are shaded more attractively.

d. Click **Find & Select** in the Editing group and click **Replace**. Type **410** in the **Find what box**. Type **411** in the **Replace with box**, click **Replace All**, and then click **OK** when notified that Excel has made seven replacements. Click **Close** in the *Find and Replace* dialog box.

You discovered that you consistently typed an incorrect area code. You used Find and Replace to make the corrections quickly.

e. Save the workbook as **f01h5Stp4Contributors_LastFirst** in the Office Records folder you created. Exit Excel, if necessary. Submit your files based on your instructor's directions.

Insert Tab Tasks

As its title implies, the Insert tab enables you to insert, or add, items into a file. Much of the Insert tab is specific to the particular application, with some commonalities to other Office applications. Word's Insert tab includes text-related commands, whereas Excel's is more focused on inserting such items as charts and tables. Word allows you to insert apps from the Microsoft app store, so you could add an application such as Merriam-Webster Dictionary. Both Word and Excel allow you to insert Apps for Office to build powerful Web-backed solutions. PowerPoint's Insert tab includes multimedia items and links. Despite their obvious differences in focus, all Office applications share a common group on the Insert tab—the Illustrations group. In addition, all Office applications enable you to insert headers, footers, text boxes, and symbols. Those options are also found on the Insert tab in various groups, depending on the particular application. In this section, you will work with common activities on the Insert tab, including inserting online pictures.

Inserting Objects

With few exceptions, all Office applications share common options in the Illustrations group of the Insert tab. PowerPoint places some of those common features in the Images group. You can insert pictures, shapes, and *SmartArt*. SmartArt is a diagram that presents information visually to effectively communicate a message. These items are considered objects, retaining their separate nature when they are inserted in files. That means that you can select them and manage them independently of the underlying document, worksheet, or presentation.

After an object has been inserted, you can click the object to select it or click anywhere outside the object to deselect it. When an object is selected, a border surrounds it with handles, or small dots, appearing at each corner and in the middle of each side. Figure 1.49 shows a selected object, surrounded by handles. Unless an object is selected, you cannot change or modify it. When an object is selected, the Ribbon expands to include one or more contextual tabs. Items on the contextual tabs relate to the selected object, enabling you to modify and manage it.

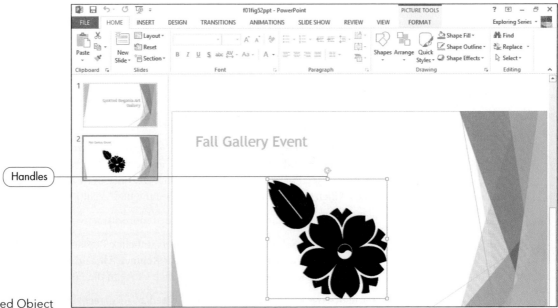

FIGURE 1.49 Selected Object

You can resize and move a selected object. Place the mouse pointer on any handle and drag (when the mouse pointer looks like a two-headed arrow) to resize the object. Be careful! If you drag a side handle, the object is likely to be skewed, possibly resulting in a poor image. Instead, drag a corner handle to proportionally resize the image. To move an object, drag the object when the mouse pointer looks like a four-headed arrow.

Insert Pictures

STEP 2 >> Documents, worksheets, and presentations can include much more than just words and numbers. You can easily add energy and additional description to the project by including pictures and other graphic elements. Although a *picture* is usually just that—a digital photo—it is actually defined as a graphic element retrieved from storage media such as a hard drive or a CD. A picture could actually be a clip art item that you saved from the Internet onto your hard drive.

The process of inserting a picture is simple.

1. Click in the project where you want the picture to be placed. Make sure you know where the picture that you plan to use is stored.
2. Click the INSERT tab.
3. Click Pictures in the Illustrations group (or Images group in PowerPoint). The Insert Picture dialog box is shown in Figure 1.50. You can also use Online Pictures to search for and insert pictures.
4. Navigate to where your picture is saved and click Insert (or simply double-click the picture).

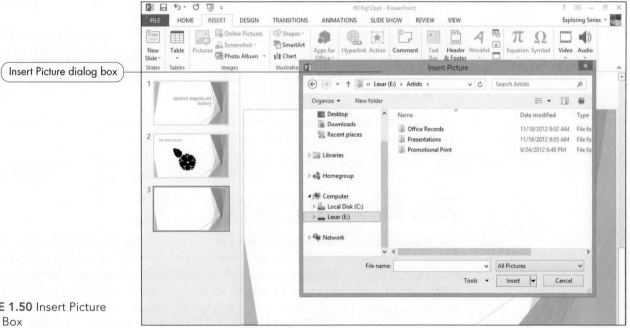

FIGURE 1.50 Insert Picture Dialog Box

In addition, on some slide layouts, PowerPoint displays Pictures and Online Pictures buttons that you can click to search for and select a picture for the slide.

Insert and Modify SmartArt

The SmartArt feature enables you to create a diagram and to enter text to provide a visual representation of data. To create a SmartArt diagram, choose a diagram type that fits the purpose: List, Process, Cycle, Hierarchy, Relationships, Matrix, Pyramid, and Picture. You can get additional SmartArt diagrams at Office.com. To insert a SmartArt object, do the following:

1. Click the INSERT tab.
2. Click SmartArt in the Illustrations group to display the Choose a SmartArt Graphic dialog box.
3. Click the type of SmartArt diagram you want in the left pane of the dialog box.
4. Click the SmartArt subtype from the center pane.
5. Preview the selected SmartArt and subtype in the right pane and click OK.

Once you select the SmartArt diagram type and the subtype, a Text pane opens in which you can enter text. The text you enter displays within the selected object. If the SmartArt diagram contains more objects than you need, click the object and press Delete.

The SmartArt Tools Design tab enables you to customize the design of a SmartArt diagram. You can modify the diagram by changing its layout, colors, and style. The layout controls the construction of the diagram. The style controls the visual effects, such as embossing and rounded corners of the diagram. The SmartArt Tools Format tab controls the shape fill color, border, and size options.

Insert and Format Shapes

You can insert a shape to add a visual effect to a worksheet. You can insert various types of lines, rectangles, basic shapes (such as an oval, a pie shape, or a smiley face), block arrows, equation shapes, flowchart shapes, stars and banners, and callouts. You can insert shapes, such as a callout, to draw attention to particular worksheet data. To insert a shape, do the following:

1. Click the INSERT tab.
2. Click Shapes in the Illustrations group.
3. Select the shape you want to insert from the Shapes gallery.
4. Drag the cross-hair pointer to create the shape in the worksheet where you want it to appear.

After you insert the shape, the Drawing Tools Format tab displays so that you can change the shape, apply a shape style with fill color, and adjust the size.

Review Tab Tasks

As a final touch, you should always check a project for spelling, grammatical, and word usage errors. If the project is a collaborative effort, you and your colleagues might add comments and suggest changes. You can even use a thesaurus to find synonyms for words that are not quite right for your purpose. The Review tab in each Office application provides all these options and more. In this section, you will learn to review a file, checking for spelling and grammatical errors. You will also learn to use a thesaurus to identify synonyms.

Reviewing a File

As you create or edit a file, you will want to make sure no spelling or grammatical errors exist. You will also be concerned with wording, being sure to select words and phrases that best represent the purpose of the document, worksheet, or presentation. On occasion, you might even find yourself at a loss for an appropriate word. Not to worry. Word, Excel, and PowerPoint all provide standard tools for proofreading, including a spelling and grammar checker and a thesaurus.

Check Spelling and Grammar

STEP 1 » In general, all Office applications check your spelling and grammar as you type. If a word is unrecognized, it is flagged as misspelled or grammatically incorrect. Misspellings are identified with a red wavy underline, grammatical problems are underlined in green, and word usage errors (such as using *bear* instead of *bare*) have a blue underline. If the word or phrase is truly in error—that is, it is not a person's name or an unusual term that is not in the application's dictionary—you can correct it manually, or you can let the software correct it for you. If you right-click a word or phrase that is identified as a mistake, you will see a shortcut menu similar to that shown in Figure 1.51. If the application's dictionary can make a suggestion as to the correct spelling, you can click to accept the suggestion and make the change. If a grammatical rule is violated, you will have an opportunity to select a correction. However, if the text is actually correct, you can click Ignore or Ignore All (to bypass all occurrences of the flagged error in the current document). Click *Add to Dictionary* if you want the word to be considered correct whenever it appears in all documents. Similar selections on a shortcut menu enable you to ignore grammatical mistakes if they are not errors.

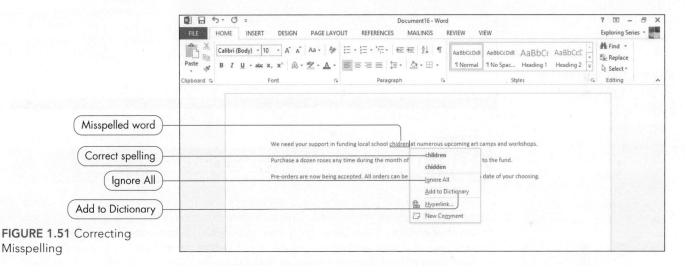

FIGURE 1.51 Correcting Misspelling

You might prefer the convenience of addressing possible misspellings and grammatical errors without having to examine each underlined word or phrase. To do so, click Spelling & Grammar in the Proofing group on the Review tab. Beginning at the top of the document, each identified error is highlighted in a pane similar to Figure 1.52. You can then choose how to address the problem by making a selection from the options in the pane.

Spelling pane

FIGURE 1.52 Checking for Spelling and Grammatical Errors

Many Office settings are considered **_default_** options. Thus, unless you specify otherwise, the default options are in effect. One such default option is the automatic spelling and grammar checker. If you prefer to enable and disable certain options or change default settings in an Office application, you can click the FILE tab and select Options. From that point, you can work through a series of categories, selecting or deselecting options at will. For example, if you want to change how the application corrects and formats text, you can select or deselect settings in the Proofing group.

Use the Thesaurus

As you write, there will be times when you are at a loss for an appropriate word. Perhaps you feel that you are overusing a word and want to find a suitable substitute. The Thesaurus is the Office tool to use in such a situation. Located in the Proofing group on the Review tab, Thesaurus enables you to search for synonyms, or words with similar meanings. Select a word and click Thesaurus in the Proofing group on the Review tab. A task pane displays on the right side of the screen, and synonyms are listed similar to those shown in Figure 1.53. You can also use the Thesaurus before typing a word to find substitutes. Simply click Thesaurus and type the word for which you are seeking a synonym in the Search box. Press Enter or click the magnifying glass to the right of the Search box for some suggestions. Finally, you can also identify synonyms when you right-click a word and point to Synonyms (if any are available). Click any word from the options offered to place it in the document.

Thesaurus pane

FIGURE 1.53 Thesaurus

Page Layout Tab Tasks

When you prepare a document or worksheet, you are concerned with the way the project appears onscreen and possibly in print. Unlike Word and Excel, a PowerPoint presentation is usually designed as a slide show, so it is not nearly as critical to concern yourself with page layout settings. The Page Layout tab in Word and Excel provides access to a full range of options such as margin settings and page orientation. In this section, you will identify page layout settings that are common to Office applications.

Because a document is most often designed to be printed, you will want to make sure it looks its best in printed form. That means that you will need to know how to adjust margins and how to change the page orientation. Perhaps the document or spreadsheet should be centered on the page vertically or the text should be aligned in columns. By adjusting page settings, you can do all these things and more. You will find the most common page settings, such as margins and page orientation, in the Page Setup group on the Page Layout tab. For less common settings, such as determining whether headers should print on odd or even pages, you can use the Page Setup dialog box.

Changing Margins

A *margin* is the area of blank space that displays to the left, right, top, and bottom of a document or worksheet. Margins are evident only if you are in Print Layout or Page Layout view or if you are in the Backstage view, previewing a document to print. To set or change margins, click the Page Layout tab. As shown in Figure 1.54, the Page Setup group enables you to change such items as margins and orientation. To change margins:

1. Click Margins in the Page Setup group on the PAGE LAYOUT tab.
2. If the margins that you intend to use are included in any of the preset margin options, click a selection. Otherwise, click Custom Margins to display the Page Setup dialog box in which you can create custom margin settings.
3. Click OK to accept the settings and close the dialog box.

You can also change margins when you click Print on the File tab.

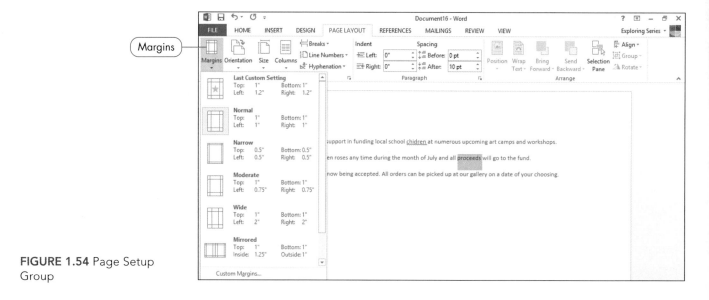

FIGURE 1.54 Page Setup
Group

Changing Page Orientation

STEP 3 >> Documents and worksheets can be displayed in *portrait* orientation or in *landscape*. A page displayed or printed in portrait orientation is taller than it is wide. A page in landscape orientation is wider than it is tall. Word documents are usually more attractive displayed in portrait orientation, whereas Excel worksheets are often more suitable in landscape. To select page orientation, click Orientation in the Page Setup group on the Page Layout tab (see Figure 1.55). Orientation is also an option in the Print area of the Backstage view.

Using the Page Setup Dialog Box

The Page Setup group contains the most commonly used page options in the particular Office application. Some are unique to Excel, and others are more applicable to Word. Other less common settings are available in the Page Setup dialog box only, displayed when you click the Page Setup Dialog Box Launcher. The subsequent dialog box includes options for customizing margins, selecting page orientation, centering vertically, printing gridlines, and creating headers and footers, although some of those options are available only when working with Word; others are unique to Excel. Figure 1.55 shows both the Excel and Word Page Setup dialog boxes.

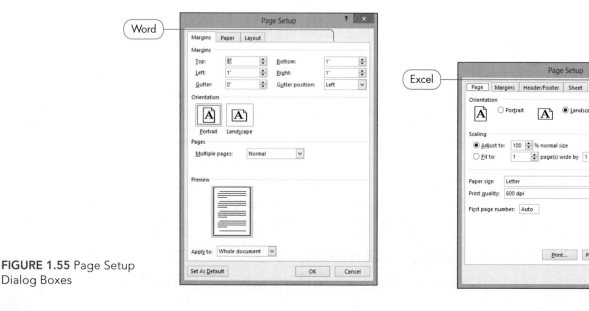

FIGURE 1.55 Page Setup
Dialog Boxes

Quick Concepts ✓

1. Give two ways to resize an object, such as a picture, that has been inserted in a document. *p. 61*

2. Often, an Office application will identify a word as misspelled that is not actually misspelled. How can that happen? If a word is flagged as misspelled, how can you correct it (or ignore it if it is not actually an error)? *p. 63*

3. Give two ways to change a document from a portrait orientation to landscape. Identify at least one document type that you think would be better suited for landscape orientation rather than portrait. *p. 66*

4. What dialog box includes options for selecting margins, centering vertically, and changing page orientation? *p. 66*

Hands-On Exercises

Watch the Video for this Hands-On Exercise!

MyITLab®
HOE6 Training

6 Insert Tab Tasks, Page Layout Tab Tasks, and Review Tab Tasks

A series of enrichment programs at the Spotted Begonia Art Gallery is nearing kickoff. You are helping plan a ceremony to commemorate the occasion. To encourage interest and participation, you will edit a PowerPoint presentation that is to be shown to civic groups, the local retiree association, and to city and county leaders to solicit additional funding. You know that pictures add energy to a presentation when used appropriately, so you will check for those elements, adding whatever is necessary. A major concern is making sure the presentation is error free and that it is available in print so that meeting participants can review it later. As a reminder, you also plan to have available a handout giving the time and date of the dedication ceremony. You will use the Insert tab to work with illustrations and the Review tab to check for errors, and you will use Word to generate an attractive handout as a reminder of the date.

Skills covered: Check Spelling and Use the Thesaurus • Insert Pictures • Change Margins and Page Orientation

STEP 1 ≫ CHECK SPELLING AND USE THE THESAURUS

As you check the PowerPoint presentation that will be shown to local groups, you make sure no misspellings or grammatical mistakes exist. You also use the Thesaurus to find a suitable substitution for a word you feel should be replaced. Refer to Figure 1.56 as you complete Step 1.

FIGURE 1.56 Project Presentation

a. Navigate to the Start screen. Scroll across the tiles, if necessary, and click **PowerPoint 2013**. Click **Open Other Presentations**. Open *f01h6Programs* and save the document as **f01h6Programs_LastFirst** in the Promotional Print folder (a subfolder of Artists) you created.

The PowerPoint presentation opens, with Slide 1 shown in Normal view.

b. Click the **SLIDE SHOW tab** and click **From Beginning** in the Start Slide Show group to view the presentation. Click to advance from one slide to another. After the last slide, click to return to Normal view.

c. Click the **REVIEW tab** and click **Spelling** in the Proofing group. Correct any words that are misspelled by clicking the correction and clicking Change or Ignore in the Spelling pane. Click **Change** to accept *Creativity* on Slide 2, click **workshops** and click **Change** on Slide 3, and click **Change** to accept *Thank* for Slide 5. Refer to Figure 1.56. Click **OK** when the spell check is complete and close the pane.

d. Click **Slide 2** in the Slides pane on the left. Double-click the bulleted word *Creativity*, click **Thesaurus** in the Proofing group, point to *Imagination* in the Thesaurus pane, click the arrow to the right of the word, and then select **Insert**.

The word *Creativity* is replaced with the word *Imagination*.

e. Click the **Close (X) button** in the top-right corner of the Thesaurus pane.

f. Save the presentation.

STEP 2 ≫ INSERT PICTURES

Although the presentation provides the necessary information and encourages viewers to become active participants in the enrichment programs, you believe that pictures might make it a little more exciting. Where appropriate, you will include a picture. Refer to Figure 1.57 as you complete Step 2.

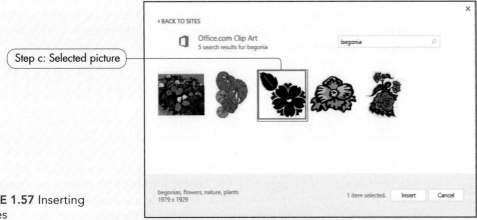

Step c: Selected picture

FIGURE 1.57 Inserting Pictures

a. Click **Slide 2** in the Slides pane on the left, if necessary. Click the **INSERT tab** and click **Online Pictures** in the Images group.

The Insert Pictures pane displays on the screen.

> **TROUBLESHOOTING:** You can add your own pictures to slides using the Pictures command. Or you can copy and paste images directly from a Web page.

b. Type **begonia** in the **Office.com Clip Art search box** and press **Enter**.

You will identify pictures that may be displayed on Slide 2.

c. Click to select the black flower shown in Figure 1.57 or use a similar image. Click **Insert**.

The picture may not be placed as you would like, but you will move and resize it in the next substep as necessary. Also, notice that the picture is selected, as indicated by the box and handles surrounding it.

> **TROUBLESHOOTING:** It is very easy to make the mistake of inserting duplicate pictures on a slide, perhaps because you clicked the image more than once in the task pane. If that should happen, you can remove any unwanted picture by clicking to select it and pressing Delete.

d. Click a corner handle—the small square on the border of the picture. Make sure the mouse pointer appears as a double-headed arrow. Drag to resize the image so that it fits well on the slide. Click in the center of the picture. The mouse pointer should appear as a four-headed arrow. Drag the picture slightly to the right corner of the slide. Make sure the picture is still selected (it should be surrounded by a box and handles). If it is not selected, click to select it.

> **TROUBLESHOOTING:** You may not need to perform this substep if the picture came in as desired. Proceed to the next substep if this occurs.

e. Click **Slide 5** in the Slides pane on the left. Click the **INSERT tab** and select **Online Pictures**. Type **happy art** in the **Office.com Clip Art search box** and press **Enter**. Click the **Three handprints picture** and click **Insert**.

A picture is placed on the final slide.

f. Click to select the picture, if necessary. Drag a corner handle to resize the picture. Click the center of the picture and drag the picture to reposition it in the bottom-right corner of the slide, as shown in Figure 1.57.

> **TROUBLESHOOTING:** You can only move the picture when the mouse pointer looks like a four-headed arrow. If instead you drag a handle, the picture will be resized instead of moved. Click Undo on the Quick Access Toolbar and begin again.

g. Click **Slide 3**. Click the **INSERT tab**, click **Online Pictures**, and then search for **school art**. Select and insert the picture named **Art Teacher working with student on a project in school**. Using the previously practiced technique, resize the image height to **3.9"** and position as necessary to add the picture to the right side of the slide.

h. Save the presentation and exit PowerPoint. Submit your file based on your instructor's directions.

STEP 3 ≫ CHANGE MARGINS AND PAGE ORIENTATION

You are ready to finalize the flyer promoting the workshops, but before printing it you want to see how it will look. You wonder if it would be better in landscape or portrait orientation, so you will try both. After adjusting the margins, you are ready to save the flyer for later printing and distribution. Refer to Figure 1.58 as you complete Step 3.

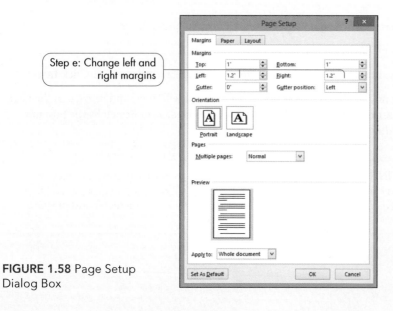

Step e: Change left and right margins

FIGURE 1.58 Page Setup Dialog Box

a. Navigate to the Start screen. Scroll across the tiles, if necessary, and click **Word 2013**. Click **Open Other Documents**. Open *f01h6Handout* and save the document as **f01h6Handout_ LastFirst** in the Promotional Print folder (a subfolder of Artists) you created.

b. Click the **PAGE LAYOUT tab**, click **Orientation** in the Page Setup group, and then select **Landscape** to view the flyer in landscape orientation.

   You want to see how the handout will look in landscape orientation.

c. Click the **FILE tab**, click **Print**, and then click **Next Page** and click **Previous Page** (right- and left-pointing arrows at the bottom center of the preview page).

   The second page of the handout shows only the last two bullets and the contact information. You can see that the two-page layout is not an attractive option.

d. Click the **Back arrow** in the top-left corner. Click **Undo** on the Quick Access Toolbar. Click the **FILE tab** and click **Print**.

   The document fits on one page. Portrait orientation is a much better choice for the handout.

e. Click the **Back arrow** in the top-left corner. Click the **PAGE LAYOUT tab** if necessary, click **Margins** in the Page Setup group, and then select **Custom Margins**. Click the **spin arrow** beside the left margin box to increase the margin to **1.2**. Similarly, change the right margin to **1.2**. Refer to Figure 1.58. Click **OK**.

f. Save the document and exit Word. Submit your file based on your instructor's directions.

Chapter Objectives Review

After reading this chapter, you have accomplished the following objectives:

1. **Log in with your Microsoft account.**
   - Your Microsoft account connects you to all of Microsoft's Internet-based resources.

2. **Identify the Start screen components.**
   - The Start screen has a sleek, clean interface that is made up of tiles and Charms.

3. **Interact with the Start screen.**
   - Customize the Start screen to access programs and apps.

4. **Access the desktop.**
   - Simplified to accommodate mobile devices, laptops, and desktops.

5. **Use File Explorer.**
   - Understand and customize the interface: Change the view to provide as little or as much detail as you need.
   - Work with groups on the Navigation Pane: Provides access to all resources, folders, and files.

6. **Work with folders and files.**
   - Create a folder: A well-named folder structure can be created in File Explorer or within a program as you save a file.
   - Open, rename, and delete folders and files: File Explorer can be used to perform these tasks.
   - Save a file: When saving a file for the first time, you need to indicate the location and the name of the file.

7. **Select, copy, and move multiple files and folders.**
   - Select multiple files and folders: Folders and files can be selected as a group.
   - Copy and move files and folders: Folders and the files within them can be easily moved to the same or a different drive.

8. **Identify common interface components.**
   - Use the Backstage view and the Quick Access Toolbar: The Backstage view can perform several commands.
   - Familiarize yourself with the Ribbon: Provides access to common tasks.
   - Use the status bar: The status bar provides information relative to the open file and quick access to View and Zoom level options.

9. **Get Office Help.**
   - Use Office Help: The Help button links to online resources and technical support.
   - Use Enhanced ScreenTips: Provides the purpose of a command button as you point to it.
   - Get help with dialog boxes: Use the Help button in the top-right corner of a dialog box to get help relevant to the task.

10. **Open a file.**
    - Create a new file: A document can be created as a blank document or with a template.
    - Open a file using the Open dialog box: Previously saved files can be located and opened using a dialog box.
    - Open a file using the Recent Documents list: Documents that you have worked with recently display here.
    - Open a file from the Templates list: Templates are a convenient way to save time when designing a document.

11. **Print a file.**
    - Check and change orientation or perform other commands related to the look of your file before printing.

12. **Close a file and application.**
    - Close files you are not working on to avoid becoming overwhelmed.

13. **Select and edit text.**
    - Select text to edit: Commit to memory: "Select, then do."
    - Use the Mini toolbar: Provides instant access to common formatting commands after text is selected.
    - Apply font attributes: These can be applied to selected text with toggle commands.
    - Change the font: Choose from a set of fonts found within all Office applications.
    - Change the font size, color, and attributes: These commands are located in the Font group on the Ribbon.

14. **Use the Clipboard group commands.**
    - Copy formats with the Format Painter: Copy formatting features from one section of text to another.
    - Move and copy text: Text can be selected, copied, and moved between applications or within the same application.
    - Use the Office Clipboard: This pane stores up to 24 cut or copied selections for use later on in your computing session.

15. **Use the Editing group commands.**
    - Find and replace text: Finds each occurrence of a series of characters and replaces them with another series.
    - Use advanced find and replace feature: Change the format of every occurrence of a series of characters.

16. **Insert objects.**
    - Insert pictures: You can insert pictures from a CD or other media, or from an online resource such as Office.com.
    - Insert and modify SmartArt: Create a diagram and to enter text to provide a visual of data.
    - Insert and format shapes: You can insert various types of lines and basic shapes.

17. **Review a file.**
    - Check spelling and grammar: All Office applications check and mark these error types as you type for later correction.
    - Use the Thesaurus: Enables you to search for synonyms.

18. **Use the Page Setup dialog box.**
    - Change margins: You can control the amount of blank space that surrounds the text in your document.
    - Change margins and page orientations, and create header and footers.

Key Terms Matching

Match the key terms with their definitions. Write the key term letter by the appropriate numbered definition.

a. Backstage view
b. Charms
c. Cloud storage
d. Find
e. Font
f. Format Painter
g. Group
h. Mini toolbar
i. Navigation Pane
j. Operating system

k. Quick Access Toolbar
l. Ribbon
m. OneDrive
n. Snip
o. Snipping Tool
p. Start screen
q. Subfolder
r. Tile
s. Windows 8.1.1
t. Windows 8.1.1 app

1. _____ A tool that copies all formatting from one area to another. **p. 49**

2. _____ Software that directs computer activities such as checking all components, managing system resources, and communicating with application software. **p. 2**

3. _____ A task-oriented section of the Ribbon that contains related commands. **p. 25**

4. _____ An app used to store, access, and share files and folders. **p. 2**

5. _____ Any of the several colorful block images found on the Start screen that when clicked takes you to a program, file, folder, or other Windows 8.1.1 app. **p. 3**

6. _____ A component of Office 2013 that provides a concise collection of commands related to an open file. **p. 23**

7. _____ A tool that displays near selected text that contains formatting commands. **p. 46**

8. _____ A level of folder structure indicated as a folder within another folder. **p. 10**

9. _____ An application specifically designed to run in the Start screen interface of Windows 8.1.1. **p. 3**

10. _____ A command used to locate each occurrence of a series of characters. **p. 52**

11. _____ A Windows 8.1.1 accessory program that allows you to capture a screen display so that you can save, annotate, or share it. **p. 5**

12. _____ What you see after starting your Windows 8.1.1 computer and entering your username and password. **p. 2**

13. _____ Provides handy access to commonly executed tasks such as saving a file and undoing recent actions. **p. 23**

14. _____ A Microsoft operating system released in 2012 that is available on laptops, desktops, and tablet computers. **p. 2**

15. _____ A component made up of five icons that provide similar functionality to the Start button found in previous versions of Windows. **p. 3**

16. _____ The captured screen display created by the Snipping Tool. **p. 5**

17. _____ The long bar located just beneath the title bar containing tabs, groups, and commands. **p. 25**

18. _____ Provides access to computer resources, folders, files, and networked peripherals. **p. 11**

19. _____ A technology used to store files and to work with programs that are stored in a central location on the Internet. **p. 2**

20. _____ A character design or the way characters display onscreen. **p. 45**

Multiple Choice

1. The Recent Documents list shows documents that have been previously:
   (a) Printed.
   (b) Opened.
   (c) Saved in an earlier software version.
   (d) Deleted.

2. Which of the following File Explorer features collects related data from folders and gives them a single name?
   (a) Network
   (b) Favorites
   (c) Libraries
   (d) Computer

3. When you want to copy the format of a selection but not the content, you should:
   (a) Double-click Copy in the Clipboard group.
   (b) Right-click the selection and click Copy.
   (c) Click Copy Format in the Clipboard group.
   (d) Click Format Painter in the Clipboard group.

4. Which of the following is *not* a benefit of using OneDrive?
   (a) Save your folders and files in the cloud.
   (b) Share your files and folders with others.
   (c) Hold video conferences with others.
   (d) Simultaneously work on the same document with others.

5. What does a red wavy underline in a document, spreadsheet, or presentation mean?
   (a) A word is misspelled or not recognized by the Office dictionary
   (b) A grammatical mistake exists
   (c) An apparent word usage mistake exists
   (d) A word has been replaced with a synonym

6. When you close a file:
   (a) You are prompted to save the file (unless you have made no changes since last saving it).
   (b) The application (Word, Excel, or PowerPoint) is also closed.
   (c) You must first save the file.
   (d) You must change the file name.

7. Live Preview:
   (a) Opens a predesigned document or spreadsheet that is relevant to your task.
   (b) Provides a preview of the results of a choice you are considering before you make a final selection.
   (c) Provides a preview of an upcoming Office version.
   (d) Enlarges the font onscreen.

8. You can get help when working with an Office application in which one of the following areas?
   (a) Help button
   (b) Status bar
   (c) The Backstage view
   (d) Quick Access Toolbar

9. The *Find and Replace* feature enables you to do which of the following?
   (a) Find all instances of misspelling and automatically correct (or replace) them
   (b) Find any grammatical errors and automatically correct (or replace) them
   (c) Find any specified font settings and replace them with another selection
   (d) Find any character string and replace it with another

10. A document or worksheet printed in landscape orientation is:
    (a) Taller than it is wide.
    (b) Wider than it is tall.
    (c) A document with 2" left and right margins.
    (d) A document with 2" top and bottom margins.

Practice Exercises

1 Designing Web Pages

You have been asked to make a presentation to the local business association. With the mayor's renewed emphasis on growing the local economy, many businesses are interested in establishing a Web presence. The business owners would like to know a little bit more about how Web pages are designed. In preparation for the presentation, you need to proofread and edit your PowerPoint file. This exercise follows the same set of skills as used in Hands-On Exercises 1–6 in the chapter. Refer to Figure 1.59 as you complete this exercise.

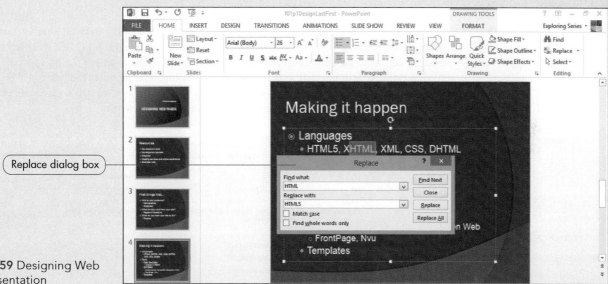

FIGURE 1.59 Designing Web Pages Presentation

a. Click **File Explorer** on the taskbar and select the location where you save your files. Click the **HOME tab** and click **New folder** in the New group. Type **Designing Web Pages** and press **Enter**.

Take a snip, name it **f01p1DesignSnip_LastFirst**, and then save it in the Designing Web Pages folder. Close File Explorer.

b. Point to the bottom-right corner of your screen to display the Charms and click the **Start charm**. Scroll if necessary and click **PowerPoint 2013** to start PowerPoint. Open *f01p1Design* and save it as **f01p1Design_LastFirst** in the Designing Web Pages folder. In Slide 1, drag to select the text *Firstname Lastname* and type your own first and last names. Click an empty area of the slide to cancel the selection.

c. Click the **REVIEW tab** and click **Spelling** in the Proofing group. In the Spelling pane, click **Change** or **Ignore** to make or not make a change as needed. Most identified misspellings should be changed. The words *KompoZer* and *Nvu* are not misspelled, so you should ignore them when they are flagged. Click **OK** to end the spell check.

d. Click the **SLIDE SHOW tab**. Click **From Beginning** in the Start Slide Show group. Click each slide to view the show and press **Esc** on the last slide.

e. Click **Slide 2** in the Slides pane on the left. Drag to select the *Other tools* text and press **Backspace** on the keyboard to delete the text.

f. Click **Slide 4** in the Slides pane. Click the **HOME tab** and click **Replace** in the Editing group. Type **HTML** in the **Find what box** and **HTML5** in the **Replace with box**. Click **Find Next**. Read the slide and click **Replace** to change the first instance of *HTML*. Refer to Figure 1.59. Click **Close**.

g. Click **Replace** in the Editing group. Type **CSS** in the **Find what box** and **CSS5** in the **Replace with box**. Click **Replace All** and click **OK**. Click **Close**.

h. Drag to select the *FrontPage, Nvu* text and press **Backspace** on the keyboard to delete the text.

i. Press **Ctrl+End** to place the insertion point at the end of *Templates* and press **Enter**. Type **Database Connectivity** to create a new bulleted item.

j. Click the **FILE tab** and click **Print**. Click the **Full Page Slides arrow** and click **6 Slides Horizontal** to see a preview of all of the slides as a handout. Click the **Back arrow** and click the **HOME tab**.

k. Click **Slide 1** in the Slides pane to move to the beginning of the presentation.

l. Drag the **Zoom slider** on the status bar to the right to **130%** to magnify the text. Then use the **Zoom Slider** to return to **60%**.

m. Save and close the file. Submit your files based on your instructor's directions.

2 ## Upscale Bakery

You have always been interested in baking and have worked in the field for several years. You now have an opportunity to devote yourself full time to your career as the CEO of a company dedicated to baking cupcakes, pastries, and catering. One of the first steps in getting the business off the ground is developing a business plan so that you can request financial support. You will use Word to develop your business plan. This exercise follows the same set of skills as used in Hands-On Exercises 1, 3, 4, and 5 in the chapter. Refer to Figure 1.60 as you complete this exercise.

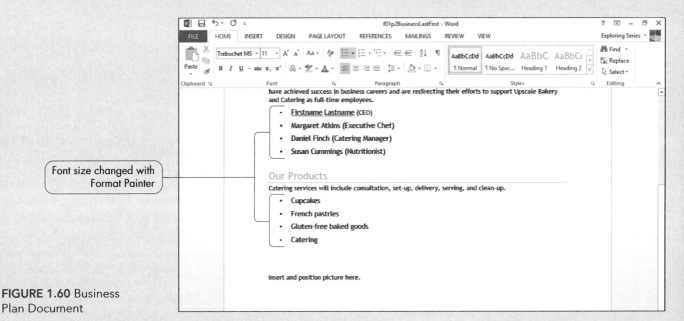

FIGURE 1.60 Business Plan Document

a. Click **File Explorer** on the taskbar and select the location where you save your files. Click the **HOME tab** and click **New folder** in the New group. Type **Business Plan** and press **Enter**.

Take a snip, name it **f01p2BusinessSnip_LastFirst**, and save it in the Business Plan folder. Close File Explorer.

b. Point to the bottom-right corner of your screen to display the Charms and click the **Start charm**. Scroll if necessary and click **Word 2013** to start Word. Open *f01p2Business* and save it as **f01p2Business_LastFirst** in the Business Plan folder.

c. Click the **REVIEW tab** and click **Spelling & Grammar** in the Proofing group. Click **Change** for all suggestions.

d. Drag the paragraphs beginning with *Our Staff* and ending with *(Nutritionist)*. Click the **HOME tab** and click **Cut** in the Clipboard group. Click to the left of *Our Products* and click **Paste**.

e. Select the text *Your name* in the first bullet and replace it with your first and last names. Select that entire bullet and use the Mini toolbar to use Live Preview to see some other Font sizes. Then click **11** to increase the size.

f. Double-click the **Format Painter** in the Clipboard group on the HOME tab. Drag the Format Painter to change the other *Our Staff* bullets to **11**. Drag all four *Our Products* bullets. Click the **Format Painter button** to toggle it off and click outside of the text to deselect it. Refer to Figure 1.60.

g. Select the last line in the document, which says *Insert and position picture here.*, and press **Delete**. Click the **INSERT tab** and click **Online Pictures** in the Illustrations group.

- Click in the **Office.com Clip Art search box**, type **Cupcakes**, and then press **Enter**.
- Select **Cupcake with a single birthday candle** or select any image and click **Insert**. Do not deselect the image.
- Click the **PICTURE TOOLS FORMAT tab**, if necessary, click the **More button** in the Picture Styles group, and then click the **Soft Edge Rectangle** (sixth from the left on the top row).
- Click outside the picture.

h. Click the **FILE tab** and click **Print**. Change *Normal Margins* to **Moderate Margins**. Click the **Back arrow**.

i. Click the picture and click **Center** in the Paragraph group on the HOME tab.

j. Save and close the file. Submit your files based on your instructor's directions.

3 Best Friends Pet Care

You and a friend are starting a pet sitting service and have a few clients already. Billing will be a large part of your record keeping, so you are planning ahead by developing a series of folders to maintain those records. This exercise follows the same set of skills as used in Hands-On Exercises 1, 2, and 5 in the chapter. Refer to Figure 1.61 as you complete this exercise.

FIGURE 1.61 Best Friends Pet Care

a. Click **File Explorer** on the taskbar and select the location where you save your files. Click the **Home tab** and click **New folder** in the New group. Type **Best Friends** and press **Enter**.

b. Double-click **Best Friends** in the Content pane to open the folder. Create new subfolders as follows:

- Click the **Home tab** and click **New folder** in the New group. Type **Business Letters** and press **Enter**.
- Click the **Home tab** and click **New folder** in the New group. Type **Billing Records** and press **Enter**. Compare your results to Figure 1.61. Take a snip and name it **f01p3FriendsSnip_LastFirst**. Save it in the Billing Records subfolder of the Best Friends folder. Close File Explorer.

c. Navigate to the Start screen and click on **Word 2013**. Click **Open Other Documents** and open *f01p3Friends*. Save it as **f01p3Friends_LastFirst** in the Business Letters subfolder of the Best Friends folder.

d. Use *Find and Replace* to replace the text *Your Name* with your name by doing the following:

- Click **Replace** in the Editing group on the HOME tab.
- Type **Your name** in the **Find what box**. Type your first and last names in the **Replace with box**.
- Click **Replace** and click **OK**. Close the *Find and Replace* dialog box. Close, save changes to the document, and exit Word.

e. Click **File Explorer** on the taskbar so that you can rename one of your folders:

- Click **Computer** in the Navigation Pane.
- In the Content pane, navigate to the drive where you earlier created the Best Friends folder. Double-click the **Best Friends folder**.
- Right-click **Billing Records**, click **Rename**, type **Accounting Records**, and then press **Enter**.

f. Take a snip and name it **f01p3FolderSnip_LastFirst**. Save it in the Business Letters subfolder of the Best Friends folder. Submit your files based on your instructor's directions.

Mid-Level Exercises

1 Reference Letter

You are an instructor at a local community college. A student has asked you to provide her with a letter of reference for a job application. You have used Word to prepare the letter, but now you need to make a few changes before it is finalized.

a. Open File Explorer. Create a new folder named **References** in the location where you are saving your student files. Take a snip, name it **f01m1ReferencesSnip_LastFirst**, and save it in the References folder. Close File Explorer.

b. Start Word. Open *f01m1Letter* and save it in the References folder as **f01m1Letter_LastFirst**.

c. Select the date and point to several font sizes in the Mini toolbar. Use the Live Preview to compare them. Click **11**.

d. Double-click the date and use the **Format Painter** to change the rest of the letter to font size 11.

e. Apply bold to the student's name, *Stacy VanPatten*, in the first sentence.

f. Correct all errors using Spelling & Grammar. Her last name is spelled correctly. Use the Thesaurus to find a synonym for *intelligent* and replace wih **gifted**. Change the *an* to *a* just before the new word. Replace each occurrence of *Stacy* with **Stacey**.

g. Move the last paragraph—beginning with *In my opinion*—to position it before the second paragraph—beginning with *Stacey is a gifted*.

h. Move the insertion point to the beginning of the document.

i. Change the margins to **Narrow**.

j. Preview the document as it will appear when printed.

k. Save and close the file. Submit your files based on your instructor's directions.

2 Medical Monitoring

You are enrolled in a Health Informatics program of study in which you learn to manage databases related to health fields. For a class project, your instructor requires that you monitor your blood pressure, recording your findings in an Excel worksheet. You have recorded the week's data and will now make a few changes before printing the worksheet for submission.

a. Open File Explorer. Create a new folder named **Medical** in the location where you are saving your student files. Take a snip, name it **f01m2MedicalSnip_LastFirst**, and save it in the Medical folder. Close File Explorer.

b. Start Excel. Open *f01m2Tracker* and save it as **f01m2Tracker_LastFirst** in the Medical folder.

c. Preview the worksheet as it will appear when printed. Change the orientation of the worksheet to **Landscape**. Preview the worksheet again.

d. Click in the cell to the right of *Name* and type your first and last names. Press **Enter**.

e. Change the font of the text in **cell C1** to **Verdana**. Use Live Preview to try some font sizes. Change the font size to **20**.

f. Check the spelling for the worksheet.

 **DISCOVER**

g. Get help on showing decimal places. You want to increase the decimal places for the values in **cells E22, F22, and G22** so that each value shows two places to the right of the decimal. Use Excel Help to learn how to do that. You might use *Increase Decimals* as a Search term. When you find the answer, select the three cells and increase the decimal places to **2**.

h. Click **cell A1** and insert a picture of your choice related to blood pressure. Be sure the image includes content from Office.com. Resize and position the picture so that it displays in an attractive manner. Format the picture with **Soft Edges** set to **4 pt**. Change the margins to **Wide**.

i. Open the Backstage view and adjust print settings to print two copies. You will not actually print two copies unless directed by your instructor.

j. Save and close the file. Submit your files based on your instructor's directions.

3 Today's Musical Artists

COLLABORATION CASE

CREATIVE CASE ★

With a few of your classmates, you will use PowerPoint to create a single presentation on your favorite musical artists. Each student must create at least one slide and then all of the slides will be added to the presentation. Because everyone's schedule is varied, you should use either your Outlook account or OneDrive to pass the presentation file among the group.

a. Open File Explorer. Create a new folder named **Musical** in the location where you are saving your student files. Take a snip, name it **f01m3MusicalSnip_LastFirst**, and then save it in the Musical folder. Close File Explorer.

b. Start PowerPoint. Create a new presentation and save it as **f01m3Music_GroupName** in the Musical folder.

c. Add one slide that contains the name of the artist, the genre, and two or three interesting facts about the artist.

d. Insert a picture of the artist or clip art that represents the artist.

e. Put your name on the slide that you created. Save the presentation.

f. Pass the presentation to the next student so that he or she can perform the same tasks and save the presentation before passing it on to the next student. Continue until all group members have created a slide in the presentation.

g. Save and close the file. Submit your file based on your instructor's directions.

Beyond the Classroom

Fitness Planner

RESEARCH CASE

You will use Microsoft Excel to develop a fitness planner. Open *f01b2Exercise* and save it as **f01b2Exercise_LastFirst**. Because the fitness planner is a template, the exercise categories are listed, but without actual data. You will personalize the planner. Change the orientation to **Landscape**. Move the contents of **cell A2** (*Exercise Planner*) to **cell A1**. Click **cell A8** and use the Format Painter to copy the format of that selection to **cells A5** and **A6**. Increase the font size of **cell A1** to **26**. Use Excel Help to learn how to insert a header and put your name in the header. Begin the fitness planner, entering at least one activity in each category (warm-up, aerobics, strength, and cool-down). Submit as directed by your instructor.

Household Records

DISASTER RECOVERY

FROM SCRATCH

Use Microsoft Excel to create a detailed record of your household appliances and other items of value that are in your home. In case of burglary or disaster, an insurance claim is expedited if you are able to itemize what was lost along with identifying information such as serial numbers. You will then make a copy of the record on another storage device for safekeeping outside your home (in case your home is destroyed by a fire or weather-related catastrophe). Connect a flash drive to your computer and then use File Explorer to create a folder on the hard drive titled **Home Records**. Design a worksheet listing at least five fictional appliances and electronic equipment along with the serial number of each. Save the workbook as **f01b3Household_LastFirst** in the Home Records folder. Close the workbook and exit Excel. Use File Explorer to copy the Home Records folder from the hard drive to your flash drive. Use the Snipping Tool to create a full-screen snip of the screen display. Save it as **f01b3Disaster_LastFirst** in the Home Records folder. Close all open windows and submit as directed by your instructor.

Meetings

SOFT SKILLS CASE

FROM SCRATCH

After watching the Meetings video, you will use File Explorer to create a series of folders and subfolders to organize meetings by date. Each folder should be named by month, day, and year. Three subfolders should be created for each meeting. The subfolders should be named **Agenda**, **Handouts**, and **Meeting Notes**. Use the Snipping Tool to create a full-screen snip of the screen display. Save it as **f01b4Meetings_LastFirst**. Submit as directed by your instructor.

Capstone Exercise

You are a member of the Student Government Association (SGA) at your college. As a community project, the SGA is sponsoring a Stop Smoking drive designed to provide information on the health risks posed by smoking cigarettes and to offer solutions to those who want to quit. The SGA has partnered with the local branch of the American Cancer Society as well as the outreach program of the local hospital to sponsor free educational awareness seminars. As the secretary for the SGA, you will help prepare a PowerPoint presentation that will be displayed on plasma screens around campus and used in student seminars. You will use Microsoft Office to help with those tasks.

Manage Files and Folders

You will open, review, and save an Excel worksheet providing data on the personal monetary cost of smoking cigarettes over a period of years.

  a. Create a folder called **SGA Drive**.

  b. Start Excel. Open *f01c1Cost* from the student data files and save it in the SGA Drive folder as **f01c1Cost_LastFirst**.

  c. Click **cell A10** and type your first and last names. Press **Enter**.

Modify the Font

To highlight some key figures on the worksheet, you will format those cells with additional font attributes.

  a. Draw attention to the high cost of smoking for 10, 20, and 30 years by changing the font color in **cells G3 through I4** to **Red**.

  b. Italicize the Annual Cost cells (**F3** and **F4**).

  c. Click **Undo** on the Quick Access Toolbar to remove the italics. Click **Redo** to return the text to italics.

Insert a Picture

You will add a picture to the worksheet and then resize it and position it.

  a. Click **cell G7** and insert an online picture appropriate for the topic of smoking.

  b. Resize the picture and reposition it near cell B7.

  c. Click outside the picture to deselect it.

Preview Print, Change Page Layout, and Print

To get an idea of how the worksheet will look when printed, you will preview the worksheet. Then you will change the orientation and margins before printing it.

  a. Preview the document as it will appear when printed.

  b. Change the page orientation to **Landscape**. Click the **PAGE LAYOUT tab** and change the margins to **Narrow**.

  c. Preview the document as it will appear when printed.

  d. Adjust the print settings to print two copies. You will not actually print two copies unless directed by your instructor.

  e. Save and close the file.

Find and Replace

You have developed a PowerPoint presentation that you will use to present to student groups and for display on plasma screens across campus. The presentation is designed to increase awareness of the health problems associated with smoking. The PowerPoint presentation has come back from the reviewers with only one comment: A reviewer suggested that you spell out Centers for Disease Control and Prevention, instead of abbreviating it. You do not remember exactly which slide or slides the abbreviation might have been on, so you use *Find and Replace* to make the change quickly.

  a. Start PowerPoint. Open *f01c1Quit* and save it in the SGA Drive folder as **f01c1Quit_LastFirst**.

  b. Replace all occurrences of *CDC* with **Centers for Disease Control and Prevention**.

Cut and Paste and Insert a Text Box

The Mark Twain quote on Slide 1 might be more effective on the last slide in the presentation, so you will cut and paste it there in a text box.

  a. On Slide 1, select the entire Mark Twain quote by clicking on the placeholder border. When the border is solid, the entire placeholder and its contents are selected.

  b. On Slide 22, paste the quote, reposition it more attractively, and then format it in a larger font size.

Check Spelling and Change View

Before you call the presentation complete, you will spell check it and view it as a slide show.

  a. Check spelling. The word *hairlike* is not misspelled, so it should not be corrected.

  b. View the slide show and take the smoking quiz. Click after the last slide to return to the presentation.

  c. Save and close the presentation. Exit PowerPoint. Submit both files included in this project as directed by your instructor.

Introduction to PowerPoint

Creating a Basic Presentation

Konstantin Chagin/Shutterstock

OBJECTIVES AFTER YOU READ THIS CHAPTER, YOU WILL BE ABLE TO:

1. Use PowerPoint views p. 85
2. Type a speaker note p. 90
3. Save as a slide show p. 90
4. Plan a presentation p. 95
5. Assess presentation content p. 98
6. Review the presentation p. 99

7. Insert media objects p. 105
8. Add a table p. 106
9. Use animations and transitions p. 106
10. Insert a header or footer p. 109
11. Run and navigate a slide show p. 116
12. Print in PowerPoint p. 119

CASE STUDY | Be a Trainer

You teach employee training courses for the Training and Development department of your State Department of Human Resources. You begin each course by delivering an electronic presentation. The slide show presents your objectives for the course, organizes your content, and aids your audience's retention. You prepare the presentation using Microsoft Office PowerPoint 2013.

Because of the exceptional quality of your presentations, the director of the State Department of Human Resources has asked you to prepare a new course on presentation skills. In the Hands-On Exercises for this chapter, you will work with two presentations for this course. One presentation will focus on the benefits of using PowerPoint, and the other will focus on the preparation for a slide show, including planning, organizing, and delivering.

Introduction to PowerPoint

You can use Microsoft PowerPoint 2013 to create an electronic slide show or other materials for use in a professional presentation. A *slide* is the most basic element of PowerPoint (similar to a page being the most basic element of Microsoft Word). Multiple slides may be arranged to create a presentation, called a *slide show*, that can be used to deliver your message in a variety of ways: you can project the slide show on a screen as part of a presentation, run it automatically at a kiosk or from a DVD, display it on the World Wide Web, or create printed handouts. A *PowerPoint presentation* is an electronic slide show saved with a .pptx extension after the file name.

Figure 1.1 shows a PowerPoint presentation with slides containing content, such as text, online pictures, and images. The presentation has a consistent design and color scheme. It is easy to create presentations with consistent and attractive designs using PowerPoint.

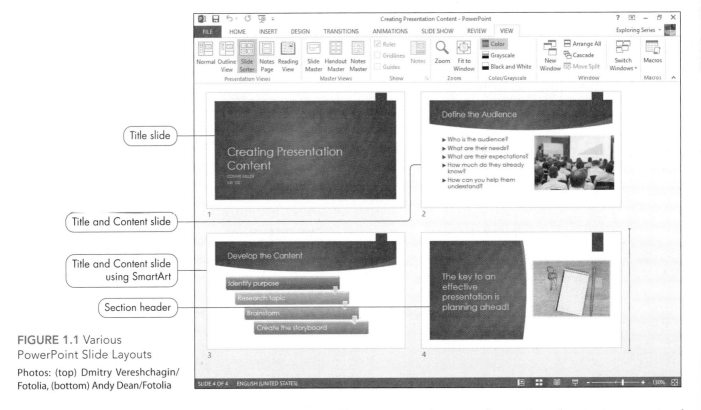

FIGURE 1.1 Various PowerPoint Slide Layouts

Photos: (top) Dmitry Vereshchagin/Fotolia, (bottom) Andy Dean/Fotolia

In this section, you will start your exploration of PowerPoint by viewing a previously completed presentation so that you can appreciate the benefits of using PowerPoint. You will modify the presentation and add identifying information, examine PowerPoint views to discover the advantages of each view, and save the presentation.

TIP · Polish Your Delivery

The speaker is the most important part of any presentation. Poor delivery will ruin even the best presentation. Speak slowly and clearly, maintain eye contact with your audience, and use the information on the slides to guide you. Do not just read the information on the screen, but expand on each sentence or image to give your audience the intended message.

Using PowerPoint Views

STEP 1 >> Figure 1.2 shows the default PowerPoint view, *Normal view*, with two panes that provide maximum flexibility in working with the presentation. The pane on the left side of the screen shows *thumbnails* (slide miniatures), and the Slide pane on the right displays the current slide. This is where you make edits to slide content.

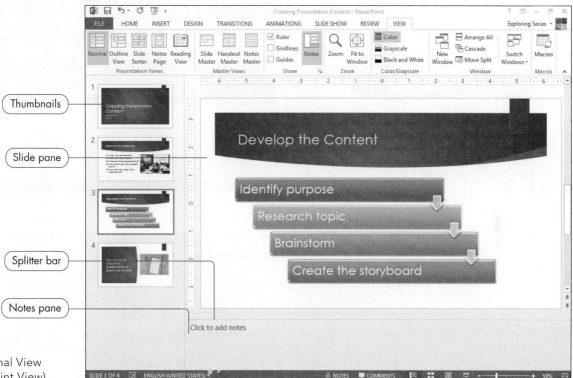

FIGURE 1.2 Normal View (Default PowerPoint View)

TIP **Showing the Notes Pane**

When you open PowerPoint, the Notes pane may be hidden from view. The Notes pane is where you enter notes pertaining to the slide or the presentation. You can change the size of these panes by dragging the splitter bar that separates one pane from another. To show the pane, click the View tab, and then click Normal in the Presentation Views group. Alternatively, you can click Notes on the status bar.

Figure 1.3 shows PowerPoint's *status bar*, which contains the slide number and options that control the view of your presentation: Notes button, Comments button, View buttons, a Zoom slider, the Zoom level button, and the *Fit slide to current window* button. The status bar is located at the bottom of your screen and can be customized. To customize the status bar, right-click it, and then click the options you want displayed from the Customize Status Bar list.

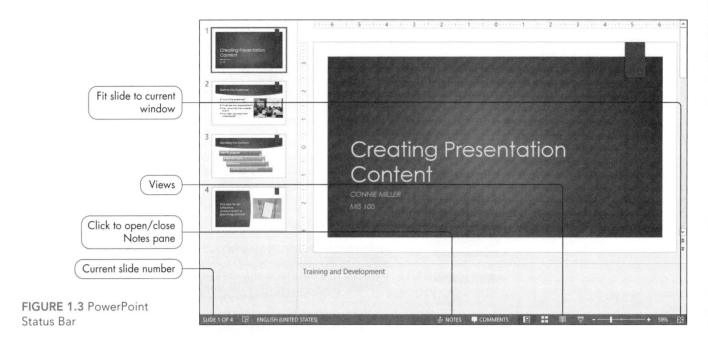

Fit slide to current window

Views

Click to open/close Notes pane

Current slide number

FIGURE 1.3 PowerPoint Status Bar

While in Normal view, you can hide the left pane to expand the Slide pane so that you can see more detail while editing slide content. To hide the left Thumbnails pane, drag the splitter bar that separates one pane from another until you see the word *Thumbnails* appear. You can also hide the Notes pane at the bottom by clicking the Notes button in the Status bar. Figure 1.4 shows an individual slide in Normal view with the Thumbnails pane and the Notes pane closed. You can restore the view by clicking the View tab and clicking Normal in the Presentation Views group.

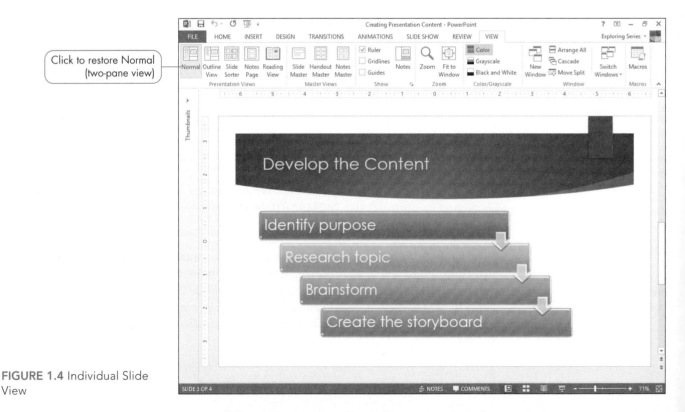

Click to restore Normal (two-pane view)

FIGURE 1.4 Individual Slide View

PowerPoint offers views in addition to Normal view, including Outline View, Slide Sorter view, Notes Page view, Reading View, and Slide Show view. Access Outline View, Slide Sorter, Notes Page, and Reading View from the Presentation Views group on the View tab. Access options for the Slide Show view from the Start Slide Show group on the Slide Show tab. For quick access, many of these views are available on the status bar.

Outline View is used when you would like to enter text into your presentation using an outline. In other words, rather than having to enter the text into each placeholder on each slide separately, you can type the text directly into an outline. Figure 1.5 shows an example of the Outline View.

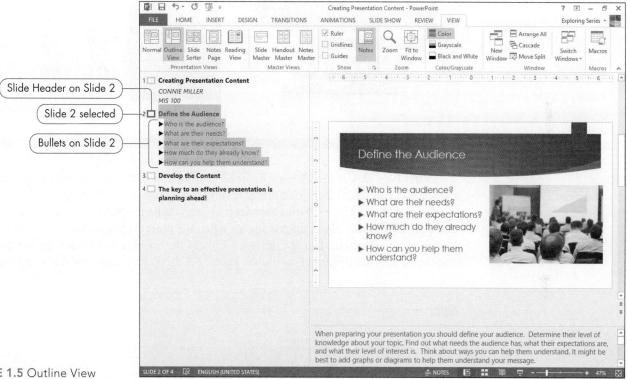

FIGURE 1.5 Outline View

Slide Sorter view displays thumbnails of your presentation slides, which enables you to view multiple slides simultaneously (see Figure 1.6). This view is helpful when you wish to change the order of the slides or to delete one or more slides. You can set transition effects (the way the slides transition from one to another) for multiple slides in Slide Sorter view. If you are in Slide Sorter view and double-click a slide thumbnail, PowerPoint returns the selected slide to Normal view. To rearrange slides in Slide Sorter view:

1. Move the mouse pointer over the slide thumbnail of the slide you wish to move.
2. Drag the slide to the new location.

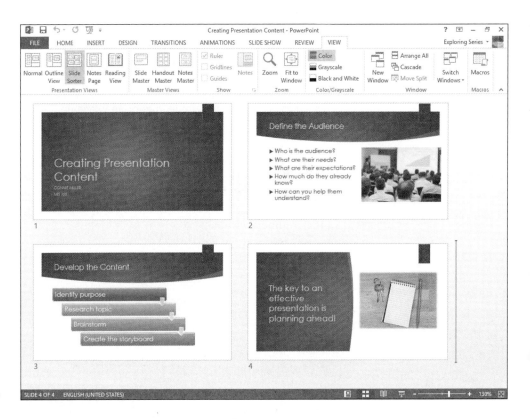

FIGURE 1.6 Slide Sorter View

Notes Page view is used when you need to enter and edit large amounts of text to which the speaker can refer when presenting. If you have a large amount of technical detail in the speaker notes, you can use Notes Page view to print audience handouts that include the slide and associated notes. Notes do not display when the presentation is shown (except when the Presenter view is used), but are intended to help the speaker remember the key points or additional information about each slide. Figure 1.7 shows an example of the Notes Page view.

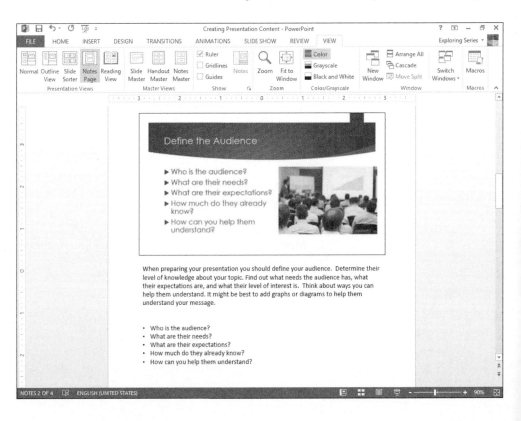

FIGURE 1.7 Notes Page View

Reading View is used to view the slide show full screen, one slide at a time. Animations and transitions are active in the Reading View. A title bar including the Minimize, Maximize/Restore (which changes its name and appearance depending on whether the window is maximized or at a smaller size), and Close buttons is visible, as well as a modified status bar (see Figure 1.8). In addition to View buttons, the status bar includes navigation buttons for moving to the next or previous slide, as well as a menu for accomplishing common tasks such as printing. Press Esc to quickly return to the previous view.

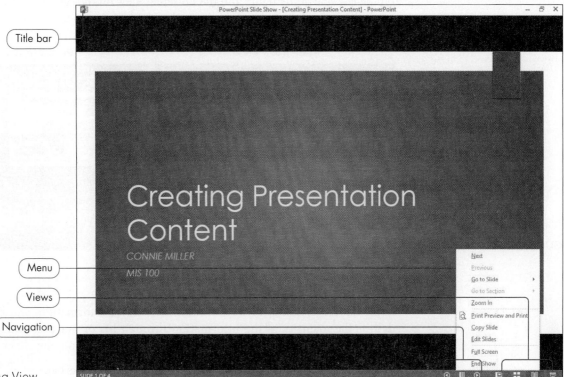

FIGURE 1.8 Reading View

Slide Show view is used to deliver the completed presentation full screen to an audience, one slide at a time, as an electronic presentation (see Figure 1.9). The slide show can be presented manually, where the speaker clicks the mouse to move from one slide to the next, or automatically, where each slide stays on the screen for a predetermined amount of time, after which the next slide appears. A slide show can contain a combination of both methods for advancing to the next slide. You can insert transition effects to impact the look of how one slide moves to the next. To end the slide show, press Esc.

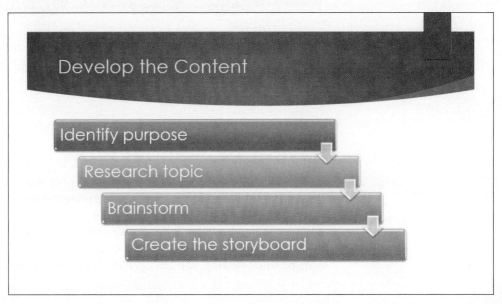

FIGURE 1.9 Slide Show View

Presenter view is a specialty view that delivers a presentation on two monitors simultaneously. Typically, one monitor is a projector that delivers the full-screen presentation to the audience; the other monitor is a laptop or computer so that the presenter can see the slide, speaker notes, and a thumbnail image of the next slide. This enables the presenter to move between slides as needed, navigate to the previous or next slide using arrows, or write on the slide with a marker. A timer displays the time elapsed since the presentation began so that the presenter can keep track of the presentation length. Figure 1.10 shows the audience view on the left side of the figure and the Presenter view on the right side. To use Presenter view, select the Use Presenter View option in the Monitors group under the Slide Show tab.

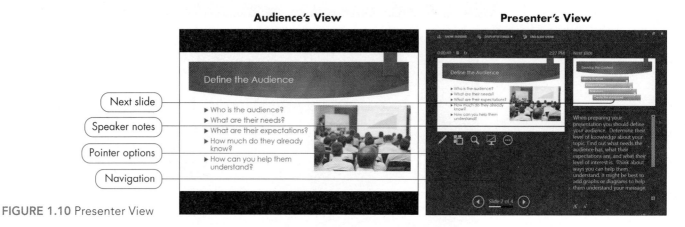

FIGURE 1.10 Presenter View

Typing a Speaker Note

Slides should contain only a minimum amount of information, and the speaker should deliver the majority of the information through his or her presentation. Consequently, speaker notes can be a most useful tool when giving a presentation. To create a speaker note:

STEP 2 »

1. If the Notes pane is not visible, click Notes on the status bar.
2. Drag the splitter bar between the Slide pane and the Notes pane up to expand the Notes pane.
3. Click in the Notes pane to begin typing. To modify the text, click the HOME tab and apply formatting using the tools in the Font and Paragraph groups.

TIP   Format a Speaker Note

The speaker's notes can be formatted much like a Word document. You can create bulleted lists and italicize or bold key words you want to feature, among other things to help you stay organized and on track with your presentation. Not all text modifications will be visible in the Normal view or in the Presenter view. To see modifications such as font and font size, switch to the Notes Page view.

Saving As a Slide Show

STEP 3 »

PowerPoint presentations are saved with a .pptx file extension and opened in Normal view so that you can make changes to the presentation. You can save your presentation as a *PowerPoint show* with a .ppsx extension by using the Save As command. This file type will open the presentation in Slide Show view and is best for distributing an unchangeable version of a completed slide show to others for viewing. Whereas the .ppsx file cannot be changed while viewing, you can open the file in PowerPoint and edit it.

1. Describe the main advantage for using each of the following views: Normal view, Notes Page view, Slide Sorter view, and Slide Show view. ***pp. 85–89***

2. Explain the difference between a PowerPoint presentation (.pptx) and a PowerPoint show (.ppsx). ***p. 90***

3. Discuss the purpose of a speaker note. ***p. 90***

Hands-On Exercises

Watch the Video for this Hands-On Exercise!

MyITLab®
HOE1 Training

1 Introduction to PowerPoint

You have been asked to create a presentation on the benefits of PowerPoint for the Training and Development department. You decide to view an existing presentation to determine if it contains material you can adapt for your presentation. You view the presentation, add a speaker note, and then save the presentation as a PowerPoint show.

Skills covered: Open, View, and Save a Presentation • Type a Speaker Note • Save as a PowerPoint Show

STEP 1 》 OPEN, VIEW, AND SAVE THE PRESENTATION

In this step, you open and save the slide show created by your colleague. You will also review your presentation. You experiment with various methods of advancing to the next slide and then return to Normal view. As you use the various methods of advancing to the next slide, you find the one that is most comfortable to you and then use that method as you view slide shows in the future. An audio clip of audience applause will play when you view Slide 4: The Essence of PowerPoint. You will want to wear a headset if you are in a classroom lab so that you do not disturb classmates.

    a. Start PowerPoint and open the *p01h1Intro* file.

    b. Save the file as **p01h1Intro_LastFirst**.

> **TROUBLESHOOTING:** If you make any major mistakes in this exercise, close the file, open *p01h1Intro* again, and then start this exercise over. When you save files, use your last and first names. For example, as the PowerPoint author, I would name my presentation *p01h1Intro_RutledgeAmy*.

    c. Click **Slide Show** on the status bar.

        The presentation begins with the title slide, the first slide in all slide shows. The title has an animation assigned, so it comes in automatically.

    d. Press **Spacebar** to advance to the second slide and read the slide.

        The title on the second slide automatically wipes down, and the arrow wipes to the right.

    e. Position the pointer in the bottom-left corner side of the slide, and click the **right arrow** in the Navigation bar to advance to the next slide. Read the slide content.

        The text on the third slide, and all following slides, has the same animation applied to create consistency in the presentation.

    f. Click the **left mouse button** to advance to the fourth slide, which has a sound icon displayed on the slide.

        The sound icon on the slide indicates sound has been added. The sound has been set to come in automatically so you do not need to click anything for the sound to play.

> **TROUBLESHOOTING:** If you do not hear the sound, your computer may not have a sound card or your sound may be muted.

    g. Continue to navigate through the slides until you come to the end of the presentation (a black screen).

    h. Press **Esc** to return to Normal view.

STEP 2 ≫ TYPE A SPEAKER NOTE

In this step, you add a speaker note to a slide to help you remember to mention some of the many objects that can be added to a slide. You also view the note in Notes view to see how it will print. Refer to Figure 1.11 as you complete Step 2.

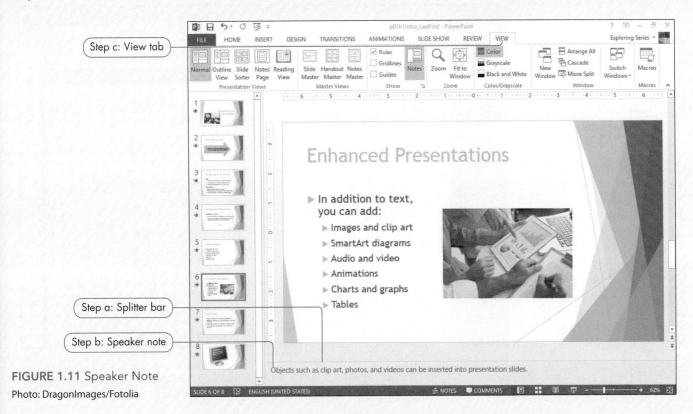

FIGURE 1.11 Speaker Note

Photo: DragonImages/Fotolia

a. Click the **Slide 6 thumbnail** and drag the splitter bar between the Slide pane and the Notes pane up to expand the Notes pane, if necessary.

Slide 6 is selected, and the slide displays in the Slide pane.

TROUBLESHOOTING: If the Notes pane is not visible, click Notes on the Status bar.

---

b. Type **Objects such as clip art, photos, and videos can be inserted into presentation slides.** in the **Notes pane**.

c. Click the **VIEW tab** and click **Notes Page** view in the Presentation Views group.

The slide is shown at a reduced size and the speaker note is shown below the slide.

d. Click **Normal** in the Presentation Views group.

This returns the presentation to the Normal view.

e. Save the presentation.

You want to save the slide show as a PowerPoint show so that it opens automatically in Slide Show view rather than Normal view. Refer to Figure 1.12 as you complete Step 3.

Step c: Opens in Slide Show view

Step c: PowerPoint presentation file

FIGURE 1.12 Saving a Presentation as a PowerPoint Show

a. Click the **FILE tab**, click **Save As**, click **Browse**, select the file location where it is to be saved, click **Save as type**, and then select **PowerPoint Show**.

b. Leave the file name *p01h1Intro_LastFirst* for the PowerPoint show.

Although you are saving this file with the same file name as the presentation, it will not overwrite the file, as it is a different file type.

c. Click **Save**.

You have created a new file, a PowerPoint Show, in your folder. A gray icon is used to indicate the PowerPoint Show file that opens in Slide Show view. The orange icon listed is used to indicate the PowerPoint Presentation file. See Figure 1.12 to view these icons.

d. Close the *p01h1Intro_LastFirst* presentation and submit based on your instructor's directions. Exit PowerPoint.

Presentation Creation

You are ready to create your own presentation by choosing a theme, adding content, and applying formatting. You should create the presentation by adding the content first and then applying formatting so that you can concentrate on your message and its structure without getting distracted by the formatting of the presentation.

Planning a Presentation

Creating an effective presentation requires advance planning. First, determine the goal of your presentation. An informative presentation could notify the audience about a change in policy or procedure. An educational presentation could teach an audience about a subject or a skill. Sales presentations are often persuasive calls to action to encourage the purchase of a product, but they can also be used to sell an idea or process. A goodwill presentation could be used to recognize an employee or acknowledge an organization. You could even create a certificate of appreciation using PowerPoint.

Next, research your audience—determine their level of knowledge about your topic. Find out what needs the audience has, what their expectations are, and what their level of interest is.

After determining your purpose and researching your audience, brainstorm how to deliver your message. Before using your computer, you may wish to sketch out your thoughts on paper to help you organize them. After organizing your thoughts, add them as content to the slide show, and then format the presentation.

In this section, you will create a visual plan called a *storyboard*. You will also learn to polish your presentation by using layouts, applying design themes, and reviewing your presentation for errors.

Prepare a Storyboard

A *storyboard* is a visual plan for your presentation that helps you plan the direction of your presentation. It can be a very rough draft that you sketch out while brainstorming, or it can be an elaborate plan that includes the text and objects drawn as they would appear on a slide.

A simple PowerPoint storyboard is divided into sections representing individual slides. The first block in the storyboard is used for the title slide. Subsequent blocks are used to introduce the topics, develop the topics, and then summarize the information. Figure 1.13 shows a working copy of a storyboard for planning presentation content. The storyboard is in rough-draft form and shows changes made during the review process. A blank copy of the document in Figure 1.13 has been placed on the student CD should you wish to use this for presentation planning. The PowerPoint presentation shown in Figure 1.14 incorporates the changes.

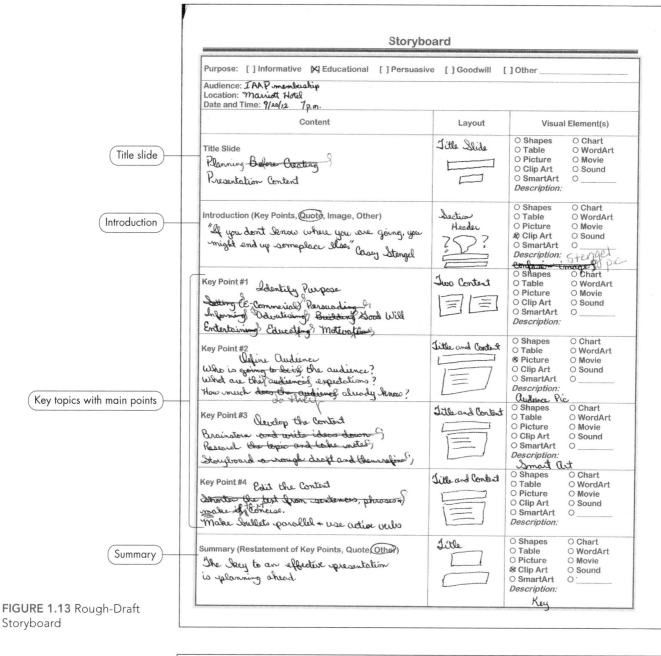

FIGURE 1.13 Rough-Draft
Storyboard

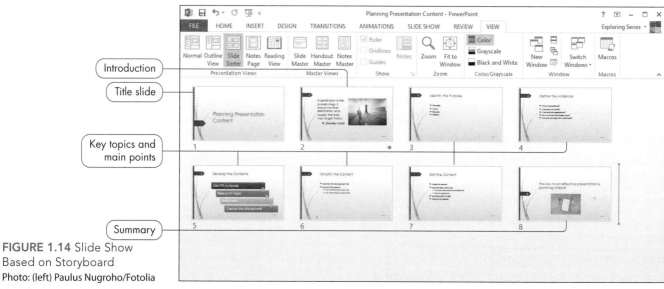

FIGURE 1.14 Slide Show
Based on Storyboard
Photo: (left) Paulus Nugroho/Fotolia

Begin with a Theme or Template

When you first open PowerPoint 2013, you are presented with the opportunity to choose from several themes. A **theme** is a file that includes the formatting elements like a background, a color scheme, and slide layouts that position content placeholders. Some presentations, or **templates**, include suggestions for how to modify the slide show, whereas others include ideas about what you could say to inform your audience about your topic. PowerPoint 2013 has added widescreen themes in addition to the standard sizes to accommodate widescreen monitors and wide-format projectors. If you don't want to use one of the pre-created, widescreen themes, you can choose to open a different presentation.

Once you have chosen a theme, you will see the variants for the theme. A **variant** is a variation of the theme design you have chosen. Each variant uses different color palettes and font families. Figure 1.15 shows the Ion theme with four variant options for this theme. Click Create to choose your theme and begin your presentation. Even though you choose your theme first, your decision is not final as you can always change a theme later. (To change a theme or variant, click the Design tab. Additional themes and variants will display.)

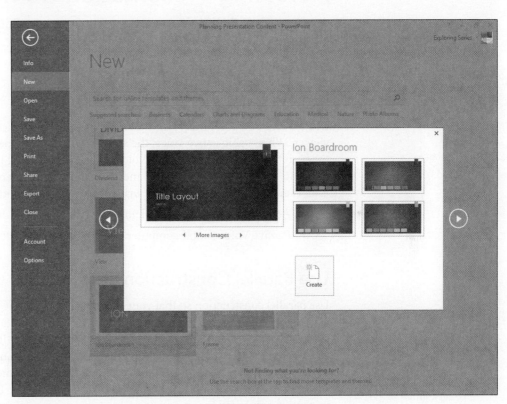

FIGURE 1.15 Ion Theme with Variant Options

Create a Title Slide and Introduction

The title slide should have a short title that indicates the purpose of the presentation. Try to capture the title in two to five words. The title slide should also contain information such as the speaker's name and title, the speaker's organization, the organization's logo, and the date of the presentation. This information is typically included in the subtitle placeholder.

After the title slide, you may want to include an introduction slide that will get the audience's attention. The introduction could be a list of topics covered in the presentation, a thought-provoking quotation or question, or an image that relates to the topic. Introduction slides can also be used to distinguish between topics or sections of the presentation.

Create the Main Body of Slides

The content of your presentation follows the title slide and the introduction. Each key thought should be a separate slide with the details needed to support that thought. Present the details as bullets or a short paragraph that relates to the content. When determining the content, ask yourself what you want your audience to learn and remember. Support the content with facts, examples, charts or graphs, illustrations, images, or video clips.

Create the Conclusion

End your presentation with a summary or conclusion that reviews the main points, restates the purpose of the presentation, or invokes a call to action. You may also want to repeat your contact information at the end of the presentation so the audience knows how to follow up with any questions or needs.

Assessing Presentation Content

After you create the storyboard, review what you wrote. Edit your text to shorten complete sentences to phrases that you can use as bulleted points by eliminating excess adverbs and adjectives and using only a few prepositions.

Use Active Voice

Review and edit the phrases so they begin with active voice when possible to involve the viewer. When using active voice, the subject of the phrase performs the action expressed in the verb. In phrases using passive voice, the subject is acted upon. Passive voice needs more words to communicate your ideas and can make your presentation seem flat. The following is an example of the same thought written in active voice and passive voice:

- Active Voice: Students need good computer skills for problem solving.
- Passive Voice: Good computer skills are needed by students for problem solving.

Use Parallel Construction

Use parallel construction so that your bullets are in the same grammatical form to help your audience see the connection between your phrases. If you start your first bullet with a noun, start each successive bullet with a noun; if you start your first bullet with a verb, continue with verbs. Parallel construction also gives each bullet an equal level of importance and promotes balance in your message. In the following example, the fourth bullet is not parallel to the first three bullets because it does not begin with a verb. The fifth bullet shows the bullet in parallel construction.

- Find a good place to study.
- Organize your study time.
- Study for tests with a partner.
- Terminology is important so learn how to use it properly. (Incorrect)
- Learn and use terminology properly. (Correct)

Follow the 7 × 7 Guideline

Remember, the slides will be read by your audience, not you. Therefore, you should not put entire paragraphs on your slides. Keep the information on your slides concise. You will expand on the slide content when delivering your presentation with the use of notes. Follow the 7 × 7 guideline, which suggests that you use no more than seven words per line and seven lines per slide. Although you may be forced to exceed this guideline on occasion, follow it as often as possible.

After you complete the planning and review process, you are ready to prepare the PowerPoint slide show to use with your presentation.

Use Slide Layouts

 PowerPoint provides a set of predefined slide *layouts* that determine the position of the objects or content on a slide. Slide layouts contain several combinations of placeholders. When you click the New Slide arrow on the Home tab, a gallery from which you can choose a layout displays. All of the layouts except the Blank layout include placeholders. *Placeholders* are objects that hold specific content, such as titles, subtitles, or images. Placeholders determine the position of the objects on the slide.

After you select a layout, click a placeholder to add your content. When you click a placeholder you can edit it. The border of the placeholder becomes a dashed line and you are able to enter content. If you click the dashed line placeholder border, the placeholder and its content are selected. The border changes to a solid line. Once selected, you can drag the placeholder to a new position or delete the placeholder. Any change you make impacts all content in the placeholder. Unused placeholders in a layout do not show when you display a slide show.

A new, blank presentation includes a title slide layout with a placeholder for the presentation title and subtitle. Add new slides using the layout from the layout gallery. By default, text on slides following the title slide appears as bullets.

TIP | Using Bullets

To increase or decrease indents for bulleted items, use Tab. To increase an indent, press Tab. To decrease an indent, hold down Shift+Tab.

You can change the layout of an existing slide by dragging placeholders to a new location or by adding new placeholders and objects. To format the text in the slide, use the controls in the Paragraph group found on the Home tab. You can make basic edits such as changing font, color, and size by using these controls.

TIP | New Slide Button

The New Slide button has two parts, the New Slide button and the New Slide arrow. Click the New Slide arrow when you want to choose a layout from the gallery. Click New Slide, which appears above the New Slide arrow, to quickly insert a new slide. If you click New Slide when the Title slide is selected, the new slide uses the Title and Content layout. If the current slide uses any layout other than Title slide, the new slide uses the same layout.

Reviewing the Presentation

After you create the presentation, check for spelling errors and incorrect word usage. Nothing is more embarrassing or can make you appear more unprofessional than a misspelled word enlarged on a big screen.

 Use a four-step method for checking spelling in PowerPoint. First, read the slide content after you enter it. Second, use the Spelling feature located in the Review tab to check the entire presentation. Third, ask a friend or colleague to review the presentation. Finally, display the presentation in Slide Show view or Reading View and read each word on each slide out loud. Although proofreading four times may seem excessive, it will help ensure your presentation is professional.

 Proofing Options

The Spelling feature, by default, does not catch contextual errors like *to*, *too*, and *two*, but you can set the Proofing options to help you find and fix this type of error. To modify the proofing options, click File and click Options. Click Proofing in the PowerPoint Options window and click Check Grammar and Spelling. With this option selected, the spelling checker will flag contextual mistakes with a red wavy underline. To correct the error, right-click the flagged word and select the proper word choice.

Use the Thesaurus

As you create and edit your presentation, you may notice that you are using one word too often, especially at the beginning of bullets. Use the Thesaurus so your bulleted lists do not constantly begin with the same word and so you make varied word choices.

Reorder Slides

As you develop your presentation, you may realize that your need to reorder your slides. This can easily be done using the Slide Sorter view. To reorder slides:

STEP 5 »
1. Click the VIEW tab.
2. Click Slide Sorter in the Presentation Views group.
3. Select the slide you wish to move and drag the slide to the new location.
4. Double-click any slide to return to the Normal view.

Quick Concepts

1. Identify the three advanced planning steps you should follow before adding content to a slide show. ***p. 95***

2. Define "storyboard" and describe how a storyboard aids you in creating a slide show. ***p. 95***

3. Describe two guidelines you should follow when assessing your slide content. ***p. 98***

4. Explain the difference between a slide layout and a presentation theme. ***pp. 97 and 99***

2 Presentation Creation

To help state employees learn the process for presentation creation, you decide to give them guidelines for determining content, structuring a slide show, and assessing content. You create a slide show to deliver these guidelines.

Skills covered: Create a New Presentation and Edit the Title Slide • Add New Slides • Use Spell Check and the Thesaurus • Modify Text and Layout • Reorder Slides

STEP 1 ≫ CREATE A NEW PRESENTATION AND EDIT THE TITLE SLIDE

You are creating a Training and Development presentation for your employees. As you progress through the steps, you will add and edit several slides. You begin by choosing the Ion theme with a specific variation color.

    a. Start PowerPoint.

    b. Choose the **Retrospect theme** with the **orange variant**. Click **Create**.

    c. Save the presentation as **p01h2Content_LastFirst**.

    d. On the title slide, click in the **title placeholder** and type **Creating Presentation Content**.

    e. Type your name in the **subtitle placeholder**.

    f. Click **Notes** on the status bar. Add the text **Training and Development** to the **Notes pane**.

    g. Save the presentation.

STEP 2 ≫ ADD NEW SLIDES

You continue creating your presentation by adding a second slide with the Title and Content layout. After adding a title to the slide, you create a bulleted list to develop your topic. After adding the presentation content, you proofread the presentation to ensure no errors exist. Refer to Figure 1.16 as you complete Step 2.

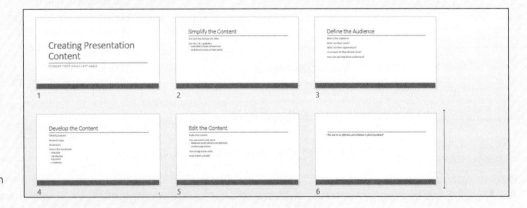

FIGURE 1.16 New Slides with Text Content

    a. Click **New Slide** in the Slides group on the HOME tab.

        The new Slide 2 contains two placeholders: one for the title and one for body content. You can insert an object, such as a table or image, by clicking a button in the center of the content placeholder. To enter text in a list, type the text in the content placeholder.

    b. Type **Simplify the Content** in the **title placeholder**.

c. Click in the **content placeholder** below the title placeholder, type **Use one main concept per slide**, and then press **Enter**.

By default, the list level is the same as the previous level. Notice that the Retrospect theme does not automatically place bullets into the body of the presentation.

d. Type **Use the 7 × 7 guideline** and press **Enter**.

e. Click **Increase List Level** in the Paragraph group.

The list level indents, the font size is reduced, and a bullet appears indicating this is a subset of the main level.

f. Type **Limit slide to seven or fewer lines** and press **Enter**.

g. Type **Limit lines to seven or fewer words**. (Do not include the period.)

By default, the list level is the same as the previous level.

h. Click **New Slide** in the Slides group four times to create four more slides with the Title and Content layout.

i. Type the following text in the appropriate slide. Use **Increase List Level** and **Decrease List Level** in the Paragraph group to change levels.

Slide	Slide Title	Content Data
3	Define the Audience	Who is the audience?
		What are their needs?
		What are their expectations?
		How much do they already know?
		How can you help them understand?
4	Develop the Content	Identify purpose
		Research topic
		Brainstorm
		Create the storyboard
		Title slide
		Introduction
		Key points
		Conclusion
5	Edit the Content	Make text concise
		Use consistent verb tense
		Eliminate excess adverbs and adjectives
		Use few prepositions
		Use strong active verbs
		Keep bullets parallel
6		The key to an effective presentation is planning ahead!

j. Save the presentation.

STEP 3 ≫ USE SPELL CHECK AND THE THESAURUS

It is important to proofread your presentation, making sure that you did not make any errors in spelling or grammar. Additionally, it is important not to use the same words too frequently. In this step, you check for spelling errors and substitute the word *key* for the word *main*.

a. Click **Spelling** in the Proofing group on the REVIEW tab and correct any errors. Carefully proofread each slide.

The result of the spelling check depends on how accurately you entered the text of the presentation.

b. On Slide 2, use the Thesaurus to change *main* in the first bulleted point to **key** and click the **Close (X) button** on the Thesaurus.

c. Save the presentation.

STEP 4 ≫ MODIFY TEXT AND LAYOUT

You want to end the slide show with a statement emphasizing the importance of planning and decide to modify the text and layout of the slide to give it more emphasis. You also leave space on the slide so that later you can add clip art. Refer to Figure 1.17 as you complete Step 4.

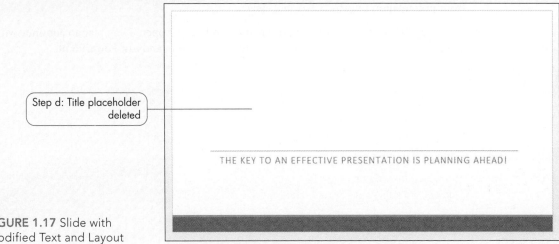

Step d: Title placeholder deleted

THE KEY TO AN EFFECTIVE PRESENTATION IS PLANNING AHEAD!

FIGURE 1.17 Slide with Modified Text and Layout

a. Click the **Slide 6 thumbnail** in the Slides pane.

b. Click the **HOME tab** and click **Layout** in the Slides group.

c. Click **Section Header** from the Layout gallery.

The layout for Slide 6 changes to the Section Header layout. The Section Header layout can be used on any slide in a slide show if its format meets your needs.

d. Click the border of the title placeholder and press **Delete**.

The dotted line border becomes a solid line, which indicates the placeholder is selected. Pressing Delete removes the placeholder and the content of that placeholder.

e. Click the **subtitle placeholder** and click **Center** in the Paragraph group on the HOME tab.

The layout of Slide 6 has now been modified.

f. Save the presentation.

STEP 5 ≫ REORDER SLIDES

You notice that the slides do not follow a logical order. You change the slide positions in Slide Sorter view. Refer to Figure 1.18 as you complete Step 5.

Step b: Original Slide 2 is now Slide 5

FIGURE 1.18 Reordered Slide Show

a. Click the **VIEW tab** and click **Slide Sorter** in the Presentation Views group.

b. Select **Slide 2** and drag it before the summary (last) slide so that it becomes Slide 5.

   After you drop the slide, all slides renumber.

c. Double-click **Slide 6**.

   Your presentation returns to Normal view.

d. Save the *p01h2Content_LastFirst* presentation and keep it open if you plan to continue with the next Hands-On Exercise. If not, close the presentation and exit PowerPoint.

Presentation Enhancement

You can strengthen your slide show by adding graphics and media objects that relate to the message and support the text. PowerPoint enables you to include a variety of visual objects to add impact to your presentation. You can add online pictures, WordArt (stylized letters), sound, animated clips, and video clips to increase your presentation's impact. You can add tables, charts and graphs, and SmartArt diagrams created in PowerPoint, or you can insert objects that were created in other applications, such as a chart from Microsoft Excel or a table from Microsoft Word. You can add animations and transitions to catch the audience's attention. You can also add identifying information on slides or audience handouts by adding headers and footers.

In this section, you will add a table to organize data in columns and rows. You will insert clip art objects that relate to your topics and will move and resize the clip art. You will apply transitions to control how one slide changes to another and add animations to text and clip art to add visual interest. You will finish by adding identifying information in a header and footer.

Inserting Media Objects

Adding media objects such as pictures, clip art, audio, and/or video is especially important in PowerPoint, as PowerPoint is a visual medium. In addition to using the Insert tab to insert media objects in any layout, the following layouts include specific buttons to quickly insert objects:

- Title and Content
- Two Content
- Comparison
- Content with Caption
- Picture with Caption

STEP 2 » Clicking the Pictures icon in the content placeholder (or the Pictures button on the Insert tab) opens a dialog box you can use to browse for picture files on your hard drive or a removable storage device. Clicking Online Pictures opens the Insert Pictures dialog box that allows you to search Office.com Clip Art or elsewhere on the World Wide Web. Figure 1.19 displays the layout buttons.

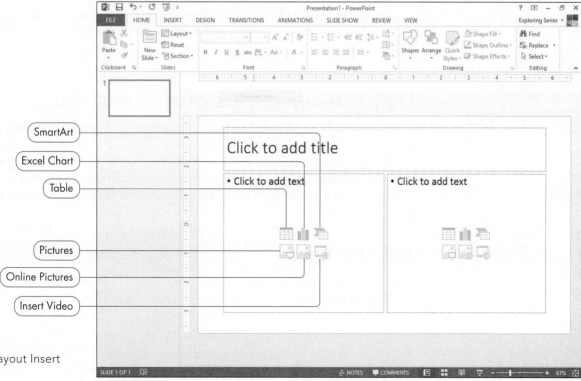

FIGURE 1.19 Layout Insert Buttons

Adding a Table

A *table* organizes information in columns and rows. Tables can be simple and include just a few words or images, or they can be more complex and include structured numerical data.

STEP 1 »

To create a table on a new slide, you can select any layout, click the Insert tab, click Table in the Tables group, and then specify the number of rows and columns you would like to have. You can also click the Insert Table icon on any slide layout that includes it. Figure 1.20 shows a table added to a slide. Once a table is created, you can resize a column or a row by positioning the pointer over the border you wish to resize and then dragging the border to the desired position.

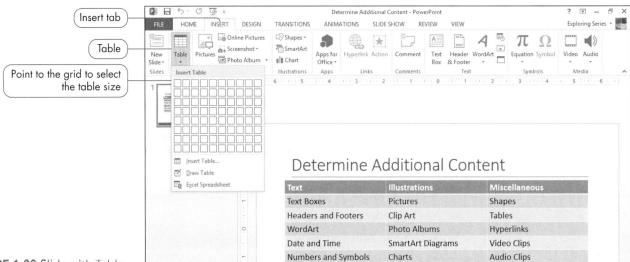

FIGURE 1.20 Slide with Table

TIP Movement within a Table

The insertion point will show you where the text you type will appear in the table. Use the arrow keys or click anywhere in the table to move the insertion point to a new cell. You can also use the Tab key to move the insertion point. Press Tab to move to the next cell or press Shift+Tab to move to the previous cell. Pressing Ctrl+Tab inserts an indent within the cell. Pressing Tab in the last cell of a table creates a new blank row at the end of the table.

Using Animations and Transitions

An *animation* is a movement that controls the entrance, emphasis, exit, and/or path of objects on a slide. A *transition* is a specific animation that is applied as a previous slide is replaced by a new slide while displayed in Slide Show view or Reading View. Animating objects can help focus the audience's attention on an important point, can control the flow of information on a slide, and can help you keep the audience's attention. Transitions provide visual interest as the slides change.

Animate Objects

You can animate objects using a variety of animations, and each animation can be modified by changing its effect options. The effect options available for animations are determined by the animation type. For example, if you choose a Wipe animation, you can determine the direction of the wipe. If you choose an Object Color animation, you can determine the color to be added to the object. Keep animations consistent for a professional presentation.

STEP 4 To apply an animation to text or other objects, do the following:

1. Select the object you want to animate.
2. Click the ANIMATIONS tab.
3. Click More in the Animation group to display the Animation gallery.
4. Click an animation type to apply.
5. Click Effect Options to display any available options related to the selected animation type.

The slide in Figure 1.21 shows an animation effect added to the picture. A tag with the number 1 is attached to the picture to show that it will run first. A quote on the slide (not pictured) has a number 2 to show that it will play after the first animation.

FIGURE 1.21 Animation Gallery

The slide in Figure 1.22 shows Fly In animation effects added to the quotation and name line. Tags with the numbers 2 and 3 are attached and are shaded pink to show that they are selected. The Effect Options gallery for the Fly In Effect is open so that a direction for the image to fly in from can be selected. Click Preview in the Preview group to see all animations on the slide play. You can also see the animations in Reading View and in Slide Show view. Slides that include an animation display a star icon beneath the slide when viewing the slides in Slide Sorter view.

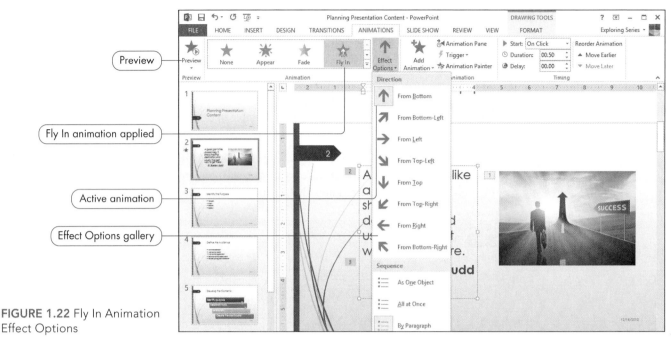

FIGURE 1.22 Fly In Animation Effect Options

PowerPoint's Animation Painter feature lets you copy an animation from one object to another. To use the Animation Painter, select an object with an animation applied, click Animation Painter in the Advanced Animation group on the Animations tab, and then click the text or object to which you want to apply the animation.

Apply Transitions

STEP 3 Transitions are selected from the *Transition to This Slide* group on the Transitions tab. You can select from the basic transitions displayed or from the Transition gallery. To display the Transition gallery, click the More button in the *Transition to This Slide* group on the Transitions tab. Figure 1.23 displays the Transition gallery and the available transitions in the following groups: Subtle, Exciting, and Dynamic Content. Click Effect Options in the *Transition to This Slide* group to see any effects that can be applied to the transition.

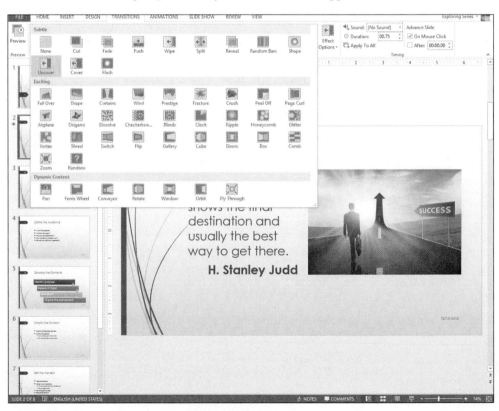

FIGURE 1.23 Transition Gallery

TIP **Slide Sorter View and Transitions**

Transition effects and transition effect options also can be applied from the Slide Sorter view. Applying transitions in Slide Sorter view is helpful when you want to apply the same transition to multiple slides. Do so by selecting the slides prior to applying the effect.

After you choose a transition effect, you can select a sound to play when the transition takes effect. You can choose the duration of the transition in seconds, which controls how quickly the transition takes place. You can also control whether the transition applies to all the slides or just the current slide. The sound can be added by choosing an option in the Sound menu found in the Timing group on the Transitions tab.

Another determination you must make is how you want to start the transition process. Use the Advance Slide options in the Timing group to determine whether you want to manually click or press a key to advance to the next slide or if you want the slide to automatically advance after a specified number of seconds. You can set the number of seconds for the slide to display in the same area.

To delete a transition, click the Transitions tab and click None in the *Transition to This Slide* group. If you wish to remove all transitions, click the Transitions tab, click None in the *Transition to This Slide* group, and then click *Apply to All* in the Timing group.

 TIP **Effectively Adding Transitions, Animations, and Sound**

When you select your transitions, sounds, and animations, remember that too many transition and animation styles can be distracting. The audience will be wondering what is coming next rather than paying attention to your message. The speed of the transition is important, too—very slow transitions will lose the interest of your audience. Too many sound clips can be annoying. Consider whether you need to have the sound of applause with the transition of every slide. Is a typewriter sound necessary to keep your audience's attention, or will it grate on their nerves if it is used on every word? Ask someone to review your presentation and let you know of any annoying or jarring elements.

Inserting a Header or Footer

The date of the presentation, the presentation audience, a logo, a company name, and other identifying information are very valuable, and you may want such information to appear on every slide, handout, or notes page. Use the *Header and Footer* feature to do this. A **header** contains information that generally appears at the top of pages in a handout or on a notes page. A **footer** contains information that generally appears at the bottom of slides in a presentation or at the bottom of pages in a handout or on a notes page. Because the slide master (Slide Master View) of the theme controls the placement of the header/footer elements, you may find headers and footers in various locations on the slide.

STEP 5 To insert text in a header or footer, do the following:

1. Click the INSERT tab.
2. Click Header & Footer in the Text group.
3. Click the Slide tab or the *Notes and Handouts* tab.
4. Click desired options and enter desired text, if necessary.
5. Click *Apply to All* to add the information to all slides or pages, or if you are adding the header or footer to a single slide, click Apply.

Figure 1.24 shows the Slide tab of the *Header and Footer* dialog box.

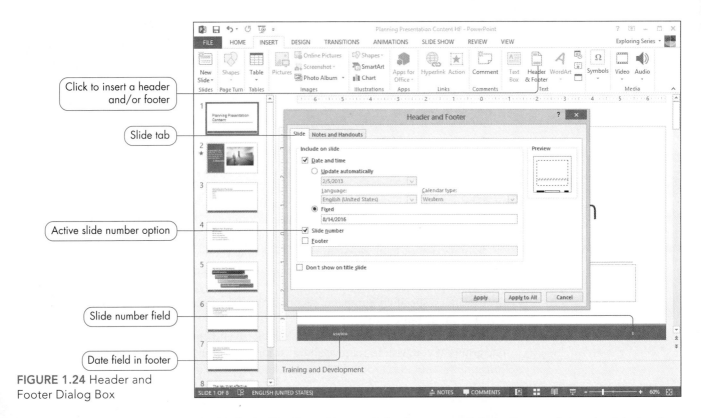

Click to insert a header and/or footer

Slide tab

Active slide number option

Slide number field

Date field in footer

FIGURE 1.24 Header and Footer Dialog Box

With the *Header and Footer* dialog box open, click the *Date and time* check box to insert the current date and time signature. Click *Update automatically* if you wish the date to always be current. Once you select *Update automatically*, you can select the date format you prefer. Alternatively, you can choose the option to enter a fixed date to preserve the original date, which can help you keep track of versions. Click the Slide Number check box to show the slide number on the slide. Click in the Footer box to enter information. The Preview window allows you to see the position of these fields. Always note the position of the fields, as PowerPoint layouts vary considerably in *Header and Footer* field positions. If you do not want the header or footer to appear on the title slide, select *Don't show on title slide*.

The *Notes and Handouts* tab gives you an extra field box for the Header field. Because this feature is used for printouts, the slides are not numbered, but the pages in the handout are. As you activate the fields, the Preview window shows the location of the fields. The date and time are located on the top right of the printout. The Header field is located on the top left. The page number is located on the bottom right, and the Footer field is on the bottom left.

Quick Concepts

1. Explain why adding media objects to a PowerPoint slide show is important. *p. 105*

2. How does a table organize information? *p. 106*

3. Describe three benefits that can occur when objects are animated in a slide show. *p. 106*

4. Give an example of when you would use the *Update automatically* option in the *Header and Footer* feature. When would you use the *Fixed date* option? *p. 110*

Hands-On Exercises

Watch the Video for this Hands-On Exercise!

MyITLab®
HOE3 Training

3 Presentation Enhancement

You decide to strengthen the slide show by adding objects. You know that adding clip art and additional information in a table will help state employees stay interested and retain information. You insert a table, add clip art, apply a transition, and animate the objects you have included. Finally, you enter a slide footer and a *Notes and Handouts* header and footer.

Skills covered: Add a Table • Insert Online Pictures • Apply a Transition • Animate Objects • Create a Handout Header and Footer

STEP 1 >> ADD A TABLE

To organize the list of objects that can be added to a PowerPoint slide, you create a table on a new slide. Listing these objects as bullets would take far more space than a table takes. Refer to Figure 1.25 as you complete Step 1.

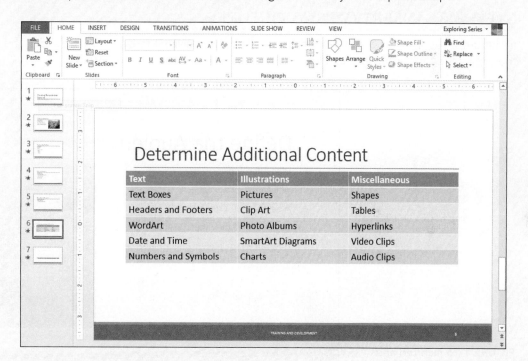

FIGURE 1.25 PowerPoint Table

a. Open *p01h2Content_LastFirst* if you closed it after the last Hands-On Exercise and save it as **p01h3Content_LastFirst**, changing *h2* to *h3*.

> TROUBLESHOOTING: If you make any major mistakes in this exercise, you can close the file, open *p01h2Content_LastFirst* again, and then start this exercise over.

b. Click **Slide 5** and click **New Slide** in the Slides group.

A new slide with the *Title and Content* layout is inserted after Slide 5.

c. Click the **title placeholder** and type **Determine Additional Content**.

d. Click **Insert Table** in the content placeholder in the center of the slide.

The Insert Table dialog box opens.

e. Set the number of columns to **3** and the number of rows to **6** and click **OK**.

PowerPoint creates the table and positions it on the slide. The first row is formatted differently from the other rows so that it can be used for column headings.

f. Click the top-left cell in the table and type **Text**. Press **Tab** to move to the next cell and type **Illustrations**. Press **Tab**, type **Miscellaneous**, and then press **Tab** to move to the next row.

g. Type the following text in the remaining table cells, pressing **Tab** after each entry.

Text Boxes	Pictures	Shapes
Headers and Footers	Clip Art	Tables
WordArt	Photo Albums	Hyperlinks
Date and Time	SmartArt Diagrams	Video Clips
Numbers and Symbols	Charts	Audio Clips

h. Save the presentation.

STEP 2 ≫ INSERT ONLINE PICTURES

In this step, you insert clip art from Office.com and then resize it to better fit the slide. The clip art you insert relates to the topic and adds visual interest. Refer to Figure 1.26 as you complete Step 2.

Step b: Clip art inserted

FIGURE 1.26 Inserted and Resized Clip Art

a. Display **Slide 2**, click **Layout** on the HOME tab, and then click the **Two Content layout**.

Changing the layout for this slide will better accommodate the photo you will add in the next step.

b. Click the **Online Pictures icon** in the right content placeholder, click the **Office.com Clip Art search box**, and then type the keyword **audience**. Press **Enter**. Select the image shown in Figure 1.26. Click **Insert**.

> **TROUBLESHOOTING:** If you cannot locate the picture shown in Figure 1.26, choose another photo showing an audience.

c. Save the presentation.

STEP 3 >> APPLY A TRANSITION

To add motion when one slide changes into another, you apply a transition to all slides in the presentation. You select a transition that is not distracting but that adds emphasis to the title slide. You will also include a sound as the transition occurs. Refer to Figure 1.27 as you complete Step 3.

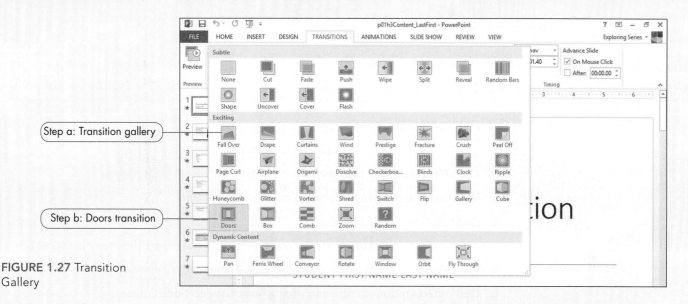

FIGURE 1.27 Transition Gallery

a. Click the **TRANSITIONS tab** and click **More** in the *Transition to This Slide* group.

   The Transition gallery displays.

b. Click **Doors** under *Exciting*.

   The transition effect will apply to all of the slides in the presentation. Notice that a star has been added next to the thumbnail of any slide where a transition has been applied.

c. Click **Apply to All** in the Timing group.

d. Select the **Slide 1 thumbnail**, click the **Sound arrow** in the Timing group, and then select **Push**.

   The Push sound will play as Slide 1 enters when in Slide Show view.

e. Click **Preview**.

   The Transition effect will play along with the sound for the first slide.

> **TROUBLESHOOTING:** If you are completing this activity in a classroom lab, you may need to plug in headphones or turn on speakers to hear the sound.

f. Save the presentation.

STEP 4 >> ANIMATE OBJECTS

You add animation to your slide show by controlling how individual objects such as lines of text or images enter or exit the slides. Refer to Figure 1.28 as you complete Step 4.

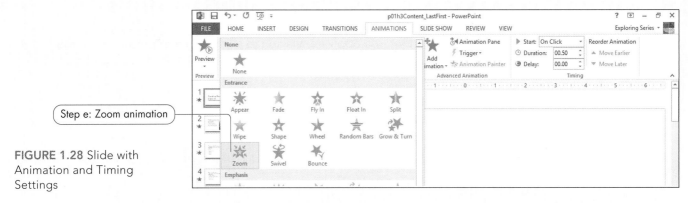

Step e: Zoom animation

FIGURE 1.28 Slide with Animation and Timing Settings

a. Select the **title placeholder** on Slide 1.

b. Click the **ANIMATIONS tab** and click **More** in the Animation group.

c. Click **Float In** (under *Entrance*).

The Float In animation is applied to the title placeholder.

d. On Slide 2, select the clip art image.

You decide to apply and modify the Zoom animation and change the animation speed.

e. Click **More** in the Animation group and click **Zoom** (under *Entrance*).

f. Click **Effect Options** in the Animation group and select **Slide Center**.

The clip art now grows and zooms from the center of the slide.

g. Save the presentation.

STEP 5 ≫ CREATE A HANDOUT HEADER AND FOOTER

Because you are creating this presentation for the Training and Development department, you include this identifying information in a slide footer. You also decide to include your personal information in a Notes and Handouts header and footer. Refer to Figure 1.29 as you complete Step 5.

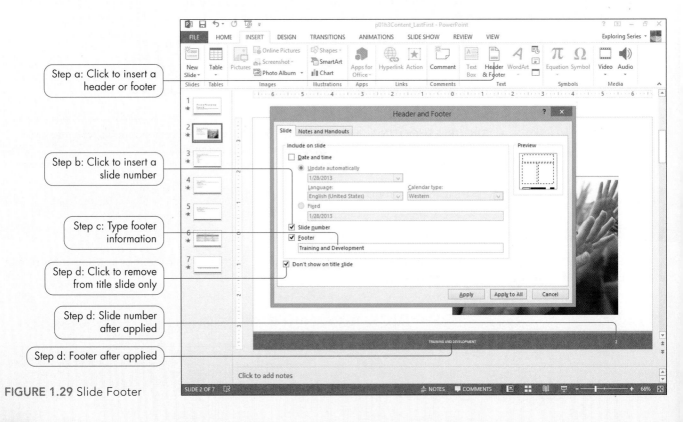

Step a: Click to insert a header or footer

Step b: Click to insert a slide number

Step c: Type footer information

Step d: Click to remove from title slide only

Step d: Slide number after applied

Step d: Footer after applied

FIGURE 1.29 Slide Footer

a. Click the **INSERT tab** and click **Header & Footer** in the Text group.

The Header and Footer dialog box opens, with the Slide tab active.

b. Click **Slide number**.

The slide number will now appear on each slide. Note the position of the slide number in the Preview window: top right of the slide. The template determined the position of the slide number.

c. Click the **Footer check box** and type **Training and Development**.

Training and Development will appear on each slide. Note the position of the footer in the Preview window: bottom right of the slide.

d. Click **Don't show on title slide** and click **Apply to All**.

The slide footer displays at the bottom right on all slides except the title slide.

e. Save the **p01h3Content_LastFirst** presentation and keep it open if you plan to continue to the next Hands-On Exercise. Close the file and exit PowerPoint if you will not continue with the next exercise at this time.

Navigation and Printing

STEP 1 » In the beginning of this chapter, you opened a slide show and advanced one by one through the slides by clicking the mouse button. Audiences may ask questions that can be answered by going to another slide in the presentation. As you respond to the questions, you may find yourself needing to jump back to a previous slide or needing to move to a future slide. You may even find that during your presentation you wish to direct your audience's attention to a single area of a slide (a new feature of PowerPoint 2013). PowerPoint's navigation options enable you to maneuver through a presentation easily.

To help your audience follow your presentation, you can choose to provide them with a handout. Various options are available for audience handouts. Be aware of the options, and choose the one that best suits your audience's needs. You may distribute handouts at the beginning of your presentation for note taking or provide your audience with the notes afterward.

In this section, you will run a slide show and navigate within the show. You will practice a variety of methods for advancing to new slides or returning to previously viewed slides. You will annotate slides during a presentation and will change from screen view to black-screen view. Finally, you will print handouts of the slide show.

Running and Navigating a Slide Show

PowerPoint provides multiple methods to advance through the slide show. You can also go backward to a previous slide, if desired. Use Table 1.1 to identify the navigation options, and then experiment with each method for advancing and going backward. Find the method that you are most comfortable using and stay with that method.

TABLE 1.1 Navigation Options

Navigation Option	Navigation Method
Advance Through the Slide Show	Press the Spacebar.
	Press Page Down.
	Press N for next.
	Press → or ↓.
	Press Enter.
Return to a Previous Slide or Animation	Right-click and choose Previous from the shortcut menu.
	Press Page Up.
	Press P for previous.
	Press ← or ↑.
	Press Backspace.
End the Slide Show	Press Esc.
Go to a Specific Slide	Type the slide number and press Enter.
	Right-click, point to See All Slides, and then click the slide desired.
Zoom into a Specific Area of a Slide	Right-click, point to Zoom In, and then choose the desired area of the slide.
	To zoom out, press Esc.

If an audience member asks a question that is answered in another slide on your slide show, you can go to that specific slide by using the See All Slides command. The See All Slides command is found on the shortcut menu, which displays when you right-click anywhere on the active slide during your presentation. The See All Slides command displays all of your slides so you can easily identify and select the slide to which you want to go. This shortcut menu also lets you end the slide show as well as access other features.

If an audience member asks you a question that is best explained by a graph or diagram you have on a slide in your presentation, you can zoom in on a single section of the slide to answer the question. To enlarge a section of a slide on the screen, do the following:

1. Navigate to the slide.
2. Click the magnifying glass icon. This will bring up a highlighted rectangular area on your slide.
3. Move the rectangular box over the area of the slide you want to emphasize. (Figure 1.30 shows the rectangular box.)
4. Click Esc to return to Normal view.

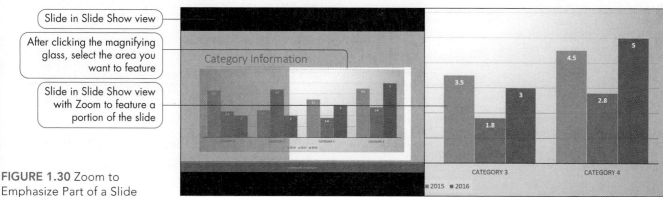

FIGURE 1.30 Zoom to Emphasize Part of a Slide

Practice the following delivery tips to gain confidence and polish your delivery.

Before the presentation:

- Practice or rehearse your PowerPoint presentation at home until you are comfortable with the material and its corresponding slides.

- Do not read from a prepared script or your PowerPoint Notes. Presenting is not karaoke. Know your material thoroughly. Glance at your notes infrequently. Never post a screen full of small text and then torture your audience by saying, "I know you can't read this, so I will …"

- Arrive early to set up so you do not keep the audience waiting while you manage equipment.

- Have a backup in case the equipment does not work: Overhead transparencies or handouts work well.

- If appropriate, prepare handouts for your audience so they can relax and participate in your presentation rather than scramble taking notes.

- Make sure your handouts acknowledge and document quotes, data, and sources.

During the presentation:

- Speak to the person farthest away from you to be sure the people in the last row can hear you. Speak slowly and clearly.

- Vary your delivery. Show emotion or enthusiasm for your topic. If you do not care about your topic, why should the audience?

- Pause to emphasize key points when speaking.

- Look at the audience, not at the screen, as you speak to open communication and gain credibility.

- Use the three-second guide: Look into the eyes of a member of the audience for three seconds and then scan the entire audience. Continue doing this throughout your presentation. Use your eye contact to keep members of the audience involved.

- Blank the screen by typing B or W at any time during your presentation when you want to solicit questions, comments, or discussion.

- Do not overwhelm your audience with your PowerPoint animations, sounds, and special effects. These features should not overpower you and your message, but should enhance your message.

After the presentation:

- Thank the audience for their attention and participation. Leave on a positive note.

Annotate the Slide Show

STEP 2 >> You may find it helpful to add *annotations* (notes or drawings) to your slides during a presentation. To add written notes or drawings, do the following:

1. Right-click a slide in Slide Show view.
2. Point to Pointer Options.
3. Click Pen or Highlighter.
4. Hold down the left mouse button and write or draw on the screen.

If you want to change the ink color for the Pen or Highlighter, right-click to bring up the shortcut menu, point to Pointer Options, and then click your pen type and ink color. To erase what you have drawn, press E. Your drawings or added text will be clumsy efforts at best, unless you use a tablet computer that includes a stylus and drawing screen. With each slide, you must again activate the drawing pointer, in order to avoid accidentally drawing on your slides. The annotations you create are not permanent unless you save the annotations when exiting the slide show and then save the changes upon exiting the file. You may want to save the annotated file with a different file name from the original presentation.

Rather than annotate a slide, you may simply want to point to a specific section of the screen. The laser pointer feature will allow you to do this. To use the laser pointer, do the following:

1. Right-click a slide in Slide Show view.
2. Point to Pointer Options.
3. Click Laser Pointer.
4. Move the mouse to the desired position.
5. Press Esc to end the laser pointer.

 TIP **Annotating Shortcuts**

Press Ctrl+P to change the pointer to a drawing pointer while presenting, and click and draw on the slide, much the same way your favorite football announcer diagrams a play. Use Page Down and Page Up to move forward and backward in the presentation while the annotation is in effect. Press Ctrl+A to return the mouse pointer to an arrow.

Printing in PowerPoint

A printed copy of a PowerPoint slide show can be used to display speaker notes for reference during the presentation, for audience handouts or a study guide, or as a means to deliver the presentation if there were an equipment failure. A printout of a single slide with text on it can be used as a poster or banner. Figure 1.31 shows the print options. Depending on your printer and printer settings, your button names may vary. To print a copy of the slide show using the default PowerPoint settings, do the following:

1. Click the FILE tab.
2. Click Print.
3. Click Printer to choose the print device you want to use.
4. Click Print All Slides to select the print area and range.
5. Click Full Page Slides to select the layout of the printout.
6. Click to select Collated or Uncollated.
7. Click Color to select color, grayscale, or pure black and white.
8. Click Print.

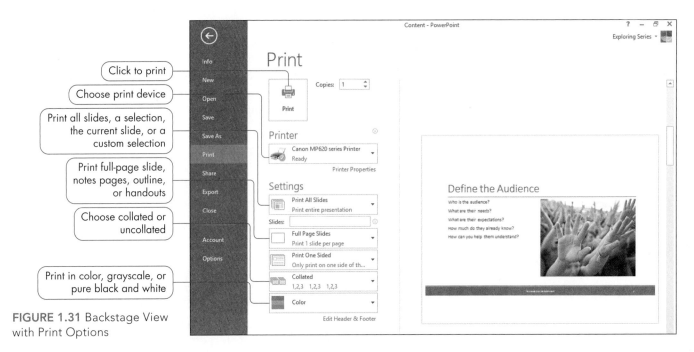

Click to print

Choose print device

Print all slides, a selection, the current slide, or a custom selection

Print full-page slide, notes pages, outline, or handouts

Choose collated or uncollated

Print in color, grayscale, or pure black and white

FIGURE 1.31 Backstage View with Print Options

Print Full Page Slides

Use the Print Full Page Slides option to print the slides for use as a backup or when the slides contain a great deal of detail the audience needs to examine. You will be grateful for the backup if your projector bulb blows out or if your computer quits working during a presentation.

If you are printing the slides on paper smaller than the standard size, be sure to change the slide size and orientation before you print. By default, PowerPoint sets the slides for landscape orientation for printing so that the width is greater than the height (11" × 8 1/2"). If you are going to print a flyer or overhead transparency, however, you need to set PowerPoint to portrait orientation, to print so that the height is greater than the width (8 1/2" × 11").

To change your slide orientation:

1. Click the DESIGN tab.
2. Click Slide Size in the Customize group.
3. Click Customize Slide Size.
4. Click Portrait or Landscape in the *Slides* section. Here, you can also change the size of the slide as well as the orientation. If you want to create a custom size of paper to print, enter the height and width.

After you click the File tab and click Print, you can determine the color option with which to print.

- Color: prints your presentation in color if you have a color printer or grayscale if you are printing on a black-and-white printer.
- Grayscale: prints in shades of gray, but be aware that backgrounds do not print when using the Grayscale option. By not printing the background, you make the text in the printout easier to read and you save a lot of ink or toner.
- Pure Black and White: prints in black and white only, with no gray color.

When you click Full Page Slides, several print options become available:

- Frame Slides: puts a black border around the slides in the printout, giving the printout a more polished appearance.
- Scale to Fit Paper: ensures that each slide prints on one page even if you have selected a custom size for your slide show, or if you have set up the slide show so that it is larger than the paper on which you are printing. If you have applied shadows to text or objects, click High Quality so that the shadows print.
- Print Comments and Ink Markup: prints any comments or annotations. This option is active only if you have used this feature.

Print Handouts

STEP 3>>
The principal purpose for printing handouts is to give your audience something they can use to follow and take notes on during the presentation. With your handout and their notes, the audience has an excellent resource for the future. Handouts can be printed with one, two, three, four, six, or nine slides per page. Printing three handouts per page is a popular option because it places thumbnails of the slides on the left side of the printout and lines on which the audience can write on the right side of the printout. Figure 1.32 shows the option set to Handouts and the *Slides per page* option set to 6.

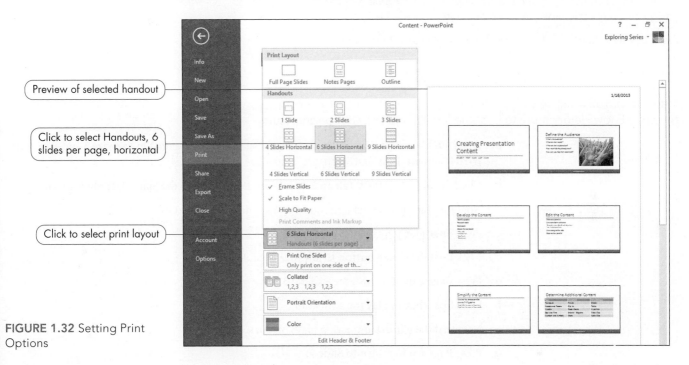

Preview of selected handout

Click to select Handouts, 6 slides per page, horizontal

Click to select print layout

FIGURE 1.32 Setting Print Options

Print Notes Pages

If you include charts, technical information, or references in a speaker note, you will want to print a Notes Page if you want the audience to have a copy. To print a specific Notes Page, change the print layout to Notes Pages and click the Print All Slides arrow. Click Custom Range and enter the specific slides to print.

Print Outlines

You may print your presentation as an outline made up of the slide titles and main text from each of your slides if you only want to deal with a few pages. The outline generally gives you enough detail to keep you on track with your presentation, but does not display speaker notes.

Quick **Concepts**

1. How do you access the *Go to Slide* command when displaying a slide show, and what does it do? *p. 116*

2. Discuss three presentation delivery do's and three presentation don'ts. *p. 118*

3. Describe at least three uses for a printed copy of a PowerPoint slide show. *p. 119*

Hands-On Exercises

Watch the Video for this Hands-On Exercise!

MyITLab®
HOE4 Training

4 Navigation and Printing

To prepare for your presentation to Training and Development department employees, you practice displaying the slide show and navigating to specific slides. You also annotate a slide and print audience handouts.

Skills covered: Start a Slide Show • Annotate a Slide • Print Audience Handouts

STEP 1 ≫ START A SLIDE SHOW

In this step, you practice various slide navigation techniques to become comfortable with their use. You also review the Slide Show Help feature to become familiar with navigation shortcuts.

a. Open *p01h3Content_LastFirst* if you closed it at the end of Hands-On Exercise 3 and save it as **p01h4Content_LastFirst**, changing *h3* to *h4*.

b. Click the **SLIDE SHOW tab** and click **From Beginning** in the Start Slide Show group.

   Note the transition effect and sound you applied in Hands-On Exercise 3.

c. Press **Spacebar** to display the animation.

d. Click the **left mouse button** to advance to Slide 2.

e. Press **Page Down** to advance to Slide 3.

f. Press **Spacebar** to play the animation.

   Note that the clip art animation plays on click.

g. Press **Page Up** to return to Slide 2.

h. Click the **Magnifying glass icon** and zoom in only on the text for Slide 2.

i. Press **Enter** to advance to Slide 3.

j. Press **N** to advance to Slide 4.

k. Press **Backspace** to return to Slide 3.

l. Press the number **5** and press **Enter**.

   Slide 5 displays.

m. Press **F1** and read the Slide Show Help window showing the shortcut tips that are available during the display of a slide show. Practice moving between slides using the shortcuts shown in Help.

n. Close the Help window.

STEP 2 ≫ ANNOTATE A SLIDE

You practice annotating a slide using a pen, and then you remove the annotations. You practice darkening the screen and returning to the presentation from the dark screen.

    a. On Slide 3, press **Ctrl+P**.

        The mouse pointer becomes a pen.

    b. Circle and underline the words *Research topic* on the slide.

    c. Press **E**.

        The annotations erase.

    d. Press **B**.

        The screen blackens.

    e. Press **B** again.

        The slide show displays again.

    f. Press **Esc** to end annotations.

    g. Press **Esc** to end the slide show.

STEP 3 ≫ PRINT AUDIENCE HANDOUTS

To enable your audience to follow along during your presentation, you print handouts of your presentation. You know that many of the audience members will also keep your handouts for future reference.

    a. Click the **FILE tab** to display the Backstage view and click **Print**.

    b. Click **Full Page Slides** and select **4 Slides Horizontal** in the *Handouts* section.

> **TROUBLESHOOTING:** If you have previously selected a different print layout, Full Page Slides will be changed to that layout. Click the arrow next to the displayed layout option.

    c. Click **Print** to print the presentation if requested by your instructor.

    d. Save and close the file, and submit based on your instructor's directions.

Chapter Objectives Review

After reading this chapter, you have accomplished the following objectives:

1. **Use PowerPoint views.**
   - Slide shows are electronic presentations that enable you to advance through slides containing content that will help your audience understand your message.
   - Normal view displays either thumbnail images or an outline in one pane, the slide in one pane, and a Notes pane.
   - Slide Sorter view displays thumbnails of slides to enable you to organize your presentation.
   - Outline View enables you to easily create a presentation from an outline.
   - Notes Page view displays a thumbnail of the slide and speaker notes.
   - Slide Show view displays the slide show in full-screen view for an audience.
   - Presenter view gives the presenter options such as a timer and notes, whereas the audience views the full-screen presentation.

2. **Type a speaker note.**
   - Slides should contain only a minimum amount of information, and the speaker should deliver the majority of the information throughout the presentation.
   - Speaker notes can be added to the PowerPoint presentation to provide the speaker with additional notes, data, or other comments that will be useful during the presentation.

3. **Save as a slide show.**
   - You can save a presentation as a slide show, so that when the file opens it is in Slide Show mode. Slide shows cannot be edited and are saved with the file extension .ppsx.

4. **Plan a presentation.**
   - Prepare a storyboard: Organize your ideas on a storyboard, and then create your presentation in PowerPoint.
   - Create a title slide and introduction: The title slide should have a short title that indicates the purpose. An introduction slide will get the audience's attention.
   - Create the main body of slides: The content of your presentation follows the title slide and the introduction.
   - Create the conclusion: End your presentation with a summary or conclusion that reviews the main points, restates the purpose, or invokes a call to action.

5. **Assess presentation content.**
   - Use active voice: Review and edit the phrases so they begin with active voice when possible.
   - Use parallel construction: Use parallel construction so that your bullets are in the same grammatical form.

   - Follow the 7 × 7 guideline: Use no more than seven words per line and seven lines per slide.
   - When you add a slide, you can choose from a set of predefined slide layouts that determine the position of the objects or content on a slide.
   - Placeholders hold content and determine the position of the objects on the slide.
   - Reorder slides: You can easily reorder your slides using the Slide Sorter view.

6. **Review the presentation.**
   - Use the Spelling and Thesaurus features, and review the presentation in Normal and Slide Show views to ensure no errors exist.

7. **Insert media objects.**
   - Media objects such as clip art, images, movies, and sound can be added to enhance the message of your slides and to add visual interest.

8. **Add a table.**
   - Tables organize information in rows and columns.

9. **Use animations and transitions.**
   - Animate objects: Animations control the movement of an object on the slide.
   - Apply transitions: Transitions control the movement of slides as one slide changes to another.

10. **Insert a header or footer.**
    - Headers and footers are used for identifying information on the slide or on handouts and note pages. Header and footer locations vary depending on the theme applied.

11. **Run and navigate a slide show.**
    - Various navigation methods advance the slide show, return to previously viewed slides, or go to specific slides.
    - Slides can be annotated during a presentation to add emphasis or comments to slides.

12. **Print in PowerPoint.**
    - Print handouts: Handouts print miniatures of the slides using 1, 2, 3, 4, 6, or 9 slide thumbnails per page.
    - Print notes pages: Notes Page method prints a single thumbnail of a slide with its associated notes per page.
    - Print outlines: Outline View prints the titles and main points of the presentation in outline format.

Key Terms Matching

Match the key terms with their definitions. Write the key term letter by the appropriate numbered definition.

a. Animation
b. Annotation
c. Layout
d. Normal view
e. Notes Page view
f. Placeholder
g. PowerPoint presentation
h. PowerPoint show
i. Presenter view
j. Reading View

k. Slide
l. Slide show
m. Slide Show view
n. Slide Sorter view
o. Status bar
p. Storyboard
q. Theme
r. Thumbnail
s. Transition
t. Variant

1. _____ Defines containers, positioning, and formatting for all of the content that appears on a slide. **p. 99**

2. _____ The default PowerPoint view, containing two panes that provide maximum flexibility in working with the presentation. **p. 85**

3. _____ A container that holds content. **p. 99**

4. _____ The movement applied to an object or objects on a slide. **p. 106**

5. _____ The most basic element of PowerPoint, analogous to a page in a Word document. **p. 84**

6. _____ A note or drawing added to a slide during a presentation. **p. 118**

7. _____ Located at the bottom of the screen, this contains the slide number, a spell check button, and options that control the view of your presentation. **p. 85**

8. _____ Used to view a slide show full screen, one slide at a time. **p. 89**

9. _____ A presentation saved with a .pptx extension. **p. 84**

10. _____ A method to deliver your message in a variety of ways using multiple slides. **p. 84**

11. _____ Used if the speaker needs to enter and edit large amounts of text for reference in the presentation. **p. 88**

12. _____ Uses a .ppsx extension. **p. 90**

13. _____ A specialty view that delivers a presentation on two monitors simultaneously. **p. 90**

14. _____ A variation of the theme you have chosen, using different color palettes and font families. **p. 97**

15. _____ Used to deliver a completed presentation full screen to an audience, one slide at a time. **p. 89**

16. _____ A slide miniature. **p. 85**

17. _____ A specific animation that is applied when a previous slide is replaced by a new slide. **p. 106**

18. _____ Displays thumbnails of your presentation slides, allowing you to view multiple slides simultaneously. **p. 87**

19. _____ A visual design that helps you plan the direction of your presentation slides. **p. 95**

20. _____ A collection of formatting choices that includes colors, fonts, and special effects. **p. 97**

Multiple Choice

1. Which of the following will display a list of shortcuts for navigating when presenting a slide show?

    (a) F1

    (b) F11

    (c) Ctrl+Enter

    (d) Esc

2. What is the name for PowerPoint's predefined slide arrangements?

    (a) Placeholder views

    (b) Slide layouts

    (c) Slide guides

    (d) Slide displays

3. What is the term for a variation of the theme using different color palettes and font families?

    (a) Palette

    (b) Design

    (c) Variant

    (d) Layout

4. When making a presentation that includes a large detailed table, which print method should you use?

    (a) Handout, 6 Slides Horizontal

    (b) Outline

    (c) Notes Pages

    (d) Full Page Slide

5. Which of the following components are contained in Normal view?

    (a) Slide Sorter pane, Thumbnails pane, and Reading pane

    (b) Thumbnails pane, Slide pane, and Reading pane

    (c) Thumbnails pane and Slide pane

    (d) Slide pane, Notes pane, and Slide Sorter pane

6. What view is the best choice if you want to reorder the slides in a presentation?

    (a) Presenter view

    (b) Reading View

    (c) Slide Sorter view

    (d) Slide Show view

7. Regarding themes, which of the following is a *true* statement?

    (a) A theme must be applied before slides are created.

    (b) The theme can be changed after all of the slides have been created.

    (c) Themes control placeholder location but not fonts and backgrounds.

    (d) Placeholders positioned by a theme cannot be moved.

8. In reference to content development, which of the following points is *not* in active voice and is not parallel to the others?

    (a) Identify the purpose of the presentation.

    (b) Storyboards are used to sketch out thoughts.

    (c) Brainstorm your thoughts.

    (d) Research your topic.

9. The animation effect that controls how one slide changes to another slide is called:

    (a) Transition.

    (b) Timing.

    (c) Animation.

    (d) Advance.

10. During a slide show, which of the following would best be used to focus audience attention on a specific object?

    (a) Put nothing on the slide but the object.

    (b) Apply an animation to the object.

    (c) Use the Pen tool to circle the object.

    (d) Apply a transition to the object.

Practice Exercises

1 Student Success

The slide show you create in this practice exercise covers concepts and skills that will help you be successful in college. You create a title slide, an introduction, four slides containing main points of the presentation, and a conclusion slide. Then, you review the presentation and edit a slide so that the text of the bulleted items is parallel. Finally, you print a title page to use as a cover and notes pages to staple together as a reference. This exercise follows the same set of skills as used in Hands-On Exercises 1–4 in the chapter. Refer to Figure 1.33 as you complete the exercise.

FIGURE 1.33 Student Success Strategies

Photo: falcn/Fotolia

a. Open PowerPoint.

b. Click the **Facet theme**. Click the variant with the dark blue background (bottom-right corner) and click **Create**.

c. Save the presentation as **p01p1Success_LastFirst**.

d. Click the **Slide 1 thumbnail**. Click the **INSERT tab**, click **Header & Footer** in the Text group, and then click the **Notes and Handouts tab** in the *Header and Footer* dialog box. Make the following changes:

- Select the **Date and time check box** and click **Update automatically** (if necessary).
- Click to select the **Header check box** and type your name in the **Header box**.
- Click the **Footer check box** and type your instructor's name and your class name in the **Footer box**. Click **Apply to All**.

e. On Slide 1, click in the **title placeholder** and type **Student Success Strategies**. Click in the **subtitle placeholder** and type your name.

f. Click **New Slide** in the Slides group on the HOME tab to create a new slide (Slide 2) for the introduction of the slide show. Type **Tips for College Success** in the **title placeholder** and type the following bulleted text in the **content placeholder**:

- **Class attendance**
- **Be organized**
- **Read your textbook**
- **Use available services**

g. Click **New Slide** in the Slides group on the HOME tab to create a new slide (Slide 3) for the first main point of the slide show. Type **Step 1: Attend Class** in the **title placeholder** and type the following bulleted text in the **content placeholder**:

- **Attend class**
- **Complete assignments**
- **Participate in discussions**
- **Take notes**

h. Click **Notes** on the status bar. Type the following in the **Notes pane**: **When you miss class, you lose the opportunity to listen to the lecture, take notes, participate in discussions, and you also miss assignments, quizzes, and tests.**

i. Click **New Slide** in the Slides group on the HOME tab to create a new slide (Slide 4) for the second main point of the slide show. Type **Step 2: Be Organized** in the **title placeholder** and enter the following bulleted text in the **content placeholder**:

- **Use a planner**
- **Keep all notes and handouts in a binder**
- **Save all papers and projects**
- **Get classmates' contact information**
- **Set up a study space**

j. Type the following in the **Notes pane** for Slide 4: **Record every assignment, quiz, and exam date in a planner. Keep all returned papers, quizzes, to use as a resource for studying for a final exam and as a record of your grades for the course.**

k. Click the **New Slide arrow** in the Slides group on the HOME tab. Click **Two Content** to create a new slide (Slide 5) for the third main point of the slide show. Type **Step 3: Read Your Textbook** in the **title placeholder** and enter the following text in the **content placeholder** on the left side of the slide following the title:

- **Scan**
- **Read**
- **Review**

l. Click the **Online Pictures icon** in the content placeholder on the right side of the slide. Type **textbook** in the **Office.com Clip Art box**. Press **Enter**. Click an image of stacked textbooks on the slide, as shown in Figure 1.34, and click **Insert** to insert the image.

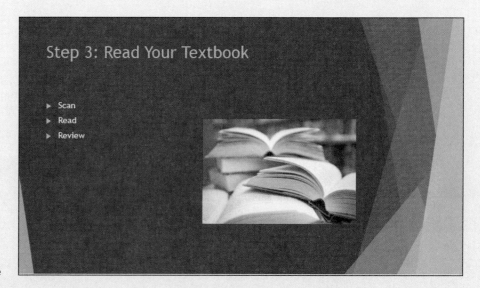

FIGURE 1.34 Inserted Image

TROUBLESHOOTING: If you cannot locate the image in Figure 1.34, select another clip art image of a textbook or textbooks. Expand your search terms to include other result types if necessary.

m. Type the following in the **Notes pane: Read the chapter summary and review questions. Next, read the entire chapter for detail and to increase your comprehension.**

n. Click the **New Slide arrow** in the Slides group on the HOME tab. Click **Title and Content** to create a new slide (Slide 6) for the last main point of the slide show. Type **Step 4: Use Available Services** in the **title placeholder**.

o. Click the **Insert Table icon** in the content placeholder. Set *Number of columns* to **2** and *Number of rows* to **7**. Click **OK**. Type the following text in the columns, pressing **Tab** after each entry except the last:

Class Assistance	Other Assistance
Tutors	Academic Advisor
Libraries	Clubs/Activities
Honors Programs	Counseling
Computer Labs	Financial Aid
Accessibility Services	Health Services
Testing Centers	Placement

p. Type the following in the **Notes pane** for Slide 6: **You can use campus facilities like computer labs without charge because typically the cost is covered through fees you pay. You can also get questions answered and problems resolved by talking to personnel in campus offices.**

q. Click the **New Slide arrow** in the Slides group on the HOME tab. Click **Title Slide** to create a new slide (Slide 7) for the conclusion slide of the slide show. Type **Being self-disciplined is the key to being a college success story!** in the **title placeholder**. Select the border of the subtitle placeholder and press **Delete**.

r. Review Slide 2 and note that the slide bullets are not in parallel construction. The first bulleted point needs to be changed to active voice. Select **Class attendance** and type **Attend class**.

s. Click the **TRANSITIONS tab** and click **More** in the *Transition to This Slide* group. Click **Push** in the Transition gallery.

t. Click **Apply to All** in the Timing Group.

u. Click the **FILE tab**, click **Print**, and then click in the box marked *Slides*. Type **2-7** as the slide range. Click **Full Page Slides** and select **Notes Pages**. Click **Frame Slides** and click **Print**, if your instructor asks you to submit printed slides.

v. Staple the title page you printed to the front of the Notes Pages to use as a cover page, if your instructor asked you to print this exercise.

w. Click the **REVIEW tab** and click **Spelling**. Click **Save** to save the presentation. Click the **FILE tab**, click **Save As**, and then choose the location where you will save the file. In the Save As dialog box, change the *Save as type* to **PowerPoint Show** and click **Save**. Close the presentation. Submit files based on your instructor's directions.

2 Tips for a Successful Presentation

FROM SCRATCH

Your employer is a successful author who has been asked by the local International Association of Administrative Professionals (IAAP) to give tips for presenting successfully using PowerPoint. He created a storyboard of his presentation and has asked you to create the presentation from the storyboard. This exercise follows the same set of skills as used in Hands-On Exercises 2 and 3 in the chapter. Refer to Figure 1.35 as you complete this exercise.

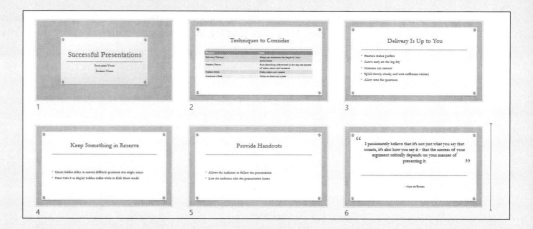

FIGURE 1.35 Successful Presentations

a. Open PowerPoint.

b. Select the **Organic** theme, select the variant in the bottom-right corner, and then click **Create**.

c. Save the presentation as **p01p2Presenting_LastFirst**.

d. Click the **INSERT tab**, click **Header & Footer**, and then click the **Notes and Handouts tab** in the *Header and Footer* dialog box.

  • Click to select the **Date and time check box** and click **Update automatically**, if necessary.
  • Click to select the **Header check box** and type your name in the **Header box**.
  • Click to select the **Footer check box** and type your instructor's name and your class name. Click **Apply to All**.

e. On Slide 1, click in the **title placeholder** and type **Successful Presentations**. Click in the **subtitle placeholder** and type your instructor's name. Press **Enter**. On the new line, type your name.

f. Click the **HOME tab** and click **New Slide** in the Slides group.

g. Click in the **title placeholder** and type **Techniques to Consider**.

h. Click the **Insert Table icon** in the content placeholder and enter **2** columns and **5** rows.

i. Type the following information in the table cells, pressing **Tab** after each item except the last.

Feature	Use
Rehearse Timings	Helps you determine the length of your presentation
Header/Footer	Puts identifying information on the top and bottom of slides, notes, and handouts
Hidden Slides	Hides slides until needed
Annotate a Slide	Writes or draws on a slide

j. Click the **HOME tab** and click **New Slide** in the Slides group. Type **Delivery Is Up to You** in the title placeholder.

k. Click in the **content placeholder** and type the following bulleted text:

  • **Practice makes perfect**
  • **Arrive early on the big day**
  • **Maintain eye contact**
  • **Speak slowly, clearly, and with sufficient volume**
  • **Allow time for questions**

l. Click **New Slide** and type **Keep Something in Reserve** in the **title placeholder**.

m. Click in the **content placeholder** and type the following bulleted text:

  • **Create hidden slides to answer difficult questions that might occur**
  • **Press Ctrl+S while in Slide Show view to display hidden slides**

n. Click **New Slide** and type **Provide Handouts** in the **title placeholder**.

o. Click in the **content placeholder** and type the following bulleted text:

- **Allows the audience to follow the presentation**
- **Lets the audience take the presentation home**

p. Click the **New Slide arrow** and click **Quote with Caption**.

q. Type **I passionately believe that it's not just what you say that counts, it's also how you say it - that the success of your argument critically depends on your manner of presenting it.** in the title placeholder.

r. Click the **center placeholder** and press **Delete**.

s. Type - **Alain de Botton** in the **bottom placeholder**.

t. Click the **REVIEW tab** and click **Spelling** in the Proofing group. Accept *Lets* in Slide 5, if necessary. Review the presentation in Slide Show view to fix any spelling errors.

u. Click the **SLIDE SHOW tab** and click **From Beginning** in the Start Slide Show group. Press **Page Down** to advance through the slides. When you reach the last slide of the slide show, press the number **3** and press **Enter** to return to Slide 3.

v. Right-click, point to *Pointer Options*, and then click **Highlighter**. Highlight **Speak slowly, clearly, and with sufficient volume**.

w. Press **Page Down** to advance through the remainder of the presentation. Press **Esc** when you reach the black slide at the end of the slide show and click **Keep** to keep your slide annotations.

x. **Save** the presentation. Close the file and submit based on your instructor's directions.

Mid-Level Exercises

1 Planning Presentation Content

Brainstorming a topic and creating a storyboard with ideas is the first step in slide show development. After creating the slide show from a storyboard, however, the information should be accessed and edited so that the final slide show is polished and professional. In this exercise, you create a slide show from a storyboard and then edit the slide show following the tips contained in the content.

a. Open PowerPoint. Create a new presentation, applying the design theme of your choice to the presentation. Save the presentation as **p01m1Refine_LastFirst**.

b. Create the following slides with the content contained in the following table:

Slide Number	Slide Layout	Slide Title	Slide Content
1	Title	Refining Presentation Content	(type your name) (type your class)
2	Title and Content	Principles for Refining Content	• Simplify content • Reduce text • Edit text • Make text readable • Emphasize main points • Create consistency • Create a mood with color

3	Title and Content	Simplify Content	• Plan 3 to 5 text slides per major concept
			• Use one main concept per slide
			• Use 7 × 7 guideline
			  • Limit slide to 7 or fewer lines
			  • Limit words in lines to 7 or fewer

4	Title and Content	Reduce Text	• First Edit
			  • Reduce paragraph text to sentences
			• Second Edit
			  • Reduce sentences to phrases
			• Third Edit
			  • Edit phrase text

5	Title and Content	Edit Text	• Make text concise • Use consistent verb tense • Use strong, action verbs • Use few adverbs and adjectives • Use few prepositions

6	Title and Content	Make Text Readable	• Consider font attributes
			  • Font style
			  • Font size
			• Choose a typeface that depicts the content
			• Limit the number of fonts on slide

7	Title and Content	Emphasize Main Points	• Use images and objects that relate to topic • Animate text and charts • Use bullets for items of equal importance • Use numbers for ranking or sequencing

Slide Number	Slide Layout	Slide Title	Slide Content
8	Title and Content	Create Consistency	• Use same fonts, sizes, and attributes
			• Apply consistent alignment
			• Use same paragraph spacing
			• Utilize color scheme
9	Two Content	Create a Mood with Color	*(In the left placeholder)*
			• Yellow—Optimism, Warmth
			• White—Peace, Quiet
			• Green—Growth
			• Red—Action, Enthusiasm
			• Blue—Calm, Traditional
			• Black—Power, Strength
			• Grey—Neutral
10	Title Slide	The key to success is to make certain your slide show is a visual aid and not a visual distraction.	Dr. Joseph Sommerville
			Peak Communication Performance

c. Show the slide number on the slides. Apply to all slides except on the title slide. (Note: the slide number will appear at the top of the slides for this theme.)

d. On Slide 9, insert a clip art image in the empty placeholder that illustrates the concept of color. Add other visual objects if you choose, but make sure the objects enhance the message.

e. Review the slide show and adjust font size, image size, and placeholder location until all elements fit attractively and professionally on the slides.

f. Assign the transition of your choice to all slides in the slide show, and then animate at least one individual object of your choice.

g. Save the presentation. Close the file and submit based on your instructor's directions.

2 Wireless Network Safety

You volunteer at the local community center. You have been asked to present to a group of young teens about staying safe when using wireless computer networks. You have researched the topic and using your notes you are ready to prepare your presentation.

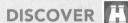

a. Open PowerPoint and start a new presentation. Apply the design theme of your choice. Save the presentation as **p01m2Wifi_LastFirst**.

b. Add **WiFi Safety** as a footer on all slides except the title slide. Also include an automatically updated date and time and a slide number. (Note: The placement of Wifi Safety footer text, dates, and slide numbers will vary based on the theme chosen.)

c. Create a *Notes and Handouts* header with your name and a footer with your instructor's name and your class name. Include the current date. Apply to all.

d. On the title slide, add the title **WiFi Safety** in the **title placeholder**. Type **Keeping Your Personal Information Safe** in the **subtitle placeholder**.

e. Insert a new slide using the **Two Content layout**. Type **Wireless Fidelity (WiFi)** as the title.

f. Type the following into the **left content placeholder**:
   • **Uses radio waves to exchange data wirelessly via a computer network**
   • **Commonly found at coffee shops and other public places**
   • **Also called hotspots**

g. Add a clip art photograph to the right content placeholder: Search for **WiFi** in the Office.com clip art box. Insert the photo of your choosing. Move the photo so it is positioned attractively.

h. Insert a new slide using the **Title and Content layout** as the third slide in the presentation. Type **WiFi Hotspot Security** as the title.

i. Type the following into the **content placeholder**:

- **Avoid unsecured networks if possible**
- **Don't access confidential information**
- **Set network locations to "Public"**
- **Keep firewall and antivirus software up-to-date**

j. Click **Notes** on the status bar. Add the following text to the **Notes pane**:

Although a number of threats exist when using public WiFi hotspots, there are several ways you can protect yourself and your computer.

k. Insert a new slide using the **Blank layout** as the fourth slide in the presentation.

l. Click the **INSERT tab**, click **Table**, and then draw a table with four rows and four columns. Type the following text in the table.

Threat	Explanation
Identity Theft	Criminal act involving the use of your personal information for financial gain.
Hacking	Unauthorized access to a computer or network.
Malware	Software programs that are designed to be harmful. A virus is a type of malware.

m. Position the table attractively on the page.

n. Apply the **Fade transition** from the Subtle category to all slides in the slide show.

o. Add the **Bounce animation** from the Entrance category to the content placeholder and the image on Slide 2. Set the animations so they bounce at the same time.

p. Move Slide 4 so that it becomes Slide 3.

q. Review the presentation and correct any errors you find.

r. Print the handouts, three per page, framed.

s. Save the presentation. Close the file and submit based on your instructor's directions.

---

3 | Creating a Free Web Site and Blog for Your PowerPoint Experiences

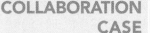

Web 2.0 technologies make it easy for people to interact using the Internet. Web applications often combine functions to help us create our online identity, share information, collaborate on projects, and socialize. In this exercise, you will create an online identity for your use in your PowerPoint class, share information about your PowerPoint experience with others, and get to know a few of your classmates. You will create a Web site for use during your PowerPoint class, add information to the pages in your Web site, and then share the address of your site with others. You will also visit the Web sites of others in your class.

a. Open a Web browser and go to **www.weebly.com**.

b. Enter your full name as the Username in the Sign Up box, enter your e-mail address, and then enter a password.

c. Select the text in the Welcome to Weebly box and enter a title for your Web site as follows: use your first name followed by PPT to indicate this is your PowerPoint site, select the Education category, and then Class Project for your site type.

d. Select **Use a Subdomain of Weebly.com** in the Choose Your Website Domain box to set up the address where people will find your Web site online. Using a subdomain of Weebly.com is free. Click **Continue**. You have created your Web site and you should note your Web site address as you will be sharing this address with your instructor and/or selected classmates.

e. Select the **Elements tab**, if necessary, and drag elements from the top bar to the page to create your site. Add an element that can be used to introduce yourself to others (such as Paragraph with Title or Paragraph with Picture). Also, add a contact form so other students can get in touch with you if they have a comment or question.

f. Click the **Design tab** and select the Design theme of your choice for your site.

g. Click the **Pages tab** and click **Add Blog**. Click in the **Page Name box**, select **Blog Remove!**, type the name you want to use for your blog, and then click **Save Settings**. The left panel of the screen now shows that your Web site has two pages: your home page and your blog site.

h. Edit your blog by adding text that explains your previous experience with PowerPoint and why you have registered for this class. Search YouTube for a video about PowerPoint or presentation skills. Create a second blog entry about what you learned and include the link for others to view if interested.

i. Publish your Web site. Type the security words in the verification box as requested. Click the **X** in the Website Published box to finish.

j. Exchange Web site addresses with at least three other students in your class. Visit your classmates' Web sites and use the contact form on their Home pages to leave your information and a comment. Then, revisit your Web site to see what comments your classmates entered.

k. E-mail your instructor the Web site address you created in step e so your instructor can visit your site.

Beyond the Classroom

Taking Online Courses

RESEARCH CASE

FROM SCRATCH

Many colleges and universities are offering online courses as an alternative to face-to-face classroom instruction. Use the Internet to research the pros and cons of taking a class online, explain why some courses may be better suited to this format, and discuss some strategies to succeed in an online course. Create a storyboard on paper or using Microsoft Word. Include a title slide and at least four slides related to this topic. Include a summary reviewing the success strategies. Choose a theme, transitions, and animations. Insert at least one appropriate clip art image. Include slide notes as necessary. Create a handout header with your name, page numbers, and the current date. Include a handout footer with your instructor's name and your class name. Review the presentation to ensure there are no errors by viewing each slide in Slide Show view. Print as directed by your instructor. Save the presentation as **p01b2OnlineSuccess_LastFirst**. Close the file and submit based on your instructor's directions.

Polishing a Business Presentation

DISASTER RECOVERY

A neighbor has created a slide show to present to a local business explaining his company's services. He has asked you to refine the slide show so it has a more professional appearance. Open *p01b3Green* and save the file as **p01b3Green_LastFirst**. View the slide show. Note that the text is difficult to read because of a lack of contrast with the background, there are capitalization errors and spelling errors, the bulleted points are not parallel, and images are positioned and sized poorly. Select and apply a design theme and a colors scheme. Modify text following the guidelines presented throughout this chapter. Reposition placeholders as needed. Size and position the images in the presentation or replace them with your choice of images. Text may be included in speaker notes to emphasize visuals, if desired. Apply a transition to all slides. Add a minimum of two animations. Make other changes you choose. Create a handout header with your name and the current date. Include a handout footer with your instructor's name and your class name. Review the presentation to ensure there are no errors by viewing each slide in Slide Show view. Save your file and then save it again as a PowerPoint show. Close the file and submit based on your instructor's directions.

Preparing for an Interview

SOFT SKILLS

FROM SCRATCH

Research the profession you are most interested in pursuing upon graduation. Create a storyboard on paper or using Microsoft Word outlining job search strategies for the profession. Then, create a PowerPoint presentation based on this outline. Include a title slide and at least four slides related to this topic. Choose a theme, transitions, and animations. Insert at least one appropriate clip art image. Include slide notes on most slides as necessary. Create a handout header with your name and the current date. Include a handout footer with your instructor's name and your class name. Review the presentation to ensure there are no errors by viewing each slide in Slide Show view. Print as directed by your instructor. Save the presentation as **p01b3Search_LastFirst**. Close the file and submit based on your instructor's directions.

Gamerz is a successful retail store. The company sells video games as well as traditional games such as puzzles and board games, and is renowned for hosting game nights and competitions. Gamerz is a place where customers can find gaming resources, supplies, gaming news, and a good challenge. The store has been in operation for six years and has increased its revenue and profit each year. The partners are looking to expand their operation and need to prepare a presentation for an important meeting with financiers.

Create a Title Slide

You add your name to the title slide, apply a theme, and create a slide for the Gamerz mission statement.

a. Open *p01c1Capital* and save it as **p01c1Capital_ LastFirst**.

b. Create a *Notes and Handouts* header with your name and a footer with your instructor's name and your class name. Include the current date. Apply to all.

c. On Slide 1, replace *Your name* in the **subtitle place-holder** with your name.

d. Apply the **Retrospect design theme** with the gray background variant.

e. Insert a new slide using the **Title Only layout** after Slide 1. Type the following in the **title placeholder**: **Gamerz provides a friendly setting in which customers can purchase game equipment and resources as well as participate in a variety of challenging gaming activities.**

f. Change the font size to **30 pt** and apply **Italic**.

Create Tables to Display Sales Data

You create tables to show the increase in sales from last year to this year, the sales increase by category, and the sales increase by quarters.

a. On Slide 5, create a table of six columns and three rows. Type the data from Table 1 below in your table.

b. Format the table text font to **20 pt**. Center align the column headings and right align all numbers. Position the table on the slide so it is approximately centered.

c. On Slide 6, create a table of five columns and three rows. Type the data from Table 2 below in your table and apply the same formatting to this table that you applied in step b.

d. Check the spelling in the presentation, and review the presentation for any other errors. Fix anything you think is necessary.

e. View the presentation, and as you navigate through the slides, note that the presentation plan included the mission statement as the introduction slide, included supporting data in the body of the presentation, and included a plan for the future as the conclusion (summary) slide.

Add Clip Art and Animation

Gamerz uses a video game controller in its logo. You use a video game controller on the title slide to continue this identifying image.

a. On Slide 1, open Online Pictures. Use **video game controller** as your search keyword in the Office.com Clip Art search box and locate the image of a video game controller. Size and position the image appropriately.

b. Use the same clip art of a video game controller on the last slide of your slide show. Position the clip in the bottom-right portion of your slide, and increase its size.

c. On Slide 4, select the **Our first year was profitable box** and apply the **Fly In entrance animation**.

d. Select the **Our second year was significantly better box** and apply the **Fly In entrance animation**. Change the Start option to **After Previous**.

TABLE 1

Year	New Video Games	Used Video Games	Board Games	Puzzles	Events
Last Year	$120,200	$90,200	$75,915	$31,590	$25,755
This Year	$128,200	$110,700	$115,856	$38,540	$46,065

TABLE 2

Year	Qtr 1	Qtr 2	Qtr 3	Qtr 4
Last Year	$64,761	$55,710	$34,292	$72,101
This Year	$75,594	$68,497	$69,057	$119,551

Use Presentation View

You proofread the presentation in Slide Show view and check the animations. You print a handout with four slides per page.

a. Start the slide show and navigate through the presentation.

b. Annotate the conclusion slide, *The Next Steps*, by underlining *detailed financial proposal* and circling *two* and *ten* with a red pen.

c. Exit the presentation and keep the annotations.

d. Save and close the file, and submit based on your instructor's directions.

Presentation Development

CHAPTER 2

Konstantin Chagin/Shutterstock

Planning and Preparing a Presentation

OBJECTIVES | AFTER YOU READ THIS CHAPTER, YOU WILL BE ABLE TO:

1. Create a presentation using a template p. 140
2. Modify a presentation based on a template p. 142
3. Create a presentation in Outline view p. 148
4. Modify an outline structure p. 149
5. Print an outline p. 151
6. Import an outline p. 156

7. Reuse slides from an existing presentation p. 156
8. Use sections p. 160
9. Examine slide show design principles p. 161
10. Modify a theme p. 163
11. Modify the slide master p. 164

CASE STUDY | The Wellness Education Center

The Wellness Education Center at your school promotes overall good health to students and employees. The director of the Center has asked you to create two slide shows that she can use to deliver presentations to the campus community.

You create a presentation to inform campus groups about the Center by downloading a template with a wellness theme from Microsoft Office Online. You modify several of the layouts the template provides to customize the template to your needs. To concentrate on the content of the slides, you use the Outline view to enter slide text and edit the presentation outline.

You create a second presentation for the Center using an outline the director created in Microsoft Word. You import the outline, supplement it with slides you reuse from another presentation, and divide the presentation into sections. Using standard slide show design guidelines, polish the presentation by editing the content and the theme.

Templates

One of the hardest things about creating a presentation is getting started. You may have a general idea of what you want to say but not how to organize your thoughts. Or you may know what you want to say but need help designing the look for the slides. PowerPoint's templates enable you to create professional-looking presentations and may even include content to help you decide what to say. In this section, you will learn how to create a presentation using a template that you modify to fit your needs.

Creating a Presentation Using a Template

A *template* is a file that includes the formatting elements like a background, a theme with a color scheme and font selections for titles and text boxes, and slide layouts that position content placeholders. Some templates include suggestions for how to modify the template, whereas others include ideas about what you could say to inform your audience about your topic. These suggestions can help you learn to use many of the features in PowerPoint.

PowerPoint offers templates for you to use. You can quickly and easily download additional professional templates in a variety of categories. These templates were created by Microsoft, a Microsoft partner, or a member of the Microsoft community. For example, you can select a suggested search term or type your own search term in the Search box. Then you can filter by category to narrow your search further. For example, you can download a template for a renewable energy presentation created by a Microsoft partner, an active listening presentation created by a Microsoft community member, or a business financial report created by Microsoft. Figure 2.1 shows four PowerPoint templates.

Food pyramid presentation template

Wedding photo album template widescreen

Marketing plan template with graph

Health and fitness presentation template widescreen

FIGURE 2.1 Templates

TIP Searching for a Template

When you search for a template, you are searching those located on your computer as well as online from Microsoft.com. With Office 2013, templates are no longer installed on your computer with the program but rather are located online. Consequently, your computer must be connected to the Internet to search for Office 2013 templates.

When you create a new presentation, you typically choose a template with a theme and variant that suits your project. To begin a presentation using a template, do the following:

1. Start PowerPoint.
2. Click one of the suggested search terms or click in the search box and type the text for which you would like to search. Press Enter.

   For example, you may wish to search for Marketing templates, and thus you would type *Marketing* as your search term.
3. Click a template or theme to preview it in a new window.
4. Click Create to open the template.

Figure 2.2 displays the Backstage view of *Templates and Themes*. Your view may show different template options, as Microsoft frequently updates the available templates.

Enter a search term or terms here to find templates

Click one of the suggested searches

Click to start a Blank Presentation

FIGURE 2.2 Templates and Themes

You can filter your results further by using one of the filter categories on the right side of the screen. For example, Figure 2.3 shows a Photo Albums template search further narrowed to presentations with the criteria of Family. Depending on your search criteria, you may also see non–PowerPoint templates in your search results.

Search results using the suggested search term "Photo Albums"

Category filters are used to further narrow the search

FIGURE 2.3 Template Categories

TIP · Searching by Template Dimensions

In the category list, you can search by 4:3 for templates with the typical screen dimensions or 16:9 for widescreen templates. Since most screens and televisions have moved to the widescreen format, you may wish to choose the 16:9 dimension size.

Click once on the template to preview the template. Double-click the template to open the presentation. In Figure 2.4, the Family Photo Album template is selected. The title slide for the template displays in the new screen. You can view the other slides in the template by clicking the More Images arrows. Click Create to select the template or click the left or right red arrows to preview other templates.

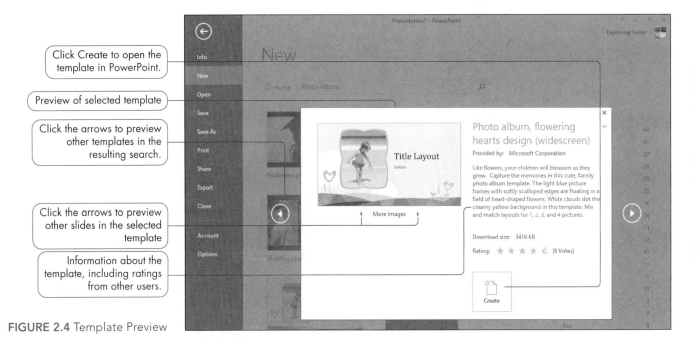

FIGURE 2.4 Template Preview

Modifying a Presentation Based on a Template

 The templates you download may have custom layouts unique to that particular template. After you download a template, you can modify it, perhaps by changing a font style or size, moving or deleting a placeholder, or moving an object on the slide. After you modify the presentation, you can save it and use it repeatedly. The ability to save these changes can save you a tremendous amount of time, because you will not have to redo your modifications the next time you use the presentation.

Quick **Concepts** ✓

1. Is a template the same thing as a theme? Why or why not? *p. 140*

2. Why might someone use a template rather than start from a blank presentation? *p. 140*

3. What are some of the categories of templates available in PowerPoint 2013? *p. 141*

Hands-On Exercises

Watch the Video for this Hands-On Exercise!

MyITLab®
HOE1 Training

1 Templates

To promote the Wellness Education Center at your school, you decide to create a presentation that can be shown to campus groups and other organizations to inform them about the Center and its mission.

Skills covered: Create a New Presentation Based on a Template • Modify a Placeholder • Modify a Layout • Add Pictures and Modify a Caption

STEP 1 ≫ CREATE A NEW PRESENTATION BASED ON A TEMPLATE

You begin the Wellness Education Center presentation by looking for a template that is upbeat and that will represent the idea that being healthy makes you feel good. You locate the perfect template (a photo album with warm sunflowers on the cover) from the Photo Albums category. You open a new presentation based on the template and save the presentation. Refer to Figure 2.5 as you complete Step 1.

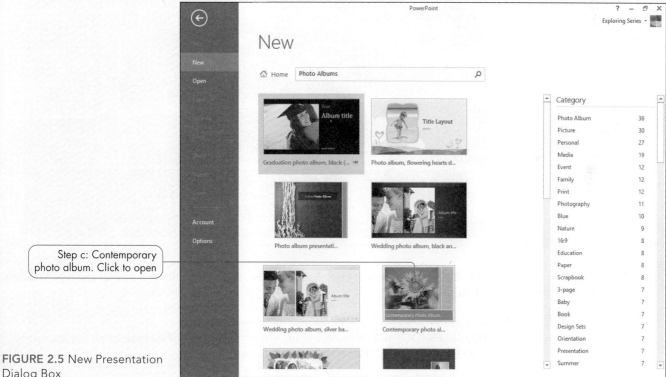

FIGURE 2.5 New Presentation Dialog Box

a. Start PowerPoint.

b. Click the **Photo Albums** category in Suggested searches.

Thumbnails of sample Photo Album templates will display.

c. Click **Contemporary photo album** and click **Create** in the Preview window.

d. View the slide show and read each of the instructions included in the template.

Templates may include instructions for their use or tips on the content that may be added to create a specific presentation. For example, Slide 2 includes instructions to follow for adding your own pages to the album.

e. Click the **INSERT tab** and click **Header & Footer** in the Text group. Click the **Notes and Handouts tab** in the Header and Footer dialog box. Create a handout header with your name and the current date and a handout footer with your instructor's name and your class. Include the current date. The page number feature can remain active. Click **Apply to All**.

f. Save the presentation as **p02h1Center_LastFirst**.

STEP 2 ≫ MODIFY A PLACEHOLDER

The template you selected and downloaded consists of a Title Slide layout you like, but the text in the placeholders needs to be changed to the Wellness Center information. You edit the title slide to include the Center's name and slogan. You also modify the title placeholder to make the Center's name stand out. Refer to Figure 2.6 as you complete Step 2.

Step b: Modified subtitle placeholder text

Step a: Modified title placeholder text

FIGURE 2.6 Edited Title Slide

a. On Slide 1, select the text *Contemporary Photo Album* in the title placeholder and type **Wellness Education Center**.

> **TROUBLESHOOTING:** If you make any major mistakes in this exercise, close the file, open *p02h1Center_LastFirst* again, and then start this exercise over.

b. Click the subtitle text *Click to add date or details* and type **Dedicated to Promoting Healthy Lifestyles!**.

c. Select the title text and click **Italic** and **Text Shadow** in the Font group on the HOME tab.

The template's title placeholder is modified to make the title text stand out.

d. Save the presentation.

STEP 3 » MODIFY A LAYOUT

The Contemporary Photo Album template includes many layouts designed to create an interesting photo album. Although the layout you selected conveys the warm feeling you desire, the layouts need to be modified to fit your needs. You modify a section layout and add a new slide with the layout of your choice. You also delete unnecessary slides. Refer to Figure 2.7 as you complete Step 3.

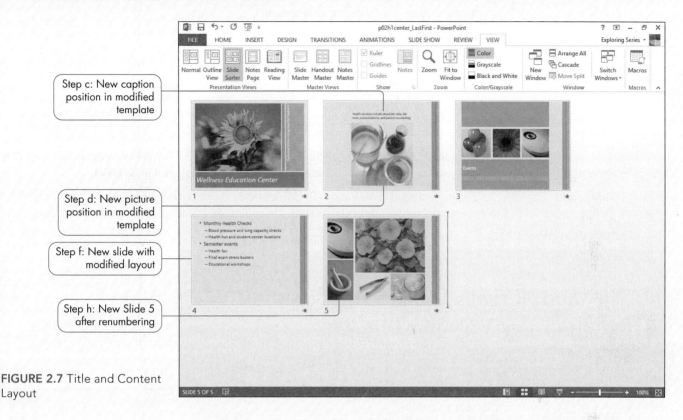

Step c: New caption position in modified template

Step d: New picture position in modified template

Step f: New slide with modified layout

Step h: New Slide 5 after renumbering

FIGURE 2.7 Title and Content Layout

a. On Slide 2, replace the sample text with **Health services include physician care, lab tests, immunizations, and patient counseling.**

b. Click the **Layout arrow** in the Slides group and click the **Square with Caption layout**.

Note that the Contemporary Photo Album template has many more layouts than the default Office Theme template. The number of layouts provided with a template varies, so always check to see your options.

c. Click the caption and drag the caption to the top of the picture (not above it). As you drag, you will notice red line guides appear to help you as you move the object.

Shift constrains the movement of the caption as you drag so that the new position of the caption is aligned left with its original position.

d. Select the picture and drag the picture below the caption.

The template layout is modified to show the caption above the picture.

e. On Slide 3, select the placeholder text that reads *Choose a layout...*, and then type **Events**. Delete the subtitle text.

When you delete existing text in a new template placeholder, it is replaced with instructional text such as *Click to add subtitle*. It is not necessary to delete this text, as it will not display when the slide show is viewed.

f. Click the **New Slide arrow** and click the **Title and Content layout**.

> **TROUBLESHOOTING:** Clicking the New Slide arrow opens the Layout gallery for you to select a layout. Clicking New Slide directly above the New Slide arrow creates a new slide using the layout of the current slide.

g. Delete the title placeholder in the new slide and drag the content placeholder to the top of the slide. Enter the following information:

- **Monthly Health Checks**
  - **Blood pressure and lung capacity checks**
  - **Health Hut and Student Center locations**
- **Semester Events**
  - **Health fair**
  - **Final exam stress busters**
  - **Educational workshops**

h. Click the **VIEW tab** and click **Slide Sorter** in the Presentation Views group. Hold down **Ctrl** and click to dual select the **Slide 5** and **Slide 6 thumbnails** and press **Delete**.

The presentation now contains five slides. After you make the deletions, the remaining slides are renumbered, and the slide that becomes Slide 5 is a collage of images from the template.

i. Click **Normal** in the Presentation Views group.

j. Save the presentation.

STEP 4 ≫ ADD PICTURES AND MODIFY A CAPTION

You decide to add a slide using one of the template's layouts to add a picture of a Wellness Center room and the nursing staff. You modify the layout by deleting a caption placeholder and changing the size of another. Refer to Figure 2.8 as you complete Step 4.

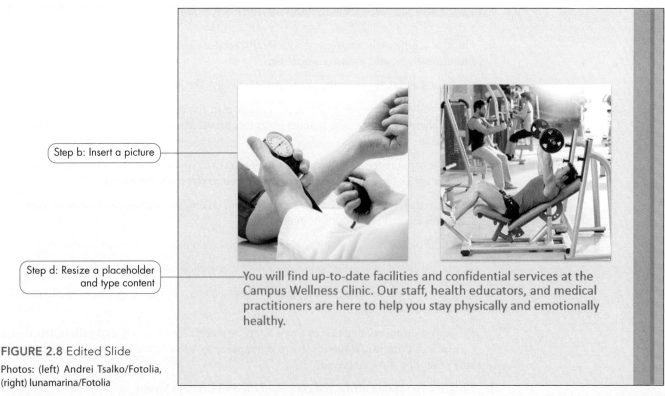

Step b: Insert a picture

Step d: Resize a placeholder and type content

You will find up-to-date facilities and confidential services at the Campus Wellness Clinic. Our staff, health educators, and medical practitioners are here to help you stay physically and emotionally healthy.

FIGURE 2.8 Edited Slide

Photos: (left) Andrei Tsalko/Fotolia, (right) lunamarina/Fotolia

a. On Slide 4, click the **New Slide arrow** on the HOME tab and click **2-Up Square with Caption**.

A new slide is created. The layout includes two picture placeholders and two caption placeholders.

b. Select the **left picture placeholder** and click **Online Pictures** on the INSERT tab. In the **Office.com Clip Art search box**, type **Blood Pressure Check**, press **Enter**, and then insert a picture of your choice.

The image is added to the placeholder.

c. Select the **right picture placeholder** and click **Online Pictures** on the INSERT tab. In the **Office.com Clip Art search box**, type **Gym**, press **Enter**, and then insert a picture of your choice.

TROUBLESHOOTING: Clicking the icon in the center of the picture placeholder will open the Insert Picture dialog box. If this happens, press Cancel. Select somewhere in the white space around the icon to select the placeholder. Once the placeholder is selected, you will be able to continue with the instructions for adding an Online Picture.

---

d. Delete the right caption placeholder and select the remaining caption placeholder. Click the **FORMAT tab** located under *DRAWING TOOLS*. In the size group, change the width to **7.7"**. The caption placeholder will now be the length of both pictures.

e. Type the following in the **caption placeholder: You will find up-to-date facilities and confidential services at the Campus Wellness Clinic. Our staff, health educators, and medical practitioners are here to help you stay physically and emotionally healthy.**

f. Spell check and save the presentation. Keep the presentation open if you plan to continue with Hands-On Exercise 2. If not, save and close the presentation, and exit PowerPoint.

Outlines

An *outline* organizes text using a *hierarchy* with main points and subpoints to indicate the levels of importance of the text. When you use a storyboard to determine your content, you create a basic outline. An outline is the fastest way to enter or edit text for a presentation. Think of an outline as the road map you use to create your presentation. Rather than having to enter the text in each placeholder on each slide separately, you can type the text directly into an outline, and it will populate into the slides automatically.

In this section, you will add content to a presentation in Outline view. After creating the presentation, you will modify the outline structure. Finally, you will print the outline.

Creating a Presentation in Outline View

STEP 1 ▶ To create an outline for your presentation you must be in *Outline view*. To change to Outline view:

1. Click the VIEW tab.
2. Click Outline View in the Presentations Views group.

In Outline view, the presentation is displayed as a list of all slides that illustrates the hierarchy of the titles and text in each individual slide. Beside each slide is a slide number, next to which is a slide icon, followed by the slide title if the slide contains a title placeholder. The slide title is bolded. Slide text is indented under the slide title. A slide with only an image (no text) will not have a title in the outline and will display only the slide number and icon.

One benefit of working in Outline view is that you get a good overview of your presentation without the distraction of design elements, and you can move easily from one slide to the next. You can copy text or bullets from one slide to another and rearrange the order of the slides or bullets. Outline view makes it easy to see relationships between points and to determine where information belongs. Figure 2.9 shows a portion of a presentation in Outline view.

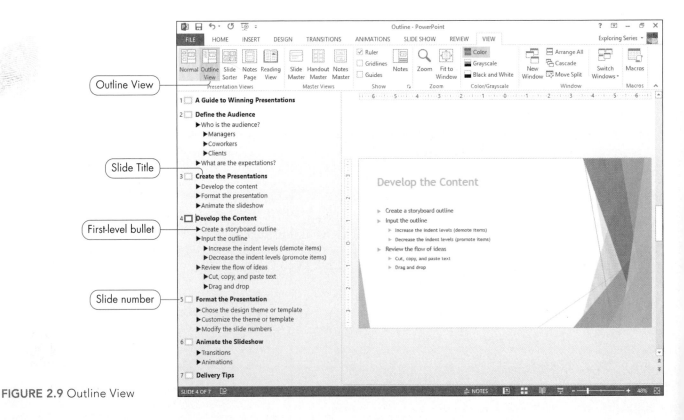

FIGURE 2.9 Outline View

PowerPoint accommodates nine levels of indentation, although you will likely only use two or three per slide. Levels make it possible to show hierarchy or relationships between the information on your slides. The main points appear on Level 1; subsidiary items are indented below the main point to which they apply, and their font size is decreased.

You can promote any item to a higher level or demote it to a lower level, either before or after the text is entered, by clicking Increase List Level or Decrease List Level in the Paragraph group on the Home tab. When designing your slides, consider the number of subsidiary or lower-level items you add to a main point; too many levels within a single slide make the slide difficult to read or understand because the text size becomes smaller with each additional level.

TIP | Changing List Levels in an Outline

As a quick alternative to using Increase and Decrease List Level commands on the Home tab, press Tab to demote an item or press Shift+Tab to promote an item.

On Slide 4 in Figure 2.9, the title of the slide, *Develop the Content*, appears immediately after the slide number and icon. The first-level bullet, *Create a storyboard outline*, is indented under the title. The next first-level bullet, *Input the outline*, has two subsidiary, or second-level, bullets. The following bullet, *Review the flow of ideas*, is moved back to Level 1, and it also has two subsidiary bullets.

STEP 2 >> Outline view can be an efficient way to create and edit a presentation. To use the Outline view to create a presentation, use the Outline pane located on the left:

1. Press Enter to create a new slide or bullet at the same level.
2. Press Tab to demote or Shift+Tab to promote items as you type to create a hierarchy of information on each slide.
3. Use the Cut, Copy, and Paste commands in the Clipboard group on the HOME tab to move and copy selected text.

Modifying an Outline Structure

Because Outline view shows the overall structure of your presentation, you can use it to move bullets or slides until your outline's organization is refined. You can collapse or expand your view of the outline contents to see slide contents or just slide titles. A *collapsed outline* view displays only slide icons and the titles of the slides, whereas the *expanded outline* view displays the slide icon, the title, and the content of the slides. You can collapse or expand the content in individual slides or in all slides.

Figure 2.10 displays a collapsed view of the outline displaying only the icon and title of each slide. When a slide is collapsed, a wavy line appears below the slide title, letting you know additional levels exist but are not displayed. The collapsed view makes it easy to move slides. To move a slide, position the pointer over a slide icon until the pointer changes to a four-headed arrow, and then drag the icon to the desired position.

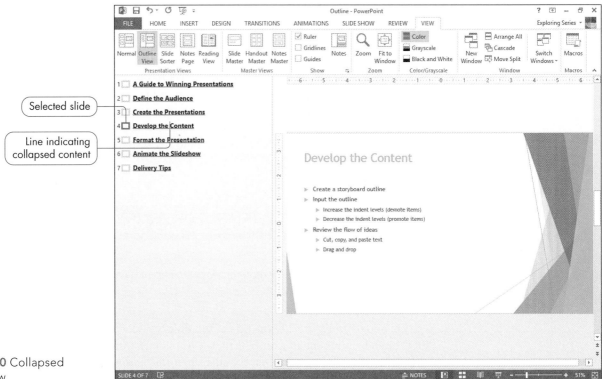

FIGURE 2.10 Collapsed Outline View

STEP 3

To collapse or expand a slide:

1. In the Outline pane, double-click the slide icon. Doing this action expands the slide contents in the pane.
2. Right-click the text following an icon to display a shortcut menu with options for collapsing or expanding the selected slides or all slides.

Figure 2.11 shows the shortcut menu options.

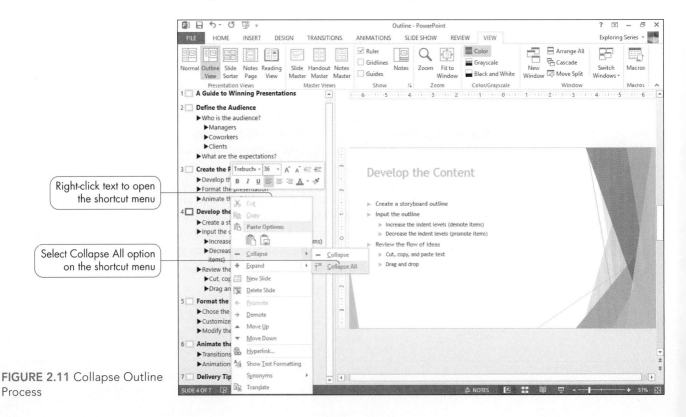

FIGURE 2.11 Collapse Outline Process

Printing an Outline

You can print an outline in either expanded or collapsed view. Figure 2.12 displays a preview of an expanded view of the outline ready to print. The slide icon and slide number will print with the outline. To print the outline, do the following:

1. Click the FILE tab.
2. Click Print.
3. Click Full Page Slides, Notes Pages, or Outline (whichever displays) to open a gallery of printing choices.
4. Click Outline.
5. Click Print.

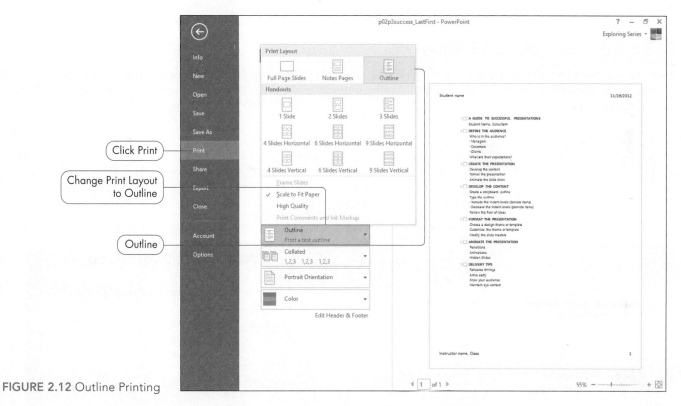

FIGURE 2.12 Outline Printing

Quick Concepts

1. What is a hierarchy? *p. 148*

2. What are two benefits of creating a presentation in Outline view? *p. 148*

3. Why would you collapse the view of an outline while in Outline view? *p. 149*

Hands-On Exercises

Watch the Video for this Hands-On Exercise!

MyITLab®
HOE2 Training

2 Outlines

The Wellness Center sponsors a Walking Wellness group to help campus members increase their physical activity and cardiovascular fitness. The director of the Wellness Center believes that joining a group increases a member's level of commitment and provides an incentive for the member to stay active. She asks you to edit the slide show you created in Hands-On Exercise 1 to include information about the walking group.

Skills covered: Use Outline View • Edit the Outline • Modify the Outline Structure and Print

---

STEP 1 ≫ USE OUTLINE VIEW

Because you want to concentrate on the information in the presentation rather than the design elements, you use Outline view. You add the information about the walking group as requested by the director. Refer to Figure 2.13 as you complete Step 1.

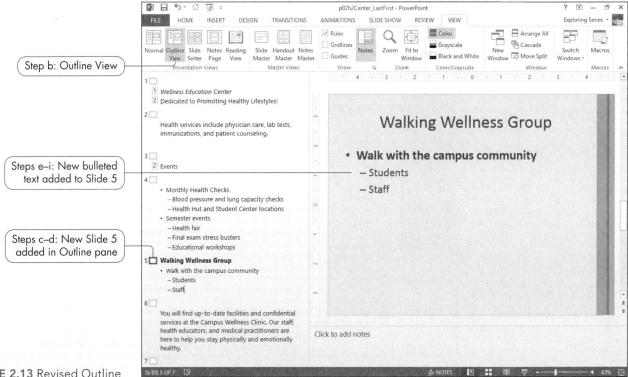

FIGURE 2.13 Revised Outline

a. Open *p02h1Center_LastFirst*, if necessary, and save the presentation as **p02h2Ccenter_LastFirst**, changing *h1* to *h2*.

b. Click the **VIEW tab** and click **Outline View** in the Presentation Views group.

Note that each slide in the presentation is numbered and has a slide icon. Slides 1 through 5 include text on the slides. Slide 6 contains images only, so no text is displayed in the outline.

c. Click at the end of the last bullet on Slide 4 and press **Enter**.

The text in the outline is also displayed on the slide in the Slide pane. The insertion point is now positioned to enter text at the same level as the previous bullet point. To create a new slide at a higher level, you must decrease the indent level.

d. Click **Decrease List Level** in the Paragraph group on the HOME tab twice.

A new Slide 5 is created, the previous Slide 5 is renumbered as Slide 6, Slide 6 is renumbered as Slide 7, etc.

e. Type **Walking Wellness Group** and press **Enter**.

Pressing Enter moves the insertion point to the next line and creates a new slide, Slide 6.

f. Press **Tab** to demote the text in the outline.

The insertion point is now positioned to enter bulleted text.

g. Type **Walk with the campus community** and press **Enter**.

h. Press **Tab** to demote the bullet and type **Students**.

Students becomes Level 3 text.

i. Press **Enter** and type **Staff**.

j. Save the presentation.

STEP 2 ➤➤ EDIT THE OUTLINE

While proofreading your outline, you discover that you did not identify one of the campus community groups. Finally, you notice that you left out one of the most important slides in your presentation: why someone should walk. You edit the outline and make these changes. Refer to Figure 2.14 as you complete Step 2.

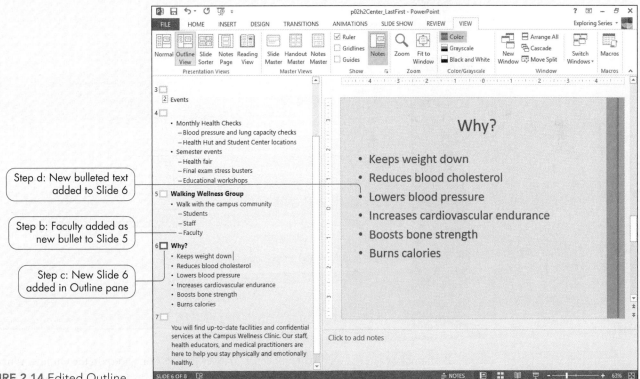

FIGURE 2.14 Edited Outline

a. Click at the end of the word *Staff* on Slide 5 of the outline.

b. Press **Enter** and type **Faculty**.

> **TROUBLESHOOTING:** If your text does not appear in the correct position, check to see if the insertion point was in the wrong location. To enter a blank line for a new bullet, the insertion point must be at the end of an existing bullet point, not at the beginning.

c. Press **Enter** and press **Shift+Tab** twice.

Pressing Shift+Tab promotes the text to create a new Slide 6.

d. Using the Outline pane, type the information for Slide 6 as shown below:

Why?

- **Keeps weight down**
- **Reduces blood cholesterol**
- **Lowers blood pressure**
- **Increases cardiovascular endurance**
- **Boosts bone strength**
- **Burns calories**

e. Save the presentation.

STEP 3 ≫ MODIFY THE OUTLINE STRUCTURE AND PRINT

The director of the Wellness Clinic has reviewed the slide show and made several suggestions about its structure. She feels that keeping weight down belongs at the bottom of the list of reasons for walking and asks you to reposition it. Refer to Figure 2.15 as you complete Step 3.

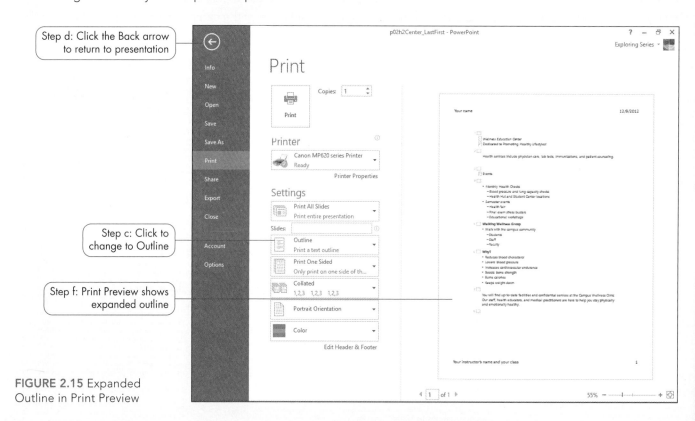

FIGURE 2.15 Expanded Outline in Print Preview

a. Position the pointer over the first bullet, *Keeps weight down*, on Slide 6 in the Outline. When the mouse pointer looks like a four-headed arrow, click and drag the text until it becomes the last bullet on the slide.

b. Right-click the Slide 6 text, point to *Collapse*, and then click **Collapse All**.

Only the slide titles will be shown in the Outline.

c. Click the **FILE tab**, click **Print**, and then click the **Full Page Slides arrow**, if necessary. Click **Outline**.

A preview of the collapsed outline shows in the Preview pane. Because so few slides contain titles, the collapsed outline is not helpful.

d. Click the **back arrow** to return to the presentation.

The Outline pane is once again visible.

e. Right-click any text visible in the Outline pane, point to *Expand*, and then select **Expand All**.

f. Click the **FILE tab** and click **Print**.

The Outline Print Layout is retained from step d and the expanded outline shows in the Preview pane.

g. Click the **back arrow** to return to the presentation.

h. Spell check the presentation. Save and close the presentation, and submit based on your instructor's directions.

Data Imports

You can add slides to a presentation in several ways if the content exists in other formats, such as an outline in Word or slides from other presentations. PowerPoint can create slides based on Microsoft Word outlines (.docx or .doc formats) or outlines saved in another word-processing format that PowerPoint recognizes. You can import data into a slide show to add existing slides from a previously created presentation. This is a very efficient way to add content to a slide show.

In this section, you will learn how to import an outline into a PowerPoint presentation and how to add slides from another presentation into the current presentation.

Importing an Outline

Outlines created in Microsoft Word created specifically in an outline format can be imported to quickly create a PowerPoint presentation. To create an outline in Word, you must click the View tab, click Outline, and then enter your text. A list in Word that was not created in the Outline view will not import easily to PowerPoint.

PowerPoint recognizes outlines created and saved in *rich text format (.rtf)*, a file format you can use to transfer formatted text documents between applications such as word-processing programs and PowerPoint. You can even transfer documents between different platforms such as Macintosh and Windows. The structure and most of the text formatting are retained when you import the outline into PowerPoint.

PowerPoint also recognizes outlines created and saved in a *plain text format* (which uses the file extension *.txt*), a file format that retains text without any formatting. Because .txt outlines have no saved hierarchical structure, each line of the outline becomes a slide. Another alternative is to import a Web document (.htm), but in this case all the text from the file appears in one placeholder on one slide. Avoid saving outlines you create in these formats, but if you receive an outline in a .txt or .htm format, you can create a hierarchy in PowerPoint without having to retype the text.

 To create a new presentation from an outline, do the following:

1. Click the New Slide arrow on the HOME tab.
2. Click *Slides from Outline*.
3. Locate and select your file and click Insert.

TIP Problems Importing a Word Outline

If you import a Word document that appears to be an outline and after importing, each line of the Word document becomes a title for a new slide, the Word document is actually a bulleted list rather than an outline. These two features are separate and distinct in Word and do not import into PowerPoint in the same manner. Open the bulleted list in Word in the Outline View, apply outline formatting, save the file in the RTF format, and then re-import it to PowerPoint.

Reusing Slides from an Existing Presentation

You can reuse slides from an existing PowerPoint presentation when creating a new presentation. To import existing slides without having to open the other file, do the following:

1. Click the New Slide arrow in the Slides group on the HOME tab.
2. Click Reuse Slides.

3. Click Browse, click Browse File, and then navigate to the folder containing the presentation that has the slides you want to use.

4. Click Open.

5. Click a slide to add it to the presentation or right-click any slide and select Insert All Slides to add all of the slides to the presentation.

By default, when you insert a slide into the presentation, it takes on the formatting of the open presentation. If the new slides do not take on the formatting of the open presentation, select the imported text in Outline view and click Clear all Formatting in the Font group of the Home tab. It will format the slides using the active theme. If you wish to retain the formatting of the original presentation, click the *Keep source formatting* check box at the bottom of the Reuse Slides pane, shown in Figure 2.16.

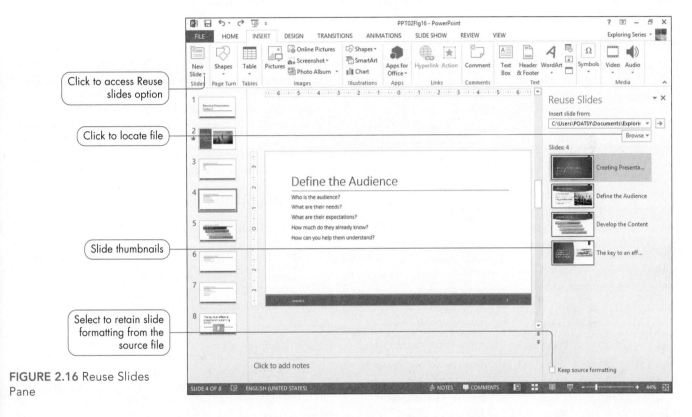

FIGURE 2.16 Reuse Slides Pane

Quick **Concepts**

1. What are the two types of text formats for outlines that PowerPoint recognizes? *p. 156*

2. Do you need to have another presentation open to reuse its content in your current presentation? *p. 156*

3. When you insert a slide into a presentation, what formatting does it use—the formatting from the open presentation or its original formatting? *p. 157*

Hands-On Exercises

3 Data Imports

The director of the Wellness Clinic is impressed with the clinic overview presentation you created. She gives you an electronic copy of an outline she created in a word-processing software package and asks if you can convert it into a slide show. You create a slide show from the outline and then supplement it with content from another slide show.

Skills covered: Import a Rich Text Format Outline • Reuse Slides from Another Presentation

---

STEP 1 ≫ IMPORT A RICH TEXT FORMAT OUTLINE

The director of the Wellness Clinic saves an outline for a presentation in rich text format. You import the outline into PowerPoint to use as the basis for a presentation about the clinic, its mission, and the services it provides to students, staff, and faculty. Refer to Figure 2.17 as you complete Step 1.

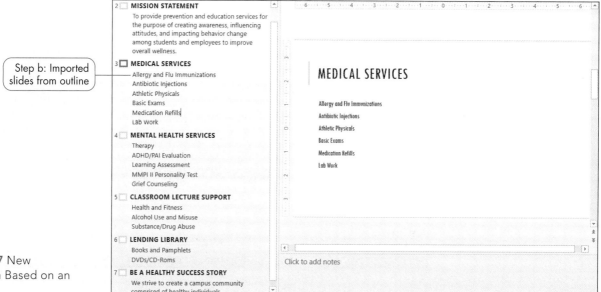

FIGURE 2.17 New Presentation Based on an Outline

a. Click the **FILE tab**, click **New**, and then double-click **Blank Presentation**.

A new blank presentation opens.

b. Click the **New Slide arrow**, click **Slides from Outline**, and then navigate to the location of your Chapter 2 student data files.

c. Browse and open file *p02h3MedOutline*.

The outline is opened and new slides are added to the presentation.

d. Click the **VIEW tab** and click **Outline View** in the Presentation Views group.

The outline retains its hierarchy. Each slide has a title and bulleted text.

e. Create a handout header with your name and a handout footer with your instructor's name and your class. Include the current date.

f. Apply the **Integral theme** to all slides.

The Integral theme adds a subtle blue line next to the title.

g. Save the presentation as **p02h3Mission_LastFirst**.

STEP 2 >> REUSE SLIDES FROM ANOTHER PRESENTATION

While reviewing the Wellness Center presentation, you realize you do not have a title slide or a final slide inviting students to contact the Center. You reuse slides from another presentation created for the Center containing slides that would fit well in this presentation. Refer to Figure 2.18 as you complete Step 2.

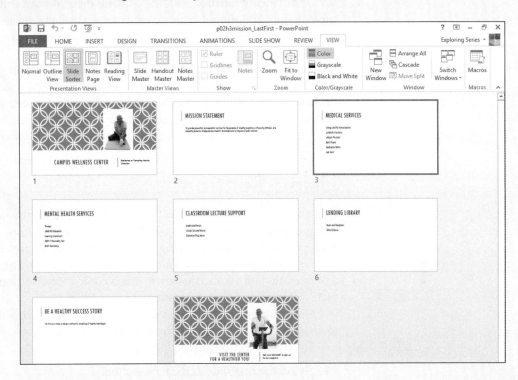

FIGURE 2.18 Reused Slides Added to Presentation

a. On Slide 1, click the **New Slide arrow** in the Slides group on the HOME tab. Click **Reuse Slides** at the bottom of the New Slides gallery.

b. Click **Browse**, click **Browse File**, and then locate your student data files. Select *p02h3Wellness.pptx*, and then click **Open**.

> **TROUBLESHOOTING:** If you do not see the *p02h3Wellness* file, click *Files of type* and select All PowerPoint Presentations.

c. Click the **Keep source formatting check box** at the bottom of the Reuse Slides pane.

   With Keep source formatting selected, the images and design of the slides you reuse will transfer with the slide.

d. Click the first slide (*Campus Wellness…*) in the Reuse Slides pane.

   The slide is added to your presentation after the current slide, Slide 1.

e. Delete the blank title slide that is currently Slide 1.

   The newly reused slide needs to be in the Slide 1 position to serve as the title slide of your presentation.

f. Click the **Slide 7 icon** (*BE A HEALTHY SUCCESS STORY*) in the original presentation.

g. Click **Slide 7** in the Reuse Slides pane and close the Reuse Slides pane.

h. Keep the presentation open if you plan to continue with the next Hands-On Exercise. If not, save and close the presentation, and exit PowerPoint.

Design

When working with the content of a presentation, it can be helpful to work with the blank Office Theme. Working in the blank template lets you concentrate on what you want to say. After you are satisfied with the content, then you can consider the visual aspects of the presentation. You should evaluate many aspects when considering the visual design of your presentation. Those aspects include layout, background, typography, color, and animation, as well as dividing the content into sections.

Because the majority of people using PowerPoint are not graphic artists and do not have a strong design background, Microsoft designers created a variety of methods to help users deal with design issues. Using these features, you can create a slide show using a professional design and then modify it to reflect your own preferences. Before doing so, however, you need to consider some basic visual design principles for PowerPoint.

Using Sections

Content organization is an effective design element. Content divided into *sections* can help you group slides meaningfully. When you create a section, it is given the name *Untitled Section*. You will want to change the section name to give it a meaningful name, which enables you to jump to a section quickly. For example, you may be creating a slide show for a presentation on geothermal energy. You could create sections for Earth, plate boundaries, plate tectonics, and thermal features.

Slide sections can be collapsed or expanded. Use either Normal view or Slide Sorter view to create sections. Figure 2.19 shows a section added to a presentation in Normal view.

STEP 1 » To create a section, do the following:

1. Select the first slide of the new section.
2. Click Section in the Slides group on the HOME tab.
3. Click Add Section.
4. Right-click Untitled Section and select Rename Section.
5. Type a new name for the section.

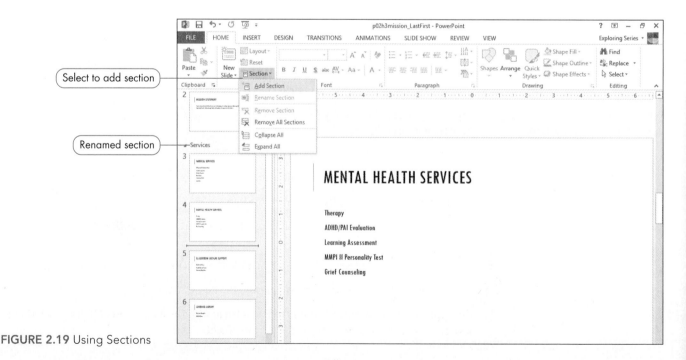

FIGURE 2.19 Using Sections

Examining Slide Show Design Principles

STEP 2 » When applied to a project, universally accepted design principles can increase its appeal and professionalism. Some design aspects may be applied in specific ways to the various types of modern communications: communicating through print media such as flyers or brochures, through audio media such as narrations or music, or through a visual medium such as a slide show. The following reference table focuses on principles that apply to slide shows and examines examples of slides that illustrate these principles.

REFERENCE Slide Show Design Principles

Example	Design Tip
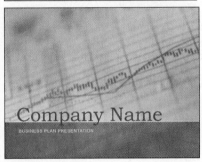**FIGURE 2.20** Examples of Templates Appropriate for Different Audiences	• **Choose design elements appropriate for the audience.** Consider the audience's background. A presentation to elementary students might use bright, primary colors and cartoon-like clip art. Fonts should be large and easy to read. For an adult audience, choose muted earth tones and use photographs rather than cartoon-like clip art to give the slide show a more professional appearance. Figure 2.20 shows design examples suitable for grade school and business audiences, respectively. Photo: (top) Stasys Eidiejus/Fotolia
**FIGURE 2.21** Examples of a Cluttered Design (top) and a Clean Design (bottom)	• **Keep the design neat and clean.** This principle is often referred to as KISS: Keep it sweet and simple! Figure 2.21 shows an example of a cluttered and a clean design. Avoid using multiple fonts and font colors on a slide. Do not use more than three fonts on a slide. Avoid using multiple clip art images. Use white space (empty space) to open up your design. Photos: (top, left) AnnaPa/Fotolia, (top, right) fuumiing/Fotolia, (bottom) .shock/Fotolia

Example	Design Tip

Example

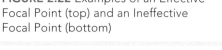

FIGURE 2.22 Examples of an Effective Focal Point (top) and an Ineffective Focal Point (bottom)

Design Tip

- **Create a focal point that leads the viewer's eyes to the critical information on the slide.**
  The focal point should be the main area of interest. Pictures should always lead the viewer's eyes to the focal point, not away from it. Images should not be so large that they detract from the focal point, unless your goal is to make the image the focal point. Figure 2.22 illustrates examples of ineffective and effective focal points.

Photos: (top) Photoroller/Fotolia, (bottom) vgstudio/Fotolia

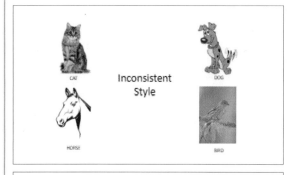

FIGURE 2.23 Examples of Disjointed (top) and Unified (bottom) Design Elements

- **Use unified design elements for a professional look.**
  Visual unity creates a harmony between the elements of the slide and between the slides in the slide show. Unity gives the viewer a sense of order and peace. Create unity by repeating colors and shapes. Use clip art in only one style. Figure 2.23 shows a disjointed and a unified design.

Photos: (top, clockwise from top left) DenisNata/Fotolia, JoeyBear/Fotolia, donyanedomam/Fotolia, master24/Fotolia; (bottom, clockwise from top right) DoraZett/Fotolia, Anna Sedneva/Fotolia, Julia Remezova/Fotolia

FIGURE 2.24 Sans Serif (left) and Serif (right) Fonts

- **Choose fonts appropriate for the output of your presentation.**
  If a presentation is to be delivered through a projection device, consider using sans serif fonts with short text blocks. If your presentation will be delivered as a printout, consider using serif fonts. Serif fonts help guide the reader's eyes across the page. You may use longer text blocks in printed presentations. Figure 2.24 displays an example of a sans serif font—a font that does not have serifs, or small lines, at the ends of letters. It also shows an example of a serif font with the serifs on the letter *S* circled. Decorative fonts are also available but should be used sparingly. When choosing a font, remember that readability is critical in a presentation.

Example	Design Tip
Text Guidelines • <u>Do not underline text.</u> • DO NOT USE ALL CAPS. • Use **bold** and *italics* sparingly. • Avoid text that leaves one word on a line on its own. • Avoid using multiple spaces after punctuation. Space once after punctuation in a text block. Spacing more can create rivers of white. The white "river" can be very distracting. The white space draws the eye from the message. It can throb when projected. **FIGURE 2.25** Appropriate and Inappropriate Text Examples	• **Do not underline text.** Underlined text is harder to read, and it is generally assumed that underlined text is a hyperlink. • **Avoid using all capital letters.** In addition to being difficult to read, words or phrases in all caps are considered to be "yelling" at the audience. • **Use italics and bold sparingly.** Too much emphasis through the use of italics and bold is confusing and makes it difficult to determine what is important. • **Avoid creating lines of text that leave a single word hanging on a line of its own.** Modify the placeholder size so that more than one word is on a subsequent line. • **Use just one space after punctuation in text blocks.** Using more than one space can create distracting white space in the text block. Figure 2.25 illustrates these principles.
Title Text ▸ Title text should be in title case and 36pt or more ▸ Bulleted text should be in sentence case and 28pt or more **FIGURE 2.26** Readable Text Guidelines	• **Make text readable.** Title text should use title case and be 36 pt or higher. Bulleted text should be in sentence case and be 28 pt or higher. Figure 2.26 illustrates readable text.

Remember that these design principles are guidelines. You may choose to avoid applying one or more of the principles, but you should be aware of the principles and carefully consider why you are not following them. If you are in doubt about your design, ask a classmate or colleague to review the design and make suggestions. Fresh eyes can see things you might miss.

Modifying a Theme

STEP 3 ▶ Themes can be modified once they have been applied. You can change the variants, colors, fonts, and effects used in the theme. You can even change the background styles. Each of these options is on the Design tab, and each has its own gallery. Figure 2.27 shows the locations for accessing the galleries.

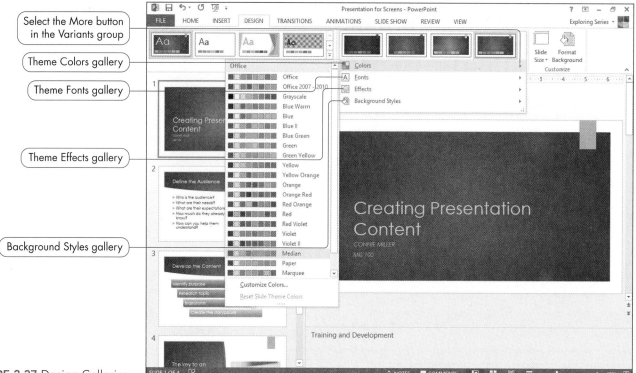

Labels on figure:
- Select the More button in the Variants group
- Theme Colors gallery
- Theme Fonts gallery
- Theme Effects gallery
- Background Styles gallery

FIGURE 2.27 Design Galleries

Each PowerPoint theme includes a *Colors gallery*, a gallery that provides a set of colors with each color assigned to a different element in the theme design. Once the theme is selected, you can click Colors to display the built-in gallery. Click one of the Theme Colors to apply it. You can even create your own color theme set by clicking Customize Colors at the bottom of the gallery.

Selecting a font for the title and another for the bullets or body text of your presentation can be difficult. Without a background in typography, determining which fonts go together well is difficult. The *Fonts gallery* is a gallery that pairs a title font and a body font. Click any of the samples in the Fonts gallery, and the font pair is applied to your theme.

The *Effects gallery* displays a full range of special effects that can be applied to all shapes in the presentation. Using effects aids you in maintaining a consistency to the appearance of your presentation. The gallery includes effects such as a soft glow, soft edges, shadows, or three-dimensional (3-D) look.

You can change the background style of the theme by accessing the *Background Styles gallery*, a gallery containing backgrounds consistent with the selected Theme Colors. Simply changing your background style can liven up a presentation and give it your individual style.

Some of the themes include background shapes to create the design. If the background designs interfere with other objects on the slide, such as tables, images, or charts, you can select Hide Background Graphics by clicking Format Background, and the background shapes will not display for that slide.

To access these galleries, do the following:

1. Click the DESIGN tab.
2. In the Variants group, click More and choose the gallery you wish to change (Colors, Fonts, Effects, or Background Styles).

Modifying the Slide Master

STEP 4 >> You can further modify and customize your presentation through the slide master. *Masters* control the layouts, background designs, and color combinations for handouts, notes pages, and slides, giving the presentation a consistent appearance. By changing the masters, you make selections that affect the entire slide show and the supporting materials. This is more efficient than changing each slide in the presentation. The design elements you already know about, such as themes and layouts, can be applied to each type of master. Masters control the consistency of your presentations, notes, and handouts. Slide masters can be reused in other presentations. In this section, you learn how to modify the slide masters. Specifically, you will learn how to customize the slide master and slide layouts controlled by the slide master.

Each of the layouts available to you when you choose a design theme has consistent elements that are set by a ***slide master*** containing design information. The slide master is the top slide in a hierarchy of slides based on the master. As you modify the slide master, elements in the slide layouts related to it are also modified to maintain consistency. A slide master includes associated slide layouts such as a title slide layout, various content slide layouts, and a blank slide layout. The associated slide layouts designate the location of placeholders and other objects on slides as well as formatting information.

To modify a slide master or slide layout based on a slide master, do the following:

1. Click the VIEW tab.
2. Click Slide Master in the Master Views group.
3. Click the slide master at the top of the list or click one of the associated layouts.
4. Make modifications.
5. Click Close Master View in the Close group on the SLIDE MASTER tab.

In Slide Master view, the slide master is the larger, top slide thumbnail shown in the left pane. The Title Slide Layout is the second slide in the pane. The number of slides following it varies depending upon the template. Figure 2.28 shows the Organic Theme Slide Master and its related slide layouts. The ScreenTip for the slide master indicates it is used by one slide because the slide show is a new slide show composed of a single title slide.

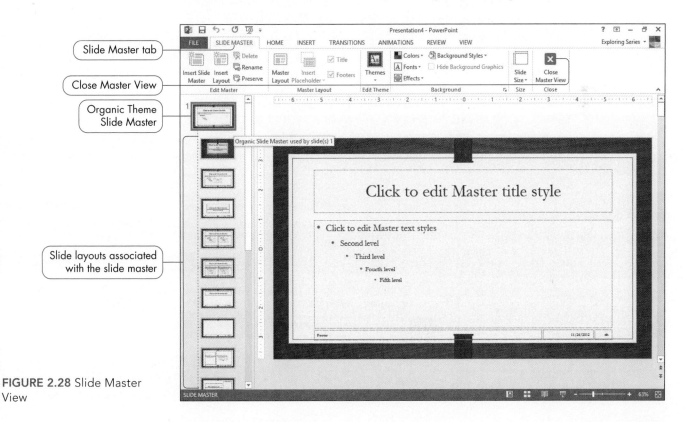

FIGURE 2.28 Slide Master View

The slide master is the most efficient way of setting the fonts, color scheme, and effects for the entire slide show. For example, you may wish to add a small company logo to the right corner of all slides. To set these choices, click the slide master thumbnail in the slide pane to display the slide master. The main pane shows the placeholders for title style, text styles, a date field, a footer field, and a page number field. Double-click the text in the Master title style or any level of text in the Master text styles placeholder and modify the font appearance. You can also make adjustments to the footer, date, and page number fields.

You can move and size the placeholders on the slide master. The modifications in position and size will be reflected on the associated slide layouts. This may conflict with some of the slide layout placeholders, however. The placeholders can be moved on the individual slide layouts as needed.

Quick
Concepts

1. How are sections in a presentation similar to tabs in a binder? ***p. 160***

2. Locate a PowerPoint presentation online and then use the Slide Show Design Principles described in this chapter to identify principles the creator used or failed to use. ***p. 161***

3. Which elements of a theme can be modified? Why would you modify a theme? ***p. 163***

Hands-On Exercises

Watch the Video for this Hands-On Exercise!

MyITLab®
HOE4 Training

4 Design

The director of the Wellness Center plans to add more content to the Campus Wellness Center mission presentation. To help her organize the content, you create sections in the slide show. You apply your knowledge of design principles to make the text more professional and readable. Finally, you change the theme and make modifications to the presentation through the slide master.

Skills covered: Create Sections • Apply Design Principles • Modify a Theme • Modify the Slide Master

STEP 1 >> CREATE SECTIONS

After reviewing the Campus Wellness Center mission slide show, you decide to create four sections organizing the content. Refer to Figure 2.29 as you complete Step 1.

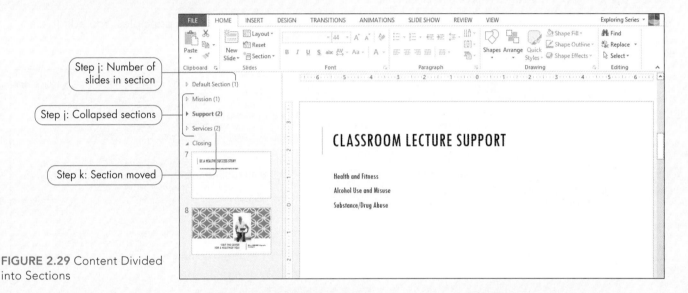

FIGURE 2.29 Content Divided into Sections

a. Open *p02h3Mission_LastFirst*, if necessary, and save the presentation as **p02h4Mission_LastFirst**, changing *h3* to *h4*.

b. Click the **VIEW tab**, click **Normal**, and then click the **Slide 2 icon**.

c. Click **Section** in the **Slides group** on the HOME tab and select **Add Section**.

    A section divider is positioned between Slide 1 and Slide 2 in the Slides tab. It is labeled *Untitled Section*.

d. Right-click the **Untitled Section divider** and select **Rename Section**.

    The Rename Section dialog box opens.

e. Type **Mission** in the **Section name box** and click **Rename**.

    The section divider name changes and displays in the Slides tab.

f. Create a new section between Slides 2 and 3.

g. Right-click **Untitled Section**, click **Rename**, and then name the section **Services**.

h. Right-click between Slide 4 and Slide 5, click **Add Section**, and then rename the section **Support**.

i. Right-click between **Slide 6** and **Slide 7** and create a section named **Closing**.

The slide show content is divided into logical sections.

j. Right-click any section divider and select **Collapse All**.

The Slides tab shows the four sections you created: *Mission*, *Services*, *Support*, and *Closing*, as well as the *Default* section. Each section divider displays the section name and the number of slides in the section.

k. Right-click the **Support section** and click **Move Section Up**.

The *Support* section and all its associated slides are moved above the *Services* section.

l. Right-click any section divider and click **Expand All**.

m. Click the **VIEW tab** and click **Slide Sorter** in the Presentation Views group.

Slide Sorter view displays the slides in each section.

n. Click **Normal** in the Presentation Views group. Save the presentation.

STEP 2 ➤➤ APPLY DESIGN PRINCIPLES

You note that several of the slides in the presentation do not use slide show text design principles. You edit these slides so they are more readable. Refer to Figure 2.30 as you complete Step 2.

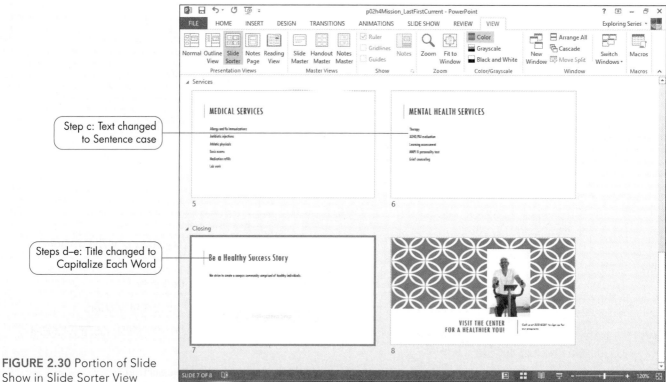

FIGURE 2.30 Portion of Slide Show in Slide Sorter View

a. On Slide 3, select the text below the title placeholder, click the **Change Case arrow** in the **Font group** of the HOME tab, and then select **Sentence case**.

The text now meets the guideline and is more readable.

b. Change the text below the titles in Slides 4, 5, and 6 to **Sentence case**.

c. On Slide 4, change the second line to **DVDs/CDs**.

Always proofread to ensure that the case feature accurately reflects proper capitalization.

d. On Slide 7, select the **title text**, click **Change Case** in the Font group, and then click **Capitalize Each Word**.

Each word in the title begins with a capital letter.

e. Change the uppercase *A* in the title to a lowercase *a*.

Title case capitalization guidelines state that only significant parts of speech of four or more letters should be capitalized. Minor parts of speech including articles and words shorter than four letters should not be capitalized.

f. Click the **VIEW tab** and click **Slide Sorter** in the Presentation Views group.

Note the sentence case in the *Services* section.

g. Save the presentation.

STEP 3 ≫ MODIFY A THEME

Although you are satisfied with the opening and closing slides, you think the main body of slides should be enhanced. You decide to change the theme and then modify the new theme to customize it. Refer to Figure 2.31 as you complete Step 3.

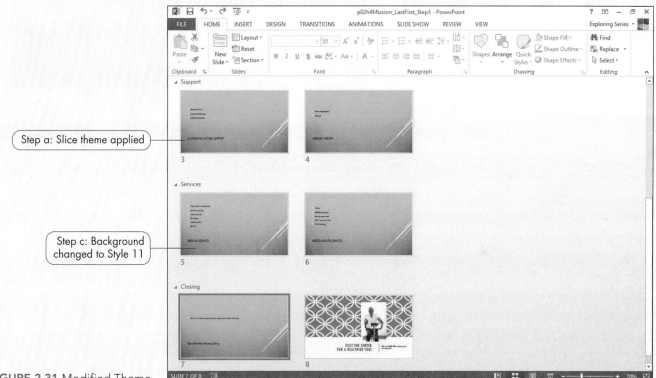

FIGURE 2.31 Modified Theme

a. Click the **DESIGN tab** and click **Slice** in the Themes gallery.

The Slice theme, which provides a new background, is applied to the slide show except for the title and conclusion slides.

b. Click the **DESIGN tab** and click **More** in the Variants group.

The Variants Gallery opens.

c. Select **Background Styles** and click **Style 11**.

d. Save the presentation.

STEP 4 ≫ MODIFY THE SLIDE MASTER

You want to add the Campus Wellness Center logo to slides 2 through 7 using the slide master. Refer to Figure 2.32 as you complete Step 4.

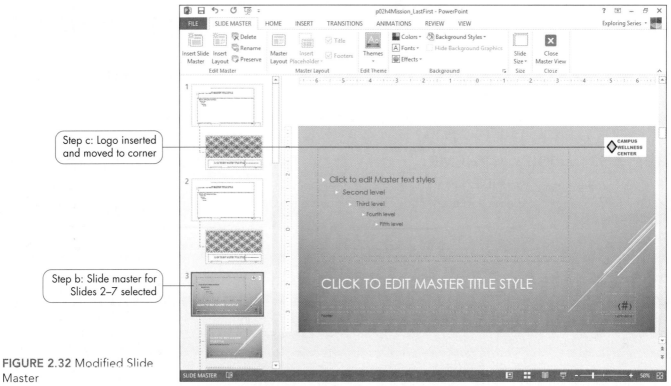

Step c: Logo inserted and moved to corner

Step b: Slide master for Slides 2–7 selected

FIGURE 2.32 Modified Slide Master

a. Click the **VIEW tab** and click **Slide Master** in the Master Views group.

Note the masters labeled 1 and 2. These masters control the first and last slides of the presentation.

b. Click the slide master thumbnail next to the number 3.

The third slide master controls slides 2 through 7.

c. Click the **INSERT tab** and click **Pictures**. Locate *p02h4Logo.jpg* picture file in the student files folder and click **Insert**.

The Campus Wellness Center logo is inserted.

d. Move the logo to the top right corner of the slide master.

e. Click the **SLIDE MASTER tab**. Click **Close Master View** in the Close group.

Observe that the logo has been inserted on Slides 2 through 7 in the presentation.

f. Spell check the presentation. Save and close the file, and submit based on your instructor's directions.

Chapter Objectives Review

After reading this chapter, you have accomplished the following objectives:

1. **Create a presentation using a template.**
   - Using a template saves time and enables you to create a more professional presentation.
   - Templates incorporate a theme, a layout, and content that you can modify.
   - You can download templates from Office.com or elsewhere on the Web.

2. **Modify a presentation based on a template.**
   - You can modify the structure of a template. The structure is modified by changing the layout of a slide.
   - To change the layout, drag placeholders to new locations or resize placeholders.

3. **Create a presentation in Outline view.**
   - When you use a storyboard to determine your content, you create a basic outline.
   - Entering your presentation in Outline view enables you to concentrate on the content of the presentation and saves time because you can enter information efficiently without moving from placeholder to placeholder.

4. **Modify an outline structure.**
   - Because Outline view helps you see the structure of the presentation, you are able to see where content needs to be strengthened or where the flow of information needs to be revised.
   - If you decide a slide contains content that would be presented better in another location in the slide show, use the Collapse and Expand features to easily move it.
   - By collapsing the slide content, you can drag the slide to a new location and then expand it.
   - To move individual bullet points, cut and paste the bullet points, or drag and drop them.

5. **Print an outline.**
   - An outline can be printed in either collapsed or expanded form to be used during a presentation.

6. **Import an outline.**
   - You can import any outline that has been saved in a format PowerPoint can read.
   - In addition to a Word outline, you can use the common generic formats rich text format and plain text format.

7. **Reuse slides from an existing presentation.**
   - Slides that have been previously created can be reused in new slide shows for efficiency and continuity.

8. **Use sections.**
   - Sections help organize slides.
   - Each section can be named to help identify the contents of the sections.
   - Sections can be collapsed or expanded.

9. **Examine slide show design principles.**
   - Using basic slide show principles and applying the guidelines make presentations more polished and professional.

10. **Modify a theme.**
    - In addition to layouts, a template includes themes that define its font attributes, colors, and backgrounds.
    - Themes can be changed to customize a slide show.

11. **Modify the slide master.**
    - A slide master controls the design elements and slide layouts associated with the slides in a presentation.

Key Terms Matching

Match the key terms with their definitions. Write the key term letter by the appropriate numbered definition.

a. Background styles gallery
b. Collapsed outline
c. Colors gallery
d. Effects gallery
e. Expanded outline
f. Fonts gallery
g. Hierarchy

h. Master
i. Outline
j. Outline view
k. Plain text format (.txt)
l. Slide Master
m. Rich text format (.rtf)
n. Template

1. _____ A file that incorporates a theme, a layout, and content that can be modified. **p. 140**

2. _____ A method of organizing text in a hierarchy to depict relationships. **p. 148**

3. _____ Indicates levels of importance in a structure. **p. 148**

4. _____ Shows the presentation in an outline format displayed in levels according to the points and any subpoints on each slide. **p. 148**

5. _____ Displays only the slide number, icon, and title of each slide in Outline view. **p. 149**

6. _____ Displays the slide number, icon, title, and content of each slide in Outline view. **p. 149**

7. _____ A file format that retains structure and most text formatting when transferring documents between applications or platforms. **p. 156**

8. _____ A file format that retains only text but no formatting when transferring documents between applications or platforms. **p. 156**

9. _____ Provides a set of colors for every available theme. **p. 164**

10. _____ Contains font sets for the content. **p. 164**

11. _____ Includes a range of effects for shapes used in the presentation. **p. 164**

12. _____ Provides both solid color and background styles for application to a theme. **p. 164**

13. _____ The top slide in a hierarchy of slides based on the master. **p. 165**

14. _____ Controls the layouts, background designs, and color combinations for handouts, notes pages, and slides, giving the presentation a consistent appearance. **p. 164**

Multiple Choice

1. A template is a format that can be modified and incorporates all of the following *except*:

   (a) Theme.
   (b) Layout.
   (c) Margins.
   (d) Content.

2. To create a presentation based on a template, click the:

   (a) FILE tab and search for a template.
   (b) FILE tab, click New, and then search for a template.
   (c) INSERT tab and select Add Template.
   (d) DESIGN tab and select New.

3. What is the advantage to collapsing the outline so only the slide titles are visible?

   (a) Transitions and animations can be added.
   (b) Graphical objects become visible.
   (c) More slide titles are displayed at one time, making it easier to rearrange the slides in the presentation.
   (d) All of the above.

4. Which of the following is *true*?

   (a) The slide layout can be changed after the template has been chosen.
   (b) Themes applied to a template will not be saved with the slide show.
   (c) Placeholders downloaded with a template cannot be modified.
   (d) Slides cannot be added to a presentation after a template has been chosen.

5. Which of the following is the fastest and most efficient method for reusing a slide you have customized in another presentation?

   (a) Open the slide, delete the content, and then enter the new information.
   (b) Save the custom slide and reuse it in the new presentation.
   (c) Open the slide and cut and paste the placeholders to a new slide.
   (d) Drag the placeholders from one slide to the next.

6. Which of the following is not an efficient method for adding existing content to a presentation?

   (a) Retype the content from an existing slide show into a new slide show.
   (b) Insert content by adding slides from an outline.

   (c) Copy and paste slides from an existing slide show into a new slide show.
   (d) Insert content by reusing slides.

7. All of the following are true *except*:

   (a) Pressing TAB demotes a bullet point from the first level to the second level.
   (b) Pressing SHIFT+TAB promotes a bullet point from the second level to the first level.
   (c) Pressing SHIFT+TAB demotes a bullet point from the first level to the second level.
   (d) Pressing Increase List Level demotes a bullet point from the first level to the second level.

8. Which of the following is *not* true of sections?

   (a) Sections can be renamed.
   (b) Sections can be created in Normal view or Slide Sorter view.
   (c) Sections can be collapsed.
   (d) A slide show can be divided into only six logical sections.

9. Which of the following formats cannot be imported to use as an outline for a presentation?

   (a) .jpg
   (b) .docx
   (c) .txt
   (d) .rtf

10. You own a small business and decide to institute an Employee of the Month award program. Which of the following would be the fastest way to create the award certificate with a professional look?

    (a) Enter the text in the title placeholder of a slide, change the font for each line, and then drag several clip art images of awards onto the slide.
    (b) Select a Theme, modify the placeholders, and then enter the award text information.
    (c) Create a table, enter the award text in the table, and then add clip art.
    (d) Access Microsoft Office Online and download an Award certificate template.

Practice Exercises

1 | Certificate of Excellence

Figure 2.33 displays a Certificate of Excellence, created from a template downloaded from Microsoft Office Online for K&H Design, a small concrete design shop. You are the owner of K&H Design, and you want to present your employee, Juan Carlos Sanchez, with the Certificate of Excellence. This exercise follows the same set of skills as used in Hands-On Exercises 1 and 4 in the chapter. Refer to Figure 2.33 as you complete this exercise.

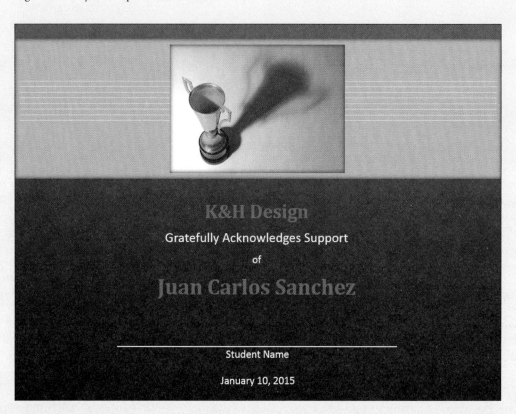

FIGURE 2.33 Downloaded and Modified Template

a. Start PowerPoint. Click in the **Search online templates and themes search box**. Search for **Certificate of appreciation**.

   Thumbnails of sample templates will display.

b. Click **Certificate of appreciation to donor** and click **Create** in the Preview pane.

c. Save the file as **p02p1Donor_LastFirst**.

d. Create a *Notes and Handouts* header with your name and a footer with your instructor's name and your class. Include the current date set to update automatically. The page number feature can remain active. Click **Apply to All**.

e. Select the text *Organization Name* and type **K&H Design**.

f. Select the text *Name* and type **Juan Carlos Sanchez**.

g. Select the box containing the words *Presenter Name and Title* and replace the text with your first and last names.

h. Select the text *Date* and type today's date.

i. Click the **DESIGN tab** and click **More** in the Variants group. Select **Background Styles** and click **Style 12** (third row, fourth column).

j. Save and close the file, and submit based on your instructor's directions.

2 Classic Photo Album

You enjoy using your digital camera to record nature shots during trips you take on weekends. You decide to store these pictures in an electronic slide show that you can display for your family. You use the Classic Photo Album template. This exercise follows the same set of skills as used in Hands-On Exercises 1 and 4 in the chapter. Refer to Figure 2.34 as you complete this exercise.

Modified title

Modified template layout

FIGURE 2.34 Classic Photo Album in Slide Sorter View

Photos: Paul Moore/Fotolia

a. Start PowerPoint.

b. Click **Photo Albums** at the end of the row of Suggested searches.
   Thumbnails of sample templates will display.

c. Click **Classic photo album** and click **Create**.

d. Save the presentation file as **p02p2Album_LastFirst**.

e. Create a *Notes and Handouts* header with your name and a footer with your instructor's name and your class. Include the current date set to update automatically. The page number feature can remain active. Click **Apply to All**.

f. Select the word *CLASSIC* in the **title placeholder** of the first slide and type **Nature**.

g. Change the case of the title to **Capitalize Each Word**.

h. Replace the text in the **subtitle placeholder**, *Click to add date and other details*, with **Favorite Pictures in 2016**.

i. Click the **New Slide arrow** to display the Layout gallery.

j. Click the **Portrait with Caption layout** to add a new Slide 2.

k. Click the **picture icon**, locate the image *p02p2Nature* from your student data files, and then click **Insert**.

l. Click in the **caption placeholder** and type **Our way is not soft grass, it's a mountain path with lots of rocks. But it goes upwards, forward, toward the sun.** Press **Enter** twice and type **Ruth Westheimer**.

m. On Slide 3, read the text in the placeholder and click anywhere in the text.

n. Click the border of the caption placeholder and press **Delete** to remove the content. Select the placeholder again and press **Delete** to remove the placeholder. Modify the layout of the slide by dragging the picture placeholder to the right side of the slide.

o. Select the **Slide 4 thumbnail**, click **Layout** in the Slides group, and then click the **2-Up Landscape with Captions layout** to apply it to the slide.

p. Select the extra photograph (the smaller one) and press **Delete**. Select a border surrounding one of the caption placeholders and press **Delete**. Repeat selecting and deleting until all caption placeholders have been deleted. Delete the CHOOSE A LAYOUT placeholder.

q. Select the **Slide 5 thumbnail**, hold down **Ctrl**, and select the **Slide 7 thumbnail** in the Slides tab, and then press **Delete** to delete Slides 5 and 7 entirely.

r. Click the **SLIDE SHOW tab** and click **From Beginning** in the Start Slide Show group to view your presentation. Note the variety of layouts. Press **Esc** when you are done viewing the presentation.

s. Save and close the file, and submit based on your instructor's directions.

3 A Guide to Successful Presentations

Your community's Small Business Development Center (SBDC) asks you to provide training to local small business owners on preparing and delivering presentations. You create an outline and then supplement it by reusing slides from another presentation and by adding slides from an outline. Because the slides come from different sources, they have different fonts, and you change the fonts to match, one of the design principles discussed in the chapter. You create sections to organize the presentation and then polish the presentation by adding and modifying a theme. This exercise follows the same set of skills as used in Hands-On Exercises 2–4 in the chapter.

a. Create a new, blank presentation. Click the **VIEW tab** and click **Outline View**. Click next to the Slide 1 icon and type **A Guide to Winning Presentations**. Press **Enter** and press **Tab**. Type your name and add the title **Consultant**.

b. Save the new presentation as **p02p3Success_LastFirst**.

c. Create a *Notes and Handouts* header with your name and a footer with your instructor's name and your class. Include the current date set to update automatically. The page number feature can remain active.

d. Click the **New Slide arrow** in the Slides group, click **Slides from Outline**, locate *p02p3TipsOutline* in your student data files, and then click **Insert**.

e. Switch to Outline view, select the word *Winning* on Slide 1, and type **Successful**.

f. Click at the end of the last bulleted text on Slide 3, press **Enter**, and then press **Shift+Tab** to create a new Slide 4. Type **Develop the Content** and press **Enter**.

g. Press Tab, type **Create a storyboard outline**, and then press **Enter**.

h. Type **Type the outline** and press **Enter**.

i. Press **Tab** to create a subpoint and type **Increase the indent levels (demote items)**. Press **Enter**.

j. Type **Decrease the indent levels (promote items)** and press **Enter**.

k. Press **Shift+Tab** to return to the previous level and type **Review the flow of ideas**.

l. Click at the end of the last bulleted text on Slide 4 and click the **New Slide arrow** in the Slides group.

m. Click **Reuse Slides** at the bottom of the gallery to open the Reuse Slides pane. Click **Browse**, click **Browse File**, select *p02p3Reuse*, and then click **Open**.

> **TROUBLESHOOTING:** If you do not see the *p02p3Reuse* file, change the *Files of type* option to All PowerPoint Presentations.

n. Double-click each of the slides in the Reuse Slides pane to insert the slides into the slide show. Close the Reuse Slides pane.

o. Press **Ctrl+A** to select all text in the outline, change the font to **Calibri (Body)**, and then deselect the text.

p. Right-click any bullet point to collapse, point to *Collapse*, and then select **Collapse All**.

q. Drag the Slide 5 icon below the Slide 7 icon.

r. Right-click one of the slide titles, point to *Expand*, and then select **Expand All**.

s. Click the **VIEW tab**, click **Normal**, and then click the **DESIGN tab**. Click **More** in the Themes group and click **Integral**. Choose the green variant (the second variant from the left).

t. On Slide 2, click the **HOME tab**, click **Section**, and then select **Add Section**.

u. Right-click **Untitled Section**, select **Rename Section**, select **Untitled Section** (if necessary), and then type **Create**. Click **Rename**.

v. Repeat steps t and u to create a section named **Refine** before Slide 5 and a section named **Deliver** before Slide 7.

w. Click **VIEW tab** and click **Slide Master**. Click the top slide (numbered Slide 1) in the slide pane.

x. Click the **INSERT tab** and click **Pictures**. Locate *p02p3PresenterLogo* and click **Insert**. Move the image to the bottom-right corner of the slide. Click the **SLIDE MASTER tab** and click **Close Master View**.

y. Click the **FILE tab**, click **Print**, click **Full Page Slides**, and select **Outline**. View the outline in the Preview pane and press **Cancel** to close the Print dialog box.

z. Save and close the file, and submit based on your instructor's directions.

1 Nutrition Guide

You have been asked to help create a presentation for a local Girl Scout troop that is featuring good nutrition as its theme for the month. You locate a Microsoft Office Online template for nutrition that has some fun animations that you think the young girls will enjoy. Since you've given similar presentations, you decide to reuse basic slide content you've previously created on standard nutritional guidelines supported by the U.S. Department of Agriculture. Lastly, you modify the presentation using the Slide Master so all the changes are easily implemented to all slides.

a. Start PowerPoint, and in **Search online templates and themes box**, type **Nutrition**.

b. Select **Health nutrition presentation** and click **Create**.

c. Save the presentation as **p02m1Food_LastFirst**.

d. Create a *Notes and Handouts* header with your name and a footer with your instructor's name and your class. Include the current date.

e. View the slides in Slide Show view.

f. You notice that there are cute animations on the first and last slides, but some modifications need to be made.

g. On Slide 1, replace the word *Fruit* in the triangle with **Food**.

h. Click Slide 6 and make a similar change, replacing *Fruit* with **Food**.

i. Make the following changes to Slide 1:
- Replace *Feb – 2010* with the current month and year.
- Replace *Title of the Presentation* with **Nutritional Guide**.
- Delete the subtitle of the presentation.

j. Delete Slides 2 through 5.

k. Click the **New Slide arrow** in the Slides group of the HOME tab and select **Reuse Slides**.

l. Browse to locate and select the *p02m1Diet* presentation from the student data files in the Reuse Slides pane.

m. Select all seven slides in the Reuse Slides pane. Close the Reuse Slides pane.

n. Move Slide 2 so it becomes the last slide of the presentation.

o. Click the **VIEW tab** and click **Slide Master** from the Master Views group.

p. Click the top slide in the left pane and make the following changes to the Title and Content Layout slide master:
- Select the five levels of text in the content placeholder, click the **Font Color arrow** in the Mini Toolbar, select the **Eyedropper**, and then click the grapes image in the bottom-right corner to select the color of the grapes.
- Select the text in the title (*Click to edit Master title style*), click the **Font Color arrow** in the Mini Toolbar, select **Lime, Text 1, Darker 25%** (fifth row, second column).
- Increase the font size of the slide title to **36**.
- Change *www.funFruit.com* to **www.funFood.com** in the bottom-right corner of the slide.
- Click the center text box at the bottom of the slide, delete *Coming to Fruition*, and then type **for Everyone**.
- Close the Slide Master and close the Reuse Slides pane.

q. View Slides 2 through 8 to ensure the changes in the slide master are reflected in the slides.

r. Select Slide 9 and make the following changes
- Replace *Pears, not for squares* with **Food is fun for everyone!**
- Delete the text box content.

s. Save and close the file, and submit based on your instructor's directions.

2 Go Digital

CREATIVE CASE

FROM SCRATCH

The local senior citizens' center has asked you to speak on photography. The center has many residents interested in learning about digital photography. You decide to create a presentation with sections on learning the advantages of a digital camera, choosing a camera, taking pictures with a digital camera, and printing and sharing photos. In this exercise, you begin the presentation by creating the sections and completing the content for the first section.

a. Create a new blank PowerPoint presentation and create slides from the *p02m2Outline.docx* outline. Save the slide show as **p02m2Digital_LastFirst**.

b. Apply the **Wisp theme** to the slides.

c. Delete the blank Slide 1 and change the layout of the new Slide 1 to **Title Slide**.

d. Review the presentation in PowerPoint's Outline view and add the following information as the last bullets on Slide 2:
   - **Instant feedback**
   - **Sharing**

e. Promote the text *Free Experimentation* on Slide 4 so that it creates a new slide.

> **TROUBLESHOOTING:** If you cannot select a bullet, place your insertion point at the end of the bullet and click to select the bulleted line.

f. Select all text in Outline view and click **Clear All Formatting** in the Font group on the HOME tab.

g. Open the Reuse Slides pane and browse to locate and open the *p02m2Slides* presentation. Click the last slide in the original presentation. Right-click any slide and click **Insert All Slides**. The new slides should be inserted as Slides 6 and 7. Close the Reuse Slides pane.

h. Select **More in the Variants Gallery** on the DESIGN tab and change the presentation font to **Corbel**. Using the Colors gallery, change the presentation colors to **Red**.

i. Return to Normal view.

j. Create a section between Slides 1 and 2 named **Advantages**.

k. Create a section after Slide 7 named **Choosing a Digital Camera**.

DISCOVER

l. Use the Web to research things to consider when purchasing a digital camera. Be sure to include the major types of cameras available.

m. Insert a new Slide 8 in the **Choosing a Digital Camera** section to explain your findings.

n. Create a *Notes and Handouts* header with your name and a footer with your instructor's name and your class. Include the current date.

o. Save and close the file, and submit based on your instructor's directions.

3 Using Social Technologies for Ideas and Resources

OLLABORATION CASE

FROM SCRATCH

Social networking enables us to connect with others who share common interests via the Internet. Social networking also helps businesses connect with their customers. Give an overview of some of the popular social media technologies such as Facebook, Twitter, LinkedIn, etc. and discuss how businesses can utilize them to engage their customers. Choose a business that interests you and discuss which social media technologies it uses and how they are used to connect with its customers. In this exercise, you will visit Microsoft's Office.com website, download a template from the Design Gallery, modify the template with your information, and then post the PowerPoint presentation you create to a Web site for others to view.

a. Access the Internet and go to http://office.microsoft.com/en-us/templates. Click **PowerPoint**. Click to see all available PowerPoint 2013 templates.

b. The page you view displays a series of slides created by Microsoft and some of its partners. Microsoft provides these slides as an exclusive benefit for its users. Click the thumbnail to see further details about the presentation.

c. Select one of the presentations and download the slides to the location you use to store your files for this class. Save the file as **p02m3Resources_GroupName**. Open the saved slide show and modify the slides so they reflect your information and ideas. Be sure to follow the design principles discussed in the chapter. Your presentation should be approximately 6–9 slides in length, including the title and credit slides. Delete any unnecessary slides found in the template. Make sure you create a final slide that credits the source for the slide design. Provide the URL for the location from where you downloaded the presentation.

d. Load your edited presentation to an online location for others to review. Upload your presentation to your Microsoft OneDrive account or use another method for sharing your presentation with your instructor and classmates. (If you do not already have a OneDrive account, you can create a free account at https://onedrive.live.com.)

e. Invite three classmates to go to the site, view the presentation you saved, and then add a comment about your presentation. If using OneDrive, to add comments, click the **Comment button** in PowerPoint Online. If you saved to another online storage location, share the location with three classmates and ask them to download the presentation. After viewing the presentation, ask them to e-mail you with their comments.

f. Visit three of your classmates' presentations from their storage locations. Leave a comment about their presentations or e-mail your classmates, sharing a comment about their presentations.

g. Review the comments of your classmates.

h. Submit based on your instructor's directions.

Social Media Marketing

RESEARCH CASE

FROM SCRATCH

You have a bright, creative, and energetic personality, and you are using these talents in college as a senior majoring in marketing. You hope to work in social media marketing. The Marketing 405 course you are taking this semester requires every student to create a social media marketing plan for a fictional company and to present an overview of the company to the class. This presentation should include the company purpose, the company's history, and past and present projects—all of which you are to "creatively invent." Include a final slide giving the resources you used to create your presentation.

Search Office.com for an appropriate template to use in creating your presentation. Research what a social media marketing campaign entails, and use what you learn to add your own content to comply with the case requirements. Add clip art, transitions, and animations as desired. Organize using sections. Create a handout header with your name and a handout footer with your instructor's name and your class. Include the current date. Save the presentation as **p02b2Marketing_LastFirst** and submit as directed by your instructor.

Michigan, My State

DISASTER RECOVERY

Your sister spent a lot of time researching and creating a presentation on the state of Michigan for a youth organization leader and team members. She does not like the presentation's design and has asked for your help. You show her how to download the state history report presentation template from Office.com, Presentations category, Academic subcategory. Save the new presentation as **p02b3State_LastFirst**. Reuse her slides, which are saved as *p02b3Michigan*. Cut and paste the images she gathered into the correct placeholders and move bulleted text to the correct slide. Resize placeholders as needed. You tell your sister that mixing clip art with pictures is contributing to the cluttered look. Choose one format based on your preference. Create new slides with appropriate layouts as needed. You remind her that although federal government organizations allow use of their images in an educational setting, your sister should give proper credit if she is going to use their data. Give credit to the State of Michigan's Web site for the information obtained from Michigan.gov (http://michigan.gov/kids). Give credit to the U.S. Census Bureau (www.census.gov) for the Quick Facts. Finalize the presentation by deleting unneeded slides, adding appropriate sections, modifying themes, proofreading, and applying transitions. Create a handout header with your name and a handout footer with your instructor's name and your class. Include the current date. Print the outline as directed by your instructor. Save the presentation and submit as directed by your instructor.

Time Management Skills

SOFT SKILLS CASE

FROM SCRATCH

Time management is an important skill for both students and professionals. Review the time management lesson found at the following Web site: http://www.gcflearnfree.org/jobsuccess/2. Using Word in Outline View, create an outline discussing the major points of the lesson. Your outline should have four headings with supporting bullets for each. Create a PowerPoint presentation based on your outline and add design elements to enhance your presentation. Be sure to follow the design rules discussed in this chapter. Add a small clock or hourglass to one corner of your slides using the slide master. Create a handout header with your name and a handout footer with your instructor's name and your class. Include the current date. Save the presentation as **p02b4TimeManagement_LastFirst** and submit as directed by your instructor.

Capstone Exercise

Your neighbors in your small southwestern subdivision are concerned about drought, fire danger, and water conservation. You volunteer to gather information about possible solutions and share the information with them in a PowerPoint presentation at the next neighborhood association meeting. In this capstone project, you concentrate on developing the content of the presentation.

Design Template

You download an Office.com template to create the basic design and structure for your presentation, save the presentation, and create the title slide.

a. Create a new presentation using one of the available templates. Search for the template using the search term **Ecology** and locate and download the **Ecology photo panels template**.

b. Save the presentation as **p02c1Wise_LastFirst**.

c. Type **Conserve** as the title on the title slide.

d. Type the subtitle **Waterwise Landscaping**.

e. Delete the blank Slides 7 through 11.

f. Create a handout header with your name and a handout footer with your instructor's name and your class. Include the current date. Apply to all slides.

Outline and Modifications

Based on the storyboard you created after researching water conservation on the Internet, you type the outline of your presentation. As you create the outline, you also modify the outline structure.

a. Open the Outline View.

b. Type **Waterwise Options** as the title for Slide 2.

c. Enter each of the following as Level 1 bullets for Slide 2: **Zeroscaping, Xeriscaping**. Remove the third bullet, which is blank.

d. Delete Slides 3, 4, and 5.

e. Change the layout of the new Slide 3 to **Title and Content**.

f. Type **Purpose of Landscaping** as the title for Slide 3.

g. Type each of the following as Level 1 bullets for Slide 3: **Beauty, Utility, Conservation**.

h. Add this speaker note to Slide 3: **With water becoming a limited resource, conservation has become an additional purpose of landscaping.**

i. Modify the outline structure by reversing Slides 2 and 3.

Imported Outline

You have an outline on zeroscaping that was created in Microsoft Word and a slide show on xeriscaping. You reuse this content to build your slide show.

a. Position the insertion point at the end of the outline.

b. Use the **Slides from Outline option** to insert the *p02c1Zero* outline.

c. Delete any blank slides.

d. Change the layout of Slide 4 to **Picture with Caption**.

e. Insert *p02c1Zeropic* in the **picture placeholder**.

f. Position the point of insertion at the end of the outline.

g. Reuse all of the slides, using the same order, from *p02c1Xeri* to add four slides to the end of the presentation.

h. Insert *p02c1Xeripic* in the **picture placeholder** on Slide 8.

Design

The outline slides do not match the design of the other slides. You want to remove the formatting from those slides to create a uniform look. Additionally, the room in which you will be displaying the slide show is very light. You decide to darken the slides, which will increase the slide visibility. You also adjust the font size of two captions to increase their readability.

a. Select **Slides 4 through 7** in the outline and clear all formatting from the slides.

b. Change the background style for all four slides to **Style 4** (first row, fourth column).

c. Increase the font size of the title and caption text two levels on Slides 4 and 8.

d. Use the spelling checker and proofread the presentation.

Sections

To facilitate moving between the slides concerning zeroscaping and the slides concerning xeriscaping, you create sections.

a. Add a section before Slide 4 and rename it **Zeroscaping**.

b. Add a section before Slide 8 and rename it **Xeriscaping**.

c. Print the outline as directed by your instructor.

d. Save and close the file, and submit based on your instructor's directions.

Presentation Design

CHAPTER 3

Illustrations and Infographics

Konstantin Chagin/Shutterstock

OBJECTIVES | AFTER YOU READ THIS CHAPTER, YOU WILL BE ABLE TO:

1. Create shapes p. 184
2. Apply Quick Styles and customize shapes p. 189
3. Create SmartArt p. 203
4. Modify SmartArt p. 206

5. Create WordArt p. 210
6. Modify WordArt p. 210
7. Modify objects p. 217
8. Arrange objects p. 224

CASE STUDY | Illustrations and Infographics Mini-Camp

As an information technology (IT) project manager, you must often create presentations for senior management. Your presentations detail current team projects, which often require flow charts and diagrams.

This summer, you are working with several IT interns. You have been requested to introduce the interns to drawing using computer-based drawing tools, creating infographics, and working with online pictures. You decide to teach a PowerPoint mini-camp because you want to introduce the participants to PowerPoint's many tools for creating and modifying illustrations.

You begin the camp by teaching the participants how to create and modify lines and shapes, how to use shapes to create flow charts, how to use SmartArt diagrams, and how to modify online pictures to meet their needs. You also teach participants WordArt manipulation as a creative way to enhance text used in illustrations and infographics.

Shapes

Text can be very effective when giving a presentation, but sometimes it is simply not enough. Illustrations and diagrams can and usually do add additional clarity to the idea that is being presented. One type of visual element is a ***shape***, a geometric or non-geometric object used to create an illustration or to highlight information. For example, on a slide containing a list of items, you could include a quote related to the items and create the quote inside a shape to call attention to it. You can combine shapes to create complex images. Figure 3.1 shows three PowerPoint themes using shapes in each of these ways. The Striped Black Border theme uses a rectangular shape to draw attention to the information in the title placeholder. The Currency design theme uses curved lines to create an interesting design. The ListDiagram theme uses rounded rectangles to emphasize each concept.

FIGURE 3.1 Using Shapes in Themes

Infographics, a shortened term for information graphics, are visual representations of data or knowledge. Infographics typically use shapes to present complex data or knowledge in an easily understood visual representation. PowerPoint includes powerful drawing tools you can use to create lines and shapes, which are the basis for infographics. Because drawn images are created with shapes, you should learn to modify the shapes used for drawn images to meet your needs. In addition to using the drawing tools, you can enhance shapes by adding effects such as 3-D, shadow, glow, warp, bevel, and others. These effects are accessible through style galleries. Using these visual effects makes it easy for you to create professional-looking infographics to enhance your presentation.

In this section, you will create and modify various shapes and lines. You will also customize shapes and apply special effects to objects. Finally, you will learn how to apply and change outline effects.

Creating Shapes

STEP 1 》 PowerPoint provides tools for creating shapes. You can insert a multitude of standard geometric shapes such as circles, squares, hearts, or stars. You can insert equation shapes, such as + and ÷, and a variety of banners. After you create a shape, you can modify it and apply fills and special effects.

To create a shape, do the following:

1. Click the INSERT tab.
2. Click Shapes in the Illustrations group.
3. Click the shape you desire from the Shapes gallery.
4. Click the desired position in which to place the shape, or drag the cross-hair pointer to control the approximate size of the shape as desired.
5. Release the mouse button.

To resize the shape, drag any of the sizing handles that surround the shape after it is created. Figure 3.2 shows the Shapes gallery and the many shapes from which you can choose. Notice that the most recently used shapes are at the top of the list so you can conveniently reuse them.

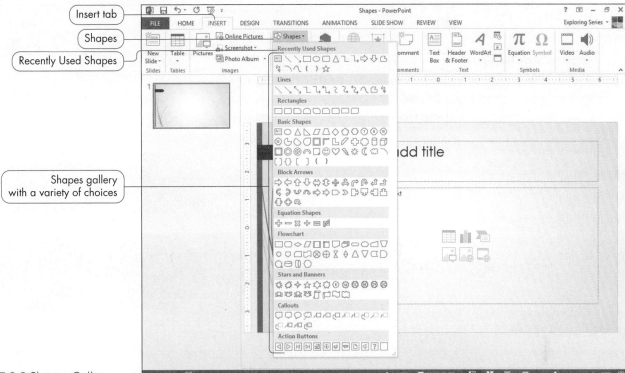

Insert tab

Shapes

Recently Used Shapes

Shapes gallery with a variety of choices

FIGURE 3.2 Shapes Gallery

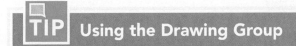

Using the Drawing Group

You can also access the Shapes gallery from the Drawing group on the Home tab. This group allows you to choose a shape, arrange its order and position, apply a Quick Style, and then change properties of the shape. If you have a widescreen monitor or if your monitor is set for a higher resolution, the Drawing group displays individual shapes instead of one Shapes command. If this is the case, click the More button to open the Shapes gallery.

The Shapes command deactivates the selected shape after you draw it once, forcing you to reselect the shape each time you want to use it. By activating the *Lock Drawing Mode* feature, you can add several shapes of the same type on your slide without selecting the shape each time.

To activate Lock Drawing Mode:

1. Right-click the shape you want to use in the Shapes gallery and select Lock Drawing Mode.

2. Click anywhere on the slide or drag to create the first shape.

3. Click or drag repeatedly to create additional shapes of the same type.

4. To release the Lock Drawing Mode, press Esc.

Figure 3.3 shows a series of squares created with the Lock Drawing Mode activated. Additionally the figure shows a basic oval and Smiley Face both located in the Basic Shapes category, and a *callout* created using the Oval Callout located in the Callouts category. A callout is a shape that includes a line with a text box that can be used to add notes, often used in cartooning. Notice that the Smiley Face shape is selected on the slide. The sizing handles display around the shape. This yellow square is an *adjustment handle* that you can drag to change the shape. If you drag the adjustment handle upward, the smile becomes a frown. Some shapes have an adjustment handle, and some do not.

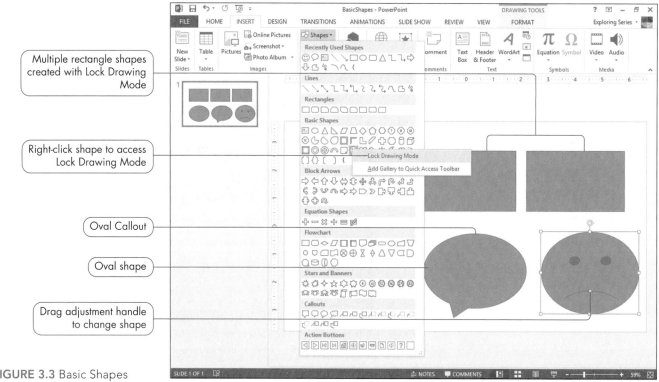

Multiple rectangle shapes created with Lock Drawing Mode

Right-click shape to access Lock Drawing Mode

Oval Callout

Oval shape

Drag adjustment handle to change shape

FIGURE 3.3 Basic Shapes

TIP | **Constrain a Shape**

A rectangle can be constrained or forced to form a perfect square, and an oval or ellipse can be constrained to form a perfect circle. To constrain a shape, press and hold Shift as you drag to create the shape.

Draw Lines and Connectors

Lines are shapes that can be used to point to information, to connect shapes on a slide, or to divide a slide into sections. Lines also are often used in slide design. To draw a straight line:

1. Select the line in the Lines category of the Shapes gallery.
2. Position the pointer on the slide where you want the line to begin.
3. Drag to create the line. Hold Shift as you drag to constrain to a perfectly horizontal, vertical, or any multiple of a 45-degree angle line.

You can also create curved lines. These may take a little practice to get the curve you want. To create a curved line:

1. Click the curve shape in the Lines category of the Shapes gallery.
2. Click the slide at the location where you want to start the curve.
3. Click again where the peaks or valleys of the curve occur and continue to click and move the mouse to shape the curve in the desired pattern.
4. Double-click to end the curve.

As you click while creating the curve, you set a point for the curve to bend around. To draw a shape that looks like it was drawn with a pen, select the Scribble shape.

In addition to drawing simple lines to create dividing lines and waves, you may need *connectors*, or lines that attach to the shapes you create. Connector lines move with shapes when the shapes are moved. The three types of connectors are straight, elbow (to create angled lines), and curved. To determine which line shapes are connectors, point to the line in the gallery and a ScreenTip will appear with the shape name, such as Curved Arrow Connector.

The first step in working with connectors is to create the shapes you want to connect with lines.

To connect shapes:

1. Create the shapes you wish to connect.
2. Select a connector line from the Lines category of the Shape gallery.
3. After you select the connector, squares appear around the previously created shapes when you move your pointer over them. These are the locations where you can attach the connector.
4. Click one of the squares to connect with the circle of the connector line that will appear on the next shape. You can also drag to control the direction and size of the connector line.
5. The two shapes are now connected. You can also connect placeholders with a connector line.

If you move a shape that is joined to another shape using a connector line, the connecting line moves with it, extending or shortening as necessary to maintain the connection. Sometimes when you rearrange the shapes, the connectors may no longer extend to the shape that was not moved, or the connectors may cross shapes and be confusing. If that happens, you can use the yellow adjustment handle located on the connector line to reshape the connectors. Select the connector lines and drag the handles to obtain a clearer path.

A *flow chart* is an illustration that shows a sequence to be followed or a plan containing steps (see Figure 3.4). For example, you could use a flow chart to illustrate the sequence to follow when implementing a new product. Connector lines join the shapes in a flow chart.

The typical flow chart sequence includes start and end points shown in oval shapes, steps shown in rectangular shapes, and decisions to be made shown in diamond shapes. Connectors with arrows demonstrate the order in which the sequence should be followed to accomplish the goal. Each shape has a label to which you can add text, indicating what the shape represents. When you select a shape and type or paste text into it, the text becomes part of the shape.

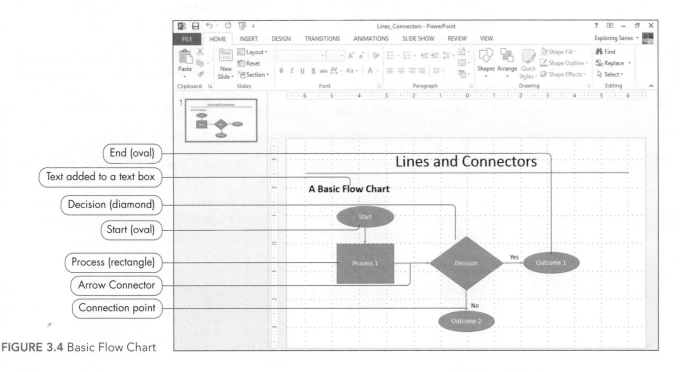

FIGURE 3.4 Basic Flow Chart

Sometimes it is necessary to add a text box to a slide. *Text boxes* can be more flexible than content placeholders or can be added to slides in which the chosen layout doesn't include a content placeholder, but text is still necessary. For example, use a text box to add a quote to a slide that is separate from the slide content placeholder. Text inside a text box can be formatted just as text in placeholders is formatted. You can even add a border, fill, shadow, or 3-D effect to the text in a text box. Figure 3.4 shows a basic flow chart created with shapes, connectors, and text boxes.

Create and Modify Freeform Shapes

A *freeform shape* is a shape that can be used to create customized shapes using both curved and straight-line segments.

To create a freeform shape:

1. Select the Freeform shape in the Lines category of the Shapes gallery and click the slide.
2. Click to draw straight lines and drag to create curves.
3. Double-click to end the freeform shape. If you end by clicking the starting point of the shape, you create a closed shape.

 TIP Create a Closed Shape

If you use the Curve, Freeform, or Scribble line tool to create a shape and end the shape at its starting point, the starting point and ending points join to create a closed shape. The advantage of joining the ends of the line and creating a closed shape is that you can include a fill, or interior content.

Sometimes, the freeform shape you have drawn is not exactly as you desired. You can modify the freeform shape to achieve the desired shape. This can be achieved through the help of a vertex. *Vertexes*, also known *as anchor points*, which are the black squares that control the curve line segments, indicate where two line segments meet or end. If you will recall, from early principles of math, it takes at least two points to define a line segment; thus you can control the shape by using the points. Click a point to move and drag it to a new position or to modify the shape's line segment curve. A vertex can be deleted if you right-click the point and select Delete Point. Either moving a vertex or deleting it will redefine the object's shape. Figure 3.5 shows a freeform shape with its vertexes displayed. Figure 3.6 shows a selected vertex dragged to a new position. When you release the left mouse button, the freeform will take the new shape.

To modify a freeform shape:

1. Select the freeform shape and click the FORMAT tab on the DRAWING TOOLS tab.
2. Click Edit Shape in the Insert Shapes group and click Edit Points.
3. To modify the freeform shape, drag one of the vertexes or one of the handles that extend from the vertex point. After you click Edit Points, right-click a vertex for additional control options.

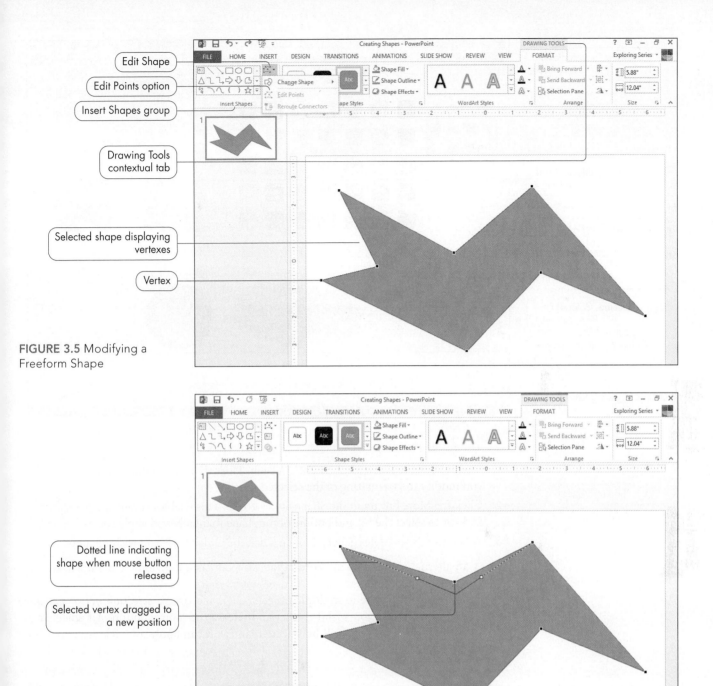

Edit Shape
Edit Points option
Insert Shapes group
Drawing Tools contextual tab
Selected shape displaying vertexes
Vertex

FIGURE 3.5 Modifying a Freeform Shape

Dotted line indicating shape when mouse button released
Selected vertex dragged to a new position

FIGURE 3.6 Moving a Vertex

Applying Quick Styles and Customizing Shapes

STEP 3 》 A *Quick Style* is a combination of different formats that can be selected from the Quick Style gallery and applied to a shape or other objects. To see how a Quick Style would look when applied, position your pointer over the Quick Style thumbnail. When you identify the style you want, click to apply the style to a selected object. Options in the gallery include edges, shadows, line styles, gradients, and 3-D effects. Figure 3.7 shows the Quick Style gallery and several shapes with a variety of Quick Styles applied to them.

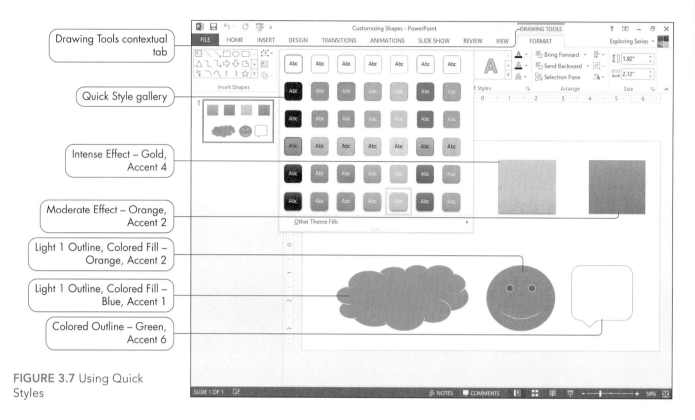

Drawing Tools contextual tab

Quick Style gallery

Intense Effect – Gold, Accent 4

Moderate Effect – Orange, Accent 2

Light 1 Outline, Colored Fill – Orange, Accent 2

Light 1 Outline, Colored Fill – Blue, Accent 1

Colored Outline – Green, Accent 6

FIGURE 3.7 Using Quick Styles

To apply a Quick Style to a shape:

1. Select the shape and click the FORMAT tab. This tab provides the tools to work with as you modify the formatting of the selected shape.
2. Click the More button in the Shape Styles group. This enables you to apply a Quick Style or to select the fill and outline of the shape manually and apply special effects.
3. When the Quick Styles gallery is open, click the Quick Style you wish to apply.

As an alternative to using the Format tab, you can click the Home tab and click Quick Styles in the Drawing group.

To apply a Quick Style to multiple objects, click and drag a *selection net* or *marquee* around all of the objects you wish to select and release the mouse button. All objects contained entirely within the net will be selected, and you can apply a Quick Style to all the objects at the same time.

> **TIP** **Selecting Multiple Objects**
>
> If objects are difficult to select with a selection net because of their placement or because they are nonadjacent, press and hold Ctrl or Shift as you click each object. While the Ctrl or Shift keys are pressed, each mouse click adds an object to the selection. When you have selected all objects, choose the style or effect you want, and it will apply only to the selected objects.

Change Shape Fills

One way to customize a shape is by changing the shape *fill*, or the interior of the shape. You can choose a solid color fill, no fill, a picture fill, a *gradient fill* (a blend of one color to another color or one shade to another shade), or a texture fill. To change the fill of a selected object, click Shape Fill in the Shape Styles group on the Format tab. The Shape Fill gallery provides color choices that match the theme colors or color choices based on Standard Colors. Figure 3.8 shows the Shape Fill options and a shape filled with the Yellow Standard Color.

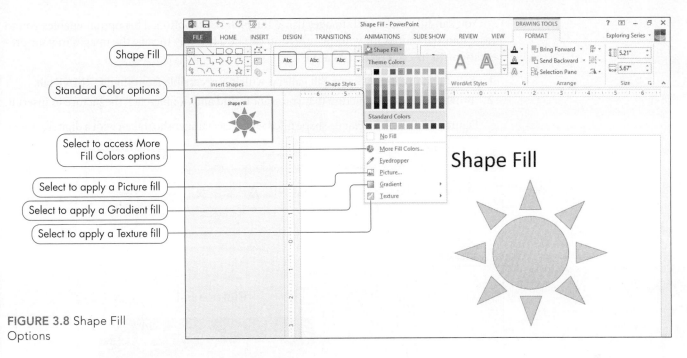

Shape Fill

Standard Color options

Select to access More Fill Colors options

Select to apply a Picture fill

Select to apply a Gradient fill

Select to apply a Texture fill

FIGURE 3.8 Shape Fill Options

If the color choices do not meet your needs, you can recreate an exact color in another part of your presentation by using the Eyedropper tool. Perhaps you want to recreate the red in the picture of a sunset you have in your presentation. To use the Eyedropper:

1. Click the shape you want to fill, click the Shape Fill arrow, and then select Eyedropper.
2. Hover over the color you want to recreate and press Enter.
3. The shape will now be filled with that color.

Alternatively, you may also select More Fill Colors to open the Colors dialog box where you can mix colors based on an RGB color model (Red Green Blue) or an HSL color model (Hue Saturation Luminosity). The default RGB color model gives each of the colors red, green, and blue a numeric value that ranges from 0 to 255. The combination of these values creates the fill color assigned to your shape. When all three RGB values are 0, you get black. When all three RGB values are 255, you get white. By using different combinations of numbers between 0 and 255, you can create more than 16 million shades of color.

The Colors dialog box also enables you to determine the amount of *transparency*, or visibility of the fill. At 0% transparency, the fill is *opaque* (or solid), while at 100% transparency, the fill is clear. The Colors dialog box enables you to drag a slider to specify the percentage of transparency. Figure 3.9 shows the Colors dialog box with the RGB color model selected, Red assigned a value of 236, Green assigned a value of 32, Blue assigned a value of 148, and a transparency set at 0%.

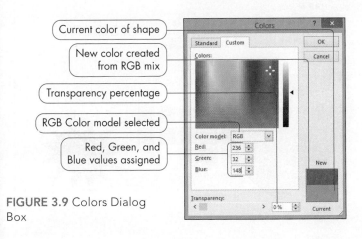

Current color of shape

New color created from RGB mix

Transparency percentage

RGB Color model selected

Red, Green, and Blue values assigned

FIGURE 3.9 Colors Dialog Box

You can fill shapes with images using the *picture fill* option. This option enables you to create unusual frames for your pictures and can be a fun way to vary the images in your presentation. To insert a picture as a fill:

1. Select Picture in the Shape Fill gallery, which is accessible from the FORMAT tab.
2. Browse to locate the picture that you want to add and double-click the picture to insert it.

Figure 3.10 shows the Plaque shape filled with a casual snapshot taken with a digital camera.

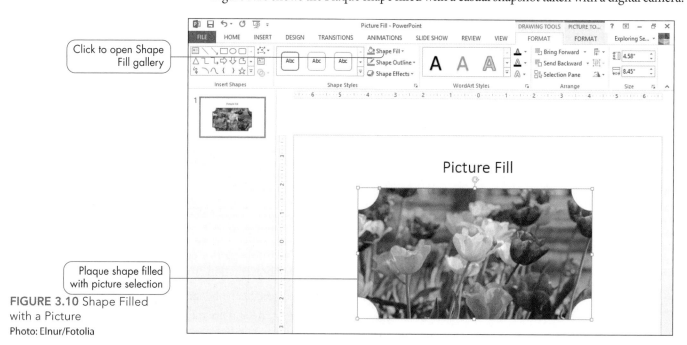

FIGURE 3.10 Shape Filled with a Picture
Photo: Elnur/Fotolia

As discussed earlier in the chapter, you can fill shapes with gradient fills, a blend of two or more colors. When you select Gradient from the Shape Fill gallery, another gallery of options opens, enabling you to select Light and Dark Variations that blend the current color with white or black in linear or radial gradients. Figure 3.11 shows the gradient options for a selected object.

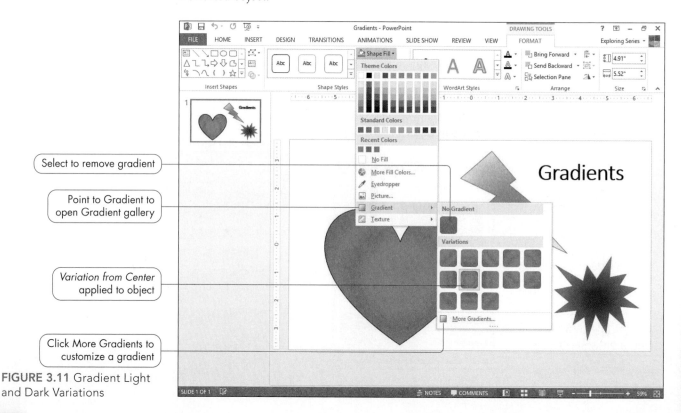

FIGURE 3.11 Gradient Light and Dark Variations

When you select More Gradients at the bottom of the Gradients gallery, the Format Shape pane displays. The Gradient fill option in the *Fill* section provides access to the Preset gradients gallery. This gallery gives you a variety of gradients using a multitude of colors to create truly beautiful impressions. Figure 3.12 shows the Preset gradients gallery.

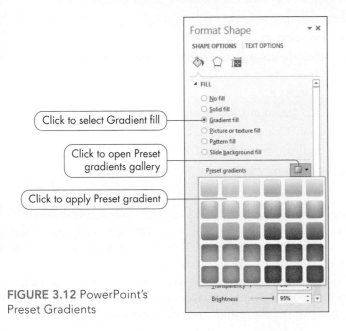

Click to select Gradient fill

Click to open Preset gradients gallery

Click to apply Preset gradient

FIGURE 3.12 PowerPoint's Preset Gradients

You can create a custom gradient in the Format Shape pane. You can select the colors to blend for the gradient, the direction and angle of the gradient, the brightness of the colors, and the amount of transparency to apply. Figure 3.13 shows a custom gradient created for a heart image.

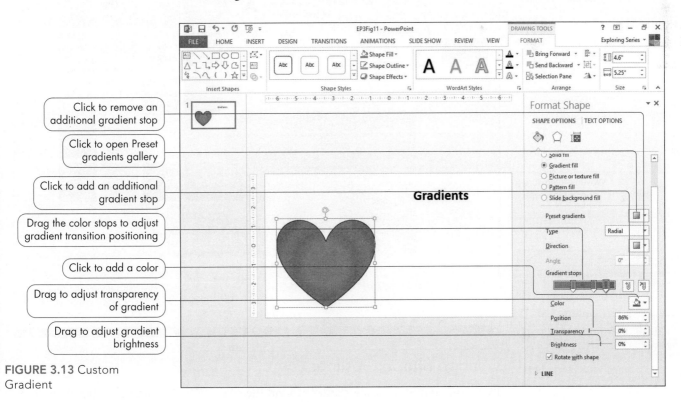

Click to remove an additional gradient stop

Click to open Preset gradients gallery

Click to add an additional gradient stop

Drag the color stops to adjust gradient transition positioning

Click to add a color

Drag to adjust transparency of gradient

Drag to adjust gradient brightness

FIGURE 3.13 Custom Gradient

To create a custom gradient:

1. Select the shape you want to contain the gradient.
2. Click the FORMAT tab.
3. Click the Format Shape dialog box launcher in the Shape Styles group.
4. Click Fill and click Gradient Fill.
5. Click the first Gradient stop to select it.
6. Click the Color arrow and select the color from Theme Colors, Standard Colors, More Colors, or the Eyedropper.
7. Click the last Gradient stop to select it.
8. Click the Color arrow and select the color from one of the color categories.
9. Click *Add gradient stop* to add an additional color if desired.
10. Drag the new gradient stop until you create the desired blend.
11. Click a gradient stop and click *Remove gradient stop* to remove a color.
12. Click Close.

Selecting *Picture or texture fill* in the Format Shape pane gives you access to common **texture fills**, such as canvas, denim, marble, or cork, which you can use to fill your object. Selecting the Texture button opens the Texture gallery, which has several options. Click the File button to navigate and insert a picture, which can be stretched to fit the shape or tiled so the picture is repeated to fill the shape. Tiled textures have seamless edges so that you cannot tell where one tile ends and another begins. To tile a picture or texture fill, select *Tile picture as texture*. Figure 3.14 shows the Texture gallery and a rectangle used as a background that contains the woven mat fill.

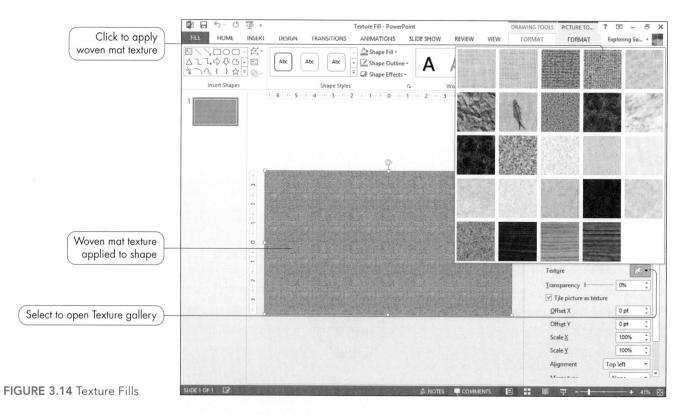

FIGURE 3.14 Texture Fills

Change Shape Outlines

By default, outlines form a border around the shape. You can modify a shape's outline by changing its color, style, or **line weight** (thickness). You can modify outlines using the Shape Styles feature accessible in the Shape Styles group or by clicking the Shape Styles dialog box launcher to open the Format Shape pane. You can customize outlines using the Shape Outline gallery options available in the Shape Styles group or the Line options in the Format Shape pane. First, select the line or object and open the Shape Outline gallery by clicking Shape Outline. The same color options used to change the color of fills are available to change the color of outlines. If you wish to remove an outline, select the No Outline option. In Figure 3.15, the outline surrounding the shape with the picture fill has been removed so that it does not detract from the image.

The width or thickness of a line is measured in *points* (pt), the smallest unit of measurement in typography. One vertical inch contains 72 pt.

To set the line width:

1. Click Shape Outline in the Shape Styles group on the DRAWING TOOLS FORMAT tab.
2. Point to Weight to display line weight choices from 1/4 pt to 6 pt.

To access additional line weight options, select More Lines to open the Format Shape pane with the Line options displayed. The Format Shape pane enables you to change the line weight using the spin arrows in the Width box or by typing the weight directly into the Width box. You can also use the Format Shape pane to create Compound type outlines, which combine thick and thin lines. Figure 3.15 displays lines and an outline for a shape in various weights.

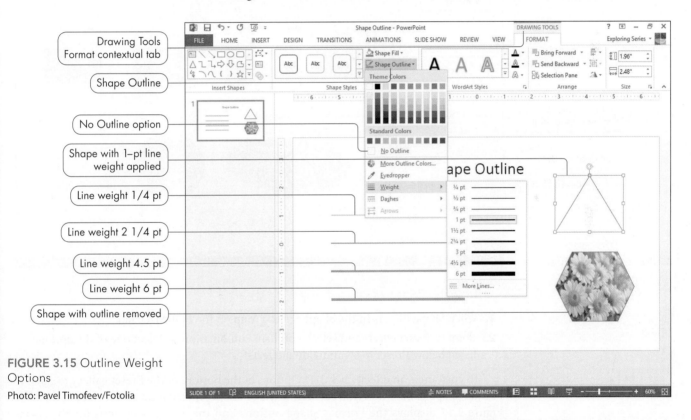

FIGURE 3.15 Outline Weight Options

Photo: Pavel Timofeev/Fotolia

For variety, you can change a solid line to a dashed line. Dashed lines make interesting boxes or borders for shapes and placeholders by using round dots, square dots, and combinations of short dashes, long dashes, and dots. To make a line or object outline dashed:

1. Select the object.
2. Click Shape Outline on the FORMAT tab.
3. Point to the Dashes option and click the desired line style.

You can add an arrowhead to the beginning or end of a line to create an arrow that points to critical information on the slide. The Shape Outline feature enables you to create many different styles of arrows using points, circles, and diamonds. To add an arrowhead:

1. Select a line.
2. Click Shape Outline on the FORMAT tab.

3. Point to the Arrows option.
4. Click the desired style.

Change Shape Effects

STEP 4 ≫ You do not need an expensive, high-powered graphics editor for special effects because PowerPoint enables you to apply many stunning effects to shapes: preset three-dimensional effects, shadow effects, reflections, glows, soft edge effects, bevels, and 3-D rotations. One of the greatest strengths of PowerPoint is its ability to immediately update any shape effects if you choose a new theme. Figure 3.16 shows an example of some of the shape effects available.

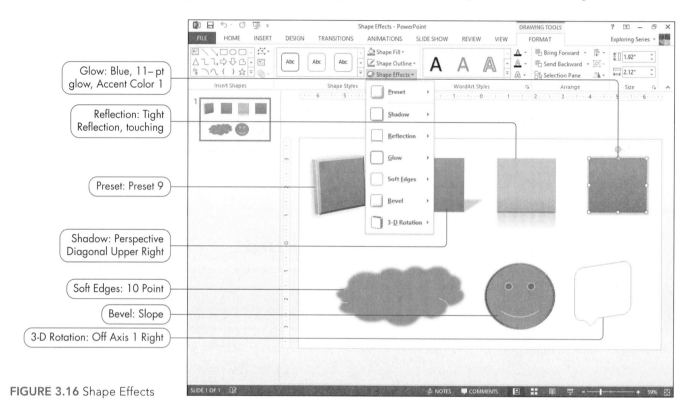

FIGURE 3.16 Shape Effects

To apply effects to a selected shape:

1. Click Shape Effects in the Shape Styles group on the FORMAT tab.
2. Point to *Preset effects* and select a built-in combination or select one of the options listed below Preset to set individual effects.

To customize an effect, click 3-D Options at the bottom of the Preset gallery to open the Format Shape pane, where you can define the bevel, depth, contour, and surface of the effect. Figure 3.17 displays the Format Shape options and the Material options for the surface of a shape.

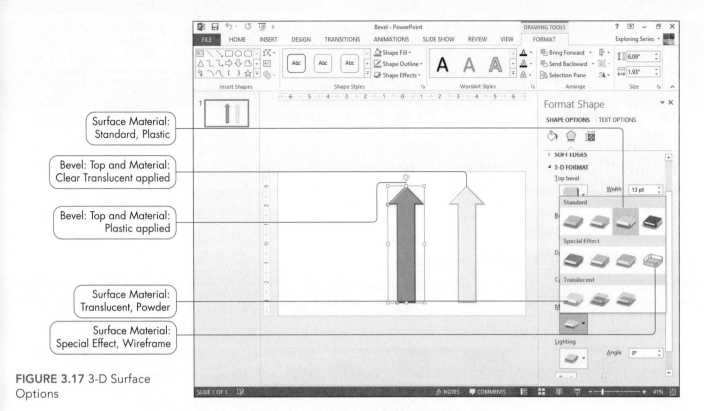

Surface Material: Standard, Plastic

Bevel: Top and Material: Clear Translucent applied

Bevel: Top and Material: Plastic applied

Surface Material: Translucent, Powder

Surface Material: Special Effect, Wireframe

FIGURE 3.17 3-D Surface Options

Quick Concepts

1. Describe the purpose and effectiveness of incorporating shapes into a presentation. *p. 184*

2. What is the value of using connector lines when creating a flow chart? *p. 187*

3. List three types of fills that can be applied to a shape. *p. 190*

Hands-On Exercises

Watch the Video for this Hands-On Exercise!

MyITLab®
HOE1 Training

1 Shapes

You begin your PowerPoint mini-camp by having the interns work with a project status report. They will create basic shapes using PowerPoint's drawing tools. You also ask the group to customize the shapes by adding styles and effects.

Skills covered: Create Basic Shapes • Draw and Format Connector Lines • Apply a Quick Style and Customize Shapes • Use Shape Effects

---

STEP 1 ≫ CREATE BASIC SHAPES

Knowing how to use a flow chart to diagram the processes or steps needed to complete a project or task is a valuable skill. To teach participants how to create multiple shapes using the Lock Drawing Mode, you have them create several ovals as part of a project flow chart. Refer to Figure 3.18 as you complete Step 1.

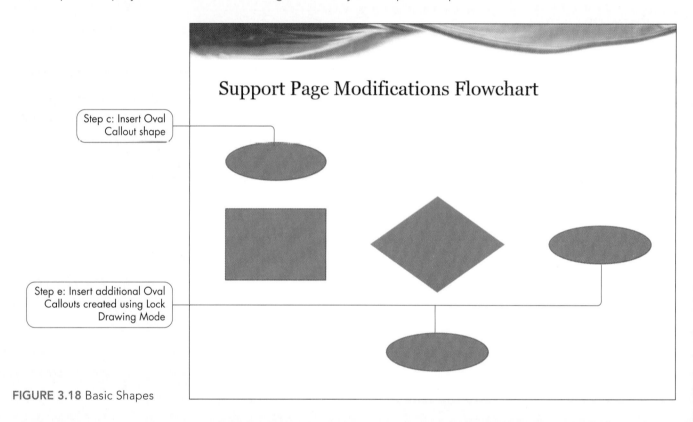

FIGURE 3.18 Basic Shapes

a. Start PowerPoint, open *p03h1Project*, and then save it as **p03h1Project_LastFirst**.

> **TROUBLESHOOTING:** If you make any major mistakes in this exercise, you can press Ctrl+Z to undo as many steps as needed, or close the file, open *p03h1Project*, and then start this exercise over.

b. On Slide 1, replace *First Name Last Name* with your name. Create a handout header with your name and a handout footer with your instructor's name and your class. Include the current date. Apply to all.

c. On Slide 6, click **Oval** in the Basic Shapes in the Drawing group on the HOME tab. Position your pointer on the top-left side of the slide above the square shape and below the title and drag to create the shape.

> **TROUBLESHOOTING:** If you do not see the Oval shape, click the More button for the Basic Shapes or click the Insert tab and click Shapes in the Illustrations group.

Do not worry about the exact placement or size of the shapes you create at this time. You will learn how to precisely place and size shapes in the steps to follow.

d. Click the **INSERT tab** and click **Shapes** in the Illustrations group. Right-click **Oval** in the Basic Shapes category and select **Lock Drawing Mode**.

You activate Lock Drawing Mode so that you can create multiple shapes of the same kind.

e. Position the pointer to the right of the diamond and drag to create the oval. Repeat this process below the diamond to mimic Figure 3.18. Press **Esc** to turn off Lock Drawing Mode.

You create two additional Oval callouts.

f. Save the presentation.

STEP 2 ≫ DRAW AND FORMAT CONNECTOR LINES

To continue building the flow chart, the mini-camp interns need to practice creating connecting lines between shapes. You also teach the group how to add a text box to a slide so they can add text, because the title only template is being used. Refer to Figure 3.19 as you complete Step 2.

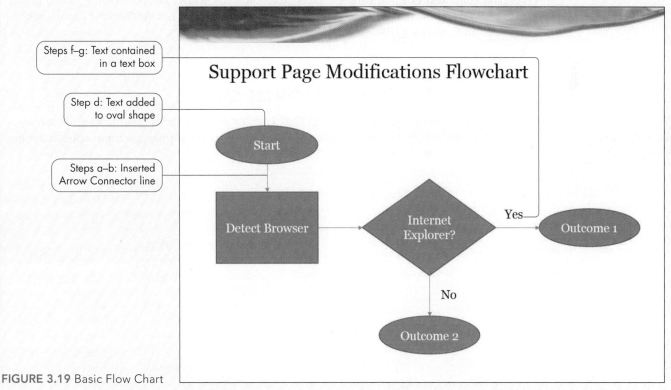

FIGURE 3.19 Basic Flow Chart

a. Click **Shapes** in the Illustrations group, click **Arrow** in the Lines category, move the cross-hair pointer over the oval on the left side of the slide, and then position the pointer on the bottom-center handle.

The shape's connector handles appear when a connector line is selected and the cross-hair pointer is moved onto the shape.

b. Drag a connecting line that attaches the bottom-center connecting handle of the oval to the top center connecting handle of the rectangle below it.

A connector arrow is placed between the oval and the rectangle. The default line weight is very thin at 1/2 pt.

c. Click **Shapes** in the Illustrations group on the FORMAT tab, right-click the **Arrow**, and then select **Lock Drawing Mode**. Create connecting arrows using the technique just practiced that will attach the rectangle to the diamond and the diamond to the two remaining ovals, as shown in Figure 3.19. Press **Esc**.

d. Right-click the oval on the top-left of the slide, select **Edit Text**, and then type **Start**.

The text you typed becomes part of the oval shape.

e. Select the square shape and type **Detect Browser**. Use either of the practiced methods to select each of the remaining shapes and type the text shown in Figure 3.19.

f. Click the **INSERT tab** and click **Text Box** in the Text group.

Clicking Text Box enables you to create text that is not contained in a shape or in a placeholder on the slide.

g. Position the pointer above the connector between the *Decision* diamond and the *Outcome 1* oval, click once, and then type **Yes**.

> **TROUBLESHOOTING:** If the text box is not positioned above the connector line between the *Decision* diamond and the *Outcome 1* oval, click the border (not the sizing handle) of the text box and drag it into position.

h. Click **Text Box** in the Insert Shapes group on the FORMAT tab, position the pointer to the right side of the connector between the *Decision* diamond and the *Outcome 2* oval, click once, and then type **No**. Reposition the text box if necessary.

i. Save the presentation.

STEP 3 ›› APPLY A QUICK STYLE AND CUSTOMIZE SHAPES

You encourage participants of the mini-camp to experiment with Quick Styles and to modify shape fills so that they are able to customize shapes. Then they set the shapes to styles of your choice to show they can meet specifications when asked. Refer to Figure 3.20 as you complete Step 3.

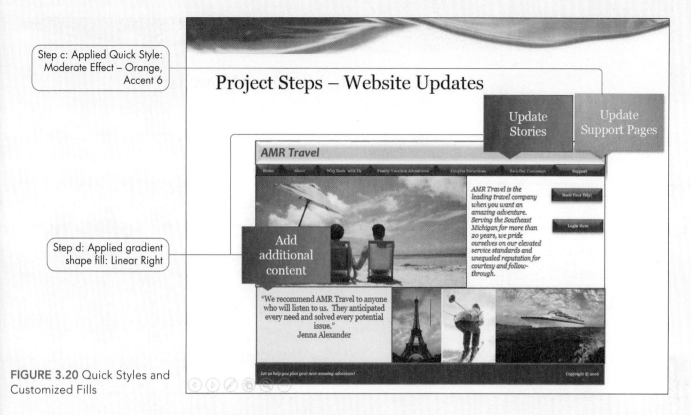

Step c: Applied Quick Style: Moderate Effect – Orange, Accent 6

Step d: Applied gradient shape fill: Linear Right

FIGURE 3.20 Quick Styles and Customized Fills

a. On Slide 5, select the far-right callout shape.

b. Click the **FORMAT tab** and click **More** in the Shape Styles group.

   The Quick Style gallery opens.

c. Move your pointer over the Quick Styles and note the changes in fill, outline, and effects to the shape as you do so. After you are through experimenting, click **Moderate Effect - Orange, Accent 6** (fifth row, seventh column). Click in an empty area to deselect the callout.

   Live Preview shows the effects on your object as you move the pointer over the Quick Style options.

d. Press and hold **Ctrl** and click the remaining two callout shapes to select them. Click the **FORMAT tab**, click **Shape Fill** in the Shape Styles group, and then click **Blue, Accent 1** (first row, fifth column). Click **Shape Fill** again, point to *Gradient*, and then click **Linear Right** under *Dark Variations*. Click **Text Fill** in the WordArt Styles group and click **White, Background 1** to change the text to a white color.

   You apply a gradient fill to more than one shape at a time.

e. Save the presentation.

STEP 4 ≫ USE SHAPE EFFECTS

PowerPoint provides many shape effects that you can use for emphasis. You ask the participants to apply effects to the flow chart shapes so they become familiar with the options available. Refer to Figure 3.21 as you complete Step 4.

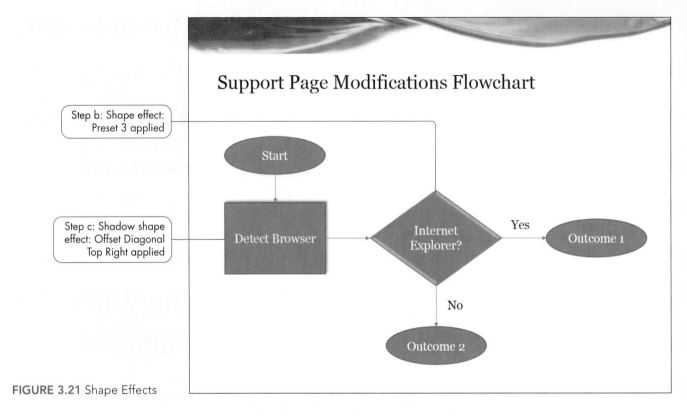

FIGURE 3.21 Shape Effects

a. Click **Slide 6** and click the diamond shape.

b. Click the **FORMAT tab**, click **Shape Effects** in the Shape Styles group, point to *Preset*, and then click **Preset 3**.

Preset 3 combines a bevel type, a depth, contours, and a surface effect.

c. Select the rectangle shape, click **Shape Effects** in the Shape Styles group, point to *Shadow*, and then click **Offset Diagonal Top Right** (Outer category).

The Offset Diagonal option applies a 4-pt soft shadow to the top right of the rectangle.

d. Spell check the presentation. Save the presentation and submit the file based on your instructor's directions. Close the file and exit PowerPoint.

SmartArt and WordArt

Diagrams are infographics used to illustrate concepts and processes. PowerPoint includes a feature to create eye-catching diagrams: SmartArt. Attention is drawn to an infographic using text created by another eye-catching PowerPoint feature: WordArt. In this section, you will create and modify SmartArt diagrams and WordArt text.

Creating SmartArt

STEP 1

The ***SmartArt*** feature enables you to create a diagram and to enter the text of your message in one of many existing layouts. SmartArt helps to create a visual representation of your information. The resulting illustration is professional looking and complements the theme you selected. You can also convert existing text to SmartArt. Figure 3.22 compares a text-based slide in the common bullet format to a second slide showing the same information converted to a SmartArt diagram. The arrows and colors in the SmartArt diagram make it easy for the viewer to understand the message and remember the concept of a cycle. It is especially effective when you add animation to each step.

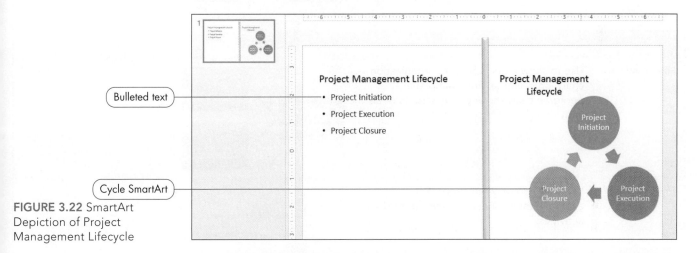

FIGURE 3.22 SmartArt Depiction of Project Management Lifecycle

A SmartArt diagram creates a layout for your information, provides a pane for quickly entering information, automatically sizes shapes and text, and gives you the ability to switch between layouts, making it easy to choose the most effective layout. Some layouts can be used for any type of information and are designed to be visually attractive, while other layouts are created specifically for a certain type of information, such as a process or hierarchy. SmartArt types include options for presenting lists of information in ordered (steps to complete a task) or unordered (features of a product) formats.

To create a SmartArt diagram, choose a diagram type that fits your message. The SmartArt gallery has nine different categories of diagrams: List, Process, Cycle, Hierarchy, Relationship, Matrix, Pyramid, Picture, and Office.com. At the top of the list of categories is All, which you can click to display the choices from all categories. Each category includes a description of the type of information appropriate for the layouts in that category. The following reference table shows the SmartArt categories and their purposes.

Type	Purpose	Sample SmartArt
List	Use to show nonsequential information. For example: a list of items to be checked on a roof each year.	Flashing / Shingles / Soffits
Process	Use to show steps in a process or a timeline. For example: the steps involved in washing a car.	Hose > Sponge > Rinse
Cycle	Use to show a continual process. For example: the recurring business cycle.	Expansion / Recovery / Downturn / Recession
Hierarchy	Use to show a decision tree, organization chart, or pedigree. For example: a pedigree chart showing the parents of an individual.	Reed J. Olsen — Ivan Olsen / Gladys Jones
Relationship	Use to illustrate connections. For example: the connections among outdoor activities.	Camping / Hiking / Fishing
Matrix	Use to show how parts relate to a whole. For example: the Keirsey Temperament Theory of four groups describing human behavior.	Rationals / Idealists / Keirsey Temperaments / Artisans / Guardians
Pyramid	Use to show proportional relationships with the largest component on the top or bottom. For example: an ecology chart.	Indirect Consumers / Direct Consumers / Producers

Type	Purpose	Sample SmartArt
Picture	Use to show nonsequential or grouped blocks of information. Maximizes both horizontal and vertical display space for shapes.	
Office.com	Miscellaneous shapes for showing blocks of information.	

Figure 3.23 shows the Choose a SmartArt Graphic dialog box. The pane on the left side shows the types of SmartArt diagrams available. Each type of diagram includes subtypes that are displayed in the center pane. Clicking one of the subtypes enlarges the selected graphic and displays it in the preview pane on the right side. The preview pane describes purposes for which the SmartArt subtype can be used effectively. Some of the descriptions include tips for the type of text to enter.

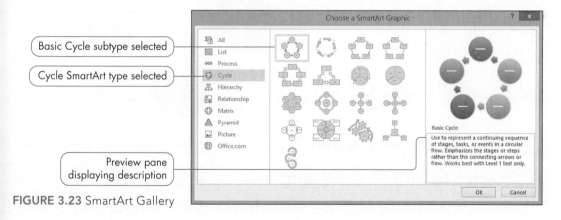

Basic Cycle subtype selected

Cycle SmartArt type selected

Preview pane displaying description

FIGURE 3.23 SmartArt Gallery

To create a SmartArt diagram:

1. Click the INSERT tab.
2. Click SmartArt in the Illustrations group.
3. Click the type of SmartArt diagram you want in the left pane.
4. Click the SmartArt subtype you want in the center pane.
5. Preview the selected SmartArt and subtype in the right pane.
6. Click OK.

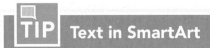

TIP | Text in SmartArt

Some SmartArt layouts allow only one level of text, while others are set up for one or two levels of text. So, if there are main and subpoints that need to be displayed, a SmartArt graphic that allows two levels of text is necessary. Also, be sure to keep the text short and limit it to key points to create a visually appealing diagram.

Once you select the SmartArt diagram type and the subtype, a **Text pane** opens in which you can enter text. If the Text pane does not open, click Text Pane in the Create Graphic group on the SmartArt Tools Design tab. The Text pane works like an outline—enter a line of text, press Enter, and then press Tab or Shift+Tab to increase or decrease the indent level. The font size will decrease to fit text inside the shape, or the shape may grow to fit the text, depending on the size and number of shapes in your SmartArt diagram. The layout accommodates additional shapes as you enter text unless the type of shape is designed for a specific number of shapes, such as the Relationship Counterbalance Arrows layout, which is designed to show two opposing ideas. If you choose a diagram with more shapes than you need, you may need to delete the extra shapes; then PowerPoint will automatically rearrange the shapes to eliminate any blank space. Figure 3.24 shows text entered into the Text pane for a Basic Cycle SmartArt diagram. Because four lines of text were entered, four shapes were created.

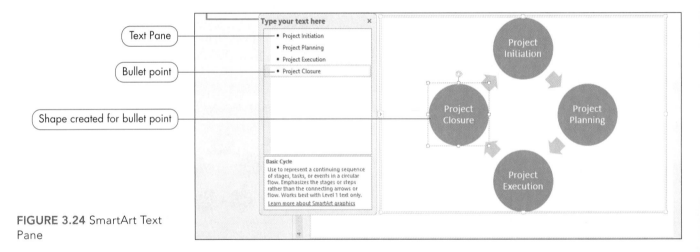

FIGURE 3.24 SmartArt Text Pane

Modifying SmartArt

You can modify SmartArt diagrams with the same tools used for other shapes and text boxes. You can reposition or resize a SmartArt diagram by dragging its borders. You also can modify SmartArt text in the Text pane just as if it is in a placeholder, or you can modify the text in the shape itself. If you need an additional shape, click to position your insertion point in the Text pane at the beginning or end of the text where you want to add a shape, press Enter, and then type the text.

An alternative method for adding shapes is to use the Add Shape command. To use the Add Shape command, do the following:

1. Click an existing shape in the SmartArt diagram.
2. Click the SMARTART TOOLS DESIGN tab.
3. Click the Add Shape arrow in the Create Graphic group.
4. Select Add Shape After, Add Shape Before, Add Shape Above, Add Shape Below, or Add Assistant when available.

SmartArt diagrams have two galleries used to enhance the appearance of the diagram, both of which are located under the SmartArt Tools Design tab in the SmartArt Styles group. One gallery changes colors, and the other gallery applies a combination of special effects.

Change SmartArt Theme Colors

STEP 2 » To change the color scheme of your SmartArt diagram, click Change Colors to display the Colors gallery (see Figure 3.25). The gallery contains Primary Theme Colors, Colorful, and Accent color schemes. Click a color variation to apply it to the SmartArt diagram.

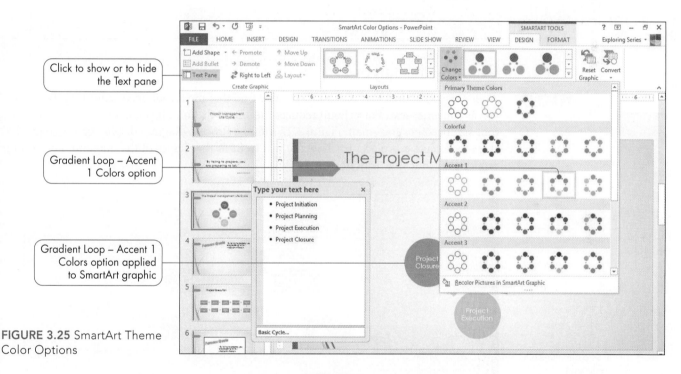

FIGURE 3.25 SmartArt Theme Color Options

Use Quick Styles with SmartArt

After creating the diagram, you can use Quick Styles to adjust the style to match other styles you have used in your presentation or to make the diagram easier to understand. To apply a Quick Style to a SmartArt diagram, click the diagram and click the Quick Style from the SmartArt Styles gallery. To see the complete gallery, click the More button in the SmartArt Styles group on the SmartArt Tools Design tab. The gallery opens and displays simple combinations of special effects, such as shadows, gradients, and 3-D effects, that combine perspectives and surface styles. Figure 3.26 displays the SmartArt Quick Styles gallery.

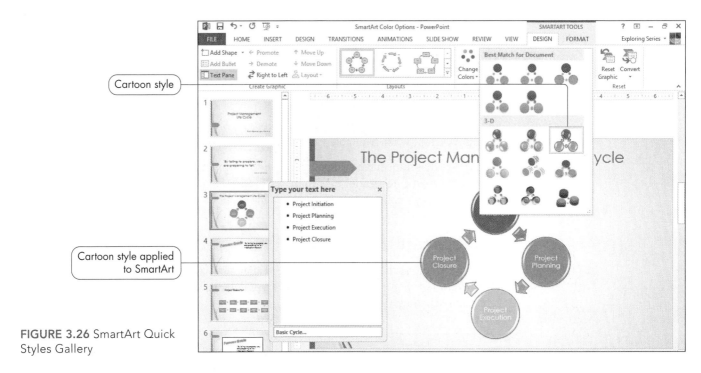

FIGURE 3.26 SmartArt Quick Styles Gallery

Labels on figure: Cartoon style; Cartoon style applied to SmartArt

Change the Layout

STEP 3 ⟫ After creating a SmartArt diagram, you may find that the layout needs adjusting. For example, as you enter text, PowerPoint reduces the size of the font. If you enter too much text, the font size becomes too small. Figure 3.27 shows a Process diagram displaying the sequential steps to execute a project. To allow the text to fit in the shapes of the diagram, PowerPoint reduced the font size to 13 pt.

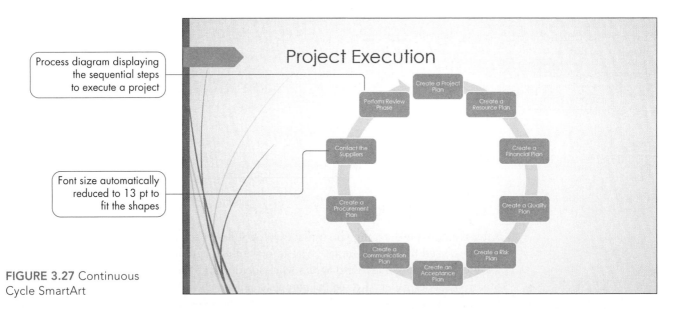

FIGURE 3.27 Continuous Cycle SmartArt

Labels on figure: Process diagram displaying the sequential steps to execute a project; Font size automatically reduced to 13 pt to fit the shapes

By adjusting the layout, you can make the Project Execution diagram easier to read. First, select the SmartArt diagram and the SmartArt Tools Design tab. Click the More button in the Layouts group to display the Layouts gallery. Layouts display the various subtypes for the SmartArt layout type currently applied. In addition, Live Preview will reflect the current color and styles applied for any layout subtype changes. Figure 3.28 shows the same process from Figure 3.27 only modified to utilize the Basic Bending Process layout.

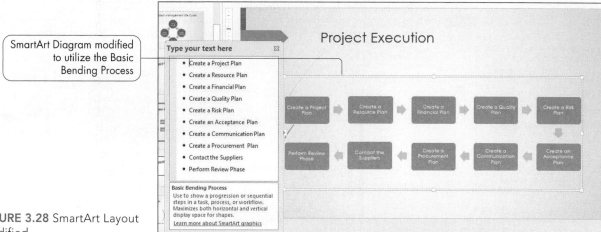

SmartArt Diagram modified to utilize the Basic Bending Process

FIGURE 3.28 SmartArt Layout Modified

Change SmartArt Type

You can change the SmartArt diagram type if you decide a different diagram would be better. The process is similar to changing the SmartArt layout subtypes. Changing the diagram type may affect the audience's perception of your diagram. For example, if you have created a list of unordered items, switching to a cycle diagram implies that a specific order to the items exists. Also, if you have customized the shapes, keep in mind that changes to colors, line styles, and fills will transfer from the old diagram to a new one. However, some effects, such as rotation, do not transfer.

To change the SmartArt diagram type:

1. Click to select the SmartArt diagram.
2. Click the More button in the Layouts group on the DESIGN tab and click More Layouts.
3. The *Choose a SmartArt Graphic* gallery opens, displaying all the layouts grouped by category. Click the type and layout you desire.

Convert Text to a SmartArt Diagram

You can also convert existing text to a SmartArt diagram by selecting the placeholder containing the text and clicking *Convert to SmartArt Graphic* in the Paragraph group on the Home tab. When the gallery opens, click the desired layout for the SmartArt diagram (see Figure 3.29).

TIP Converting Text to SmartArt

To quickly convert text to a SmartArt graphic, select the text, right-click, and then select *Convert to SmartArt*. The *Convert to SmartArt* gallery opens so you can select a SmartArt style.

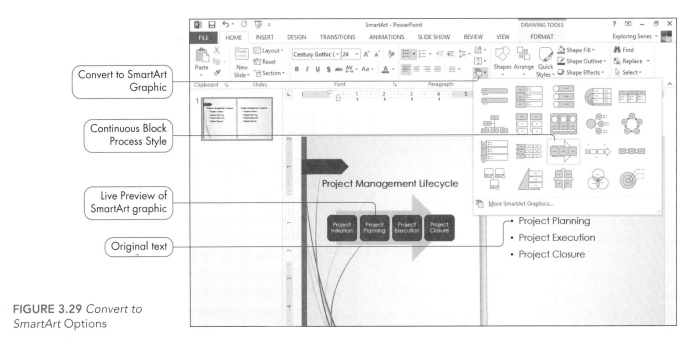

Convert to SmartArt Graphic

Continuous Block Process Style

Live Preview of SmartArt graphic

Original text

FIGURE 3.29 *Convert to SmartArt Options*

Creating WordArt

STEP 4》》   ***WordArt*** is text that uses special effects based on styles in the WordArt gallery to call attention to the text. In WordArt, special effects apply to the text itself, not to the shape surrounding the text. For example, in a WordArt graphic the text would have a 3-D reflection rather than the box surrounding the text. By applying special effects, such as curves or waves, directly to the text, you can create text that emphasizes the information for your audience.

The WordArt gallery has a variety of text styles to choose from, as well as the option to change individual settings or elements to modify the style. You can convert existing text to WordArt text, or you can create a WordArt object and then enter text.

To create WordArt:

1.   Click the INSERT tab.
2.   Click WordArt in the Text group.
3.   Click the WordArt style of your choice.
4.   Enter your text in the WordArt placeholder.

To convert existing text to a WordArt graphic:

1.   Select the text to convert to WordArt text.
2.   Click the More button in the WordArt Styles group on the FORMAT tab.
3.   Click the WordArt style of your choice.

Modifying WordArt

You can change the style of a WordArt object by clicking a Quick Style located in the WordArt Styles group on the Format tab. Alternatively, you can modify the individual elements of the WordArt by clicking Text Fill, Text Outline, or Text Effects in the WordArt Styles group. WordArt Text Effects includes a unique Transform option. Transform can rotate the WordArt text around a path or add a warp to stretch, angle, or bloat letters. Figure 3.30 shows the WordArt gallery options, and Figure 3.31 shows the warp options available in the WordArt Transform category.

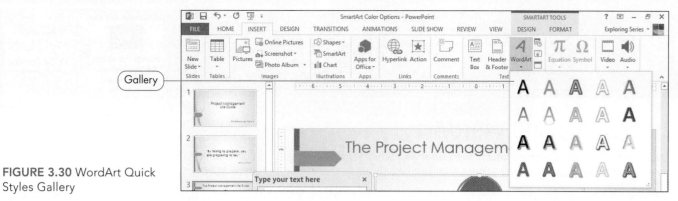

FIGURE 3.30 WordArt Quick Styles Gallery

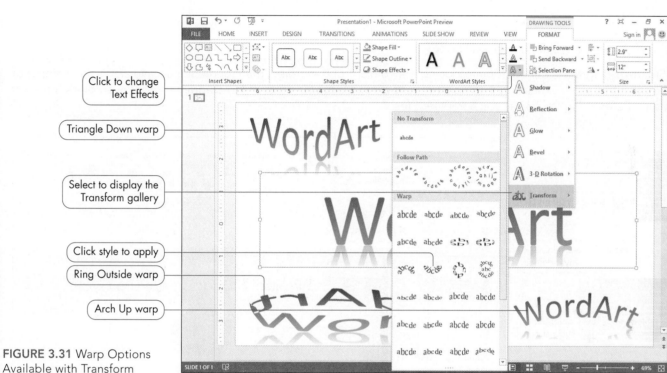

Click to change Text Effects

Triangle Down warp

Select to display the Transform gallery

Click style to apply

Ring Outside warp

Arch Up warp

FIGURE 3.31 Warp Options Available with Transform

Quick Concepts ✓

1. Which SmartArt diagram type would be most effective to show a timeline? *p. 204*

2. How does entering text in a SmartArt Text Pane work like an outline? *p. 206*

3. How would you convert existing text to a SmartArt diagram? *p. 209*

4. List three text effects that can be modified when using WordArt. *p. 210*

Hands-On Exercises

Watch the Video for this Hands-On Exercise!

MyITLab®
HOE2 Training

2 SmartArt and WordArt

To teach your mini-camp participants how to work with SmartArt and WordArt, you choose to have the group work with a presentation about a process—the water cycle. To make the slide show interesting, you have included fun, interesting water facts.

Skills covered: Create SmartArt • Modify a SmartArt Diagram • Change SmartArt Type and Modify the SmartArt Layout • Create and Modify WordArt

STEP 1 ≫ CREATE SMARTART

A SmartArt diagram is perfect for introducing the concept of the project management life cycle and is an example of a simple infographic explaining a complex concept. You teach your students to diagram using PowerPoint's SmartArt feature. Refer to Figure 3.32 as you complete Step 1.

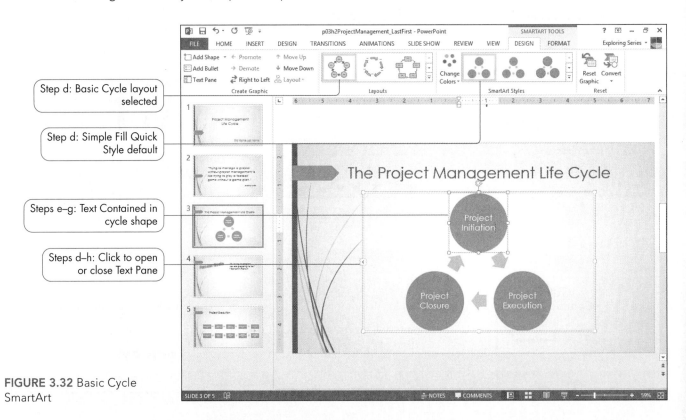

FIGURE 3.32 Basic Cycle SmartArt

a. Open the *p03h2ProjectManagement* presentation and save it as **p03h2ProjectManagement_ LastFirst**.

b. On Slide 1, replace *First Name Last Name* with your name. Create a handout header with your name and a handout footer with your instructor's name and your class. Include the current date.

c. Click **Slide 3**. Click the **INSERT tab** and click **SmartArt** in the Illustrations group.

   The *Choose a SmartArt Graphic* dialog box opens.

d. Click **Cycle**, click the subtype **Basic Cycle**, and then click **OK**.

   The Text pane opens with the insertion point in the first bullet location so that you can enter the text for the first cycle shape.

> **TROUBLESHOOTING:** If the Text pane is not displayed, click Text Pane in the Create Graphic group or click the arrow on the center-left side of the SmartArt boundary.

    e. Type **Project Initiation**.

       As you type, the font size for the text gets smaller so the text fits in the shape.

    f. Press ⬇ to move to the second bullet and type **Project Execution**. Repeat this technique to add a third bullet and type **Project Closure**.

    g. Press ⬇ to move to the blank bullet point and press **Backspace**. Repeat to remove the second blank bullet point.

       The extra shapes in the Basic Cycle SmartArt are removed.

    h. Click the **Close (X) button** on the top right of the Text pane to close it.

    i. Drag the SmartArt object down so that it does not overlap with the title.

    j. Resize the SmartArt object by selecting the outside object border, dragging the corners of the object, and then repositioning it until the object fits comfortably under the title. See Figure 3.32.

    k. Save the presentation.

STEP 2 ≫ MODIFY A SMARTART DIAGRAM

You need to modify the structure of the SmartArt diagram because a step in the cycle was omitted. The diagram could be enhanced with a color style change. You teach your participants these skills. Refer to Figure 3.33 as you complete Step 2.

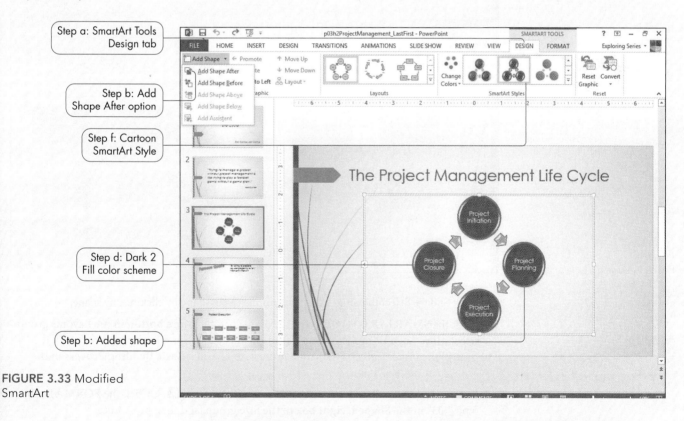

FIGURE 3.33 Modified SmartArt

    a. Click the **Project Initiation shape** and click the **SMARTART TOOLS DESIGN tab**, if necessary.

    b. Click the **Add Shape arrow** in the Create Graphic group and select **Add Shape After**.

       You have added a new shape after *Project Initiation* and before *Project Execution*.

> **TROUBLESHOOTING:** If you had clicked Add Shape, you would have automatically added a shape after the selected shape. Using the Add Shape arrow gives you a choice of adding before or after.

c. Type **Project Planning** in the new shape.

d. Click the SmartArt border to select all the shapes in the SmartArt diagram, click **Change Colors** in the SmartArt Styles group, and then click **Dark 2 Fill** in the Primary Theme Colors category.

e. Click the **More button** in the SmartArt Styles group and move the pointer over the styles.

Live Preview shows the impact each style has on the shapes and text in the SmartArt diagram.

f. Click **Cartoon** in the 3-D category (first row, third column).

This choice makes the text readable and enhances the appearance of the SmartArt diagram.

g. Save the presentation.

STEP 3 ≫ CHANGE SMARTART TYPE AND MODIFY THE SMARTART LAYOUT

Many different layouts are available for SmartArt diagrams, and you teach the mini-camp group that for an infographic to be effective, it must be understood quickly. You ask the group to note the reduced font size on the process SmartArt showing the Project Execution. You teach them to change the layout of the SmartArt to make it more effective. Refer to Figure 3.34 as you complete Step 3.

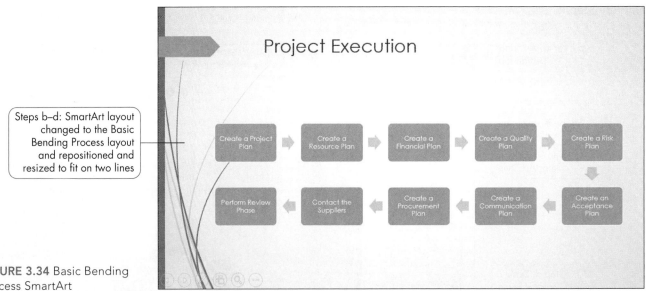

Steps b–d: SmartArt layout changed to the Basic Bending Process layout and repositioned and resized to fit on two lines

FIGURE 3.34 Basic Bending Process SmartArt

a. Click **Slide 5**. Select the **SmartArt Continuous Cycle shape** by clicking any shape.

b. Click the **SMARTART TOOLS DESIGN tab**, click the **More button** in the Layouts group, select **More Layouts** at the bottom of the Layouts gallery, and then click **Process** in the left pane of the *Choose a SmartArt Graphic* dialog box. Click **Basic Bending Process** in the center pane and click **OK**.

c. Click the **SmartArt border** to select all the shapes, if necessary. Click the **FORMAT tab**, type **4.03"** in the **Shape Height box** in the Size group, and then press **Enter**.

d. Open the Size Dialog Box Launcher. Click **POSITION** and **type 1.6"** in the **Horizontal Position box** and **2.44"** in the **Vertical Position box**.

Deselect the SmartArt diagram by clicking outside of the SmartArt.

e. Save the presentation.

STEP 4 ›› CREATE AND MODIFY WORDART

You teach the participants how to use WordArt to call attention to text and how to modify the Text effects applied to the WordArt. You also have them insert text in a text box so they can compare the options available with each method for adding text to a slide. Refer to Figure 3.35 as you complete Step 4.

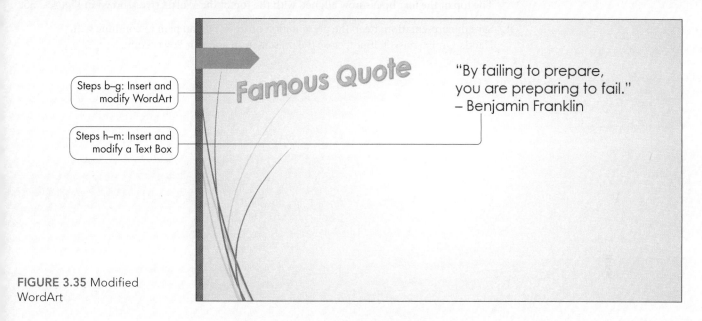

FIGURE 3.35 Modified WordArt

a. Click **Slide 4**. Click the **INSERT tab** and click **WordArt** in the Text group.

b. Click **Pattern Fill - Orange, Accent 1, 50%, Hard Shadow - Accent 1** (fourth row, third column).

   A WordArt placeholder is centered on the slide.

c. Type **Famous Quote** in the **WordArt placeholder**.

d. Click the **FORMAT tab**, if necessary, click **Text Effects** in the WordArt Styles group, and then point to *3-D Rotation*.

   The 3-D Rotation gallery opens, showing No Rotation, Parallel, Perspective, and Oblique categories.

e. Click **Off Axis 1 Right** (under Parallel category, second row, second column).

f. Type **1.5"** in the **Shape Height box** in the Size group and press **Enter**.

   The height of the WordArt shape adjusts to 1.5".

g. Open the Size Dialog Box Launcher and click **POSITION** to expand. Type **0.69"** in the **Horizontal Position box** and **1.08"** in the **Vertical Position box**. Drag the WordArt shape to the top-left corner of the slide as shown in Figure 3.35. Close the Size Dialog Box Launcher and deselect the shape.

h. Click the **INSERT tab** and click **Text Box** in the Text group.

i. Click to the bottom right of the WordArt shape and type **"By failing to prepare, you are preparing to fail." – Benjamin Franklin**.

   The text box expands to fit the text, with the result that the text is contained in one long line that flows off the slide.

j. Click the **FORMAT tab**, type **5.1"** in the **Shape Width box** in the Size group, and then press **Enter**.

k. Click the **Size Dialog Box Launcher**, click to expand the TEXT BOX options, and then click the **Wrap text in shape check box**.

l. Click the border of the text box to select all the text. Click the **HOME tab** and change the font size of the text to **28 pt**.

m. Click the **Size Dialog Box Launcher**. Click **POSITION**. Type **6.98"** in the **Horizonal Position box** and type **1.08"** in the **Vertical Position box**.

The top of the text box is now aligned with the top of the WordArt, as shown in Figure 3.35.

n. Save the presentation. Keep the presentation onscreen if you plan to continue with Hands-On Exercise 3. If not, close the presentation and exit PowerPoint.

Object Manipulation

As you add objects to your slides, you may need to manipulate them by arranging them differently on the slide or recoloring them. Perhaps you have several shapes created, and you want them to align at their left edges, or you want to arrange them by their center points and then determine the order of the shapes. You may have inserted a drawn image, and the colors used in the image do not match the color of the SmartArt on a slide. You may have added a drawn image that includes something you do not want.

In this section, you will learn to modify objects. You will isolate objects, flip and rotate objects, group and ungroup objects, and recolor the image. You will also learn to determine the order of objects and align objects to one another and to the slide.

Modifying Objects

Many clip art images are made from a series of combined shapes. You can modify existing drawings by breaking them into individual shapes and removing pieces you do not need, changing or recoloring shapes, rotating shapes, and combining shapes from several objects to create a new object. Figure 3.36 shows a picnic illustration available from Microsoft Office Online. The illustration was broken apart; the fireworks, flag, fries, and tablecloth removed; the hamburger, hotdogs, and milkshake flipped and resized; and the hamburger and chocolate milkshake recolored.

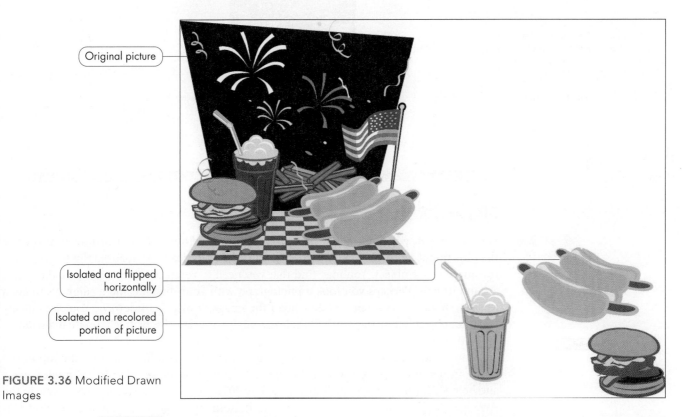

Original picture

Isolated and flipped
horizontally

Isolated and recolored
portion of picture

FIGURE 3.36 Modified Drawn
Images

STEP 1 Resizing objects is the most common modification procedure. You have learned to resize an object by dragging a sizing handle; however, you may need a more precise resizing method. For example, you use PowerPoint to create an advertisement for an automobile trader magazine, and the magazine specifies that the ad must fit in a 2" by 2" space. You can specify the exact height and width measurement of an object or adjust to a specific proportion of its original size.

The controls to resize an object to an exact measurement are found in the Size group on the Format tab or the Format pane. The Size group contains controls to change the height and width of an object quickly. The Format pane also contains boxes for entering exact measurements for shape height and width, but additionally allows you to use a precise rotation angle and to scale an object based on its original size (note that not all Online Pictures entered are added at full size).

To keep the original height and width proportions of an image, make sure the *Lock aspect ratio* check box is selected. **Aspect ratio** is the ratio of an object's width to its height. The image in Figure 3.37 was proportionally sized to more than twice its original size.

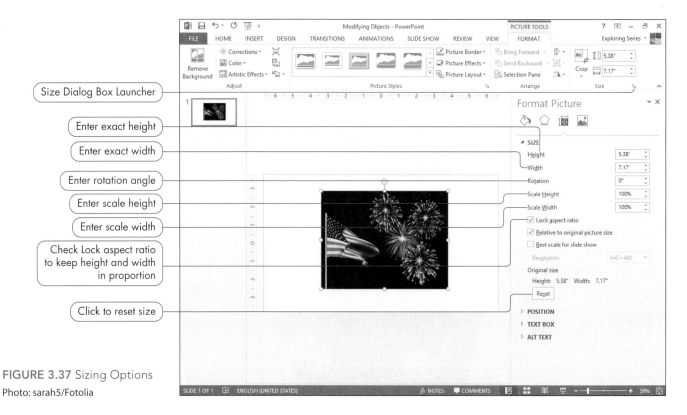

FIGURE 3.37 Sizing Options
Photo: sarah5/Fotolia

Flip and Rotate

STEP 2

Sometimes you will find that an object is facing the wrong way and you need to reverse the direction it faces, or **flip** it. You can flip an object vertically or horizontally to get a mirror image of the object. You may find that you need to **rotate** an object, or move the object around its axis. Perhaps you took a photograph with your digital camera sideways to get a full-length view, but when you download the image, it displays sideways. You can quickly rotate an object left or right 90°, flip it horizontally or vertically, or freely rotate it any number of degrees.

You rotate a selected object by dragging the rotation handle located at the top of the object in the direction you want it to rotate. To constrain the rotation to 15° angles, press and hold Shift while dragging. To rotate exactly 90° to the left or the right, click Rotate in the Arrange group on the Format tab. If you need a mirror image, click Rotate and select Flip Vertical or Flip Horizontal. You can also drag one of the side sizing handles over the opposite side and flip it. However, this method will cause distortion if you do not drag far enough to keep the height and width measurements proportional. Figure 3.38 shows rotate options and an image that has been flipped.

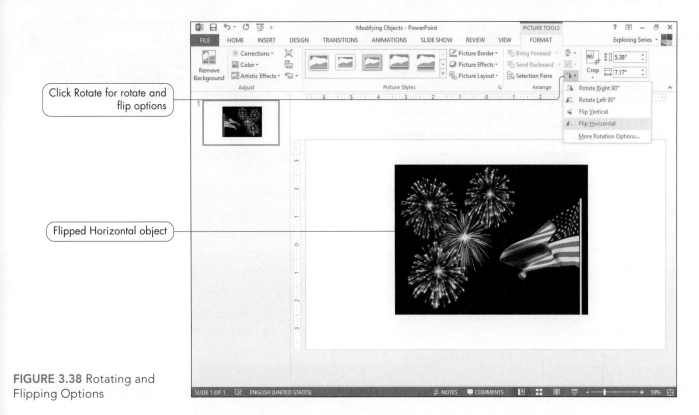

Click Rotate for rotate and flip options

Flipped Horizontal object

FIGURE 3.38 Rotating and Flipping Options

Merge Shapes

The Merge Shapes feature allows you to take shapes that you have inserted and merge them together. There are five different merging options: Union, Combine, Fragment, Intersect, and Subtract. Figure 3.39 shows the five different merging option results of a heart and a lightning bolt created using Shapes in the Insert Shapes group on the Format tab. To merge shapes:

1. Arrange the shapes so they are overlapping as desired.
2. Select the overlapping shapes by dragging a selection net around all of the shapes.
3. Click the FORMAT tab.
4. Click Merge Shapes in the Insert Shapes group.
5. Click the merge option of your choice.

TIP Using Subtract Shapes

When applying the Subtract Shapes merging option, you will have a different result depending on the shape you select first. In Figure 3.39, the heart was selected first, and the lightning bolt second.

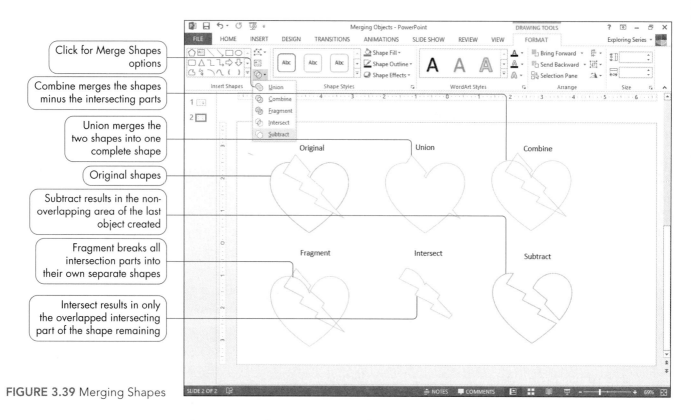

Click for Merge Shapes options

Combine merges the shapes minus the intersecting parts

Union merges the two shapes into one complete shape

Original shapes

Subtract results in the non-overlapping area of the last object created

Fragment breaks all intersection parts into their own separate shapes

Intersect results in only the overlapped intersecting part of the shape remaining

FIGURE 3.39 Merging Shapes

Group and Ungroup Objects

STEP 3 » A drawn object is usually created in pieces, layered, and then grouped to create the final image. These images can be *ungrouped*, or broken apart, so you can modify or delete the individual pieces. *Grouping* enables multiple objects to act or move as though they were a single object, whereas ungrouping separates an object into individual shapes. Grouping is different from merging a shape. Grouping simply makes it easier to move the newly grouped object or apply formatting, whereas merging may create a new object altogether.

Clip art images are typically created and saved as *vector graphics*, which are math-based. Drawing programs such as Adobe Illustrator and CorelDRAW are used to create vector graphic images. The advantage of vector files is that they retain perfect clarity when edited or resized due to the fact that the computer simply recalculates the math. Vector files also use a smaller amount of storage space compared to their pixel-based counterparts such as photographs. Many company logos or the drawn clip art images available from the Online Pictures on Microsoft.com are vector graphics, which leads to another advantage of vector images: If a vector clip art image is inserted, it is automatically a grouped image, and thus, the option to ungroup is available. This ability to ungroup (or group) the image enables you to separate the parts of the image and edit or adjust the image to tailor it to your needs.

TIP An Image That Will Not Ungroup

If your selected imported image will not ungroup for editing, it is not in a vector format. Online Pictures from Microsoft.com also contains clip art in bitmap, .jpg, .gif, and .png formats, which are not vector-based images and cannot be ungrouped.

Some non-vector graphics can be converted into drawing objects. Right-click the image on the slide and select Edit Picture if the option is available. If the option is not available, the graphic cannot be converted into a drawing object. After you select Edit Picture, a message opens asking if you want to convert the picture into a drawing object. Click Yes. This action converts the object into a vector graphic.

Once converted into a drawing object, right-click the image again, point to Group, and then select Ungroup. The object ungroups and the individual pieces are selected. Some images may have more than one grouping. The artist may create an image from individual shapes, group it, layer it on other images, and then group it again. If this occurs, the ungroup option will be available to repeat again. Figure 3.40 is an example of a complex file that has been ungrouped with some of the pieces selected.

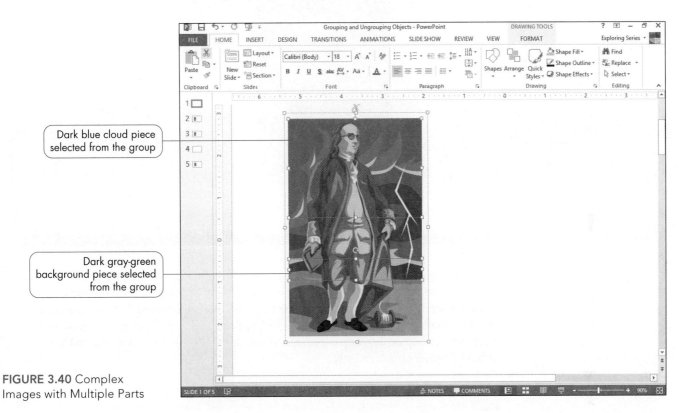

FIGURE 3.40 Complex Images with Multiple Parts

If necessary, to continue ungrouping, select the image, right-click, click Group, and then click Ungroup as many times as necessary to break the image down to all shapes. You can also select the image and click the Format tab. Click Group in the Arrange group, and if the image can be broken down further, the Ungroup option will be active with Group and Regroup grayed out. Select Ungroup, and each individual shape is surrounded by adjustment handles. Click outside of the image borders to deselect the shapes and click the individual shape you wish to change. Figure 3.41 shows a graphic that has been ungrouped. All of the individual parts are selected.

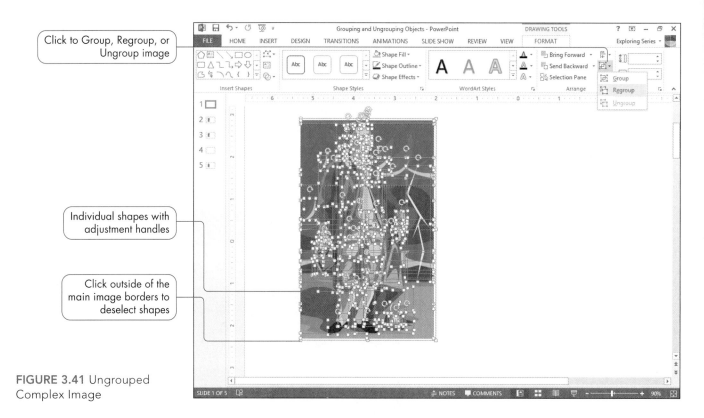

FIGURE 3.41 Ungrouped Complex Image

Labels for Figure 3.41:
- Click to Group, Regroup, or Ungroup image
- Individual shapes with adjustment handles
- Click outside of the main image borders to deselect shapes

When working with the individual shapes of an image, it is helpful to zoom in on the image. Zooming helps you make sure you have the correct shape before you make modifications. Figure 3.42 shows a selected shape that has had its fill changed to a theme color. Once you have made all of your needed changes, drag a selection net around all the shapes of the image and Group or Regroup the image. If you do not group the image, you risk moving the individual pieces inadvertently.

FIGURE 3.42 Modifying Ungrouped Shapes

Labels for Figure 3.42:
- Selected shape with Theme Color applied
- Theme Colors fill options
- Drag Zoom slider to enlarge image view

Recolor Objects

STEP 4 ≫ You can quickly change the colors in an image using the Recolor Picture option regardless of image file type, which enables you to match your image to the color scheme of your presentation without the ability or need for ungrouping the image and changing the color of each shape. You can select either a dark or a light variation of your color scheme.

You also can change the color mode of your picture to Grayscale, Sepia, Washout, or Black and White. Grayscale changes your picture up to 256 shades of gray. Sepia gives you that popular golden tone often used for an old-fashioned photo look. Washout is used to create watermarks, whereas *Black and White* is a way to reduce image color to black and white. Figure 3.43 shows an image and three variations of color.

Black and White: 50%

Washout

Original image from Online Pictures

Orange, Accent color 2 Light

FIGURE 3.43 Recoloring Objects

Photo: virinaflora/Fotolia

To change the colors of your image:

1. Select the image you want to change.
2. Click the FORMAT tab.
3. Click Color in the Adjust group.
4. Click the color variation of your choice, or select More Variations to open the Theme Colors options and select a theme color.

The Recolor gallery includes a Set Transparent Color option that is extremely valuable for creating a transparent area in many pictures. When you click Set Transparent Color, the pointer changes shape and includes an arrowhead for pointing. Move the pointer until the arrowhead is pointing directly at the color you wish to make transparent and click. The color becomes transparent so that anything underneath shows through. In Figure 3.44, the sky is set to transparent so the white background shows.

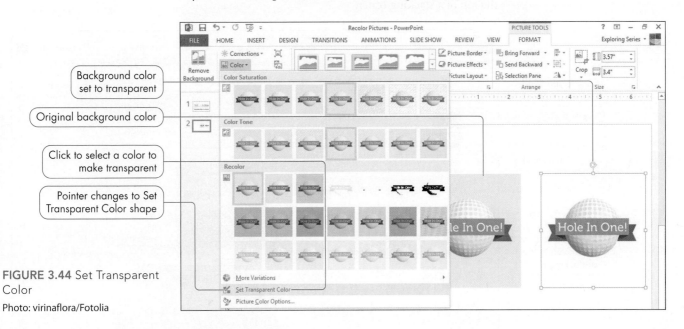

Background color set to transparent

Original background color

Click to select a color to make transparent

Pointer changes to Set Transparent Color shape

FIGURE 3.44 Set Transparent Color

Photo: virinaflora/Fotolia

Arranging Objects

When you have multiple objects such as shapes, Online Pictures, SmartArt, and WordArt on the page, it can become challenging and time consuming to arrange them. Smart Guides (discussed in Chapter 2) are good for simple alignment; however, this does not work for all situations. For more complex siutations, PowerPoint has several features to control the order and position of the objects, how the objects align to one another, and how they align to the slide. Before using any of these features, you must select the object(s). You can select the object(s) by using the **Selection Pane**. The Selection Pane, found in the Arrange group on the Format tab, contains a list of all objects on the slide. Click Selection Pane to open the Selection Pane if an object is selected. Click any object on the list to select it and make changes to it. The object you selected is highlighted in the Selection Pane. If an object is not selected, click the Home tab, click Select in the Editing group, and then select Selection Pane.

Order Objects

STEP 5 ≫

You can layer shapes by placing them under or on top of one another. The order of the layers is called the **stacking order**. PowerPoint adds shapes or other objects in a stacking order as you add them to the slide. The last shape you place on the slide is on top and is the highest in the stacking order. Drawn images are comprised of shapes that have been stacked. Once you ungroup an image and modify it, you may need to change the stacking order. You can open the Selection Pane to see the order in which objects are placed. The topmost object on the list is at the top of the stacking order.

To change the order of a stack of shapes:

1. Select a shape.
2. Click the FORMAT tab.
3. The Arrange group on the FORMAT tab includes the Bring Forward and Send Backward arrows to open a submenu for each that includes the following options:

Bring to Front	Moves the shape to the top of the stacking order
Send to Back	Moves the shape to the bottom of the stacking order
Bring Forward	Moves the shape up one layer
Send Backward	Moves the shape down one layer

Figure 3.45 shows the results of changing a square in the middle of a stacking order to the top of a stacking order.

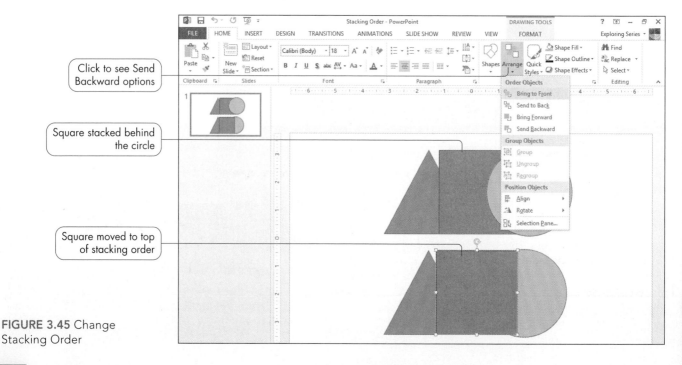

FIGURE 3.45 Change Stacking Order

You can right-click a shape and select *Bring to Front* or *Send to Back*. Using this method, you can still choose whether to move one layer or all layers. You also can open the Selection Pane, select the object, and then click the Re-order Bring Forward arrow or the Send Backward arrow to move the object up the list or down the list.

Align Objects

You can position objects precisely on the slide. For example, you can align a series of boxes at their tops or adjust the amount of space between the boxes so that they are evenly spaced. PowerPoint has rulers, a grid, and drawing guides that enable you to complete the aligning process quickly.

Each slide can display a **grid** containing intersecting lines, similar to traditional graph paper. Grids are hidden and are nonprinting, but you can display the grid to align your objects and to keep them evenly spaced. When you activate the grid, you will not see it in Slide Show view, and it will not print. Rulers can also help keep your objects aligned by enabling you to see the exact size of an object or the distance between shapes.

To view the grid and the ruler, click the View tab and click the check boxes for *Gridlines and Ruler*. To change the grid settings:

1. Click the VIEW tab.
2. Click the Show Dialog Box Launcher in the Show group.
3. Adjust the settings and click *Display grid on screen*.
4. Click OK.

By default, objects snap to the gridlines and measurement lines on the rulers. The *Snap to* feature forces an object to align with the grid by either the center point or the edge of the object, whichever is closer to the gridline. You can turn off the *Snap to* feature or change the setting so that objects snap to other objects. To change the grid settings, select an object and click the Show Dialog Box Launcher on the View tab.

Figure 3.46 displays the *Grid and Guides* dialog box options.

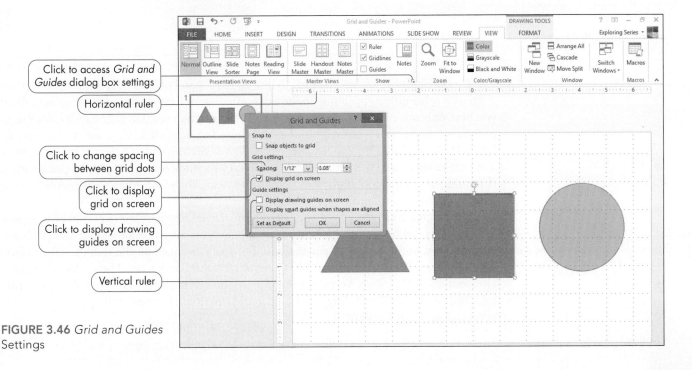

FIGURE 3.46 *Grid and Guides Settings*

Guides are nonprinting, temporary vertical or horizontal lines that you can place on a page to help you align objects or determine regions of the slide. New to PowerPoint 2013 are *SmartGuides*. You will notice the red-line SmartGuides display when you move objects on your slide. These simple guides help you quickly align objects in relation to other objects. For more precise positioning of objects, you can use guides to mark margins on a slide.

To activate guides:

1. Click the VIEW tab.
2. Click the check box next to Guides.
3. Click the Show Dialog Box Launcher.
4. Click *Display drawing guides on screen.*
5. Click OK.

When you first display the guides, you see two guides that intersect at the center of the slide (the zero setting on both the horizontal and vertical rulers). To move a guide, position your cursor over it and drag. A directional arrow will appear as well as a measurement telling you how far from the center point you are moving the guide. To create additional guides, press Ctrl+Shift while dragging. To remove guides, drag them off the slide. Figure 3.47 displays the default horizontal and vertical guides.

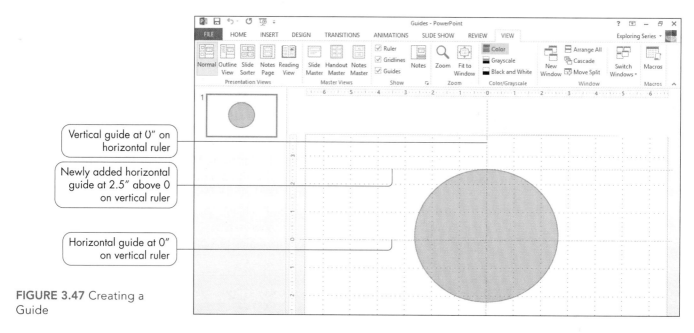

Vertical guide at 0" on horizontal ruler

Newly added horizontal guide at 2.5" above 0 on vertical ruler

Horizontal guide at 0" on vertical ruler

FIGURE 3.47 Creating a Guide

The *Align* feature makes it simple to line up shapes and objects in several ways. You can align with other objects by lining up the sides, middles, or top/bottom edges of objects. Or, if you have only one object or group selected, you can align in relation to the slide—for example, the top or left side of the slide. To align selected objects, click Align on the Format tab. When the alignment options display, select *Align to Slide* or Align Selected Objects. After you have determined whether you want to align to the slide or align objects to one another, determine which specific align option you want to use: Align Left, Align Center, Align Right, Align Top, Align Middle, or Align Bottom.

The Align feature also includes options to *distribute* selected shapes evenly over a given area. Perhaps you have shapes on the page but one is too close to another and another is too far away. You want to have an equal amount of space between all the shapes. After selecting the shapes, click Align in the Arrange group on the Format tab. Then select Distribute Horizontally or Distribute Vertically. Figure 3.48 shows three shapes that are aligned at their middles, aligned to the middle of the slide, and distributed horizontally so that the space between them is equidistant.

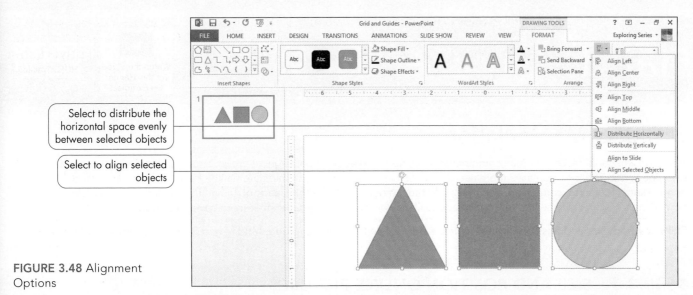

Select to distribute the horizontal space evenly between selected objects

Select to align selected objects

FIGURE 3.48 Alignment Options

Quick **Concepts** ✓

1. What is the name for the process of breaking apart an image so that individual shapes can be modified? *p. 220*

2. What PowerPoint feature allows you to quickly change the colors in an image? Why would you do this? *p. 223*

3. How are rulers, a grid, and drawing guides used when aligning objects? *p. 225*

Hands-On Exercises

Watch the Video for this Hands-On Exercise!

MyITLab®
HOE3 Training

3 Object Manipulation

Although you could teach your mini-camp participants how to size, position, align, ungroup, and use other object manipulation techniques using shapes, you have them use Online Pictures. The ability to manipulate Online Pictures by grouping and ungrouping, recoloring, combining, and using other techniques turns the thousands of Online Pictures images available from Microsoft Office Online into millions of possibilities. You want your group members to have these skills.

Skills covered: Size and Position Online Pictures • Flip Online Pictures • Ungroup, Modify, and Regroup Online Pictures • Recolor a Picture • Create and Reorder Shapes

STEP 1 ≫ SIZE AND POSITION ONLINE PICTURES

You teach your mini-camp participants to use the Size Dialog Box Launcher. You want them to be able to precisely size and position objects on the slide. Refer to Figure 3.49 as you complete Step 1.

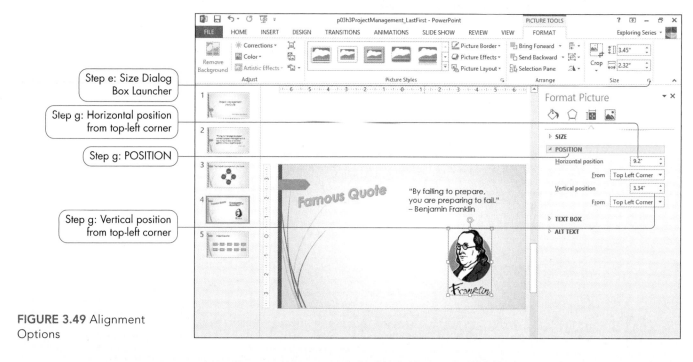

FIGURE 3.49 Alignment Options

a. Open the *p03h2ProjectManagement_LastFirst* presentation if you closed it after the previous exercise. Save the presentation as **p03h3ProjectManagement_LastFirst**, changing *h2* to *h3*.

b. Click **Slide 4**. Click the **INSERT tab** and click **Online Pictures** in the Images group.

The Insert Pictures pane opens.

c. Type **Benjamin Franklin** in the **Office.com Clip Art search box** and press **Enter**.

A few images of Benjamin Franklin display. Entering the keywords *Benjamin Franklin* narrowed your search more than if you had entered the generic keyword *Franklin*.

d. Insert the Online Pictures image of Benjamin Franklin as shown in Figure 3.49.

You have inserted the Online Pictures image in the center of Slide 4.

TROUBLESHOOTING: If you cannot locate the image in Figure 3.49, select another Online Pictures image of Benjamin Franklin. Expand your search terms to include other result types if necessary.

e. Click the **Size Dialog Box Launcher** in the Size group on the FORMAT tab.

The Format Picture pane opens with the SIZE option expanded.

f. Type **3.45"** in the **Height box** and click in the **Width box**.

Because *Lock aspect ratio* is selected, the width of the image changes to 2.32", keeping the image in proportion.

g. Click the **POSITION arrow** in the Format Picture pane to expand the options. Type **9.2"** in the **Horizontal position box**, type **3.34"** in the **Vertical position box**, press **Enter**, and then close the Format Picture pane.

The picture is moved to a new position.

h. Save the presentation.

STEP 2 ≫ FLIP ONLINE PICTURES

Rotating and flipping are both ways to angle an object on the slide. You can rotate using precise measurements or, for an imprecise method of rotation, you can rotate the object using the Rotation handle. You ask your participants to use these methods so that they are familiar with the benefits of each. Refer to Figure 3.50 as you complete Step 2.

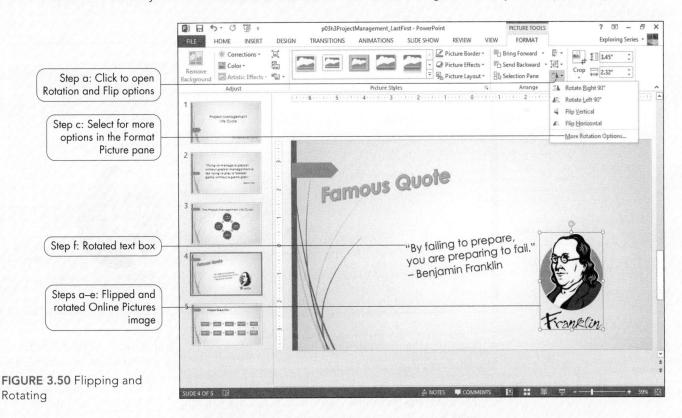

FIGURE 3.50 Flipping and Rotating

a. Click the **Benjamin Franklin image** and click **Rotate** in the Arrange group on the FORMAT tab.

The rotate and flip options appear.

b. Click **Flip Horizontal**.

c. Click **Rotate** in the Arrange group and select **More Rotation Options**.

d. Type **180** in the **Rotation box** and press **Enter**.

The picture is rotated upside down.

e. Click **Rotate** and select **Flip Vertical**. Close the Format Shape pane.

The Online Pictures picture appears to be in its original position, but the rotation angle is still set at 180°.

f. Select the text box in the top right of the slide and drag it down and to the left to the approximate center of the slide. Position the insertion point over the rotation handle and drag the rotation handle to the left until the text box is rotated to approximately match the slant in the *Famous Quote* WordArt.

> **TROUBLESHOOTING:** As you change the angle of rotation for the text box, you will need to reposition it on the slide. An easy way to make small position adjustments is to press the arrow keys on the keyboard.

g. Save the presentation.

STEP 3 ⟫ UNGROUP, MODIFY, AND REGROUP ONLINE PICTURES

Being able to change colors, remove shapes, add shapes, and group and regroup Online Pictures images are important skills you want your participants to master. You ask the participants to change the color of the letters in Franklin, move grouped items, and regroup the Ben Franklin Online Pictures image. Refer to Figure 3.51 as you complete Step 3.

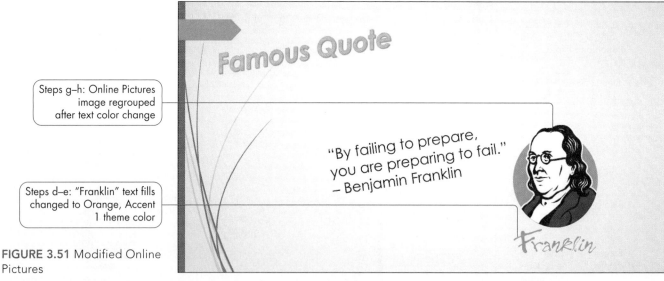

Steps g–h: Online Pictures image regrouped after text color change

Steps d–e: "Franklin" text fills changed to Orange, Accent 1 theme color

FIGURE 3.51 Modified Online Pictures

a. Right-click the **Benjamin Franklin picture** on Slide 4, select **Edit Picture**, and then click **Yes** when the Microsoft Office PowerPoint message box opens asking if you would like to convert the picture to a Microsoft Drawing Object.

The image has been converted to a drawing object and flips back to its original rotation angle.

b. Click the **FORMAT tab**, click **Group** in the Arrange group, select **Ungroup**, and then click outside the Online Pictures border.

When you ungroup the Online Pictures image, each shape comprising the image is selected and surrounded with adjustment handles. Clicking outside the border deselects the shapes so that you can select just the one you wish to modify.

c. Drag the **Zoom slider** until the image is at a level with which you are comfortable and drag the scroll bars to locate the name *Franklin* at the bottom of the Online Pictures image.

Zooming in makes selecting the individual shape you wish to modify easier.

d. Select the **F** in *Franklin*, click the **FORMAT tab** if necessary, click **Shape Fill** in the Shape Styles group, and then click **Orange, Accent 1** (first row, fifth column).

You change the black *F* in the original Online Pictures image to a color that matches your theme color.

e. Drag a selection around all the remaining letters in *Franklin* and click the **Shape Fill button** (not the arrow) to change the fill color of the other letters to **Orange, Accent 1**.

The Shape Fill button will default to the last color selected.

f. Click the **VIEW tab** and click **Fit to Window** in the Zoom group.

g. Drag a selection net around all the shapes used to make the Benjamin Franklin Online Pictures image. It may be easier to start at the outside top-right area and drag down to the bottom-left corner area to avoid including the text box.

All the shapes are selected. Pressing Ctrl and clicking the shapes individually would be time consuming because of the many shapes involved.

h. Click the **FORMAT tab**, click **Group** in the Arrange group, and then select **Regroup**.

Because the WordArt and the text box were not part of the original group, they do not become part of the group.

i. Save the presentation.

STEP 4 ≫ RECOLOR A PICTURE

You teach your mini-camp participants to recolor an Online Pictures image so that it matches the color scheme of the presentation. Refer to Figure 3.52 as you complete Step 4.

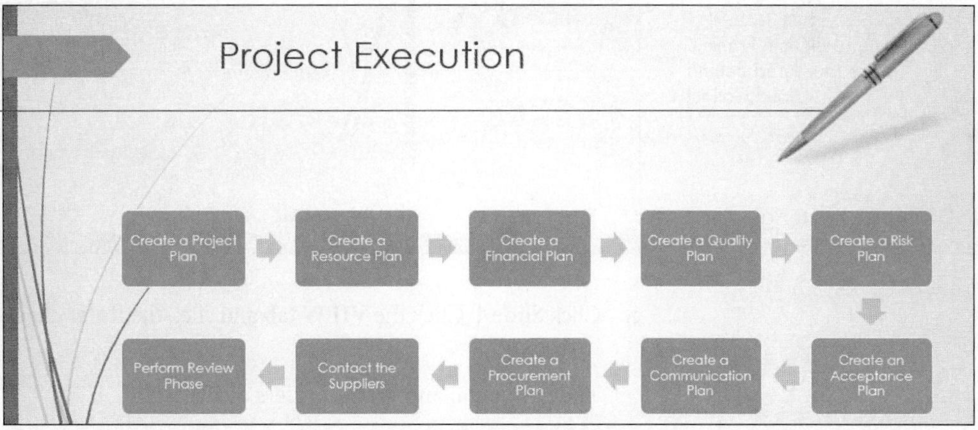

FIGURE 3.52 Recolored Pen Image

Steps c–f: Online Pictures image inserted, aligned to top-right, and recolored ballpoint pen

a. Click **Slide 5**. Click the **INSERT tab** and click **Online Pictures** in the Images group.

b. Type **Pen** in the **Office.com Clip Art search box** and press Enter.

c. Choose the gray ballpoint pen. Refer to Figure 3.52 to determine which pen to insert.

d. While the Online Picture image is selected, click the **FORMAT tab** under *PICTURE TOOLS*. In the Size group, change the height to **3"**.

The width will change to 3" automatically.

e. Click the **FORMAT tab** under *PICTURE TOOLS* again, if not already selected. Click **Align** in the Arrange group and select **Align Top** to move the object to the top of the slide. Once the Online Picture image is aligned to the top, click **Align** again and select **Align Right**.

The Online Picture image is now aligned to the top right of the slide.

f. Click **Color** in the Adjust group located under the FORMAT tab and click **Green, Accent color 6 Dark** under the Recolor category (second row, seventh column).

Online Pictures images do not need to be converted to a drawing object; you can use the picture tools to modify them. Recoloring an image can be applied to any image, and therefore it does not require Online Pictures images to be ungrouped or to be vectors.

The color of the Online Pictures image now matches the colors in the theme.

g. Save the presentation.

STEP 5 ➤➤ CREATE AND REORDER SHAPES

Being able to create and reorder shapes allows you to be creative, enabling you to create backgrounds, borders, and corners. You ask your group to create a background for three Online Pictures images, which unifies the images. Refer to Figure 3.53 as you complete Step 5.

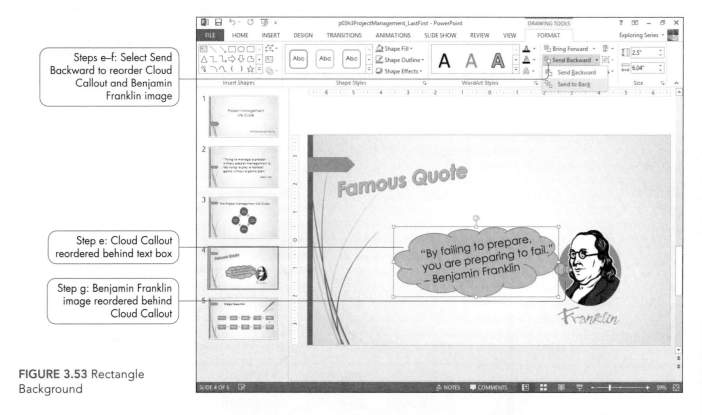

Steps e–f: Select Send Backward to reorder Cloud Callout and Benjamin Franklin image

Step e: Cloud Callout reordered behind text box

Step g: Benjamin Franklin image reordered behind Cloud Callout

FIGURE 3.53 Rectangle Background

a. Click **Slide 4**. Click the **VIEW tab** and click the **Ruler check box** in the Show group (if necessary).

The horizontal and vertical rulers display.

b. Click the **INSERT tab**, click **Shapes** in the Illustrations group, and then click the **Cloud Callout** in the Callouts category.

c. Position the cross-hair pointer on the slide so that the indicator on the ruler is at the 3.5" mark to the left of the zero point on the horizontal ruler and the 0.5" mark above the zero point on the vertical ruler.

This is the beginning point for the cloud callout.

d. Drag to the 2.5" mark to the right of the zero point on the horizontal ruler and the 2" mark below the zero point on the vertical ruler and release.

A large cloud callout shape in the theme color is created on top of the text box on the slide. You will use the cloud callout as a background for the Online Pictures image. Currently, it is hiding the quote and must be reordered.

e. Drag the yellow square at the bottom of the callout shape to the 3" mark to the right of the zero point on the horizontal ruler and the 1" mark below 0 on the vertical ruler until it looks similar to the position shown in Figure 3.53.

f. Click the **FORMAT tab**, click **Shape Fill arrow** in the Shape Styles group, and then click **Orange, Accent 1, Lighter 40%** (fourth row, fifth column). Click **Send Backward** in the Arrange group of the FORMAT tab and select **Send to Back**.

g. Select the **Benjamin Franklin Online Pictures image**. Click **Send Backward** in the Arrange group and select **Send to Back**. If necessary, nudge the Franklin image and text box into position as seen in Figure 3.53.

h. Save and submit the file based on your instructor's directions. Close the file and exit PowerPoint.

Chapter Objectives Review

After reading this chapter, you have accomplished the following objectives:

1. **Create shapes.**
   - You can use shapes to highlight information, as a design element, as the basis for creating illustrations, or to contain information in infographics.
   - Draw lines and connectors: Lines are shapes that can be used to point to information, or to divide a slide into sections. Connectors are lines that attach to the shapes you create and move with shapes when the shapes are moved.
   - Create and modify freeform shapes: PowerPoint provides tools for creating, sizing, and positioning shapes. A freeform shape is a shape that can be used to create customized shapes using both curved and straight-line segments. Sometimes, the freeform shape you have drawn is not exactly as you desired. You can modify the freeform shape to achieve the desired shape through the help of a vertex. Vertexes are the black squares that control the curve line segments, indicating where two line segments meet or end.

2. **Apply Quick Styles and customize shapes.**
   - Change shape fills: A shape can be customized by changing its default fill to another color, to a picture, to a gradient, to a texture, or to no fill.
   - Change shape outlines: The shape outline color, weight, or dash style can be modified.
   - Change shape effects: Special effects such as shadows, reflections, and glows may be added.
   - Applying a Quick Style enables you to apply preset options.

3. **Create SmartArt.**
   - SmartArt graphics are diagrams that present information visually to effectively communicate your message.
   - SmartArt can be used to create effective infographics.
   - You can convert text to a SmartArt diagram.

4. **Modify SmartArt.**
   - Change SmartArt theme colors: SmartArt diagrams can be modified to fit nearly any color scheme.
   - Use Quick Styles with SmartArt: After creating the diagram, you can use Quick Styles to adjust the style to match other styles you have used in your presentation or to make the diagram easier to understand.
   - Change the layout: Once a SmartArt diagram type has been chosen, it can easily be converted to another type.
   - Change SmartArt type: You can change the SmartArt diagram type if you decide a different type would be better.

   - Convert text to a SmartArt diagram: Bullets and other text can be converted directly to a SmartArt diagram.
   - SmartArt can be modified to include additional shapes, to delete shapes, to apply a SmartArt style, to revise the color scheme, or to add special effects.
   - The direction of the SmartArt can be changed.
   - SmartArt can be resized and repositioned.

5. **Create WordArt.**
   - WordArt is text with decorative effects applied to draw attention to the text.
   - Select a WordArt style and type the text you desire.

6. **Modify WordArt.**
   - WordArt can be modified by transforming the shape of the text and by applying special effects and colors.
   - Text created as WordArt can be edited.
   - Among the many special effects available are 3-D presets and rotations.

7. **Modify objects.**
   - Flip and rotate: An object may be flipped horizontally or vertically, or rotated by dragging its green rotation handle.
   - Merge shapes: The Merge Shapes feature allows you to take shapes that you have inserted and merge them together. There are five different merging options: Union, Combine, Fragment, Intersect, and Subtract.
   - Group and ungroup objects: Vector images can be ungrouped so basic shapes can be customized, and objects can be regrouped so they can be moved as one object.
   - Recolor objects: Pictures can be recolored by changing their color mode or by applying dark or light variations of a theme color or custom color.

8. **Arrange objects.**
   - Objects are stacked in layers.
   - The object at the top of the layer is the one that fully displays, while other objects in the stack may have some portions blocked.
   - Order objects: The stacking order of shapes can be reordered so that objects can be seen as desired.
   - Align objects: Features such as rulers, grids, guides, align, and distribute can be used to arrange objects on a slide and arrange objects in relation to one another.

Key Terms Matching

Match the key terms with their definitions. Write the key term letter by the appropriate numbered definition.

a.	Adjustment handle	**k.**	Infographic
b.	Aspect ratio	**l.**	Line weight
c.	Callout	**m.**	Lock Drawing Mode
d.	Connector	**n.**	Picture fill
e.	Distribute	**o.**	Selection net
f.	Flow chart	**p.**	SmartArt
g.	Freeform shape	**q.**	Stacking order
h.	Gradient fill	**r.**	Texture fill
i.	Group	**s.**	Vector graphic
j.	Guide	**t.**	Vertex

1. _____ Inserts an image from a file into a shape. **p. 192**

2. _____ A blend of two or more colors or shades. **p. 190**

3. _____ A marquee that selects all objects in an area you define by dragging the mouse. **p. 190**

4. _____ A yellow square that enables you to modify a shape. **p. 185**

5. _____ Enables the creation of multiple shapes of the same type. **p. 185**

6. _____ An illustration showing the sequence of a project or plan. **p. 187**

7. _____ A visual representation of data or knowledge. **p. 184**

8. _____ A line shape that is attached to and moves with other shapes. **p. 186**

9. _____ Diagram that presents information visually to effectively communicate a message. **p. 203**

10. _____ Refers to keeping an object's proportion the same with respect to width and height. **p. 218**

11. _____ Combines two or more objects. **p. 220**

12. _____ Point where a curve ends or the point where two line segments meet in a freeform shape. **p. 188**

13. _____ To divide or evenly spread shapes over a given area. **p. 226**

14. _____ Inserts a texture such as marble into a shape. **p. 194**

15. _____ A shape that combines both curved and straight lines. **p. 188**

16. _____ A shape that includes a text box you can use to add notes. **p. 185**

17. _____ The order of objects placed on top of one another. **p. 224**

18. _____ An object-oriented graphic based on geometric formulas. **p. 220**

19. _____ A straight horizontal or vertical line used to align objects. **p. 226**

20. _____ The width or thickness of a line. **p. 194**

Multiple Choice

1. Which of the following is text that has a decorative effect applied?

   (a) Text box

   (b) WordArt

   (c) Text pane

   (d) SmartArt

2. To rotate a shape on your slide:

   (a) Do nothing, because shapes cannot be rotated.

   (b) Drag one of the corner adjustment handles.

   (c) Double-click the lightning bolt and enter the number of degrees to rotate.

   (d) Drag the handle at the top of the image.

3. Which of the following is a reason for ungrouping a drawn object?

   (a) To resize the group as one piece

   (b) To move the objects as one

   (c) To add text on top of the group

   (d) To be able to individually change shapes used to create the composite image

4. Which of the following is a reason for grouping shapes?

   (a) To be able to change each shape individually

   (b) To create a relationship diagram

   (c) To move or modify the objects as one

   (d) To connect the shapes with connectors

5. You have inserted an Online Pictures image of the ocean with a sailboat on the right side. If you flip the image vertically, what would the resulting image look like?

   (a) The image would show right side up, but the sailboat would be on the left side.

   (b) The image would be upside down with the sailboat pointing down.

   (c) The image would be rotated 270°, and the sailboat would be at the top.

   (d) The image would be rotated 90°, and the sailboat would be on the bottom.

6. You have items needed for a camping trip in a bullet placeholder. Which of the following SmartArt diagrams would you use to display the data as an infographic?

   (a) Hierarchy

   (b) Cycle

   (c) List

   (d) Relationship

7. Which of the following is *not* available from the SmartArt gallery?

   (a) Data table

   (b) Horizontal bullet list

   (c) Process graphic

   (d) Cycle matrix

8. Which of the following might be a reason for changing the stacking order of shapes?

   (a) To show a relationship by placing shapes in front of or behind each other

   (b) To hide something on a shape

   (c) To uncover something hidden by another shape

   (d) All of the above

9. Which of the following is used to show a continual process?

   (a) Hierarchy

   (b) Matrix

   (c) Cycle

   (d) Relationship

10. Which of the following may be used to add emphasis to text on a slide?

    (a) Apply a WordArt Quick Style to the selected text.

    (b) Create the text using the WordArt feature.

    (c) Apply a Text Effect to the selected text.

    (d) All of the above

Practice Exercises

1 Cloud Computing Infographic

To help explain cloud computing to employees, you decide to create an infographic using a SmartArt Hierarchy diagram. You want the infographic to show the three categories of cloud computing: IaaS (Infrastructure-as-a-Service), PaaS (Platform-as-a-Service), and SaaS (Software-as-a-Service). You also want to show common providers in each category to help employees recognize the differences in the categories. This exercise follows the same set of skills as used in Hands-On Exercise 2 in the chapter. Refer to Figure 3.54 as you complete this exercise.

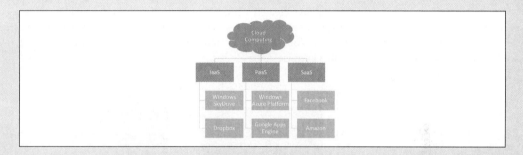

FIGURE 3.54 Cloud Computing Infographic

a. Open a blank presentation file and save it as **p03p1Cloud_LastFirst**. Create a *Notes and Handouts* header with your name and a footer with your instructor's name and your class. Include the current date.

b. Click the **HOME tab** and click **Layout** in the Slides group. Select the **Blank layout**.

c. Click the **INSERT tab** and click **SmartArt** in the Illustrations group. Click **Hierarchy** in the left pane of the *Choose a SmartArt Graphic* dialog box. Click **Lined List** (fourth row, third column) and click **OK**.

d. Change the size of the shape by doing the following:
   - Click the **FORMAT tab**, click **Size**, and then click the **Size Dialog Box Launcher** to open the Format Shape pane.
   - Click the SmartArt shape.
   - Click in the **Height box** and type **6.5"**.
   - Click in the **Width box** and type **8"**.
   - Click the **POSITION arrow**, if necessary, and type **2.8"** in the **Horizontal position box** and **0.5"** in the **Vertical position box**.
   - Close the Format Shape pane.

e. Click the **DESIGN tab** and click **Text Pane** in the Create Graphic group to open the text pane (if necessary).

f. Type **Cloud Computing** in the first bulleted level in the Text pane.

g. Select the second bullet point and type **IaaS**. Press **Enter**, press **Tab**, and then type **Windows OneDrive**. Press **Enter** and type **Dropbox**. Press **Enter**.

h. Press **Shift+Tab** and type **PaaS**. Press **Enter**, press **Tab**, and then type **Windows Azure Platform**. Press **Enter** and type **Google Apps Engine**.

i. Select the first [Text] bullet point and type **SaaS**. Select the remaining [Text] bullet point, press **Tab**, and then type **Facebook**. Press **Enter** and type **Amazon**.

j. Close the Text pane.

k. Click the **More button** in the Layouts group on the DESIGN tab and click **Organization Chart** (first row, first column).

l. Click **Change Colors** in the SmartArt Styles group and click **Colorful Range - Accent Colors 2 to 3**.

m. Click the **More button** in the SmartArt Styles group and click **White Outline** in the *Best Match for Document* section.

n. Select the **Cloud Computing shape** and click the **FORMAT tab**. Click **Change Shape** in the Shapes group and click **Cloud** in the *Basic Shapes* section. Click **Larger** in the Shapes group six times.

o. Apply the **Fill - White, Outline - Accent 1, Shadow WordArt style** to the Cloud Computing text box. Then, apply the **Tight Reflection, touching Reflection Text Effect** to the WordArt.

p. Save and close the file. Submit based on your instructor's directions.

2 Principles of Pilates

You have created a slide show about Pilates for your Pilates instructor to show prospective students. You use infographics, shapes, and Online Pictures to share his message. This exercise follows the same set of skills as used in Hands-On Exercises 1–3 in the chapter. Refer to Figure 3.55 as you complete this exercise.

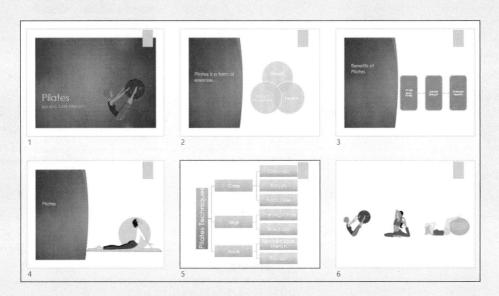

FIGURE 3.55 Pilates, Strengthening the Core

a. Open *p03p2Pilates* and save it as **p03p2Pilates_LastFirst**.

b. Create a handout header with your name and a handout footer with your instructor's name and your class. Include the current date.

c. Click **Slide 2**. Click the placeholder containing the bullet points and click the **HOME tab**.

d. Click **Convert to SmartArt** in the Paragraph group and click **Basic Venn**.

e. Click **Change Colors** in the SmartArt Styles group. Click **Transparent Gradient Range - Accent 1** in the *Accent 1* section.

f. Click **Slide 3**. Click the **INSERT tab**, click **Shapes** in the Illustrations group, and then select **Double Arrow** in the *Lines* section. Drag an arrow from the right-center connecting point on the *Whole Body Fitness* shape to the left-center connecting point on the *Creates Strength* shape. Repeat this step to create a connector between the *Creates Strength* shape and the *Increases Flexibility* shape.

g. Click **Slide 5**. Select the **Hierarchy SmartArt** and click the **SMARTART TOOLS DESIGN tab**.

h. Select the **Core shape** and click the **Add Shape arrow** in the Create Graphic group. Select **Add Shape Below** and type **Plank Pose**.

i. Click the **More button** in the Layouts group on the DESIGN tab and select **More Layouts**. Click **Horizontal Multi-Level Hierarchy** in the Hierarchy category.

j. Click **Intense Effect** in the SmartArt Styles group.

k. Click **Slide 1**. Select the image, click the **FORMAT tab**, and then click **Color** in the Adjust group. Click **Sepia** in the Recolor variations category (first row, third column).

l. Click **Slide 4**. Right-click the image and select **Edit Picture**. Click **Yes** to convert the picture into a drawing object. Select the image again.

m. Click the **FORMAT tab** and click **Group** in the Arrange group. Select **Ungroup**.

n. Click the **VIEW tab** and click **Zoom** in the Zoom group. Select **200%** and click **OK**. Deselect the shapes and select the circle.

o. Click the **FORMAT tab** and click **Shape Fill**. Select **Lime, Accent** 1 (top row, fifth column).

p. Click **Fit to Window** in the Zoom group.

q. Drag a selection net around all the shapes comprising the clip art image, click the **FORMAT tab**, click **Group** in the Arrange group, and then select **Regroup**.

r. Click the **INSERT tab** and click **Shapes** in the Illustrations group. Click **Freeform** in the *Line* section.

s. Click approximately 0.5" from the foot of the woman to create the first point of a freeform shape you create to resemble a mat (see Figure 3.55).

t. Click approximately 0.5" from the right hand of the woman to create the second point of the freeform shape.

u. Click approximately 1/4" vertically and horizontally from the bottom right of the slide.

v. Click approximately 1/4" vertically and horizontally from the bottom left of the slide.

w. Click the starting point of the freeform shape to complete the shape.

x. Click the **FORMAT tab**, click the **Send Backward arrow**, and then select **Send to Back**.

y. Click **Slide 6**. Line up the three figures in a horizontal line beginning with the woman with the red ball and ending with the woman with the purple ball. Drag a selection net around all the images and click the **FORMAT tab**. Click **Align,** click **Align Middle**. Click **Align,** click **Distribute Horizontally** to evenly distribute the images.

z. View the slide show. Save and close the file, and submit based on your instructor's directions.

Mid-Level Exercises

1 SmartArt and Online Pictures Ideas

To help you become familiar with the SmartArt Graphic gallery and the types of information appropriate for each type of diagram, you create a slide show of "SmartArt ideas." You also manipulate clip art. In this activity, you work extensively with sizing, placement, and fills.

a. Open *p03m1Ideas* and save it as **p03m1Ideas_LastFirst**. On Slide 1, replace *First Name Last Name* with your name.

b. Create a handout header with your name and a handout footer with your instructor's name and your class. Include the current date.

c. View the gridlines.

d. Click **Slide 2**. Insert a **Vertical Box List SmartArt diagram** (second row, second column in the List category) and make the following modifications:
- Apply the **Subtle Effect** from SmartArt Styles.
- Type the following list items into the **Text Pane**:
  - **List**
  - **Process**
  - **Cycle**
  - **Hierarchy**
  - **Relationship**
  - **Matrix**
  - **Pyramid**
  - **Picture**
- Change the text font size to **24 pt**.
- Size the SmartArt diagram to 7" wide and drag it so that it is at the horizontal center of the slide using the grid to help you determine placement.
- Align the bottom border of the SmartArt diagram with the last line of the gridline.

e. Click **Slide 3**. Convert the text to an **Upward Arrow SmartArt diagram** and make the following modifications:
- Apply the **Simple Fill SmartArt Style**.
- Change the height of the SmartArt diagram to **6.17"** and the width to **10"**.
- **Align Center** the diagram. Then **Align Middle** the diagram.

f. Click **Slide 4**. Insert a **Diverging Radial SmartArt diagram** and make the following modifications:
- Apply the **3-D Polished SmartArt Style**.
- Change the SmartArt colors to **Colorful - Accent Colors** (first row, first column in the *Color* section).
- Type **Residential College** as the center hub and type **Build Community**, **Promote Personal Growth**, and **Support Academic Success** as the spokes around the hub. Remove the extra shape.
- Set the height of the SmartArt to **5.5"** and the width to **6.67"**.

g. Click **Slide 5**. Insert a **Horizontal Hierarchy SmartArt diagram** (third row, fourth column in the Hierarchy category) and make the following modifications:
- Apply the **Flat Scene SmartArt Style**.
- Type **School of Business** as the first-level bullet in the **Text Pane**. Enter **M&M** and **DIS** as the second-level bullets and type the following in the third-level bullets: **Marketing**, **Management**, **MIS**, and **POM**.
- Click **Right to Left** in the Create Graphic group to change the orientation of the diagram.
- Drag the borders of the SmartArt graphic until it fits the page and the text is large enough to read.

 **h.** Click **Slide 6**. Insert a **Basic Venn SmartArt diagram** (tenth row, fourth column in the Relationship category) and make the following modifications:
- Type the following as three bullets in the **Text Pane**: **Anesthesiology**, **Nurses**, and **Surgeon**.
  - Insert a picture fill in the *Anesthesiology* shape using an Online Picture with *Doctor* as the key term.

- Insert a picture fill in the *Nurses* shape using an Online Picture with *Nurse* as the key term.
- Insert a picture fill in the *Surgeon* shape using an Online Picture with *Surgeon* as the key term.
- Recolor all images using the **Grayscale variation**.
- Format the SmartArt text with the **Fill - White, Outline - Accent 2, Hard Shadow - Accent 2 Style**.
- Set the height of the SmartArt to **4.5"** and the width to **5.5"**.
- Use the grid to center the Venn diagram in the available space.

i. Click **Slide 7**. Insert a **Basic Matrix SmartArt diagram** (first row, first column in the Matrix category) and make the following modifications:

- Apply the **Subtle Effect SmartArt Style**.
- Change the colors to **Colorful - Accent Colors**.
- Type the following text in the **Text Pane**:
  - **Urgent & Important**
  - **Not Urgent & Important**
  - **Urgent & Not Important**
  - **Not Urgent & Not Important**

j. Click **Slide 8**. Insert a **Basic Pyramid SmartArt diagram** (first row, first column in the Pyramid category) and make the following modifications:

- Apply the **Subtle Effect SmartArt Style**.
- Enter a blank space at the top pyramid level and add the following text to the remaining levels. You will add the text for the top pyramid level in a text box in a later step so that the font in the SmartArt is not reduced to a difficult-to-read font size.
  - **Esteem**
  - **Belonging and Love**
  - **Safety**
  - **Biological Needs**
- Drag the border of the SmartArt diagram until it fills the available white space on the slide. Deselect the pyramid.
- Create a text box on the top left of the slide and type **Self-Actualization** in the **text box**. Change the font size to **39 pt**. Drag the text box so it is centered over the top of the empty pyramid.
- Apply the **Fill - Brown, Text 1, Shadow WordArt Style** to the text box *Maslow's Hierarchy of Needs*.
- Apply the **Deflate Transform Text Effect** to the WordArt text.

k. Click **Slide 9**. Ungroup the complex clip art image until all grouping is undone. Make the following changes:

- Change the color of the bird so it is red.
- Regroup the pieces of the clip art image.

l. View the slide show. Save and close the file, and submit based on your instructor's directions.

2 The Arts

CREATIVE CASE

A presentation created by a local arts volunteer can be improved using shapes and SmartArt. You will update the presentation using the Organic design theme, Inset SmartArt style.

a. Open *p03m2Perform* and save it as **p03m2Perform_LastFirst**. Create a *Notes and Handouts* header with your name and a footer with your instructor's name and your class. Include the current date.

b. Click **Slide 4**. Select the bulleted text and convert it to a **Process Arrows SmartArt diagram** available in the Process SmartArt category. Apply the **Polished SmartArt Style** available in the 3-D category.

c. Click **Slide 5**. Select the existing SmartArt diagram and change the layout to a **Segmented Pyramid** in the Pyramid SmartArt category. Apply the **Inset SmartArt Style** available in the 3-D category. Resize the SmartArt to fit the available area and horizontally center the SmartArt.

d. Click **Slide 6**. Create an **Organization Chart SmartArt diagram** available in the Hierarchy category. The top level of management is the *Executive Committee*. The Executive Committee has the following subcommittees: **Finance Committee**, **Program Committee**, and **Marketing Committee**.

e. Add two shapes beneath each. Add the following committees to the Finance Committee: **Investments** and **Financial Oversight**. Add the following committees to the Program Committee: **Grants** and **Distribution**. Add the following committees to the Marketing Committee: **Public Relations** and **Fundraising**.

f. Apply the **Inset SmartArt Style** available in the 3-D category.

 g. Click **Slide 7**. Insert your choice of music clip art. Ungroup the clip art image and change the fill color of several shapes to theme colors. Resize and position the image as appropriate. Regroup the clip art.

> **TROUBLESHOOTING:** If you choose an image that you cannot ungroup and modify, choose another image.

h. Use the Freeform tool or Curve tool to create a shape that covers the title, subtitle, and the clip art image. Move the shape you created to the back so all other objects on the slide are visible. Edit the shape fill and outline, and move the objects on the slide until you are satisfied with your slide.

i. Save and close the presentation, and submit based on your instructor's directions.

3 Learning from an Expert

COLLABORATION CASE

Video-sharing sites such as YouTube.com make it possible to learn from PowerPoint industry experts as well as everyday PowerPoint users. You can learn through step-by-step instructions or by inspiration after seeing others use PowerPoint. The video source may also refer you to a professional Web site that will provide you with a wealth of tips and ideas for creating slide shows that move your work from ordinary to extraordinary. In this exercise, you will view a YouTube video featuring the work of Nancy Duarte, a well-known PowerPoint industry expert. After viewing the video and related Web site, you will use shapes and animation to recreate one of the effects in Duarte's presentation. Finally, you will post the slide you created to your Web site and blog about your experience. Note: This exercise assumes you have done the collaboration exercise for Chapter 1. If you have not completed that exercise, use OneDrive.com or another method for sharing your presentation with your instructor and classmates.

a. Access the Internet and go to www.youtube.com. Search for the video *Duarte Design's Five Rules for Presentations by Nancy Duarte*. View the video, click the supporting link beneath the video (http://blog.duarte.com/), and note the additional resources available to viewers of the video. Close the Web site.

b. Advance to 2:29 in the video clip on YouTube and rewatch Duarte's Rule 4—Practice Design Not Decoration.

c. Open *p03m3Duarte.pptx*, which contains the slide *Duarte's Rule 4*. Apply animations to the shapes and text contained in the file to reproduce the effect of Duarte's slide. If you prefer, create your own slide reproducing any of Duarte's rules for effective presentations and animate it as desired. Save the file as **p03m3Duarte_LastFirst**.

d. Load your animated slide to your Weebly Web site if you completed Collaboration Exercise 1. Open the site and click the Multimedia link on the Elements tab. Drag the File element to your home page and upload the *p03m3Duarte_LastFirst* file. If you are not using the Weebly.com site created during Collaborative Exercise 1, upload your animated slide to OneDrive.com or another online storage site.

e. Create a blog entry about this experience if you are using the Weebly.com site created in Collaborative Exercise 1. Discuss Duarte's rules and whether you have seen good examples and/or bad examples of these rules used in presentations. Ask three classmates to go to your Weebly Web site, view the presentation you saved, and then add a comment about your presentation or blog entry. If you saved to OneDrive.com or another online storage location, share the location with three classmates and ask them to download the presentation. Ask your classmates to view the presentation and ask them to e-mail you with their comments.

f. Visit three of your classmates' Web sites after the due date for this exercise and use the contact form on their home pages to leave your information and a comment about their presentations or blogs. Revisit your Web site to see what comments your classmates entered. Or, download and view three of your classmates' animated slides from the storage location they used.

g. E-mail your instructor your Web site address or storage location so your instructor can review your presentation.

Beyond the Classroom

Predators

RESEARCH CASE

FROM SCRATCH

Create a presentation about a predator of your choice, such as a shark or lion. After an appropriate title slide, include an introduction slide using a Pyramid SmartArt that shows the levels in a food chain. Use the following levels from top level to bottom level to create the pyramid: **Predators**, **Secondary Consumers**, **Primary Consumers**, and **Primary Producers**. The food chain is shown as a pyramid to show that meat-eating predators at the top of the food chain are more rare than plant-eating primary consumers, which are more rare than primary producers such as plants. Type a speaker note for the introduction slide that summarizes how the levels of the food chain work. After the introductory slide, research the predator of your choice and include a minimum of four slides sharing information about the predator. For example, create a presentation about sharks that could include where sharks are located, their classification, their prey, their hunting methods and tools, and their conservation status. Add at least one additional slide that includes shapes and add shape effects to the shapes. Include speaker notes to clarify information. On the title slide, add a title using WordArt of your choice. Apply a design theme and modify it as desired. In addition to the Food Chain Pyramid, include several Online Pictures images or pictures in appropriate locations. Add a transition and animations to enhance the show. Include a *Notes and Handouts* header with your name and a handout footer with your instructor's name and your class. Save your presentation as **p03b2Predator_LastFirst**. Submit based on your instructor's directions.

My Nation

DISASTER RECOVERY

Your student teaching supervisor has asked you to change the presentation she created about America's symbols to make it more visually and emotionally interesting for her students. If you desire, you may select another country, but be sure to include the inspirational symbols of the country you choose. Open *p03b3Symbols* or create your own presentation and save the new presentation as **p03b3Symbols_ LastFirst**. Apply the design theme of your choice and change other themes as desired. Add shapes, SmartArt, pictures, and clip art to add visual interest. Text can be moved to speaker notes, if desired, so that you can showcase symbols. Align and order objects attractively. Finalize the presentation by proofreading and applying transitions and animations. Create a *Notes and Handouts* header with your name and a footer with your instructor's name and your class. Include the current date. Save the presentation and submit based on your instructor's directions.

Personal Financial Management

SOFT SKILLS CASE

FROM SCRATCH

Research personal financial management practices. You may wish to use one of the lessons found on CNN Money: http://money.cnn.com/magazines/moneymag/money101/. Then, create a PowerPoint presentation based on your research. Include a title slide and at least five slides related to the topic you have chosen. Choose a theme, transitions, and animations. Insert at least one appropriate clip art image and incorporate a SmartArt diagram into your presentation to better demonstrate your point. Also incorporate WordArt into your presentation. Include slide notes on most slides as necessary and add your sources to the notes. Create a handout header with your name and the current date. Include a handout footer with your instructor's name and your class name. Review the presentation to ensure there are no errors. Save the presentation as **p03b4Money_LastFirst** and submit based on your instructor's directions.

Capstone Exercise

You began a presentation on waterwise landscaping and concentrated on the content of the presentation. You decide to use the SmartArt feature to create infographics to demonstrate a process and to incorporate shapes to demonstrate concepts.

Create a "Fire Aware" Landscape

You decide to create shapes to explain the concept of creating zones to protect a home from fire and indicate the depth of the zones on the landscape. You stack three oval shapes to create the zones, and you use a combination of text boxes and online pictures to create the landscape. Refer to Figure 3.57 as you complete this exercise.

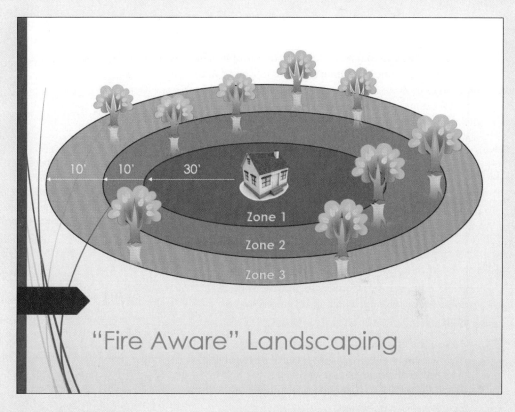

FIGURE 3.57 Fire Aware Landscaping

Photo: aey/Fotolia

a. Open *p03c1Xeri* and save it as **p03c1Xeri_LastFirst**. Create a handout footer with your name and your class.

b. Click **Slide 12**. Insert an oval shape in the approximate center of the blank area of the slide. This will be the center oval in a stack of ovals used to define the zones. Apply the following modifications to the shape:

   - Change the Shape Fill, under more colors, to a custom RGB color: **Red:51, Green:102, and Blue:0**, and a **Transparency** of **50%**.
   - Change the oval size to a height of **1.67"** and width of **5"**.

c. Make a copy of the oval you created in step b. Change the second oval size to a height of **2.92"** and width of **7.08"**.

d. Make a third copy of the oval. Change the third oval size to a height of **4"** and width of **9"**.

e. Select the largest oval and send to back. Select the middle-sized oval and send backward so that the smallest oval is the top layer, followed by the middle and largest ovals.

f. Select all three ovals and **Align Center** and **Align Middle**. Using the *POSITION* section in the Format Shapes Pane, group the three ovals so they will move as one. Position the group at horizontal position **0.58"** from the top-left corner and vertical position **1.33"** from the top-left corner.

g. Insert a text box, type **Zone 1**, and then drag it to the bottom center of the small oval. Apply the **Fill - Sky Blue, Background 2, Inner Shadow WordArt Style** to the text. Make two copies of the text box and edit them to read *Zone 2* and *Zone 3*. Drag **Zone 2** to the bottom center of the medium-sized oval and drag **Zone 3** to the bottom center of the large oval.

h. **Align Center** the text boxes.

i. Locate and insert an online picture of a house, and position it in the center of Zone 1. Size it appropriately.

j. Create an arrow that begins near the left edge of the house image and points left to the edge of the Zone 1 oval (see Figure 3.57). Create another arrow that begins near the end of the first arrow and ends at the edge of the Zone 2 oval, and a similar arrow for Zone 3. Set the weight for the arrows at **1 pt**. Set the arrow color to **White, Background 1**.

k. Create three text boxes and center one above each arrow. Label the Zone 1 text box **30'** and label the Zone 2 and 3 text boxes **10'**. Format the text color to **White, Background 1**.

l. Locate and insert an online picture of a tree. Duplicate it multiple times and position a few trees in Zone 2 and more trees in Zone 3. Position smaller trees toward the top of the zones and larger trees nearer the bottom of the zones. Refer to Figure 3.57, but your tree and tree placement can vary.

Convert Text to SmartArt

To add visual interest to slides, you go through the slide show and convert some of the bulleted lists to SmartArt graphics.

a. Click **Slide 2**. Convert the bulleted text to a **Basic Venn SmartArt graphic**.

b. Click **Slide 3**. Select the **Waterwise Options bulleted text** and convert it to a **Converging Arrow SmartArt graphic**. Apply the following modifications to the graphic:

- Resize the graphic so that the arrows almost touch in the middle to show the convergence of the methods around the theme of conserving water.
- Align the SmartArt diagram in the middle of the horizontal space for *Waterwise Options*.
- Apply the **Polished SmartArt Style** to arrows.

c. Select the **Wildfire Aware Options bulleted text** and convert it to a **Continuous Arrow Process SmartArt graphic** to indicate that the creation of defensible landscaping leads to zones. Apply the **Polished SmartArt Style** and change the text color for each text block in the arrow to **White, Background 1**.

Create SmartArt

You have a list of waterwise landscaping principles that you decide would present well as a SmartArt list.

a. Add a new slide after Slide 12 using a **Title Only layout**.

b. Type **Principles for Waterwise Landscaping** in the **title placeholder**. Change the title font size to **29 pt** and resize the placeholder so the title displays on one line.

c. Insert a text box and type **Tips from the Office of Community Services, Fort Lewis College** inside. Center the text under the title.

d. Insert a **Vertical Bracket List SmartArt** to show the steps, or work flow, in the waterwise landscaping process. Type the text in the following table in the **Text Pane**. The number should be at Level 1, and the process text should be at Level 2.

Number	Process Text
1	Develop Landscape Plan
2	Condition Your Soil
3	Limit Lawn Size
4	Irrigate Efficiently
5	Use Appropriate Plants
6	Apply Mulches
7	Maintain

Convert Text to WordArt

The last graphic you want to insert is a WordArt object. After inserting the WordArt, you will apply an animation scheme.

a. Click **Slide 1** and select the title.

b. Apply the **Pattern Fill - Dark Blue, Accent 3, Narrow Horizontal, Inner Shadow WordArt Style** to the title.

c. Apply the **Fill - Dark Blue, Accent 3, Angle Bevel Style** to the subtitle.

d. Apply the **Fly In animation** to the title and apply the **Fade animation** to the subtitle.

e. Check the spelling in the slide show and accept or correct all spellings on the slide.

f. View the slide show. Save and close the file, and submit based on your instructor's directions.

PowerPoint Rich Media Tools

CHAPTER 4

Konstantin Chagin/Shutterstock

Enhancing with Multimedia

CASE STUDY | Engagement Album

Your sister was recently married. As a gift to the couple, you decide to create two memory slide shows to celebrate. The first slide show will feature images of the couple in a few engagement photos and on their honeymoon in Europe. The second slide show will display photos taken during a family vacation.

As you prepare the first slide show, you edit the images using PowerPoint's Picture Tools. Each slide in the first slide show is created individually, and each image is manipulated individually. You download an image from the Internet representing the couple's honeymoon and insert a video of fireworks recorded by the groom during the honeymoon. You insert a fireworks sound clip and music file to complement the fireworks display. Finally, you create the second slide show, a family vacation, using PowerPoint's Photo Album feature. You utilize the Photo Album options for image manipulation.

Pictures

Multimedia refers to multiple forms of media, such as text, graphics, sound, animation, and video, that are used to entertain or inform an audience. You can use any of these types of media in PowerPoint by placing the multimedia object on a slide. You already have placed text and graphics in presentations, and you have applied animations to objects and transitions to slides. In this chapter, you will expand your experience with multimedia by inserting pictures, sound, and video in slides.

Multimedia graphics include clip art, objects created using drawing programs, diagrams and illustrations, pictures or photographs, scanned images, and more. You have worked extensively with clip art, diagrams, and illustrations. In this section, you will concentrate on pictures.

Pictures are bitmap images that computers can read and interpret to create a photorealistic image. Unlike clip art ***vector images***, which are created by mathematical statements, ***bitmap images*** are created by bits or pixels placed on a grid or map. In a bitmap image, each pixel contains information about the color to be displayed. A bitmap image is required to have the realism necessary for a photograph. Think of vector images as connect-the-dots and bitmap images as paint-by-number, and you begin to see the difference in the methods of representation.

Each type of image has its own advantages and disadvantages. Vector graphics can be sized easily and still retain their clarity but are not photorealistic. Bitmap images represent a much more complex range of colors and shades but can become pixelated (individual pixels are visible and display square edges for a "jaggies" effect) when they are enlarged. A bitmap image can also be a large file, so ***compression***, a method applied to data to reduce the amount of space required for file storage, may be applied. The compression may be lossy (some data may be lost when decompressed) or lossless (no data is lost when decompressed).

TIP | Compression: Lossy Versus Lossless

Depending on the image's use, you may want to choose a specific image format so that images don't appear pixelated when enlarged. Certain formats can be either lossy or lossless. Lossy compression reduces a file by permanently eliminating certain data, especially redundant data. This makes the file size smaller. However, when the file is uncompressed, only a part of the original data is still there. Pixelation may not even be noticeable for certain image uses, so it might not be an issue. The JPEG image file, a common format, is an image that has lossy compression.

Alternatively, with lossless compression, data that was originally in the file remains after the file is uncompressed. All of the information is completely restored. The Graphics Interchange File (GIF) is an image format that provides lossless compression.

Figure 4.1 displays a pumpkin created as a vector image and one created as a bitmap image. Note the differences in realism. The boxes show a portion of the images enlarged. Note the pixilation, or jaggedness, in the enlarged portion of the bitmap image.

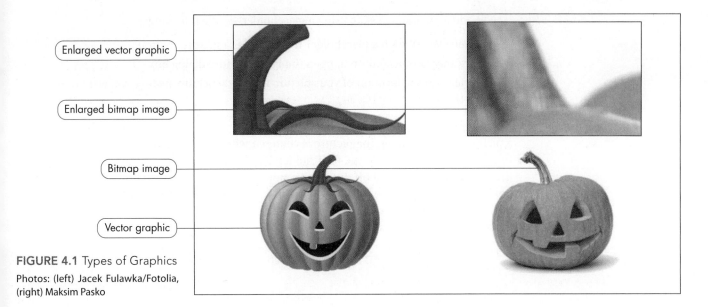

FIGURE 4.1 Types of Graphics
Photos: (left) Jacek Fulawka/Fotolia, (right) Maksim Pasko

Labels on figure:
- Enlarged vector graphic
- Enlarged bitmap image
- Bitmap image
- Vector graphic

Inserting a Picture

PowerPoint does not have to be all bullets; a good image can be more memorable than a simple list of words. You can accomplish this task by scanning and saving a photograph or piece of artwork, by downloading images from a digital camera, by downloading a previously created bitmap image from Office.com Clip Art or the Internet, or by creating an image in a graphics-editing software package like Adobe Photoshop. Table 4.1 displays the types of graphic file formats that you can add to a PowerPoint slide in alphabetical order by file extension.

TABLE 4.1 Types of Graphic File Formats Supported by PowerPoint

File Format	Extension	Description
Windows Bitmap (Device Independent Bitmap)	.bmp, .dib	A representation consisting of rows and columns of dots. The value of each dot is stored in one or more bits of data. Uncompressed and creates large file size.
Windows Enhanced Metafile	.emf, .wmf	A Windows 32-bit file format.
Graphics Interchange Format	.gif	Limited to 256 colors. Effective for scanned images such as illustrations rather than for color photographs. Good for line drawings and black-and-white images. Supports transparent backgrounds.
Joint Photographic Experts Group	.jpg, .jpeg	Supports 16 million colors and is optimized for photographs and complex graphics. Format of choice for most photographs on the Web. Uses lossy compression.
Macintosh PICT	.pict, .pic, .pct	Holds both vector and bitmap images. PICT supports 8 colors; PICT2 supports 16 million colors.
Portable Network Graphics	.png	Supports 16 million colors. Approved as a standard by the World Wide Web Consortium (W3C). Intended to replace .gif format. Uses lossy compression.
Tagged Image File Format	.tif, .tiff	Best file format for storing bitmapped images on personal computers. Can be any resolution. Lossless image storage creates large file sizes. Not widely supported by browsers.
Microsoft Windows Metafile	.wmf	A Windows 16-bit file format.

STEP 1 »

To add a picture to a slide using a placeholder, do the following:

1. Select a layout with a placeholder that includes a Pictures button.
2. Click the Pictures button to open the Insert Picture dialog box.
3. Navigate to the location of your picture files and click the picture you want to use.
4. Click Insert.

Figure 4.2 shows two examples of placeholders with Pictures buttons. When you insert a picture in this manner, the picture is centered within the placeholder frame and is sometimes cropped to fit within the placeholder. This effect can cause unwanted results, such as the tops of heads cropped off. If this situation occurs, undo the insertion, enlarge the placeholder, and then repeat the steps for inserting an image. Use this method sparingly, however, because any changes you make to the slide master or theme may not appear correctly once those changes are applied.

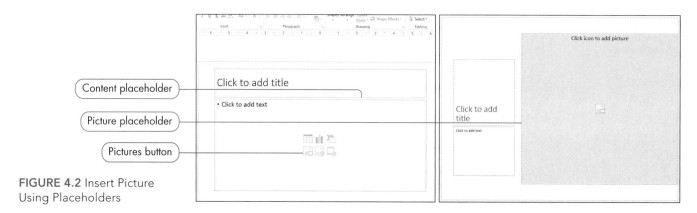

FIGURE 4.2 Insert Picture Using Placeholders

Another way to insert an image is to click Pictures on the Insert tab. The advantage of this method is that your image comes in at full size rather than centered and cropped in a placeholder, and you do not need a picture placeholder. You can then resize the image to fit the desired area. The disadvantage is the time you spend resizing and positioning the image.

To add a picture using the Insert tab, do the following:

1. Click the INSERT tab.
2. Click Pictures in the Images group.
3. Navigate to the location of your picture files and click the picture you want to use.
4. Click Insert.
5. Adjust the size and position of the picture as necessary.

TIP | Adding Images Using File Explorer

If you are adding multiple images to a slide show, you can speed up the process by inserting images directly from File Explorer. Open File Explorer and navigate to the folder where the images are located. Position the File Explorer window next to the PowerPoint window and drag the images from the Explorer window onto the slides of your choice.

Transforming a Picture

Once you insert a picture onto a slide, PowerPoint provides powerful tools that you can use to adjust the image. Found on the Picture Tools Format tab (see Figure 4.3), Picture Tools are designed to adjust an image background, correct image problems, manipulate image color, or add artistic or stylized effects. You can also arrange, crop, or resize an image using Picture

Tools. Additionally, when you right-click on the picture and select Format Picture, you will open the Format Picture task pane, where you can also access these same tools.

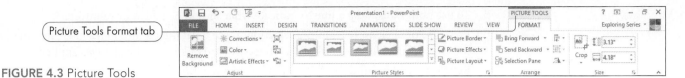

Picture Tools Format tab

FIGURE 4.3 Picture Tools

Remove a Picture Background

The Remove Background tool in the Adjust group on the Format tab enables you to remove portions of a picture you do not want to keep. Rather than have a rectangle-shaped picture on your slide, you can have an image that flows into the slide. When you select a picture and click the Remove Background tool, PowerPoint creates an automatic marquee selection area in the picture that determines the *background*, or area to be removed, and the *foreground*, or area to be kept. PowerPoint identifies the background selection with magenta coloring. You can then adjust PowerPoint's automatic selection by marking areas you want to keep, marking areas you want to remove, and deleting any markings you do not want. You can discard any changes you have made or keep your changes. Figure 4.4 shows a picture in which the Remove Background tool has created a marquee identifying the foreground and background.

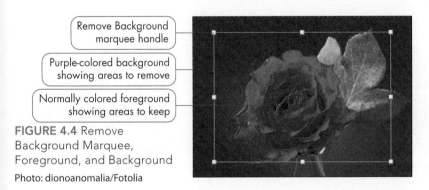

Remove Background marquee handle

Purple-colored background showing areas to remove

Normally colored foreground showing areas to keep

FIGURE 4.4 Remove Background Marquee, Foreground, and Background

Photo: dionoanomalia/Fotolia

Once the background has been identified by the marquee, you can refine the marquee size and shape so that it contains everything you want to keep without extra areas. To resize the marquee:

1. Drag a marquee handle (the same process you use to resize clip art).
2. Refine the picture further by using the tools available on the Background Removal tab (see Figure 4.5).

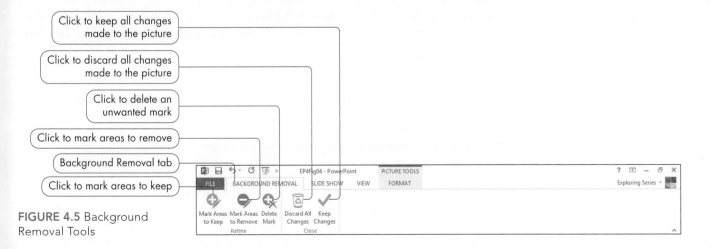

Click to keep all changes made to the picture

Click to discard all changes made to the picture

Click to delete an unwanted mark

Click to mark areas to remove

Background Removal tab

Click to mark areas to keep

FIGURE 4.5 Background Removal Tools

3. Use the *Mark Areas to Keep* tool to add to the foreground, which keeps the area.

4. Use the *Mark Areas to Remove* tool to add to the background, which eliminates the area.

5. To use both tools, drag a line to indicate what should be added or removed.

6. Press Esc or click away from the selection to see what the picture looks like. Note that the thumbnail also shows what the image will look like with the changes applied.

7. Return to Background Removal and continue working with your picture. Figure 4.6 shows a resized marquee with enlarged areas marked to show areas to keep and to remove. Figure 4.7 shows the flower picture with the background removed.

Line used to determine areas of picture to remove

Resized marquee

Line used to determine areas of picture to keep

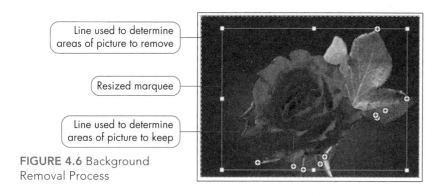

FIGURE 4.6 Background Removal Process

FIGURE 4.7 Background Removed from Flower

Correct a Picture

PowerPoint 2013 includes Corrections, a set of tools in the Adjust group. As well as being able to adjust brightness and contrast as in previous versions, you can now soften or sharpen a picture. You can see what a correction will look like by previewing it in Live Preview.

You can enhance a picture by *sharpening* it—bringing out the detail by making the boundaries of the content more prominent. Or you may want to *soften* the content—blur the edges so the boundaries are less prominent. Sharpening a picture can make it clearer, but oversharpening can make the picture look grainy. Softening is a technique often used for a more romantic image or to make skin appear softer, but applying too much blur can make the picture difficult to see.

STEP 2 »

To sharpen or soften a picture, do the following:

1. Select the picture.

2. Click the FORMAT tab.

3. Click Corrections in the Adjust group.

4. Point to the thumbnails in the *Sharpen/Soften* section to view the corrections in Live Preview.

5. Click the thumbnail to apply the degree of correction you want.

You can make fine adjustments to the amount of sharpness and softness you apply to a picture. To make adjustments, follow Steps 1–3 on the previous page and click Picture Corrections Options at the bottom of the gallery. The Format Picture pane opens. Drag the *Sharpness* slider or enter a percentage in the box next to the slider. Figure 4.8 shows the Corrections gallery, a picture that has been softened, and a picture that has been sharpened.

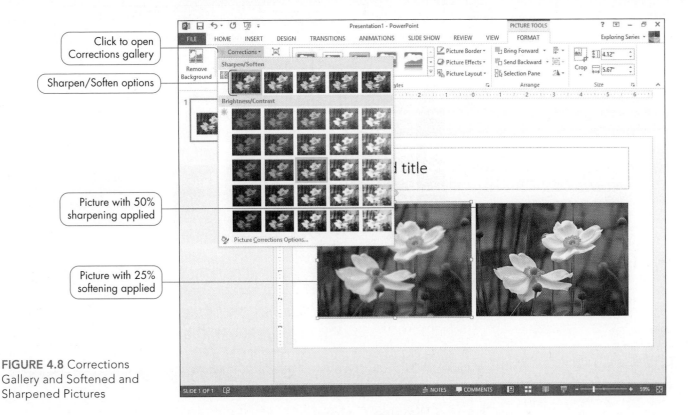

FIGURE 4.8 Corrections Gallery and Softened and Sharpened Pictures

The **brightness** (lightness or darkness) of a picture is often a matter of individual preference. You might need to change the brightness of your picture for reasons other than preference, however. For example, sometimes printing a picture requires a different brightness than is needed when projecting an image. This situation occurs because during printing, the ink may spread when placed on the page, making the picture darker. Or, you might want a picture as a background and need to reduce the brightness so that text will show on the background.

Contrast refers to the difference between the darkest area (black level) and lightest area (white level). If the contrast is not set correctly, your picture can look washed out or muddy; too much contrast, and the light portion of your image will appear to explode off the screen or page. Your setting may vary depending on whether you are going to project the image or print it. Projecting impacts an image because of the light in the room. In a very light room, the image may seem to need a greater contrast than in a darker room, and you may need to adjust the contrast accordingly. Try to set your control for the lighting that will appear when you display the presentation.

To adjust the brightness and contrast of a picture, do the following:

1. Select the picture.
2. Click the FORMAT tab.
3. Click Corrections in the Adjust group.
4. Point to the thumbnails in the *Brightness/Contrast* section to view the corrections in Live Preview.
5. Click the thumbnail to apply the degree of correction you want.

You can make fine adjustments to the amount of brightness or contrast you apply. To make adjustments, follow Steps 1–3 above and click Picture Corrections Options at the bottom of the gallery. The Format Picture task pane opens. Drag the Brightness and Contrast sliders until you get the result you want or enter percentages in the boxes next to the sliders. Figure 4.9 shows the Corrections gallery displaying the original picture as well as the same picture that has been adjusted for brightness.

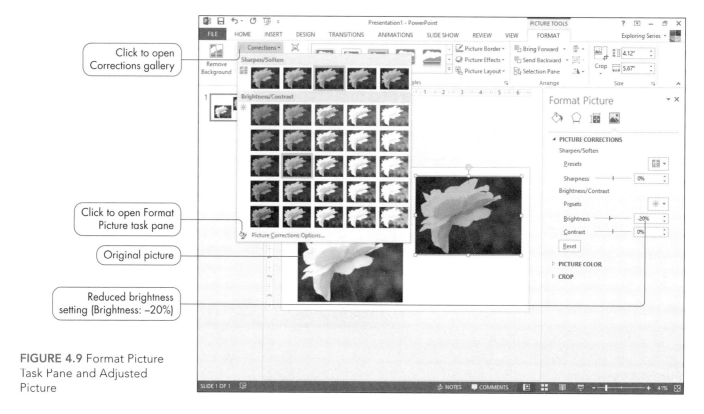

FIGURE 4.9 Format Picture Task Pane and Adjusted Picture

Change Picture Color

You can change the colors in your picture by using PowerPoint's color tools. To access the color tools, do the following:

1. Select the picture.
2. Click the FORMAT tab.
3. Click Color in the Adjust group.
4. Point to the thumbnails in the gallery to view the corrections in Live Preview.
5. Click the thumbnail to apply the color effect you want.

You can change a picture's *saturation* or the intensity of the colors in an image. A high saturation level makes the colors more vivid, whereas 0% saturation converts the picture to grayscale. Figure 4.10 shows a picture at its original (100%) intensity and with various levels of intensity.

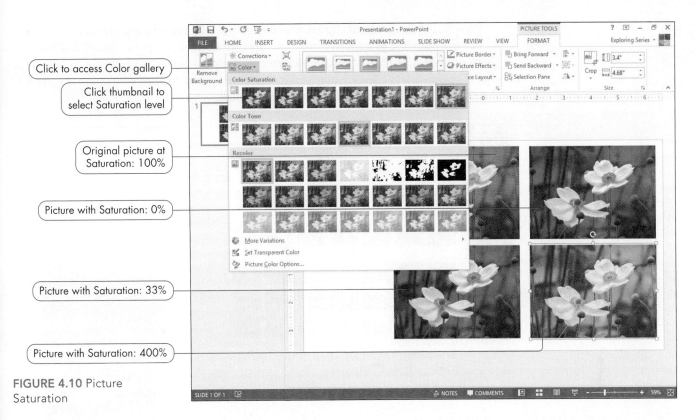

Click to access Color gallery

Click thumbnail to select Saturation level

Original picture at Saturation: 100%

Picture with Saturation: 0%

Picture with Saturation: 33%

Picture with Saturation: 400%

FIGURE 4.10 Picture Saturation

The *tone*, or temperature, of a color is a characteristic of lighting in pictures. It is measured in *kelvin* (K) units of absolute temperature. Lower color temperatures are cool colors and appear blueish white, whereas higher color temperatures are warm colors and appear yellowish to red. PowerPoint enables you to increase or decrease a picture's temperature to enhance its details. Point to a thumbnail to see the amount of temperature in Kelvin units that would be applied. Figure 4.11 shows a picture with its original cooler tone and a copy of the picture at a higher temperature with a warmer tone.

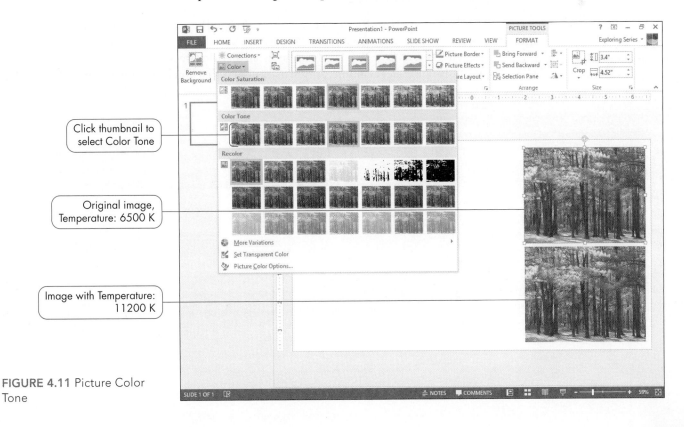

Click thumbnail to select Color Tone

Original image, Temperature: 6500 K

Image with Temperature: 11200 K

FIGURE 4.11 Picture Color Tone

Previously, you *recolored* clip art illustrations by changing multiple colors to two colors. You can use the same process to recolor pictures. You can click a preset thumbnail from the gallery or click More Variations to pick from additional colors. To return a picture to its original color, click the No Recolor preset thumbnail under the *Recolor* section. Figure 4.12 shows a picture with the Sepia Recolor preset applied.

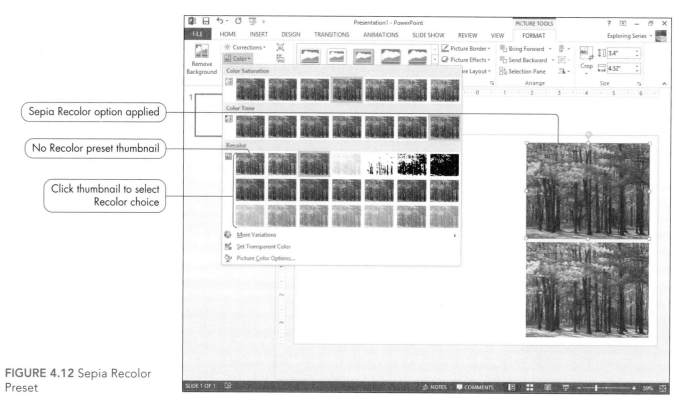

FIGURE 4.12 Sepia Recolor Preset

Use Artistic Effects

PowerPoint's artistic effects enable you to change the appearance of a picture so that it looks like it was created with a marker, as a pencil sketch or watercolor painting, or using other effects. Use Live Preview to see how an artistic effect changes your picture. You can apply only one effect at a time. Any artistic effects that you have previously applied are lost when you apply a new effect. Figure 4.13 shows a Glow Edges artistic effect applied to a picture.

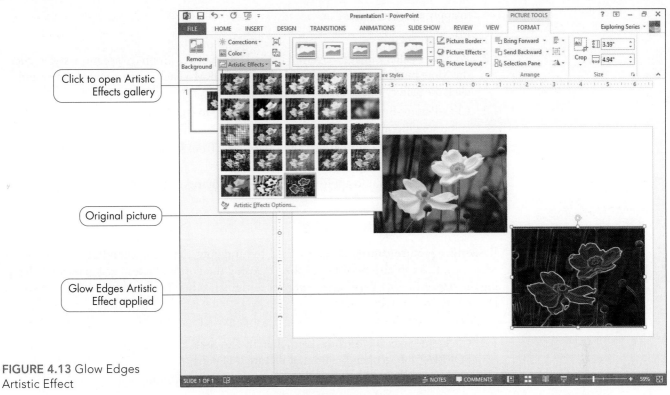

Click to open Artistic Effects gallery

Original picture

Glow Edges Artistic Effect applied

FIGURE 4.13 Glow Edges Artistic Effect

STEP 3 ▸▸

To use an artistic effect, do the following:

1. Select the picture.
2. Click the FORMAT tab.
3. Click Artistic Effects in the Adjust group.
4. Point to the thumbnails in the gallery to view the artistic effects in Live Preview.
5. Click the thumbnail of the artistic effect you want to use.

Apply Picture Styles

With Picture Styles, you can surround your picture with attractive frames, soften the edges of pictures, add shadows to the edges of pictures, apply 3-D effects to pictures, and add glossy reflections below your pictures. Many other effects are possible with Picture Styles, and when you consider that each of these effects can be modified, your creative opportunities are endless! Figure 4.14 shows a few of the possibilities.

Snip Diagonal Corner, White Picture Style applied

Bevel Perspective Left, White Picture Style applied

Metal Oval Picture Style Applied

FIGURE 4.14 Picture Style Applications

To apply a picture style:

1. Select the picture.
2. Point to a gallery image displayed in the Picture Styles group (to see more styles, click the More button) on the PICTURE TOOLS FORMAT tab to see a Live Preview and click the gallery image to select the picture style.
3. Click Picture Border in the Picture Styles group to enable you to select your border color, weight, or dash style.
4. You can use the Picture Effects option to select from Preset, Shadow, Reflection, Glow, Soft Edges, Bevel, and 3-D Rotation effects.
5. Use Picture Layout to apply your picture to a SmartArt diagram.

Resize or Crop a Picture

Resizing a picture can be accomplished by dragging the sizing handles for the image. Moreover, this can also be accomplished by using the Format Picture task pane and changing the size of the picture to a percent of the original. When *Lock aspect ratio* is checked, the image is resized proportionally.

To resize a picture:

1. Click the Size Dialog Box Launcher in the Size group on the PICTURE TOOLS FORMAT tab to open the Format Picture task pane.
2. Click in the Scale Height or Scale Width box, select 100, and then type the new size.

Cropping a picture using the Crop tool lets you eliminate unwanted portions of an image, focusing the viewer's attention on what you want him or her to see. Remember that if you crop an image and try to enlarge the resulting picture, pixelation may occur that reduces the quality of the image. Figure 4.15 shows a picture with the areas to be cropped from view displayed in gray.

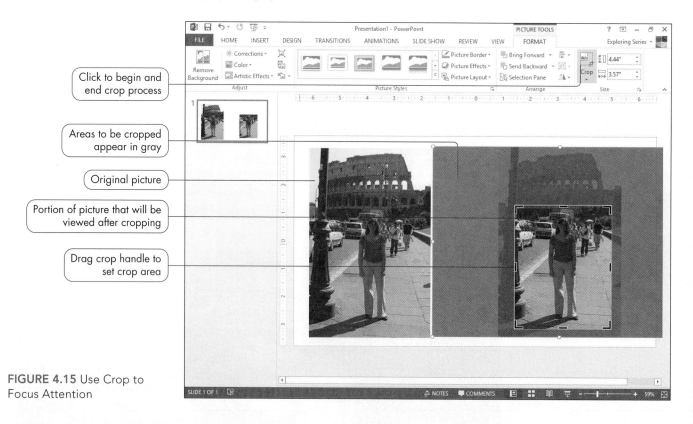

FIGURE 4.15 Use Crop to Focus Attention

To crop a picture, do the following:

1. Select the picture.
2. Click the FORMAT tab.
3. Click Crop in the Size group.
4. Position the mouse pointer over a cropping handle and drag inward to eliminate the portion of the image you do not want to view. Use a corner handle to crop in two directions at once.
5. Repeat Step 4 for the remaining sides of the picture.
6. Click Crop again to toggle it off.

When you crop a picture, the cropped portion does not display on the slide, but it is not removed from the presentation file. This is helpful in case you decide later to reset the picture to its original state. When you crop an image, because the unwanted portions of the image are not deleted, the file size is not reduced. Use the Compress Pictures feature to reduce the file size of the image, or all images at once, to reduce the file size of the presentation.

Compress Pictures

When you add pictures to your PowerPoint presentation, especially high-resolution pictures downloaded from a digital camera, the presentation file size dramatically increases. It may increase to the point that the presentation becomes slow to load and sluggish to play. The increase in the file size depends on the resolution of the pictures you add. Use the Compress Pictures feature to eliminate a large part of this problem. The Compress Pictures feature is in the Adjust group on the Picture Tools Format tab.

The Compress Pictures feature can help you manage large image files by changing the resolution of pictures and by permanently deleting any cropped areas of a selected picture. By default, you apply compression to only the selected image. If you remove the check, all pictures in the presentation are compressed. You select the amount of compression applied by determining your output. Select 220 pixels per inch (ppi) to ensure you will obtain a good quality printout. Select 150 ppi, however, if you will be displaying the slide show only onscreen or using it for a Web page. Select 96 ppi if you plan to e-mail the slide show. Figure 4.16 shows the Compress Pictures dialog box.

Click to open Compress Pictures dialog box

Compression applied only to the selected image

FIGURE 4.16 Picture Compression Options

Create a Background from a Picture

Pictures can make appealing backgrounds if they are transparent enough that text on top of them can be easily read. Picture backgrounds personalize your presentation. To use a photograph as a background, use the Format Background command rather than the Insert Picture feature. Using Insert Picture involves more time because when the picture is inserted it must be resized and the order of the objects on the screen has to be changed to prevent the photograph from hiding placeholders. Figure 4.17 shows an image inserted using Insert Picture that must be resized if it is to be used as a background. It hides the placeholders, so it needs to be positioned at the back and its transparency must be adjusted. Figure 4.18 shows the same picture as Figure 4.17, but in this figure, it was inserted as a background. It is automatically placed behind placeholders and resized to fit the slide, and the transparency is adjusted.

If the background image is too busy or not transparent enough, it can make the presentation difficult to read or distract the audience. You may need to test several images and settings if its color does not contrast enough with the text.

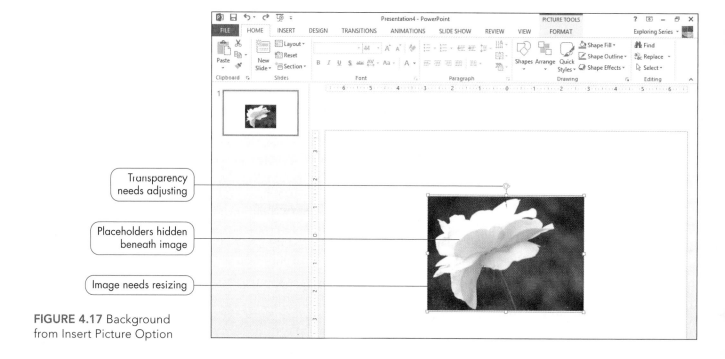

FIGURE 4.17 Background from Insert Picture Option

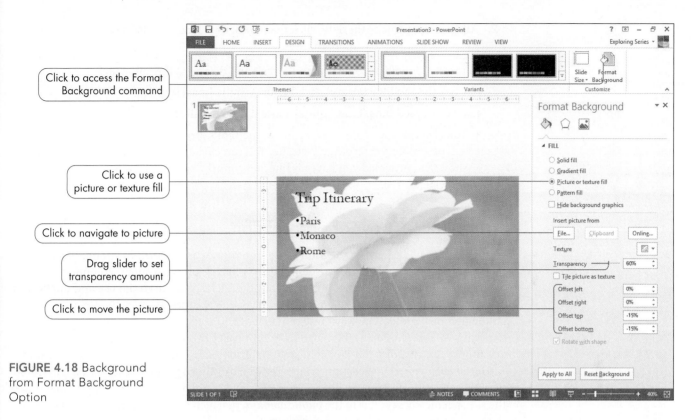

Click to access the Format Background command

Click to use a picture or texture fill

Click to navigate to picture

Drag slider to set transparency amount

Click to move the picture

FIGURE 4.18 Background from Format Background Option

To create a background from a picture using the Background command, do the following:

1. Click the DESIGN tab.
2. Click Format Background in the Customize group. The Format Background task pane displays.
3. Click *Picture or texture fill*.
4. Click File and navigate to the location where your picture is stored.
5. Click the picture file and click Insert.
6. Adjust the transparency for the picture.
7. Click Close to apply the picture background to the current slide or click *Apply to All* to apply it to all slides in the presentation.

The task pane also includes options for moving the picture by offsetting it to the left or right or the top or bottom, and for adjusting the transparency amount.

Using the Internet as a Resource

In this chapter, you will use the Internet as a resource for pictures, video, and audio. PowerPoint interacts with the Internet in three important ways:

1. You can download resources from any Web page for inclusion in a PowerPoint presentation. Note, however, that some images may not be used without permission or license from the creator.
2. You can insert hyperlinks into a PowerPoint presentation and click those links to display the associated Web page in your browser.
3. You can convert any PowerPoint presentation into a Web page.

STEP 5 >>   Regardless of how you choose to use a photograph, your first task is to locate the required image. To download an image:

1. Right-click the image to display a shortcut menu and select Save Picture As to save the file. (This command may vary among Web broswers.)

2. Alternatively, when you right-click the photograph, you can also select Copy to copy the picture onto the Clipboard.

To insert a downloaded picture in PowerPoint, do any of the following:

- Click the INSERT tab and click Pictures in the Images group.
- If you copied the picture, simply paste it onto the slide.
- You also can click Insert Hyperlink in the Links group on the INSERT tab to insert a hyperlink to the resource Web site. You can click the hyperlink during the slide show, and provided you have an Internet connection, your browser will display the associated page.

Understand Copyright Protection

A *copyright* provides legal protection to a written or artistic work, including literary, dramatic, musical, and artistic works such as poetry, novels, movies, songs, computer software, and architecture. It gives the author of a work the exclusive right to the use and duplication of that work. A copyright does not protect facts, ideas, systems, or methods of operation, although it may protect the way these things are expressed.

The owner of the copyright may sell or give up a portion of his or her rights; for example, an author may give distribution rights to a publisher and/or grant movie rights to a studio. *Infringement of copyright* occurs anytime a right held by the copyright owner is violated without permission of the owner. Anything on the Internet should be considered copyrighted unless the site specifically says it is in the *public domain*, in which case the author is giving everyone the right to freely reproduce and distribute the material, thereby making the work owned by the public at large. A work also may enter the public domain when the copyright has expired. Facts themselves are not covered by copyright, so you can use statistical data without fear of infringement. Images are protected unless the owner gives his or her permission for downloading.

TIP Using Media Elements

Photos, clip art, fonts, sounds, and videos available from Microsoft and its partners through Office.com are part of Microsoft's Media Elements and are copyright protected by Microsoft. To see what uses of Media Elements are prohibited, go to http://www.office.com and search for *What Uses of Photos, Clip Art, and Font Images are Prohibited?*

The answer to what you can use from the Web depends on many things, including the amount of the information you reference, as well as the intended use of that information. It is considered fair use, and thus not an infringement of copyright, to use a portion of a work for educational or nonprofit purposes, or for critical review or commentary. In other words, you can use quotes, facts, or other information from the Web in an educational setting, but you should cite the original work in your footnotes, or list the resource on a bibliography page or slide. The following reference table presents guidelines for students and teachers to help determine what multimedia can be used in an educational project based on the Proposal for Fair Use Guidelines for Educational Multimedia created in 1996. These guidelines were created by a group of publishers, authors, and educators who gathered to interpret the Copyright Act of 1976 as it applies to educational and scholarly uses of multimedia. You should note that although these guidelines are part of the Congressional Record, they are not law. They can, however, help you determine when you can use multimedia materials under Fair Use principles in a noncommercial, educational use.

REFERENCE Multimedia Copyright Guidelines for Students and Teachers

The following guidelines are based on Section 107 of the U.S. Copyright Act of 1976 and the Proposal for Fair Use Guidelines for Educational Multimedia (1996), which sets forth fair use factors for multimedia projects. These guidelines cover the use of multimedia based on Time, Portion, and Copying and Distribution Limitations. For the complete text of the guidelines, see www.uspto.gov/web/offices/dcom/olia/confu/confurep.pdf.

General Guidelines

- Student projects for specific courses may be displayed and kept in personal portfolios as examples of their academic work.
- Students in specific courses may use multimedia in projects with proper credit and citations. Full bibliographic information must be used when available.
- Students and teachers must display copyright notice if copyright ownership information is shown on the original source. Copyright may be shown in a sources or bibliographic section unless the presentation is being used for distance learning. In distance learning situations, copyright must appear on the screen when the image is viewed.
- Teachers may use media for face-to-face curriculum-based instruction, for directed self-study, in demonstrations on how to create multimedia productions, for presentations at conferences, and for distance learning. Teachers may also retain projects in their personal portfolios for personal use such as job interviews or tenure review.
- Teachers may use multimedia projects for educational purposes for up to two years, after which permission of the copyright holder is required.
- Students and teachers do not need to write for permission to use media if it falls under multimedia guidelines unless there is a possibility that the project could be broadly distributed at a later date.

Text Guidelines

- Up to 10 percent of a copyrighted work, or up to 1,000 words, may be used, whichever is less.
- Up to 250 words of a poem, but no more than five poems (or excerpts) from different poets or an anthology. No more than three poems (or excerpts) from a single poet.

Illustrations

- A photograph or illustration may be used in its entirety.
- Up to 15 images, but no more than 15 images from a collection.
- No more than 5 images of an artist's or photographer's work.

Motion Media

- Up to 10 percent of a copyrighted work or 3 minutes, whichever is less.
- Clip cannot be altered in any way.

Music and Sound

- Up to 10 percent of a copyrighted musical composition, not to exceed 30 seconds.
- Up to 10 percent of a sound recording, not to exceed 30 seconds.
- Alterations cannot change the basic melody or fundamental character of the work.

Distribution Limitations

- Multimedia projects should not be posted to unsecured Web sites.
- No more than two copies of the original may be made, only one of which may be placed on reserve for instructional purposes.
- A copy of a project may be made for backup purposes, but may be used only when the original has been lost, damaged, or stolen.
- If more than one person created a project, each person may keep only one copy.

In the following Hands-On Exercise, you will insert pictures (bitmap images) into slides, both with and the use of content placeholders. You will use Picture Tools to remove a background from an image, to soften and sharpen an image, and to adjust the brightness, contrast, saturation, and tone of a picture. You will apply a picture style and modify its effects. You will crop a picture and compress all the images in the slide show. You will also create a background for a slide from a picture. Finally, you will learn about using the Internet as a resource for images and review the Fair Use guidelines relating to student use of media downloaded from the Internet. You will download a picture from the Internet and insert the picture into a slide show.

Quick Concepts

1. What is the difference between bitmap images and vector graphics? Name one advantage and disadvantage of each type of graphic. **p. 248**

2. Why would you compress an image? **p. 259**

3. List five ways to transform an image by using PowerPoint's Picture Tools. **p. 250**

4. What is infringement of copyright? What is "fair use?" **p. 262**

Hands-On Exercises

Watch the Video
for this Hands-
On Exercise!

MyITLab®
HOE1 Training

1 Pictures

You decide to create a memories slide show for your sister and her husband, who were recently married. You include their engagement and honeymoon pictures.

Skills covered: Insert Pictures and Remove a Background • Correct a Picture and Change Picture Color • Apply an Artistic Effect and a Picture Style • Create a Background from a Picture, Crop and Compress • Insert a Picture from the Internet

STEP 1 ≫ INSERT PICTURES AND REMOVE A BACKGROUND

You start the memory album with a picture from the couple's engagement. Because the Title Slide layout does not include a placeholder for content, you add a picture using the *Insert Picture from File* feature. You then insert images into content placeholders provided in the album layout. Refer to Figure 4.19 as you complete Step 1.

Steps e–f: Resized and positioned image

Step g–i: Image inserted and background removed

AMY AND DAN | September 9th

Steps m–n: Images inserted using content placeholders

FIGURE 4.19 Inserted Pictures

a. Open *p04h1Memory* and save it as **p04h1Memory_LastFirst**.

> **TROUBLESHOOTING:** If you make any major mistakes in this exercise, you can close the file, open *p04h1Memory* again, and then start this exercise over.

b. Create a handout header with your name and a handout footer with your instructor's name and your class. Apply to all slides. Include the current date.

c. On Slide 1, click the **INSERT tab** and click **Pictures** in the Images group.

   You add a picture using the Insert Picture command because the Title Slide layout does not include a placeholder for content. The Insert Picture dialog box opens.

d. Locate the *p04h1Mem1.jpg* picture in the *p04h1Memory_Media* folder and click **Insert**.

   The picture is inserted and centered on the slide.

e. Click the **Size Dialog Box Launcher** in the Size group on the FORMAT tab to open the Format Picture task pane. Click in the **Scale Height box**, select **100**, and then type **96**. Press **Enter**.

   Typing 96 in the Scale Height box automatically sets the Scale Width to 96% because the *Lock aspect ratio* check box is selected.

f. Click **POSITION** in the Format Picture task pane and set the **Horizontal Position** to **1.00"** from the Top Left Corner. Set the **Vertical Position** to **0.11"** from the Top Left Corner. Click the **Close (X) button**.

g. Click the **INSERT tab**, click **Pictures** in the Images group, and then locate and insert *p04h1Mem2.jpg*.

h. Click **Remove Background** in the Adjust group on the FORMAT tab.

   A marquee that includes most of the flower appears around the image. Some petals are cut off and need to be added back in.

i. Drag the left-center, left-bottom, and right-center sizing handles of the marquee as necessary until all petals and the stem are included in the picture (see Figure 4.20).

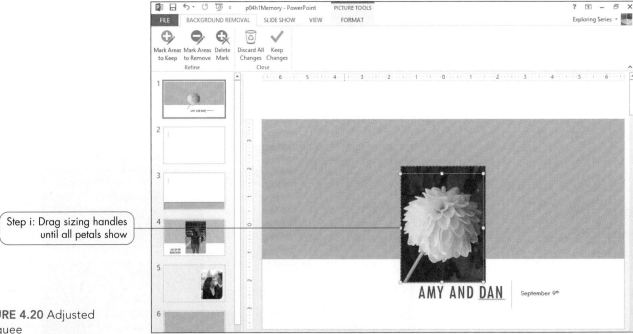

Step i: Drag sizing handles until all petals show

FIGURE 4.20 Adjusted Marquee

j. Click **Keep Changes** in the Close group on the BACKGROUND REMOVAL tab.

   The background is removed from the flower.

k. Click the **Size Dialog Box Launcher** in the Size group to open the Format Picture task pane and remove the check in the **Relative to original picture size check box** in the *SIZE* section. Click in the **Scale Height box** and type **50**. Press **Enter**.

l. Click **POSITION** in the Format Picture task pane, if necessary, and set the **Horizontal Position** to **11.59"** from the Top Left Corner. Set the **Vertical Position** to **4.79"** from the Top Left Corner. Click the **Close (X) button** to close the Format Picture task pane.

The flower is now positioned in the right lower section of the slide. Refer to Figure 4.19.

m. Click **Slide 2**. Click **Pictures** in the large content placeholder on the left side of the slide. Click the *p04h1Mem3.jpg* file to select it and click **Insert**.

n. Use the Pictures buttons in the two small content placeholders on the right side of the screen to insert *p04h1Mem4.jpg* and *p04h1Mem5.jpg* into your presentation.

Note that the images were centered inside the placeholders.

o. Save the presentation.

STEP 2 » CORRECT A PICTURE AND CHANGE PICTURE COLOR

You want to include two pictures of the couple in the memory album, but the pictures were taken in different lighting conditions. You decide to use PowerPoint's correction tools to enhance the pictures. You also change the color tone of a picture to warm it up to match the warm color of the background graphic color on the slide where it appears. Refer to Figure 4.21 as you complete Step 2.

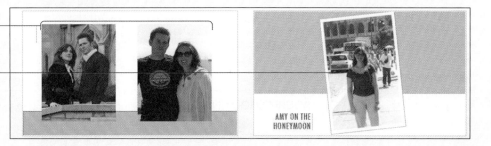

Steps b–c: Apply Brightness/Contrast

Steps e–f: Adjust temperature and apply picture style

FIGURE 4.21 Picture Correction and Color Tone Adjustment

a. Click **Slide 3**. Click the **Pictures button** in the content placeholders to insert *p04h1Mem6.jpg* into the left placeholder and *p04h1Mem7.jpg* into the right placeholder.

b. Select the image on the left and click **Corrections** in the Adjust group on the FORMAT tab. Click **Brightness: –20% Contrast: +20%** (fourth row, second column of the *Brightness/Contrast* section).

The image becomes slightly darker, and the increased contrast brings out the picture detail.

c. Select the image on the right and click **Corrections** in the Adjust group on the FORMAT tab. Click **Brightness: –20% Contrast: 0% (Normal)** (third row, second column of the *Brightness/Contrast* section).

The image becomes more contrasted, and the brightness is reduced.

d. Click **Slide 4** and select the picture of the woman.

e. Click **Color** in the Adjust group and click **Temperature: 11200 K** in the Color Tone gallery. Next, click **Corrections** in the Adjust group and click **Brightness: +40% Contrast: 0%** (third row, fifth column).

The cooler tones in the image are converted to warmer tones, which casts a gold hue over the picture. The picture is also brighter, emphasizing the colosseum in the background.

f. Click the **More button** in the Picture Styles group and click **Rotated, White**.

g. Save the presentation.

STEP 3 » APPLY AN ARTISTIC EFFECT AND A PICTURE STYLE

The title slide includes a picture of the couple that you want to stand out. The Artistic Effects gallery includes many picture effects, and the Picture Styles gallery includes a variety of Picture Border effects. You decide to experiment with the options available in the galleries to see the impact they have on the title slide picture. You also apply an artistic effect. Refer to Figure 4.22 as you complete Step 3.

Steps c–e: Artistic effects and picture styles applied to image

Steps f–i: Artistic effects and picture styles applied to image

AMY AND DAN | September 9th

FIGURE 4.22 Applied Artistic Effect and Picture Styles

a. Click **Slide 1**, select the picture of the couple, and then click the **FORMAT tab**, if necessary.

b. Click **Artistic Effects** in the Adjust group.

The Artistic Effects gallery opens. Point to the effects and watch how each effect impacts the image.

> **TROUBLESHOOTING:** Some of the artistic effects involve extensive changes, so expect a slowdown as the preview is created.

c. Click **Texturizer** (fourth row, second column).

A light texture is applied to the picture.

d. Click the **More button** in the Picture Styles group.

The Picture Styles gallery opens. Point to the styles and watch how each style impacts the image.

e. Click **Center Shadow Rectangle**.

A gray shadow displays evenly around the picture.

f. Click the **HOME tab**, click **Format Painter** in the Clipboard group, and then click the **flower picture**.

You copied the artistic effect and picture style and applied them to the flower.

g. Select the picture of the couple again and click the **FORMAT tab**.

h. Click **Picture Border** in the Picture Styles group and click **Brown, Text 2** (first row, fourth column) in the *Theme Colors* section.

i. Click **Picture Effects** in the Picture Styles group, point to *Bevel*, and then click **Cool Slant** (first row, fourth column of the *Bevel* section).

The Bevel effect is applied to the outer edges of the picture.

j. Save the presentation.

STEP 4 >> CREATE A BACKGROUND FROM A PICTURE, CROP, AND COMPRESS

The honeymooners stayed in a suite with a gorgeous view of a garden, and you want to include a picture of one of the flowers as the background setting of a picture of the honeymooners. Refer to Figure 4.23 as you complete Step 4.

Steps b–e: Fill background with picture

Steps h–j: Crop the image

FIGURE 4.23 Background from a Picture

a. Click the **DESIGN tab**.

b. Click **Slide 5** and click **Format Background** in the Customize group.

  The Format Background task pane displays.

c. Click the **Hide background graphics check box** in the Format Background task pane.

d. Click **Picture or texture fill** and click **File** to open the Insert Picture dialog box.

e. Select *p04h1Mem8.jpg*, click **Insert**, and then close the Format Background task pane.

f. Examine the picture on the far right of the slide.

g. Click the **VIEW tab** and click **Ruler** in the Show group, if necessary.

  Activating the ruler will make it easier for you to determine the area to crop.

h. Select the picture, click the **FORMAT tab**, and then click **Crop** in the Size group.

i. Drag the top-left corner down and to the right until the vertical ruler reaches approximately the +2 1/2" mark and the horizontal ruler reaches approximately the +2" mark.

  The resulting size of the image is 5.81" high and 4.25" wide—yours may differ.

j. Click **Crop** in the Size group again to crop the area from view and to turn off the Crop feature.

k. Select the cropped picture and click the **FORMAT tab**, if necessary.

l. Click **Compress Pictures** in the Adjust group.

  The Compress Pictures dialog box opens.

m. Click **Use document resolution** in the *Target output* section.

n. Click the **Apply only to this picture check box** to deselect it.

  You need to compress all the pictures you have used in the presentation to reduce the presentation file size, not just the selected picture.

o. Click **OK**.

The portions of the image that were cropped from view are deleted, and all pictures in the slide show are compressed.

p. Save the presentation.

STEP 5 ≫ INSERT A PICTURE FROM THE INTERNET

The couple visited Rome, Italy, during their honeymoon, so you want to insert a picture of the Colosseum to end the slide show. You insert an image from Image*After, a Web site that provides pictures free for personal or commercial use. Refer to Figure 4.24 as you complete Step 5.

FIGURE 4.24 Hyperlink to ImageAfter.com

a. Click **Slide 6**. Note the text *Image*After* (imageafter.com) is a hyperlink.

The hyperlink will display if you view the presentation in Slide Show view.

b. Right-click the link and select **Open Hyperlink** to launch the Web site in your default browser.

> **TROUBLESHOOTING:** If you are not connected to the Internet, the hyperlink will not work. Connect to the Internet and repeat step b.

The Image*After Web site displays thumbnails of images pertaining to the Colosseum in Rome.

c. Click the thumbnail of your choice to display a larger image. Right-click the image, select **Copy**, and then close the browser.

The Copy command may be named something else depending on the Web browser you are using.

d. Right-click anywhere on Slide 6 and paste the image using the Picture paste option in the submenu.

e. Depending on the size of the image you insert, you may need to adjust the image size to appropriately fit in the presentation.

f. Drag the picture to position it on the left side of the slide, leaving the Image*After text box visible.

The Image*After text box should be visible to give credit to the image source.

g. Save the presentation. Keep the presentation open if you plan to continue with the next Hands-On Exercise. If not, close the presentation and exit PowerPoint.

Video

With video added to your project, you can greatly enhance and reinforce your story, and your audience can retain more of what they see. For example, a video of water tumbling over a waterfall would stir the emotions of a viewer far more than a table listing the number of gallons of water falling within a designated period of time. Anytime you can engage a viewer's emotions, he or she will better remember your message.

In this section, you will learn the types of video file formats that PowerPoint supports, examine the options available when using video, and insert a video clip into the memories presentation.

Adding Video

Table 4.2 displays the common types of video file formats you can add to a presentation, listed in alphabetical order by file extension. Different file formats use different types of *codec* (coder/decoder) software, which use algorithms to compress or code videos, and then decompress or decode the videos for playback. Video playback places tremendous demand on your computer system in terms of processing speed and memory. Using a codec reduces that demand. In order for your video file to be viewed correctly, the video player must have the appropriate software installed and the correct version of the software. Even though your video file extension is the same as the one listed in Table 4.2 or in Help, the video may not play correctly if the correct version of the codec software is not installed.

TABLE 4.2 Types of Video File Formats Supported by PowerPoint		
File Format	**Extension**	**Description**
Windows Media File	.asf	**Advanced Streaming Format** Stores synchronized multimedia data. Used to stream audio and video content, images, and script commands over a network.
Windows Video File	.avi	**Audio Video Interleave** Stores sound and moving pictures in Microsoft Resource Interchange File Format (RIFF).
Movie File	.mpg or .mpeg	**Moving Picture Experts Group** Evolving set of standards for video and audio compression developed by the Moving Picture Experts Group. Designed specifically for use with Video-CD and CD-i media.
Adobe Flash Media	.swf	**Flash Video** File format generally used to deliver video over the Internet. Uses Adobe Flash Player.
Windows Media Video File	.wmv	**Windows Media Video** Compresses audio and video by using Windows Media Video compressed format. Requires minimal amount of storage space on your computer's hard drive.

When you add video to your presentation, you can *embed* the video and store the video within the presentation, or you can *link* to the video, which creates a connection from the presentation to another location such as a storage device or Web site. The advantage of embedding video is that a copy of the video file is placed in the slide, so moving or deleting the original video will not impact your presentation. The advantage of linking a video file is that your presentation file size is smaller. A linked video is stored in its own file. Another advantage of linking over embedding is that the presentation video is updated automatically if the original video object is changed. One caution for using a linked video from a file—the video is not part of the presentation, and if you save the presentation file to a different location, such as a flash drive, you must make sure you save the video to the new location, too. If you change the location of the video, you must make sure to change the link to the video file in the presentation.

STEP 1 »

To insert a video in a presentation, do the following:

1. Click the INSERT tab.
2. Click Video in the Media group.
3. Click *Video on My PC*.
4. Browse, locate, and select the video you want to use in the presentation.
5. Click Insert to insert the video in your presentation or click the Insert arrow and select *Link to File* to link the video to your presentation.

PowerPoint 2013 has made it even easier to add online video, such as a video from YouTube, to a presentation. You can search for an online video from within PowerPoint, and the video will be inserted directly into your slide. You can then move the video to the location on the slide or resize the video just as you would a photograph. Figure 4.25 shows the search box options for Online Video. Video can be inserted from anywhere on the Web, your OneDrive account (if you have video saved there), YouTube, or from a Web site where you have been given the embed code for the video.

Figure 4.26 shows the results of the TED video search. The search term *TED Talks* in the YouTube Search box was used for the search. (TED.com is a popular Web site for videos relating to technology, entertainment, and design.) These videos can also be viewed from TED.com.

FIGURE 4.25 Online Video Search Options

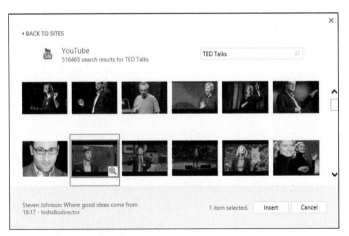

FIGURE 4.26 Search Results for YouTube Search

To search for and insert an online video in a presentation, do the following:

1. Click the INSERT tab.
2. Click Video in the Media group.
3. Click Online Video.

4. Browse, locate, and select the video you want to use in the presentation.

5. Click Insert to insert the video in your presentation.

You can also embed video from an online Web site. When you embed video from the online site, you have to copy and paste the embed code from the online site into the *From a Video Embed Code* box. Figure 4.27 shows embed code inserted into PowerPoint's *From a Video Embed Code* box. If you have embedded video from an online site, you must be connected to the Internet when you display the presentation.

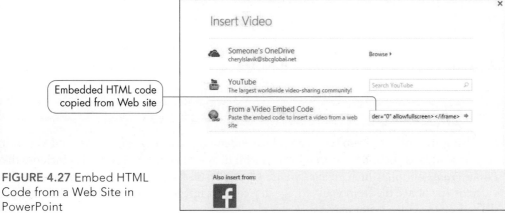

Embedded HTML code copied from Web site

FIGURE 4.27 Embed HTML Code from a Web Site in PowerPoint

To insert embed code from an online video site, do the following:

1. Locate video on an online video site.

2. Copy the embed code.

3. Click the INSERT tab in PowerPoint.

4. Click Video in the Media group.

5. Click Online Video.

6. Paste the embed HTML code into the *From a Video Embed Code* box.

7. Click Insert.

Whether you have inserted your own video or video from a Web site, the video will include a Media Controls bar with a Play/Pause button, a Move Back button, a Move Forward button, a time notation, and a Mute/Unmute control slider. The Move Back and Move Forward buttons aid you when editing your own video. The Media Controls bar is shown in Figure 4.28.

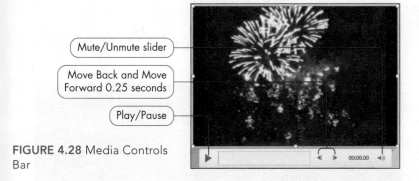

Mute/Unmute slider

Move Back and Move Forward 0.25 seconds

Play/Pause

FIGURE 4.28 Media Controls Bar

Using Video Tools

PowerPoint includes wonderful tools for working with video. You can format the video's brightness and contrast, color, and style. You can apply most artistic image effects, add or remove bookmarks, trim the video, and set fade in or fade out effects. When you select an inserted video, the Video Tools tab displays with two tabs: the Format tab and the Playback tab.

Format a Video

The Format tab includes options for playing the video for preview purposes, adjusting the video, applying a style to the video, arranging a video on the slide, and cropping and sizing the video. Figure 4.29 displays the Video Tools Format tab. Some of these tools will not work with embedded Web site videos.

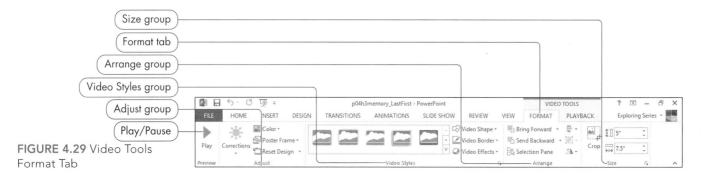

FIGURE 4.29 Video Tools Format Tab

Using the Adjust group, you can adjust video contrast and brightness, and you can recolor a video as you did when you worked with images. The Adjust group also includes the *Poster Frame* option, which enables you to choose a still frame (or image) from within the video or any image file from your storage device. This image is displayed on the PowerPoint slide when the video is not playing.

STEP 2 ≫

To create a poster frame from a video, do the following:

1. Click Play in the Preview group to display the video.
2. Pause the video when the frame you want to use as the poster frame appears.
3. Click Poster Frame in the Adjust group.
4. Click Current Frame.

To create a poster frame from an image stored in your storage device, do the following:

1. Click Poster Frame in the Adjust group.
2. Click *Image from File*.
3. Locate and select desired image.
4. Click Insert.

Figure 4.30 shows a video using with a Poster Frame option set to the current frame.

FIGURE 4.30 Poster Frame Option

The Style effects available for images are also available for videos. In addition to the styles in the Video Styles gallery, you can edit the shape of a video, change the border of the video, and add video effects such as Shadow, Reflection, Glow, Soft Edges, Bevel, and 3-D Rotation. Figure 4.31 shows a video formatted to fit a PowerPoint shape, with a gray border and reflection added.

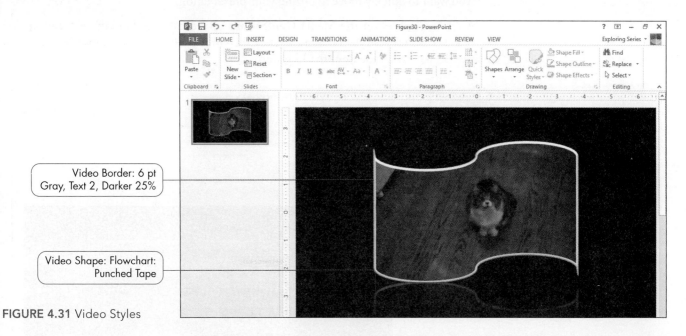

Video Border: 6 pt
Gray, Text 2, Darker 25%

Video Shape: Flowchart:
Punched Tape

FIGURE 4.31 Video Styles

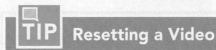

TIP Resetting a Video

To discard all formatting changes from a selected video, click the Reset Design arrow in the Adjust group on the Format tab and select Reset Design or Reset Design & Size.

Set Video Playback Options

The Playback tab includes options used when viewing a video. These tools can be used to bookmark, edit, and control the video, and can eliminate the need to use any outside video-editing software for basic video-editing functions. Figure 4.32 displays the Video Tools Playback tab.

Playback tab

Set Video Options

Set Fade In and
Fade Out duration

Click to open Trim
Video dialog box

Click to Add or
Remove Bookmark

Play/Pause

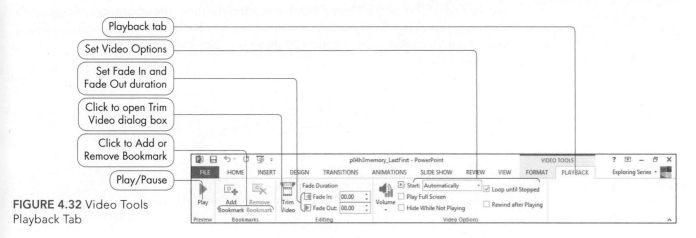

FIGURE 4.32 Video Tools
Playback Tab

You can use bookmarks to mark specific locations in a video, making it possible to quickly advance to the part of the video you want to display or to trigger an event in an animation.

STEP 3》

To bookmark a video, do the following:

1. Select the video and click the PLAYBACK tab.
2. Click Play on the Media Control bar. Pause the video at the desired frame.
3. Click Add Bookmark in the Bookmarks group when the video reaches the location you want to quickly move to during your presentation.

A circle displays on the Media Control bar to indicate the bookmark location (see Figure 4.33). To remove the bookmark, click the circle on the Media Control bar and click Remove Bookmark in the Bookmarks group.

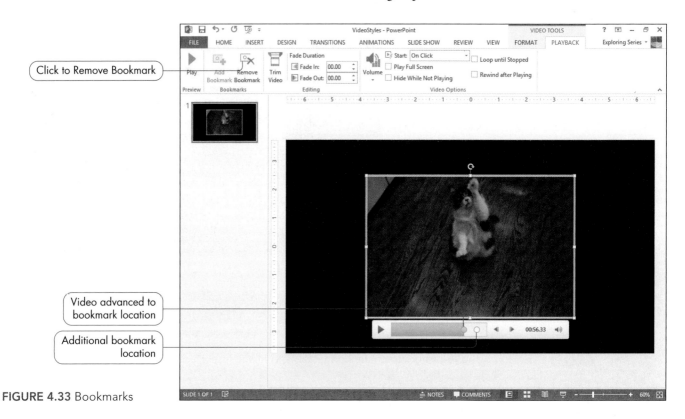

FIGURE 4.33 Bookmarks

PowerPoint enables you to perform basic video editing by enabling you to determine the starting and ending of a video and set a Fade In and Fade Out duration. In the Trim Video dialog box, which you access in the Editing group on the Playback tab, you can use the Trim option to specify the Start Time and End Time for a video, or you can drag the Start marker and the End marker on the Timing slide bar to select the time. The advantage to dragging the markers is that as you drag, you can view the video. Any bookmarks you set will also display in the Trim Video dialog box. Figure 4.34 shows the Trim Video dialog box.

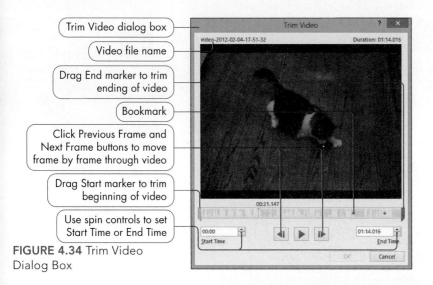

Trim Video dialog box

Video file name

Drag End marker to trim ending of video

Bookmark

Click Previous Frame and Next Frame buttons to move frame by frame through video

Drag Start marker to trim beginning of video

Use spin controls to set Start Time or End Time

FIGURE 4.34 Trim Video Dialog Box

To set a Fade In or Fade Out duration, click the spin arrows or enter an exact time in the appropriate boxes in the Editing group on the Playback tab. If you have selected a poster frame for your video, the poster frame will fade into the first frame of your video.

The Video Options group of the Playback tab enables you to control a variety of display options. You can control the volume of the video by clicking the Volume arrow and selecting Low, Medium, or High. You can also mute any sound attached to the video.

The Video Options group also enables you to determine whether the video starts on the click of the mouse (the default setting) or automatically when the slide displays. You can choose to play the video at full screen, hide the video when it is not playing, loop continuously until you stop the playback, and rewind after playing.

Quick Concepts

1. What is a video codec, and why is it usually necessary? *p. 271*

2. Explain the difference between embedding a video and linking a video. *p. 271*

3. Why would you add a bookmark to a video? *p. 275*

2 Video

In Europe, the couple recorded some fireworks displayed during a sports event. The groom gave you a copy of the fireworks video because you think it would be an excellent finale to the slide show. You insert the video, add a photo frame, and set the video playback options.

Skills covered: Insert a Video from a File • Format a Video • Set Video Playback Options

---

STEP 1 ≫ INSERT A VIDEO FROM A FILE

You create a copy of the previous presentation and insert the fireworks video. Refer to Figure 4.35 as you complete Step 1.

FIGURE 4.35 Inserted Windows Media Video File

a. Open the *p04h1Memory_LastFirst* presentation and save it as **p04h2Memory_LastFirst**, changing *h1* to *h2*.

b. Click **Slide 7**. Click the **INSERT tab** and click Video in the Media group.

c. Select **Video on My PC**, open the *p04h1Memory_Media* folder, select *p04h2Fireworks.wmv*, and then click **Insert**.

d. Save the presentation.

STEP 2 ≫ FORMAT A VIDEO

The first image of the video shows the fireworks in the beginning stages. You decide to use a poster frame of the fireworks while they are fully bursting so the slide has an attractive image on display before the video begins. You also decide that a shape removing the edges of the video would be an improvement. Finally, you add a shadow video effect. Refer to Figure 4.36 as you complete Step 2.

Step b: Poster Frame set to fireworks fully bursting

Step c: Hexagon shape applied

Step d: Perspective Diagonal Lower Left shadow applied

FIGURE 4.36 Formatted Video File

a. Click **Move Forward 0.25 Seconds** on the Media Controls bar located beneath the video to advance the video to the frame at 2.00 seconds.

b. Click the **FORMAT tab**, if necessary, click **Poster Frame** in the Adjust group, and then click **Current Frame**.

The frame you selected becomes the poster frame and displays on the slide.

c. Click **Video Shape** in the Video Styles group and click **Hexagon** in the Basic Shapes category.

The video shape changes to a hexagon.

d. Click **Video Effects**, point to *Shadow*, and then click **Perspective Diagonal Lower Left** in the Perspective category.

The shadow displays in a hexagon shape with a perspective view.

e. Click the **SLIDE SHOW tab** and click **From Current Slide** in the Start Slide Show group.

Slide 7 opens with the video displayed on the slide. The poster frame shows the fireworks at full cascade with the video shadow.

f. Move the pointer to the bottom of the video to display the Media Controls bar and click **Play**. Press **Esc** when you are finished.

g. Save the presentation.

STEP 3 ≫ SET VIDEO PLAYBACK OPTIONS

The last burst of fireworks does not finish its crescendo, so you decide to trim away this last portion of the video. Because you do not want the viewers of the presentation to have to click to begin the video, you change the start setting to start automatically. You decide to loop the video to play continuously until stopped because it is so short. Refer to Figure 4.37 as you complete Step 3.

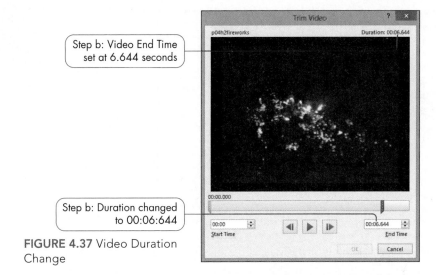

Step b: Video End Time set at 6.644 seconds

Step b: Duration changed to 00:06:644

FIGURE 4.37 Video Duration Change

a. Select the video object, if necessary, click the **PLAYBACK tab**, and then click **Trim Video** in the Editing group.

The Trim Video dialog box opens.

b. Drag the red **End Time marker** on the slider until *00:06.644* appears in the End Time box, or type **00:06.644** in the **End Time box**, and click **OK**.

The duration of the video changes from 7.755 seconds to 6.644 seconds.

c. Click the **Start arrow** in the Video Options group and select **Automatically**.

d. Select the **Loop until Stopped check box** in the Video Options group.

The fireworks video will continue to play until you advance to end the slide show.

e. Click the **SLIDE SHOW tab** and click **From Beginning** in the Start Slide Show group.

Advance through the slide show. Note the video plays in the hexagon shape.

f. Save the presentation. Keep the presentation open if you plan to continue with the next Hands-On Exercise. If not, close the presentation and exit PowerPoint.

Audio

Audio can draw on common elements of any language or culture—screams, laughs, sobs—to add excitement, provide a pleasurable background, set the mood, or serve as a wake-up call for the audience. Harnessing the emotional impact of sound in your presentation can transform your presentation from good to extraordinary. On the other hand, use sound incorrectly, and you can destroy your presentation, leaving your audience confused or distracted. Keep in mind the guideline emphasized throughout this book—any object you add to the presentation should enhance, not detract from, your message.

In this section, you will review the methods for inserting sound and tips for each method. You insert sound from the Insert Audio dialog box or saved audio file and learn how to determine the number of times a sound clip plays, the number of slides through which the sound plays, and the method for launching the sound.

Adding Audio

Your computer needs a sound card and speakers to play audio. In a classroom or computer laboratory, you will need a headset or headphones/earbuds for playback so that you do not disturb other students. You can locate and play sounds and music from the Insert Audio dialog box, or from a hard drive, flash drive, or any other storage device. You can also record your own sounds, music, or narration to play from PowerPoint.

Insert Audio from a File

Table 4.3 lists the commonly used types of audio file formats supported by PowerPoint, listed in alphabetical order by extension.

TABLE 4.3 Commonly Used Audio File Formats Supported by PowerPoint

File Format	Extension	Description
MIDI File	.mid or .midi	**Musical Instrument Digital Interface** Standard format for interchange of musical information between musical instruments, synthesizers, and computers.
MP3 Audio File	.mp3	**MPEG Audio Layer 3** Sound file that has been compressed by using the MPEG Audio Layer 3 codec (developed by the Fraunhofer Institute).
Windows Audio File	.wav	**Wave Form** Stores sounds as waveforms. Depending on various factors, one minute of sound can occupy as little as 644 kilobytes or as much as 27 megabytes of storage.
Windows Media Audio File	.wma	**Windows Media Audio** Sound format used to distribute recorded music, usually over the Internet. Compressed using the Microsoft Windows Media Audio codec.

STEP 1》 To insert audio from a file, do the following:

1. Click the INSERT tab.
2. Click Audio in the Media group.
3. Click *Audio on My PC*.
4. Browse, locate, and select the desired file.
5. Click Insert.

A gray speaker icon representing the file displays in the center of the slide with a Media Controls bar beneath it. The same controls are available when you select audio as when you select video.

Add Audio from Office.com Clip Art

You can search for and insert Office.com Clip Art files, which include a number of royalty-free sounds. These audio files are typically short in duration.

To insert sound from an Online Site:

1. Click the INSERT tab, click Audio in the Media Group, and then click Online Audio.
2. When the search box opens, enter a term in the Office.com Clip Art box and press Enter.
3. Point to a sound clip in the results pane to display a tip showing the length of the sound track.
4. Hover over the clip to hear a preview.
5. Select the desired clip and click Insert.

> **TIP** Hiding the Sound Icon During a Presentation
>
> When audio is added to a presentation, the sound icon shows on the slide. You may not want the icon to display during the presentation, however. To hide the icon during a presentation, click the icon, click the Audio Tools Playback tab, and select Hide During Show in the Audio Options group.

Record and Insert Audio

Sometimes you may find it helpful to add recorded audio to a slide show. Although you could record music, *narration* (spoken commentary) is more common. One example of a need for recorded narration is when you want to create a self-running presentation, such as a presentation displaying in a kiosk at the mall or online. Other examples include creating an association between words and an image on the screen for a presentation to a group learning a new language and vocabulary building for young children. Rather than adding a narration prior to a presentation, you could create the narration during the presentation. For example, recording the discussion and decisions made during a meeting would create an archive of the meeting.

Before creating the narration, keep in mind the following:

- Your computer will need a sound card, speakers, and a microphone.
- Comments on selected slides may be recorded rather than narrating the entire presentation.
- Voice narration takes precedence over any other sounds during playback, making it possible for a voice to play over inserted audio files.
- PowerPoint records the amount of time it takes you to narrate each slide, and if you save the slide timings, you can use them to create an automatic slide show.
- You can pause and resume recording during the process.

To record audio, do the following:

1. Click the INSERT tab.
2. Click Audio in the Media group.
3. Click Record Audio.
4. Click Record (see Figure 4.38).
5. Record your message.
6. Click Stop.
7. Click Play to check the recording.
8. Type a name for the recording and click OK.

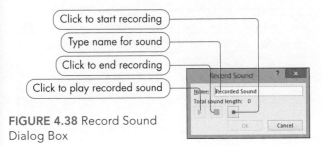

FIGURE 4.38 Record Sound Dialog Box

- Click to start recording
- Type name for sound
- Click to end recording
- Click to play recorded sound

TIP **Create Notes of Your Narration**

A transcript of your narration should be available for those in your audience who are hearing impaired. Providing the transcript lets this audience gain from your presentation, too. Put the transcript in the Notes pane and print the notes to provide a transcript.

Changing Audio Settings

When the icon for an inserted audio clip is selected, the Audio Tools tab appears with two tabs: Format and Playback. The Format tab is not relevant, as it provides options relating to images. The Playback tab provides options for playing and pausing the audio clip, adding a bookmark, trimming, fading in and out, adjusting volume, determining starting method, hiding the audio icon while playing, looping, and rewinding after playing. All of these features work similarly to the video features, except that the *Trim audio* feature provides an audio time line rather than a video preview window.

Animate an Audio Sequence

Although the Playback tab gives you only two options for starting—On Click or Automatically—you have other options available through the Timing group on the Animations tab. You can choose whether the audio plays with a previous event or after a previous event; for example, you can have the audio play as a picture appears or after.

STEP 2 ≫   To set the audio to play with or after a previous event:

1. Select the sound icon.
2. Click the ANIMATIONS tab.
3. Click the Start arrow in the Timing group.
4. Click With Previous or After Previous.

The Timing group on the Animations tab also includes a Delay spin box that you can use to delay the play of an audio clip (see Figure 4.39).

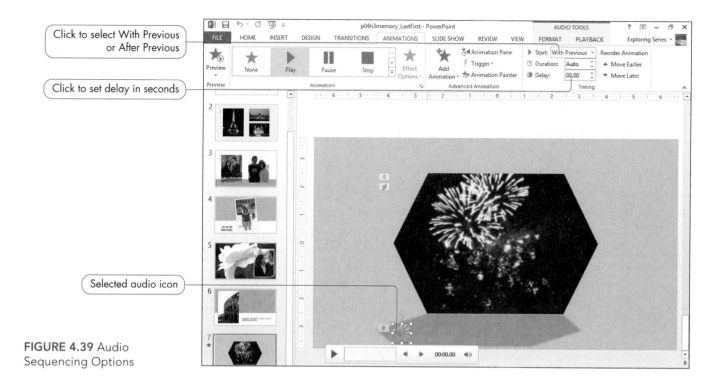

Labels in figure:
- Click to select With Previous or After Previous
- Click to set delay in seconds
- Selected audio icon

FIGURE 4.39 Audio Sequencing Options

Play a Sound over Multiple Slides

By default, audio plays until it ends or until the next mouse click. If you are playing background music, this means the music ends when you click to advance to the next slide.

To continue audio over multiple slides, do the following:

1. Select the sound icon and click the ANIMATIONS tab.
2. Click Animation Pane in the Advanced Animation group.
3. Select the sound you want to continue over multiple slides.
4. Click the arrow to the right of the sound.
5. Click Effect Options.
6. Click the After option in the *Stop playing* section of the Effect tab.
7. Enter the number of slides during which you want the sound to play (see Figure 4.40).

If the background music stops before you get to the last slide, use the Loop Until Stopped feature to keep the sound repeating. Click the Playback tab and click the Loop Until Stopped check box in the Audio Options group.

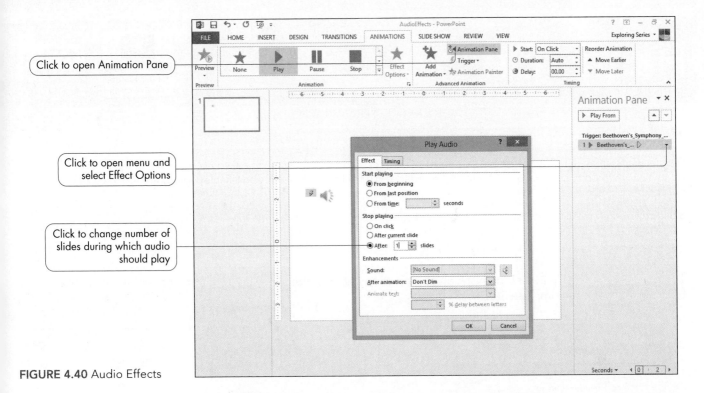

Click to open Animation Pane

Click to open menu and select Effect Options

Click to change number of slides during which audio should play

FIGURE 4.40 Audio Effects

TIP Play Across All Slides

You can set an audio clip to play across slides easily by clicking the Playback tab and selecting the Play Across Slides check box. This option does not let you set the number of slides over which you want the audio to play, however.

Quick
Concepts ✓

1. What are the three methods for inserting audio into a presentation? *p. 281*

2. Describe a situation where a narrated PowerPoint presentation would be advisable. *p. 282*

3. What audio options are available from the Audio Tools Playback tab? *p. 283*

Hands-On Exercises

Watch the Video
for this Hands-
On Exercise!

MyITLab®
HOE3 Training

3 Audio

You decide to create a background mood for the memories presentation by inserting a favorite audio clip of the bride—Beethoven's Symphony No. 9. You also want to experience the full effect of the fireworks finale slide by adding the sounds of fireworks exploding.

Skills covered: Add Audio from a File • Change Audio Settings • Insert Sound from Office.com Clip Art

STEP 1 >> ADD AUDIO FROM A FILE

The bride is a classically trained pianist, so you decide to enhance the slide show with one of her favorite pieces. Refer to Figure 4.41 as you complete Step 1.

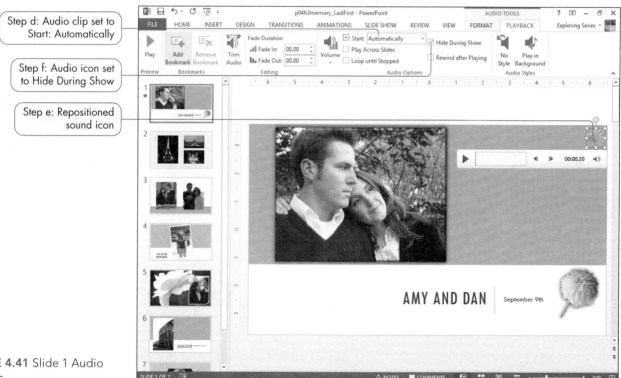

FIGURE 4.41 Slide 1 Audio Settings

a. Open the *p04h2Memory_LastFirst* presentation if you closed it after the last exercise and save it as **p04h3Memory_LastFirst**, changing *h2* to *h3*.

> **TROUBLESHOOTING:** To complete this exercise, it is best that you have a sound card and speakers. Even if this equipment is not available, however, you can still perform these steps to gain the knowledge.

b. Click **Slide 1**. Click the **INSERT tab**, click **Audio** in the Media group, and then select **Audio on My PC**.

The Insert Audio dialog box opens.

c. Locate the *p04h1Memory_Media* folder, select **Beethoven's_Symphony_No_9**, and then click **Insert**.

The sound icon and Media Controls bar are displayed in the center of the slide.

d. Click the **PLAYBACK tab**, click the **Start arrow** in the Audio Options group, and then select **Automatically**.

e. Drag the **sound icon** to the top-right corner of the slide.

f. Click the **Hide During Show check box** in the Audio Options group.

g. Click **Play** in the Preview group.

h. Save the presentation.

STEP 2 » CHANGE AUDIO SETTINGS

Because PowerPoint's default setting ends a sound file when a slide advances, the Beethoven file is abruptly cut off when you advance to the next slide. You adjust the sound settings so the file plays continuously through all slides in the slide show. Refer to Figure 4.42 as you complete Step 2.

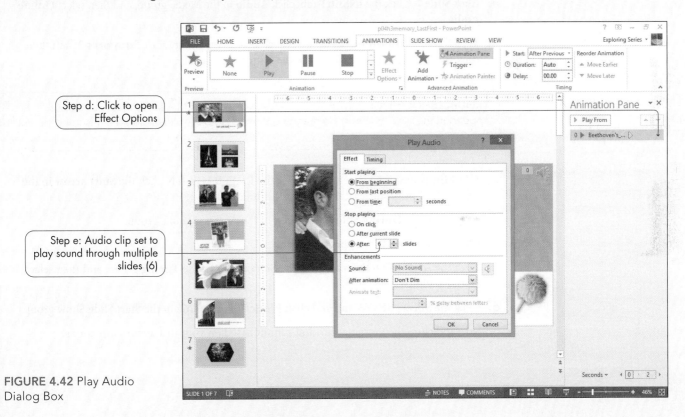

FIGURE 4.42 Play Audio Dialog Box

a. Click the **SLIDE SHOW tab** and click **From Beginning** in the Start Slide Show group. Advance through the slides and end the slide show.

Note that the sound clip on Slide 1 discontinues playing as soon as you click to advance to the next slide.

b. Select the **sound icon** on the top-right of Slide 1.

c. Click the **ANIMATIONS tab** and click **Animation Pane** in the Advanced Animation group.

d. Click the **Beethoven's Symphony sound arrow** in the animation list and select **Effect Options**.

e. Click **After** in the *Stop playing* section, type **6** in the box, and then click **OK**. Close the Animation Pane.

f. Save the presentation.

g. Play the slide show and note the music plays through the sixth slide.

STEP 3 ≫ INSERT SOUND FROM OFFICE.COM CLIP ART

The sound of fireworks exploding would make the finale slide more effective. You locate a fireworks audio clip, add it to the fireworks slide, set it to start automatically, and set it to loop until the presentation ends. After adding the audio clip, you modify its setting so it plays concurrently with the video. You move the audio icon so that it does not block the view of the fireworks. You also hide the audio icon during the presentation. Refer to Figure 4.43 as you complete Step 3.

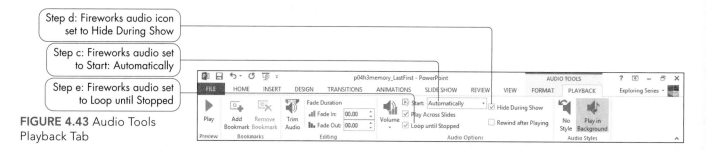

FIGURE 4.43 Audio Tools Playback Tab

Step d: Fireworks audio icon set to Hide During Show

Step c: Fireworks audio set to Start: Automatically

Step e: Fireworks audio set to Loop until Stopped

a. Click **Slide 7**. Click the **INSERT tab**, click **Audio** in the Media group, and then select **Online Audio**.

b. Type the keyword **fireworks** in the **Search box**, press **Enter**, click **Fireworks 2**, and then click **Insert**. Drag the sound icon to the bottom-left corner.

> **TROUBLESHOOTING:** If the sound clip speaker icon and Media Controls bar do not appear on the slide, you may be dragging the clip onto the slide instead of inserting the clip.

c. Select the **sound icon** if necessary, click the **PLAYBACK tab**, click the **Start arrow** in the Audio Options group, and then select **Automatically**.

d. Click the **Hide During Show check box** in the Audio Options group.

e. Click the **Loop until Stopped check box**.

f. Click the **ANIMATIONS tab**, click the **Start arrow** in the Timing group, and then select **With Previous.**

g. Click the **SLIDE SHOW tab** and click **From Current Slide** in the Start Slide Show group.

h. Save and close the presentation, and submit based on your instructor's directions.

Photo Albums

PowerPoint has a Photo Album feature designed to speed up the album creation process. This feature takes the images you select and arranges them on album pages based on selections you make.

In this section, you will use the Photo Album feature to create an album and use the feature settings to customize your album.

Creating a Photo Album

A PowerPoint *Photo Album* is a presentation that contains multiple pictures that are imported and formatted through the Photo Album feature. Because each picture does not have to be formatted individually, you save a considerable amount of time. The photo album in Figure 4.44 took less than two minutes to create and assign a theme. Because a four-per-page layout was selected, images were reduced to fit the size of the placeholder. This setting drastically reduced the size of some images.

Album layout, four per page
Album Title page automatically created
Banded theme

FIGURE 4.44 PowerPoint Photo Album

STEP 1 ❯❯

To create a photo album, do the following:

1. Click the INSERT tab.
2. Click Photo Album in the Images group.
3. Click File/Disk.
4. Navigate to your pictures and select the pictures to include in the album.
5. Click Insert.
6. Select the Photo Album options you want.
7. Click Create.

If you click the Photo Album arrow, you may choose between creating a new album and editing a previously created album. When you select the pictures you want to include in the album, do not worry about the order of the pictures. You can change the order later. Once an album has been created, you can edit the album settings by clicking the Photo Album arrow in the Images group on the Insert tab and selecting Edit Photo Album.

TIP **Creating Family Albums**

After creating an album, add transitions and you have a beautiful presentation for a family gathering or special event. Loop the presentation and let it run so people can watch as they desire. Burn the presentation to a CD and send it as a holiday greeting.

Setting Photo Album Options

Using the photo album features can save you some time formatting and setting various design options. Several tools allow you to do things such as selecting picture order, rotating images, changing contrast and brightness, inserting captions for your photos, and finally selecting an album layout. Figure 4.45 shows the location of these tools. Each is discussed in detail in the following sections.

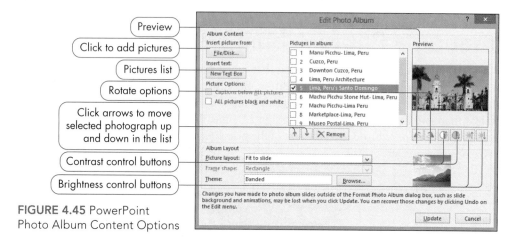

FIGURE 4.45 PowerPoint Photo Album Content Options

Selecting Pictures and Setting the Picture Order

After pictures are selected, they will display in a list in the *Album Content* section of the Photo Album dialog box. Click the name of a picture to display a preview to help you determine the order of pictures in the album.

To set the picture order:

1. Use the *Move up* arrow and the *Move down* arrow to reposition a selected photograph.
2. Use Ctrl or Shift to select more than one image.
3. Delete any unwanted photographs by selecting them and clicking Remove.

If you have downloaded photographs from a digital camera, you may need to rotate some images. Click the check box of the photo you want to rotate and click the rotate left or rotate right button. Rotate buttons are included in the *Album Content* section under the image preview.

Changing Picture Contrast and Brightness

STEP 2 Contrast and brightness controls enable you to fine-tune your pictures. To set the contrast or brightness:

1. Click the check box next to the photo you want to modify.
2. Click the contrast or brightness controls until the photo is modified as desired.

Inserting Captions

The New Text Box button allows you to insert a text box with the photo caption in the album. The text placeholder is the same size as the placeholders for pictures. The *Captions below ALL pictures* option will not become available until you choose an album layout, which is discussed next. When this option is active, the file name of the picture displays as a caption below the picture in the album. You can modify the caption text once the album is created.

Setting an Album Layout

STEP 3 »

The *Album Layout* section of the Photo Album dialog box gives many options for personalizing the album. First, you can select a Picture layout: a single picture fitted to a full slide; one, two, or four pictures on a slide; or one, two, or four pictures and a title placeholder per slide. When you fit a single picture per slide, the image is maximized on the slide.

STEP 4 »

You can select from a variety of frame shapes in the *Album Layout* section. Options include rectangles, rounded rectangles, simple black or white frames, a compound black frame, a center shadow rectangle, or a soft edge rectangle.

STEP 5 »

You can apply a theme for the background of your album while in the Photo Album dialog box. This helps to personalize the album. If you are in a networked lab situation, it may be difficult to navigate to the location where themes are stored. If this is the case, create the album and in the main PowerPoint window, click the Design tab, click the More button in the Themes group, and then select your theme from the gallery.

Quick Concepts ✓

1. What advantages does the Photo Album feature offer? *p. 289*

2. List two image transformation tools available in the *Album Content* section of the Photo Album dialog box. *p. 290*

3. Describe one way to personalize an album. *p. 291*

4 Photo Albums

The bride and groom also took a trip to Peru, capturing photos of the gorgeous scenery. You prepare a photo album to help them preserve their memories. You take the time to improve the picture quality by adjusting the brightness and contrast. You also apply an album layout, apply frame shapes, and apply a theme to further personalize the album.

Skills covered: Create an Album, Select and Order Pictures • Adjust Contrast and Brightness • Set Picture Layout • Select Frame Shape • Edit Album Settings and Apply a Theme

STEP 1 ≫ CREATE AN ALBUM, SELECT AND ORDER PICTURES

You have a folder in which you have saved the images you want to use for the vacation album. In this step, you add the images to the album and order the images by the date during which the trip was taken. Refer to Figure 4.46 as you complete Step 1.

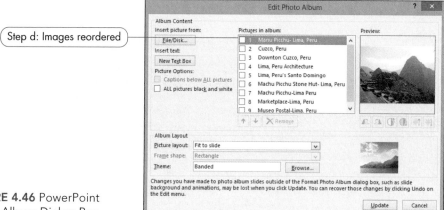

FIGURE 4.46 PowerPoint Photo Album Dialog Box

a.   Open a new blank presentation. Click the **INSERT tab** and click **Photo Album** in the Images group.

The Photo Album dialog box opens.

b.   Click **File/Disk**. Open the *p04h4Album_Media* folder.

c.   Click one of the files in the list, press **Ctrl+A** to select all pictures in the folder, and then click **Insert**.

The list of pictures displays in the *Pictures in album* box.

d.   Click to select the *Manu Picchu- Lima, Peru* picture and click the **Move up arrow** to reposition the picture so that it is the first picture in the list. Refer to Figure 4.46 to ensure your images are in the correct order and click **Create**.

STEP 2 ≫ ADJUST CONTRAST AND BRIGHTNESS

The Photo Album feature includes buttons that enable you to adjust the contrast and brightness of images without having to access PowerPoint's Picture Tools. You use the Photo Album buttons to adjust the contrast in one of the Isle of Skye pictures. Refer to Figure 4.47 as you complete Step 2.

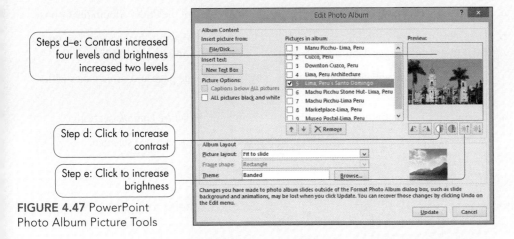

Steps d–e: Contrast increased four levels and brightness increased two levels

Step d: Click to increase contrast

Step e: Click to increase brightness

FIGURE 4.47 PowerPoint Photo Album Picture Tools

a. Click the **Photo Album arrow** located in the Images group under the INSERT tab.

b. Select Edit Photo Album.

> **TROUBLESHOOTING:** If the list of photos does not display, you have selected the Photo Album button and not the Photo Album arrow.

c. Select **Lima, Peru's Santo Domingo** by placing a check mark in its check box in the **Pictures in album list**.

d. Click **Increase Contrast** (third button from the left) four times.

e. Click **Increase Brightness** (fifth button from the left) twice.

The adjusted image can be viewed in the Preview window. If you had changed brightness only, the image would be washed out.

STEP 3 ≫ SET PICTURE LAYOUT

You change the layout of the album pages to four pictures per page. Then, to help identify the location the image was taken from during the trip, you include captions. Refer to Figure 4.48 as you complete Step 3.

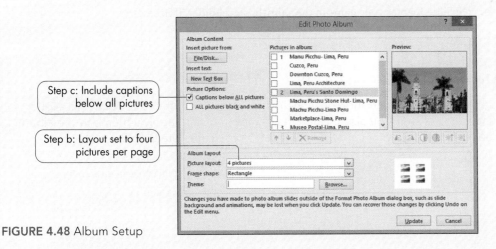

Step c: Include captions below all pictures

Step b: Layout set to four pictures per page

FIGURE 4.48 Album Setup

a. Click the **Picture layout arrow** in the *Album Layout* section of the Photo Album dialog box.

b. Click each of the layouts and view the layout in the Album Layout Preview window on the right (below the larger Album Content Preview window) and select **4 pictures**.

Clicking *4 pictures* will create an album of four pages—a title page and three pages with pictures.

c. Click the **Captions below ALL pictures check box** in the *Picture Options* section.

Captions below ALL pictures only becomes available after the layout is selected.

STEP 4 ▶▶ SELECT FRAME SHAPE

You decide to use a simple white frame to enhance the pictures taken during the trips. Refer to Figure 4.49 as you complete Step 4.

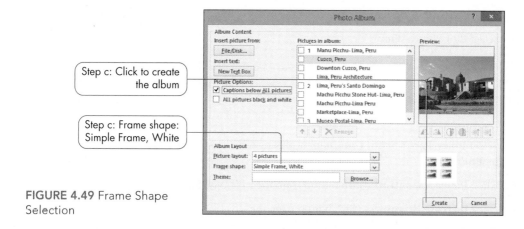

FIGURE 4.49 Frame Shape Selection

a. Click the **Frame shape arrow** in the *Album Layout* section.

b. Select each of the frames and view the layout in the Preview window on the right.

c. Select **Simple Frame, White** and click **Update**.

d. Create a handout header with your name and a handout footer with your instructor's name and your class. Include the current date.

e. On Slide 1, enter your name in the **subtitle placeholder**, if necessary.

f. Save the presentation as **p04h4Album_LastFirst**.

STEP 5 ▶▶ EDIT ALBUM SETTINGS AND APPLY A THEME

You decide to edit your album settings so that you include only one picture per page rather than four. This allows more space for the pictures to show more detail. You also change the frame shape and apply a theme to the album. Finally, you correct one of the captions for an image. Refer to Figure 4.50 as you complete Step 5.

Step b: Layout changed to 1 per page

Step c: Frame changed to Center Shadow Rectangle

Step d: Banded theme with Orange Variant applied

FIGURE 4.50 Slides 1–9 of the Revised Photo Album

a. Click the **INSERT tab**, click the **Photo Album arrow** in the Images group, and then select **Edit Photo Album**.

The Edit Photo Album dialog box opens displaying the current settings, which you may now change.

b. Click the **Picture layout arrow** and select **1 picture**. If necessary, delete any blank slides.

c. Click the **Frame shape arrow** and select **Center Shadow Rectangle**. Click **Update**.

The pictures now display one per page.

d. Click the **DESIGN tab**, apply **Banded theme** in the Themes group, and then click the **Orange Variant** in the Variants group.

e. Click **Slide 4**. Edit the text box to correct the spelling of *Downtown*.

The text box caption below the image has been corrected, since the picture file name was misspelled.

f. Save and close the file, and submit based on your instructor's directions.

Chapter Objectives Review

After reading this chapter, you have accomplished the following objectives:

1. **Insert a picture.**
   - Pictures are in a bitmap format and are photorealistic portrayals.
   - They can be inserted using the Insert Picture option, which centers the image on the slide, or by using placeholders that center and crop the image inside the placeholder.

2. **Transform a picture.**
   - Pictures can be transformed in a variety of ways, including removing the background, applying corrections, changing colors, applying artistic effects and picture styles, and cropping.
   - Remove a background: The Remove Background tool enables you to remove portions of a picture you do not want to keep.
   - Correct a picture: You can enhance a picture by sharpening or softening it, or you can increase or decrease a picture's brightness and contrast.
   - Change picture color: Use the color tools to adjust the saturation and tone of your pictures.
   - Use artistic effects: With artistic effects you can change the appearance of a picture so that it looks like it was created with a marker, as a pencil sketch, and more.
   - Apply picture styles: You can surround your picture with attractive frames, soften the edges of pictures, add shadows to the edges of pictures, apply 3-D effects to pictures, add glossy reflections, and more.
   - Resize or crop a picture: You can resize pictures or crop them to remove unwanted portions of the image.
   - Compress pictures: Pictures can be compressed to save file storage space.
   - Create a background from a picture: Pictures can make appealing backgrounds when you adjust the transparency.

3. **Use the Internet as a resource.**
   - The Internet can be extremely valuable when searching for information for a presentation.
   - Understand copyright protection: Although students and teachers have rights under the Fair Use Act, care should be taken to honor all copyrights.
   - Before inserting any information or clips into your slide show, research the copyright ownership.
   - To be safe, contact the Web site owner and request permission to use the material.
   - Any information used should be credited and include hyperlinks when possible, although attribution does not relieve you of the requirement to honor copyrights.

4. **Add video.**
   - You can insert video located on your hard drive or storage device or YouTube, or embed HTML coding from an online site.

5. **Use Video Tools.**
   - PowerPoint includes video editing tools.

   - Format a video: You can adjust the brightness and contrast, recolor, set a poster frame, select a style, and arrange and size a video.
   - Set video playback options: You can also add a bookmark, trim, set a fade in and fade out effect, control the volume, determine how to start the video, set the video to play full screen, hide the video when not playing, loop until stopped, rewind after playing, and show media controls.

6. **Add audio.**
   - Audio catches audience attention and adds excitement to a presentation.
   - Take care when adding sound that it enhances your message rather than detracts from it.
   - Insert audio from a file: PowerPoint supports many different audio file formats that enable you to include sounds with your presentation.
   - Add audio from Office.com clip art: Office.com provides a number of short, royalty-free sounds.
   - Record and insert audio: You may find it helpful to add recorded audio to a slide show by using narration (spoken commentary).

7. **Change audio settings.**
   - Animate an audio sequence: You can also add a bookmark, trim, set a fade in and fade out effect, control the volume, and determine how to start audio.
   - You can hide the speaker icon when not playing, loop until stopped, rewind after playing, and show media controls.
   - Play a sound over multiple slides: By default, audio plays during one slide and stops when you advance to a new slide, but it can be set to play over multiple slides.

8. **Create a Photo Album.**
   - When you have multiple images to be inserted, using the Photo Album feature enables you to quickly insert the images into a slide show.
   - After identifying the images you want to use, you can rearrange the order of the pictures in the album.
   - You also can choose among layouts for the best appearance.

9. **Set Photo Album options.**
   - Select pictures and set the picture order: PowerPoint enables you to determine the order of pictures in the album.
   - Album options for contrast and brightness enable you to make image changes without having to leave the Photo Album dialog box.
   - In addition to adjusting contrast and brightness, you can change the pictures to black and white.
   - Insert captions: File names can be turned into captions for the pictures.
   - Set an album layout: A frame shape can be selected and a theme applied to complete the album appearance.

Key Terms Matching

Match the key terms with their definitions. Write the key term letter by the appropriate numbered definition.

a. Background
b. Bitmap image
c. Brightness
d. Compression
e. Contrast
f. Copyright
g. Cropping
h. Embed
i. Foreground
j. Link

k. Multimedia
l. Narration
m. Photo Album
n. Poster frame
o. Public domain
p. Recolor
q. Saturation
r. Sharpening
s. Softening
t. Tone

1. _____ An image created by bits or pixels placed on a grid to form a picture. **p. 248**

2. _____ Spoken commentary that is added to a presentation. **p. 282**

3. _____ Process of changing picture colors to a new temperature. **p. 256**

4. _____ Temperature of a color. **p. 255**

5. _____ The intensity of a color. **p. 254**

6. _____ Enhances the edges of the content in a picture to make the boundaries more prominent. **p. 252**

7. _____ Legal protection afforded to a written or artistic work. **p. 262**

8. _____ To store an object from an external source within a presentation. **p. 271**

9. _____ The difference between the darkest and lightest areas of a picture. **p. 253**

10. _____ The process of eliminating any unwanted portions of an image. **p. 258**

11. _____ The rights to a literary work or property owned by the public at large. **p. 262**

12. _____ Method applied to data to reduce the amount of space required for file storage. **p. 248**

13. _____ The portion of the picture that is kept, which is also the main subject of the picture. **p. 251**

14. _____ Multiple forms of media used to entertain or inform an audience. **p. 248**

15. _____ Presentation containing multiple pictures organized into album pages. **p. 289**

16. _____ The portion of a picture that is removed because it is not desired in the picture. **p. 251**

17. _____ A connection from the presentation to another location such as a storage device or Web site. **p. 271**

18. _____ The frame that displays on a slide when a video is not playing. **p. 274**

19. _____ Blurs the edges of the content in a picture to make the boundaries less prominent. **p. 252**

20. _____ The lightness or darkness of a picture. **p. 253**

Multiple Choice

1. Which of the following file formats supports transparent backgrounds, is limited to 256 colors, and is effective for scanned images such as illustrations rather than color photographs?

   (a) .bmp

   (b) .jpg

   (c) .gif

   (d) .tiff

2. Which of the following is *not* permitted for a student project containing copyrighted material?

   (a) The student markets the project on a personal Web site.

   (b) Only a portion of copyrighted material is used, and the portion was determined by the type of media used.

   (c) The student receives permission to use copyrighted material to be distributed to classmates in the project.

   (d) The educational project is produced for a specific class and then retained in a personal portfolio for display in a job interview.

3. Which of the following Picture Tools would help you manage large image files by permanently deleting any cropped areas of a selected picture and by changing the resolution of the pictures?

   (a) Brightness

   (b) Contrast

   (c) Recolor

   (d) Compress Pictures

4. Which of the following picture adjustments is *not* found in the corrections tools?

   (a) Sharpness

   (b) Contrast

   (c) Tone

   (d) Soften

5. Which of the following stores sound and moving pictures in Microsoft Resource Interchange File Format (RIFF)?

   (a) .gif

   (b) .wmv

   (c) .avi

   (d) .bmp

6. All of the following can be used to play a selected sound clip for preview *except*:

   (a) Click Play/Pause on the Media Controls bar.

   (b) Click Play in the Preview group on the Audio Tools Playback tab.

   (c) Click the blue bar on the right side of the clip in the Insert Audio dialog box and select Preview/Properties.

   (d) Click Play in the Preview group on the Audio Tools Playback tab.

7. Which of the following is a *false* statement regarding recording a narration?

   (a) Narrations cannot be paused during recording.

   (b) You can pause and resume recording during the process.

   (c) PowerPoint records the amount of time it takes you to narrate each slide.

   (d) Voice narration takes precedence over any other sounds during playback.

8. The Photo Album dialog box enables you to make all of the following edits to pictures *except*:

   (a) Rotate.

   (b) Contrast.

   (c) Crop.

   (d) Brightness.

9. Which of the following formatting options is *not* available for video?

   (a) Brightness

   (b) Cropping

   (c) Background Removal

   (d) Soft Edges

10. Audio Playback tools enable you to do all of the following *except*:

    (a) Add a bookmark.

    (b) Fade the audio in.

    (c) Rewind after playing.

    (d) Apply an artistic effect.

1 Geocaching Slide Show

The slide show in Figure 4.51 is designed to be used with a presentation introducing a group to the sport of geocaching. Geocaching became a new sport on May 2, 2000, when 24 satellites around the globe stopped the intentional degradation of GPS signals. On May 3, Dave Ulmer hid a bucket of trinkets in the woods outside Portland, Oregon, and the sport was born! It continues to grow at remarkable speed. Your geocaching presentation is designed to teach the basics of taking something, leaving something, and signing the logbook. This exercise follows the same set of skills as used in Hands-On Exercises 1 and 3 in the chapter. Refer to Figure 4.51 as you complete this exercise.

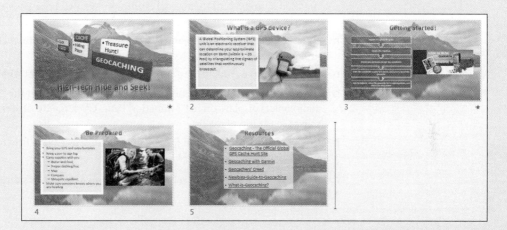

FIGURE 4.51 Geocaching Slide Show

Photo: tupatu76/Fotolia

a. Open the *p04p1Cache* slide show and save it as **p04p1Cache_LastFirst**.

b. Create a handout header with your name and a handout footer with your instructor's name and your class. Include the current date.

c. Click the **DESIGN tab** in any slide and click **Format Background** in the Customize group to open the Format Background task pane.

d. Click **Picture or texture fill**, click **Online...**, type **mountain lake** in the **Office.com Clip Art search box**, and press **Enter**. Select the photo shown in the background of Figure 4.51 (or a similar photo) and click **Insert**. Drag the **Transparency slider** to 30% or type **30** in the **Transparency box**. Click **Apply to All** and click **Close** to close the Format Background task pane.

e. Click **Slide 2**. Click the **Pictures button** in the right placeholder. In the *p04p1Cache_Media* folder, click and examine the **p04p1gps picture**. Click **Insert** and examine the image on Slide 2 and note the resizing of the placeholder to keep the image in proportion.

f. Click **Color** in the Adjust group and change the **Color Saturation** to **0%**.

g. Click the border of the text box on the left side of the slide, click the **HOME tab**, click **Format Painter** in the Clipboard group, and then click the **gps picture**.

h. Open your browser and type **garminuk.geocaching.com** in the address bar to open the *Geocaching with Garmin* Web site. Right-click **Geocaching with Garmin** and select **Save background as**. Save the image as **p04p1garminlogo** (used with permission) to your student data folder for this chapter. Close your browser.

> **TROUBLESHOOTING:** The Save Background As option is available in Internet Explorer. If you are using Firefox, click View Background Image and right-click and save the image. If you are using another browser, right-click the image and select the appropriate option from the menu.

i. Click **Slide 3**. Click the **Pictures button** in the placeholder on the right. Locate the *p04p1garmin-logo* image and click **Insert**.

j. Click **Slide 4**. Click the picture of the geocachers and click the **FORMAT tab**. Click **Artistic Effects** in the Adjust group and select **Paint Strokes**.

k. Click **Slide 1**. If you are able to record narration in your computer lab, click the **INSERT tab**, click the **Audio arrow** in the Media group, and then select **Record Audio**. Click the red **Record Sound button** and read the Speaker Note at the bottom of Slide 1. When finished reading, click the blue **Stop button** and click **OK**. If you are not able to record narration, proceed to step l.

l. If you are not able to record narration in your computer lab, click **Insert**, click the **Audio arrow** in the Media group, and then select **Audio on My PC**. Locate *p04p1Narration* in the p04p1Cache_ Media folder and click **Insert**.

m. Click the **PLAYBACK tab** and select the **Hide During Show check box** in the Audio Options group. Drag the audio icon to the top right of the slide.

n. Click the **Start arrow** in the Audio Options group and select **Automatically**.

o. Click the **ANIMATIONS tab** and click **Animation Pane** in the Advanced Animation group. The audio object displays on the Animation Pane. Click the **Re-Order up arrow** until the sound object moves to the top of the list.

p. Click the **Start arrow** in the Timing group and select **With Previous**. Close the Animation Pane.

q. View the slide show.

r. Save and close the file, and submit based on your instructor's directions.

2 Geocaching Album

FROM SCRATCH

Geocachers are asked to share their geocaching experience in the geocache logbook. The *Geocaching — The Official Global GPS Cache Hunt Site* includes some easy steps for logging a geocache find and even enables you to upload a photo with your log entry. Often, geocachers also put their geocaching stories, photos, and videos online in the form of slide shows using a variety of software packages. In this exercise, you create a geocache slide show quickly and easily using the PowerPoint Photo Album feature and add video and text to the slide show. This exercise follows the same set of skills as used in Hands-On Exercises 2 and 4 in the chapter. Refer to Figure 4.52 as you complete this exercise.

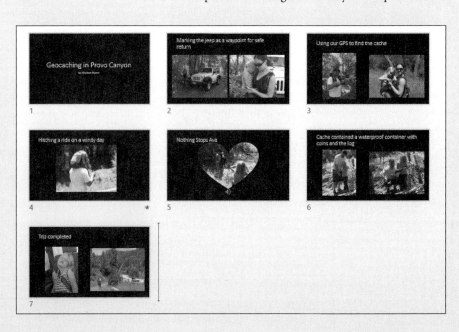

FIGURE 4.52 Geocaching Album

a. Open a new blank presentation. Click the **INSERT tab** and click **Photo Album** in the Images group.

b. Click **File/Disk** in the *Insert picture from* section, open the p04p2Geo_Media folder, click one of the files, and then press **Ctrl+A** to select all pictures in the folder. Click **Insert**.

c. Select *p04p2Img3* in the *Pictures in album* section and click **Rotate Right** (second option from the left). Repeat to rotate *p04p2Img5* and *p04p2Img8* to the right.

d. Click the **Picture layout arrow** in the *Album Layout* section and select **2 pictures with title**.

e. Click the **Frame shape arrow** in the *Album Layout* section and select **Center Shadow Rectangle**.

f. Click **Create** and save the album as **p04p2Geo_LastFirst**.

g. Create a handout header with your name and a handout footer with your instructor's name and your class. Include the current date.

h. Click **Slide 1**, if necessary. Change the title to **Geocaching in Provo Canyon**. Change the subtitle to include your name, if necessary.

i. Click the **DESIGN tab**, click the **More button** in the Themes group, and then click the **Office Theme Dark theme**.

j. Enter the following slide titles:

Slide 2   Marking the jeep as a waypoint for safe return
Slide 3   Using our GPS to find the cache
Slide 4   Cache contained a waterproof container with coins and the log
Slide 5   Trip completed

k. Click **Slide 3**. Click the **HOME tab**, click the **New Slide arrow**, and then select **Title Only**. Change the title of the slide to **Hitching a ride on a windy day**.

l. Click the **Insert tab**, click the **Video arrow** in the Media group, and then select **Video on My PC**. Click *p04p2Vid1* from the p04p2Geo_Media folder and click **Insert**.

m. Click the **PLAYBACK tab** and click **Trim Video** in the Editing group. Type **00:17.491** in the **Start Time box** and click **Play**. Type **00:22.337** in the **End Time box** and click **OK**.

n. Type **00.01** in the **Fade Out box** in the Editing group.

o. Click the **Start arrow** in the Video Options group and select **Automatically**.

p. Click the **FORMAT tab** and move to the video frame at 4.75 seconds. Click **Poster Frame** in the Adjust group and select **Current Frame**.

q. Insert a new Title Only slide, change the title to **Nothing Stops Ava**, and then insert *p04p2Vid2* from the p04p2Geo_Media folder.

r. Click the **PLAYBACK tab** and click **Move Forward 0.25 Seconds** on the Media Controls bar to advance the video to the frame at 14 seconds. Click **Add Bookmark** in the Bookmarks group.

s. Click the **FORMAT tab**, click **Video Shape** in the Video Styles group, and then click **Heart** in the Basic Shapes gallery.

t. Click **Slide 7**, click the **INSERT tab**, click **Audio** in the Media group, and then click **Online Audio**. Type the keyword **lullaby**, and press **Enter**. Click the **Music Box Melody**. Click **Insert**.

u. Drag the audio icon to the bottom of the screen.

v. Select one of the images in your album, click the **FORMAT tab**, click **Compress Pictures** in the Adjust group, and then click the **Apply only to this picture check box** to deselect it. Click **OK**.

w. View the slide show. On Slide 5, point to the Media Controls bar, click the bookmark, and then click **Play** to begin the video at the bookmark site.

x. Save and close the file, and submit based on your instructor's directions.

3 Accident Record

FROM
SCRATCH

You are involved in an accident on your bullet bike on the way to school one morning. You take pictures with your cell phone to keep a record of the damage to send to your insurance agent. You decide the quickest way to assemble the photographs is to create a Photo Album that is suitable for sending by e-mail. You then edit the Photo Album to include a text box so that you have a location in which to enter the accident details. This exercise follows the same set of skills as used in Hands-On Exercises 1 and 4 in the chapter. Refer to Figure 4.53 as you complete this exercise.

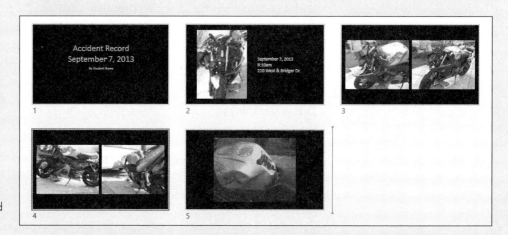

FIGURE 4.53 Accident Record Compressed for E-Mail

a. Open a blank presentation document, click the **INSERT tab**, and then click **Photo Album** in the Images group.

b. Click **File/Disk**, navigate to the p04p3Accident_Media folder, press **Ctrl+A**, and then click **Insert**.

c. Click **Create** to create the album and save the album as **p04p3Accident_LastFirst**.

d. Review the slides and note that each picture is placed on its own slide, that the photograph is dark in Slide 6, and that the photograph of the bullet bike is sideways in Slide 7.

e. Click the **INSERT tab**, click the **Photo Album arrow**, and then select **Edit Photo Album**.

f. Select the **p04p3Accident6 picture** and click the **Move up arrow** to reposition it so that it is the first picture in the *Pictures in album* list.

g. Click the **Rotate left button** once to rotate the picture so that the bullet bike is upright.

h. With *p04p3Accident6* still selected, click **New Text Box**.

i. Select **p04p3Accident5**, click the **Increase Contrast button** five times, and then click the **Increase Brightness button** seven times.

j. Click the **Picture layout arrow** in the *Album Layout* section and click **2 pictures**.

k. Click the **Frame shape arrow** in the *Album Layout* section and select **Center Shadow Rectangle**.

l. Click **Update**.

m. Create a handout header with your name and a handout footer with your instructor's name and your class. Include the current date.

n. Move to Slide 1 and change the Photo Album title to **Accident Record** on one line and **September 7, 2016** on the following line. Change the subtitle to include your name, if necessary.

o. Move to Slide 2, select the words *Text Box*, and then type the following information:
   - **September 7, 2016**
   - **8:10 a.m.**
   - **210 West & Bridger Dr.**

p. Select the image on Slide 5 and click the **FORMAT tab**. Change the height to **6"** in the Size group. The width automatically adjusts to 8".

q. Click **Align** in the Arrange group and click **Align Center**. Click **Align** in the Arrange group again and click **Align Middle**.

r. With the image still selected, click **Compress Pictures** in the Adjust group and deselect the **Apply only to this picture check box** so all pictures in the album will be compressed.

s. Click **E-mail** in the *Target output* section and click **OK**.

t. Spell check the presentation. Save and close the file, and submit based on your instructor's directions.

Mid-Level Exercises

1 ATV for Sale

FROM SCRATCH

You have enjoyed riding your four wheeler ATV but now decide that you want to sell it to purchase a snowmobile. Using PowerPoint, you create a flyer advertising the four wheeler that you can reproduce to hang on bulletin boards at the college. Refer to Figure 4.54 as you complete this exercise.

FIGURE 4.54 ATV Sales Flyer

Photo: (top, left) marinini/Fotolia

a. Open a blank presentation and save it as **p04m1Flyer_LastFirst**.

b. Create a handout header with your name and a handout footer with your instructor's name and your class. Include the current date.

c. Change the layout to **Blank layout**.

d. Insert the *p04m1Atv1* image located in your student files in the p04m1Flyer_Media folder. Drag the image so that it aligns with the top edge of the page.

e. Insert a WordArt object in the Text group by clicking the **INSERT tab**, clicking **WordArt, Gradient Fill - Gray** (second row, first column), and then typing **FOUR WHEELER ATV**. Apply the Text Effect **Tight Reflection, touching** (first row, first column under *Reflection Variations*).

f. Center the text below the picture.

g. Click the **INSERT tab**, click **Online Pictures** to locate the *For Sale* sign shown in Figure 4.54, and then insert the image.

h. Change the scale of the *For Sale* image to 75% of its original size. Position the *For Sale* sign in the top-left corner.

i. Create a text box and type **Call 702-555-1212**. Apply a WordArt Style to the text using the FORMAT tab: **WordArt Fill - Orange, Accent 2, Outline - Accent 2** (first row, third column). Change the font size to **28 pt**.

j. Insert the *p04m1Atv2* image located in your student files in the p04m1Flyer_Media folder. Drag the image so that the image borders align with the bottom-right corner of the flyer.

k. Adjust the sharpness of the image to **+50%**. Adjust the brightness and contrast to **Brightness: +40% Contrast: +40%**.

l. Create a text box and type the following information inside it:

Year: 2005

Usage: 195 hours, 754 miles

Color: Hunter Green

Price: $4,395

m. Change the font size of the text box to **24 pt**. Position the text box below the *Call 702-555-1212* text.

n. Compress all the photographs on the flyer.

o. Spell check the presentation. Save and close the file, and submit based on your instructor's directions.

2 Impressionist Paintings

In this exercise, you will use the Internet to obtain images of paintings by some of the masters of the Impressionist style. The paintings may be viewed at the Web Museum (www.ibiblio.org/wm/paint) that is maintained by Nicolas Pioch for academic and educational use. On the Famous Artworks exhibition page, click the Impressionism Theme (or search for Impressionist paintings or painters).

a. Open the *p04m2Painting* presentation and save it as **p04m2Painting _LastFirst**.

b. Create a handout header with your name and a handout footer with your instructor's name and your class. Include the current date. On Slide 1, change the subtitle *First Name Last Name* to your name.

c. View the slide show and click the hyperlink to *The Web Museum* on Slide 1 to open the Famous Artworks exhibition. Locate the images you will copy and paste into the slide show.

d. When you locate a painting, click the thumbnail image to enlarge it, then right-click it and save the image to a new folder on your storage device named **Impressionist Paintings**. If necessary, change the name of the file to include the artist and the name of the painting. Repeat this process until you have saved each of the images of the paintings shown in the table below and close the browser.

Slide #	Artist	Title
Slide 1	Alfred Sisley	*Autumn: Banks of the Seine near Bougival*
Slide 2	Claude Monet	*Impression: soleil levant*
Slide 4	Edgar Degas	*Ballet Rehearsal*
Slide 5	Claude Monet	*Waterlilies, Green Reflection, Left Part*
Slide 6	Berthe Morisot	*The Artist's Sister at a Window*
Slide 7	Pierre-Auguste Renoir	*On the Terrace*

 e. Return to your slide show. Insert the picture for Slide 1 as a background and insert each of the remaining pictures on the appropriate artist's slide. Resize and position the images as needed. Use picture styles. You do not need to compress the images, as they are already low resolution.

f. Change the font on the Slide 1 Subtitle Placeholder to **White Bold**.

g. Insert an audio clip of your choice in Slide 1. As an alternative to providing your own audio clip, search for the keyword **classical** in the Insert Audio dialog box. Find *Nocturne in Es-Dur* in the search results and insert it in Slide 1.

h. Position the audio icon on the slide and hide it during show. Loop the audio clip and set the song so it plays continuously across slides and does not stop with the next mouse click.

 **i.** Insert a blank slide after Slide 7. Search the Web for a video clip on Impressionist art, copy the embed code for the video, and then insert the embed code in PowerPoint. Apply a **Video Style** and choose other video settings as desired.

j. Spell check the presentation. Save and close the file, and submit based on your instructor's directions.

3 Red Butte Garden

FROM
SCRATCH

You visited Red Butte Garden, a part of the University of Utah, and enjoyed the natural gardens and the botanical garden. You want to create a Photo Album of the pictures you took that day.

a. Create a new Photo Album and insert all of the pictures in the p04m3Garden_Media folder.

b. Remove the *p04m3Img1* (Red Butte Garden & Arboretum) picture.

c. Locate *p04m3Img2*, increase the brightness six times, and then increase the contrast twice.

d. Locate *p04m3Img14*, increase the brightness twice, and then increase the contrast six times.

e. Apply a **2 pictures layout** and the **Simple Frame, White frame** shape style.

f. Create the album and save it as **p04m3Garden_LastFirst**.

g. Create a handout header with your name and a handout footer with your instructor's name and your class. Include the current date.

h. Edit the album so only one picture per page displays and click **Update**.

i. Insert *p04m3Img1* as the background for Slide 1 and remove the title and subtitle placeholders.

j. Move Slide 2 to the end of the slide show and apply the **Paint Brush Artistic Effect**.

k. Click **Slide 14**. Apply a **Sharpen: 50% correction**.

l. Apply the **Reveal transition** on any slide and set the advance to automatically advance after **00:02:00**. Apply to all slides.

m. Save and close the file, and submit based on your instructor's directions.

4 Collaborating on a Group Project

COLLABORATION CASE

In this exercise, you will collaborate with two to three students from your class to create a PowerPoint presentation advertising a product. Your group will determine the product you want to sell. Be inventive! Find an existing product that you can use as a prop to represent your new product (see example in second paragraph). Create a storyboard for that product and use a digital camera or cell phone to capture images for the product. You will upload your version of the pictures to a location all team members can access, such as a OneDrive account. You will then view your team's pictures, download the ones you want to use, and create a presentation based on the storyboard—each group member prepares his or her own storyboard and presentation. Only the images are shared. You will insert the images you want to use in the slides. You will edit the images as needed. You will create a final slide that lists all of the team members in your group. Finally, you will upload your version of the presentation to your Web site and blog about your experience.

For example, after talking using chat technology, a group decides to use green mouthwash as their product. But rather than have it represent mouthwash, they are going to use it as a "brain enhancer." They create a storyboard that lists Slide 1 as a Title and Content slide using the image of the mouthwash and the name of the product—Brain ++. For the second slide, they decide to illustrate the problem by having a picture of a person holding a test paper with the grade F plainly visible. For the third slide, they decide to illustrate the solution by having the same person pretending to drink the Brain ++. The fourth slide demonstrates the result by showing the same person holding a test paper with the grade A plainly visible. The last slide lists all members of the group. Note: This exercise assumes you have done the Collaboration exercise for Chapter 1. If you have not completed that exercise, use OneDrive.com or another method for sharing your presentation with your instructor and classmates.

a. Create a group with two to three class members and exchange contact information so you will be able to message each other. For example, have each member create a Microsoft account, a Yahoo! account, a Facebook account, or use Oovoo or some other text or video chat technology.

b. Determine, as a group, the product you will be advertising and its use. Discuss the story line for your product with the group, then each member should create a storyboard.

c. Each member should use a digital camera or cell phone to take pictures of the product.

d. Upload your images to OneDrive, which will allow all group members to access the pictures.

e. View all of the images your group uploaded, determine which ones you want to use in your presentation, and then download those images.

f. Create a PowerPoint presentation and insert the product images into slides following the storyboard you created. Edit the slides and images as needed. Enhance slides as desired.

g. Save the completed presentation as **p04m4Product_GroupName** to OneDrive.

h. Create a blog posting about this experience, or write an essay using Microsoft Word. Was collaborating with others through a chat tool a good experience or was it difficult? What did you like about the experience? How could it have been improved? How easily did your group reach agreement on your product?

i. If you stored your presentation on OneDrive, share the folder with your instructor so he or she can download and view the presentation.

Beyond the Classroom

Zeroscaping Versus Xeriscaping

RESEARCH CASE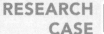

While on a trip through the Southwest, you took pictures of zeroscaping examples. You plan to use them in an existing slide show on waterwise landscaping. You want to know more about xeriscaping, however, so you research xeriscaping online. One site, XericUtah (xericutah. com), has beautiful images of xeriscaping, so you contact them and receive permission to use images from their Web site.

Open *p04b2Landscape* and save it as **p04b2Landscape_LastFirst**. Add a handout header with your name and a handout footer with your instructor's name and your class. Include the current date. Research zeroscaping and xeriscaping online and include the Web sites on a Resources slide at the end of the slide show. Please remember that giving credit to your source does not mean you are released from copyright requirements. Create several speaker notes with information you find during your research. Use the zeroscaping images located in the p04b2Landscape_Media folder where appropriate, but visit xericutah.com to obtain images for the xeriscaping portion of the slide show. Use a xeriscaping picture for the background of the Title slide. You may change the template and add animations as desired. Add an audio clip and set it to play across all slides. Insert a related video on its own slide. Save and close the file, and submit based on your instructor's directions.

Cascade Springs Ecosystem

DISASTER RECOVERY

You and another fifth-grade teacher are working together to create slide shows for your science students. The other teacher visited Cascade Springs, took pictures, and created a PowerPoint Photo Album of the pictures. Open *p04b3Springs* and save the new presentation as **p04b3Springs_LastFirst**. Review the album and read the speaker notes created from National Forest Service signs available to hikers to help them understand the fragile ecosystem. Your role is to review the presentation created by the album and determine which slides and speaker notes to keep. When necessary, rotate images. You may also change the template or slides as desired. If it is possible to record narration in your classroom lab, read and record shortened versions of at least three speaker notes and add the audio files to the slides. If you are unable to record the narration, insert the audio files in the p04b3Springs_Media folder in appropriate locations. Set the audio files to play when the sound icon is clicked. This allows a teacher to determine if he or she wants to use recordings during the presentation or lecture himself or herself. Finalize the presentation by proofreading, applying transitions and animations, and testing sound icons to ensure they work properly. Compress all images to Screen Target Output. Finally, create a handout header with your name and a handout footer with your instructor's name and your class. Include the current date. Save the album and submit as directed by your instructor.

Dress for Success

SOFT SKILLS CASE

FROM SCRATCH

First impressions are important when job hunting, so it is essential to dress professionally. Professions and companies vary, but following a basic set of rules will ensure that you make a good impression. Watch the Soft Skills Dress for Success Video on myITlab or as provided by your instructor. Create a PowerPoint presentation with photos to demonstrate the dos and don'ts. You may choose to create your presentation for either men, women, or both combined. Apply several of the photo-editing techniques discussed in the chapter to the photos. Indicate your modifications in the speaker notes on each slide. Locate a video to coincide with this topic and insert the video on its own slide. Add a handout header with your name and a handout footer with your instructor's name and your class. Include the current date. Be sure to include the Web sites on a Resources slide at the end of the slide show. Please remember that giving credit to your source does not mean you are released from copyright requirements. Finalize the presentation by proofreading, applying transitions and animations, and testing sound icons to ensure they work properly. Compress all images to Screen Target Output. Save the presentation as **p04b4Dress_LastFirst** and submit as directed by your instructor.

Capstone Exercise

Your parents recently visited Washington, DC. You volunteer to create a slide show that they can e-mail to family and friends. You use a modified version of Microsoft's Contemporary Photo Album template. The album has been modified to use a Green theme. In this activity, you will create the content, insert the photos, modify the photos, add sound, and insert a video clip of the soldier in Arlington. All media for this activity are located in the p04c1DC_Media folder.

Insert Pictures

Using template layouts and picture placeholders, you insert photos of the city. You modify template placeholders for better fit.

a. Open the file named *p04c1DC* and save it as **p04c1DC_LastFirst**.

b. Create a handout header with your name and a handout footer with your instructor's name and your class. Include the current date.

c. Click **Slide 1**, if necessary. Locate the p04c1DC_Media folder and insert *p04c1DC1* into the picture placeholder.

d. Change the subtitle to your first and last name.

e. Click **Slide 2** and insert *p04c1DC2*. Replace the caption *Click to add title* with **World War II Memorial**.

f. Click **Slide 3**. Insert *p04c1DC3* in the picture placeholder and replace the caption Click to add text with **The Capitol Building**.

g. Crop out the vehicles in the bottom of the photo of the Capitol building. Reposition the photo as needed.

h. Click **Slide 4**. Change the layout to **Left Two Pictures with Caption**.

i. Replace the text in the title placeholder with **Washington Monument and Lincoln Memorial** and delete the subtitle placeholder. Insert *p04c1DC4* in the left picture placeholder and insert *p04c1DC5* in the right placeholder.

j. Click **Slide 5**. Replace the text in the caption placeholder with **Arlington National Cemetery**. Insert *p04c1DC6* in the top-left picture placeholder, insert *p04c1DC7* in the top-right placeholder, insert *p04c1DC8* in the bottom-left placeholder, and then insert *p04c1DC9* in the bottom-right placeholder.

k. View and save the presentation.

Apply and Modify a Picture Style, Change Images

The pictures on Slides 1 and 4 would stand out better if they had a frame. You apply and modify a Picture Style.

a. Click **Slide 4**. Select the left picture and apply the **Metal Oval picture style**.

b. Apply the **Preset 5 Picture Effect** to the left picture (second row, first column).

c. Use the Format Painter to copy the effects applied to the left photo and apply them to the photo on the right.

d. Click **Slide 1** and select the picture. Apply the **Rotated, White picture style** and apply the **Watercolor Sponge artistic effect**.

e. Save the presentation.

Adjust and Compress Images

Some pictures on Slide 5 need the brightness, contrast, and color tones adjusted. You use Picture Tools to adjust the pictures, and you apply an e-mail compression to all photographs.

a. Click **Slide 5**, select the bottom-left picture, and then increase the image brightness **+20%**.

b. Select the top-left picture, set the saturation to **200%**, and then set the color tone to **7200 K**.

c. Compress all images for e-mail output.

d. Save the presentation.

Insert a Video and Add Sound

You insert a video clip of the changing of the guard for the Tomb of the Unknown Soldier and modify the settings. Finally, you add a soft music clip that plays continuously through all slides.

a. Click **Slide 6**. Add the title text **Changing of the Guard**. Center the text.

b. Search for and insert a YouTube video showing the changing of the guard at Arlington National Cemetery. Resize the video to a height of **5"**.

c. Set the video to play automatically.

d. Change the Video Options to **Hide While Not Playing** and to **Rewind after Playing**.

e. Click **Slide 1**. Search for an audio clip using **yankee doodle** as the keyword for your search.

f. Insert *Yankee Doodle 2* on Slide 1 and have it **Play across Slides** and start **Automatically**.

g. Hide the audio icon during the show.

h. Spell check the presentation. Save and close the file, and submit based on your instructor's directions.

Create a Photo Album

Your friend asks you for a printed copy of all of the images. You prepare a photo album and print it.

a. Create a New Photo Album using the images in the p04c1DC_Media folder.

b. Rearrange the pictures so they appear in the following order: DC1, DC3, DC2, and then the remaining pictures in numerical order.

c. Create the album using two pictures per slide and a **Simple Frame, White frame shape**.

d. Save the album as **p04c1Washington_LastFirst**.

e. Delete the last slide.

f. Create a handout header with your name and a handout footer with your instructor's name and your class. Include the current date.

g. Apply *DC1* at 50% transparency as the background image for the title slide.

h. Modify the title on the Title Slide to **Washington Sights** and type your name in the subtitle. Change the text color to **Black**. Bold the text.

i. Spell check the presentation. Save and close the file, and submit based on your instructor's directions.

Infographics

CHAPTER 5

Creating Text Charts, Tables, and Graphs

Konstantin Chagin/Shutterstock

CASE STUDY | Healthy Living: Antioxidants

The county health department is sponsoring a health fair, and you have been invited to present a session on antioxidants. Studies show there is a correlation between eating food rich in antioxidants and better overall health, so you want to share this information with others.

You prepare a poster that quickly and efficiently communicates the message that antioxidants promote good health and invites participants to enter the room for more information. After preparing the poster, you work on the PowerPoint presentation and decide to present information about top foods rich in antioxidants in tables so the information is neatly organized. Finally, you decide to add a graph displaying the antioxidant levels in "superfoods" and format a graph displaying the top 20 common food sources of antioxidants.

Text-Based Charts

In today's electronic environment, information is readily and quickly available, which makes it easy to feel overwhelmed. Common infographics that aid you in organizing and understanding information include text-based charts and statistical charts and graphs. ***Text-based charts*** primarily arrange and organize information with text to illustrate relationships among words, numbers, and/or graphics. These charts communicate relationships both verbally and visually. Statistical charts and graphs use points, lines, circles, bars, or other shapes to visually communicate numerical relationships, such as changes in time or comparisons.

Posters, large printed items that are displayed to advertise or publicize, and hanging signs printed on paper, vinyl, or cloth are used for advertising and publicizing. Both can be created in PowerPoint as text-based charts. Tables are another common type of text-based chart. Though text can communicate a message by its appearance (typeface, color, size, style, contrast), it can also communicate a message by how it is positioned or arranged. Therefore, when you design a text-based chart you need to carefully plan how the information is arranged within the chart and fully utilize formatting tools. Figure 5.1 shows an example of a text-based chart—a banner that has been printed locally on vinyl for durability. Once created in PowerPoint, a text-based chart can be uploaded to an online printing service to be mounted on foam backing for display or printed to use as handouts. Both can be delivered by the printing service for distribution at a function or event.

Event advertisement

FIGURE 5.1 Common Use for Text-Based Charts
Photo: Domas Balys/Fotolia

Figure 5.2 shows a PowerPoint table template illustrating a classic example of a relationship between numbers. This example, a simple multiplication table, is used to teach multiplication in an elementary school classroom. The table shows the product derived when a number in the column heading is multiplied by a number in the row heading. Notice that the intersection of the first row and the first column shows the multiplication operator.

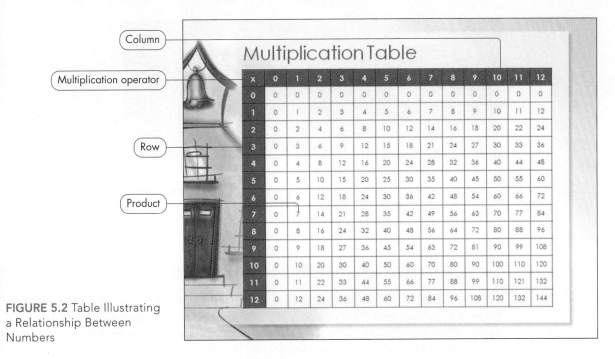

FIGURE 5.2 Table Illustrating a Relationship Between Numbers

Figure 5.3 shows another PowerPoint table template. This example illustrates a more complex relationship. Text, color, and font size, along with cell shading and arrow graphics, are used to guide the viewer through the process.

Process Steps for Sales to Consumers

SOLUTION SELLING® SALES PROCESS STEPS	Phase 1 Prospecting	Phase 2 Qualifying	Phase 3 Proposal	Phase 4 Decision	Phase 5 Repeat Business
SALES PROCESS ACTIVITIES AND MILESTONES	Generate new prospects (via referrals, networking, trade associations, conferences) Look at existing customer base for opportunities	Probe and assess needs with decision-maker Qualify the buyer Create a buying vision that maps product/service to business needs	Demonstrate to decision-maker your ability to meet their needs Ask for the business Issue the proposal	Negotiate Close the sale	Complete the work (deliver the product/service) Follow-up with the customer
OUTCOMES/GOALS	Initial sponsor identified	Buying vision and access to decision-maker	Value demonstrated and proposal submitted	Signed contract	Satisfied customer (repeat business, reference)
JOB AIDS	Business Development Prompter Customer Reference Story Competitive Points List	Product/Service Benefit Statement Follow-Up to Product/Service Sales Call (informal)	Product/Service Evaluation Plan	Rebuttals to Negotiation Roadblocks Give-Get List for Negotiation Tradeoffs Negotiation Tracker	Product/Service Satisfaction Tracker Sale Follow-Up Letter
CUSTOMER BUYING PROCESS	Identify needs	Determine requirements	Evaluate options	Negotiate	Implement and evaluate success

FIGURE 5.3 Table Illustrating a Complex Relationship Between Steps in a Process

Figure 5.4 displays an attention-grabbing banner announcing a local sporting event. For large banners or for posters printed on material other than paper, you can send your file to a commercial printing service.

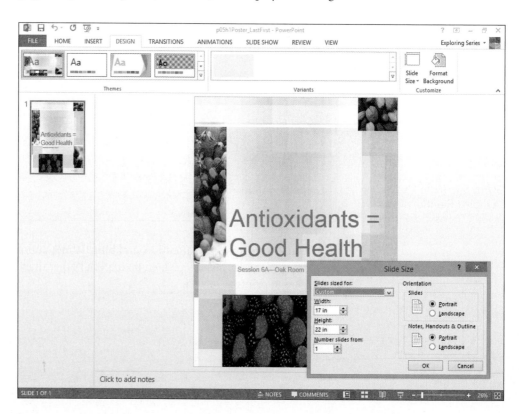

FIGURE 5.4 Banner Created in PowerPoint

Photos: (left) Alexey Buravtsoff/ Fotolia, (right) Seamartini Graphics/ Fotolia

In this section, you will learn how to create a poster and a banner. You will also learn how to create and draw a table in a slide. Finally, you will learn how to design a table to effectively communicate and organize your ideas.

Creating a Poster or a Banner

Although graphic professionals use other tools for professional print jobs, you can create banners or posters with PowerPoint. You create the poster or banner on a single slide. An important part of planning for a poster or banner is to consider how you will print the slide because this often determines how you format the single slide. Consider the printer when determining margins. Printers have margins beyond which text and graphics will not print. For commercial printing, it is important to identify all specifications, such as width and height of the finished product, not just margins. Also, when printing wide-format banners or posters, the printer may not support large-sized sheets of paper. If your printer does not support banner- or poster-sized paper, you can submit the file to a local or online printing service.

STEP 1

Use the Page Setup command to design the size of your poster or banner. With the Page Setup command, you can create documents that range from wide-format text-based documents, such as posters and banners, to small banners that appear at the tops of Web pages. The poster in Figure 5.5 is a standard size for uploading to an online printing service. The page setup for this poster, 17" × 22", also displays in the figure.

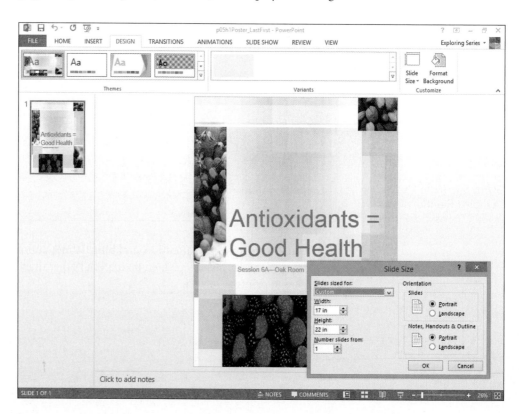

FIGURE 5.5 17" × 22" Poster Created in PowerPoint

After opening PowerPoint and opening a file, you can access the Page Setup command on the Ribbon. To use the Page Setup command, do the following:

1. Click the DESIGN tab.
2. Click Slide Size in the Customize group.
3. Select Custom Slide Size.
4. Click the first option, the *Slides sized for* arrow, and click to select the slide size based upon the desired output.
5. Next, use the Width and Height spin arrows to further adjust the size or, if a desired option is not available in the *Slides sized for* box, to create a custom-sized output.
6. On the right side of the Slide Size dialog box, choose the orientation for Slides and for Notes, Handouts & Outline based upon the desired output.
7. If you have chosen Custom and clicked OK, you may be prompted to adjust content or scale. Choose Maximize or Ensure Fit based upon the desired output.

TIP | Web Page Banners

The Banner option in the *Slides sized for* area is 8" × 1"—an ideal size for a Web banner that displays across the top of a Web page.

Drawing a Table

Tables are a form of text-based chart that organizes information into a highly structured grid (up to 75 rows and columns). Because tables are such a common way to present information, they can be created in PowerPoint, Word, Excel, and Access. If you create a table in Word, Excel, or Access, you can then insert it into a PowerPoint slide. Previously, you inserted a table by using the Insert feature to automatically create a table grid. In this section, you create tables by manually drawing the grid.

If the table design requires multiple cell heights and widths or diagonal borders, using the Pencil tool to draw the table can save time.

To draw a table, do the following:

1. Click the INSERT tab and click the *Add a Table* arrow in the Tables group.
2. Select Draw Table.
3. Drag the pencil to define the outer table boundary.
4. Click Draw Table in the Draw Borders group on the TABLE TOOLS DESIGN tab.
5. Drag the pencil to draw the column and row borders inside the table.
6. Click Eraser in the Draw Borders group on the TABLE TOOLS DESIGN tab and drag the eraser across the border between the two cells you wish to join.
7. Press Esc to finish drawing your table.

TIP | Distribute Table Space Equally

You do not need to be exact when drawing a table because the Layout tab includes buttons that distribute the width of the columns or the height of the rows so that they are uniformly spaced. To distribute columns or rows, select the cells you want to equalize and click Distribute Columns or Distribute Rows in the Cell Size group on the Layout tab.

Creating a Table Structure

Think carefully about the structure of a table before you create it to maximize the impact of the data it will contain. Tables should convey essential facts that supplement the message in the presentation but should omit distracting details. The table should be easy to understand and consistent with other objects in the presentation.

A table needs a title to communicate its purpose. Keep the title short, but ensure that it gives enough information to accurately identify the table's purpose. Use a subtitle to give further information about the purpose, if necessary, but it should be in a smaller font size. The top row of the table body usually contains **column headers** to identify the contents of the columns. Column headers should be distinguishable from cell contents. Set the headers off by using color, bold font, italics, or a larger font than you use for the table body cells. Make sure that the font size of the column headers is not larger than the title and subtitle.

> **TIP Merge Cells to Create a Title Row**
>
> To create a title row that stretches across several cells, select the cells to merge, and then click Merge Cells in the Merge group on the Layout tab. You can also use the Eraser tool on the Table Tools Design tab to erase the border between the cells or right-click selected cells and click Merge Cells.

The first column of a table, or the **stub column**, typically contains the information that identifies the data in each row. The last row of a table can be used for totals, a note, or source information. Use a smaller font size for the note or source, but make sure it is still large enough to be readable.

You can use table and cell borders to help clarify the information. Typically, horizontal borders are used to set off the title and subtitle from the headings and to set off headings from the table body. Vertical borders help define the columns. Figure 5.6 shows a basic table structure with the table elements identified. Bold is used to emphasize the table title and column headings. Font sizes vary depending on the table element, but the note or source-information row uses the smallest font size. One of the columns is shaded in blue and one of the rows is shaded in pale pink to help identify the differences. This is for illustration purposes only—this is not a table style. The intersection of the column and row, or the cell, is shaded in purple. The table is boxed, or surrounded by borders, and borders surround each cell. A heavier border is used to set off the title information from the column headings, the column headings from the body of the table, and the note information from the rest of the table.

Table Title		
Subtitle		
Stub Heading	**Column Heading**	**Column Heading**
Stub (Row Heading)	cell	
Stub (Row Heading)		
Stub (Row Heading)		
Stub (Row Heading)		
Note or Source Information		

FIGURE 5.6 Table Elements

Format Table Elements

The formatting of table elements is no longer as rigid as in years past unless you are preparing a table to adhere to specific guidelines such as American Psychological Association (APA) style. If this is the case, be sure to check a style guide for the style requirements and format the table per the guidelines. Otherwise, use type size, type style (bold, italics), alignment, or color to distinguish the table elements from one another. Remember to use design effects to clarify, not decorate.

Simplify Table Data

Table data on a slide should be as simple as possible to convey the message. Just as you limit text in bullets, limit the number of entries in tables to keep the font size large enough to read. For example, rather than listing 30 items in a table, list the top 5. Consider providing the audience with a printed Word table if you want them to have a list of all 30 items.

Another way to simplify data is to shorten numbers by rounding them to whole numbers. An alternative to this is to show numbers with a designation stating that the number is in thousands or millions. How you align the numbers in a cell depends on the type of data the cell contains. For example, numbers that do not have a decimal point can be right-aligned, or they can align on the decimal point if one exists. Occasionally you may have to left-align or center text in other columns. Generally speaking, however, you want to keep the alignment consistent throughout the table.

Change Row Height, Column Width, and Table Size

The row height or column width can be changed to accommodate information or to call attention to a cell, row, or column. For example, title rows are often taller than the rows containing body cells. To quickly adjust row height or column width, position the pointer over the target border of a row or column until the pointer changes into a sizing pointer and drag the border to adjust the row or column to the desired height or width. For a more precise change, use the Table Row Height or Table Column Width features in the Cell Size group on the Layout tab. You can also adjust the size by clicking the spin box arrows or by entering an exact size in the box.

You can resize the table manually by dragging a corner or middle sizing handle. Dragging the top- or bottom-middle handles changes the table height, whereas dragging the left- or right-middle handles changes the table width. Dragging a corner handle while holding down Shift sizes the table in both the vertical and horizontal directions simultaneously. To set a specific size for the table, specify Height or Width in the Table Size group of the Table Tools Layout tab.

Align Text Within Cells, Rows, and Columns

The Alignment group on the Layout tab includes features that not only align the contents of a cell horizontally and vertically but also change the direction of the text by rotating it or changing its orientation. You can even change the margins inside the cell. First, select the text you want to align in a single cell, row, or column. Then, to align text, click one of the alignment buttons in the Alignment group on the Layout tab. To align text horizontally, select Align Left, Center, or Align Right. To align vertically, select Align Top, Center Vertically, or Align Bottom.

To change the direction of the text within a cell, row, or column, click Text Direction and select from the options. To rotate the text, select *Rotate all text 90 degrees* (text positioned vertically facing to the right) or select *Rotate all text 270 degrees* (text positioned vertically facing to the left). To change the text orientation from horizontal to vertical for each individual character, select Stacked.

You can change internal margins from a default of 0.05" for top and bottom margins and 0.1" for left and right margins to no margins, narrow margins, and wide margins. To change the cell margins, click Cell Margins in the Alignment group and click an option from the Cell Margins gallery. Click Custom Margins at the bottom of the gallery to set each margin individually. Figure 5.7 shows a table with text rotated 270 degrees within a column.

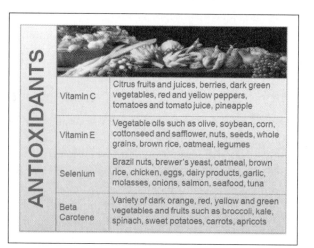

ANTIOXIDANTS		
	Vitamin C	Citrus fruits and juices, berries, dark green vegetables, red and yellow peppers, tomatoes and tomato juice, pineapple
	Vitamin E	Vegetable oils such as olive, soybean, corn, cottonseed and safflower, nuts, seeds, whole grains, brown rice, oatmeal, legumes
	Selenium	Brazil nuts, brewer's yeast, oatmeal, brown rice, chicken, eggs, dairy products, garlic, molasses, onions, salmon, seafood, tuna
	Beta Carotene	Variety of dark orange, red, yellow and green vegetables and fruits such as broccoli, kale, spinach, sweet potatoes, carrots, apricots

FIGURE 5.7 Rotated Text Within a Column

Quick **Concepts**

1. What type of relationships in the displayed data do statistical charts or graphs communicate? *p. 314*

2. Explain how text-based charts show relationships. *p. 314*

3. List the purposes of a table title and subtitle. *p. 318*

Hands-On Exercises

1 Text-Based Charts

You prepare a poster that visitors at the county health fair can see as they walk by the room in which you are presenting. After preparing the poster, your focus turns to the work on the PowerPoint presentation that will be delivered. Information about top foods rich in antioxidants will be presented and neatly organized in tables.

Skills covered: Create a Poster • Draw a Table • Create Table Structure

STEP 1 ≫ CREATE A POSTER

The poster you prepare will be displayed outside your room to communicate the simple message that antioxidants promote good health. You also want the poster to follow the same design as the antioxidant slide show already created, so you use the slide-show title slide as the basis for the poster and resize it to a standard poster size. Finally, you print a scaled-down version of the poster as a record of the presentation. Refer to Figure 5.8 as you complete Step 1.

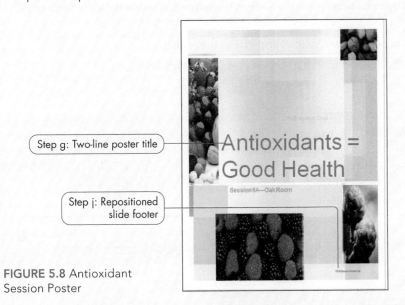

FIGURE 5.8 Antioxidant Session Poster

a. Open *p05h1Poster* and save it as **p05h1Poster_LastFirst**.

> **TROUBLESHOOTING:** If you make any major mistakes in this exercise, you can close the file, open *p05h1Poster* again, and then start this exercise over.

b. Create a handout header with your name and a handout footer with your instructor's name and your class. Include the current date.

c. Click the **DESIGN tab**, click **Slide Size** in the Customize group, and then select **Custom Slide Size**.

d. Select the existing number for *Width* and change it to **17**.

e. Select the existing number for *Height* and change it to **22**.

The *Slides sized for* box changes to Custom. Orientation changes to portrait for the *Slides* option and the *Notes, Handouts & Outline* option because the height of the slide is now greater than its width.

f. Click **OK**. Click **Maximize** and note the change in orientation.

The Maximize options scale the slide to show the entire slide. The Ensure Fit option scales the slide to fit in the window.

g. Select the **title placeholder** and type **Antioxidants = Good Health**.

h. Change the font size of the title placeholder to **144 pt**.

The session title is split into two lines. It is important to use a font large enough to be viewed easily by health-fair participants.

i. Create a slide footer that reads **2016 County Health Fair**. Click **Apply**.

By default, the slide footer is positioned at the bottom center of the slide, which makes it very difficult to read.

j. Click the **footer placeholder** to select it. Hold down **Shift** to constrain the movement horizontally and drag the slide footer border straight across to the right side of the poster so that it is positioned under the picture of the artichokes with the right border of the placeholder on the edge of the slide.

This new position increases the readability of the footer.

k. Click the **FILE tab** and click **Print**.

The Preview display may show only a portion of the poster because the poster size is larger than the typical printer paper size.

l. Click the **Full Page Slides arrow** in the *Settings* section and, if necessary, click **Scale to Fit Paper** to ensure a check appears next to this option.

The poster can now be printed to the paper size in the printer.

m. Save and close the file, and submit based on your instructor's directions.

STEP 2 ⟫ DRAW A TABLE

With the poster done, you open the Antioxidants = Healthy Living slide show you want to use during your health-fair presentation. You have sketched out a plan for an antioxidant table that lists a vitamin or mineral and some foods that include this antioxidant type. You realize that because of the varied columns and rows, the most efficient way to create the table is to draw it. Refer to Figure 5.9 to see the table structure that will result when you complete Step 2.

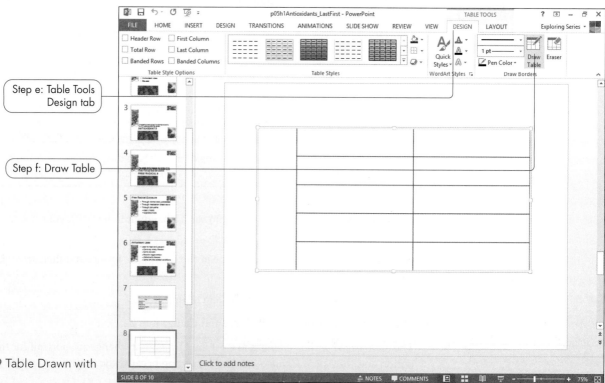

FIGURE 5.9 Table Drawn with Pencil

a. Open *p05h1Antioxidants* and save it as **p05h1Antioxidants_LastFirst**

b. Create a handout header with your name and a handout footer with your instructor's name and your class. Include the current date.

c. Click the **VIEW tab** and click the **Ruler check box** in the Show group to display the ruler, if necessary.

   The horizontal and vertical rulers display for use in creating a table.

d. Click **Slide 7** to create a new slide after Slide 7. Click the **HOME tab**, click the **New Slide arrow**, and then click **Blank**.

e. On new Slide 8, click the **DESIGN tab** and click **Format Background** in the Customize group. Click the **Hide background graphics check box** in the Format Background pane. Close the Format Background pane.

f. Click the **INSERT tab**, click **Table** in the Tables group, and then select **Draw Table**.

   The pointer changes to a pencil.

g. Use the ruler as a guide to draw a table starting at 4" to the left of the zero mark on the horizontal ruler and 2.5" above the zero mark on the vertical ruler. End the table at 4" to the right of the zero mark on the horizontal ruler and 2.5" below the zero mark on the vertical ruler.

   The outer border of the table is created.

h. Click the **TABLE TOOLS DESIGN tab**, if necessary, and click **Draw Table** in the Draw Borders group.

i. Drag the pencil down to create a column border, beginning at approximately 1" on the horizontal ruler. Release the mouse button as soon as you see the complete border appear.

   Inches are measured from the top-left edge of the table.

> **TROUBLESHOOTING:** If a new table is created in this step, you may have dragged the pencil outside of the table boundaries. Click Undo on the Quick Access Toolbar and select Draw Table in the Draw Borders group on the Table Tools Design tab. Beginning inside the table borders, drag the pencil straight down and release it when you see the complete border.

j. Drag a row border beginning from the first column right border to the right boundary of the table approximately 1" from the top boundary.

k. Drag three more row borders without worrying whether the rows are exactly the same height at this time.

   Your table now contains five rows to the right of the first column.

l. Split the new rows of the table into two columns by dragging a vertical border.

   Your table now contains three columns.

m. Press **Esc** to deactivate the table-drawing mode.

n. Select the center cell and the right cell in the top row, click the **LAYOUT tab**, and then click **Distribute Columns** in the Cell Size group.

   The width of the selected cells is distributed equally.

o. Select all five rows that were created by drawing the four borders in steps j and k.

p. Click **Distribute Rows** in the Cell Size group.

   The height of the selected cells is distributed equally.

q. Select the center column and click **Center** in the Alignment group.

   Any text typed into the center column is centered horizontally in the cells.

r. Select the center and right columns and click **Center Vertically** in the Alignment group.

Any text typed into the two right column cells is centered vertically.

s. Save the presentation.

You save the table and will add the content in Hands-On Exercise 2.

STEP 3 ›› CREATE TABLE STRUCTURE

You review the Antioxidants = Healthy Living slide show and note that the table on Slide 7 does not include a title row or column headings. Without this information, the data in the table are meaningless. You create structure in the table by adding a row for a title and by adding headers to the columns. Refer to Figure 5.10 as you complete Step 3.

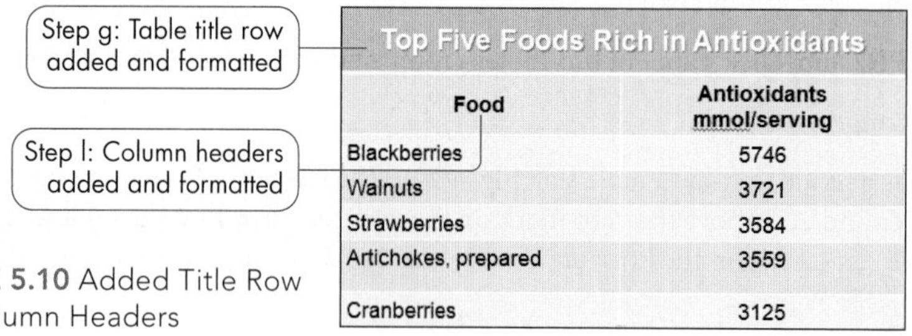

Step g: Table title row added and formatted

Step l: Column headers added and formatted

FIGURE 5.10 Added Title Row and Column Headers

Top Five Foods Rich in Antioxidants	
Food	**Antioxidants mmol/serving**
Blackberries	5746
Walnuts	3721
Strawberries	3584
Artichokes, prepared	3559
Cranberries	3125

a. On Slide 7, select the table. Click the **TABLE TOOLS DESIGN tab** and click **Draw Table** in the Draw Borders group.

b. Drag the pencil horizontally through the blank row at the top of the table.

A new row is created above *Blackberries*. You now have two blank rows available that you can use to create and format the table title and column headings.

> **TROUBLESHOOTING:** If a new table is created in this step instead of a new row, click Undo on the Quick Access Toolbar and drag the pencil through the row without touching the border of the existing table.

c. Press **Esc** to exit Draw Table mode and select both cells in the top row of the table.

d. Click the **LAYOUT tab** and click **Merge Cells** in the Merge group.

The selected cells merge into one cell for the table title. The table title is formatted with a white font color for emphasis.

e. Type the title **Top Five Foods Rich in Antioxidants** in the title row.

The wording of the title now clearly defines the table's purpose.

f. Click **Center** in the Alignment group and click **Center Vertically** in the Alignment group.

g. Change the Height value in the Cell Size group to **0.6"**.

The Cell Size group is located in the center of the Ribbon. Be careful to not use the Table Size group on the right end of the Ribbon.

h. Select the title and change the font size to **24 pt**. Click the **TABLE TOOLS DESIGN tab**, click the **Text Effects arrow** in the WordArt Styles group, point to *Shadow*, and then click **Offset Diagonal Bottom Right** (the first option under *Outer*) to add a text shadow.

The formatting of the title enhances the title message.

i. Type **Food** in the left cell of the blank row 2 and press **Tab**. Type **Antioxidants mmol/ serving** in the right cell of the blank row 2.

j. Select the column headings in row 2 and apply bold.

The column heading for the second column wraps to fit the text on two lines in the cell.

k. Click the **LAYOUT tab** and click **Center** in the Alignment group.

l. Click **Center Vertically** in the Alignment group.

m. Save the presentation. Keep the presentation open if you plan to continue with the Hands-On Exercise 2. If not, close the presentation and exit PowerPoint.

Table Design

After you create a table, you may find that its appearance or structure must be modified to ensure the tabular information can be quickly read and understood. In this section, you will learn how to set a background fill; change table borders and effects; insert and delete columns and rows; and adjust text within cells, rows, and columns—all with the goal of making information meaningful to the audience.

Because tables may be created in other software applications, you may choose to import or paste the table into PowerPoint and modify it. In this section, you will learn how to share information between applications.

Formatting Table Components

To change the appearance of a table, you may choose to apply formatting to table components, such as the header or total rows, or use the tools in the Table Style Options group on the Table Tools Design tab. You can change table components using a *table style*, a combination of formatting choices for table components based on the theme of the presentation.

STEP 1 ⟩ Whether you choose to format and customize the individual style options or apply a full table style, you should understand the different types of formatting available. Table 5.1 shows what is formatted when a table style is applied to a table component.

TABLE 5.1	Table Components and Table Style Formatting Options
Header Row	Formats the row used for the table title or column headers
Total Row	Formats the last row in the table and displays column totals
First Column	Formats the stub (first column) differently than other columns
Last Column	Formats the last column differently than the other columns
Banded Rows	Formats even rows differently than odd rows
Banded Columns	Formats even columns differently than odd columns

To apply a style option to a selected table, click the check box next to the style option name in the Table Style Options group on the Table Tools Design tab. To apply a table style from the Table Styles gallery that impacts all of the formatting options based on the theme of the presentation, click the More button in the Table Styles group. This gallery displays the Best Match for Document at the top of the gallery along with Light, Medium, and Dark styles. Note that at the bottom of the Quick Styles gallery there is an option to clear the table of all styles. It does not remove individual attributes such as bold if those attributes were applied separately, however. Figure 5.11 shows the Table Styles group and the Table Quick Styles gallery.

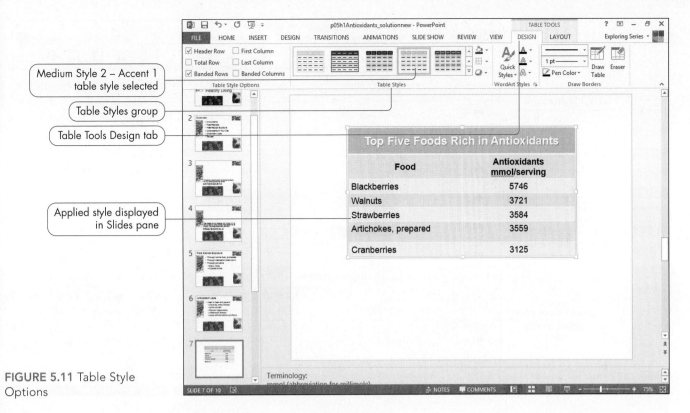

Medium Style 2 – Accent 1 table style selected

Table Styles group

Table Tools Design tab

Applied style displayed in Slides pane

FIGURE 5.11 Table Style Options

Set a Background Fill

To add an interesting element to the background of the table or selected cells, you can change the background fill style. To change the background fill style, do the following:

1. Select the cells in which you want a background change.
2. Click the TABLE TOOLS DESIGN tab.
3. Click the Shading arrow in the Table Styles group.
4. Select from Theme, Standard Colors, Picture, Gradient, Texture, or Table Background or use the eyedropper tool to pick a color from another object.

Another way to change these background attributes is to right-click in the cell or selected cells in which you want the background change and click Format Shape to display the Format Shape pane. The main advantage of using the right-click method is that the Format Shape pane enables you to choose multiple options including shape and text options, which are not available through the Table Styles group.

You can easily add a picture as the background attribute. To add a picture background to a table cell, do the following in the Format Shape pane:

1. Right-click the cell and select Format Shape.
2. If necessary, click Shape Options.
3. Click the Fill & Line button and click the *Picture or texture fill* option.
4. Click Online under *Insert picture from*.
5. Enter a keyword to search for the picture you want to insert. Locate the picture and click Insert.
6. Click Close to close the Format Shape pane.

You can also insert a clip art image or photo by clicking File instead of clicking Online. The Insert Picture dialog box opens. Navigate and locate the desired image and click Insert (alternatively, double-click the image file). Click Close. Figure 5.12 has an added column to the left of the Food column that uses a picture of berries from Microsoft's Clip Art as a background fill for the top food listing and displays the Format Shape pane options.

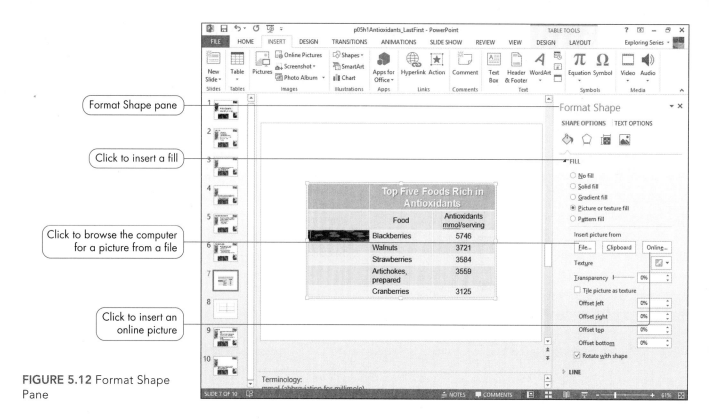

FIGURE 5.12 Format Shape Pane

Callout labels on figure:
- Format Shape pane
- Click to insert a fill
- Click to browse the computer for a picture from a file
- Click to insert an online picture

Change Table Borders

Change border style, weight, and color by using the pen options located in the Draw Borders group on the Table Tools Design tab. The Pen Style option changes the style of the line used to draw borders and includes options for dotted and dashed lines. The Pen Weight option changes the width of the border, and the Pen Color option changes the color of the border.

After selecting the style, weight, and color of a border, click the border you want to change with the pencil. You can also drag to create additional borders with the pencil. If you have multiple borders to change, however, it is faster to use the Borders button in the Table Styles group on the Table Tools Design tab. Select the cell or cells you want to affect, or select the entire table. You can choose to have no border; all cells bordered; only outside borders; only inside borders; just a top, bottom, left, or right border; inside horizontal or vertical borders; or diagonal down or up borders.

Apply a Table Special Effect

Special effects may be added to a cell, selected cells, or a table. To apply one of the effects, click Effects in the Table Styles group on the Table Tools Design tab. Three effects options include Cell Bevel, Shadow, and Reflection. Pointing to one of these options opens that effect's gallery. As with other galleries, you can preview the effects on the selected cells or the table to view the impact of the effects before committing to a choice. The gallery also includes a No option for each effect that removes any previously applied effects. Figure 5.13 shows four tables: the original table with the default style settings, a table with the Riblet bevel effect applied to all cells, a table with the Perspective Diagonal Upper Left shadow effect, and a table showing a Full Reflection, touching reflection style.

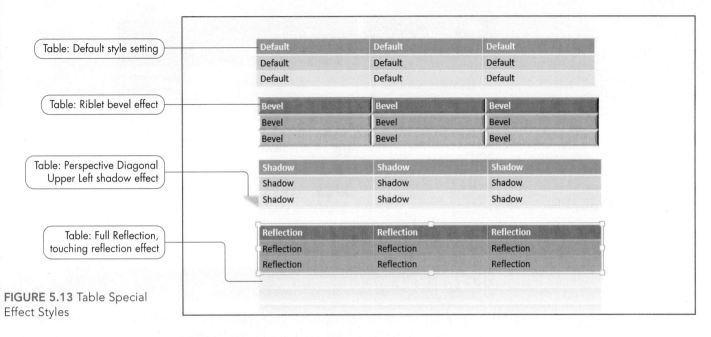

Table: Default style setting

Table: Riblet bevel effect

Table: Perspective Diagonal Upper Left shadow effect

Table: Full Reflection, touching reflection effect

FIGURE 5.13 Table Special Effect Styles

Changing Table Layout

After creating a table, or even while creating it, you can use the tools on the Table Tools Layout tab to change the layout of the table by inserting or deleting columns and rows. View Gridlines is also included on the Layout tab in the Table group, which is a toggle button that enables you to show or hide the table gridlines.

Insert Columns and Rows

STEP 2 ❯❯

You can add a row or a column to your table. To control where the row appears, click in a cell next to where you want to add the new row. Click Insert Above or Insert Below in the Rows & Columns group on the Layout tab. If you want the new row to appear at the bottom of a table, click in the last cell of the table and press Tab. The process is similar for inserting a column to the left or right of an existing column: click in a cell next to where you want the new column, and then click Insert Left or Insert Right in the Rows & Columns group on the Layout tab. As an alternative to using the Layout tab, you can right-click in a selected cell, click Insert on the context menu that displays, and then click one of the insert columns or insert rows options.

Delete Columns and Rows

To delete selected columns and rows, click Delete in the Rows & Columns group on the Layout tab and click Delete Columns, Delete Rows, or Delete Table. You can also right-click in selected cells, click Delete on the Mini toolbar, and then click Delete Columns, Delete Rows, or Delete Table. Figure 5.14 displays two tables: an original table and the same table after modifications. The theme style was changed. The modified table no longer contains a top row with a picture fill. A column was added to the left, and a clip art image was inserted in each of the resulting cells. Finally, a row was added to the bottom of the table so source information could be included.

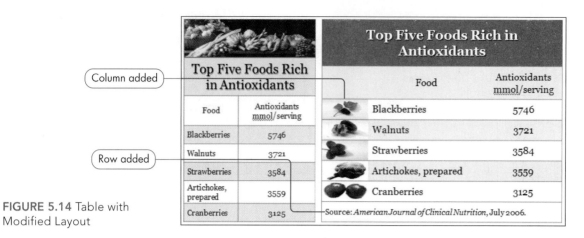

Column added

Row added

FIGURE 5.14 Table with Modified Layout

TIP | **Use the Eraser Tool**

You can quickly merge cells by clicking the Eraser tool located in the Draw Borders group on the Table Tools Design tab, and then use the Eraser tool to click the border you want to remove.

Sharing Information Between Applications

PowerPoint's table features can handle simple tables well, but if a table requires calculations, create it in Excel to take advantage of Excel's powerful data features. After creating the table, you can embed the Excel worksheet in a presentation slide as an object or link the slide to the Excel worksheet or a Word table. ***Object linking and embedding (OLE)*** lets you insert an object created in one application into a document created in another application.

STEP 3 » Linking an object differs from embedding an object. To understand the differences, you need to understand four key terms used in the object linking and embedding process (see Table 5.2).

TABLE 5.2 Object Linking and Embedding Key Terms

Key Term	Definition
Source application	The application you used to create the original object, such as Word or Excel
Destination application	The application into which the object is being inserted, such as PowerPoint
Source file	The file that contains the original table or data that is used or copied to create a linked or embedded object, such as a Word document or an Excel worksheet
Destination file	The file that contains the inserted object, such as a PowerPoint presentation with an Excel worksheet embedded in it

If you create a table in Excel and paste it into a PowerPoint slide, Excel is the source application and PowerPoint is the destination application. The Excel file containing the table is the source file for the object. Once you insert the table object into PowerPoint, the PowerPoint presentation is the destination file. The simplest way to transfer any object is to copy it within the source application, and then paste it into the destination application. This embeds the copied object into the application.

An ***embedded object*** becomes a part of the destination file, and, once inserted, the object is no longer a part of the source file. An embedded object does not maintain a connection to the source file or source application in which the object was created. For example, a cell range of data copied from Excel and pasted into PowerPoint results in a table object displaying the data that can be edited as a table. Changes to the table data in PowerPoint do not change the source cells within the original Excel file. The PowerPoint table tool options appear on the Ribbon when the data is selected in PowerPoint, and the table is treated as any other table of data.

In the case of a chart created in Excel, the default option to paste creates a linked object. You would need to choose the option to paste as a picture to embed the chart into PowerPoint without a link to the source file. The PowerPoint Ribbon would display picture tool options. Figure 5.15 shows a PowerPoint presentation with an embedded table. It is important to note that if you edit the embedded table, the source document (an Excel document in this example) is *not* changed.

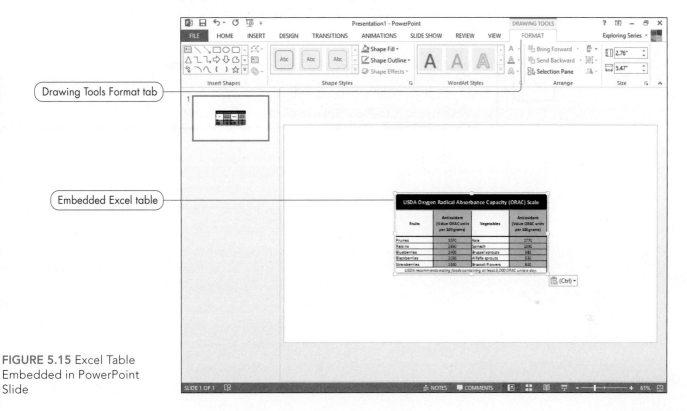

FIGURE 5.15 Excel Table Embedded in PowerPoint Slide

If you link an object, the information is stored in the source file, and the object in the destination file is updated when you modify it in the source file. When you double-click a linked object, the source application opens, and you are actually editing the source file. The changes you make in the source file display in PowerPoint. The **linked object** stores the data in the source file. The destination file stores only the location of the source file while displaying a picture or representation of the linked data from the source file. The representation in PowerPoint is only a shortcut to the source file so that changes to the source file are reflected and updated in the presentation. One advantage of linking is a smaller file size because PowerPoint stores only the link to the data needed to display the information. Another advantage is the data only needs to be changed once in the source file, and any files linked to that source file automatically update the information. However, there may be times when it is not desirable to update the data, in which case an embedded object is the desired method.

To embed a new object, do the following:

1. Open the source file.
2. Select and copy the object or data.
3. Click to make the destination PowerPoint file active and click at the insertion point.
4. Paste the object into PowerPoint.

To link a previously created object, do the following:

1. Open the source file.
2. Select and copy the object or data.
3. Click to make the destination PowerPoint file active and click at the insertion point.
4. Click the Paste arrow and click Paste Special.
5. In the Paste Special dialog box, check the *Paste link* option, choose the object type in the As box, such as a Microsoft Excel Worksheet Object, and then click OK.

Alternatively, you can link an object into PowerPoint by using the Object button in the Text group on the Insert tab. From the Insert Object dialog box, choose the *Create new* option, which links to a new file, or choose the *Create from file* option, which enables navigating (Browse) to an existing file. The *Display as icon* option displays an icon in the PowerPoint presentation, and double-clicking the icon launches the source file. Click OK when you are finished.

Quick
Concepts

1. What Ribbon tab provides table formatting options? ***p. 326***
2. Define an embedded object. ***p. 330***
3. What type of data does a linked object represent? ***p. 331***

Hands-On Exercises

Watch the Video for this Hands-On Exercise!

MyITLab®
HOE2 Training

2 Table Design

You continue revising the county health fair antioxidants presentation to make the information in the tables easy to read and to enhance their appearance.

Skills covered: Format Table Components • Change Table Layouts • Share Information Between Applications

STEP 1 ≫ FORMAT TABLE COMPONENTS

You enhance the table on Slide 7 by changing the table style to a clean, clear style. You add a column to the table, and then format the cells in the column to include pictures of the food mentioned in the middle column. As a final step, you add a row to the table so that you can acknowledge a source. Refer to Figure 5.16 as you complete Step 1.

Step p: Vertically centered text

Steps i–j: Photographs added

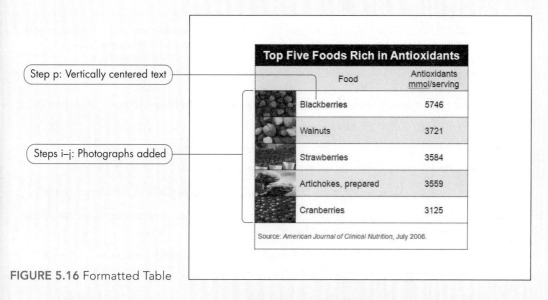

Top Five Foods Rich in Antioxidants		
	Food	Antioxidants mmol/serving
	Blackberries	5746
	Walnuts	3721
	Strawberries	3584
	Artichokes, prepared	3559
	Cranberries	3125
Source: American Journal of Clinical Nutrition, July 2006.		

FIGURE 5.16 Formatted Table

a. Open the *p05h1Antioxidants_LastFirst* slide show, if necessary. Save the slide show as **p05h2Antioxidants_LastFirst**, changing the *h1* to *h2*.

b. On Slide 7, select the table. Click the **TABLE TOOLS DESIGN tab**, click the **More button** in the Table Styles group, and then select **Medium Style 1 - Accent 4** (first row, fifth column, Medium category).

Medium Style 1 - Accent 4 includes a Header Row style and a Banded Rows style. The black font color can be easily read.

TIP Control Table Style Options

The Table Style Options group in the Table Tools Design tab is where you can turn on or turn off the various style options that control table styles.

c. Click in any of the cells in the first column, click the **LAYOUT tab**, and then click **Insert Left** in the Rows & Columns group.

A new column is inserted to the left of the Food column.

d. Select both cells in the top row and click **Merge Cells** in the Merge group.

e. Click in the new left column, click in the **Width box** in the Cell Size group, type **1.2**, and then press **Enter** to apply the change. Change the width of the middle column to **3"** and the width of the right column to **2"**.

f. Select the last five rows of the table (exclude the title and column heading rows), click in the **Height box** in the Cell Size group, and then type **.75**.

g. Click in the cell to the left of *Blackberries* and right-click.

h. Click **Format Shape** to open the Format Shape pane, click **Fill & Line** (image of bucket), if necessary, and then click **Fill** to open the fill options. Click the **Picture or texture fill option** if necessary.

A texture appears in your cell.

i. Click **Online** to open the Insert Picture dialog box, type **blackberries** in the **Office.com Clip Art Search box**, and then press **Enter**. Select the photograph of the blackberries and raspberries (see Figure 5.16) that appears in the search results and click **Insert** to close the Insert Picture dialog box. Close the Format Shape pane.

TROUBLESHOOTING: If you do not see a photograph of blackberries and raspberries, you may not have Internet access. Substitute a clip art image if you are not able to access the Internet.

---

j. Repeat steps h and i to insert photographs in the cells to the left of *Walnuts, Strawberries, Artichokes*, and *Cranberries*.

k. Position the pointer in the last cell of the table and press **Tab**.

A new row is created with the properties of the row above it.

l. Select the cells in the newly created last row and click **Merge Cells** in the Merge group.

m. Right-click the merged cell to display the Format Shape pane, if necessary. Click **No Fill** in the Format Shape pane and click **Close**.

n. Type **Source:** *American Journal of Clinical Nutrition,* **July 2006**. Be sure to apply italic formatting to the text as shown. Select the text and change the font size to **14 pt**.

o. Drag the table (at the border edge) to reposition to the approximate vertical center of the slide.

p. Select **rows 3 through 8** and click **Center Vertically** in the Alignment group on the LAYOUT tab.

q. Save the presentation.

STEP 2 ≫ CHANGE TABLE LAYOUTS

As you work with the design of the tables in your slide show, you often find that changing the structure of a table requires that you change the formatting of a table and vice versa. Each choice you make entails making further choices as you refine the presentation. In this exercise, you continue refining the tables in your antioxidants presentation. Refer to Figure 5.17 as you complete Step 2.

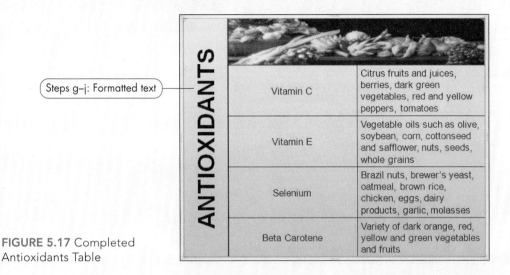

Steps g–j: Formatted text

FIGURE 5.17 Completed Antioxidants Table

a. Select the table on Slide 8. Click the **TABLE TOOLS DESIGN tab**, click the **More button** in the Table Styles group, and then click **Themed Style 1 - Accent 4** (first row, fifth column, *Best Match for Document* category).

b. Click **Eraser** in the Draw Borders group and click the vertical border that splits row 1 into two cells. (Do not click the border that divides columns 2 and 3 for the remaining rows.) Press **Esc**.

   The border disappears, and the cells merge into one.

c. Click in the top row. Click the **Shading arrow** in the Table Styles group and click **Picture**.

d. Click **Browse** in the Insert Picture dialog box, locate and select *p05h2Fruits.jpg*, and then click **Insert**.

   The image is resized to fit the row.

e. Click the **LAYOUT tab**, change the row height to **1.2"**, and then press **Enter**.

f. Enter the remaining data, as shown in Figure 5.17, without worrying about the text size or position.

g. Click in **column 1**, click **Text Direction** in the Alignment group, and then click **Rotate all text 270°**.

h. Click **Center Vertically** in the Alignment group.

i. Select the **Antioxidants text** in column 1, change the font size to **44 pt**, and then click **Center** for the alignment. Click the **TABLE TOOLS DESIGN tab**. Click **Effects** in the Table Styles group and click **Shadow** and **Offset Bottom** (under *Outer*).

j. Click the **First Column option** in the Table Style Options group.

   Activating the First Column table style bolds the text in the first column and creates a bold black border between the first column and the remaining columns.

k. Drag the table to the approximate vertical and horizontal center of the slide.

l. Save the presentation.

You have an Excel file that contains data for the USDA Oxygen Radical Absorbance Capacity (ORAC) Scale that you want to include in the presentation. Rather than re-create this information, you insert a linked copy of the table in your presentation. Refer to Figure 5.18 as you complete Step 3.

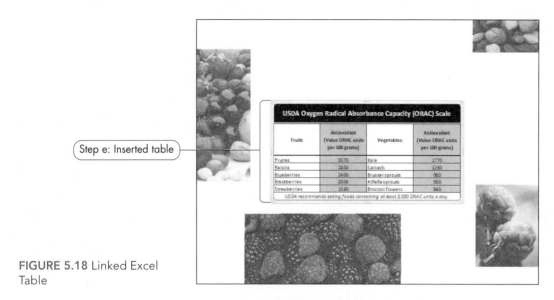

Step e: Inserted table

FIGURE 5.18 Linked Excel Table

a. Create a new slide after Slide 8 using the Blank layout.

b. Open *p05h2Orac.xlsx* and save the file as **p05h2Orac_LastFirst.xlsx**.

c. Select the **range A1:D8** to select all the table data in the Excel file. Click **Copy** in the Clipboard group on the HOME tab (or press **Ctrl+C**).

d. Click the PowerPoint file on the Windows taskbar to make the presentation the active file. Click the **Paste arrow** in the Clipboard group on the HOME tab and click **Paste Special**.

e. Click the **Paste link option** in the Paste Special dialog box. Click **Microsoft Excel Worksheet Object** in the As box, if necessary, and then click **OK**.

A copy of the Excel table is inserted into your presentation. The copy is a shortcut link to the original data file so that changes to the source data file are reflected in your presentation.

f. Close the Excel file. Double-click the table object in the presentation.

The source application, the Microsoft Excel file, opens for editing.

g. Select **row 2** in Excel, click the **Font Color arrow**, and then select **Red** under *Standard Colors*.

The column headings in the linked table change to reflect the editing you performed in Excel.

h. Observe the color change to the column headings in the presentation. Save the changes in the Excel file. Close Excel.

i. Save the presentation. Keep the presentation open if you plan to continue with the Hands-On Exercise 3. If not, close the presentation and exit PowerPoint.

Statistical Charts and Graphs

Statistical charts and graphs help you communicate numerical relationships more effectively than using words to describe them. A chart or graph can compare data and show trends or patterns. Summarizing information in a chart or graph helps your audience understand and retain your message.

In this section, you will identify chart types and elements. Then you will learn how to create and insert a chart in a slide.

Identifying Chart Types and Elements

PowerPoint includes tools to create professional-looking charts. You can even save your chart as a template so you can apply the same formatting to new charts of the same type. When you create a chart using PowerPoint, you enter the information in an Excel workbook. The Excel worksheet you use to create the chart is then embedded in your presentation.

Whereas the term *chart* can refer to visual displays of information such as tables, maps, lists, SmartArt diagrams, and others, the term *graph* is specific to a chart that displays a relationship between two sets of numbers plotted as data points with coordinates on a grid. These two terms have become synonymous and are used interchangeably now. Microsoft Office applications use the term *chart* to describe the charts and graphs provided for your use.

Before beginning to create a chart, think about the information you are presenting and determine what message you want to convey using a chart. Are you representing changes over time? Are you comparing or summarizing data? Are you representing a single series or multiple series? What type of chart will your audience understand quickly?

Select Basic Chart Types

Each of the basic chart types has appropriate uses. Choose the type that portrays your message most effectively. The chart should be clear and easy to read and should present enough detail to provide the audience with an understanding of your message without overwhelming people with detail. Generally, audiences can easily understand the commonly used charts, such as pie, line, column, and bar charts.

Office includes a wide variety of charts: column charts, line charts, pie charts, bar charts, area charts, XY (scatter) charts, stock charts, surface charts, doughnut charts, bubble charts, and radar charts. The most common purposes of some of these charts are listed in Table 5.3. For greater detail on the available chart types, including chart subtype information, enter chart types in the Search box for PowerPoint Help and click the hyperlink for Available chart types.

TABLE 5.3 Reference Chart Purposes

Type	Series Type	Purpose	Sample Chart
Pie chart	Single-series	Use to show proportions of a whole. Slices are proportioned to show the relative size of each piece. Information is from data arranged in only one column or row.	
Doughnut chart	Multi-series	Use to show the relationship of parts to a whole like a pie chart but can contain more than one data series. The doughnut contains a hole in the center. Information is from data arranged only in columns or rows.	
Column chart	Single- or multi-series	Use to show data changes over a period of time or comparisons among items. Information is arranged in columns or rows and is used to plot the chart using a horizontal and a vertical axis. Categories are typically organized along the horizontal axis and values along the vertical axis. The information is displayed in vertical columns. Shapes other than vertical bars can be used for the columns, including 3-D bars, cylinders, cones, and pyramids.	
Line chart	Single- or multi-series	Use to display a large number of data points over time. Ideal for showing trends over equal time intervals such as months, quarters, or years. Information is arranged in columns or rows on a worksheet and set against a common scale. Category information is distributed evenly along the horizontal axis, and all value information is distributed evenly along the vertical axis. The information is displayed as individual points linked by lines.	
Bar chart	Single- or multi-series	Use to show comparisons between items. Information is arranged in columns or rows on a worksheet the same as in a column chart, but the bars stretch horizontally instead of vertically.	
Area chart	Single- or multi-series	Use to emphasize the magnitude of change over time. Draws attention to the total value across a trend. Basically, a line graph with the area below the plotted lines filled in. Information is arranged in columns or rows on a worksheet.	
XY (scatter) chart	Single- or multi-series	Use to show the relationships among the numeric values in several data series, or plot two groups of numbers as one series of XY coordinates. This shows distributions, groupings, or patterns. A scatter chart plots two variables, one of which is plotted on the horizontal (X) scale and one of which is plotted on the vertical (Y) scale.	

Type	Series Type	Purpose	Sample Chart
Stock chart	Single- or multi-series	Use to show fluctuations or the range of change between the high and low values of a subject over time. Commonly used to show fluctuation of stock prices, but can be used for fluctuations in temperature or scientific data. Data must be arranged in columns or rows in a specific order on the worksheet. To create a simple high-low-close stock chart, data must be arranged with High, Low, and Close entered as column headings, in that order.	
Surface chart	Single- or multi-series	Use to plot a surface using two sets of data. Colors indicate areas that are in the same range of values. Information is arranged in columns or rows on a worksheet. This is similar to a line graph but with a dimensional effect added.	
Bubble chart	Single- or multi-series	Use to show relationships like an XY (scatter) chart, but uses three values instead of two. The third value determines the size of the bubble. Bubble charts should not be used to show absolute quantities, as the scales are relative. Information is arranged in columns on the worksheet so that X values are listed in the first column and corresponding Y values and bubble size values are listed in adjacent columns.	
Radar chart	Multi-series	Use to compare the aggregate values of three or more variables represented on axes starting from the same point, like the spokes on a wheel. Enables you to use multiple criteria. Information is arranged in columns or rows on a worksheet.	

Identify Chart Elements

When you enter the data for your table in an Excel workbook, the cells that contain numeric values are called data points. A **data series** contains the data points representing a set of related numbers. The data series can be a **single-series data series** (representing only one set of data) or a **multiseries data series** (representing data for two or more sets of data). For example, you would plot the profits for a store in Destin, Florida, on a single-series chart, and the profits for stores in Destin, Fort Walton Beach, and Pensacola, Florida, on a multi-series chart.

A pie chart is an example of a single-series chart. With the whole represented as a circle, a pie chart shows the proportional relationship of each segment to the whole. A fill may be applied to each segment, or slice, or applied to the entire pie. A **label** identifies data in a chart—for example, in a pie chart, the label identifies the slices in the pie. The slices can be labeled with the series name, category name, value, or percentage. The labels can be centered, positioned inside a slice, positioned outside of the slice, or positioned according to the Best Fit option, which is based on the amount of text inside the label. Leaders are lines used to connect the label to the slice of pie. Though it is preferable to have the labels within a pie slice, often they do not fit. In that case, leaders become necessary to avoid possible confusion. Exploded pie charts emphasize data by separating, or exploding, a slice or slices from the pie.

Figure 5.19 shows a pie chart with a single series—the assets of a charitable foundation. The chart includes a title and labels indicating the category names and the percentage each slice of the pie contributes to the total. The Trusts slice is exploded for emphasis. The **chart area** (the chart and all of its elements) is bounded by the placeholder borders, whereas the **plot area** (the area representing the data) is defined by a bounding box comprised of single lines.

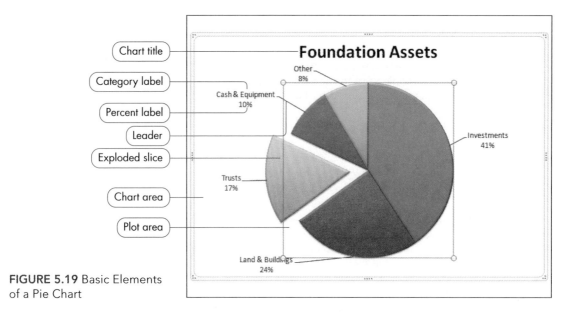

FIGURE 5.19 Basic Elements of a Pie Chart

The remaining chart types available in Office are plotted on a coordinate system and may be single-series or multiseries charts. The chart is created by plotting data points between two reference lines, or scales, called axes. The **X-axis** is the horizontal axis and usually contains the category information, such as products, companies, or intervals of time. The **Y-axis** is the vertical axis and usually contains the values or amounts. Three-dimensional charts have a third axis, the **Z-axis**, used to plot the depth of a chart. Axes can be given titles to describe what the data represent. Note that some chart types, such as pie charts, do not have axes.

Gridlines, lines that extend from the horizontal or vertical axes, can be displayed to make the chart data easier to read and understand. Tick marks are short lines on the axes that mark the category and value divisions. Data points plotted on the chart are indicated by data markers, or graphical representations such as bars, dots, or slices that can be enhanced with lines, filled areas, or pictures. To help identify the data series, a **legend** assigns a format or color to each data series and then displays that information with the data series name. Legends are only necessary for multiseries charts. Figure 5.20 shows the basic elements of a column chart.

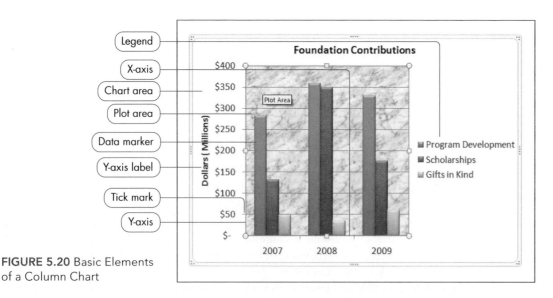

FIGURE 5.20 Basic Elements of a Column Chart

Creating and Inserting a Chart

To create a chart, start by clicking the Chart icon in a content placeholder or by clicking the Insert tab, and then clicking Chart in the Illustrations group. The Insert Chart dialog box opens with two panes. The left pane contains the chart types, and the right pane contains chart styles, or subtypes, and a preview of the selected chart type. Figure 5.21 displays the default chart type, a column chart, in the left pane and the default chart style, Clustered Column, in the right pane.

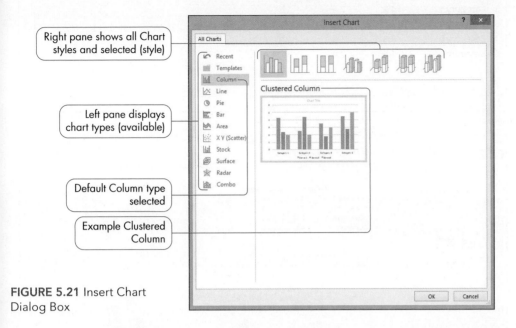

Right pane shows all Chart styles and selected (style)

Left pane displays chart types (available)

Default Column type selected

Example Clustered Column

FIGURE 5.21 Insert Chart Dialog Box

STEP 1 »

STEP 3 »

After selecting the chart type and style, click OK. Microsoft Excel opens with a worksheet containing sample data, and the PowerPoint presentation contains a chart based on the sample data. The title of the Excel workbook is *Chart in Microsoft PowerPoint*. Replace the sample data with your own data, and the PowerPoint chart updates to reflect the updated information. The Excel worksheet contains a grid of rows and columns. When you type in a cell, you replace the sample data, and your data point is created in your chart. When you enter the data, you might need to change the row heights or column widths to fit the data. If pound signs display (#####) in a cell, it means there is not enough room in the cell to display the data. To increase the width of the column, position the pointer on the line to the right of the column heading, and then double-click to adjust the column width automatically. To resize the chart data range, drag the bottom-right corner of the range. When you finish entering the data, click the Close (X) button in Excel and view the chart embedded in PowerPoint.

> ### TIP Delete the Sample Chart Data
>
> To quickly delete the sample data in a chart, click the Select All button (the intersection between the column designations and the row designations), which is located in the top left of the worksheet. This selects all of the cells in the worksheet. Once they are selected, press Delete on the keyboard.

If you close Excel and then need to edit the data the chart is based upon, click the chart, click the Chart Tools Design tab, and then click Edit Data in the Data group. The Excel worksheet reopens so you can edit your data. When you are done editing, click the Close button on the Excel worksheet to return to PowerPoint. Figure 5.22 shows an Excel worksheet, and Figure 5.23 shows the associated chart created in PowerPoint.

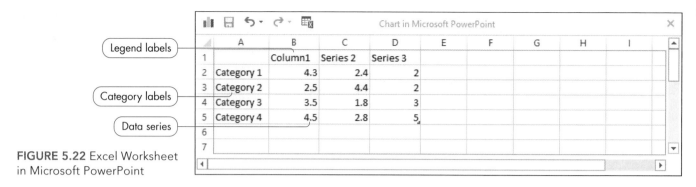

FIGURE 5.22 Excel Worksheet in Microsoft PowerPoint

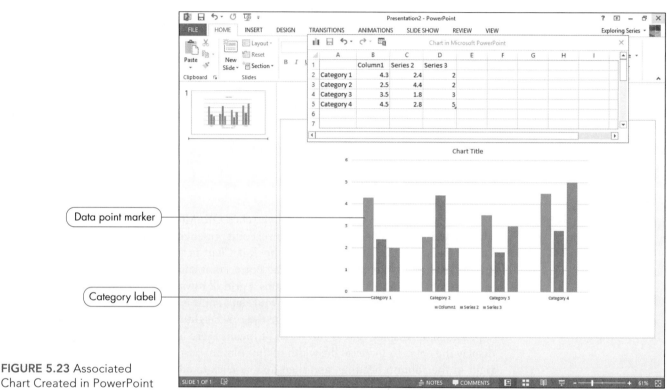

FIGURE 5.23 Associated Chart Created in PowerPoint

Switching Row and Column Data

By default, a chart is plotted based on the series data displayed in the columns of the worksheet and the column headings displayed in the legend. Because of this, the chart in Figure 5.23 emphasizes the changes in each category over three series. You can switch the emphasis if you want to emphasize the changes by year rather than by category. To do so, click Switch Row/Column in the Data group on the Design tab in PowerPoint.

STEP 2>>

The chart shown in Figure 5.23 is at its most basic level. Charts should be modified and formatted to ensure that the chart conveys the intended message. For example, without a descriptive title or labels, it is impossible to tell the purpose of the chart or what the amounts represent. In Hands-On Exercise 3, you create a basic pie chart and a column chart, and then in the next section, you explore modifications and formatting changes that complete your chart.

Quick Concepts ✓

1. Statistical charts and graphs are used to communicate what type of data? *p. 337*

2. List the type of data relationships represented by a column chart. *p. 338*

3. A pie chart is used to represent what type of data? *p. 338*

3 Statistical Charts and Graphs

Although antioxidants are available in common foods, some foods are referred to as superfruits because of the high level of antioxidants per serving. You want to show the audience at the county health fair a comparison of the antioxidant levels in a top "common" food and some of the superfruits. You create a chart to illustrate this comparison and also create a chart to show the ideal percentage of each food group in an average diet.

Skills covered: Create and Edit a Basic Column Chart • Switch the Row and Column Data • Create a Basic Pie Chart

STEP 1 ≫ CREATE AND EDIT A BASIC COLUMN CHART

You create a clustered column chart to compare the antioxidant levels in foods. While proofreading the chart, you notice an incorrect amount and a missing fruit, so you edit the chart. Refer to Figure 5.24 as you complete Step 1.

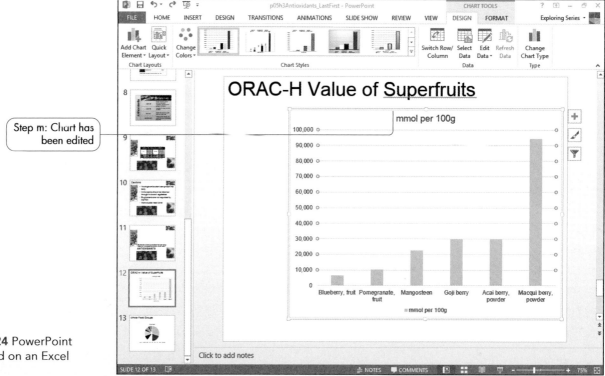

FIGURE 5.24 PowerPoint Chart Based on an Excel Worksheet

a. Open the *p05h2Antioxidants_LastFirst* slide show, if necessary. Save the slide show as **p05h3Antioxidants_LastFirst**, changing the *h2* to *h3*.

b. Insert a new slide after Slide 11 using the Title and Content layout.

c. On the new Slide 12, type **ORAC-H Value of Superfruits** in the **title placeholder**. Click outside the title placeholder.

d. Click the **DESIGN tab**, click **Format Background** in the Customize group, and then click the **Hide background graphics option** in the Format Background pane. Close the Format Background pane.

e. Click the **Insert Chart icon** on the slide. Note the default setting of Column chart, Clustered Column subtype, in the Insert Chart dialog box. Click **OK**.

   Excel opens with sample data.

f. Replace the worksheet data with the following data:

	mmol per 100g
Blueberry, fruit	6,500
Mangosteen	22,500
Goji berry	10,000
Acai berry, powder	30,000
Macqui berry, powder	94,500

g. Drag the bottom-right corner of the chart data range to resize the range to fit the data you just entered and exclude any remaining sample data.

   Series 2 and Series 3 of the sample data are not needed, and the data do not display on the PowerPoint chart once you resize the range to fit the data. If you want to clean up the source data file, the unwanted sample Series 2 and Series 3 data can be deleted.

h. Close the Excel worksheet and return to PowerPoint.

i. Click the **CHART TOOLS DESIGN tab**, if necessary, and click the **Edit Data arrow** in the Data group. Click **Edit Data in Excel 2013**. Maximize the Excel window.

   Excel opens, displaying the chart data again.

j. Click the **row 3 indicator** (Mangosteen row), right-click, and then click **Insert**.

   A new row 3 is inserted above the original row 3.

k. Type **Pomegranate, fruit** in **cell A3**, press **Tab**, and then type **10,500**.

l. Click in **cell B5**, type **30,000**, and then press **Enter**.

m. Close the Excel worksheet and return to PowerPoint.

n. Save the presentation.

STEP 2 ≫ SWITCH THE ROW AND COLUMN DATA

After evaluating the graph, you decide that you want the list of superfruits in the legend. You will swap the data from a single-series data set to a multiseries data set. Refer to Figure 5.25 as you complete Step 2.

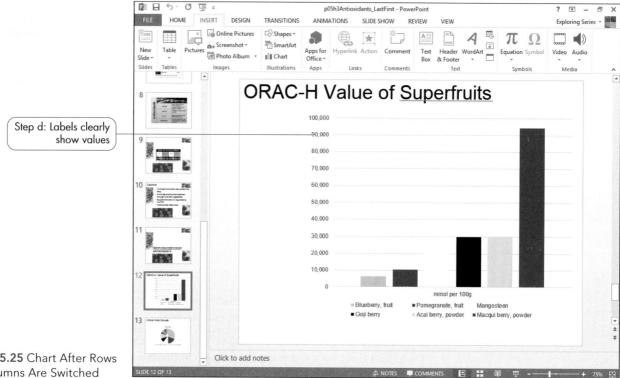

FIGURE 5.25 Chart After Rows and Columns Are Switched

a. Select the chart (if necessary).

b. Click **Select Data** in the Data group on the CHART TOOLS DESIGN tab.

The Select Data Source dialog box opens, as does Excel. The Legend Entries (Series) pane shows the *mmol per 100g* series entry, and the Horizontal (Category) Axis Labels display the food category.

c. Click **Switch Row/Column**.

The Legend Entries (Series) pane now displays the food categories, and the Horizontal (Category) Axis Labels pane now displays the *mmol per 100g* entry (see Figure 5.26).

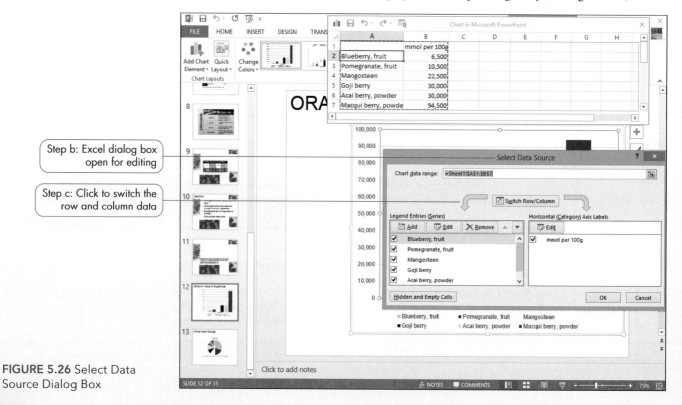

FIGURE 5.26 Select Data Source Dialog Box

d. Click **OK** and close the Excel worksheet.

> The data markers (bars) now clearly show that *Maqui berry, powder* exceeds the other superfruit ORAC-H values. Two of the markers display the same color, so a modification is necessary. You will correct this problem in Hands-On Exercise 4.

e. Save the presentation.

STEP 3 ≫ CREATE A BASIC PIE CHART

Because antioxidants are available from so many different food sources, you decide that, as part of the summary, you will discuss the ideal percentage of each food group in an average diet. As you discuss each food group, you will suggest foods in that group that contain antioxidants. You create a basic pie chart displaying the food groups as an aid for this discussion. Refer to Figure 5.27 as you complete Step 3.

FIGURE 5.27 Basic Pie Chart

a. Create a new slide after Slide 12 using the Title Only layout.

b. Type **Whole Food Groups** in the **title placeholder**. Click outside of the title placeholder.

c. Click the **DESIGN tab**, click **Format Background** in the Customize group, and then click the **Hide background graphics** option in the Format Background pane. Close the Format Background pane.

d. Click the **INSERT tab** and click **Chart** in the Illustrations group.

> The Insert Chart dialog box opens.

e. Click **Pie** in the left pane and click **OK**.

> The default pie chart type is automatically selected, and Excel opens with sample pie chart data.

f. Enter the following data for your pie chart in Excel.

	Percentage
Grains	30
Veggies	20
Meat	10
Nuts	10
Fruit	10
Dairy	5
Oils	5
Eggs	5
Legumes	5

Because a pie chart is a single-series chart, only one data series (Percentage) is entered.

g. Drag the bottom-right corner of the chart data range to resize the range to fit the data you just entered, if necessary.

> **TROUBLESHOOTING:** If you close Excel before resizing the range, not all the categories will display. Click Edit Data in the Data group on the Chart Tools Design tab to reopen Excel and resize the range to fit all categories.

h. Close the Excel worksheet.

A basic pie chart is displayed in PowerPoint. The chart needs to be modified because duplicate colors exist, and the white slice disappears into the background. You will make these modifications in Hands-On Exercise 4.

i. Save the presentation. Keep the presentation open if you plan to continue with Hands-On Exercise 4. If not, close the presentation and exit PowerPoint.

Chart Modification

Charts should be modified and formatted to ensure that the message is conveyed quickly and accurately. Adding a chart title or subtitle, axis titles, data labels, or a legend can help clarify the message, but you must balance the need for clarity with the need for simplicity. This can be a challenge, so ask a classmate or coworker to review your chart and describe their understanding of what your message is.

In addition, review your chart data to see if the numbers can be shortened by showing them as thousands, millions, or other values. If you shorten the numbers on the value axis (Y-axis), you must include an axis label identifying the axis as "in thousands" or "in millions." If you want your audience to see the actual data upon which the chart is based, you can show the data table with or without a legend.

In this section, you will learn how to change a chart type, change a chart layout, and format chart elements.

Changing a Chart Type

After creating the chart, you can experiment with other chart types to see which chart type conveys the message most effectively. For example, you may find that due to the number of bars created by the data, your column chart is cluttered and difficult to read. Changing the chart type to a line chart may show the same information in a clean, easy-to-understand format.

Changing the chart subtype may be enough to emphasize the desired point. Each of the chart types available includes subtypes or variations. Changing the subtype can give the chart a totally different look or can change the purpose of the chart dramatically. The variations include changing from 2-D formatting to 3-D formatting, stacking the data, changing the marker shape, and exploding slices, to name a few.

STEP 1 》 To change the chart type or subtype, do the following:

1. Select the chart.
2. Click the CHART TOOLS DESIGN tab.
3. Click Change Chart Type in the Type group.
4. Click the chart type you want from the left pane or the chart subtype from the right pane.
5. Click OK.

Changing the Chart Layout

Each chart type has predefined layouts that you can quickly apply to your chart. Although you can change each element of the layout individually by manually selecting a style for the individual elements, using a predefined layout keeps your charts consistent and maintains a professional feel to your presentation. To apply a predefined layout, select your chart and click the Chart Tools Design tab. Click Quick Layout in the Chart Layouts group and select the desired layout.

STEP 2 》 To change the layout manually, click the Chart Tools Design tab. Click Add Chart Element in the Chart Layouts group, choose the chart element you want to change, and then select one of the predefined options or click More Options at the bottom of the list. For example, the legend can be moved to predefined locations in the chart. Figure 5.28 shows a sample chart with the legend located at the bottom of the chart.

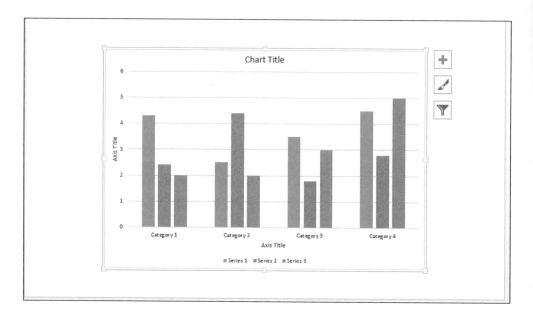

FIGURE 5.28 Chart with Legend Located at the Bottom of the Chart

1. Select the chart.
2. Click the DESIGN tab.
3. Click Add Chart Element.
4. Click Legend.
5. Click Bottom.

A chart layout generally includes a title, axis titles, and a legend. You can modify each of these elements manually by clicking each element from the Add Chart Element options.

PowerPoint determines the measurement or increments on the chart's Y-axis automatically based on the data entered in the worksheet. However, you can change the measurement used—but be careful when changing the measurements of the axes. Changing the Y-axis measurement to a smaller increment can exaggerate the data peaks and valleys displayed in the chart. Changing the measurements to larger increments can flatten or smooth out the data peaks and valleys. Additionally, when the measurements use Excel's Auto feature, they automatically adjust if you make changes to the data to which the maximum and minimum values need to adapt. By contrast, manual measurements do not adapt unless manual readjustments are applied; thus, changes to the Excel data may also require additional changes to the axis measurements for the chart.

To change the chart axis, click the Design tab and click Add Chart Element in the Chart Layouts group. Click Axes, select the axis options you wish to change, and then make the desired changes.

Formatting Chart Elements

To change chart elements such as the fill of a bar in a bar chart, select the element by either clicking it or choosing the element from the list available when you click the Chart Elements arrow in the Current Selection group on the Format tab. You can change shape fills, outline styles, and shape effects on the chart objects just as you changed shapes in SmartArt. After selecting the element, choose Shape Fill, Shape Outline, or Shape Effects from the Shape Styles group on the Format tab.

STEP 3 ❯❯

To make multiple formatting changes to an element, click Format Selection in the Current Selection group on the Format tab. This opens the Format pane for the element you have selected. Depending on that element, you can change the fill, border color, border styles, shadow, and 3-D format simply by clicking options such as Fill & Line, Effects, or Series, and choosing the formatting in the Format pane.

Quick Concepts ✓

1. How can you ensure that a chart conveys your message quickly and accurately? *p. 348*

2. Why would you want to use a predefined layout for your chart? *p. 349*

3. Name three components of a chart's layout. *p. 350*

Hands-On Exercises

Watch the Video for this Hands-On Exercise!

MyITLab®
HOE4 Training

4 Chart Modification

In your final review of the county health fair presentation, you modify the charts you have created to change a chart type for ease of reading and to correct problems with chart layouts and elements.

Skills covered: Change a Chart Type • Change a Chart Layout • Format Chart Elements

STEP 1 ≫ CHANGE A CHART TYPE

The chart on Slide 12 contains data about the amount of antioxidants per 100 grams of superfruit. You decide to convert the chart into a bar chart so that the viewer can read down a list to quickly identify the superfruit providing the most antioxidants. Refer to Figure 5.29 as you complete Step 1.

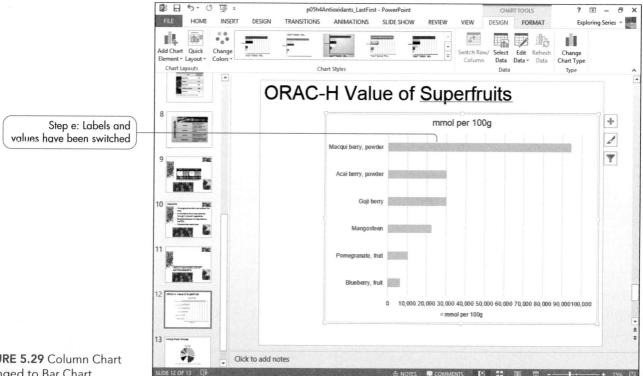

Step e: Labels and values have been switched

FIGURE 5.29 Column Chart Changed to Bar Chart

a. Open *p05h3Antioxidants_LastFirst*, if necessary. Save the presentation as **p05h4Antioxidants_ LastFirst**, changing the *h3* to *h4*.

b. On Slide 12, select the chart.

c. Click the **CHART TOOLS DESIGN tab** and click **Change Chart Type** in the Type group.

d. Select **Bar** as the chart type and accept the default subtype. Click **OK**. Reselect the chart if necessary.

The column chart type changes to the bar chart type.

e. Click **Select Data** in the Data group, click **Switch Row/Column**, click **OK**, and then close Excel.

The superfruits are listed down the vertical axis, and the values are displayed along the horizontal axis. The legend displays but is unnecessary because of the chart title.

f. Save the presentation.

STEP 2 ≫ CHANGE A CHART LAYOUT

You decide that including data labels would help the county health fair viewers understand the data. You change the layout of the bar chart so that the labels are easily added and also decide to change the fill of the bars by applying a style to make them more visible when projected. Refer to Figure 5.30 as you complete Step 2.

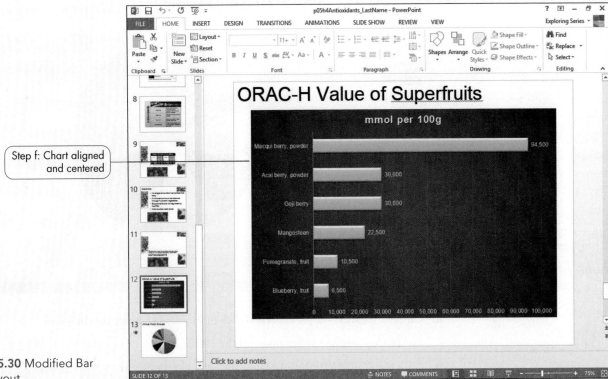

FIGURE 5.30 Modified Bar Chart Layout

a. On Slide 12, select the chart, if necessary.

b. Click the **CHART TOOLS DESIGN tab**, click **Quick Layout** in the Chart Layouts group, and then click **Layout 2**.

Layout 2 puts data labels at the outside ends of the bars and removes the horizontal axis. Layout 2 also moves the legend underneath the chart title. The legend is unnecessary and will be addressed in the next instruction.

c. Click **Add Chart Element** in the Chart Layouts group, click **Legend**, and then select **None**.

The legend is deleted.

d. Click **More** in the Chart Styles group on the CHART TOOLS DESIGN tab and click **Style 7**.

A dark background is applied to make the chart more readable and to add contrast.

e. Click the border of the chart if necessary, click the **FORMAT tab**, and then change the width of the chart to **9"** in the Size group.

f. Click **Align Objects** in the Arrange group and click **Align Middle**. Click **Align Objects** again and click **Align Center**.

g. Save the presentation.

STEP 3 ›› FORMAT CHART ELEMENTS

After reviewing the pie chart on Slide 13, you decide several elements of the chart need to be formatted. The white slice blends with the background, so the color style of the chart needs to be changed. You also want the category name and percentage on the inside end of each pie slice. Finally, because you want to discuss each food group with the county health fair attendees, you apply an animation to bring the slices in one at a time. Refer to Figure 5.31 as you complete Step 3.

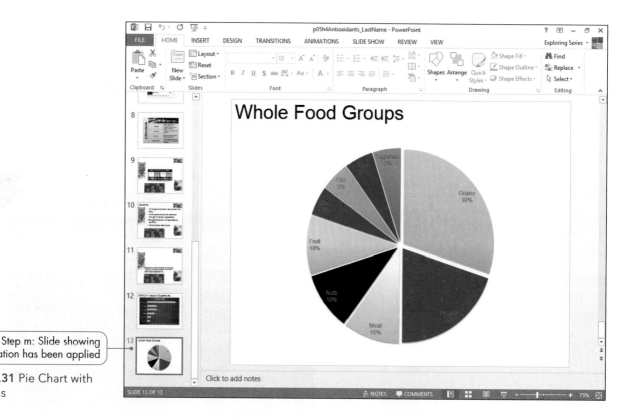

Step m: Slide showing animation has been applied

FIGURE 5.31 Pie Chart with Animations

a. On Slide 13, select the **pie chart** and click the border to activate the chart area.

The chart is selected rather than just the pie slices.

b. Click the **FORMAT tab** and change the height of the chart to **6.7"** in the Size group.

The change in the chart height moves part of the chart off the slide.

c. Click **Align Objects** in the Arrange group and click **Align Bottom**. Click **Align Objects** again and click **Align Center**.

The bottom chart border aligns with the bottom of the slide.

d. Click any slice of the pie and click **Quick Layout** in the Chart Layouts group on the CHART TOOLS DESIGN tab.

Clicking a slice of the pie once selects all slices of the pie.

> **TROUBLESHOOTING:** If you double-click a pie slice, the Format Data Point pane opens. Click Close and the pie slice is selected.

e. Click **Layout 1** (first row, first column) in the Quick Layout group.

The category name and the percentage now appear at the end of each pie slice. Because of the color scheme, some labels are not visible.

f. Click the **CHART TOOLS DESIGN tab**, click **More** in the Chart Styles group, and then click **Style 5** (first row, fifth column). Click one of the data labels on a pie slice once to select all the data labels. Click the **FORMAT tab**, click the **Text Fill arrow** in the WordArt Styles group, and then click **Red** under *Standard Colors*.

The text is changed to a theme style that coordinates with the presentation. The previous black text color was difficult to see on some of the slices, but the red color makes it easier to read the text on all the slices.

g. Select the legend on the bottom of the pie chart and press **Delete**.

The legend is unnecessary when data labels are used.

h. Select the title *Percentage* at the top of the chart and press **Delete**.

The title is unnecessary because the percent symbol appears next to the percentage displayed on each pie slice.

i. Click the **ANIMATIONS tab**, click **More** in the Animation group, and then click **Zoom** (Entrance category).

j. Click **Effect Options** in the Animation group.

The Effect Options gallery opens.

k. Click **Slide Center** in the Vanishing Point category.

l. Click **Effect Options** again and click **By Category** in the Sequence category.

m. Click **Preview** in the Preview group.

Each pie slice now individually zooms out from the center of the pie when the slide show plays.

n. Save and close the file, and submit based on your instructor's directions.

Chapter Objectives Review

After reading this chapter, you have accomplished the following objectives:

1. **Create a poster or a banner**
   - Text-based charts convey relationships among words, numbers, or graphics.
   - Posters and banners are specialized text-based charts.
   - Poster and banner files can be uploaded to an online printing service or delivered to a local printing company to be printed on special-sized paper.

2. **Draw a table**
   - Tables are text-based charts that organize information, making it possible to more easily see relationships among words, numbers, or graphics.
   - Tables can be inserted by specifying the number of columns and rows needed or by drawing the table.
   - When you have multiple cell heights and widths, drawing a table can be an efficient method to use.

3. **Create a table structure**
   - Make the table data as simple as possible to convey your message.
   - Change row height, column width, and table size to accommodate your information or call attention to it.
   - Align text within cells, rows, and columns to enhance the readability of the data.

4. **Format table components**
   - Set a background fill to add interest to the background of a table using the background fill style.
   - You can easily change border style, weight, and color.
   - You can add special effects to a cell, selected cells, or a table.

5. **Change table layout**
   - You can insert rows above or below an existing row, or insert columns to the left or right of an existing column.
   - You can delete rows or columns to change the overall layout of a table.

6. **Share information between applications**
   - Tables created in Word or Excel can be embedded in or linked to a PowerPoint presentation.
   - Embedding creates a larger file than linking because linking simply places a copy of the table into the presentation and all editing takes place in the source application.

   - Other objects, such as charts, can also be linked to or embedded in a presentation.

7. **Identify chart types and elements**
   - Choose the type of chart that best portrays your message.
   - The chart area is made up of the chart and all its elements.
   - The plot area contains the data.

8. **Create and insert a chart**
   - PowerPoint charts are based on Excel worksheets.
   - Information is entered into a worksheet and plotted to create the PowerPoint presentation.
   - The Insert Chart dialog box enables you to select the chart type and the chart style you want to use.

9. **Switch row and column data.**
   - Switch row and column data to change emphasis.
   - Charts should be modified and formatted to ensure that the chart conveys the intended message.

10. **Change a chart type**
    - Each chart type organizes and emphasizes data differently.
    - You can experiment with chart styles after creating a chart. Select the one that conveys the intended message of the chart.

11. **Change the chart layout**
    - Use a predefined layout to keep your charts consistent and maintain a professional feel for your presentation.
    - You can also edit the layout manually by choosing from chart title and axis title options, legend options, data label options, data table options, and axes and gridline options and by changing backgrounds in chart elements.

12. **Format chart elements**
    - The shape style (fill, outline, and effects) can be changed for individual chart elements.
    - You can also use the Format Selection option to affect a current selection, which enables you to choose from fill, border color, border styles, shadow, and 3-D format options.

Key Terms Matching

Match the key terms with their definitions. Write the key term letter by the appropriate numbered definition.

a. Bar chart
b. Chart area
c. Column chart
d. Data series
e. Destination file
f. Embedded object
g. Gridline
h. Label
i. Legend
j. Line chart

k. Linked object
l. Multiseries data series
m. Object linking and embedding (OLE)
n. Pie chart
o. Single-series data series
p. Source file
q. Stub column
r. Text-based chart
s. X-axis
t. Y-axis

1. _____ The file that contains an inserted object, such as a PowerPoint presentation with an Excel worksheet embedded in it. **p. 330**

2. _____ A part of the destination file that is updated when the source file is updated because the information is stored in the source file but displayed as the object in the destination file. **p. 331**

3. _____ A chart that shows a relationship between words, numbers, and/or graphics and arranges and organizes information by text. **p. 314**

4. _____ A data series representing data for two or more sets of data. **p. 339**

5. _____ A part of the destination file that, once inserted, no longer maintains a connection to the source file or source application in which the object was created. **p. 330**

6. _____ The horizontal axis, which usually contains the category information, such as products, companies, or intervals of time. **p. 340**

7. _____ A type of chart used to show comparisons among items, where the information is displayed horizontally. **p. 338**

8. _____ A line that extend from the horizontal or vertical axes and that can be displayed to make the chart data easier to read and understand. **p. 340**

9. _____ A type of chart used to show proportions of a whole. **p. 338**

10. _____ A feature that enables you to insert an object created in one application into a document created in another application. **p. 330**

11. _____ A type of chart used to show changes over time or comparisons among items where the information is displayed vertically. **p. 338**

12. _____ A data series representing only one set of data. **p. 339**

13. _____ The first column of a table that typically contains the information that identifies the data in each row. **p. 318**

14. _____ A chart element found in multiseries charts that helps identify the data series, assigns a format or color to each data series, and then displays that information with the data series name. **p. 340**

15. _____ The vertical axis, which usually contains the values or amounts. **p. 340**

16. _____ The file that contains the original table or data that is used or copied to create a linked or embedded object, such as a Word document or an Excel worksheet. **p. 330**

17. _____ A chart element that identifies data in the chart. **p. 339**

18. _____ The chart and all of its elements, bounded by the placeholder borders. **p. 339**

19. _____ A type of chart used to display a large number of data points over time. **p. 338**

20. _____ A chart element that contains the data points representing a set of related numbers. **p. 339**

Multiple Choice

1. The graphical representation you would use to communicate a relationship between numerical data such as a comparison in sales over years is a:

   (a) Photograph.

   (b) Statistical chart or graph.

   (c) SmartArt diagram.

   (d) Text-based chart.

2. A stub column is the:

   (a) Title that appears at the top of a table describing the table contents.

   (b) Data points representing a set of related numbers.

   (c) First column of the table.

   (d) Last row of the table.

3. What is the chart element that identifies data in the chart?

   (a) Gridline

   (b) Legend

   (c) Label

   (d) Data series

4. A PowerPoint slide displaying a table object that is a copy or representation of a file stored in Excel that does not get updated displays what type of object?

   (a) Embedded object

   (b) Linked object

   (c) Included object

   (d) Outsourced object

5. Which of the following is not a true statement regarding creating charts for display in a PowerPoint presentation?

   (a) When you create a chart in PowerPoint, you use an Excel worksheet to enter the data you wish to plot.

   (b) When you create a chart in PowerPoint, you use an Access database to enter the data you wish to plot.

   (c) You can create a chart by clicking the chart icon in a content placeholder.

   (d) You can paste a copy of an Excel chart into a PowerPoint slide by using the Paste Special command.

6. The purpose of a legend is to identify:

   (a) The type of information defined by the X-axis.

   (b) The type of information defined by the Y-axis.

   (c) The chart type.

   (d) What marker colors and patterns represent.

7. To represent the portion of time you spend studying versus the time you spend on other activities in a day, which chart type should you use to show their proportions relative to a 24-hour time period?

   (a) Pie

   (b) Radar

   (c) Line

   (d) Column

8. To show the growth of student enrollment at your college over the past 20 years, the best choice for your chart type would be:

   (a) Pie.

   (b) Bar.

   (c) Line.

   (d) Column.

9. To compare the sales of three sales representatives for the past two years, the best choice for your chart type would be:

   (a) Pie.

   (b) Column.

   (c) Line.

   (d) Doughnut.

10. What is the name of the table object that is part of the destination file and is updated when the source file is updated?

    (a) Linked object

    (b) Embedded object

    (c) Multiseries data series

    (d) X-axis

Practice Exercises

1 Coffee Club Poster

FROM SCRATCH

You are designing a poster to advertise the Saturday Morning Coffee Club at the 1st and Main Coffee House. The poster will be stapled to bulletin boards and placed in the store to remind customers of the event. The owner wants the poster to be simple but eye-catching, so you decide to create a poster that announces the ongoing event with general information. Once the poster is designed, you plan to take the file to a local print shop for reproduction, but before doing so you need a copy for the owner to review. You print a copy scaled to fit a standard 8.5" × 11" page. This exercise follows the same set of skills as used in Hands-On Exercise 1 in the chapter. Refer to Figure 5.32 as you complete this exercise.

Event advertisement

FIGURE 5.32 Scaled Advertising Poster

a. Begin a new presentation using the Retrospect theme and save it as **p05p1CoffeeClub_LastFirst**.

b. Create a handout header with your name and a handout footer with the file name, your instructor's name, and your class. Include the current date.

c. Click **Layout** in the Slides group on the HOME tab and click **Picture with Caption**.

d. Click the **DESIGN tab**, click **Slide Size** in the Customize group, and then select **Custom Slide Size** to open the Slide Size dialog box.

e. Select the existing number for *Width* and type **17**.

f. Select the existing number for *Height* and type **22**. Note that the *Slides sized for* option now displays *Custom* as its paper size and the Orientation is now set to *Portrait* for Slides and for Notes, Handouts & Outlines. Click **OK** and click **Maximize**.

g. Click the **INSERT tab** and click **Online Pictures**. Locate a picture online and click **Insert**. Drag the picture as needed to make it fit the placeholder.

h. Click the picture, if necessary, and click **More** in the Picture Styles group on the PICTURE TOOLS FORMAT tab.

i. Click **Simple Frame, Black** in the Picture Styles group.

j. Click the **title placeholder** and type the following information. Press **Enter** after each line (see Figure 5.32).

   Saturday Morning Coffee Club at

   1st and Main Coffee House

k. Click the **text placeholder** and type the following information. Press **Enter** after each line (see Figure 5.32).

Join us each Saturday for Coffee and Tea specials.

Local artists, authors, or musicians will present their current works!

9:00 a.m.–12:00 noon

l. Click the **FILE tab**, click **Print**, click the **Full Page Slides arrow**, and then click **Handouts, 1 Slide**.

m. Click the **1 Slide arrow** and click **Scale to Fit Paper**, if necessary. Click **Print**.

The poster prints on the size of paper loaded in the printer. Because desktop printers generally have a nonprintable region, the poster may have a white border surrounding it. Because you printed a handout instead of the full-page slide, the header and footer further reduce the size of the poster.

n. Save and close the file, and submit based on your instructor's directions.

2 Garden Club Presentation

Gardening is a seasonal activity. Each season demands specific tasks to be completed, depending on the climate zone. Some gardens require bulbs to be planted a few seasons prior to the bloom period, and some plants can be added to the garden once spring has arrived. You have been asked to create a presentation explaining this planning process. This exercise follows the skills practiced in Hands-On Exercise 2. Refer to Figure 5.33 as you complete this skill.

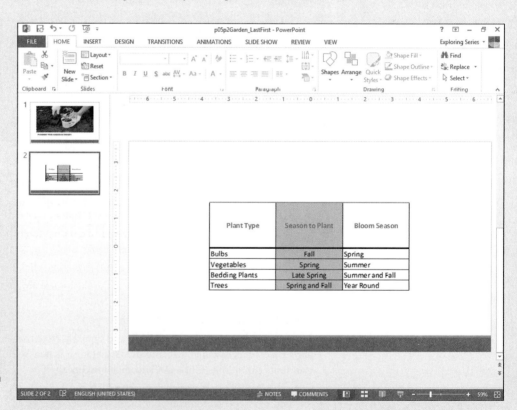

FIGURE 5.33 Planning Your Garden Activities Presentation

Photo: JackF/Fotolia

a. Open *p05p2Garden* and save the presentation as **p05p2Garden_LastFirst**.

b. Create a handout header with your name and a handout footer with your instructor's name and your class. Include the current date.

c. Open *p05p2Activities.xlsx* and save the file as **p05p2Activities_LastFirst.xlsx**.

d. Select the **range A2:C6** to select all the table data in the Excel file. Click **Copy** in the Clipboard group on the HOME tab (or press **Ctrl+C**).

e. Click the PowerPoint file on the Windows taskbar to make the presentation the active file. Click **Slide 2**. Click the **Paste arrow button** in the Clipboard group on the HOME tab and click **Paste Special**.

f. Click the **Paste link option** in the Paste Special dialog box. Click **Microsoft Excel Worksheet Object** in the As box, if necessary, and click **OK**.

g. Close the Excel file. Double-click the table object in the presentation.

h. Select **row 2** in Excel, click the **Font Color arrow**, and then select **Blue** under *Standard Colors*.

i. Observe the color change to the column headings in the presentation. Save the changes in the Excel file and close Excel.

j. Drag the bottom-right corner of the table to enlarge the table in the presentation. Click the **FORMAT tab** and click **Align Objects** in the Arrange group. Click **Align Center** and click **Align Middle**. Save and close the file, and submit based on your instructor's directions.

3 Savings Chart

No matter what stage of life you are in—a student, a recent college graduate, a newlywed, a new parent, or a retiree—you may want to create a savings account to help you reach some kind of goal. One way to accomplish this is to determine the amount you need, and then break it down into regular contributions necessary to reach your goal amount. A key idea to remember is that the more time you give your money to grow, the less money you have to invest. In this exercise, you begin a presentation on savings by creating a chart. This exercise follows the same set of skills as used in Hands-On Exercises 3 and 4 in the chapter. Refer to Figure 5.34 as you complete this exercise.

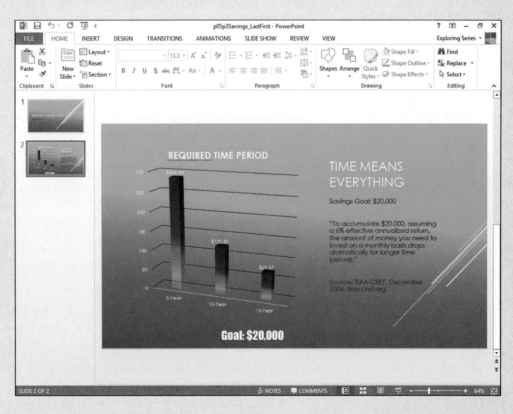

FIGURE 5.34 Savings Presentation

a. Create a new presentation based on the Slice template available in the New Presentation window. Save the presentation as **p05p3Savings_LastFirst**.

b. Create a handout header with your name and a handout footer with your instructor's name and your class. Include the current date.

c. Create a title slide, if necessary. Type **Putting Time to Work** as the title and **Saving for the Future** as the subtitle.

d. Add a new slide using the *Content with Caption* layout.

e. Click the **title placeholder** and type **Time Means Everything**. Select the text and increase the font size to **32 pt**.

f. Click the **text placeholder** on the right side of the slide below the title and type **Savings Goal: $20,000**.

g. Press **Enter** twice and type **"To accumulate $20,000, assuming a 6% effective annualized return, the amount of money you need to invest on a monthly basis drops dramatically for longer time periods."**

h. Size the text placeholder to change the height to **3.5"**. Click to place the insertion point at the end of the last sentence typed. Press **Enter** twice and type **Source: TIAA-CREF, December 2006, tiaa-cref.org**.

i. Click the **Insert Chart icon** in the *Click to add text* placeholder on the left side of the slide.

j. Click **OK** to insert the default Clustered Column chart.

k. Clear the current sample data. Enter the following information and resize the chart data range as needed to fit the data entered. Close Excel.

	Required Time Period
5-Year	286.44
10-Year	122.50
15-Year	69.37

l. Click **More** in the Chart Styles group and click **Style 9**.

m. Click **Add Chart Element** in the Chart Layouts group, click **Legend**, and then select **None**.

n. Click **Add Chart Element** in the Chart Layouts group, click **Data Labels**, and then click **Outside End**.

o. Click one of the data labels at the top of a bar to select all labels and click the **FORMAT tab**. Click **Format Selection** in the Current Selection group. In the Format Data Labels pane, click the **Label Options icon** under the LABEL OPTIONS tab heading. Click **Number** in the bottom pane options to expand it. Click the list arrow under *Category* and click **Currency**. Close the pane.

p. Insert a new text box positioned beneath the X-axis and type **Goal: $20,000** Resize and reposition the text box as necessary. Change the font to **Impact, 28 pt**.

q. Select the chart, click **Change Chart Type** in the Type group on the CHART TOOLS DESIGN tab, and then click **3-D Clustered Column** in the Column category. Click **OK**.

r. Save and close the file, and submit based on your instructor's directions.

1 School Spirit Banner

You belong to a student organization that prepares posters and banners for school activities. Next Saturday, your team, the Tazewell Tigers, faces the Ukiah Lions at Jefferson Field. You prepare a banner for this event. Refer to Figure 5.35 as you complete this exercise.

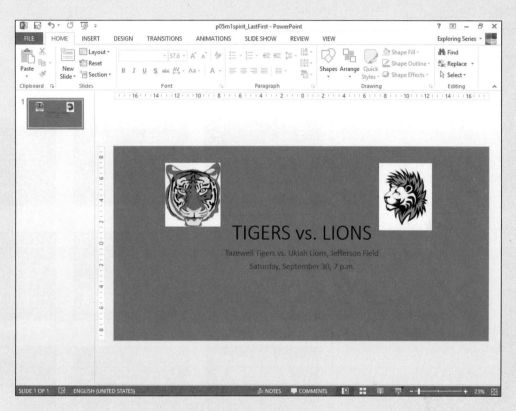

FIGURE 5.35 Example of a School Spirit Banner

a. Save a blank presentation as **p05m1Spirit_LastFirst**.

b. Create a handout header with your name and a handout footer with your instructor's name and your class. Include the current date.

c. Create a custom page size of 36" × 18", a standard size for small banners.

d. Type **TIGERS vs. LIONS** as the slide title using the font of your choice.

e. Create a two-line subtitle. Type **Tazewell Tigers vs. Ukiah Lions, Jefferson Field** as the first line of the subtitle. Type **Saturday, September 30, 7 p.m.** as the second line of the subtitle.

 f. Insert the clip art images of your choice to represent the Tigers and the Lions. If you want, you may replace the tiger and lion mascots with the mascots of your choice, making sure you also change the team names in the subtitle.

g. Arrange the clip art and placeholders on the page as you see fit. Make any other changes such as additional text and a background change as desired.

h. Save and close the file, and submit based on your instructor's directions.

2 Request for Venture Capital

You put together a presentation for a successful retail store owned by three close friends. They wish to expand their operation by requesting venture capital. Instead of creating PowerPoint tables, you decide to link to a worksheet that already contains sales data. Refer to Figure 5.36 as you complete this exercise.

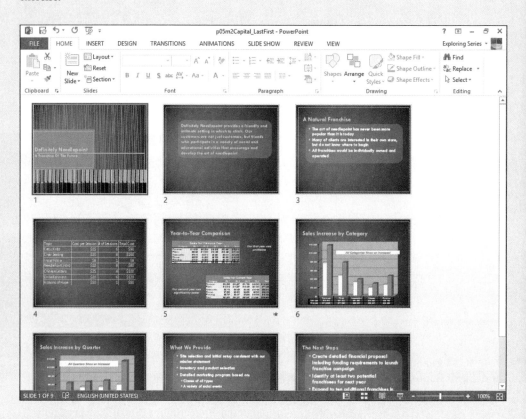

FIGURE 5.36 Microsoft Excel Objects in a Presentation

Photo: toey19863/Fotolia

a. Open *p05m2Capital* and save it as **p05m2Capital_LastFirst**.

b. Create a handout header with your name and a handout footer with your instructor's name and your class. Include the current date.

c. Open the *p05m2Sales* Excel workbook and save it as **p05m2Sales_LastFirst**.

d. Copy the data in the Previous Year tab for the range A1:F8 in Excel, switch to PowerPoint, and then paste the data as a picture on Slide 5. Change the table size height to **2"**. Drag the worksheet object to the left of the text *Our first year was profitable* and under the slide title.

e. Copy the data in the Current Year tab for the range A1:F8 in Excel, switch to PowerPoint, and then paste the data to the same slide (Slide 5), keeping the source formatting. Change the table size by locking the aspect ratio and change the table height to **2"**. Drag the worksheet object to the right of the text *Our second year was significantly better*.

f. Copy the *Increase by Category* Excel chart and paste (with Use Destination Theme & Embed Workbook selected) to Slide 6 in the presentation. Resize the chart area height to **5.5"**. Reposition the chart below the slide title. Change the font size for the vertical axis and the horizontal data table axis to **12 pt** and the font color to **White, Text 1**.

g. Copy the *Increase by Quarter* Excel chart and paste (with Use Destination Theme & Embed Workbook selected) to Slide 7 in the presentation. Size the chart area height to **5.5"**. Reposition the chart below the slide title. Change the vertical and horizontal data table axis font size to **12 pt** and the font color to **White, Text 1**.

h. Use PowerPoint's Insert Object feature to create a new object on Slide 4: a new Microsoft Excel Worksheet. Create the following table in Excel cells A1:D8 and use a formula in cell D2 to calculate the *Cost per Session* × *# of Sessions* for Celtic Knits. Auto fill the formula down to cell D8 to copy the formula for the range D2:D8 (to allow enable Excel to figure the total cost of the class for each topic). Format column D as **Currency**.

Topic	Cost per Session	# of Sessions	Total Cost
Celtic Knits	$15	6	=PRODUCT(B2:C2)
Chair Seating	$20	8	
Initial Pillow	$8	1	
NeedlePoint Intro	$10	8	
Chinese Letters	$25	4	
Embellishment	$20	6	
Ribbons of Hope	$50	1	

i. Resize the Excel window to fit the data cell range. Resize the columns to fit data by double-clicking the right column border. Change the font size to **16 pt** and change the font color to **White, Background 1**.

j. Exit Excel and size the new Excel object to a width of **8.25"** in PowerPoint. Resize columns widths as necessary.

k. Apply **Align Center** and **Align Middle** to the new Excel object.

l. Save and close the file, and submit based on your instructor's directions.

3 | Social Networking for Businesses

You and a classmate have been assigned to create a presentation about a subject that interests you personally. Together, you have decided to create the presentation about the use of social networking in business. Create a new presentation using the Ion theme available in the Themes palette and save it as **p05m3Social_LastFirst**. Each of you must research two different types of social networking that are often used. Find as much information as you can about how companies use social networking to communicate with their customers and the number of customers or users that each social network has in a least four major countries.

Create the following slides: (1) a Title slide, (2) two Content with Caption slides, and (3) a Picture with Caption slide. Create a title and subtitle as appropriate on the Title slide. Briefly describe each of the social-network advertising options and add a descriptive chart or table for the two types of social networking on the Content with Caption slides. Finally, summarize your social networking research and add an image that enhances your presentation on the final slide in the presentation.

Winter Sports

RESEARCH CASE

FROM SCRATCH

You decide to get away next week and indulge in your favorite winter sports—snowboarding and skiing. You research current daily snowfall and the price of a lift ticket at your favorite winter location. Because you are also studying charting in your Basic Computer Applications class, you decide to practice your charting skills by creating a line graph showing the new snowfall for the past seven days at your favorite location. You also create a bar chart showing the price of full-day lift tickets. You may choose to add additional slides, if desired.

Visit any site on the Internet you choose and gather the data you need to complete the charts. Create a presentation, and then save it as **p05b2Winter_LastFirst**. Enter the data for each of the charts in worksheets, and then format the charts in an attractive, easy-to-read format. Create a handout header with your name and a footer with your instructor's name and class. Include the date. Apply appropriate titles and labels as needed to ensure that the chart is easily and accurately understood. Include a slide that lists the resources you used for the data. Save and close the file, and submit based on your instructor's directions.

Chart Improvements

DISASTER RECOVERY

The presentation *p05b3Tips* includes four charts that confuse the message they are supposed to deliver. In some cases, the wrong chart type has been applied, and in others the formatting of the chart is distracting. In the Notes pane of each slide, design tips are given that you can read to help you identify the errors in the chart. Open the file and immediately save it as **p05b3Tips_LastFirst**. Read the notes associated with each slide, and then edit the chart on the slide so it incorporates the tips. Make all modifications necessary to create a professional, easy-to-understand chart. Even if you do not complete this exercise, you should read the design tips in this slide show. Save and close the file, and submit based on your instructor's directions.

Job Search Strategies

SOFT SKILLS CASE

Research the profession you are most interested in pursuing after graduation, and then create a presentation. One slide should outline two key job-search strategies for your chosen profession. Another slide should illustrate some data for expected job growth in the profession as an embedded chart or table. The last slide should provide a typical job description or want ad for your profession. Save and close the presentation, and submit based on your instructor's directions.

Capstone Exercise

A Kiss of Chocolate is a successful spa and lounge dedicated to the appreciation of chocolate and its benefits. The operation has been so successful in its five years of operation that the owners opened two additional locations and are now considering franchising. They are meeting with officers of a franchising corporation, which offers strategic corporate, management, and marketing services for franchisers. The franchising representatives have asked for an overview of the services and products of A Kiss of Chocolate, sales for this year and last year, a year-to-year comparison, and charts showing the increase. The owners of A Kiss of Chocolate ask for your help in preparing the presentation for the meeting.

Create a Poster

The owners of A Kiss of Chocolate have reserved a meeting room at a local conference center. They want a large, foam-backed poster on an easel next to the conference room door. They ask you to prepare the poster, and then they will have a local company print it.

a. Open *p05c1Spaposter* and save it as **p05c1Spaposter_LastFirst**.

b. Create a handout header with your name and a handout footer with the file name, your instructor's name, and your class. Include the current date.

c. Change the width of the page to **17"** and the height of the page to **22"** in the Page Setup dialog box. Click **OK**. Click **Maximize**.

d. Type **Gardenia Room, 9 a.m**. in a new text box.

e. Change the default text color to **Light Yellow, Text 2**. Apply bold to the text.

f. Position the left top edge of the new text box at 1" horizontal and 10" vertical positions from the top left corner.

g. Print a copy of the poster as a handout, one per page, using the *Scale to Fit Paper* option.

h. Save and close the file, and submit based on your instructor's directions.

Create a Day Spa Packages Table

Some slides of the A Kiss of Chocolate slide show have been created, including an introduction to the spa, products available for sale in the gift store, services available in the spa, and chocolate desserts and drinks available in the lounge. Now you insert a table showing the packages available in the Day Spa.

a. Open *p05c1Spashow* and save it as **p05c1Spashow_LastFirst**.

b. Create a new slide following Slide 4 using the *Title and Content* layout.

c. Type the title **Day Spa Packages**.

d. Create a four-column, five-row table. Do not worry about width or height of rows or columns.

e. Type the following column headings: **Package**, **Length**, **Cost**, **Services**.

f. Fill in the table using the following information (the table will exceed the slide, but you will format the table to fit in the next step):

A Kiss of Chocolate	1.5 hours	$160	Spa Rain Shower, Full-Body Mint Chocolate Exfoliation, 45-Minute Peppermint-Chocolate Massage
A Chocolate Hug	1.5 hours	$160	Hot Stone Treatment with Warm Raspberry-Chocolate Oil, Hydrating Body Wrap, 45-Minute Peppermint-Chocolate Massage
The Chocolate Dip	2 hours	$175	Mint-Chocolate Soufflé Body Mask, Full-Body Mint Chocolate Exfoliation, Hydrating Body Wrap, Raspberry-Chocolate Shower
Chocolate Decadence	3 hours	$300	Hot Stone Treatment with Warm Raspberry-Chocolate Oil, Raspberry-Chocolate Shower, Full-Body Mint Chocolate Exfoliation, Mint-Chocolate Soufflé Body Mask, 50-Minute Peppermint-Chocolate Massage

Modify Table Structure and Format Table

The table structure needs to be modified so the table fits on the slide. You also format the table to obtain the desired appearance.

Size the table and apply a table style. Refer to Figure 5.37 while completing this step.

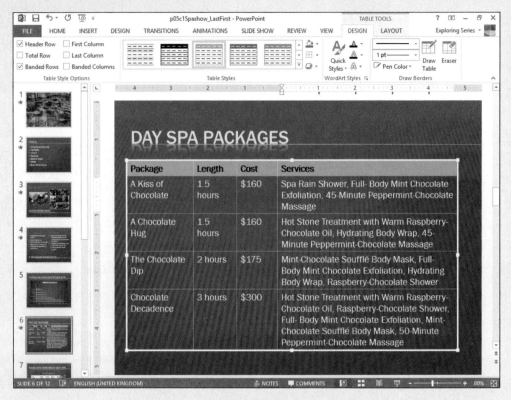

FIGURE 5.37 Day Spa Packages Table

Photos: (Slide 1) happysunstock/ Fotolia, (Slide 3, left) gtranquillity/ Fotolia, (Slide 3, right) BeTa-Artworks/ Fotolia

a. Change the table structure by dragging the first three column borders until they closely fit the column headings.

b. Set the table size to a height of **5.01"** and a width of **9"**.

c. Apply the **Light Style 2 - Accent 1 table style** (second row, second column, Light category) to the table.

d. Arrange the table so that it is centered horizontally on the slide and does not block the slide title.

Link Excel Tables and Charts

A Kiss of Chocolate's owners have tables and charts showing sales figures for this year and the previous year. These figures show that all three branches of A Kiss of Chocolate have increased revenue and profit each year, and the charts emphasize the data. Refer to Figure 5.38 while completing this step.

a. Create a Title Only slide after Slide 5 and type **Sales Have Increased at Each Spa** as the title.

b. Open the *p05c1Spasales* workbook in Excel, save it as **p05c1Spasales_LastFirst.xlsx**, and then move to the worksheet containing the sales data for the previous year. Copy the data and paste it into Slide 6 of the presentation. Change the Paste options to **Keep Source Formatting**.

c. Repeat step b to paste the worksheet data for the current year into Slide 6.

d. Size the two worksheets on Slide 6 to a height of **2.5"** and a width of **8"**.

e. Arrange the two tables attractively on the slide.

f. Create a Title Only slide after Slide 6 and type **All Stores Show an Increase** as the title of the new Slide 7. Link the *Increase by Store* Excel chart to the new slide.

g. Size the chart to a height of **4.5"** and a width of **7.5"**.

h. Align the chart in the center of the slide.

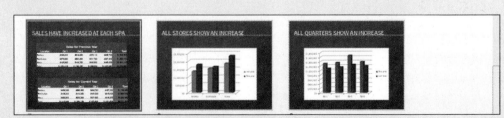

FIGURE 5.38 Linked Excel Sales Data

i. Create a Title Only slide after Slide 7 and type **All Quarters Show an Increase** as the title of the new Slide 8. Link the *Increase by Quarter* Excel chart to the new slide.

j. Size the chart to a height of **4.5"** and a width of **7.5"**.

k. Align the chart in the center of the slide.

Create a Bar Chart

Because you serve dark and milk chocolate desserts and drinks in the Chocolate Lounge, you decide to add a slide to support the idea that chocolate intake may be healthy. You create a bar chart to show the amount of antioxidants in a serving of chocolate in comparison to other foods that contain antioxidants.

a. Create a *Title and Content* slide after Slide 4 and type **Chocolate Contains Antioxidants** as the title of the new Slide 5.

b. Create a bar chart using the default Clustered Bar type with the following data:

Dark Chocolate	9080
Cocoa	8260
Prunes	5570
Milk Chocolate	3200
Raisins	2830
Blueberries	2400
Blackberries	2036
Strawberries	1540

c. Add **ORAC Units per Serving** for the title. Size the chart to a height of **5"** and a width of **8.5"**.

d. Align the chart in the center of the slide

Modify and Format a Bar Chart

You modify and format the bar chart to improve the appearance. Refer to Figure 5.39 while completing this step.

a. Remove the legend.

b. Apply **Chart Style 7** to the chart.

c. Click **Add Chart Element** in the Chart Layouts group, select **Data Labels**, and choose **More Data Label Options**.

d. Click **Number**, set the options to **General**.

e. Add a **Glow Shape Effect** to the plot area series using the **Orange, 8 pt glow, Accent color 1**.

f. Save and close the file, and submit based on your instructor's direction.

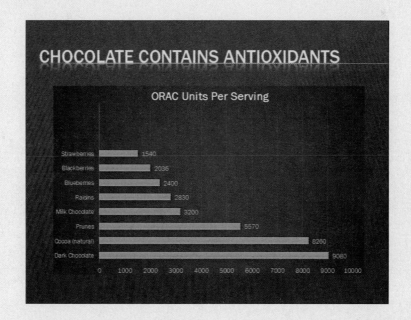

FIGURE 5.39 Chocolate Antioxidants Bar Chart

Interactivity and Advanced Animation

CHAPTER 6

Engaging the Audience

Konstantin Chagin/Shutterstock

OBJECTIVES AFTER YOU READ THIS CHAPTER, YOU WILL BE ABLE TO:

1. Insert and use hyperlinks p. 372
2. Add action buttons p. 376
3. Use a trigger p. 379
4. Apply multiple animations to an object p. 390
5. Apply a motion path animation p. 391
6. Specify animation settings and timing p. 394
7. Animate text p. 396
8. Use the Animation Pane p. 397

CASE STUDY | Teaching Aids

As the teaching assistant for a computer literacy instructor, you prepare numerous teaching aids to help students. You modify a presentation in a quiz format to help students review charts and graphs. The existing presentation includes slides that display a question and a list of choices. You insert sound action buttons so that if a student answers correctly, the student hears applause; if the student answers incorrectly, the student hears feedback indicating it is an incorrect choice. You add action buttons for students to use to navigate through the presentation and hyperlinks to open a reference table and an assignment. You include your e-mail address in the slide show in case the students need to contact you.

After modifying the Charts and Graphs presentation, you modify a presentation designed to help the computer literacy students understand PowerPoint's advanced animation features. You create animation examples for students to view.

Hyperlinks and Action Buttons

A typical PowerPoint presentation is a *linear presentation*. In a linear presentation, each slide is designed to move one right after another, and the viewer or audience progresses through slides, starting with the first slide and advancing sequentially until the last slide is reached. If you add *interactivity*, or the ability to branch nonsequentially, to another part of the presentation based on decisions made by a viewer or audience, you create a *non-linear presentation*. Adding interactivity by involving your audience in your presentation helps capture interest and retain attention. The flexibility and spontaneity of a non-linear presentation typically frees you to become more conversational with the audience, which leads to even more interaction.

You can add interactivity by creating *hyperlinks* that branch to slides or other locations containing additional information or by adding *action buttons*. An action button is a ready-made button designed to serve as an icon that can initiate an action when clicked, pointed to, or run over with the mouse. Figure 6.1 demonstrates the linear versus non-linear navigation options in a presentation. In the non-linear slide show, Slide 1 could include a menu option enabling the viewer to choose any of the remaining five slides, and the remaining slides could be designed to enable the viewer to navigate back to the first slide or to other related slides.

In this section, you will add interactivity to a slide show by adding hyperlinks, action buttons, and a trigger.

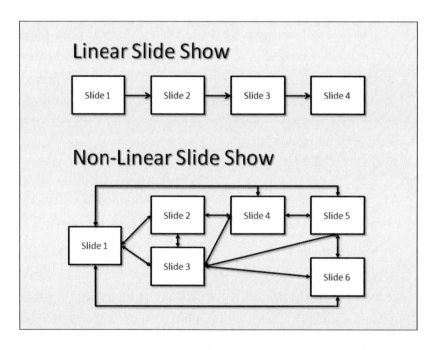

FIGURE 6.1 Linear Versus Non-Linear Navigation Options in a Presentation

Inserting and Using Hyperlinks

You can insert a hyperlink to enable a presenter to tailor the flow and content of a presentation based on audience questions or to enable single viewers to navigate through a slide show at their own pace, visiting the slides desired to gain more information in areas of interest or to review as needed. To activate a hyperlink, display the presentation in Slide Show view or Reading view and position the mouse pointer over a hyperlink; the mouse pointer becomes a hand pointer. If the hyperlink is attached to text, the text color will be different from regular text and the text will be underlined. Click the hyperlink and you jump to a new location. The first time you click a hyperlink, the color of the hyperlink changes so that you know the link has been accessed previously. The colors assigned to the unused link and the used link are set by the theme you have applied to your slide show.

STEP 6 PowerPoint enables you to attach a hyperlink to any selected object such as text, shapes, images, charts, and even SmartArt or WordArt. The hyperlink can link to a(n):

- Existing file
- Web page
- Slide in the open presentation
- New document
- E-mail address

Regardless of where you want the user to be able to move, the process for inserting a hyperlink is similar. To insert a hyperlink, do the following:

1. Select the object or text you want the link attached to.
2. Click the INSERT tab.
3. Click Hyperlink in the Links group.
4. Click the type of link you want in the *Link to* pane on the left side of the Insert Hyperlink dialog box.
5. Select and add any additional desired options and information related to the link location you selected.
6. Click OK.

> ### TIP Using Other Methods to Insert Hyperlinks
>
> You can also use the keyboard shortcut Ctrl+K or you can right-click the selected object or text and select Hyperlink from the shortcut menu to open the Insert Hyperlink dialog box.

Link to an Existing File or Web Page

When the Insert Hyperlink dialog box opens, *Link to Existing File or Web Page* is the default selection. If you are attaching the *link to* text and you selected the text before opening the dialog box, the text appears in the *Text to display* box at the top of the dialog box. If you did not pre-select text, the word to the right of the insertion point displays. You can delete any text that appears and enter the text you want to display on your slide in this box.

Often, hyperlinks link to Web pages. At the bottom of the dialog box is an Address box where you enter the **uniform resource locator (URL)**, or Web address, of the Web page you wish to link to. If you know the URL, you can type it in the box, but it is better to copy and paste a link to avoid errors caused by misspelling or incorrect punctuation.

If you do not know the URL, you can find it in one of several ways. If you visited the page recently, click Browsed Pages to show a list of the Web sites you have recently visited. Click the address from the list of URLs shown. You can also click *Browse the Web* (located below the *Text to display* box) to open your browser and navigate to the desired Web page. When you locate the page, click the PowerPoint icon on the Windows taskbar to return to PowerPoint. The URL displays in the Address box in the Insert Hyperlink dialog box. Lastly, you can copy the URL from the Web page address box by selecting the address and pressing Ctrl+C, closing the browser, and then pasting the URL in the Address box by pressing Ctrl+V.

Figure 6.2 shows how you would create a link to the Yellowstone National Park Web site. The text is selected so that a link to the Web site giving information about the park can be attached. The Insert Hyperlink dialog box is open and recently browsed pages are displayed. The hyperlink to the National Park Service Web site is shown in the Address box.

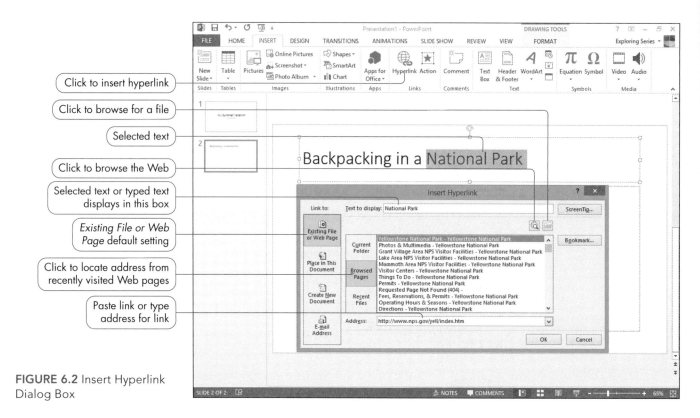

The labels on the figure read:

- Click to insert hyperlink
- Click to browse for a file
- Selected text
- Click to browse the Web
- Selected text or typed text displays in this box
- Existing File or Web Page default setting
- Click to locate address from recently visited Web pages
- Paste link or type address for link

FIGURE 6.2 Insert Hyperlink Dialog Box

If you want to link to a file stored on your computer or other storage device, from the Insert Hyperlink dialog box, click Current Folder, Recent Files, or *Browse for File* to navigate to the location of the desired file. If you know the exact file name and location, you can type it in the dialog box instead of browsing to locate the file. When you click the link during your presentation, the application in which the file was created opens and your file displays.

TIP Linking Picture Files

What if you have a company logo that you want to use in all presentations you create? Every time you insert the logo, the picture file is embedded multiple times in a presentation, wasting storage space on your drive. Rather than embed the picture, you can create a picture link to keep your PowerPoint file sizes much smaller. To create a picture link, click the Insert tab and click Pictures in the Images group. Browse for the picture you want and, instead of clicking Insert, click the Insert arrow and select *Link to File*. PowerPoint inserts a link to the picture instead of embedding the picture file in your slide show. The link stores the entire path to the file, the location of the picture, and the picture size. Always save your objects to the same folder and storage device where you store your presentation. Then, link to that location so that the link will not be broken when you present. If you ever change the logo, you replace the old logo file with the new logo file in the same location and with the same file name. When a presentation is opened that is linked to the picture, the new logo appears, so you do not have to replace the logo in every presentation.

Link to a Slide in the Open Presentation

Sometimes, you may want to create a link to another slide in a presentation. For example, you may create a menu of topics that are covered in the presentation. When you click a menu option, the presentation jumps to the slide containing the related content. Each topic slide should also include a link back to the menu. You can use links to branch to the slides that focus on your audience's anticipated questions or comments.

To create a link to another slide in the presentation, select *Place in This Document* from the Insert Hyperlink dialog box. The list of slides in the slide show displays. Select the slide to which you wish to link and click OK to close the dialog box (see Figure 6.3).

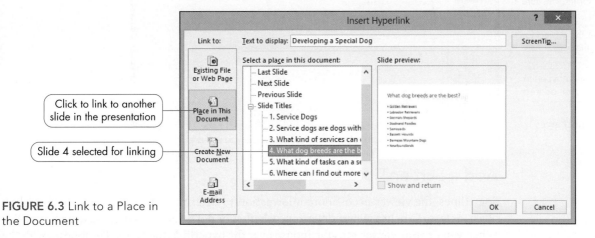

FIGURE 6.3 Link to a Place in the Document

Link to a New Document

In a training presentation, you may find it helpful to open a program and demonstrate a feature. Clicking the Create New Document option in the Insert Hyperlink dialog box enables you to do this. Use this option to create a hyperlink to a new PowerPoint presentation or other document. Browse to locate a file using the Change button or enter a file name and designate the location for the new presentation. You can specify whether you want to open the new presentation immediately for editing or to edit later. Figure 6.4 shows the options for creating a new presentation with the file name *Abilities* and opening it for immediate editing.

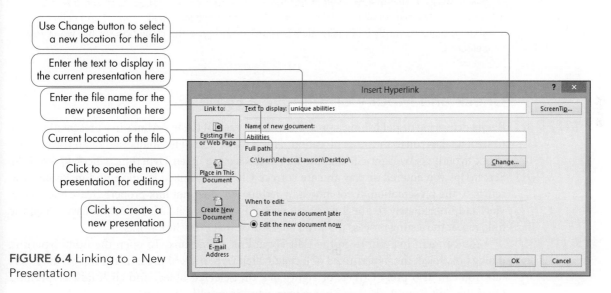

FIGURE 6.4 Linking to a New Presentation

Link to an E-Mail Address

STEP 1 To add an e-mail link to a slide, select the E-mail Address option in the Insert Hyperlink dialog box and type the address in the *E-mail address* box. As you type, the protocol designator *mailto:* is automatically added before the e-mail address. Creating an e-mail link enables your viewer to contact you for more information and is especially helpful if you post your presentation on the Web. You can add any text on the slide, such as *Contact me for further information*, by typing it on the slide and selecting it or by typing the text in the *Text to display* box. Add a subject for the e-mail to help you identify incoming mail. Alternatively, you can type your e-mail address directly on the slide, and PowerPoint automatically formats it as a link for you. Figure 6.5 displays the *E-mail address* options in the Insert Hyperlink dialog box.

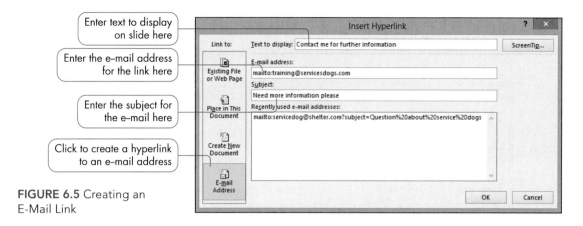

Enter text to display on slide here

Enter the e-mail address for the link here

Enter the subject for the e-mail here

Click to create a hyperlink to an e-mail address

FIGURE 6.5 Creating an E-Mail Link

Add a ScreenTip

Sometimes, the viewer needs more information to determine the purpose of the hyperlink object or text. To help a viewer determine whether or not to click a hyperlink, use a ScreenTip. When you or your viewer rolls the mouse over the hyperlink, the *ScreenTip* appears with the additional information.

To add a ScreenTip to a hyperlink, click ScreenTip in the Insert Hyperlink dialog box. The Set Hyperlink ScreenTip dialog box opens. Type the text you want to display in the box.

TIP **Adding Definitions to Technical Terms**

ScreenTips are an excellent way to define technical or new terms in a presentation. To use a ScreenTip in this manner, select the term in the text on your slide, click the Insert tab, and then click Hyperlink in the Links group. Link to *Place in This Document* and select the slide you are currently in. Finally, click ScreenTip and type the definition for the word you selected.

Check and Modify or Remove a Hyperlink

STEP 7 Before delivering or publishing a presentation, test each of the hyperlinks in a presentation view to see if it takes you to the proper location. This is the preferred technique, although you can also check hyperlinks by right-clicking the link and selecting Open Hyperlink. Check to see if the ScreenTips you entered display and are correct. Close each linked location, and make sure you return to the presentation. If you find a hyperlink that does not link properly, leave Slide Show view and immediately fix the link so you do not forget to do it later. Once you have edited the link, repeat the testing process until you are assured that every link works.

You can edit hyperlinks in the Edit Hyperlink dialog box. To open the Edit Hyperlink dialog box, select the hyperlinked object and click Hyperlink in the Links group on the Insert tab. You can also press Ctrl+K or right-click the selected object and click Edit Hyperlink. Once the Edit Hyperlink dialog box opens, you can modify the existing hyperlink.

To remove a hyperlink, click Remove Link in the Edit Hyperlink dialog box or right-click the selected object and click Remove Hyperlink from the shortcut menu. If you delete the object to which a hyperlink is attached, the hyperlink is also deleted.

Adding Action Buttons

Another way to add interactivity is by using an action button that, when you click, point to, or run the mouse over it, initiates an action. Action buttons can contain shapes such as arrows and symbols. In addition to being a hyperlink to another location, action buttons can display information, movies, documents, sound, and the Help feature. *Custom buttons* can be created and set to trigger unique actions in a presentation. Action buttons are excellent tools for navigating a slide show and are especially useful if you want to create a presentation for a *kiosk*, an interactive computer terminal available for public use, such as on campus, at a mall, or at a trade show. An interactive slide show is perfect for a kiosk display.

TIP Using Action Buttons for Navigation

Slide Show view includes default action buttons on the bottom-left of a slide that return to the previous slide, advance to the next slide, activate a pen tool, open Slide Sorter view, zoom, or display a shortcut menu. If your presentation will be used by multiple users with varied skill levels, you may want to use the default buttons. If, however, you wish to provide your users with additional choices, you may want to create custom buttons.

Table 6.1 lists the 12 different ready-made action buttons that PowerPoint includes in the Shapes gallery.

TABLE 6.1 PowerPoint Ready-Made Action Buttons

Action Button Icon	Name	Default Button Behavior
◁	Back or Previous button	Moves to previous slide
▷	Forward or Next button	Moves to next slide
◁	Beginning button	Moves to the first slide in the slide show
▷	*End button*	Moves to the last slide in the slide show
🏠	*Home button*	Moves to the first slide of the slide show by default but can be set to go to any slide
ⓘ	Information button	Can be set to move to any slide in the slide show, a custom show, a URL, another presentation, or another file in order to reveal information
↩	Return button	Returns to previous slide view regardless of the location in the slide show
🎞	*Movie button*	Can be set to play a movie file
🗎	Document button	Can be set to load a document in the application that was used to create it
🔊	Sound button	Can be set to play a sound when clicked
?	*Help button*	Can be set to open the Help feature or a Help document
☐	Custom button	Can be set to move to a slide in the slide show, a custom show, a URL, another PowerPoint presentation, a file, or a program; also can be set to run a macro, add an action to an object, or play a sound

To insert an action button, do the following:

STEP 3 ≫ 1. Click the INSERT tab.

2. Click Shapes in the Illustrations group. The Shapes gallery can also be accessed from
STEP 4 ≫   the HOME tab by clicking Shapes in the Drawing group.

3. Click the action button you want in the *Action Buttons* section of the Shapes gallery.

STEP 5 ≫ 4. Click the desired location to create the button on the slide (or click and drag to control the button size).

5. Select the Mouse Click or Mouse Over tab in the Action Settings dialog box.
6. Select desired options in the Action Settings dialog box.
7. Click OK.

Figure 6.6 shows the Action Buttons displayed in the Shapes gallery with the action button designed to return to the beginning of the slide show selected.

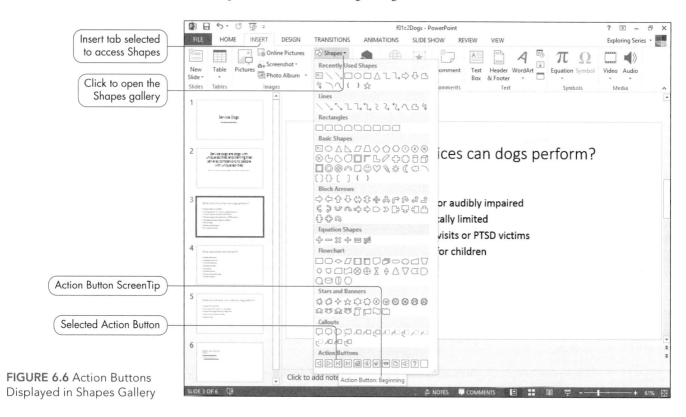

STEP 2» **TIP** **Attaching Actions to Objects**

Actions can be associated with any object, not just an action button. Select an object, click the Insert tab, and then click Action in the Links group. The Action Settings dialog box opens so that you can select the type of action and how you want the action to be initiated.

When you release the mouse button after creating an action button, the Action Settings dialog box opens. Click the *Mouse Click or Mouse Over* tab to select how to initiate the action. Regardless of which method you select, the action options are the same. You can choose to have the action button hyperlink to another location in the slide show, a Custom Show, a URL, another PowerPoint presentation, or another file. An action button can even initiate a new program. To link to a specific slide in the slide show, click the *Hyperlink to* arrow and select a slide from the list. To have the action button run a specific program, click *Run program* and browse to locate the program you wish to open. You can also program the action button to run a macro or to add an action to an object. Figure 6.7 shows the settings for an action button that returns to the first slide.

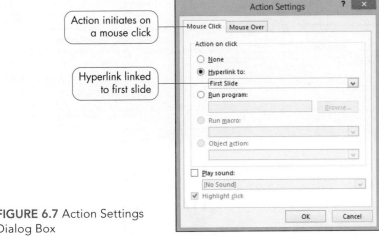

Action initiates on a mouse click

Hyperlink linked to first slide

FIGURE 6.7 Action Settings Dialog Box

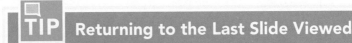

TIP **Returning to the Last Slide Viewed**

The Return action button returns you to the last slide you viewed, regardless of its location in the presentation. The Previous button takes you to the slide preceding the slide you are currently viewing.

Add Sound to an Object

Sound can be added to a hyperlink attached to an object to capture your audience's attention or to add emphasis to the subject of the link. To attach a sound to a hyperlink, click the *Play sound* check box in the Action Settings dialog box. Click the *Play sound* arrow and select the sound you want to play when the object is clicked or moused over during the show. To assign a sound file you have saved to your computer, scroll to the bottom of the list, click Other Sound, browse for the sound, and then select it.

Using a Trigger

Another way to introduce interactivity into your presentation is through the use of a trigger. A *trigger* launches an animation that takes place when you click an associated object or a bookmarked location in a media object. An *animation* is an action used to draw interest to an object in a presentation. For example, you can use text as a trigger. The trigger is set up so when you click the text, an image appears. Triggers are a fun way to add interactivity to presentations—the viewer clicks a trigger to see a surprise element. Remember this key point about triggers: a trigger must use animation.

Figure 6.8 displays a slide with a trigger. The Animation Pane is open on the right side of the slide and shows the object and the animation or action associated with the trigger. The trigger is attached to the words *Thank you.* The slide is interactive because the viewer initiates the process by clicking the trigger.

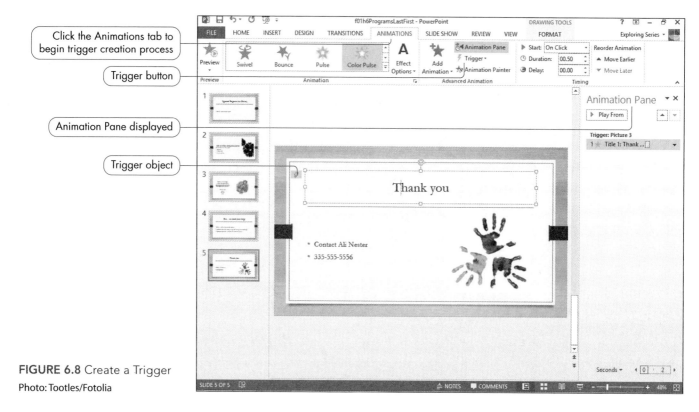

Click the Animations tab to begin trigger creation process

Trigger button

Animation Pane displayed

Trigger object

FIGURE 6.8 Create a Trigger

Photo: Tootles/Fotolia

To set up a trigger, do the following:

1. Select the object that will serve as the trigger.
2. Click the ANIMATIONS tab.
3. Add the animation effect of your choice from the Animation group.
4. Click Trigger in the Advanced Animation group.
5. Select the *On Click of* or *On Bookmark* option to determine how the animation is triggered.
6. Select the object or bookmark that will launch the animation from the displayed list.

TIP Using Games for Quizzes

Microsoft includes a Quiz Show template that includes sample quiz layouts such as True or False, Multiple Choice, and more. You can locate it by searching the templates available. You can also go to the Internet and use a search engine to search for *PowerPoint Games*. Create a storyboard to plan the slides you will need for the quiz and the interactive elements required by your plan. A standard quiz presentation would probably contain slides to introduce the test, directions, questions, feedback slides, and an ending slide.

The answers to the questions would link to the feedback slides, and the *correct* feedback slide would link to the next question. The *incorrect* feedback slide would link to the same question slide so the viewer could try again.

Quick Concepts

1. What is a presentation that enables the user to progress through the slides using action buttons and hyperlinks? ***p. 372***
2. What are the main advantages of adding an e-mail link to a presentation? ***p. 375***
3. Which type of event is a trigger used to launch in a presentation? ***p. 379***

Hands-On Exercises

Watch the Video for this Hands-On Exercise!

MyITLab®
HOE1 Training

1 Hyperlinks and Action Buttons

One of your responsibilities as a teaching assistant is to provide materials for a computer literacy class. You create a presentation to help students review charts and graphs in a quiz format. Students answer questions and receive feedback on whether they selected a "correct" or "incorrect" answer. Students can also open a reference guide and an assignment from the presentation.

Skills covered: Insert and Edit an E-Mail Hyperlink • Add an Action to a Clip Art Object • Create and Edit Sound Action Buttons • Create Action Buttons for Navigation • Create a Custom Action Button • Insert and Use Hyperlinks • Test Hyperlinks

---

STEP 1 >> INSERT AND EDIT AN E-MAIL HYPERLINK

The following table displays the storyboard used in creating the Charts and Graphs Review presentation. The storyboard notes all interactive elements you want to include in the presentation. You will modify this slide show to add the interactive elements. You will begin by inserting your e-mail address so that, if necessary, a student could contact you with questions. Refer to the table below to add the following interactive elements to the slides in the presentation.

Slide	Content	Interactive Element
1	Title Slide	None
2	Directions	• E-mail hyperlink
		• Four navigation buttons: Beginning, Back or Previous, Forward or Next, End
3	Speaker Test	Clip art object with sound action attached
4	Question One	• Four sound action buttons (one for each answer)
		• Chart with animation trigger
		• Four navigation buttons: Beginning, Back or Previous, Forward or Next, End
5	Question Two	• Four sound action buttons (one for each answer)
		• Chart with animation trigger
		• Four navigation buttons: Beginning, Back or Previous, Forward or Next, End
6	Ending Slide	• Existing file hyperlink
		• Four navigation buttons: Beginning, Back or Previous, Forward or Next, End

a. Open *p06h1Review* and save it as **p06h1Review_LastFirst**.

> **TROUBLESHOOTING:** If you make any major mistakes in this exercise, you can close the file, open *p06h1Review* again, and then start this exercise over.

b. Create a handout header with your name and a handout footer with your instructor's name and your class. Include the current date.

c. On Slide 2, position the insertion point after the colon following *contact*, press the **Spacebar**, type your e-mail address, and then press the **Spacebar**.

Because PowerPoint recognizes the format of an e-mail address, it creates an automatic hyperlink to your e-mail.

d. Right-click your e-mail address and click **Edit Hyperlink**.

e. Click in the **Subject box**, type **Charts and Graphs Review Question**, and then click **OK**.

f. Save the presentation.

Hands-On Exercise 1   381

STEP 2 ≫ ADD AN ACTION TO A CLIP ART OBJECT

Because the quiz review slide show uses audio cues to indicate whether a student answers the question correctly, it is important for the student to have a working headset. You will create an action attached to a clip art image of a headset so the student can test to see if his or her headset is working. Refer to Figure 6.9 as you complete Step 2.

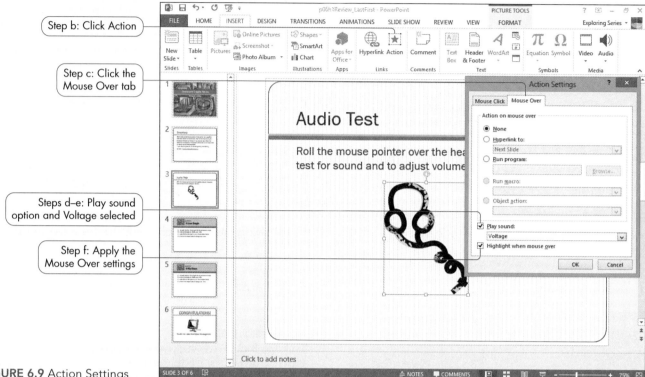

FIGURE 6.9 Action Settings

a. On Slide 3, select the **headset picture** and click the **INSERT tab**.

b. Click **Action** in the Links group.

> The Action Settings dialog box opens so that you can assign an action to the selected clip art image.

c. Click the **Mouse Over tab**, if necessary.

> By selecting the Mouse Over tab, you assign any applied actions to occur when the mouse moves over the selected object.

d. Click the **Play sound check box** and click the **list arrow**.

> PowerPoint includes a variety of sounds you can attach to objects, or you can select the Other Sound option and browse to locate a sound you have saved.

e. Click **Voltage**.

f. Click the **Highlight when mouse over check box**, if necessary, and click **OK**.

> With this option selected, the clip art image will be surrounded by a border when the mouse rolls over the top of it, which makes it easy to note the mouse-over area.

TROUBLESHOOTING: You will not be able to hear the voltage sound or see the highlight border unless you are in Slide Show view.

---

g. Save the presentation.

STEP 3 ≫ CREATE AND EDIT SOUND ACTION BUTTONS

You will create action buttons next to the answers on each of the question slides so that when clicked, the action button will play an audio response letting the student know whether he or she selected the correct answer. Refer to Figure 6.10 as you complete Step 3.

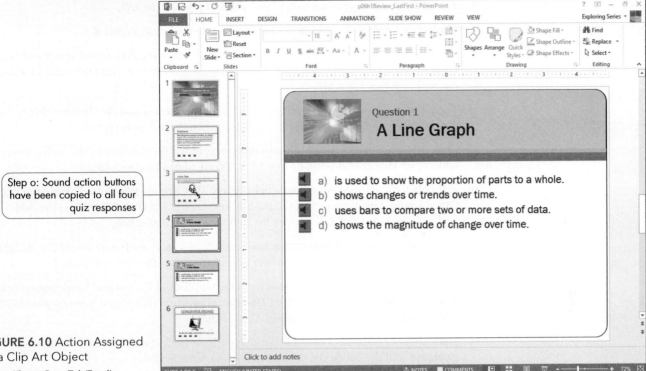

Step o: Sound action buttons have been copied to all four quiz responses

FIGURE 6.10 Action Assigned to a Clip Art Object

Photo: Kheng Guan Toh/Fotolia

a. On Slide 4, click the **INSERT tab** and click **Shapes** in the Illustrations group.

The Shapes gallery opens, and the action buttons display at the bottom of the gallery.

b. Click **Action Button: Sound**.

The Shapes gallery closes, and the pointer becomes a crosshair pointer.

c. Click in an empty portion of the slide to create the button.

Do not worry about the size or position of the button at this time. You will adjust both in a later step. The Action Settings dialog box opens to the Mouse Click tab.

d. Click the **Play sound arrow** and select **Other Sound**.

e. Locate and select the *p06h1Incorrect.wav* file.

The sound file is assigned to the action button. Because this is not the correct answer, the viewer hears *Incorrect* when the button is clicked.

f. Click **OK** to close the Add Audio dialog box and click **OK** in the Action Settings dialog box.

The action button now has sound attached to it, and the sound plays when the presentation is viewed in the Slide Show view and the Reading view.

g. Click the **FORMAT tab** with the action button still selected and click the **Size Dialog Box Launcher** in the Size group. Set **Height** to **0.35"** and **Width** to **0.35"**.

h. Click **Position** in the Format Shape pane and set **Horizontal position** to **0.5"** and **Vertical position** to **2.5"**.

Hands-On Exercise 1   383

i. Keep the sound action button selected and press **Ctrl+D** three times.

Three duplicates of the original sound action button are created. It is easier to edit duplicates than to re-create the button because the duplicates are already sized. The last duplicate created is now selected, so you will edit it first.

j. Click **Size & Properties** in the Format Shape pane. Click **Position** in the Format Shape pane and set **Horizontal position** to **0.5"** and **Vertical position** to **3.9"**.

The last duplicate you made moves into position to the left of answer *d*.

k. Right-click the selected button and click **Hyperlink**. Click the **Play sound arrow** and select **Other Sound**. Locate and select the *p06h1TryAgain.wav* file and click **OK** to close the Add Audio dialog box. Click **OK** to close the Action Settings dialog box.

The sound action button has been edited to play a different sound file. Because this is not the correct answer, the viewer hears *Try Again* when the button is clicked.

l. Click the third sound action button from the top. In the Format Shape pane, in the Position options, set **Horizontal position** to **0.5"** and **Vertical position** to **3.43"**.

m. Right-click the selected button and click **Hyperlink**. Click the **Play sound arrow** and select **Other Sound**. Locate and select the *p06h1Sorry.wav* file and click **OK** to close the Add Audio dialog box. Click **OK** to close the Action Settings dialog box.

Once again, the sound action button has been edited to play a different sound file. Because this is not the correct answer, the viewer hears *Sorry* when the button is clicked.

n. Click the second sound action button from the top, click in the **Format Shape pane**, click in the **Position options**, and then set **Horizontal position** to **0.5"** and **Vertical position** to **2.97"**. Click **Close** to close the Format Shape pane.

o. Right-click the selected button and click **Hyperlink**. Click the **Play sound arrow**, click **Applause**, and then click **OK** to close the Action Settings dialog box.

This is the correct answer, so the viewer hears applause when the button is clicked.

p. Hold down **Shift** and click to select the four sound action buttons. Press **Ctrl+C** to copy them to the Clipboard. Click **Slide 5** and press **Ctrl+V** to paste the buttons on Slide 5. Click away from the selected buttons to deselect them.

It is fastest to copy, paste, and edit the buttons to additional slides, although the sound action buttons will need to be repositioned.

q. On Slide 5, select the top sound action button (the sound action button for answer *a*), right-click, and then click **Hyperlink**. Click the **Play sound arrow**, select **Applause**, and then click **OK** to close the Action Settings dialog box.

This is the correct answer, so the viewer hears applause when the button is clicked.

r. Select the second sound action button (the sound action button for answer *b*), right-click, and then select **Hyperlink**. Click the **Play sound arrow** and select **Other Sound**. Select the *p06h1Incorrect.wav* file and click **OK** to close the Add Audio dialog box. Click **OK** to close the Action Settings dialog box.

s. Save the presentation.

STEP 4 » CREATE ACTION BUTTONS FOR NAVIGATION

You want navigation buttons with consistent placement on the slides in your slide show. You will create the buttons on one slide, and then copy and paste them to other slides. Refer to Figure 6.11 and the below table as you complete Step 4.

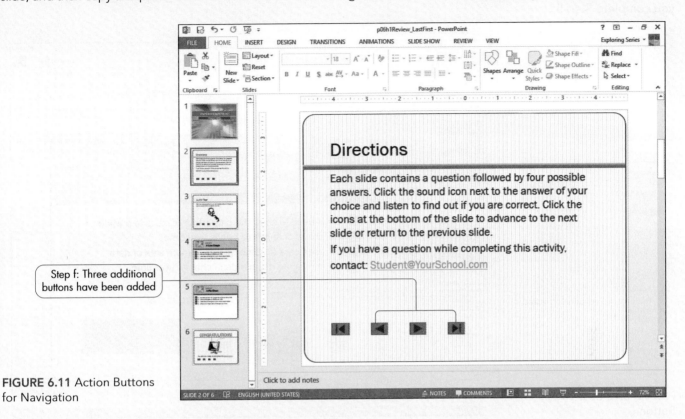

FIGURE 6.11 Action Buttons for Navigation

a. On Slide 2, click the **INSERT tab**, click **Shapes** in the Illustrations group, and then click **Action Button: Beginning** from the Action Buttons category of the Shapes gallery.

b. Click anywhere on the slide to create the action button.

The Action Settings dialog box opens, and the Beginning action button is preset to hyperlink to the first slide.

c. Click **OK**. Keep the button selected, click the **FORMAT tab** if necessary, click the **Size Dialog Box Launcher** in the Size group, and then click **Size**, if necessary.

d. Set **Height** to **0.35"** and **Width** to **0.5"**.

e. Click **Position** in the Format Shape pane and set **Horizontal position** to **0.92"** and **Vertical position** to **6.25"**.

f. Create three additional buttons using the default settings in the Action Settings dialog box and the information included in the following table:

Action Button	Height	Width	Horizontal Position	Vertical Position
Back or Previous	0.35"	0.5"	2.11"	6.25"
Forward or Next	0.35"	0.5"	3.27"	6.25"
End	0.35"	0.5"	4.46 "	6.25"

g. Select and copy the four action buttons.

h. Paste the action buttons on Slides 3 through 6.

i. Save the presentation.

STEP 5 ≫ CREATE A CUSTOM ACTION BUTTON

You want to provide students with the option of opening a Charts and Graphs Reference Guide before answering quiz questions. You will create a customizable action button for students to click to open the guide. Refer to Figure 6.12 as you complete Step 5.

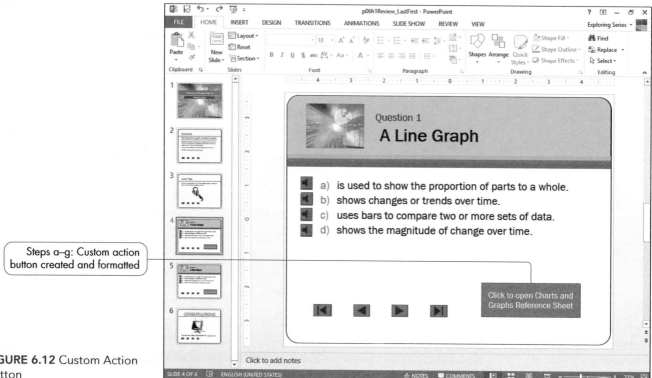

Steps a–g: Custom action button created and formatted

FIGURE 6.12 Custom Action Button

a. On Slide 4, click the **INSERT tab**, if necessary, click **Shapes** in the Illustrations group, and then click **Action Button: Custom**.

b. Click the bottom right on the slide to create an action button.

c. Click **Hyperlink to** on the Mouse Click tab in the Action Settings dialog box, click the arrow, scroll down, and then select **Other File**.

d. Locate and select the *p06h1Guide.docx* file and click **OK** to close the *Hyperlink to Other File* dialog box. Click **OK** to close the Action Settings dialog box.

e. Type **Click to open Charts and Graphs Reference Sheet** inside the selected custom action button.

f. Click the **FORMAT tab** if necessary, click the **Size Dialog Box Launcher** in the Size group, and then set **Height** to 1" and **Width** to 3".

g. Click **Position** in the Format Shape pane and set **Horizontal position** to 6" and **Vertical position** to 5.58". Click **Close**.

h. Click the border of the button object to select the entire object and text, press **Ctrl+C** to copy the custom action button, and then paste it to Slide 5.

i. Save the presentation.

STEP 6 » INSERT AND USE HYPERLINKS

After completing the review quiz, you want the students to complete an assignment on charts and graphs. To include interactivity, you will add a ScreenTip to a clip art picture that instructs the student to click the picture. You will create a hyperlink to an existing file using text in a text box. Finally, you will create a trigger that launches the text. Refer to Figure 6.13 as you complete Step 6.

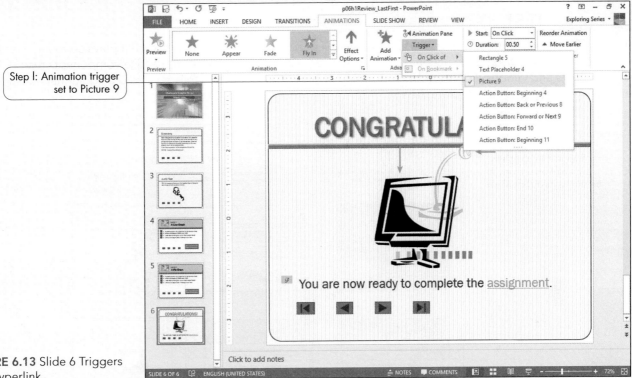

Step I: Animation trigger set to Picture 9

FIGURE 6.13 Slide 6 Triggers and Hyperlink

a. On Slide 6, select the monitor picture.

b. Click the **INSERT tab** and click **Hyperlink** in the Links group.

c. Click **Place in This Document** and click **Slide 6**.

> You are linking the monitor picture to the same location in the document so that you have access to the ScreenTip option.

d. Click **ScreenTip**, type **Click Me!** in the Set Hyperlink ScreenTip dialog box, and then click **OK**.

> The ScreenTip displays when the presentation is viewed in the Slide Show or Reading View.

e. Click **OK** to close the Insert Hyperlink dialog box.

f. Select the word *assignment* in the text box.

g. Click the **INSERT tab** if necessary and click **Hyperlink**.

h. Click **Existing File or Web Page**, click the **Browse for File button**, locate and insert *p06h1Assignment*, and then click **OK**.

i. Verify that the address for the *p06h1Assignment* file appears in the Address box and click **OK**.

> The word *assignment* is underlined, indicating it is a hyperlink.

j. Click to select the text box border, if necessary, and click the **ANIMATIONS tab**.

k. Click **Fly In** in the Animation group.

> With an animation assigned, the Trigger option is available.

l. Click **Trigger** in the Advanced Animation group, point to *On Click of*, and then click **Picture 9**.

Picture 9 (the monitor clip art) triggers the text animation when clicked in the Slide Show or Reading View.

m. Save the presentation.

STEP 7 ≫ TEST HYPERLINKS

Although it is always important to view a slide show while you are developing it to ensure it plays correctly, it is critical that a slide show with hyperlinks, action buttons, and triggers be viewed and all interactive components tested. You test the *Charts and Graphs* slide show before getting approval from your supervisor to create additional questions. Refer to Figure 6.14 as you complete Step 7.

Step a: The completed presentation is ready to be shown as a slide show

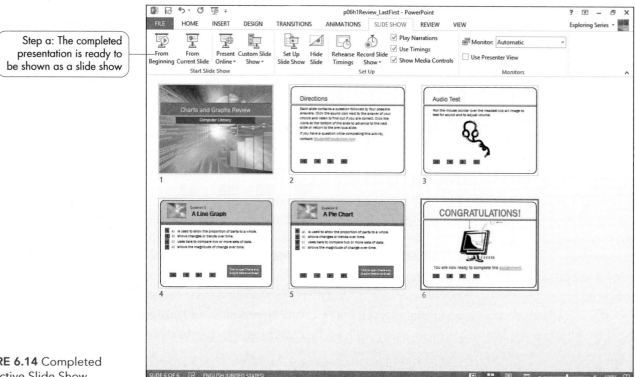

FIGURE 6.14 Completed Interactive Slide Show

a. Click the **SLIDE SHOW tab** and click **From Beginning** in the Start Slide Show group.

b. Advance to Slide 2 and click the e-mail hyperlink. Close the e-mail screen without saving.

> **TROUBLESHOOTING:** When testing sounds, you may need to adjust your volume to hear the sounds playing. You may want to use a headset if you are in a public computer lab.

c. Click the **Forward or Next action button** to move to Slide 3. Point to the headset clip art image.

> **TROUBLESHOOTING:** You will not be able to hear the Voltage sound or see the highlight border unless you are in Slide Show view. If the Voltage sound does not play when you mouse over it, exit the slide show and right-click the clip art image of the headset. Click Hyperlink, click the Mouse Over tab, and then check *Play sound*. Select Voltage from the list of sounds and click OK. Return to Slide Show mode.

d. Continue advancing through the slides in the presentation using the action buttons for navigation. Be sure to test each button.

> **TROUBLESHOOTING:** If any of the action buttons do not work, exit the slide show. In any slide, right-click the action button. Click Edit Hyperlink and check the slide showing in the *Hyperlink to:* box. If no slide is showing or if the wrong slide is showing, click the arrow and select the right slide from the list. Click OK. Copy the button and paste it on all other slides containing the button. Return to Slide Show mode.

e. On Slide 4, click each of the sound action buttons. Answer *b* should play the applause sound. The remaining sound action buttons should play a sound that indicates the choice of answer was incorrect.

> **TROUBLESHOOTING:** If any of the sound action buttons play the wrong sound, exit the slide show. Select the sound action button that plays the wrong sound, right click, and then click Hyperlink. Change the linked sound to the correct choice. Return to Slide Show mode.

f. On Slides 4 and 5, click **Click to open Charts and Graphs Reference Sheet** to open the Word document. Close the document after opening.

> **TROUBLESHOOTING:** If the Word document did not open, exit the slide show. Right-click the custom action button and click Hyperlink. Click the *Browse for File* button and locate and insert *p06h1Guide.docx*. Click OK twice. Return to Slide Show mode.

g. On Slide 5, click each of the sound action buttons. Answer *a* should play the applause sound. The remaining sound action buttons should play a sound that indicates the choice of answer was incorrect.

> **TROUBLESHOOTING:** If any of the sound action buttons plays the wrong sound, follow the Troubleshooting instructions in step e.

h. On Slide 6, point to the clip art image to view the ScreenTip.

> **TROUBLESHOOTING:** If the ScreenTip does not display, exit the slide show, right-click the image, and then click Edit Hyperlink. Click *Place in This Document*, click Slide 6, and then click ScreenTip. Type Click Me!, if necessary. Click OK twice. Return to Slide Show mode.

i. Click the image to trigger the text box animation.

> **TROUBLESHOOTING:** If the text box does not fly onto the slide, exit the slide show. Select the text box, click the Animations tab, and then check to see if the Fly In animation is assigned. Then, click Trigger in the Advanced Animation group, click *On Click of*, and then check to see if *Picture 9* is selected. Return to Slide Show mode.

j. Click **assignment** to ensure the *Charts and Graphs* assignment opens. Close the document after opening.

> **TROUBLESHOOTING:** If Word does not open and display the *p06h1Assignment.docx* file, exit the slide show. Right-click the assignment hyperlink and click Edit Hyperlink. Click the *Browse for File* button and locate and select *p06h1Assignment*. Click OK twice.

k. Save and close the file, and submit it based on your instructor's directions.

Advanced Animation

In the previous section, you used an animation trigger to control the flow of information on a slide. By fully utilizing the different types of animations and animation options, you can engage the audience's interest and direct their focus to important points in your presentation. Carefully plan animations, however, to ensure they enhance the message of the slide. Used indiscriminately, animations can be distracting to the audience.

Table 6.2 shows PowerPoint's four animation types. Each of these animation types has properties, effects, and timing that can be modified.

TABLE 6.2 PowerPoint Animation Types	
Type	**Content**
Entrance	Controls how an object moves onto or appears on a slide
Emphasis	Draws attention to an object already on a slide
Exit	Controls how an object leaves or disappears from a slide
Motion Paths	Controls the movement of an object from one position to another along a predetermined path

In this section, you will apply multiple animations to an object, modify a motion path, specify animation effects, set animation timing, control the flow of text, and fine-tune your animations using the Animation Pane.

Applying Multiple Animations to an Object

Multiple animations can be applied to an object. For example, you could apply an entrance animation that causes your company logo to fly onto a title slide, an emphasis animation that causes the logo to grow and shrink, a motion animation that causes the logo to move in a circle, and an exit animation that causes the logo to fly off the slide. You can control the timing of the animations as well as the trigger that starts the animation sequence. This complex set of animations may not be necessary, but it shows the power of the animation effects. Keep in mind, though, when you use too many animations on one object or slide, the result can be distracting and take away from the message of the object or slide.

Figure 6.15 shows multiple animations applied to a slide. Numbered animation tags indicate the order in which the animations will play.

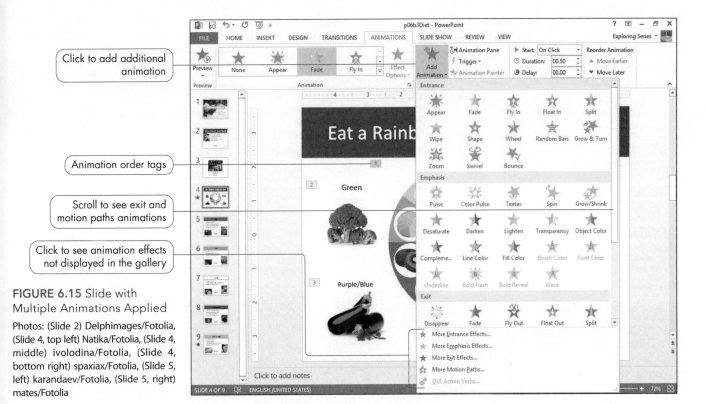

Click to add additional animation

Animation order tags

Scroll to see exit and motion paths animations

Click to see animation effects not displayed in the gallery

FIGURE 6.15 Slide with Multiple Animations Applied

Photos: (Slide 2) Delphimages/Fotolia, (Slide 4, top left) Natika/Fotolia, (Slide 4, middle) ivolodina/Fotolia, (Slide 4, bottom right) spaxiax/Fotolia, (Slide 5, left) karandaev/Fotolia, (Slide 5, right) mates/Fotolia

STEP 1 >> To add multiple animations, do the following:

1. Select the object and click the ANIMATIONS tab.
2. Apply an animation from the Animation gallery.
3. Click Add Animation in the Advanced Animation group.
4. Click an animation to apply it to the object.
5. Continue adding animations as needed.

Animation sequences should be checked as you create them to make sure they respond in the way you expect. At any time, click Preview in the Preview group to see the animation sequence in Normal view. You can also check the sequence in the Slide Show or Reading View.

Applying a Motion Path Animation

Because the eye is naturally drawn to motion, using a motion path (a predetermined path that an object follows as part of an animation) to animate an object can capture and focus a viewer's attention on key objects or text. Motion paths are linear, curved, or follow a predetermined shape. PowerPoint includes a variety of interesting motion paths such as arcs, waves, hearts, and stars. You can even draw a custom path for the object to follow.

To apply a motion path animation, do the following:

1. Select the object and click the ANIMATIONS tab.
2. Click the More button in the Animation group.
3. Scroll down to the Motion Paths category.
4. Click a motion path animation to apply it to the selected object.

Once you have applied the motion path animation to an object, the motion path appears as a dotted line on the slide. A small arrow indicates the starting point for the animation, and a red arrow with a line indicates the ending point. If it is a closed path like a circle, only the starting point displays. Figure 6.16 displays a leaf clip art image with the Turns motion path animation applied.

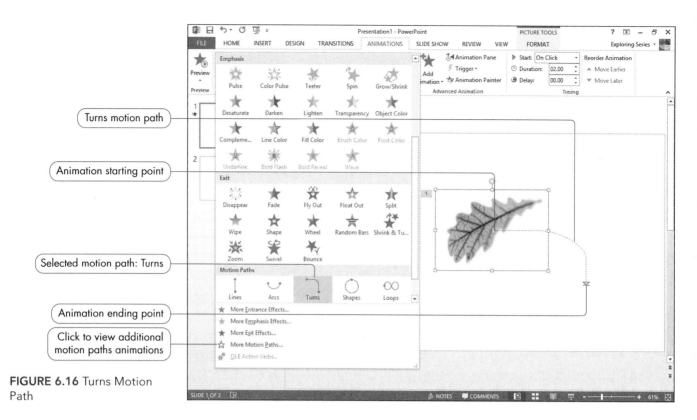

Turns motion path

Animation starting point

Selected motion path: Turns

Animation ending point

Click to view additional motion paths animations

FIGURE 6.16 Turns Motion Path

Create a Custom Path

STEP 2 ▶

A **custom path** is an animation path that can be created freehand instead of following a preset path. To draw a path in the direction and the length you determine rather than in a standard path available in the Animation gallery, select the Custom Path animation from the Animation gallery. Position the crosshair pointer in the approximate center of the object you wish to animate and drag in the direction you want the object to follow. The crosshair pointer becomes a Pencil tool that you drag until you have the desired path. Double-click to end the path.

By default, a custom path animation uses the Scribble option, which enables you to draw the path by using the mouse like a pencil. Click Effect Options in the Animation group to draw a curved or straight path. Figure 6.17 shows a custom path animation drawn using the Scribble option.

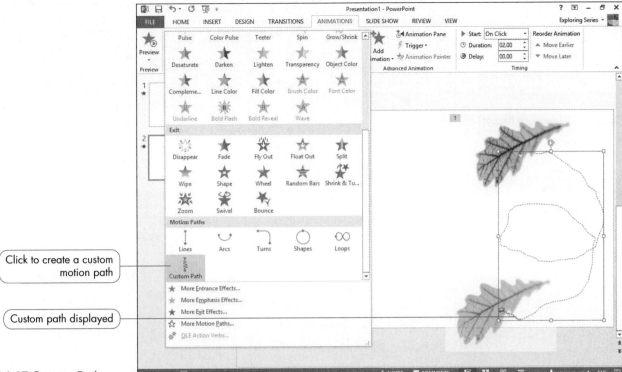

FIGURE 6.17 Custom Path

Whether you apply one of PowerPoint's motion paths or create your own, you can resize, move, or rotate the path using the same methods you use to edit a shape. To use a motion path, you choose More Motion Paths in the Animation gallery. Figure 6.18 shows a clip art image with the Stairs Down motion path applied.

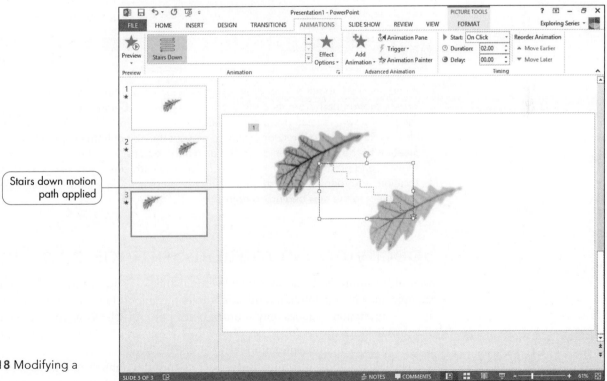

FIGURE 6.18 Modifying a Path

If you want to reshape the motion path, you must display the points that create the path. Once the points are displayed, drag a point to its new location. The path automatically adjusts. Figure 6.19 shows a custom path animation with its points displayed.

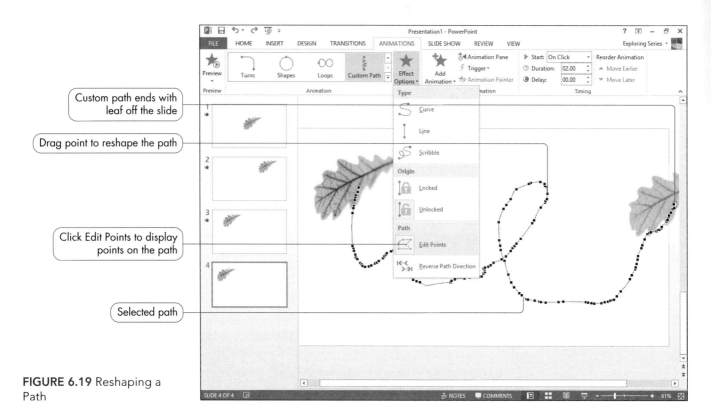

Custom path ends with leaf off the slide

Drag point to reshape the path

Click Edit Points to display points on the path

Selected path

FIGURE 6.19 Reshaping a Path

To display the points, select the path, click Effect Options in the Animation group, and then click Edit Points. Drag points on the path as needed. You can add or delete points by right-clicking the path to display the editing menu and then clicking Add Point or Delete Point.

TIP   **Reversing a Custom Path**

If you need an object to end at an exact location on a slide, it may be easier for you to draw a motion path from its ending point than from its beginning point. Once you have the path drawn, reverse the path by clicking Effect Options in the Animation group and clicking Reverse Path Direction. Then, to prevent the object from jumping from its original location to the new location when the animation begins, lock the path by clicking Effect Options and clicking Locked. If you do not lock the path, the object will show at its original location, and then its position after being reversed, causing a jerky motion. Finally, drag the object to the new beginning point.

Specifying Animation Settings and Timing

Each of the animations has associated settings that vary according to the animation. For example, the Fly Out animation includes direction, smoothing, and sound settings, whereas the Fade animation includes only sound. Some options, such as direction, are readily accessible by clicking Effect Options in the Animation group. Others such as *Bounce end* are accessed by clicking the Animation Dialog Box Launcher.

The Left motion path animation applied to the automobile clip art image in Figure 6.20 utilizes the *Smooth start* and *Smooth end* settings. The *Smooth start* and *Smooth end* settings enable an object to accelerate and decelerate along its motion path. In this figure, the clip art image speeds up at the beginning of the animation and slows down as it nears the end of its path. The automobile disappears after animating because the *After animation* setting is set to Hide After Animation.

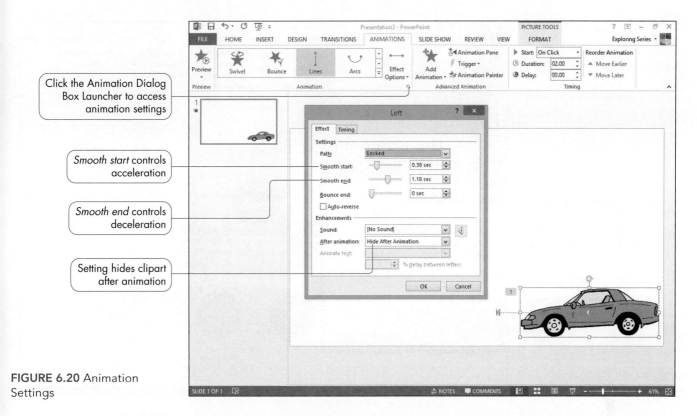

Click the Animation Dialog Box Launcher to access animation settings

Smooth start controls acceleration

Smooth end controls deceleration

Setting hides clipart after animation

FIGURE 6.20 Animation Settings

STEP 3» Attaching timing settings to animations frees you from constantly advancing to the next object and lets you concentrate on delivering your message. Previously, you have set timing options in the Timing group on the Animations tab, and that is the quickest way to set the method for starting an animation, to set the duration of an animation, and to set the delay. The Animation Dialog Box Launcher also provides access to these settings, but the dialog box it opens gives you several additional settings. You can set the number of times an animation is repeated, set the animation to rewind when it is done playing, and determine how the animation is triggered on the Timing tab of the dialog box. Figure 6.21 shows a SmartArt object with a motion path applied. In addition to animating a SmartArt object as one object, you can select individual shapes that make up the SmartArt object and animate them individually. The Circle dialog box is open, showing the Timing tab options available for the selected SmartArt object.

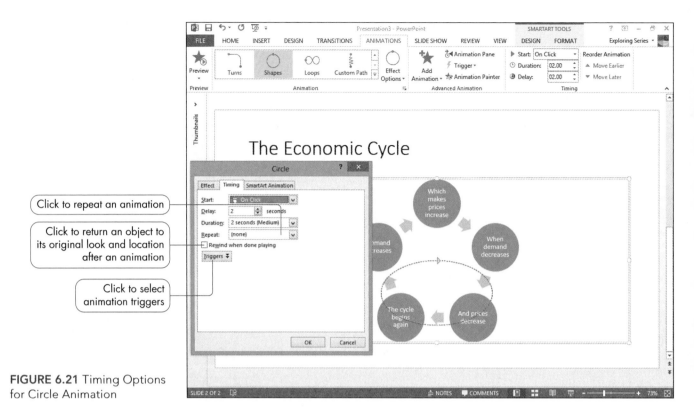

Click to repeat an animation

Click to return an object to its original look and location after an animation

Click to select animation triggers

FIGURE 6.21 Timing Options for Circle Animation

Animating Text

Although animating non-bulleted text in placeholders and text boxes uses the same method as other objects, bullet text has additional options available. These options help you keep audience attention and can keep the audience from reading ahead. You can bring text onto the slide by animating the text as one object, animating all paragraphs to come in together, and by sequencing the text animation by text outline level. A paragraph in PowerPoint can be a line of text, several lines of text or even a blank line. Whenever you press Enter to move the cursor to a new line, you create a new paragraph.

STEP 4 » To determine the animation sequence of bullet text, do the following:

1. Select the text and click the ANIMATIONS tab.
2. Apply an animation effect.
3. Click Effect Options in the Animation group.
4. Select the desired text grouping option from the Sequence list.

To assign animations beyond the first level, click the Animation Dialog Box Launcher and click the Text Animation tab. Click the *Group text* arrow and animate text up to five outline levels. Figure 6.22 shows text animated by first-level paragraphs.

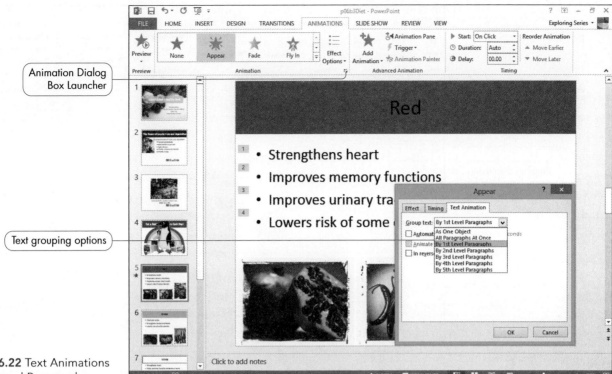

Animation Dialog Box Launcher

Text grouping options

FIGURE 6.22 Text Animations by First-Level Paragraphs

TIP Layering Text on Text

When following the 7×7 per slide text guideline, which suggest using no more than seven lines with seven words on a slide, you may find that you have more text to display on a slide than there is room available. If this happens, create two text boxes. Animate the first text box, and then click the Animation Dialog Box Launcher. Click the *After animation* arrow and click Hide After Animation. Select the second text box and animate using the Appear animation. Set the animation to play *After previous*.

Using the Animation Pane

STEP 5 As you work with complex animations, it is helpful to view the Animation Pane. The Animation Pane is similar to a summary of animation effects used. The display begins with a tag indicating how the animation starts. A *0* tag indicates the animation starts with the previous animation. A numbered tag indicates the animation begins with a mouse click, and the number indicates the animation order. No tag indicates that the animation automatically starts after the previous animation. Office 2013 has a new feature where animation effects are color-coded. For example, green indicates an entrance animation and red indicates an exit animation. An emphasis animation is coded yellow, and a motion path is coded blue.

An icon displays to the right of the tag that represents the type of animation effect applied. Next, a portion of the name of the animated object displays. Finally, a timeline displays the duration of an animation as a bar that can be used to adjust timing. To open the Animation Pane, click the Animations tab and click Animation Pane in the Advanced Animation group. To adjust animation timing, drag the edge of the animation bar. Figure 6.23 shows a slide with animated objects with the Animation Pane open.

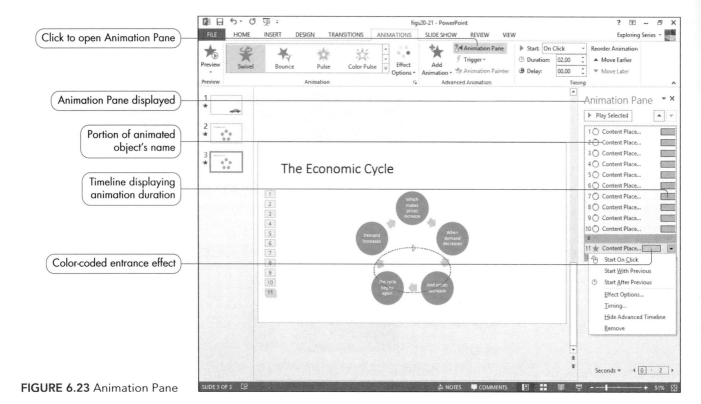

Click to open Animation Pane

Animation Pane displayed

Portion of animated object's name

Timeline displaying animation duration

Color-coded entrance effect

FIGURE 6.23 Animation Pane

Quick **Concepts**

1. Which animation effect does an Entrance animation type apply to an object? *p. 390*

2. How will applying a motion path to an object or text enhance your presentation? *p. 391*

3. What animation effects are edited and controlled in the Animation Pane? *p. 397*

Watch the Video for this Hands-On Exercise!

MyITLab®
HOE2 Training

2 Advanced Animation

In your role as the teaching assistant for the computer literacy class, you begin modifying a presentation designed to help the students understand PowerPoint's animation features. You create examples of animation for students to view.

Skills covered: Apply Multiple Animations to an Object • Create and Modify a Custom Motion Path • Specify Animation Settings and Timing • Animate Text and SmartArt • Use the Animation Pane to Modify Animations

STEP 1 ≫ APPLY MULTIPLE ANIMATIONS TO AN OBJECT

To illustrate an example of multiple animations applied to one object, you apply an entrance, emphasis, motion, and exit animation to a clip art image. After testing the animations, you use the Animation Pane to select and modify the animations. Refer to Figure 6.24 as you complete Step 1.

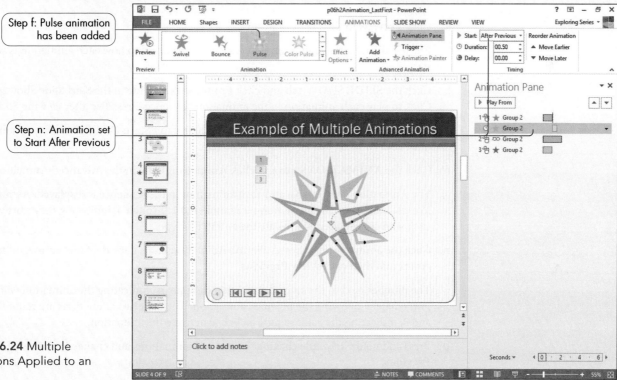

Step f: Pulse animation has been added

Step n: Animation set to Start After Previous

FIGURE 6.24 Multiple Animations Applied to an Object

a.   Open *p06h2Animation* and save it as **p06h2Animation_LastFirst**.

> **TROUBLESHOOTING:** If you make any major mistakes in this exercise, you can close the file, open *p06h2Animation* again, and then start this exercise over.

b.   Create a handout header with your name and a handout footer with your instructor's name and your class. Include the current date.

c.   On Slide 4, select the **star clip art image** and click the **ANIMATIONS tab**.

d. Click the **More button** in the Animation group and click **Grow & Turn** in the Entrance category.

The Grow & Turn animation previews, and an animation tag numbered 1 is assigned to the clip art image.

e. Click **Add Animation** in the Advanced Animation group.

f. Click **Pulse** in the Emphasis category.

The Pulse animation previews and an animation tag numbered 2 is assigned to the clip art image.

g. Click **Add Animation** in the Advanced Animation group.

h. Scroll down the Animation gallery and click **Loops** in the Motion Paths category.

The Loops animation previews, the Loops motion path displays, and an animation tag numbered 3 is assigned to the clip art image.

i. Click **Add Animation** in the Advanced Animation group.

j. Scroll down the Animation gallery and click **Shrink & Turn** in the Exit category.

The Shrink & Turn animation previews, and an animation tag numbered 4 is assigned to the clip art image.

k. Click **Preview** in the Preview group.

Preview displays the animation sequence without regard to how each animation is set to start.

l. Click the **SLIDE SHOW tab** and click **From Current Slide** in the Start Slide Show group. Click to play each animation in the animation sequence. Press **Esc** after viewing Slide 4.

Because the animations were created using the default Start: On Click timing option, you must click to start each animation in the sequence.

m. Click the **ANIMATIONS tab** and click **Animation Pane** in the Advanced Animation group.

The Animation Pane opens, and each animation in the sequence is displayed. As you point to each animation, the animations are numbered 1 through 4, indicating they start with a click, and color-coded to indicate the animation type.

n. Click the animation numbered **2** in the Animation Pane, click the **Start arrow** in the Timing group, and then click **After Previous**.

The number next to the second animation disappears, indicating the animation will activate immediately following the previous animation. The next two animations are renumbered 2 and 3, indicating they still require a click to activate the animation.

o. Press and hold **Ctrl** while clicking the last two animations and change their timings to **After Previous**.

The Animation Pane now indicates that the first animation requires a click to start. All of the numbers have disappeared, which indicates the remaining animations in the sequences will play after the previous animation is completed.

p. Test the animation sequence in Slide Show view to ensure that the animations play correctly.

q. Close the Animation Pane.

r. Save the presentation.

STEP 2 ➤➤ CREATE AND MODIFY A CUSTOM MOTION PATH

The next example of an animation in the presentation is a custom path motion animation. You will create a motion path to move a clip art image around the slide, and then you will copy the image and path to another slide and modify the path to smooth it. Refer to Figure 6.25 as you complete Step 2.

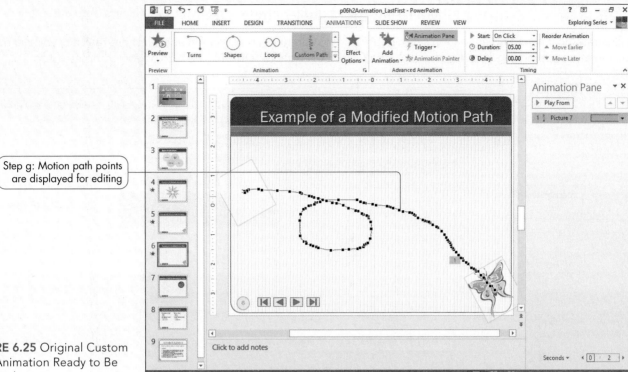

Step g: Motion path points are displayed for editing

FIGURE 6.25 Original Custom Path Animation Ready to Be Modified

a. On Slide 5, select the **butterfly clip art image**.

b. Click the **ANIMATIONS tab**, if necessary, and click the **More button** in the Animation group.

c. Click **Custom Path** in the Motion Paths category.

d. Click in the approximate center of the butterfly and drag the **Pencil tool** in a loop and off the left side of the slide. Refer to Figure 6.25. Double-click to end the path.

   The animation previews, and when the preview finishes, you see the path with its green starting point and red ending point.

e. Select **02.00** in the Duration box in the Timing Group and type **05.00**.

   Increasing the duration increases the amount of time it takes to complete the animation.

f. Copy the clip art image and paste the copy on Slide 6 using the **Use Destination Theme paste option**.

   The clip art image and its associated animation are pasted on Slide 6.

g. On Slide 6, click the **Animations tab**, if necessary, click the path, click **Effect Options** in the Animation group, and then click **Edit Points**.

   The points that create the motion path appear.

h. Click a point on the path and drag the point to a new position.

   The path reshapes based on the new point position.

i. Click a point on the path, right-click, and then click **Delete Point**.

> **TROUBLESHOOTING:** If you press Delete on the keyboard, the entire path disappears. Click Undo on the Quick Access Toolbar and repeat step i.

j. Continue to delete any points that cause a jerky animation motion, or right-click any point causing a jerky motion, and select **Smooth Point**.

k. Save the presentation.

STEP 3 » SPECIFY ANIMATION SETTINGS AND TIMING

To illustrate how changing animation settings and timing can help an animation appear more realistic, you will modify the animation settings and timing of a basketball clip art image. Refer to Figure 6.26 as you complete Step 3.

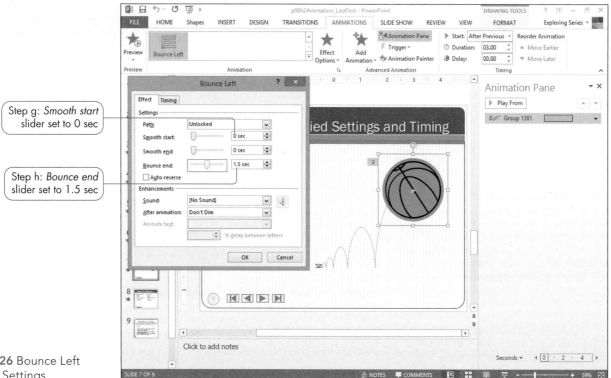

Step g: *Smooth start slider set to 0 sec*

Step h: *Bounce end slider set to 1.5 sec*

FIGURE 6.26 Bounce Left Animation Settings

a. On Slide 7, click the **basketball clip art image** to select it.

b. Click the **ANIMATIONS tab**, if necessary, click the **More button**, and then click **More Motion Paths**.

c. Click **Bounce Left** in the *Lines_Curves* section and click **OK**.

d. Click the red ending point of the animation. When the double-headed arrow displays, drag it to the left to extend the distance the animation will cover.

> **TROUBLESHOOTING:** Be sure the mouse displays as the double-headed arrow before dragging the red ending point of the animation. Otherwise, you will move the entire animation instead of extending the distance the animation will cover.

e. Click the **Duration up arrow** in the Timing group until the duration time is set at **03.00**.

  The animation will now take three seconds to complete.

f. Click the **Animation Dialog Box Launcher** in the Animation group to show additional animation effect options.

  The Bounce Left dialog box opens.

g. Drag the **Smooth start slider** to **0 sec**.

  The animation now starts at a higher speed rather than starting slowly and speeding up.

h. Drag the **Bounce end slider** to **1.5 sec** and click **OK**. (The *Smooth end* setting automatically becomes 0 sec.)

  The animation begins to slow after 1.5 seconds.

i. Click **Preview** in the Preview group.

j. Save the presentation.

STEP 4 >> ANIMATE TEXT AND SMARTART

You want to demonstrate how to control the flow of information to the computer literacy students. To do so, you will animate text and a SmartArt diagram. You will apply the Appear animation effect on text content placeholders so that students will not be distracted by movement and can concentrate on reading the text. You will apply a Shape entrance animation so that the animation shape matches the circle shapes used in the SmartArt. Refer to Figure 6.27 as you complete Step 4.

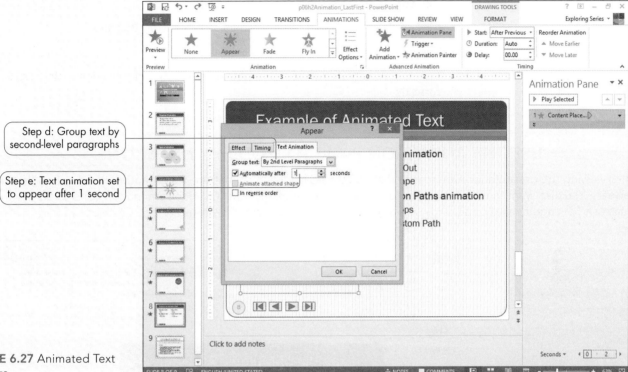

Step d: Group text by second-level paragraphs

Step e: Text animation set to appear after 1 second

FIGURE 6.27 Animated Text Settings

a. On Slide 8, click the **left content placeholder** to select it.

   Selecting text enables you to apply an animation; selecting the content placeholder is faster.

b. Click **Appear** in the *Entrance* section of the Animation group.

   Animation 1 and 2 tags appear next to the first and second first-level bullets and their associated second-level bullets.

c. Click the **Animation Dialog Box Launcher**, click the **After animation arrow**, and then click the last color option.

   Text that has been viewed dims to the new color after viewing.

d. Click the **Text Animation tab** in the Appear dialog box, click the **Group text arrow**, and then select **By 2nd Level Paragraphs**.

   First-level text and second-level text will animate one at a time.

e. Click **Automatically after**, select **0**, type **1**, and then click **OK**.

   The animation tags change to 0, indicating that they will start automatically. Preview displays the text entering, pausing for 1 second, and then dimming when the next animated text appears.

f. Click the **left content placeholder**, if necessary, click **Animation Painter**, and then click the **right content placeholder**.

   The animation timing and settings are copied to the placeholder.

g. On Slide 3, select the SmartArt diagram.

h. Click the **More button** in the Animation group and click **Shape** in the *Entrance* section.

Preview displays a Circle animation that begins at the edges of the SmartArt and moves inward to complete the shape.

i. Click **Effect Options** in the Animation group and click **Out** in the *Direction* section.

j. Click **Effect Options** in the Animation group and click **One by One** in the *Sequence* section.

Animation tags 1 through 4 appear, indicating that each object will animate individually and will start on a mouse click.

k. Click the **Start arrow** in the Timing group and click **After Previous**.

The animation tag changes to 0, indicating that the objects will animate automatically.

l. View the presentation in Slide Show view and verify that all animation settings are set correctly.

m. Save the presentation.

STEP 5 ≫ USE THE ANIMATION PANE TO MODIFY ANIMATIONS

After viewing the presentation, you realize that you would like each animation to start automatically when the slide appears. You also want to modify the timing of some animations. You will open the Animation Pane to efficiently locate and change animation settings. Refer to Figure 6.28 as you complete Step 5.

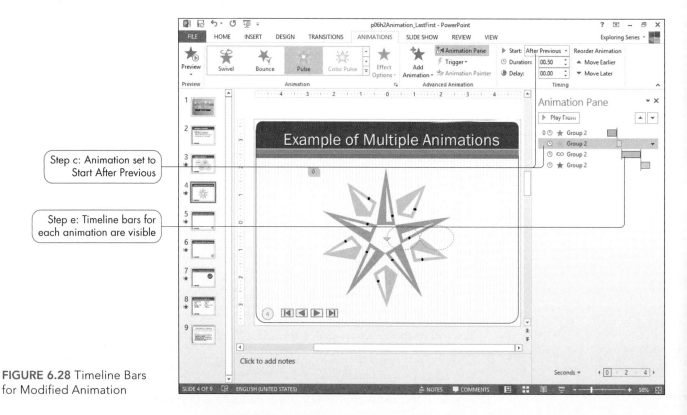

FIGURE 6.28 Timeline Bars for Modified Animation

a. Click the **ANIMATIONS tab** and click **Animation Pane** in the Advanced Animation group.

b. On Slide 4, click the **star clip art image** and notice the Animation Pane.

All animations in the Animation Pane are selected. The animation 1 tag next to the first bullet indicates that this animation plays first and requires a mouse click to launch.

c. Click the first animation in the Animation Pane to select it and click the **Start arrow** in the Timing group. Click **After Previous**.

The animation 1 tag changes to a 0.

d. Repeat step c for Slides 5 through 7.

e. On Slide 4, drag the left border of the Animation Pane to the left until the timeline bar next to each animation is visible.

The timeline bars show that each animation starts immediately after the preceding animation. The loop animation takes longer to complete than the other three animations.

f. Drag the right edge of the timeline bar for the second animation to the right until the ScreenTip displays *End: 2.6s*.

The Pulse animation duration is increased.

TROUBLESHOOTING: Be sure the mouse displays as the double-headed arrow with vertical lines in the middle. A plain double-headed arrow will not work for this task.

---

g. Click the last animation to select it, click the **Start arrow**, and then click **With Previous**.

The beginning point for the third and fourth animations align so they begin at the same time.

h. Position the pointer over the fourth animation timeline bar and drag the bar so that it begins at **3.2s**. Drag the right edge of the bar to **5.5s**.

The time the animation starts and the duration of the animation is changed.

i. Click the first animation and click **Play From** in the Animation Pane to test the animation.

j. View the presentation in Slide Show view.

k. Save and close the file, and submit it based on your instructor's directions.

Chapter Objectives Review

After reading this chapter, you have accomplished the following objectives:

1. **Insert and use hyperlinks.**
   - Hyperlinks connect two locations and can be used to add interactivity to a slide show.
   - Clicking a hyperlink takes the viewer to another slide in a slide show, to an existing file, to a Web page on the Internet, to another program, or to the screen to begin an e-mail.
   - ScreenTips can be added to hyperlinks to offer the viewer additional information.
   - Hyperlinks can be attached to any object.
   - Hyperlinks can be activated by a mouse click or a mouse over.

2. **Add action buttons.**
   - Actions are instructions to PowerPoint to perform a task such as jumping to another slide, playing a sound, or opening another program.
   - You can attach actions to any object or use an action button—a pre-made icon with actions attached.
   - Action buttons are typically used to navigate a slide show (Back or Previous button, Forward or Next button, Beginning button, End button, Home button, and Return button) or to display some type of information (Information button, Movie button, Document button, Sound button, and Help button).
   - Activate an action button with a mouse click or a mouse over.

3. **Use a trigger.**
   - A trigger is an animation option that controls when an event takes place.
   - In order for the event to take place, a viewer must click an object that has an animation trigger attached.

4. **Apply multiple animations to an object.**
   - You can apply more than one animation effect to an object.
   - Multiple animations direct the flow of information or enhance the message of a slide.

5. **Apply a motion path animation.**
   - In a motion path animation, an object follows a predetermined path to capture and focus a viewer's attention.
   - Motion paths can be linear, curved, or follow a predetermined shape.
   - Creating a Custom path motion path enables you to draw a path in any direction and of any length.
   - Add, delete, and move points on a motion path to edit it.

6. **Specify animation settings and timing.**
   - Animation settings vary according to the animation type and are modified using the Animations tab or the Animation dialog box associated with the selected animation effect.
   - Attaching timings to animations frees you from constantly advancing to the next object and lets you concentrate on delivering your message.

7. **Animate text.**
   - Animating text controls the flow of information to the audience.
   - You can bring text onto the slide by animating the text as one object, by animating all paragraphs to come in together, or by sequencing the text animation by text outline level.

8. **Use the Animation Pane.**
   - The Animation Pane provides a summary of animation effects used.
   - Tags indicate how an animation starts; the type of animation effect applied; a portion of the name of the animated object; and a timeline with bars that displays the start, end, and duration of animations.

Key Terms Matching

Match the key terms with their definitions. Write the key term letter by the appropriate numbered definition.

a. Action button
b. Animation
c. Custom button
d. Custom path
e. Emphasis
f. End button
g. Entrance
h. Exit
i. Help button
j. Home button

k. Hyperlink
l. Interactivity
m. Kiosk
n. Linear presentation
o. Motion path
p. Movie button
q. Non-linear presentation
r. ScreenTip
s. Trigger
t. Uniform resource locator (URL)

1. _____ The ability to branch or interact based on decisions made by a viewer or audience. **p. 372**

2. _____ Additional information that displays as you mouse over an object, such as a hyperlink. **p. 376**

3. _____ An action button that can be set to trigger unique actions in the presentation. **p. 376**

4. _____ A ready-made button designed to serve as an icon to which an action can be assigned. **p. 372**

5. _____ Progress through a presentation according to choices made by the viewer that determine which slide comes next. **p. 372**

6. _____ An interactive computer terminal available for public use. **p. 377**

7. _____ A predetermined path that an object follows as part of an animation. **p. 390**

8. _____ An action used to draw interest to an object in a presentation. **p. 379**

9. _____ The address of a resource on the Web. **p. 373**

10. _____ Progress through a presentation sequentially, starting with the first slide and ending with the last slide. **p. 372**

11. _____ A PowerPoint animation type that draws attention to an object already on a slide. **p. 390**

12. _____ An action button that moves to the last slide in the presentation. **p. 377**

13. _____ A connection or link that branches to another location. **p. 372**

14. _____ A PowerPoint animation type that controls how an object moves onto or appears on a slide. **p. 390**

15. _____ An action button that can be set to play a movie. **p. 377**

16. _____ An animation path that can be created freehand instead of following a preset path. **p. 392**

17. _____ An action button set to move to the first slide in the presentation. **p. 377**

18. _____ A PowerPoint animation type that controls how an object leaves or disappears from a slide. **p. 390**

19. _____ Launches an animation that takes place when the user clicks on an associated object or bookmark location in a media object. **p. 379**

20. _____ An action button that can be set to open a document with instructions or help information. **p. 377**

Multiple Choice

1. The term used for a connection from one location to another is:

   (a) Hyperlink.
   (b) Trigger.
   (c) Motion path.
   (d) Object.

2. When you click an object on the slide or when you launch an animation with a bookmark in a video and an animation effect occurs, which of the following is used?

   (a) Hyperlink
   (b) Mouse over
   (c) Action button
   (d) Trigger

3. Which of the following refers to an interactive slide show?

   (a) Sequential presentation
   (b) Linear presentation
   (c) Non-linear presentation
   (d) Abstract presentation

4. To create an action button, which tab do you click to start the process?

   (a) INSERT
   (b) DESIGN
   (c) SLIDE SHOW
   (d) VIEW

5. An alternate method for inserting or editing a hyperlink in a presentation is:

   (a) Press Ctrl+V.
   (b) Right-click the object and select Hyperlink.
   (c) Press F7.
   (d) Click the VIEW tab and choose Web Layout.

6. Which of the following is a true statement regarding multiple animations?

   (a) To add a second animation, click the INSERT tab and click Add Animation.
   (b) Multiple animations can be added to shape objects but not text objects.
   (c) Individual animations that are part of an animation sequence display in the Animation Pane.
   (d) All of the above.

7. Which of the following animation effects would enable you to change its direction setting?

   (a) Grow/Shrink
   (b) Fly In
   (c) Pulse
   (d) Appear

8. Attaching a timing setting to animations enables the presenter to more effectively:

   (a) Concentrate on delivering the message.
   (b) Close the presentation at the end.
   (c) Change timing during the presentation on the fly.
   (d) All of the above.

9. The Animation Pane includes which of the following symbols?

   (a) The letter T representing text that is animated on the slide
   (b) A direction arrow indicating the direction of the assigned animation
   (c) A clock representing whether the animation starts automatically or requires a mouse click
   (d) A symbol representing the type of animation assigned

10. Which of the following is not a type of PowerPoint animation?

    (a) Evolving
    (b) Exit
    (c) Entrance
    (d) Motion path

Practice Exercises

1 Copyright and the Law

The IT manager of your company has observed some violations of software copyright in the organization. He immediately removed the offending software but feels that perhaps it is a lack of understanding about copyright rather than deliberate theft. He has asked you, as a company trainer, to prepare and deliver a presentation about basic copyright principles for company employees. You will create a custom action button, attach sound actions, and create navigation buttons. You will link to an existing Word document with a Microsoft End User License Agreement as a sample. You will also include a link to the Microsoft volume licensing site. You will edit a hyperlink that links to a Web site with further information about copyright and copyright protection. Finally, you will add an Appear entrance animation that groups text by second-level paragraphs so the presenter can discuss each level as needed. The exercise follows the same set of skills as used in Hands-On Exercises 1 and 2 in the chapter. Refer to Figure 6.29 as you complete this exercise.

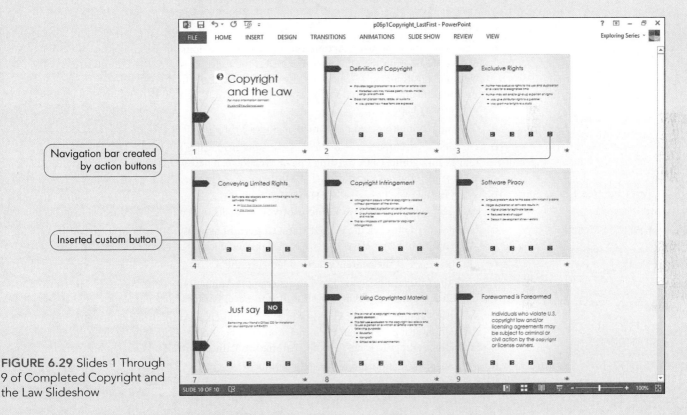

FIGURE 6.29 Slides 1 Through 9 of Completed Copyright and the Law Slideshow

a. Open *p06p1Copyright* and save it as **p06p1Copyright_LastFirst**.

b. Create a handout header with your name and a handout footer with your instructor's name and your class. Include the current date.

c. On Slide 1, position the insertion point after the colon following *contact* on the Title slide, press **Enter**, type your e-mail address, and then press **Spacebar**.

d. On Slide 7, click the **INSERT tab**, click **Shapes** in the Illustrations group, and then click **Action Button: Custom**. Click to create a button in the top right of the slide. You will size and position the button in a later step.

e. Click the **Play sound check box** on the Mouse Click tab in the Actions Settings dialog box, click the **Play sound arrow**, and then click **Other Sound**.

f. Locate and select *p06p1No.wav* and click **OK** twice.

g. Click the **FORMAT tab**, if necessary. Click the **Size Dialog Box Launcher** in the Size group and set **Height** to 1" and **Width** to 1.5". Click **POSITION** in the Format Shape pane and set **Horizontal position** to 6.25" and **Vertical position** to 1.42".

h. Type **NO** in the action button. Select the text, apply bold, and then change the font size to **40 pt**.

i. On Slide 2, click the **INSERT tab**, click **Shapes** in the Illustrations group, and then click **Action Button: Beginning**. Click to create a button near the bottom of the slide. Click **OK** to accept the default action settings.

j. Click the **FORMAT tab**, if necessary, and click the **Size Dialog Box Launcher** in the Size group to return to the Size options in the Format Shape pane. Size the button to **0.35"** by **0.35"** and position the button at a horizontal position of **6.4"** and a vertical position of **6.5"** (if necessary, refer to step g instructions). Close the dialog box.

k. Click the **FORMAT tab**, if necessary, click **Shape Fill** in the Shape Styles group, and then click **Orange, Accent 2, Lighter 60%** (third row, sixth column).

l. On Slide 2, click the **Shapes More button** in the Insert Shapes group on the FORMAT tab to create action buttons for *Back or Previous*, *Forward or Next*, and *End* (three more buttons). Repeat steps j through k to accept the default action settings for each button. Size the buttons and change the Shape Fill (step k), but do not worry about the button positions. You will position the buttons in the next step.

m. Select the left-facing arrow **Action Button: Back or Previous** and position it at **3"** horizontally and **6.5"** vertically from the top-left corner. Select the right-facing arrow **Action Button: Forward or Next** and position it at **4.7"** horizontally and **6.5"** vertically from the top-left corner. Select **Action Button: End** and position it at **8.1"** horizontally and **6.5"** vertically from the top-left corner. Close the Format Shape pane.

n. Copy all four buttons and paste them on Slides 3 through 10.

o. On Slide 4, select the text *End User License Agreement*. Click the **INSERT tab** and click **Hyperlink** in the Links group. Click **Existing File or Web Page**, if necessary, click **Browse for File**, locate and select *p06p1Eula.docx*, and then click **OK** twice.

p. Select the text *Site License*. Click **Hyperlink** in the Links group, click **Existing File or Web Page**, if necessary, and then type **www.microsoftvolumelicensing.com** in the **Address box**. Click **OK**.

q. On Slide 10, right-click the **United States Copyright hyperlink** and click **Edit Hyperlink**. Edit the Web address to **http://www.loc.gov/copyright** and click **OK**.

r. On Slide 2, select the **content placeholder**, click the **ANIMATIONS tab**, and then click **Appear**.

s. Click the **Animation Dialog Box Launcher** in the Animation group and click the **Text Animation tab**. Click the **Group text arrow**, click **By 2nd Level Paragraphs**, and then click **OK**.

t. Select the content placeholder on Slide 2, double-click **Animation Painter** in the Advanced Animation group, and then click each content placeholder in the remaining slides to copy the animation settings to each. Click the **Animation Painter button** to toggle it off when done.

u. View the presentation and test each hyperlink.

v. Save and close the file. Submit based on your instructor's directions.

2 GeGo Power!

You work in the lab of a food products company and have created several formulations of a nutritious new hot drink. You conducted a series of focus groups to study and determine consumer preferences. The focus group study also sought to determine whether consumers would be inclined to give up their morning coffee in favor of the new drink, code name "GeGo." You now want to present the results of the study to the food products company officials in the hopes they will agree to test it in the local college market in the fall. You will create a presentation that will include a study summary revealing the focus group preferences. You want to include the option to see detailed results for those who want to see them. You realize that creating a button as a trigger for the results is an excellent option. In this exercise, you will use a clip art image as the trigger button to animate the table. Finally, you will add animation. The exercise follows the same set of skills as used in Hands-On Exercise 2 in the chapter. Refer to Figure 6.30 as you complete this exercise.

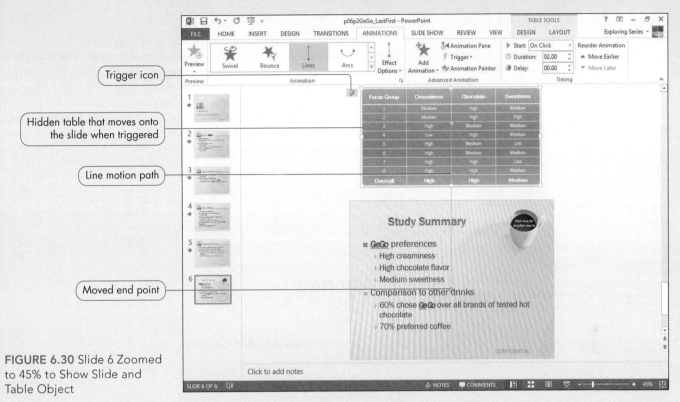

Trigger icon

Hidden table that moves onto the slide when triggered

Line motion path

Moved end point

FIGURE 6.30 Slide 6 Zoomed to 45% to Show Slide and Table Object

a. Open *p06p2GeGo* and save it as **p06p2GeGo_LastFirst.**

b. Create a handout header with your name and a handout footer with your instructor's name and your class. Include the current date.

c. On Slide 1, click the outside border of the **GeGo logo**, click the **ANIMATIONS tab**, click the **More button** in the Animation group, and then click **Zoom** under Entrance.

d. Click the **More button** in the Animation group, click **More Motion Paths**, click **Vertical Figure 8** in the *Special* section, and then click **OK**.

e. Click the **Start arrow** in the Timing group and click **With Previous**.

f. On Slide 2, click the **content placeholder** and click **Fade**.

g. Select the **content placeholder** again, double-click **Animation Painter** in the Advanced Animation group, and then click each of the **content placeholders** on Slides 3 through 5. Click the **Animation Painter** in the Advanced Animation group to turn off the feature when done.

h. On Slide 6, click the **VIEW tab**, click **Zoom** in the Zoom group, type **45%**, and then click **OK**.

   With the view reduced, a portion of a table containing the focus group results is visible at the top of the design window.

i. Click the table to select it, click the **ANIMATIONS tab**, and then click the **More button** in the Animation group.

j. Click **Lines** in the Motion Paths category to apply the animation to the table.

k. Click the red end when the double-headed arrow appears, press and hold **Shift** to constrain movement to a straight line, and then drag the red end arrow to the top of the letter *d* in the word *drinks* on the slide.

   The table descends and covers the text when triggered.

l. Click the table. Click **Trigger** in the Advanced Animation group, point to *On Click of*, and then click **Group 7**.

   Group 7 is the grouping of the hot chocolate clip art and the text box reading *Click here for detailed results*.

m. View the presentation. When Slide 6 appears, click the **hot chocolate clip art** to trigger the table animation.

n. Save and close the file, and submit it based on your instructor's directions.

1 Creative Presentation

The presentation in Figure 6.31 was created using a Microsoft Office Online template, *Presentation on brainstorming*. Because it is a presentation template, it includes suggested text to jump-start the creative process. In this exercise, you will download the template and modify it. You will add a navigation bar using custom action buttons that link to the related slides. As an alternative method for navigating, you will change the agenda items to hyperlinks that link to the associated slide. Finally, you will animate text using the animation effects and settings you select. Refer to Figure 6.31 as you complete this exercise.

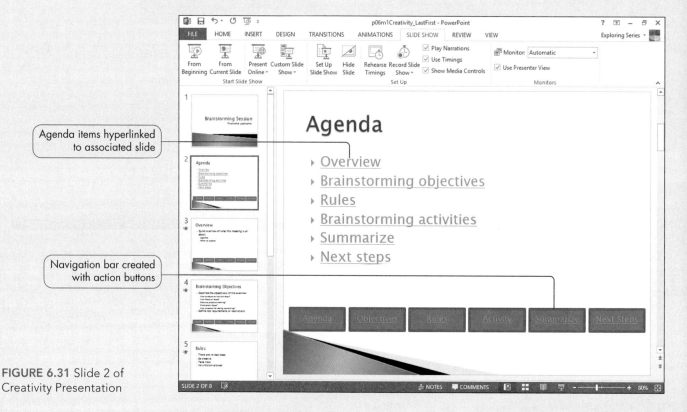

FIGURE 6.31 Slide 2 of Creativity Presentation

a. Access the New Presentation pane. Search for the *Presentation on brainstorming* template. Choose the first template in the row of options. Save the presentation as **p06m1Creativity_LastFirst**.

b. Create a handout header with your name and a handout footer with your instructor's name and your class. Include the current date.

c. On Slide 1, replace the subtitle *Your Name* with your own name.

d. On Slide 2, create a Custom Action button and click **Cancel** to bypass the Actions Setting dialog box at this time. Resize the button height to **0.59"** and **1.5"** wide. Change the Shape Fill to **Blue** (under *Standard Colors*).

e. Change the Shape Outline color to Theme Color **Indigo, Accent 5** (first row, ninth column).

f. Type **Agenda** in the action button, select the text, and then change the font size to **16 pt**.

g. Duplicate the button five times. Change the label of the duplicate buttons to **Objectives**, **Rules**, **Activity**, **Summarize**, and **Next Steps**. Position the buttons just above the slide bottom accents with Agenda as the first button and the remaining buttons listed in the order above. With all six buttons selected, align bottom and distribute the buttons horizontally.

h. Select the text on each action button and add a hyperlink to **Place in This Document** to the slide title to correspond to each of the action button titles you just created.

i. Copy the buttons and paste them on Slides 3 through 8.

j. On Slide 2, select **Overview** and add a hyperlink to Slide 3. Rather than create a return button, use the Return navigation button on the bottom left of the slide.

k. On Slide 2, continue adding hyperlinks for each agenda item to its associated slide.

l. Add the animation effects and settings you choose to the text in the presentation using a minimum of one each of the following animations: entrance, emphasis, exit, and motion path.

m. View the presentation and make any needed changes using the Animation Pane. Adjust or add additional animations, if desired.

n. Save and close the file. Submit it based on your instructor's directions.

2 Patient Assessment Flow Chart

In this exercise, you will create hyperlinks for a patient assessment flow chart for the Fire and Rescue Academy. Your task is to turn each shape in the flow chart into a clickable button with an action assigned. When clicked, the button will link to its associated slide. You will create a button to return the viewer to the flow chart after viewing a slide. You will assign a mouse-over action to a clip art image that plays the sound of an ambulance. Finally, you will add triggers to launch a sequence of animated images. Refer to Figure 6.32 as you complete this exercise.

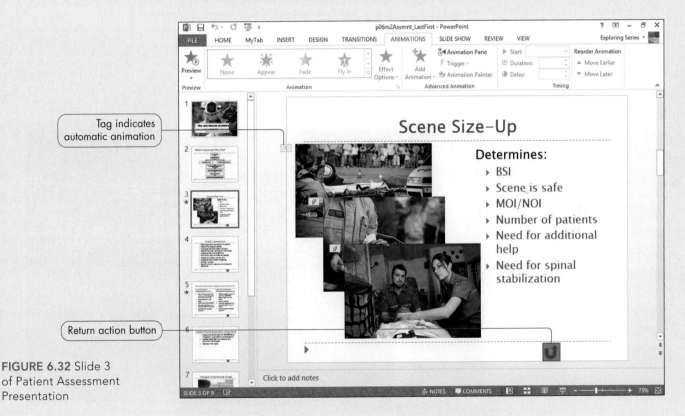

FIGURE 6.32 Slide 3 of Patient Assessment Presentation

a. Open *p06m2Assmnt* and save it as **p06m2Assmnt_LastFirst**.

b. Create a handout header with your name and a handout footer with your instructor's name and your class. Include the current date.

c. On Slide 2, select **Scene Size-Up** and add a hyperlink for the label to Slide 3.

d. Continue converting each shape label text in the Patient Assessment Flow Chart into a hyperlink to the associated slide. Note that the Focused Assessment and the Rapid Trauma Assessment labels share a common slide, Slide 5. Each of these two button labels, therefore, must link to Slide 5.

e. Enable the viewer to move quickly back to the flow chart slide by doing the following: on Slide 3, create an Action Button: Return that links to Slide 2. Resize the button to **0.5"** high by **0.5"** wide. Position it horizontally at **7.5"** from the top-left corner and vertically at **7"** from the top-left corner. Copy the button to Slides 4 through 9.

f. On Slide 7, insert a mouse-over action that plays the *p06m2Ambulance.wav* audio clip for the ambulance picture.

DISCOVER

g. Create an animation sequence for the images in Slide 3. All animations should fly in from the left. The top picture should start on click. Clicking the first image should trigger the appearance of the middle image. Clicking the middle image should trigger the appearance of the bottom image.

h. On Slide 5, use the Animation Pane to reorder the animations. The *Focused Assessment* subtitle currently appears last but should appear first, followed by its associated bullet points. The *Rapid Trauma Assessment* subtitle should appear next, followed by its associated bullet points.

i. Test each of the buttons and triggers you created in Slide Show view.

j. Edit any buttons that do not link correctly.

k. Save and close the file. Submit it based on your instructor's directions.

3 Internet History Game

COLLABORATION CASE

FROM SCRATCH

You have been assigned to work with one or more other classmates to develop an interactive PowerPoint game on some aspect of Internet history. You should begin by searching for a Microsoft PowerPoint quiz template. The quiz needs to have a variety of question types such as short answer, true/false, or another question type. Because everyone's schedule is varied, you should use either your Outlook account, another e-mail account, or OneDrive to pass the presentation file. Save the quiz as **p06m3Quiz_GroupName**. Refer to Figure 6.33 as you complete this exercise.

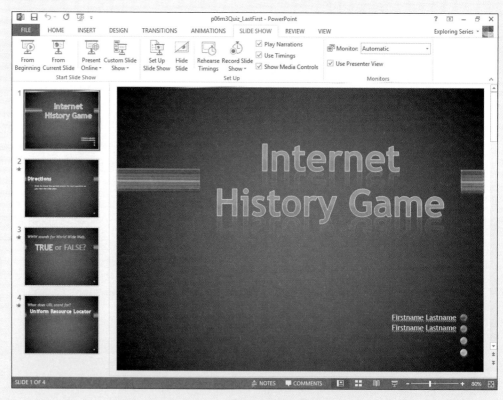

FIGURE 6.33 Interactive Game

- It will be helpful to create a storyboard to plan the slides you will need for the game and the interactive elements required by your plan.
- The first slide should contain the name of the game, your first and last names, and your partners' first and last names.
- Be sure to include a slide that gives directions for the game.
- The question slides should use animation to reveal the answers when a trigger is performed.
- Pass the presentation to the next student so that he or she can perform the same tasks, and so on.
- After all students have contributed to the presentation, submit the file as directed by your instructor.

Beyond the Classroom

Professionalism

RESEARCH CASE

FROM SCRATCH

Many professions have support organizations that are created to serve the membership and to enhance the professional growth of the members. Laurie Brems, president of the Utah Business and Computer Educators, created a slide to show Utah business educators two professional routes available for them. Following one route, educators join state and national career and technical education organizations. Following the other route, educators join the state and national business education organizations. Joining both sets of organizations ensures a business educator the greatest support network possible.

Research the professional organizations available to you in your field of interest. Create a slide that shows professional organizations from a minimum of two routes you could choose to pursue for your field of interest to illustrate the professional path(s) available to you. Include hyperlinks to the organizations. Include additional information on this slide or on additional slides in the slide show. Animate the path as desired and use the Animation Pane to adjust the duration of the animations, if necessary. Save the presentation as **p06b2Professional_LastFirst**. Create a handout header with your name and a handout footer with your instructor's name and your class. Include the current date.

Colorful Diet = Healthy Diet Presentation

DISASTER RECOVERY

You are part of a group assigned to create a presentation on healthy eating. Your group was given one hour in a computer lab to prepare, so first you sketched out a storyboard, and then you divided responsibilities. One member of the group researched the benefits of eating fruits and vegetables, and two members created the design of the presentation, including locating pictures. As information was located, it was typed into the presentation.

Open *p06b3Diet* and save it as **p06b3Diet_LastFirst**. Create a handout header with your name and a handout footer with your instructor's name and your class. Include the current date. Check the presentation design to ensure all aspects display properly and that the introduction slide, body slides, and conclusion slide appear in the correct order. Test hyperlinks, action buttons, and triggers to ensure they link properly. Edit any hyperlinks that do not link correctly. Resize the action buttons and distribute them horizontally. Apply entrance, emphasis, motion path, and exit animations to the pictures on Slide 9. Make other changes to the slide show as desired. Finally, carefully proofread the text and check the images. Remove cartoon-style images so the design is consistent.

Answering Tough Interview Questions

SOFT SKILLS CASE

FROM SCRATCH

Create a presentation that will help other students prepare to answer tough interview questions. Create a slide that lists at least five tough interview questions. Insert suggested responses to each question on a separate slide, and then create a hyperlink from the question to the slide with the appropriate answer. Apply other interactivity and advanced animations to enhance the presentation. Save and close the presentation, and submit it based on your instructor's directions.

Capstone Exercise

As a volunteer in the Campus Health Center, you are often asked to prepare presentations to run at various kiosks located around campus. The presentations vary, but all have the goal of educating students about health and safety issues. This week, you were asked to prepare a presentation based on information about the Cycle of Abuse provided to the center from the local city police department Crime Advocate Program. Refer to Figure 6.34 as you complete this capstone exercise.

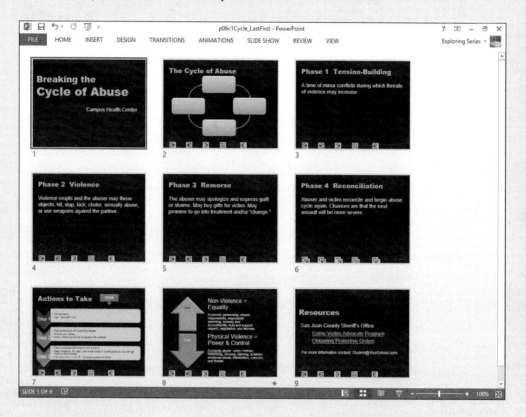

FIGURE 6.34 Animated Action Buttons and Triggers

Adding an E-Mail Address, a Web Page Hyperlink, and a Link to an Existing File

In this exercise, you will include a hyperlink to the Web site of the Crime Victim Advocate Program on the Resource slide of the presentation. You will also create a link to a Word document containing information about obtaining a protective order. You will include your e-mail address for contact information.

a. Open *p06c1Cycle* and immediately save it as **p06c1Cycle_LastFirst**.

b. Create a handout header with your name and a handout footer with your instructor's name and your class. Include the current date.

c. On Slide 9, create a hyperlink that links the text *Crime Victim Advocate Program* to http://www.sanjuancounty.org/victim_advocate.htm. Include the ScreenTip **Click to read additional information**.

d. Link the text *Obtaining Protective Orders* to the Word document *p06c1Order*.

e. Position the insertion point after the colon and space following *contact*, type your e-mail address, and then press **Spacebar**.

f. Save the presentation.

Attaching Actions to Shapes and Creating a Navigation Bar

You want to add interactivity to the slide show by enabling the viewer to click a shape in the cycle illustration on Slide 2 and then jump to a slide giving detail about the related phase. You also want the viewer to be able to easily navigate between slides, so you create a navigation bar.

a. On Slide 2, insert an action for the Tension shape so that when it is clicked, the viewer is sent to the Phase 1 Tension-Building slide.

b. Select each of the remaining shapes and convert them to action buttons that link to the appropriate slide.

c. Create an Action Button: Beginning link to Slide 2 (The Cycle of Abuse) and size it to **0.5"** high and **0.5"** wide. Set the horizontal position at **3.47"** and the vertical position at **7"**.

d. Create the following action buttons and size them to **0.5"** high and **0.5"** wide.

- Action Button: Back or Previous to a horizontal position of **0.59"** and vertical position of **7"**.
- Action Button: Return to a horizontal position of **4.96"** and vertical position of **7"**.

- Action Button: Forward or Next to a horizontal position of **0.59"** and vertical position of **7"**.
- Action Button: End

e. Set the position for Action Button: End to a horizontal position of **6.75"** and a vertical position of **7"**.

f. Copy the action buttons and paste them to Slides 3 through 9.

g. Save the presentation.

Create Animations, Action Buttons, and Triggers

To emphasize the message that physical violence equates to power and control, you will animate the information on Slide 8, convert the clip art into buttons, and then attach sound to the buttons. You will also apply a trigger to the SmartArt in Slide 7 so the viewer clicks to bring the next piece of information onscreen.

a. On Slide 8, apply a **Float In animation** to the Physical Violence = Power & Control text box. Set the animation to start **With Previous**.

b. Apply a **Fly In animation** to the *down arrow* clip art. Adjust the Effect Options so the arrow flies in **From Top**. Set the animation to start **After Previous**.

c. Apply a **Float In animation** to the *Non-Violence = Equality* text box. Set the animation to start **After Previous**.

d. Apply a **Fly In animation** to the *up arrow* clip art. Set the animation to start **After Previous**.

e. Attach a **Play sound action** to the *up arrow* clip art and set the action to play the **Chime sound**.

f. Attach a **Play sound action** to the *down arrow* clip art and set the action to play the **Explosion sound**.

g. Set a trigger to the *down arrow* clip art so that it is launched when the Physical Violence = Power & Control text box appears.

h. On Slide 7, apply a **Wipe entrance animation** to the SmartArt. Adjust the Effect Options so the steps flow from the top down and appear one by one.

i. On Slide 7, trigger the SmartArt animation using Down Arrow Callout 4.

j. Save the presentation.

Testing Hyperlinks, Action Buttons, and Triggers

Before publishing the Cycle of Abuse presentation, you know it is critical to check all hyperlinks, action buttons, and triggers to ensure they are working correctly. If a link does not work, exit the slide show and edit the link immediately so you are not relying on your memory when editing.

a. View the slide show from the beginning.

b. Click the **Tension shape** to test the action button to see if it successfully jumps to the Phase 1 Tension-Building slide.

c. Click **Action Button: Back or Previous** to see if it returns you to Slide 2.

d. Click the **Violence shape** to test the action button to see if it successfully jumps to the Phase 2 Violence slide.

e. Click **Action Button: End** to see if it successfully jumps to the Resources slide.

f. Click the **Crime Victim Advocate Program hyperlink** to see if it jumps to the San Juan County Victim Advocacy Program site. Close the browser.

g. Click the **Obtaining Protective Orders hyperlink** to see if it opens the Protective Orders information sheet. Close the browser.

h. Click **Action Button: Beginning** to see if it jumps to the menu on Slide 2.

i. Click the **Reconciliation shape** to test the action button to see if it jumps to the Phase 4 Reconciliation slide.

j. Click **Action Button: Forward or Next**.

k. Click **Click trigger** on Slide 7 until you have advanced through all steps.

l. Click the **Action Button: Forward or Next** to view Slide 8.

m. Click each arrow and listen to the associated sounds.

n. Press **Esc**.

o. Save and close the file. Submit it based on your instructor's directions.

Customization

CHAPTER 7

Customizing PowerPoint and the Slide Show

Konstantin Chagin/Shutterstock

CASE STUDY | Survival Solutions

You are the owner of Survival Solutions, a store that provides family emergency preparation supplies. You believe that preparation provides peace of mind before, during, and after an emergency. Because of your knowledge about family emergency planning and communication, you are often invited to be a guest speaker. The two topics on which you are invited to present most often are "Emergency Preparedness" and "What to Do Before, During, and After a Disaster."

To make it easier and more time efficient when you create presentations, you modify PowerPoint's settings and personalize the Ribbon to take advantage of shape tools not on the Ribbon by default. You then use the tools to create a logo for Survival Solutions. To help create recognition for your business, you modify the slide masters that control the layout and appearance of handouts, notes, and slides. You add the new logo, and then change the theme colors to match your logo colors. Finally, you create a custom show from a presentation you have used in the community so that you can have flexibility on topics based on audience request. You also control the detail displayed to the audience by hiding and unhiding slides.

PowerPoint Customization

You can become a PowerPoint power user by setting PowerPoint's options to meet your individual needs and by modifying PowerPoint's working environment to include customized tabs. Changing the default PowerPoint options can help you work more productively and smoothly, while adding a personalized tab that contains the features you use most to the Ribbon enables you to work with less effort.

In this section, you will learn how to set general options for working with PowerPoint, change how PowerPoint corrects and formats your text, customize how you save your documents, and use other more advanced options. You will also learn how to customize the Ribbon by adding a new tab containing commands that are not available on the default Ribbon. Finally, you will use the new commands to create a logo.

Setting PowerPoint Options

PowerPoint provides you with a broad range of settings that enable you to customize **PowerPoint Options** to meet your needs. To access the options, click the File tab to display the Backstage view and select Options (see Figure 7.1) to open the PowerPoint Options dialog box. Although this discussion will highlight many of the settings, you should spend time exploring all the options.

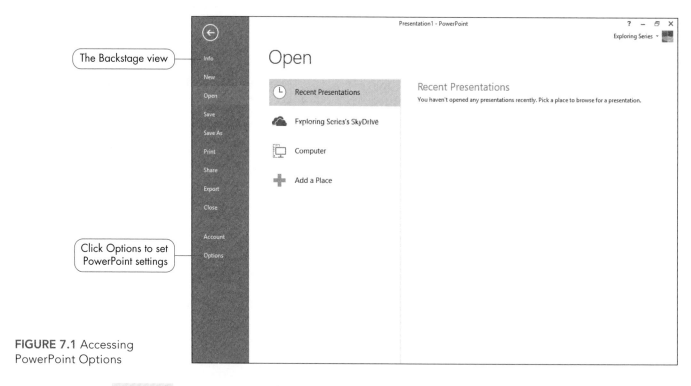

FIGURE 7.1 Accessing PowerPoint Options

STEP 1 ⟫   Figure 7.2 shows the PowerPoint Options dialog box with General options displayed.

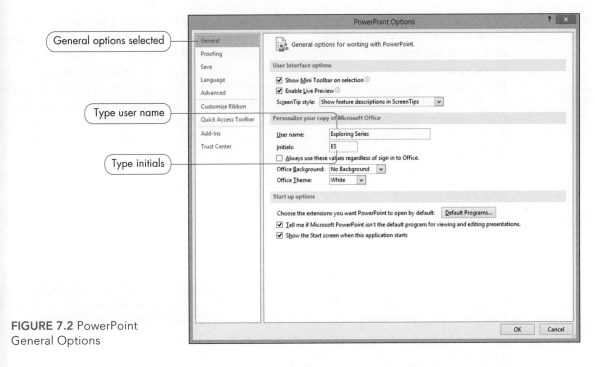

General options selected

Type user name

Type initials

FIGURE 7.2 PowerPoint
General Options

Each of the sections can help you customize your presentations.

- *User Interface options* enable you to determine whether to show the Mini Toolbar when text is selected, use Live Preview, and determine how ScreenTips display.

- *Personalize your copy of Microsoft Office* enables you to specify your name and initials. You should add your user name and initials the first time you work with PowerPoint because when you work with others on presentations, your identifying information is used to identify your comments and is included in the presentation information if you created the presentation or were the last person to modify it. Figure 7.3 shows the user's name as the author in the Backstage view Info tab because *User name* was set in General options.

- *Start up options* also enable you to specify a program choice when starting PowerPoint.

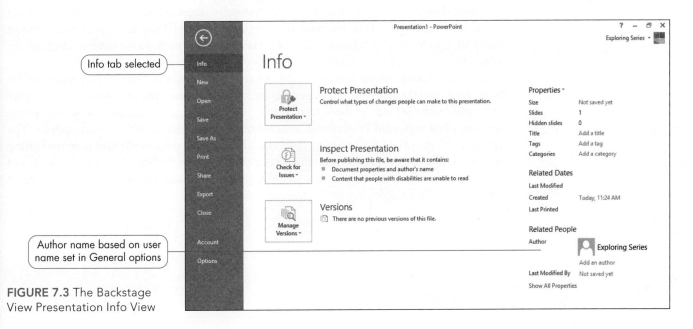

Info tab selected

Author name based on user
name set in General options

FIGURE 7.3 The Backstage
View Presentation Info View

STEP 2 »

Proofing options enable you to change how PowerPoint corrects and formats your text. Click AutoCorrect Options on the Proofing tab to open the AutoCorrect dialog box. Review each of the tab options in the dialog box to understand what PowerPoint is automatically changing as you type. Then select or deselect check boxes to apply the settings of your choice. For example, AutoCorrect automatically resizes the font of text you type as a title to fit the size of the title text placeholder. If you want the title text to be uniform on every slide, click the AutoFormat As You Type tab in the AutoCorrect dialog box if necessary and deselect the *AutoFit title text to placeholder* check box. Figure 7.4 shows the Proofing options and the AutoCorrect dialog box with the AutoFormat As You Type tab open.

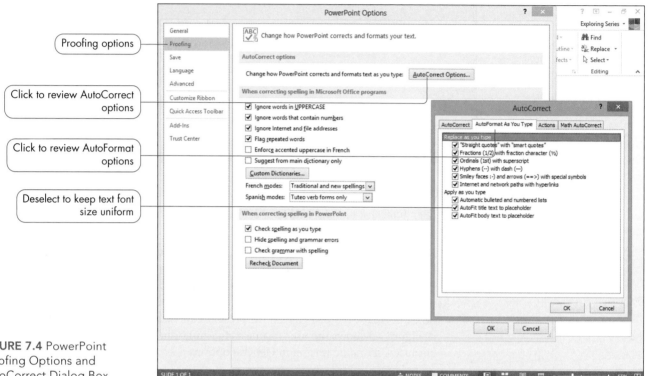

Proofing options

Click to review AutoCorrect options

Click to review AutoFormat options

Deselect to keep text font size uniform

FIGURE 7.4 PowerPoint Proofing Options and AutoCorrect Dialog Box

PowerPoint Save options enable you to customize when and where your documents are saved and can be an invaluable resource. By default, PowerPoint saves your presentation every 10 minutes so that if PowerPoint closes unexpectedly and you do not have a chance to save, you can recover the presentation. The file extension assigned to a PowerPoint presentation is *.pptx*. All but the changes you made since the last time the AutoRecover saved will be available to you the next time you open PowerPoint. The recovered presentation will display in a pane on the left side of the screen so that you can restore it. You can change the setting for how often you want PowerPoint to save your presentation using the Save options. You can also change where the program saves the AutoRecover version. To save time navigating to folders, change the location to which your presentations are saved. For example, if you always save your presentations to a folder you created for assignments, enter that location as your default file location. Figure 7.5 shows the Save options.

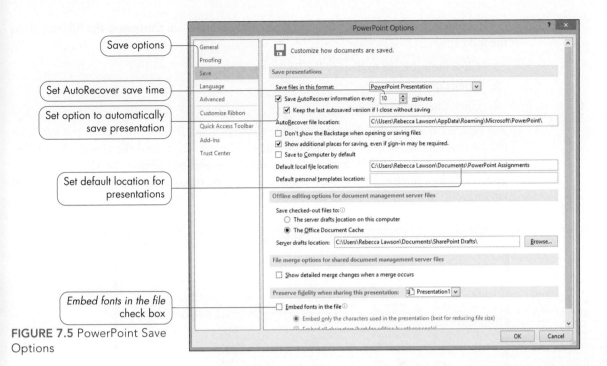

Save options

Set AutoRecover save time

Set option to automatically save presentation

Set default location for presentations

Embed fonts in the file check box

FIGURE 7.5 PowerPoint Save Options

TIP | Embed Fonts

To ensure that you have the font you need when you work on a presentation on another computer, or to ensure others reviewing and editing a presentation have access to any TrueType font you used while creating a presentation, embed the fonts in your presentation. TrueType fonts are scalable fonts supported by Windows that display and print smoothly at any point size. Click Save in the PowerPoint Options dialog box and click the *Embed fonts in the file* check box. Select the *Embed only the characters used in the presentation* option or the *Embed all characters* option. Embedding fonts increases the file size of a presentation.

Language options enable you to set the Office language used for editing, display, Help, and ScreenTips. Advanced options enable you to set your preferences for editing, cutting, copying, pasting, sizing and quality of images, setting chart data point properties, setting display options, working in Slide Show view, and printing, as well as several general options. For example, in the *Editing options* section, you can change the number of *undos* (which reverses your last action) from the default of 20 to any number from 3 to 150. The more you increase the number of undo levels, however, the more of your computer's RAM (random access memory) is used to store the undo history. If you set your undo levels to a high number, you may experience a computer slowdown.

Customizing the Ribbon

The *Customize Ribbon tab* in the PowerPoint Options dialog box enables you to create a personal tab on the Ribbon as well as modify the settings of any tab. Ribbon customization enables you to include features that are not available on the standard Ribbon. By creating a custom tab, you have access to these features as well as the features you use most often. In addition to creating a new tab, you can change the order of the tabs, change the order of the groups that appear within the tabs, and create new groups within a tab.

To customize the Ribbon, right-click the Ribbon and click *Customize the Ribbon*, or do the following:

1. Click the FILE tab to display the Backstage view.
2. Click Options.
3. Click Customize Ribbon.

Figure 7.6 shows the all of the possible *Customize the Ribbon* options on the left, with the current arrangement of the Ribbon in the right pane. To expand the view to display the groups within a tab, click + next to the group name, and to collapse the view to hide the groups, click -. To change the order of the existing tabs or groups, drag and drop a selected tab or group to a new position or use Move Up and Move Down.

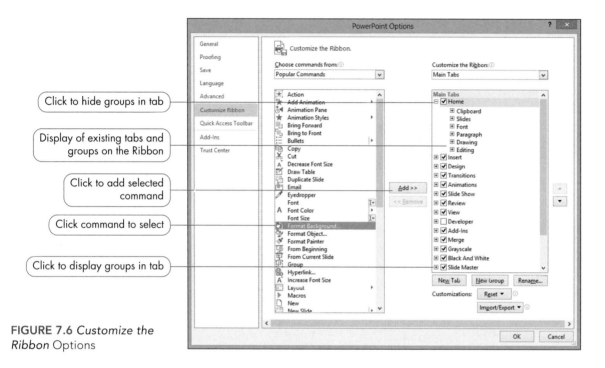

FIGURE 7.6 *Customize the Ribbon* Options

TIP Restore the Ribbon

You can restore the Ribbon to its original arrangement by clicking Reset and clicking *Reset all customizations*. Reset also enables you to reset individual Ribbon tabs.

Add a New Tab

To have access to the commands you use most, add a new tab to the Ribbon and add frequently used commands. In the *Customize the Ribbon* window, select the tab you want the new tab to appear after and click New Tab. The new tab is created and named *New Tab (Custom)*. The new tab also contains a new group named *New Group (Custom)*. To add additional groups, click New Group. You can rename tabs or groups by clicking Rename or by right-clicking the tab and selecting *Rename*. When you rename a group, you can select a colorful symbol to represent the contents of the group. Figure 7.7 shows that a new tab containing a new group has been created.

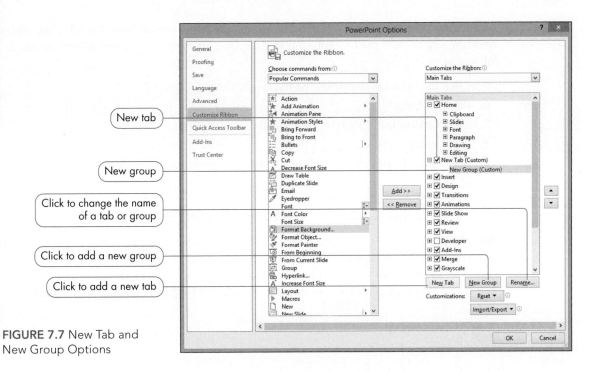

FIGURE 7.7 New Tab and New Group Options

Labels (Figure 7.7):
- New tab
- New group
- Click to change the name of a tab or group
- Click to add a new group
- Click to add a new tab

Add Commands to a Group

To add commands to an existing tab or group or to a newly created tab, click a command name on the left and click Add. Popular commands that you can add are displayed in the default view, but you can click the *Choose commands from* arrow to choose from additional commands and macros. For example, instead of using the arrow keys on the keyboard to nudge an object (move in small, precise increments), you can add the nudge commands to a group in a personalized tab. Figure 7.8 displays a customized tab with added nudge commands.

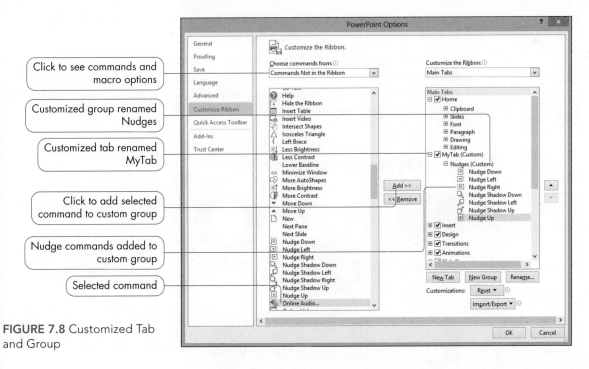

FIGURE 7.8 Customized Tab and Group

Labels (Figure 7.8):
- Click to see commands and macro options
- Customized group renamed Nudges
- Customized tab renamed MyTab
- Click to add selected command to custom group
- Nudge commands added to custom group
- Selected command

After customizing the Ribbon to maximize your productivity, you can export it as an exported Office User Interface (UI) customization file, which uses the extension

.exportedUI. Then import the file to other computers you use or share the file with others who can benefit from the custom Ribbon. To import or export a customized Ribbon, do the following:

1. Click the FILE tab to display the Backstage view.
2. Click Options.
3. Click Customize Ribbon in the left pane.
4. Click Import/Export.
5. Click *Import customization file* or *Export all customizations.*

Using Combine Shapes Commands

PowerPoint includes a set of commands that are useful when working with shapes: Combine Shapes, Intersect Shapes, Subtract Shapes, and Union Shapes. You can only access these commands by adding them to an existing tab or by creating a new tab. Figure 7.9 shows a customized tab named MyTab with a customized group named Shapes that includes the commands.

FIGURE 7.9 Custom Shapes Group Including Shape Commands

STEP 4 >> Using the Combine Shapes commands enables you to create complex shapes by joining shapes in four ways: Combine, Intersect, Subtract, or Union.

- *Combine* removes the overlapping area of two shapes.
- *Intersect* removes any area that is not overlapped.
- *Subtract* removes the shape of the second selected object from the area of the first object.
- *Union* joins selected overlapping objects so they become one shape. The shape takes on the formatting of the first shape selected.

Figure 7.10 displays two original circles that have been duplicated and joined using each of the above methods. In each case, the red circle was selected first so that the joined objects are all formatted with a red fill. The dotted outlines have been added to indicate the original areas and are not part of the result.

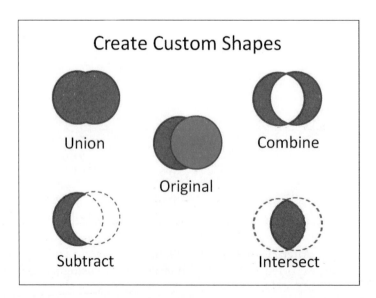

FIGURE 7.10 Combined Shapes

Quick Concepts ✓

1. What are some advantages of setting PowerPoint options? *p. 420*

2. You are working on a shared computer. How can you restore the Ribbon to its default setting? *p. 424*

3. How can you access the Combine Shapes commands? *p. 426*

Watch the Video
for this Hands-
On Exercise!

MyITLab®
HOE1 Training

1 PowerPoint Customization

You decide to modify several of PowerPoint's settings to meet your needs. Because you want to create a new logo for your store, you also create a custom Ribbon tab and add the Combine Shapes commands. You then use the Combine Shapes commands to create a logo for Survival Solutions.

Skills covered: Create User Name and Initials • Set Advanced and Proofing Options • Create a New Tab • Use Combine Shapes Commands

STEP 1 ≫ CREATE USER NAME AND INITIALS

Because you plan on working with others on several presentations, you decide to personalize your copy of Microsoft Office by adding your name and your initials. Refer to Figure 7.11 as you complete Step 1.

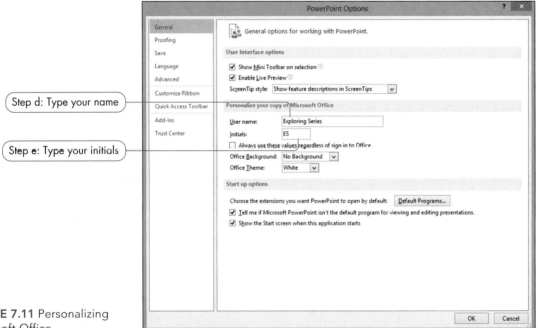

FIGURE 7.11 Personalizing Microsoft Office

a. Open the *p07h1Preparedness* presentation and save it as **p07h1Preparedness_LastFirst**.

> **TROUBLESHOOTING:** If you make any major mistakes in this exercise, you can close the file, open *p07h1Preparedness* again, and then start this exercise over.

b. Create a handout header with your name and a handout footer with your instructor's name and your class. Include the current date.

c. Click the **FILE tab** and click **Options**.

   The PowerPoint Options dialog box opens.

d. Type your name in the **User name box**, if necessary.

    e. Type your initials in the **Initials box**, if necessary.

    f. Keep the PowerPoint Options dialog box open for the next step.

> **TROUBLESHOOTING:** If you are working in a public lab, you should restore the Ribbon to its original arrangement after making changes to the Ribbon as part of these exercises.

STEP 2 ⟫ SET ADVANCED AND PROOFING OPTIONS

You decide to turn off background printing. Background printing enables you to continue working as you print but increases the print response time. Also, you use your company name, Survival Solutions, in most of the presentations you create. To minimize the chances for a typographical error, you set AutoCorrect to replace the initials "ss" with Survival Solutions. Finally, to improve the spelling checker results, you activate the *Check grammar with spelling* feature so the correct usage of words can be identified. Refer to Figure 7.12 as you complete Step 2.

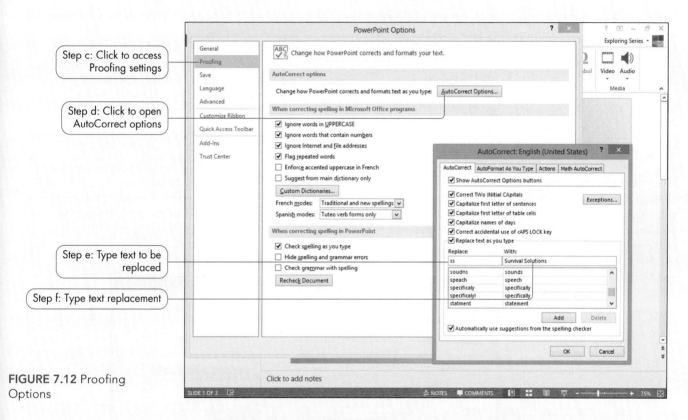

FIGURE 7.12 Proofing Options

    a. Click **Advanced** in the left pane of the PowerPoint Options dialog box.

    b. Scroll until you see the *Print* section and click the **Print in background check box** to deselect it if necessary.

       The *Print in background* option is deselected.

    c. Click **Proofing** in the left pane of the PowerPoint Options dialog box.

    d. Click **AutoCorrect Options** and click the **AutoCorrect tab**, if necessary.

       The AutoCorrect tab in the AutoCorrect dialog box opens.

    e. Type **ss** in the **Replace box**.

    f. Type **Survival Solutions** in the **With box** and click **OK**.

       Because you are only adding one text replacement, you click OK. If you wanted to add additional text replacements, you would click Add and click OK when all replacements are made.

g. Select the **Proofing tab**, if necessary. Click the **Check grammar with spelling check box** to select it if necessary and click **OK**.

The PowerPoint Options dialog box closes, and you return to Slide 1 of the presentation.

h. Click the **title placeholder**. Type **ss** and press **Spacebar** in the **title placeholder**.

Survival Solutions replaces the original placeholder text.

> **TROUBLESHOOTING:** If the text is not replaced, do the following: click the File tab, click Options, click Proofing, and then click AutoCorrect Options. Make sure the *Replace text as you type* check box is selected. Repeat steps d through f.

i. Type the following after *Survival Solutions* in the **title placeholder**: **is the write place for getting prepared.**

A wavy line displays underneath the word *write*, indicating it is the wrong word choice in this context.

j. Right-click **write** and select **right**.

The incorrect word is replaced, and the sentence is now grammatically correct.

k. Save the presentation.

STEP 3 ≫ CREATE A NEW TAB

You decide to use PowerPoint shapes to create a new logo for Survival Solutions. Because you want to combine the shapes, and because you know that you cannot access the Combine Shapes tools from the standard Ribbon, you will create a new tab customized to include a group with the Combine Shapes tools. After creating the custom tab, you will modify it to include a command to make shapes available from the new tab. Refer to Figure 7.13 as you complete Step 3.

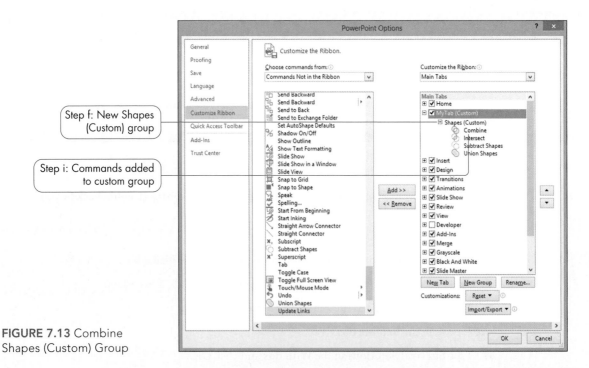

FIGURE 7.13 Combine Shapes (Custom) Group

a. Click the **FILE tab**, click **Options**, and then click **Customize Ribbon** in the PowerPoint Options dialog box.

The *Customize the Ribbon* options display in the PowerPoint Options dialog box, with the Home tab selected in the Main Tabs list.

b. Click **New Tab**.

A new tab is created in the Main Tabs list and positioned between the Home tab and the Insert tab. The tab is named *New Tab (Custom)* and contains a new group named *New Group (Custom)*.

> **TROUBLESHOOTING:** If the new tab is positioned elsewhere, click Reset, select *Reset all customizations*, and then click Yes. Repeat step b. As an alternative, you can select the new tab and click the Move Up and Move Down arrows to reposition the new tab.

c. Select **New Tab (Custom)**, click **Rename**, type **MyTab** in the **Display name box**, and then click **OK**.

The new tab displays as *MyTab (Custom)*.

d. Select **New Group (Custom)** and click **Rename**.

The Rename dialog box opens.

e. Click the **Key icon** (third row, seventh column) in the *Symbol* section; do not close the Rename dialog box.

You can display icons on the Ribbon to make it smaller if you want. Also, icons will display if your monitor has a low screen resolution setting. In either of these cases, a key icon will represent the new custom group.

f. Type **Shapes** in the **Display name box** and click **OK**.

The group displays as *Shapes (Custom)*.

g. Click the **Choose commands from arrow** and click **Commands Not in the Ribbon**.

h. Scroll down the list of commands, click **Combine Shapes**, and then click **Add**.

Combine Shapes is added to MyTab (Custom) in the Shapes (Custom) group.

i. Add the following commands to MyTab (Custom) in the Shapes (Custom) group:
- Intersect Shapes
- Subtract Shapes
- Union Shapes

j. Click **OK** to close the PowerPoint Options dialog box.

k. Click the **MyTab tab** and note that the Shapes group contains four buttons.

> **TROUBLESHOOTING:** The buttons are dimmed until two shapes are selected.

l. Right-click the **Ribbon** and click **Customize the Ribbon** so you can begin the process to insert another command on the Ribbon.

The PowerPoint Options dialog box opens.

m. Click **Shapes (Custom)** to select the group.

n. Click **Shapes** in the Popular Commands list and click **Add**.

The Shapes (Custom) group expands, and *Shapes* displays at the bottom of the list of commands contained in the group.

o. Drag **Shapes** above *Combine*.

Shapes is the first command in the reordered list.

p. Click **OK** and view the Shapes group.

The group now contains five commands.

q. Save the presentation.

After practicing using the Combine Shapes commands, you will create a new logo for Survival Solutions. You will save the new logo so that you can use it in presentations. Refer to Figure 7.14 as you complete Step 4.

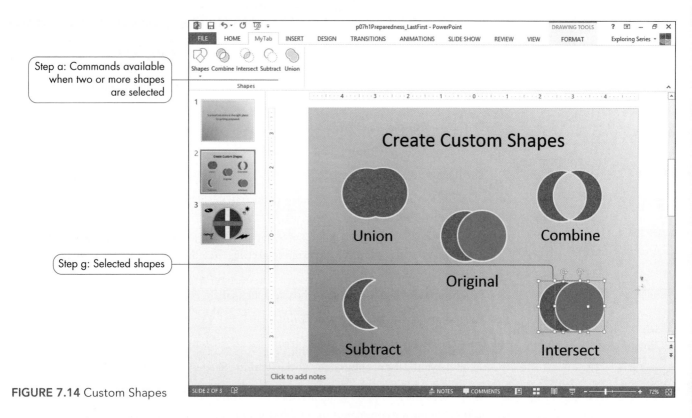

FIGURE 7.14 Custom Shapes

a. On Slide 2, select the **red circle** above the *Union* label, press and hold **Shift**, and then click the **blue circle** above the *Union* label.

The selection contains two objects.

b. Click **Union** in the Shapes group.

The circles join and become a single shape with a red fill.

> **TROUBLESHOOTING:** If the new shape is blue, the blue circle was selected first. Click Undo on the Quick Access Toolbar, click outside the circles, and then repeat steps a and b.

c. Select the **red circle** above the *Combine* label, press and hold **Shift**, and then click the **blue circle** above the *Combine* label.

d. Click **Combine** in the Shapes group.

The overlapping area of the two circles is cut out, making the background visible.

e. Select the **red circle** above the *Subtract* label, press and hold **Shift**, and then click the **blue circle** above the *Subtract* label.

f. Click **Subtract** in the Shapes group.

The overlapping area of the blue circle is cut from the red circle, creating a crescent shape.

g. Select the **red circle** above the *Intersect* label, press and hold **Shift**, and then click the **blue circle** above the *Intersect* label.

h. Click **Intersect** in the Shapes group.

The overlapping area is retained and other areas are cut from the shape.

i. On Slide 3, select the **green circle**, press and hold **Shift**, and then click the **blue circle** to add it to the selection.

j. Click **Combine** in the Shapes group.

The overlapping area of the two circles is cut out, which reveals a yellow circle that had been hidden by the shapes.

k. Select the **red rectangle**, press and hold **Shift**, and then click the vertical **yellow rectangle** to add it to the selection. Click **Union** in the Shapes group to form a red cross. Select the **green circle**, click the **FORMAT tab**, and then click **Bring Forward**.

The green circle moves to the front and becomes a border for the logo.

l. Select the **black jagged line shape** in the bottom-right corner, press and hold **Shift**, and then click the adjacent **yellow jagged line shape** to add it to the selection.

> **TROUBLESHOOTING:** If the yellow shape is difficult to select, click the View tab and click Zoom. Change the zoom setting to 200% and drag the vertical scroll button to the bottom of the vertical scroll bar and the horizontal scroll button to the far right of the horizontal scroll bar. Perform step m and click *Fit to Window* in the Zoom group.

m. Click **Intersect** in the Shapes group on the MyTab tab.

The intersection of the shapes is a thin jagged black line.

n. Copy the jagged line and paste and position it under the first line to represent the shaking that might occur during an earthquake.

o. Click a jagged line, press and hold **Shift**, and then click the other jagged line to add it to the selection. Click the **FORMAT tab** and click **Group** in the Arrange group two times.

p. Size the group to **1.3"** high by **1.85"** wide.

q. Select the **black cloud shape**, press and hold **Shift**, and then click the **yellow lightning shape** to add it to the selection.

r. Click **Subtract** in the Shapes group on the MyTab tab.

The lightning shape is subtracted from the cloud shape.

s. Drag each of the four black disaster symbols onto the yellow circle, one in each quadrant.

t. Press **Ctrl+A** to select all objects in the logo and group the objects.

The group includes the large green circle and its boundary box and sizing handles, the red cross and its boundary box and sizing handles, and each of the four disaster symbols with their boundary boxes and sizing handles. If a blank box displays on the lower left side of the slide, delete it.

u. Right-click the selected group and select **Save as Picture**. Navigate to where you are saving your student data files and type **p07h1SSLogo_LastFirst** in the **File name box**.

v. Click the **Save as type arrow**, click **PNG Portable Network Graphics Format (*.png)**, and then click **Save**.

w. Save and close the presentation, and exit PowerPoint. Submit the files as directed by your instructor.

x. Restore the Ribbon to its original arrangement if you are working in a public lab.

Master Basics

Customize a PowerPoint presentation, and you will be putting your unique creative ideas to work. Although you want to customize your slides, you still want a consistent look throughout the presentation. *Masters* control the layouts, background designs, and color combinations for handouts, notes pages, and slides, giving the presentation a consistent appearance. By changing the masters, you make selections that affect the entire slide show and the supporting materials. This is more efficient than changing each slide in the presentation. The design elements you already know about, such as themes and layouts, can be applied to each type of master. Masters control the consistency of your presentations, notes, and handouts. Slide masters can be reused in other presentations.

In this section, you learn how to modify masters. Specifically, you will learn how to customize the layout and formatting of handouts, notes, the slide master, and slide layouts controlled by the slide master.

TIP Fresh Start

Modifications to masters can be made at any time as you create the presentation, but it is best to begin with a blank presentation. This gives you a clean workspace, enabling you to concentrate on the design of your slide show, handouts, and notes.

Modifying Handout and Notes Masters

You can print handouts and notes pages of your presentation. The handouts printout displays thumbnails of the slides for audience use. The notes pages printout displays individual slides with notes and is typically used by the presenter. You might want to customize these types of printouts to display all the information you want in the position that is most advantageous.

Customize the Handout Master

The *handout master* contains the design information about the layout and formatting of audience handout pages. The handout master controls the orientation of the page; the number of slides per page; and the layout of fields such as the header, footer, date, and page number. To modify the handout master, click the View tab and click Handout Master in the Master Views group.

STEP 1 »
Click Handout Orientation in the Page Setup group to change the orientation of the handouts from portrait to landscape. You can select the number of slides you want to appear on the handouts in the Page Setup group on the Handout Master tab. Click Slides Per Page in the Page Setup group to select the number of slide thumbnails you want to print per handout page. You can also print the presentation outline from this option. Figure 7.15 shows an open handout master with *6 Slides* selected.

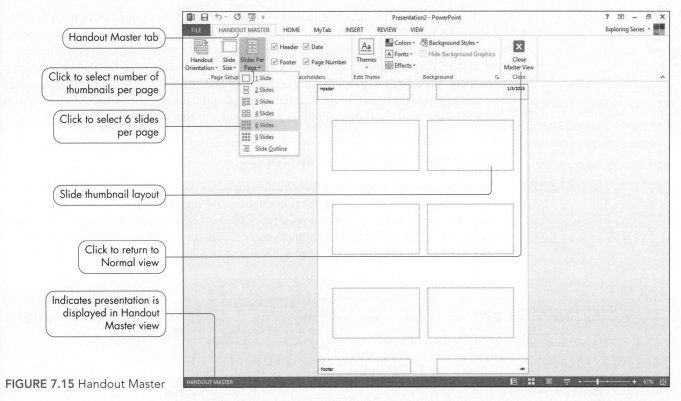

Handout Master tab

Click to select number of thumbnails per page

Click to select 6 slides per page

Slide thumbnail layout

Click to return to Normal view

Indicates presentation is displayed in Handout Master view

FIGURE 7.15 Handout Master

On the handout master, you modify the header, date, footer, or page number fields using the Placeholders group. You can omit any of these fields from the handout by deselecting the field's check box in the Placeholders group. Initially, the placeholders for the header and date fields are at the top of the page. The footer and the page number field placeholders are at the bottom of the page. You can move each placeholder by dragging it to a new location. In Figure 7.16, the date placeholder is moved to the bottom of the page. The footer is moved to the top of the page, and the page number is removed. Although the term *footer* implies that the location is always at the bottom of a page or slide, sometimes PowerPoint slide templates reposition footers at the top or on the sides.

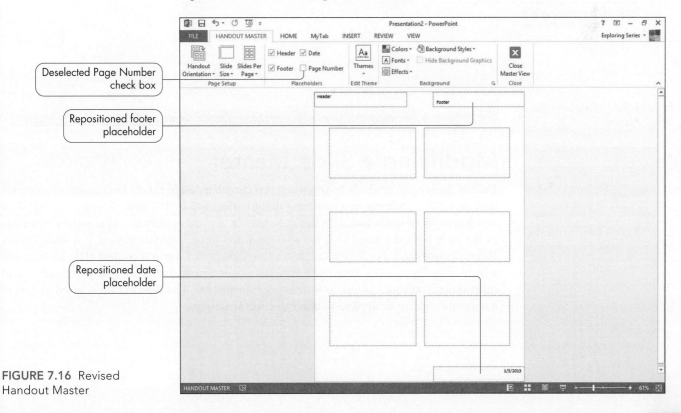

Deselected Page Number check box

Repositioned footer placeholder

Repositioned date placeholder

FIGURE 7.16 Revised Handout Master

You can modify the handout master even further using the options from the other tabs displayed on the Ribbon. For example, if you want to have a company logo on each handout page, click the Insert tab and click Pictures in the Images group. As you revise the handout master, keep in mind that the handouts are to supplement your presentation. Audience members appreciate handouts that are uncluttered and easy to read, as they often take notes on the handouts that you give them. After modifying the master, click Close Master View in the Close group on the Handout Master tab to return to Normal view.

Customize the Notes Master

STEP 2 The *notes master* contains design information for notes pages. Often, the speaker uses notes pages to prepare for and deliver the presentation and may occasionally distribute detailed notes pages to an audience. You can specify the fields, the format, and the layout of the notes master just as you did with the handout master. To modify the notes master, click the View tab and click Notes Master in the Master Views group. Figure 7.17 shows a customized notes master.

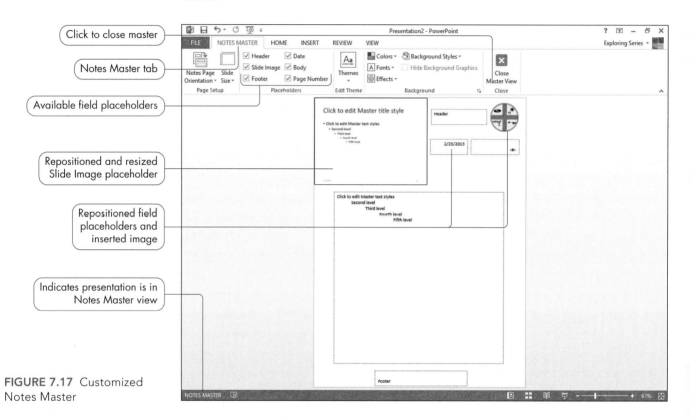

FIGURE 7.17 Customized Notes Master

Modifying a Slide Master

Each of the layouts available to you when you choose a design theme has consistent elements that are set by a *slide master* containing design information. The slide master is the top slide in a hierarchy of slides based on the slide master. As you modify the slide master, elements in the slide layouts related to it are also modified to maintain consistency. A slide master includes associated slide layouts such as a title slide layout, various content slide layouts, and a blank slide layout. The associated slide layouts designate the location of placeholders and other objects on slides as well as formatting information. The slide master is saved as part of a template and can be applied to other slide presentations.

If you want your presentation to contain two or more themes, insert a slide master for each theme. For example, you may use a different theme for different sections of the slide show. Click the View tab and click Slide Master in the Master Views group. Click Themes in the Edit Theme group and select a Built-In theme or browse for a custom theme you have saved. The theme is applied to the existing slide master and its associated layouts. Then click below the last slide layout in the Thumbnail pane. Click Themes in the Edit Theme group and select a Built-In theme or browse for a saved theme. A new slide master and its associated slide layouts are created using the new theme.

STEP 3 To modify a slide master or slide layout based on a slide master, do the following:

1. Click the VIEW tab.
2. Click Slide Master in the Master Views group.
3. Click the slide master at the top of the list or click one of the associated layouts.
4. Make modifications.
5. Click Close Master View in the Close group on the SLIDE MASTER tab.

In Slide Master view, the slide master is the larger, top slide thumbnail shown in the left pane. The Title Slide Layout is the second slide in the pane. The number of slides following it varies depending upon the template. Figure 7.18 shows the default Office Theme Slide Master and its related slide layouts. The ScreenTip for the slide master indicates it is used by one slide because the slide show is a new slide show comprised of a single title slide.

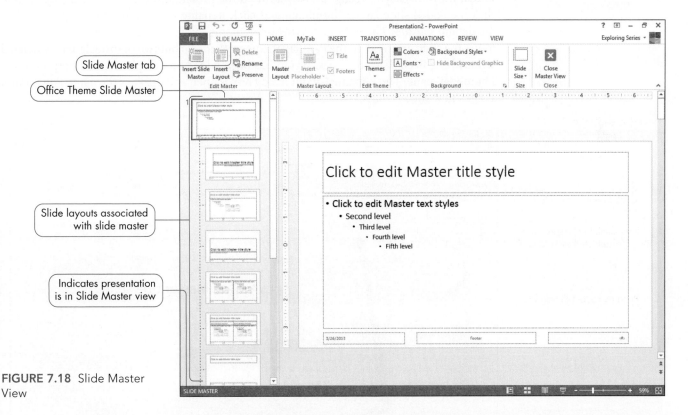

FIGURE 7.18 Slide Master View

The slide master is the most efficient way of setting the fonts, color scheme, and effects for the entire presentation. To set these choices, click the slide master thumbnail in the left pane to display the slide master. The main pane shows the placeholders for title style, text styles, a date field, a footer field, and a page number field. Double-click the text in the Master title style or any level of text in the Master text styles placeholder and modify the font appearance. You can also make adjustments to the footer, date, and page number fields.

You can move and size the placeholders on the slide master. The modifications in position and size are reflected on the associated slide layouts. This may conflict with some of the slide layout placeholders, however. The placeholders can be moved on the individual slide layouts as needed.

TIP | Slide Master Headers and Footers

As you modify the footer, date, and slide numbers on the slide master, it appears as if the information is added to the slide. This is not the case—the slide master contains formatted field placeholders and not actual information. To insert header and footer text while in the slide master, click the Insert tab and click Header & Footer in the Text group. An alternative method is to make the selections as you build the presentation in Normal view.

Delete and Add Slide Layouts

STEP 4 ≫

If you only need a limited number of layouts, delete the extras to save file size. Click the slide layout thumbnail you wish to delete and click Delete in the Edit Master group on the Slide Master tab. The Title Slide Layout cannot be deleted, but all other layouts can be removed. You can preserve a slide layout within the master even if it is not used in the presentation by clicking Insert Slide Master and clicking Preserve. If you want to add a slide layout, click Insert Layout in the Edit Master group. You should rename added slide layouts so that they are easy to recognize as you build the presentation. To rename a slide layout, click the added slide layout thumbnail and click Rename in the Edit Master group. Select the default *Custom Layout* name, type a new name, and then click Rename. Figure 7.19 shows the slide master with the Parallax theme applied. All but two of the original associated layouts have been deleted. A new layout has been added and displays at the bottom of the Thumbnail pane. The Rename Layout dialog box is open and displays the name PowerPoint assigns new slide layouts.

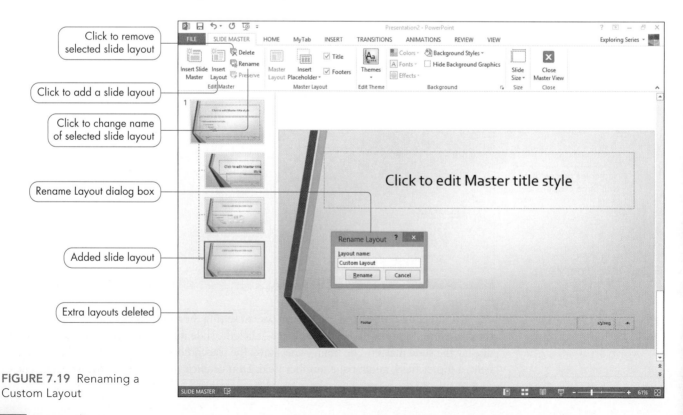

FIGURE 7.19 Renaming a Custom Layout

You can add, remove, and size placeholders on a slide layout as needed. To add a placeholder to a selected layout, click Insert Placeholder or click the Insert Placeholder arrow in the Master Layout group on the Slide Master tab. Clicking Insert Placeholder enables you to drag to create a standard content placeholder containing content buttons anywhere on the slide. Clicking the Insert Placeholder arrow enables you to create specific types of placeholders (see Figure 7.20). Once you select a type of placeholder, you can continue adding this type by clicking Insert Placeholder. To change the type, click the Insert Placeholder arrow and make a selection from the list.

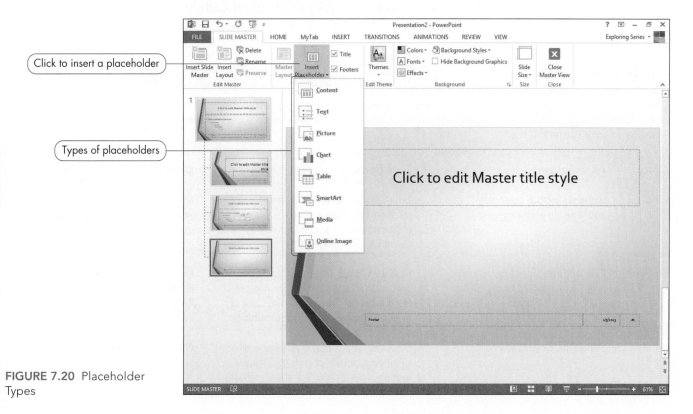

FIGURE 7.20 Placeholder Types

You may access the tabs and add objects such as images, SmartArt, shapes, and sounds. Animations can be applied to the objects, or transitions can be added to slide layouts. Elements added on a slide layout, such as a bullet list layout, appear on every slide in the presentation that uses that layout.

TIP Remove Slide Layouts and Placeholders

Select the slide thumbnail first. Click Delete in the Edit Master group on the Slide Master tab to delete the entire slide layout. If you want to remove placeholders from a slide layout, click the placeholder border and press Delete.

Customize the Slide Master Color Theme

Creating custom colors adds a creative touch to a presentation. Using the custom colors in the slide master ensures that the slide layouts maintain continuity. For example, after adding a logo to the slide master, you can use the logo colors on elements of the slide master. The associated slide layouts use the same colors.

Consider your audience and the message of your presentation as you select colors on your slide master. Look at things around you to come up with color combinations. Other PowerPoint presentations that you may see—in addition to magazines, Web sites, and other graphically designed materials—will give you a good idea of what colors work well together.

Certain color combinations work well together, and other combinations are hard to read when they are placed together. Look for combinations that provide high contrast. Think of your favorite team colors, and you are probably thinking about high-contrast color combinations. If black-and-white printouts are made for the audience, then the choice of colors for the text should provide even more contrast so the handouts are legible. Generally, the slides will be easiest to read when a dark text is placed on a lighter background. You see many presentations where the background is dark and the text is light. In making color choices, you need to consider your audience. Some members of your audience may have problems reading light text on a dark background. Additionally, if cost is an issue, printing a dark background increases the print cost due to the amount of ink needed.

REFERENCE | Color Associations

Colors can be used to attract the attention of the audience. They have a powerful effect on emotions. Colors are associated with different things. Color plays a significant role in audience response. Use this chart to select colors that support the message of your presentations.

Color	Associations	Emotions	Uses
Red	Danger, blood, strength, courage, fire, energy	Love, power, passion, rage, excitement, aggression, determination, decision making, romance, longing	Make a point or gain attention. Stimulate people into making quick decisions.
Orange	Fall, warmth, fun, joy, energy, creativity, tropics, heat, citrus fruit	Pleasure, excitement, strength, ambition, endurance, domination, happiness, enthusiasm, playfulness, determination, success, stimulation	Emphasize happiness and enjoyment. Stimulate thought. Ensure high visibility. Highlight important elements.
Yellow	Sunshine, bright, warnings	Cheerful, joy, happiness, warmth, optimism, intellect, energy, honor, loyalty, cowardice, lightheartedness, jealousy	Gain a positive response. Gain attention.
Green	Nature, calm, refreshing, money, growth, fertility	Tranquility, growth, safety, harmony, freshness, healing, restive, stability, hope, endurance, envy, jealousy	Present a new idea. Suggest safety. Promote "green" products.
Blue	Sea, sky, peace, calm, cold, impersonal, intellect, masculine, expertise, integrity	Truth, dignity, trust, wisdom, loyalty, harmony, stability, confidence, calming, tranquility, sincerity, healing, understanding, melancholy, belonging	Build trust and strength. Promote cleanliness. Suggest precision. Suppress diet.
Violet	Wealth, royalty, sophistication, intelligence, spirituality, wisdom, dignity, magic, feminine	Power, stability, luxury, extravagance, creativity, frustration, gloom, sadness	Promote children's products. Gain respect and attention.
Black	Formal, mystery, death, evil, power, elegant, prestigious, conservative, the unknown	Authority, boldness, seriousness, negativity, strength, seductiveness, evil	Emphasis. Contrast with bright colors. Ease of reading.
White	Snow, cleanliness, safety, simplicity, youth, light, purity, virginity	Perfection, distinction, enlightenment, positivity, successful, faith	Emphasis. Suggest simplicity. Promote medical products.
Gray	Neutral, science, architecture, commerce, cold	Easy-going, original, practical, solid	Complement other colors. Unify colors. Bring focus to other colors.
Brown	Earth, richness, masculine, harvest, fall	Conservative, steady, dependable, serious, stability	Build trust.

Colors convey meanings to your audience. Write the word *hot* in blue letters, and your audience will be confused. Write *hot* in red or orange, and the audience will grasp what you are trying to say. Certain colors evoke feelings. Blue, green, and violet are cool, relaxing colors. Yellow, orange, and red are invigorating, warm, action colors. If your presentation is long, using a warm color will quickly wear your audience out. The reference table shows common colors, associations people make with the colors, and emotions that are linked with the colors.

STEP 5 »

Color themes are combinations of 12 colors used for the text, lines, background, and graphics in a presentation. Color themes contain four text and background colors, six accent colors, and two hyperlink colors. Standard Office color themes may not include the color combinations that are used by your school, business, or other organization. You can customize your own color scheme in this case.

As you focus your attention on creating your own color scheme for the slide master, you have 16 million colors from which to choose. You may change any of the 12 colors used in a color theme to customize it to your needs. Avoid making each of the 12 colors completely different—choose one color family, use different shades of the colors in the family, and add two or three accent colors. Select colors that work well together. Use light and dark shades of the same color within your color scheme for a unified, professional appearance.

To customize the color theme for a slide master, do the following:

1. Click the VIEW tab.
2. Click Slide Master in the Master Views group.
3. Click the slide master thumbnail in the Slides pane.
4. Click Colors in the Background group.
5. Select a Built-In color theme or select Customize Colors.

If you select Customize Colors, the Create New Theme Colors dialog box opens showing the current theme colors. A preview of how the colors are applied on a slide is shown in a Sample pane. Click the color box next to the name of the color element that you want to change and choose a Theme color, a Standard color, or More Colors. Figure 7.21 displays the Create New Theme Colors dialog box.

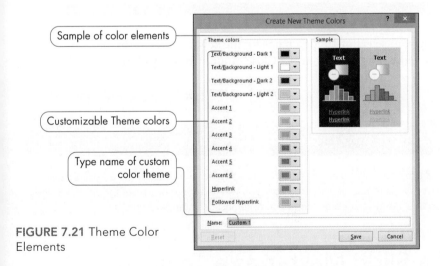

FIGURE 7.21 Theme Color Elements

The Colors dialog box that displays when you select More Colors offers two tabs for selecting colors. The Standard tab contains 127 colors and 14 shades of white to black. The Custom tab enables you to make selections based on the ***RGB*** color model, where numbers are assigned to red, green, or blue, and the mixture of red, green, or blue light creates a color representation. A zero for each represents black. The number 255 for each of the colors in the model represents white. The RGB model uses 16 million colors. Using this system, you can match any color where you know the three RGB numbers. A similar color model, ***HSL***, balances hue, saturation, and luminosity to produce a color. The numbers for black and white are represented the same way as in the RGB model.

Figure 7.22 shows the Custom tab in the Colors dialog box with the RGB color model selected. Drag the crosshairs in the Color box to the color family you wish to use, for instance green. The slider to the right of the Color box is used to select the shade of that color. If you know the RGB number, you can use the spin boxes to increase or decrease the numbers, or you can type the numbers into the boxes for each of the colors. After selecting the color, click OK to place that color into the theme. The Sample box in the Create New Theme Colors dialog box displays the current color and the new color. As you make changes to the theme element colors, look at the Sample to get an idea of how your color scheme will look on the slide.

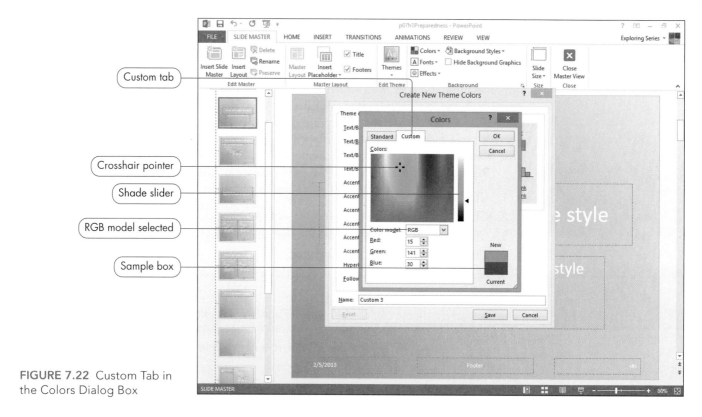

FIGURE 7.22 Custom Tab in the Colors Dialog Box

After making your selections, type a name for the new color theme in the Name box and click Save. Click Close Master View in the Close group if you have finished modifying the slide master.

TIP Monitor and Projector Differences

Monitors and projectors show colors in different ways. To avoid surprises, always test your presentation color schemes on the projector you will use for your presentation. If you are unable to do this, keep your color scheme simple and use standard colors.

Saving a Slide Master as a Template

STEP 6 >> After you modify a slide master, save the file as a template. PowerPoint saves the master as a template with an extension of *.potx* and retains the changes in the file. You can then reuse the slide master with any presentation.

To save the file as a presentation template, do the following:

1. Determine the location for your saved template.
2. Click the FILE tab and click Save As.
3. Type a file name in the *File name* box.

4. Click the *Save as type* arrow.

5. Click PowerPoint Template and click Save.

To use your custom presentation template, do the following:

1. Click the FILE tab and click Open.

2. If you saved the template to the default location, click Custom Office Templates, select your template, and then click Open.

3. If you saved the template to another location, click Open, navigate to the location, select your template, and then click Open.

Quick Concepts

1. What are the benefits of using masters? *p. 434*

2. Explain the importance of color use in your presentation. *p. 440*

3. Monitors and projectors show color in different ways. Explain how you can ensure your presentation color schemes work for both environments. *p. 442*

2 Master Basics

Because you deliver many presentations to local groups on emergency preparedness, you decide to customize a master for handouts and notes that includes your logo and contact information. Then you create a slide master and several slide layouts that you can use for presentations so people identify your business when they see your presentations and advertising.

Skills covered: Modify Handout Master • Modify Notes Master • Modify a Slide Master • Delete and Add Slide Layouts • Create a Custom Color Theme • Use the Slide Master and Template

STEP 1 ≫ MODIFY HANDOUT MASTER

At the beginning of your presentations, you will give your audience a handout of your presentation that shows four slides per page because you want the audience to have room to write notes below the slide thumbnails. For identification purposes and to save time in the future, you decide to modify the master so it includes your logo and business name. You will also reposition the date field placeholder so it appears below the header. Refer to Figure 7.23 as you complete Step 1.

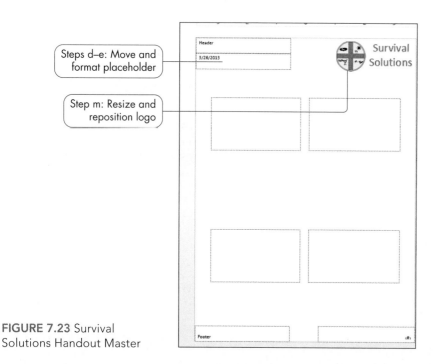

FIGURE 7.23 Survival Solutions Handout Master

a. Create a new blank presentation and save it as **p07h2Survival_LastFirst**.

b. Click the **VIEW tab** and click **Handout Master** in the Master Views group.

   The Handout Master tab opens and the master displays.

c. Click **Slides Per Page** in the Page Setup group and select **4 Slides**.

   Four slide placeholders appear on the handout for positioning purposes. You will still need to pick the number of placeholders you want to print when you are ready to print the handouts.

d. Drag the **date placeholder** immediately below the header placeholder.

e. Click the **HOME tab**, click the **date placeholder**, and then click **Align Left** in the Paragraph group.

   The Header field and the content of the date placeholder align on the left.

f. Click the **INSERT tab** and click **WordArt** in the Text group.

g. Click **Fill - Blue, Accent 1, Shadow** (first row, second column).

h. Type **Survival**, press **Enter**, and then type **Solutions**.

i. Select the text, click **Text Fill** in the WordArt Styles group, and then click **Red** in the Standard Colors category.

The text is now red.

j. Change the font size to **28 pt**.

k. Drag the WordArt to the top-right corner of the handout so that the top and right borders of the WordArt align with the top and right edges of the page.

l. Click the **INSERT tab**, click **Pictures** in the Images group, and then navigate to the location where you saved the logo you created in Hands-On Exercise 1 (*p07h1SSLogo_LastFirst*) or in your data files (*p07h2SSLogo*). Click the logo and click **Insert**.

m. Resize the logo to **1"** high by **1"** wide and drag the logo to the left of the business name.

n. Select the logo, press **Ctrl** while selecting the WordArt, and then click the **HOME tab**. Click **Copy** in the Clipboard group.

The logo and WordArt are saved together as an item to the Clipboard so that you can paste it in other locations.

o. Click the **Clipboard Dialog Box launcher** to open the Clipboard. View the copied selection in the Clipboard to ensure it was saved. Close the Clipboard.

> **TROUBLESHOOTING:** If the logo and WordArt do not appear in the Clipboard, select both objects, and then press Ctrl+C. When the copy appears in the Clipboard, close the Clipboard.

p. Click the **FILE tab** and click **Save As**. Click **Computer** and click **Browse**. Click the **Save as type arrow** and select **PowerPoint Template**. Navigate to the location where you are saving your files and name the file **p07h2SurvivalTemplate_LastFirst**. Click **Save**.

STEP 2 ≫ MODIFY NOTES MASTER

Sometimes the notes you add to your slides are very detailed and take a great deal of space. PowerPoint automatically resizes the font to fit the text to the page, which can make the text difficult to read. You will change the notes master to provide more space for notes and add your logo and business name. Refer to Figure 7.24 as you complete Step 2.

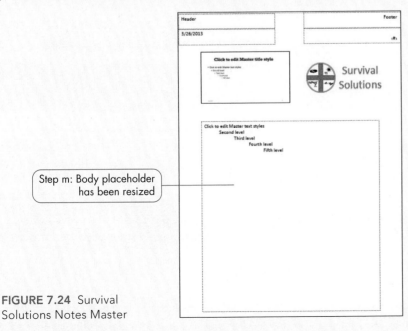

Step m: Body placeholder has been resized

FIGURE 7.24 Survival Solutions Notes Master

a. Click the **VIEW tab** and click **Notes Master** in the Master Views group.

The Notes Master tab opens and the notes master displays.

b. Click the **Slide Image placeholder**, click the **FORMAT tab**, and then click the **Size Dialog Box Launcher**. Scale the placeholder to 50% of its current size.

The placeholder reduces in size to 1.69" high by 3" wide.

c. Click **Position**. If necessary, change the **Horizontal position** to **0.75"**, change the **Vertical position** to **1.25"** from the Top Left Corner, and then click **Close**.

d. Drag the **date placeholder** beneath the header placeholder.

e. Click the **HOME tab** and click **Align Left** in the Paragraph group.

The header information and the date are left aligned.

f. Drag the **footer placeholder** to the top right of the page.

g. Right-click the **footer placeholder** and select **Format Shape**.

The Format Shape pane opens.

h. Click **TEXT OPTIONS**, click **Textbox**, change the **Vertical alignment** to **Top**, and then click **Close**.

i. Click **Align Right** in the Paragraph group.

j. Drag the **page number placeholder** beneath the footer placeholder.

k. Click the **Clipboard Dialog Box Launcher** to open the Clipboard. Select both the logo and WordArt in the list, click the arrow, and then click **Paste**. Close the Clipboard.

The objects are pasted on the Notes page.

l. Drag the logo and WordArt so they are approximately centered in the white space to the right of the Slide Image placeholder.

m. Select the **body placeholder** (the placeholder containing the text levels), click the **FORMAT tab**, and then resize the placeholder to **6.25"** high and **6"** wide.

n. Drag the **body placeholder** up until it fits on the page.

o. Click the **NOTES MASTER tab** and click **Close Master View** in the Close group.

p. Save the template.

STEP 3 » MODIFY A SLIDE MASTER

To help create the identity of your business and to build recognition for your store, you will create a Survival Solutions slide master. You will include the logo you created on the slide master and a photograph of your store on the Title Slide Master. Refer to Figure 7.25 as you complete Step 3.

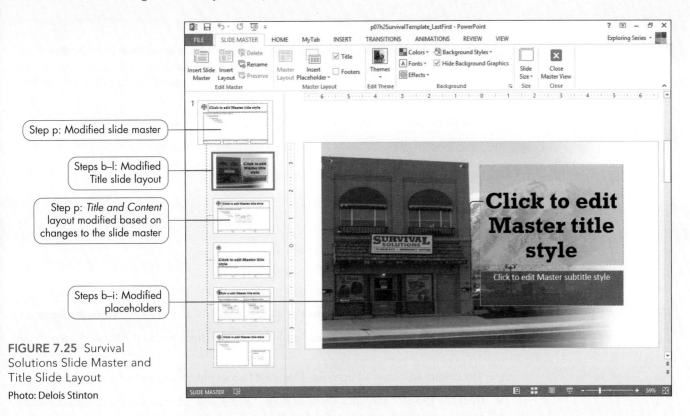

Step p: Modified slide master

Steps b–l: Modified Title slide layout

Step p: *Title and Content* layout modified based on changes to the slide master

Steps b–i: Modified placeholders

FIGURE 7.25 Survival Solutions Slide Master and Title Slide Layout

Photo: Delois Stinton

a. Click the **VIEW tab** and click **Slide Master** in the Master Views group.

The Slide Master tab opens with the Title Slide Layout selected in the thumbnails list.

> **TROUBLESHOOTING:** If you closed the template after the previous step, you will need to open the file.

b. Select the **title style placeholder**, click the **FORMAT tab**, and then click the **Size Dialog Box Launcher** in the Size group.

The Format Shape pane opens.

c. Resize the placeholder so it is **3.6"** high by **6.15"** wide.

d. Click **Position**, if necessary. Set the **Horizontal position** to **6.88"** from the Top left Corner and the **Vertical position** to **0.87"** from the Top Left Corner and click **Close**.

The placeholder moves to the right side of the slide.

e. Click the **FORMAT tab** if necessary, click **Shape Fill** in the Shape Styles group, and then do the following:

- Click **More Fill Colors**.
- Click the **Custom tab**.
- Type **206** in the **Red box**.
- Type **172** in the **Green box**.
- Type **152** in the **Blue box**.
- Type **40** in the **Transparency box**.
- Click **OK**.

The placeholder fill changes to a semitransparent fill.

f. Click the **HOME tab**, change the font to **Rockwell**, and then change the font size to **60**, if necessary. Change the font style to **Bold**.

> **TROUBLESHOOTING:** If Rockwell is not available, select any serif font available, such as Times New Roman.

g. Select the **subtitle style placeholder**, click the **FORMAT tab**, and then click the **Size Dialog Box Launcher** in the Size group. Resize the placeholder to **1.25"** high by **6.15"** wide. Position it horizontally at **6.88"** from the Top Left Corner and **4.8"** vertically from the Top Left Corner and click **Close**.

The subtitle style placeholder is positioned below the title style placeholder.

h. Click **Shape Fill** in the Shape Styles group and do the following:

- Click **More Fill Colors.**
- Click the **Custom tab.**
- Type **128** in the **Red box.**
- Type **47** in the **Green box.**
- Type **53** in the **Blue box.**
- Type **20** in the **Transparency box.**
- Click **OK.**

The placeholder fill changes to a slightly transparent brick-red fill.

i. Click the **HOME tab**, select the text, and then change the font color to **White, Background 1.**

j. Click the **SLIDE MASTER tab** and click the **Footers check box** in the Master Layout group to deselect it.

The footers are removed from the Title Slide Layout only because it is the selected layout.

k. Click the **INSERT tab**, click **Pictures** in the Images group, locate and select *p07h2Store.png* from the data files, and then click **Insert**.

l. Press ← on the keyboard once to nudge the picture to the left. Click the **Send Backward arrow** in the Arrange group on the FORMAT tab and click **Send to Back**.

The picture is positioned behind the two placeholders.

m. Click **Title Slide Layout**. Click **Hide Background Graphics** in the Background group. Select the picture and change its horizontal position to **0.63"** and vertical position to **0"**.

n. Click the **Office Theme Slide Master thumbnail**, which is located at the top of the thumbnail list.

The slide master is selected, and changes made to it will be reflected in associated slide layouts.

o. Select the **title style placeholder** and change the size to **1.38"** high by **10.55"** wide. Position it horizontally at **1.86"** and vertically at **0.42"** from the Top Left Corner.

p. Click the **HOME tab** and change the font to **Rockwell** and the font style to **Bold**, if necessary.

q. Click the **Clipboard Dialog Box launcher** to open the Clipboard. Point to the logo and WordArt in the list, click the arrow, and then click **Paste**. Delete the WordArt so only the logo remains on the slide. Close the Clipboard.

> **TROUBLESHOOTING:** If the logo and WordArt are no longer available, click the View tab, click Handout Master in the Master Views group, copy just the logo, and then return to the Slide Master view. Paste the logo on the slide master.

r. Deselect the **Lock Aspect Ratio checkbox** on the Format Picture pane. Make the following size and position modifications to the logo:

- Height: **1"**
- Width: **1"**
- Horizontal position: **0.25"** from the Top Left Corner
- Vertical position: **0.25"** from the Top Left Corner

s. Save the template.

STEP 4 ›› DELETE AND ADD SLIDE LAYOUTS

Several of the slide layouts associated with the Office Theme Slide Master you are modifying are not needed, so you will delete them. You will need a layout that includes a picture placeholder in the bottom-right corner of the slide that you will use to put pictures of supplies, however, so you create a custom layout. Refer to Figure 7.26 as you complete Step 4.

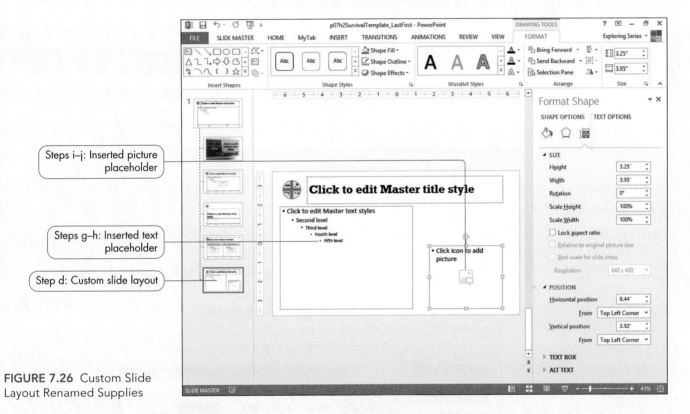

FIGURE 7.26 Custom Slide Layout Renamed Supplies

a. Click **Two Content Layout** in the thumbnail list of layouts associated with the slide master.

The Two Content layout displays.

b. Select **Delete** in the Edit Master group on the SLIDE MASTER tab.

The Two Content layout is deleted and the Comparison Layout, the next layout in the list, displays.

c. Delete the following layouts:

- Title Only
- Blank
- Content with Caption
- Picture with Caption
- Title and Vertical Text
- Vertical Title and Text

The slide master and four associated layouts remain (Title Slide, Title and Content, Section Header, and Comparison).

d. Select the last layout in the thumbnail list and click **Insert Layout** in the Edit Master group.

A new layout, Custom Layout, appears at the bottom of the list of layout thumbnails, and the slide displays in the Slide pane. The layout includes title and footers placeholders.

e. Click **Rename** in the Edit Master group and type **Supplies** in the **Layout name box** in the Rename Layout dialog box. Click **Rename**.

The name of the new layout is changed to *Supplies*.

f. Click the **Footers check box** in the Master Layout group to deselect it.

The footers at the bottom of the slide layout are removed.

g. Click the **Insert Placeholder arrow** in the Master Layout group, click **Text**, and then drag to create a text placeholder on the left side of the slide.

h. Click the **FORMAT tab** and click the **Size Dialog Box launcher** in the Size group. Resize the placeholder to **5.33"** high and **7.02"** wide. Position it horizontally at **0.42"** and vertically at **1.83"** from the Top Left Corner. Click **Close**.

The placeholder is resized and positioned on the slide.

i. Click the **SLIDE MASTER tab**, click the **Insert Placeholder arrow** in the Master Layout group, click **Picture**, and then drag to create a picture placeholder on the bottom-right of the slide.

j. Click the **FORMAT tab** and click the **Size Dialog Box launcher** in the Size group. Resize the placeholder to **3.25"** high and **3.95"** wide. Position it horizontally at **8.44"** and vertically at **3.92"** from the Top Left Corner (see Figure 7.26). Click **Close**.

k. Save the template.

STEP 5 » CREATE A CUSTOM COLOR THEME

To further refine your custom master, you will create a custom color theme using the colors in your logo and your store picture. Refer to Figure 7.27 as you complete Step 5.

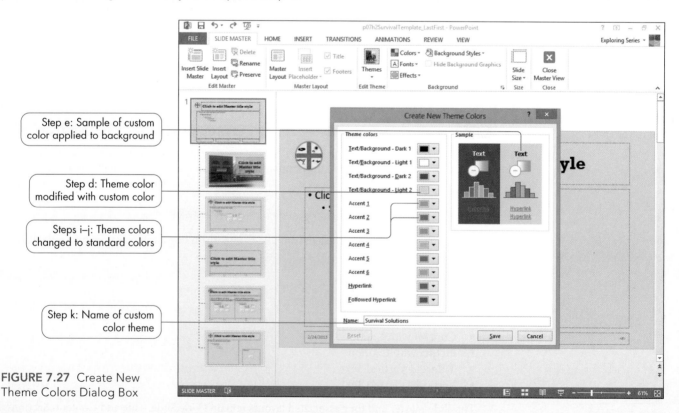

FIGURE 7.27 Create New Theme Colors Dialog Box

a. Click the **Office Theme Slide Master thumbnail** at the top of the thumbnail list.

b. Click **Colors** in the Background group.

c. Click **Customize Colors**.

The Create New Theme Colors dialog box displays the theme colors used in the Office Theme that your slide master has been using.

d. Click the **Text/Background - Light 2 arrow** and click **More Colors**.

The Colors dialog box opens with the Custom tab active.

e. Type **193** in the **Red box**, type **231** in the **Green box**, type **250** in the **Blue box**, and then click **OK**.

The Create New Theme Colors dialog box opens the custom color in the color box and in the sample.

f. Click **Save** and click **Background Styles** in the Background group.

Note that the four text and background colors from the color theme display within the 12 thumbnails, and the thumbnails in the second column show the custom color you created.

g. Click **Style 2** (first row, second column) to apply the custom color to the slide master.

h. Click **Colors** in the Background group, right-click **Custom 1**, and then select **Edit**.

The custom color theme you created opens so you can make additional modifications.

i. Select the **Accent 1 color box** and select **Green** in the Standard Colors category.

j. Select the **Accent 2 color box** and select **Red** in the Standard Colors category.

k. Type **Survival Solutions** in the **Name box** and click **Save**.

l. Click **Close Master View** in the Close group.

m. Save the template.

STEP 6 ≫ USE THE SLIDE MASTER AND TEMPLATE

To test the masters you created, you will insert slides from a Survival Solutions slide show you previously presented to a community group. You will view the slide show, and then you will preview the handout master and the notes master. Refer to Figure 7.28 as you complete Step 6.

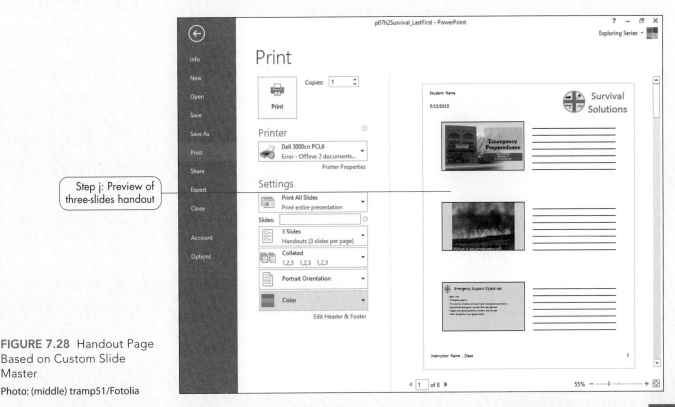

FIGURE 7.28 Handout Page Based on Custom Slide Master

Photo: (middle) tramp51/Fotolia

a. Click the **New Slide arrow** in the Slides group and select **Reuse Slides**.

The Reuse Slides task pane opens.

b. Click **Browse** in the Reuse Slides task pane and select **Browse File**.

c. Locate and select *p07h2Plan.pptx* and click **Open**.

The 24 added slides appear as thumbnails in the Reuse Slides pane.

d. Right-click any of the slides in the list and select **Insert All Slides**. Close the Reuse Slides pane.

The slides appear in the Slides pane with the slide master you created.

e. Click the **FILE tab**, click **Save As**, locate and select *p07h2Survival_LastFirst*, making sure you are saving it as a PowerPoint Presentation (.pptx file) and not as a PowerPoint Template (.potx file), and then click **Save**. Click **Yes** to confirm that you want to replace the existing file of the same name.

You will save the file using the original presentation file name so you do not overwrite the template you created. You want to be able to use the template with other presentations.

f. Create a *Notes and Handouts* header with your name and a footer with your instructor's name and your class. Include the current date.

g. Delete Slide 1.

The empty title slide is deleted, and the title slide from the inserted presentation becomes the new Slide 1.

h. Click the **VIEW tab** and click **Reading View** in the Presentation Views group. View the slide show and note the various layouts used.

i. Click the **FILE tab**, click **Print**, and then click **Full Page Slides**.

j. Click **3 Slides** in the *Handouts* section. View the preview of the handout.

k. Click **3 Slides** and click **Notes Pages** in the *Print Layout* section.

l. Scroll to view the notes for each slide.

m. Save the presentation. Keep PowerPoint open if you plan to continue with Hands-On Exercise 3. If not, exit PowerPoint.

Custom Shows

Custom shows are composed of a subset of slides assembled for a presentation. Often, a main show is developed and a number of different presentations based on the main show are created. For instance, you may plan for a 40-minute presentation only to find out at the last minute that your time has been cut to 25 minutes. Rather than show all of the slides in the presentation, moving quickly past less important slides, you can create a custom show using only the critical slides. You can also create multiple custom slide shows in a presentation that are linked so that the presentation pulls slides from each. Custom shows enable you to focus your presentation to the needs of your audience.

An alternative to creating a custom show is to designate hidden slides in a slide show. If you only have a few slides to reserve in case they are needed later, hidden slides are an alternative to creating a custom show. As you give your presentation, you can reveal hidden slides within the sequence based on your audience needs and the time constraint. You can also use hidden slides to reveal increasingly detailed slides and complex concepts as needed, or you can skip the slides without the audience being aware that you are skipping material. You will experiment with hiding slides and revealing them as you display a slide show.

In this section, you will learn how to create multiple custom shows from a single presentation and how to run and navigate a custom slide show. Finally, you will designate and display hidden slides.

Creating a Custom Slide Show

In ***basic custom shows***, you select slides from one presentation and then group them to create other presentations, enabling you to adapt a single presentation to a variety of audiences. If your original presentation contains 10 slides, you might designate the first, third, eighth, and tenth slides for one custom show and the first, fifth, and sixth slides for another. The original presentation contains all of the slides needed in the custom shows.

STEP 1 ❯❯   To create a custom show, do the following:

1. Click the SLIDE SHOW tab.
2. Click Custom Slide Show in the Start Slide Show group.
3. Select Custom Shows.
4. Click New.
5. Type a name in the *Slide show name* box.
6. Click the slide you want to include in the custom show and click Add.
7. Continue adding slides and click OK.
8. Repeat Steps 4 through 7 to create additional custom shows.

Figure 7.29 shows the Custom Shows dialog box and the Define Custom Show dialog box that opens when you click New. The dialog boxes have been rearranged so they are both visible. The slides in the original presentation are listed in the left pane of the Define Custom Show dialog box and are identified by the slide number and the title of the slide. The slides in the custom show are listed in the right pane and are numbered based on their position in the new show.

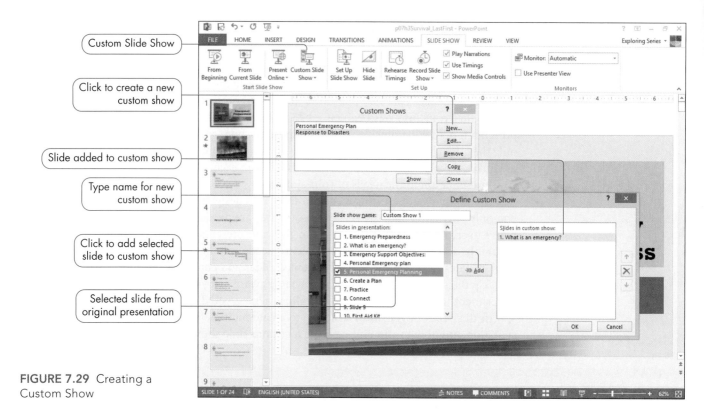

Labels on figure (left to right / top to bottom):
- Custom Slide Show
- Click to create a new custom show
- Slide added to custom show
- Type name for new custom show
- Click to add selected slide to custom show
- Selected slide from original presentation

FIGURE 7.29 Creating a Custom Show

Hyperlinked custom shows connect a main custom show to other custom shows using hyperlinks. For example, you might be giving a presentation to a group of potential students who are exploring college majors. One slide in your presentation could have links to parts of your slide show that discuss individual majors. After you quickly poll your audience, you find that everyone is interested in hearing you talk about the nursing major, while half are interested in the business major, and only one or two people want to hear about the other programs. As you present the hyperlinked show, you can decide whether to branch to the supporting shows containing other program information or not. To create a hyperlinked custom show, all of the slides must be in the same presentation. This presentation is then divided into custom shows. A hyperlinked custom show might include 10 slides from the main presentation, 3 slides from another part of the show, and 5 slides from yet another.

Create the main custom slide show, as previously described, by opening the presentation and selecting the slides that will be in the main show. Name this custom show with a unique name, such as Proposal_Links, so that you will be able to identify it later as the show that contains the hyperlinks. Create the supporting custom slide shows, as described, by selecting slides from the presentation and naming each show with a different name.

> ### TIP Main Custom Show
>
> Name the basic custom slide show with the word *Main* or *Major* as part of the name to make it easy to identify. For instance, a cooking hyperlinked custom show might be called Main Vegetable Presentation. The supporting custom slide shows might be named Cooking Beans, Peeling Tomatoes, or Roasting Vegetables.

After you create all of the custom shows, click the Home tab to return to the original presentation, if necessary. Use the Slide Thumbnail pane to select the slide in the main custom slide show that contains the hyperlinks.

1. Select the text or other object that you plan to click to view the supporting slides.
2. Click the INSERT tab and click Hyperlink in the Links group.

3. Click *Place in This Document* in the Insert Hyperlink dialog box, as shown in Figure 7.30.
4. Scroll to the bottom of the slide list where the Custom Shows list begins and click the name of the support slide show. A preview of the first slide in that show will appear in the Slide preview box.
5. Click the *Show and return* check box so that the supporting slide show will return to the main show after all of the slides have been shown.
6. Repeat these steps to set up the remaining hyperlinks.

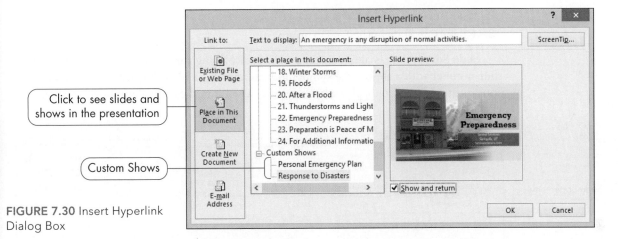

Click to see slides and shows in the presentation

Custom Shows

FIGURE 7.30 Insert Hyperlink Dialog Box

Running and Navigating a Custom Slide Show

STEP 3 »

The presentation file must be saved so that the custom show remains a subset of it. Then display the custom show from the beginning or at any time while showing the main show. To show the basic custom slide show from the beginning, do the following:

1. Open the presentation and click the SLIDE SHOW tab.
2. Click Custom Slide Show.
3. Click the name of the custom show you wish to present.

The show will begin automatically. To show the custom show during the display of the main show, right-click and select Custom Show. Then, select the title of the custom show you wish to display.

To show the hyperlinked presentation, do the following:

1. Open the presentation.
2. Click the SLIDE SHOW tab.
3. Click Custom Slide Show.
4. Select the name of the main custom slide show.

The custom presentation will begin. When a slide is reached that contains a hyperlink, click the hyperlink and continue through the supporting slides. Advance through all of the supporting slides and return to the main custom slide. Select another hyperlink if one appears on this slide or continue displaying the slides in the main custom slide show.

Designating and Displaying Hidden Slides

Although custom shows fit many needs, in some cases you may prefer to skip detailed slides in the main presentation and only show them if the audience requests additional information. Hiding slides within the sequence of the presentation depends on your ability to anticipate what your audience might ask. For example, a presentation on budgeting might include slides that speak of the budgeting process as a concept. Your audience might ask to see some actual numbers plugged into a budget. If you anticipate this question, you can create a slide with this information and hide it within the presentation. During the presentation, if no one asks to see numbers in a budget, you continue through the slide show. But if someone asks, you can show the hidden slide, and then continue through the presentation. The next time you make a presentation, the slide will again be hidden.

STEP 2

To hide a slide, do the following:

1. Select the slide you want to hide in the Slide Sorter view or in the Slides pane in Normal view.
2. Click the SLIDE SHOW tab.
3. Click Hide Slide in the Set Up group.

Slide Sorter view is active in Figure 7.31, displaying three slide numbers followed by a slide number with a slash—the symbol indicating that a slide is hidden. The thumbnail also appears grayed out. To display a hidden slide, select it in the Slide Thumbnail pane and click Hide Slide again.

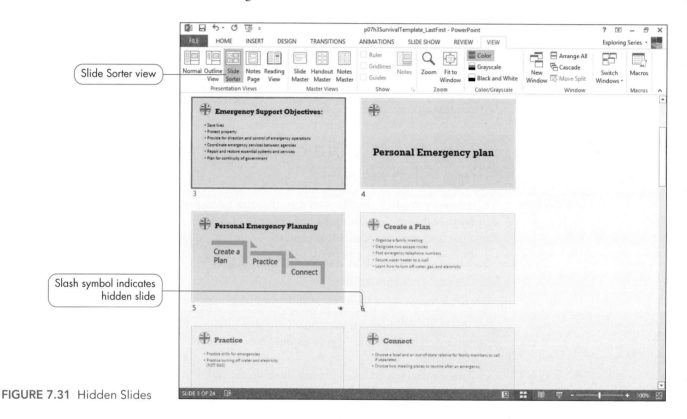

FIGURE 7.31 Hidden Slides

During the presentation, when you arrive at the location of the hidden slide, you reveal the slide by pressing H.

TIP Display a Specific Slide in Slide Show View

While in Slide Show view, if you know the slide number of a hidden slide, type the number on the keyboard and press Enter to display it. Any slide in the slide show, not just hidden slides, can be quickly displayed using this method.

As you print your slide presentation, you may decide to print the hidden slides or not. The Backstage Print view contains a check box to designate whether to print the hidden slides. It is a good idea to print the hidden slides on the notes pages for the presenter. This way, as the speech is being delivered, the presenter is reminded of the hidden slide and its content.

Quick
Concepts

1. What is the main advantage of creating a custom show? *p. 453*

2. Explain why you might want to create a hyperlinked custom show. *p. 454*

3. You decide that you want to be alerted to any hidden slides as you give your presentation. How can you print hidden slides? *p. 457*

Hands-On Exercises

 Watch the Video for this Hands-On Exercise!

 MyITLab® HOE3 Training

3 Custom Shows

The main slide show for Survival Solutions was designed so that you can create custom shows based on it to allow flexibility while presenting. You can present a custom show on how to prepare for emergencies or a custom show on responses to specific disasters depending upon audience questions and feedback. The slide show also contains several general slides that can be followed up with reserved slides containing greater detail. You will hide the detail slides and then practice navigating custom shows and displaying hidden slides.

Skills covered: Create a Custom Slide Show • Designate and Display Hidden Slides • Run and Navigate a Custom Slide Show

---

STEP 1 ≫ CREATE A CUSTOM SLIDE SHOW

You create two custom slide shows based on the main Survival Solutions presentation so that you can select the show that best meets your audience's interests. Refer to Figure 7.32 as you complete Step 1.

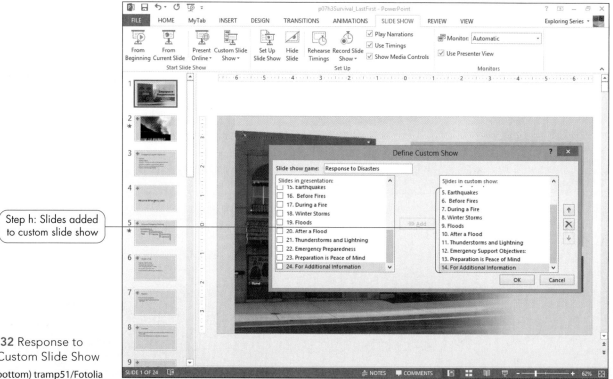

Step h: Slides added to custom slide show

FIGURE 7.32 Response to Disasters Custom Slide Show

Photo: (left, bottom) tramp51/Fotolia

a. Open *p07h2Survival_LastFirst*, if necessary, and save the presentation as **p07h3Survival_LastFirst**, changing *h2* to *h3*.

> **TROUBLESHOOTING:** Be sure you start with the correct file. Start with the Survival file, not the SurvivalTemplate file.

b. Click the **SLIDE SHOW tab** and click **Custom Slide Show** in the Start Slide Show group.

c. Select **Custom Shows** and click **New**.

The Define Custom Show dialog box opens.

d. Type **Personal Emergency Plan** in the **Slide show name box**.

e. Select **Slides 1 through 14** and **Slides 23** and **24**. Click **Add**.

Slides 1 through 14, 23, and 24 are added to the custom show. The slides are renumbered in the custom show.

> **TROUBLESHOOTING:** If you select the wrong slide, click the name of the slide on the right side of the Define Custom Show dialog box and click Remove.

f. Click **OK**.

g. Click **New** and type **Response to Disasters** in the **Slide show name box**.

h. Add the following slides in this order: 1, 2, 14, 22, 15 through 21, 3, 23, and 24.

i. Click **OK** and click **Close**.

j. Save the presentation.

STEP 2 ›› DESIGNATE AND DISPLAY HIDDEN SLIDES

To allow for differing presentation times and audience interest, you will hide slides showing detailed personal emergency planning (Slides 6–8) and storage recommendations (Slides 10–13). If time allows, you will display these slides.

a. Select the **Slide 6 thumbnail**.

b. Click the **SLIDE SHOW tab**, if necessary, and click **Hide Slide** in the Set Up group.

A slash appears through the number for the slide in the Slides tab.

c. Hide Slides 7, 8, and 10 through 13.

> **TROUBLESHOOTING:** If you hide a slide by mistake, select the slide and click Hide Slide in the Set Up group on the Slide Show tab again.

d. Click the **VIEW tab** and click **Slide Sorter** in the Presentation Views group.

Slide Sorter view displays the Hide Slide symbol on Slides 6 through 8 and 10 through 13.

e. Click **Normal**. Save the presentation.

STEP 3 ›› RUN AND NAVIGATE A CUSTOM SLIDE SHOW

To check slide order and practice displaying custom slide shows and hidden slides, you view the Personal Emergency Plan custom show.

a. Click the **SLIDE SHOW tab** and click **Custom Slide Show**.

b. Select **Personal Emergency Plan**.

c. Advance through the presentation until you reach the *Personal Emergency Planning* SmartArt diagram.

d. Click **H** on the keyboard.

Slide 6 displays, followed by Slides 7 and 8, all of which are part of a hidden sequence of slides. Then the next nonhidden slide displays, and the slide show advances through all remaining nonhidden slides. If additional hidden slides follow after this sequence, they can be displayed by pressing H on the keyboard, as in step d.

e. Advance to the end of the presentation and exit the slide show.

f. Save and close the file, and submit based on your instructor's directions.

Chapter Objectives Review

After reading this chapter, you have accomplished the following objectives:

1. **Set PowerPoint options.**
   - Set PowerPoint's options to meet your individual needs and maximize your productivity.
   - You can set options such as general working environment preferences, proofing, saving, working with languages, customizing, and many more.

2. **Customize the Ribbon.**
   - Customize the Ribbon to efficiently access PowerPoint features.
   - Create custom tabs with new groups displaying the features you use most often in one location, or move buttons and groups within the existing groups.

3. **Use Combine Shapes commands.**
   - PowerPoint includes a set of commands that are useful when working with shapes: Combine, Intersect, Subtract, and Union.
   - Combine removes the overlapping area of two shapes.
   - Intersect removes any area that is not overlapped.
   - Subtract removes the shape of the second selected object from the area of the first object.
   - Union joins selected overlapping objects so they become one shape.
   - You can only access these commands by adding them to an existing tab or by creating a new tab.

4. **Modify handout and notes masters.**
   - Masters control the consistency of your presentations, notes, and handouts.
   - A handout master controls the layout and formatting of audience handout pages.
   - The notes master controls the design information for notes pages.
   - You can customize these masters so that your printouts provide the information you want to display in the position that is most advantageous.

5. **Modify a slide master.**
   - A slide master controls the design elements and slide layouts associated with the slides in a presentation.
   - Slide layouts include a title slide layout, various content slide layouts, and a blank slide layout.
   - The layout designates the location of placeholders and other objects on the slide as well as formatting information.

6. **Save a slide master as a template.**
   - After you modify a slide master, you can save the file as a template so that you can reuse the slide master with any presentation.
   - PowerPoint saves the master as a template with an extension of .potx and retains the changes in the file.

7. **Create a custom slide show.**
   - Once a slide show is developed, you can create a number of custom slide shows based on subsets of slides from the original show.
   - Creating custom shows enables you to keep all the shows you need for various audiences within one file.
   - You can display the custom show that relates to your audience's interests.

8. **Run and navigate a custom slide show.**
   - Display a custom show from its beginning, at any time while showing the main show, or by clicking a hyperlink.
   - To show the basic custom slide show from the beginning, open the presentation, click the Slide Show tab, click Custom Slide Show, and then click the name of the custom show you wish to present. The show begins automatically.
   - To show the custom show during the main slide show, right-click and select Custom Show. Then select the title of the custom show you wish to display.
   - To display a hyperlinked custom slide show, click a link on a slide displayed during the main slide show.

9. **Designate and display hidden slides.**
   - You can create and hold slides on reserve in anticipation of audience questions. You can then hide the slide with the reserved or detailed information until the appropriate time during the presentation.
   - While presenting in Slide Show view, display a hidden slide by pressing H on the keyboard.

Key Terms Matching

Match the key terms with their definitions. Write the key term letter by the appropriate numbered definition.

<table>
<tr><td>a.</td><td>Basic custom show</td><td>j.</td><td>Master</td></tr>
<tr><td>b.</td><td>Color theme</td><td>k.</td><td>Notes master</td></tr>
<tr><td>c.</td><td>Combine</td><td>l.</td><td>PowerPoint Options</td></tr>
<tr><td>d.</td><td>Custom show</td><td>m.</td><td>.potx</td></tr>
<tr><td>e.</td><td>Customize Ribbon tab</td><td>n.</td><td>.pptx</td></tr>
<tr><td>f.</td><td>Handout master</td><td>o.</td><td>RGB</td></tr>
<tr><td>g.</td><td>HSL</td><td>p.</td><td>Slide master</td></tr>
<tr><td>h.</td><td>Hyperlinked custom show</td><td>q.</td><td>Subtract</td></tr>
<tr><td>i.</td><td>Intersect</td><td>r.</td><td>Union</td></tr>
</table>

1. _____ A grouped subset of the slides in a presentation. **p. 453**

2. _____ A color model in which the numeric system refers to the hue, saturation, and luminosity of a color. **p. 441**

3. _____ A Combine Shapes command that removes the shape of the second selected object from the area of the first object. **p. 426**

4. _____ The top slide in a hierarchy of slides that contains design information for the slides. **p. 436**

5. _____ The file extension assigned to a PowerPoint template. **p. 442**

6. _____ A numeric system for identifying the color resulting from the combination of red, green, and blue light. **p. 441**

7. _____ Contains the design information for audience handout pages. **p. 434**

8. _____ Consists of the color combinations for the text, lines, background, and graphics in a presentation. **p. 441**

9. _____ A Combine Shapes command that joins selected overlapping objects so they become one shape. **p. 426**

10. _____ Begins with a main custom show and uses hyperlinks to link between other shows. **p. 454**

11. _____ A broad range of settings that enable you to customize the environment to meet your needs. **p. 420**

12. _____ A Combine Shapes command that removes any area that is not overlapped. **p. 426**

13. _____ The file extension assigned to a PowerPoint presentation. **p. 422**

14. _____ Contains the design information for notes pages. **p. 436**

15. _____ A single presentation file from which you can create separate presentations. **p. 453**

16. _____ Contains design information that provides a consistent look to your presentation, handouts, and notes pages. **p. 434**

17. _____ A tab in the PowerPoint Options dialog box that enables you to create a personal tab on the Ribbon that includes features that are not available on the standard Ribbon. **p. 423**

18. _____ A Combine Shapes command that removes the overlapping area of two shapes. **p. 426**

Multiple Choice

1. Which of the following options can be changed in the General options within PowerPoint Options?

   (a) Image Size and Quality
   (b) User name
   (c) AutoCorrect
   (d) Customize Ribbon

2. Which of the following statements is not true regarding customizing the Ribbon?

   (a) All available PowerPoint commands are displayed on the default Ribbon.
   (b) Custom tabs and groups can be added to the Ribbon.
   (c) Tabs and groups can be renamed.
   (d) Commands can be removed from one tab and added to another.

3. The Intersect Shapes command performs which of the following functions?

   (a) Unites selected overlapping objects so they become one shape
   (b) Removes the overlapping area of two selected shapes
   (c) Removes the shape of a second selected object from the area of the first selected object
   (d) Removes any area of two selected objects that is not overlapped

4. By default, notes masters contain:

   (a) Three slide thumbnails per page.
   (b) Only a slide thumbnail and note text.
   (c) A note text, date, header, and footer.
   (d) A header, date, slide thumbnail, note text, footer, and page number.

5. Which of the following is not a true statement regarding a slide master?

   (a) A slide master controls the position of the slide thumbnail in handouts and note pages.
   (b) A slide master saved as a template can be used with multiple presentations.
   (c) A slide master is the top slide in a hierarchy of slides that stores design information and slide layouts.
   (d) A presentation can contain more than one slide master.

6. Which of the following is not a true statement about slide layouts associated with a slide master?

   (a) Slide layouts can be renamed or deleted.
   (b) Slide layouts contain the same theme (color scheme, fonts, and effects) as the slide master.
   (c) Slide layouts cannot be modified by adding additional placeholders.
   (d) Slide layouts can use either portrait or landscape orientation.

7. Custom slide shows are:

   (a) Multiple presentation files with slides copied from a main presentation file.
   (b) Subsets of slides saved in a presentation file.
   (c) Shows with a modified slide master.
   (d) Shells for building presentations.

8. Custom slide shows cannot contain:

   (a) Slides that are not a part of the original presentation.
   (b) Hyperlinks to other slide shows.
   (c) Hidden slides.
   (d) More than 10 slides.

9. Custom slide shows can be viewed using all of the following methods except by:

   (a) Clicking the SLIDE SHOW tab, clicking Custom Slide Show, and then clicking the name of the custom show.
   (b) Right-clicking in Slide Show view, selecting Custom Show, and then selecting the name of the custom show.
   (c) Pressing Ctrl+C while in Slide Show view and selecting the name of the custom show.
   (d) Clicking a hyperlink on a slide while in Slide Show view.

10. Which of the following statements is not true about hidden slides?

    (a) A hidden slide does not show when you advance from one slide to another when displaying a slide show.
    (b) A hidden slide is created using Hide Slide in the Set Up group on the SLIDE SHOW tab.
    (c) A hidden slide cannot be used during a custom slide show.
    (d) A hidden slide can be revealed when displaying a slide show by pressing H.

Practice Exercises

1 Mountain Biking Presentation

You are preparing a presentation to a local youth group about mountain bike safety and general mountain biking rules of the trail. You want the title slide to include a mountain scene with a mountain bike popping up on a trail. To begin, you will change PowerPoint options to include an AutoCorrect phrase for efficiency and to change the AutoRecover time to five minutes. You will modify the Ribbon structure you created in Hands-on Exercise 1 to add positioning features. You will use PowerPoint's Combine Shapes feature to complete the mountain scene, and then you will add and position a clip art image of a mountain bike. Finally, you will enter sample text in the title slide text and a content slide so you can view the finished handouts and notes masters. This exercise follows the same set of skills used in Hands-On Exercise 1. Refer to Figure 7.33 as you complete this exercise.

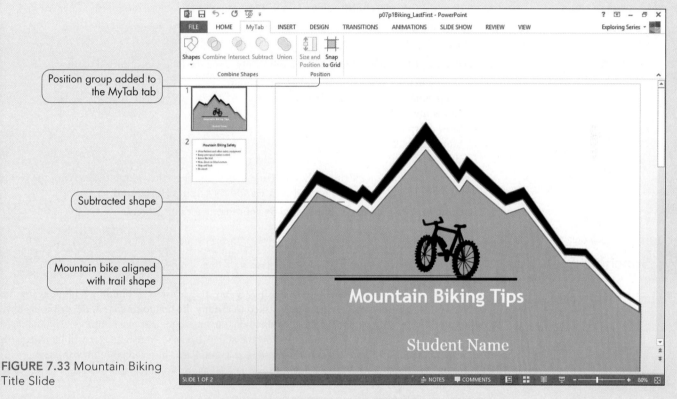

FIGURE 7.33 Mountain Biking Title Slide

a. Open *p07p1Biking* and save it as **p07p1Biking_LastFirst.pptx**.

b. Create a handout header with your name and a handout footer with the file name, your instructor's name, and your class. Include the current date.

c. Click the **FILE tab**, click **Options**, and then click **Proofing**.

d. Click **AutoCorrect Options** and click the **AutoCorrect tab**, if necessary. Type **mb** in the **Replace box** and type **Mountain Biking** in the **With box**. Click **OK**.

e. Click **Save** in the left pane, select the number in the *Save AutoRecover information every* box, and then type **5**.

f. Click **Customize Ribbon** and click **MyTab (Custom)**.

> **TROUBLESHOOTING:** If you do not have a tab named MyTab (Custom), complete Hands-On Exercise 1, Step 3.

g. Click **New Group** and click **Rename**. Type **Position** in the **Display name box** and click **OK**.

h. Select **Size and Position** in the Popular Commands list and click **Add**.

i. Click the **Choose commands from arrow** and select **Commands Not in the Ribbon**.

j. Select **Snap to Grid** and click **Add**. Click **OK**.

k. Select the **black mountain shape**, press and hold **Shift**, and then click the **orange shape** to add it to the selection. Click the **MyTab tab** and click **Subtract** in the Combine Shapes group. A jagged white line now exists where the orange shape was cut out of the black mountain shape.

l. Click the **INSERT tab**, click **Online Pictures**, type **mountain bike** in the **Office.com Clip Art box**, and then press **Enter**. Insert the clip art image shown in Figure 7.33 or another image if it is not available.

m. Drag the back wheel of the mountain bike clip art as close to the straight black trail line as possible. If the grid setting does not enable you to align the back tire with the trail, click the **MyTab tab** and click **Snap to Grid** in the Position group to deactivate it. Drag the image until the back wheel aligns with the trail line. Resize the image as desired.

n. Click in the **title placeholder** and type **mb Tips**. AutoCorrect replaces *mb* with *Mountain Biking*.

o. Type your name in the **subtitle placeholder**.

p. Add a new slide using the *Title and Content* layout.

q. Click in the **title placeholder** and type **mb Safety**. Type the following bulleted points:

- **Wear a helmet and use other safety equipment.**
- **Keep your speed under control.**
- **Know the trail.**
- **Slow down on blind corners.**
- **Stop and look.**
- **Be smart.**

r. Click the **FILE tab**, click **Print**, click **Full Page Slides**, and then click **Notes Pages**. View the Notes Pages preview. Click **Notes Pages** and click **Handouts 4 Slides Horizontal**.

s. Save and close the file, and submit based on your instructor's directions.

2 Sunshine Buildings

Your manager prepared a presentation discussing the positive features of building a home using the services of Sunshine Builders. You have been asked to modify the handouts so that the printouts have two slides per page and contain the date, company name and logo, and page number. The manager would also like the company name and logo on the slides. Because your manager will be using this same format in the future, you will save the masters as a template. This exercise follows the same set of skills as used in Hands-On Exercise 2. Refer to Figure 7.34 as you complete this exercise.

FIGURE 7.34 Handout Master

a. Open a new blank presentation and save it as **p07p2Sunshine_LastFirst.pptx**.

b. Click the **VIEW tab** and click **Handout Master** in the Master Views group.

c. Click **Slides Per Page** in the Page Setup group and select **4 Slides**.

d. Deselect the **Header check box** in the Placeholders group.

e. Select the **Page Number placeholder**, click the **MyTab tab**, and then click **Size and Position** in the Position group.

f. Set the following in the Format Shape pane and close the pane:
   - Size: Height **0.5"**, Width **1"**.
   - Position: Horizontal **3.25"** from the Top Left Corner, Vertical **9.5"** from the Top Left Corner.
   - Text Box: Vertical alignment **Top Centered**.

g. Drag the **date placeholder** to the bottom-right corner of the page, aligning its bottom border with the bottom edge of the page and the right border with the right edge of the page.

h. Click the **INSERT tab**, click **WordArt** in the Text group, click **Fill - Gold, Accent 4, Soft Bevel** (first row, fifth column), and then type **Sunshine Builders**. Drag the WordArt to the top-left corner of the page, aligning its top border with the top edge of the page and the left border with the left edge of the page.

i. Click the **INSERT tab**, click **Online Pictures** in the Images group, type **solar panel** in the **Office .com Clip Art box**, and then press **Enter**. Insert the image shown in Figure 7.34.

j. Click the **MyTab tab** and click **Size and Position** in the Position group. Set the following in the Format Picture pane and close the pane:
   - Size: Height **0.75"**, Width **0.75"**.
   - Position: Horizontal **5.75"** from the Top Left Corner, Vertical **0.1"** from the Top Left Corner.

k. Select the WordArt and clip art image, click the **HOME tab**, and then click **Copy** in the Clipboard group.

l. Click the **VIEW tab** and click **Notes Master** in the Master Views group. Deselect the **Header** and **Date check boxes** in the Placeholders group.

m. Click the **HOME tab** and click the **Clipboard Dialog Box launcher** to open the Clipboard. Point to the WordArt and clip art in the list, click the arrow, and then click **Paste**. Deselect the objects. Close the Clipboard.

n. Select the WordArt, change the font size to **48 pt**, and then drag the placeholder upward until it aligns with the left edge of the slide and is centered in the available vertical white space above the slide thumbnail.

o. Select the clip art image, click the **MyTab tab**, and then click **Size and Position** in the Position group. Set the following in the Format Picture pane and close the pane:
   - Size: Height **0.6"**, Width **0.6"**.
   - Position: Horizontal **5.75"** from the Top Left Corner, Vertical **0.25"** from the Top Left Corner.

p. Click the **VIEW tab**, click **Slide Master** in the Master Views group, and then paste the WordArt and the clip art on the Office Theme Slide Master.

q. Drag the WordArt and clip art to the top-left corner of the slide so the top border of the selection touches the top of the slide and the left border of the selection touches the left border of the slide. Close the Clipboard.

r. Select the **Master title styles placeholder**, set the following in the Format Shape pane, and then close the pane:
   - Size: Height **1.25"**, Width **8"**.
   - Position: Horizontal **1.33"** from the Top Left Corner, Vertical **1.08"** from the Top Left Corner.

s. Select the **Master text placeholder**, set the following in the Format Shape pane, and then close the pane:
   - Size: Height **4.3"**, Width **8"**.
   - Position: Horizontal **1.33"** from the Top Left Corner, Vertical **2.42"** from the Top Left Corner.

t. Click the **FILE tab** and click **Save As**. Click **Computer** and click **Browse**. Click the **Save as type arrow** and select **PowerPoint Template**. Navigate to the location where you save your solution files and name the file **p07p2SunshineTemplate_LastFirst**. Click **Save**.

u. Close the slide master. On Slide 1, type **Build Your Dream Home** in the **title placeholder** and your name in the **subtitle placeholder**. Type the following text in the notes pane: **Sunshine Builders is well known as one of the premier custom home builders in the Valley area. If innovative design, distinctive quality, and impressive value are important to you, we are your builder!**

v. Create a handout header with your name and a handout footer with the file name, your instructor's name, and your class. Include the current date.

w. Create a new slide using the *Title and Content* layout. Type **Floor Plans** in the **text placeholder** and enter the following as bullets: **Ashville, Berkeley, Cassidy, Drayton, Grayson**.

x. Add the following text in the notes pane: **One of the most exciting parts of your home-building experience is selecting your floor plan. Our floor plans reflect today's design trends.**

y. Click the **FILE tab**, click **Print**, and then click **Full Page Slides**. Click **Notes Pages** and note the preview of the printed notes pages. Click **Notes Pages** and click **2 Slides (Handouts)**. Note the preview of the handout.

z. Click **Save As**, locate *p07p2Sunshine_LastFirst.pptx*, and then click **Save**, being careful not to save the presentation over the template file. Close the file, and submit based on your instructor's directions.

3 Luxury Estates Presentation

You are a realtor selling luxury country estates. This week, you have appointments with two potential customers, so you will create a presentation using recent photographs and information about the estates you personally selected as being the most suitable. You will create custom shows for each customer including a slide personalizing the show and slides highlighting the estates. You will hide slides with cost information on each estate so they can be shown if the customer expresses an interest in the property. This exercise follows the same set of skills as used in Hands-On Exercise 3. Refer to Figure 7.35 as you complete this exercise.

FIGURE 7.35 Luxury Estates Presentation

Photos: (Slide 1) xy/Fotolia, (Slide 5, left) pics721/Fotolia, (Slide 5, right) Iriana Shiyan/Fotolia

a. Open *p07p3Luxury* and save it as **p07p3Luxury_LastFirst**.

b. Create a handout header with your name and a handout footer with your instructor's name and your class. Include the current date.

c. Click the **SLIDE SHOW tab** and click **Custom Slide Show** in the Start Slide Show group. Select **Custom Shows** and click **New**.

d. Type **Roberts** in the **Slide show name box**.

e. Select **Slides 1, 2, 4, 5, 6, 10, 11, 12**, and **19**, click **Add**, and then click **OK**.

f. Click **New** and type **Lewis** in the **Slide show name box**.

g. Select **Slides 1, 3, 7, 8, 9, 13, 14, 15, 16, 17, 18**, and **19**, click **Add**, and then click **OK**. Click **Close**.

h. Select **Slides 6, 9, 12, 15**, and **18** in the Slides pane and click **Hide Slide** in the Set Up group.

i. Click the **SLIDE SHOW tab** if necessary, click **Custom Slide Show** in the Start Slide Show tab, and then click **Roberts**.

j. Advance to Slide 5 and press **H** on the keyboard to reveal Slide 6, which is a hidden slide. Advance to the end of the presentation and exit. Repeat with the Lewis show. Advance to Slide 8 and press **H** on the keyboard to reveal Slide 9, which is a hidden slide.

k. Save and close the file, and submit based on your instructor's directions.

1 Family Reunion

You are creating a PowerPoint presentation for a family reunion and have asked family members to provide a picture labeled with names, recent family information, and the connection to your great-grandfather. You will modify PowerPoint options and the Ribbon to put the tools you need on one tab, and then combine shapes to create a family logo. You will include the logo on the handout, notes, and slide masters to create a theme. You will also modify the slide master with your preferences for a font scheme and color scheme and create three new slide layouts. You will save your work as a template so others may use it.

a. Open a blank presentation and save it as **p07m1Reunion_LastFirst.pptx**.

b. Set PowerPoint options to save AutoRecover information every **15 minutes** (Save option) and to set the default target output to **150 ppi** (Advanced option), if necessary.

c. Customize the Ribbon to put the buttons you use most on one custom tab with groups. You can modify the MyTab tab you created in previous exercises or reset the Ribbon to its original state and create a new tab with groups.

 d. Click the **Title box** and type **Our Family Reunion**. Click the **subtitle box** and add your name. Search for a clip art image using a key term such as *family* to use as your logo. After finding your logo, position it in the bottom-right corner of the slide. Copy it to the Clipboard.

e. Modify the handout and notes masters to include your logo in the position of your choice. Make at least one change to the placeholders (e.g., location, font, size) and make any other changes.

f. Display the slide master. Create a new Color theme by modifying at least two theme colors. Then, create a new Font theme by selecting a new Heading font.

g. Select the **Title Slide Layout** and insert and position a 4" by 6" picture placeholder on the slide for your great-grandfather's image. Apply a **Shape Style** as desired. Rearrange or reformat the title and subtitle placeholders to fit on the empty area of the slide.

h. Replace the title text with **Enter Great-Grandfather's Name**. Replace the subtitle text with **Enter reunion date, time, and location**.

i. Remove the date and page number placeholders from the title slide layout. Make additional design changes as desired.

j. Replace the text in the footer placeholder with your family name and the word *Reunion*. Use the *Header and Footer* dialog box on the INSERT tab to apply the footer to the title slide layout only.

k. Delete all other slide layouts. Insert a new slide layout named **Family Information**.

l. Remove the footer, date, and page number placeholders from the Family Information slide layout. Add a text placeholder that fills the blank space of the slide.

m. Copy the Family Information slide and paste it on the Slide Thumbnail pane. Rename the slide layout **Family Relationship**.

n. Remove the title and text placeholders on the Family Relationship slide layout. Insert a SmartArt placeholder that fills the blank space of the slide. Select the SmartArt options you desire.

o. Add animations and transitions as desired.

p. Click the **FILE tab** and click **Save As**. Click the **Save as type arrow** and select **PowerPoint Template**. Navigate to where you are saving your files. Name the file **p07m1ReunionTemplate_LastFirst**, and then click **Save**.

q. Click the **Slide Master tab** and click **Close Master View** in the Close group.

 r. Create a Title slide, a Family Information slide, and a Family Relationship slide using your own family information and photo or using a clip art family image and an imaginary family.

s. Create a handout header with your name and a handout footer with your instructor's name and your class. Include the current date.

t. Save the file as **p07m1Reunion_LastFirst.pptx**, being careful to save over the presentation file and not the template file. Close the presentation and submit based on your instructor's directions.

2 PTA Fundraising Shows

The PTA at the elementary school has quarterly meetings where discussions focus on plans for fundraising throughout the year. At the beginning of the year, all of the plans are put into a presentation. Two presentations cover the plans for each fundraising project. The slides contain the project description, dates, and committee assignments. One slide details the budget and is hidden during the general member meeting and displayed to the PTA board meeting. You create two custom shows that contain the title slide, the slides pertaining to the most recent project and the next project, the budget slide, and a thank-you slide.

a. Open *p07m2PTA* and save it as **p07m2PTA_LastFirst**.

b. Create a handout header with your name and a handout footer with your instructor's name and your class. Include the current date.

c. Create a custom show named **Fall Projects** using Slides 1 through 6 and 9 through 11.

d. Create a custom show named **Winter Projects** using Slides 1, 2, and 5 through 11.

e. Hide Slide 10.

f. Display the Fall Projects custom show. Show the hidden slide.

g. Display the Winter Projects custom show. Show the hidden slide.

DISCOVER

h. Use the Set Up Slide Show dialog box to display the Winter Projects custom slide show. Also set the Laser pointer color to **green**.

i. Display the entire presentation. Use the Laser pointer to draw attention to details on slides.

j. Save and close the file, and submit based on your instructor's directions.

3 Red Cliff City Agenda

COLLABORATION
CASE

As the administrative clerk for the mayor of the city, you are responsible for preparing a PowerPoint agenda presentation for every city council meeting. Because this is a task that encompasses several departments, you rely on other administrative clerks to provide pertinent information. The title slide includes meeting details, and each agenda item is listed on a single slide with the name of the person responsible for the discussion of this item. Another type of slide contains additional resources related to the agenda item, such as text, graphics, or SmartArt. You will create a slide master template so that the structure of the presentation is prepared. You will create the design of the slide master to match the city's colors and include the city logo. Each administrative clerk is responsible for providing information to you. This can be accomplished using Outlook or OneDrive. After saving the master as a template named **p07m3AgendaTemplate**, all you will have to do prior to the meeting is to put the information in the presentation using the template. Save the file as **p07m3Agenda_LastFirst**. Submit both files based on your instructor's directions.

Beyond the Classroom

Nurse Presentation

RESEARCH CASE

FROM SCRATCH

As a nurse practitioner with the Lindenberg Health Department, you spend a few hours each week talking to small groups. One week you might talk to senior citizens, and the next week you may be presenting to the faculty of the elementary school. Popular topics in the winter are colds, flu, bronchitis, and pneumonia. Most groups request information on the symptoms of these illnesses and ways to prevent getting them. After your research, you develop a presentation that contains information that will be useful to all of these groups. Use your knowledge of slide masters to create appropriate layouts. Use illustrations, images, sounds, video, animation, and transitions as appropriate. You realize that elementary school students probably are not interested in bronchitis and pneumonia, so create a custom slide show on colds and flu for this audience. Save your presentation file as **p07b2Nurse_LastFirst.pptx**.

Templates Gone Haywire

DISASTER RECOVERY

Your 14-year-old brother has been working on a presentation for his science class. He tried revising a design template but has become confused. His handouts print with a blue background, he gets blank pages when he tries to view notes pages, and the animation and transitions he applied create a mixed-up jumble of words and graphics flying all over the screen. You sit down with him and help him with the templates. You correct the handout master so that the background is white. You revise the notes page master so the placeholders necessary to display the header, slide image, and body appear, as well as the footer and page number. You make adjustments to the animations and transitions so they enhance the slide show rather than distract the audience. Open *p07b3Corrections*, make the necessary revisions, and then save it as **p07b3Corrections_LastFirst**.

Planning and Managing Your Career

SOFT SKILLS CASE

FROM SCRATCH

You will create a customized presentation that will help other students plan for and manage their careers. Create a slide that lists at least three common strategies for planning and managing careers. Suggest responses for each strategy on a separate slide, and then create a custom show for three different planning scenarios. Save and close the presentation, and submit based on your instructor's directions.

Capstone Exercise

As a volunteer docent at the Bayside Park Conservatory, you learned about plants and their care. You have specialized knowledge of exotic plants and roses. You have studied both in classes at the university. The volunteer supervisor recently observed you as you led a group through the conservatory. She approached you and requested that you speak at various gardening guild meetings throughout the state. In this capstone exercise, you will create a custom presentation demonstrating the skills learned in this chapter.

Set PowerPoint Options and Customize the Ribbon

The computer you are assigned to use while at the conservatory is one you have not used before. The person using it before you had set custom options and made Ribbon changes. You decide to change the PowerPoint Options to fit your needs, reset the Ribbon to its original state, and then customize the Ribbon to meet your needs.

a. Create a new blank presentation and save it as **p07c1Gardening_LastFirst**.

b. Create a slide footer that reads **www.bayparkconservatory .org**. Include a slide number on all slides. Do not include the slide footer and slide number on the Title slide.

c. Create a handout header with your name and a handout footer with the instructor's name and your class. Include the current date.

d. Set PowerPoint General options to include your user name and initials, if necessary.

e. Set PowerPoint Save options to AutoRecover information every 5 minutes, to keep the last autosaved version if you close without saving, and to embed fonts.

f. Reset all customizations on the Ribbon.

g. Add a custom group following the Drawing group in the HOME tab. Name the custom group **Combine Shapes**.

h. Include the following buttons from the *Commands Not in the Ribbon* list in the Combine Shapes group: Combine Shapes, Intersect Shapes, Subtract Shapes, and Union Shapes.

Combine Shapes

To add interest to the title slide, create a custom shape to frame an image of flowers in the garden.

a. Create a Round Same Side Corner Rectangle shape with the following specifications:

- Picture Fill: *p07c1Garden.jpg*.
- Size: Height **1.61"**, Width **8.5"**.
- Position: Horizontal **2.42"** from the Top Left Corner, Vertical **2.33"** from the Top Left Corner.

b. Create a Flowchart: Delay shape using the following specifications:

- Size: Height **5"**, Width **1.42"**.
- Rotation: **270°**.
- Position: Horizontal **5.96"** from the Top Left Corner, Vertical **−0.88"** from the Top Left Corner.

c. Join the rectangle shape and the flowchart shape using Union.

d. Copy the two shapes to the Clipboard.

Modify Masters and Save the Template

You decide that the frame you created belongs on the Title Slide Master. You will cut the frame from the title slide and paste it on the Title Slide Master. Then you will change the Color theme, format the master title style as WordArt, and modify the master subtitle text. Next, you will modify the handout master and the notes master. You will save the presentation as a template for reuse with other presentations.

a. Cut the frame group from the Title slide, switch to Slide Master view, and then paste the frame and flower image on the Title Slide Master.

b. Apply the **Cambria font theme**.

c. Apply the **Blue Warm color theme**. Then modify the theme by creating new theme colors using the following specifications:

Element	Red	Green	Blue
Text/Background - Dark 1	0	24	0
Text/Background - Light 1	242	242	242
Text/Background - Dark 2	0	72	0
Text/Background - Light 2	250	250	250
Accent 1	103	133	153
Accent 6	251	211	181
Hyperlink	150	210	225
Followed Hyperlink	85	5	80

d. Change the text in the title placeholder to **Place title here**.

e. Change the text in the subtitle placeholder to **Place docent name and e-mail address here**.

f. Format the slide background style using Style 5.

g. Select the **Office Theme Slide Master** and insert *p07c1Rose.png*. Align the bottom edge of the rose border with the top border of the page number placeholder.

h. Apply an **Appear animation** to the title placeholder.

i. Delete all slide layouts except for Title Slide Layout and insert two new slide layouts.

j. Select the first slide layout and rename it **Information**.

k. Replace the text in the title placeholder with **Place title here**.

l. Fill the blank portion of the slide layout with a text placeholder.

m. Select the second slide layout and rename it **Photograph**.

n. Replace the text in the title placeholder with **Place plant name here**.

o. Fill the blank portion of the slide layout with a picture placeholder.

p. Delete the bullet from the picture placeholder and replace the word *Picture* with **Place photograph here**.

q. Hide *Background Graphics* on the Title Slide Master and the Photograph Layout.

r. Apply the **Doors transition** to the Title Slide Master.

s. Switch to the Handout Master view and move the footer placeholder immediately below the header placeholder. Move the page number placeholder immediately below the date placeholder.

t. Insert *p07c1Rose.png* and modify it using the following specifications:

- Size: Height **0.71"**, Width **0.83"**.
- Position: Horizontal **3.33"** from the Top Left Corner, Vertical **0.12"** from the Top Left Corner.

u. Switch to Notes Master view and type **Slide** before the number field in the **page number placeholder**.

v. Close the Notes Master view and save the presentation as a template named **p07c1GardeningTemplate_LastFirst**.

w. Add slides to the presentation by reusing all of the slides in *p07c1Flowers.pptx*.

x. Save the presentation as **p07c1Gardening_LastFirst**, saving over the presentation you began at the beginning of this exercise. Be careful not to save over the template you created.

Set Up and Display Custom Shows

You will create two custom slide shows using a single presentation. Both will contain a title slide, information slides, and photograph slides specific to the slide show.

a. Create a custom show named **Rose Presentation** and use Slides 1, 2, 4 through 8, and 14 through 17.

b. Create a custom show named **Tropical Plants Presentation** and use Slides 1, 3, 9 through 11, and 15 through 17.

c. Display the Rose Presentation custom show.

d. Display the Tropical Plants Presentation custom show.

e. Save the presentation and close the file.

Collaboration and Distribution

CHAPTER 8

Collaborating, Preparing, Securing, and Sharing a Presentation

Konstantin Chagin/Shutterstock

OBJECTIVES AFTER YOU READ THIS CHAPTER, YOU WILL BE ABLE TO:

1. Work with comments and annotations p. 474

2. Show, hide, and print markup p. 476

3. Compare and merge presentations p. 478

4. View presentation properties p. 479

5. Check a presentation for issues p. 487

6. Protect a presentation p. 490

7. Select a presentation file type p. 500

8. Save and share a presentation p. 506

CASE STUDY | The Harbor Business Center

ACSL Development is a large, internationally owned commercial real estate development company specializing in developing properties to serve as business hubs with access to cutting-edge technology. The centers are designed to meet the demands of leading global companies. You are an intern working for the vice president of marketing, Susil Akalushi. Susil has asked you to prepare a presentation under her supervision. The presentation must describe ACSL's latest project, the Harbor Business Center, a $58.5 million, mixed-use project offering luxurious new office space that includes multiperson office suites and one-, two-, or four-person offices. Office suites are finished to a high standard with imported tile, stylish décor, and a sense of spaciousness and comfort. They include state-of-the-art communication technology. Monthly leases offer fully customizable office space, 24-hour access to the office 365 days a year, high security, access to state-of-the-art meeting facilities, and on-site banking and global messenger services. The project is centrally located two blocks from the city harbor area and one block from the state and federal courthouses.

After completing the presentation, you send it to Susil for her review. She reviews your presentation and sends it back to you with comments regarding the changes you need to make. You make the requested changes and prepare the presentation for sharing with other company employees by protecting the presentation and checking it for issues. You package the presentation so that it can be burned to a CD.

Presentation Collaboration

Collaboration is a process by which two or more individuals work together to achieve an outcome or goal. Many times, a presentation results from the collaborative efforts of a team of people. Collaborating with others in a presentation sparks the creativity and problem-solving skills of all group members, which makes the final project a better project than one in which one individual has sole responsibility. Today's technology enables you to collaborate easily with others, and Office 2013 applications include features to facilitate this process.

In this section, you will learn how to add comments, edit comments, print comments, and delete comments. You will learn how to add annotations while displaying a presentation and how to save the annotations. You will merge and compare presentations and review and manage the changes made by others. You will also view presentation properties.

Working with Comments and Annotations

After you have created your PowerPoint presentation, you may want to route it to others for review. After receiving your presentation, the *reviewer* examines the presentation and can add *comments* (text notes attached to the slide) or *annotations* (markings written or drawn on a slide for additional commentary or explanation while displaying a slide show presentation) or make additional changes. A presentation or document with comments and annotations contains *markup*. When the reviewer returns the presentation to you, you determine the changes you wish to make based on the markup in the presentation.

Add Comments

Think of comments as onscreen sticky notes that you can insert and remove as needed. You can insert comments to remind yourself of revisions you want to make or as reminders of where you are as you develop the project. If you distribute the presentation to others for review, they can add comments with suggestions. Start by clicking the Review tab and clicking New Comment in the Comments group. The Comments pane opens, and you insert a comment on the slide by typing it in a comment box. The name of the person inserting the comment is included along with the date and the reviewer's account icon. If nothing is selected, the comment icon is positioned at the top left of the slide but may be dragged to any location on the slide. If you select text or an object, or position the insertion point within text before you insert the comment, the comment icon appears next to the text or object. The Comments pane lists comments in the order they are added to the slide. To move from one comment to another, use the Previous and Next buttons in the Comments pane. You can add a new comment by clicking the New button.

 Delete All Comments

To delete all of the comments on the current slide, click the Delete arrow in the Comments group and click *Delete All Comments and Ink on This Slide*. To delete all of the comments in the presentation, click the Delete arrow and then *Delete All Comments and Ink in This Presentation*.

STEP 1 »

As you review comments, you can choose to incorporate any suggestions you agree with or to ignore any you do not wish to incorporate. Usually, you would delete a comment after your decision. This helps you determine where you are in the review process. If you are part of a work group, you may choose to leave the comments for others to see, and you may choose to reply to existing comments. To insert a comment, do the following:

1. Click the REVIEW tab.
2. Click New Comment in the Comments group. The Comments pane opens.
3. Type the comment in the comment box.
4. Click outside the box to close it.

To reply to a comment, do the following:

1. Click the comment that you want to reply to.
2. Click in the Reply text box and type your reply.
3. Press Tab when you are finished.

When you open a presentation that has new comments, a pop-up displays to alert you to the comments. To view a comment, click the comment icon on the slide or Comments on the status bar at the bottom of the screen to show the Comments pane. Comments do not display during Slide Show mode. If you want to edit an existing comment, click the comment to select it. If more than one comment is located on the slide, the fill of the selected comment icon changes color to indicate it is the active comment. Otherwise, the comment icon is simply outlined. Then click inside the comment text box in the Comments pane and edit the comment. Delete a comment by clicking Delete in the comment box or by selecting it and clicking Delete in the Comments group on the Review tab. Figure 8.1 shows the Comments pane and a slide with an open comment.

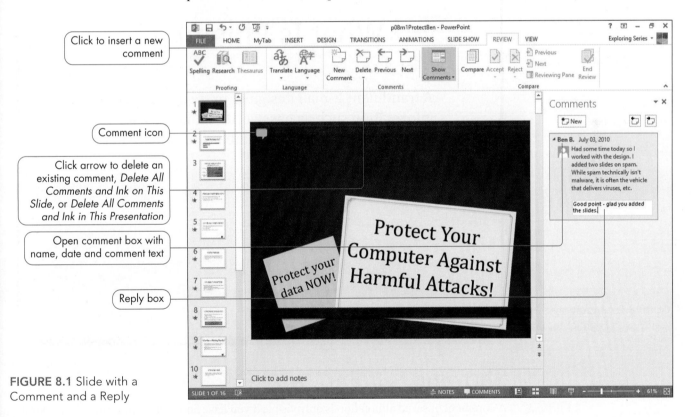

FIGURE 8.1 Slide with a Comment and a Reply

Insert Annotations

Annotations are written or drawn on a slide for additional commentary or explanation while a slide show is displayed, similar to the way a sports commentator may draw a play during the broadcast of a football game. To add an annotation while playing a slide show, right-click a slide, select Pointer Options, and then select Pen or Highlighter. Pen creates a thin line, and Highlighter creates a thick line. Drag the mouse (or your finger or stylus on a touch screen) to draw or write on the slide. To turn off the pen or highlighter, right-click, select Pointer Options, select Arrow Options, and then select Automatic. When you exit the slide show, you will be prompted to keep or discard the ink annotations.

> ### TIP | Use a Mouse as a Laser Pointer
>
> You can use your mouse as a laser pointer while displaying a presentation. This calls your audience's attention to the portion of the slide you want to emphasize without creating ink markup (annotations). To use a laser pointer, start the presentation in either Slide Show view or Reading view, press and hold Ctrl, hold down the left mouse button, and then drag the mouse to make the laser pointer appear on the slide. When you release the left mouse button, the laser pointer disappears. You can also right-click the mouse, point to Pointer Options, and then click Laser Pointer. To remove the laser pointer, return to Pointer Options and click Laser Pointer again.

Figure 8.2 shows a slide displaying in Slide Show view with the Pointer Options open and displaying annotations made with the pen and highlighter.

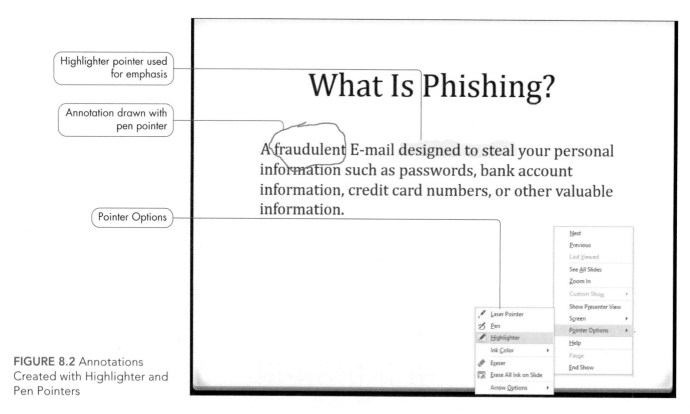

FIGURE 8.2 Annotations Created with Highlighter and Pen Pointers

Showing, Hiding, and Printing Markup

STEP 2 >> A comment or saved annotation is only visible if you have Show Markup active. Show Markup is in the Show Comments arrow in the Comments group of the Review tab. Show Markup is a toggle that displays or hides inserted comments and saved annotations. Figure 8.3 displays the active Show Markup command. The slide is displayed in Normal view. The annotations still display because they were kept when the slide show ended.

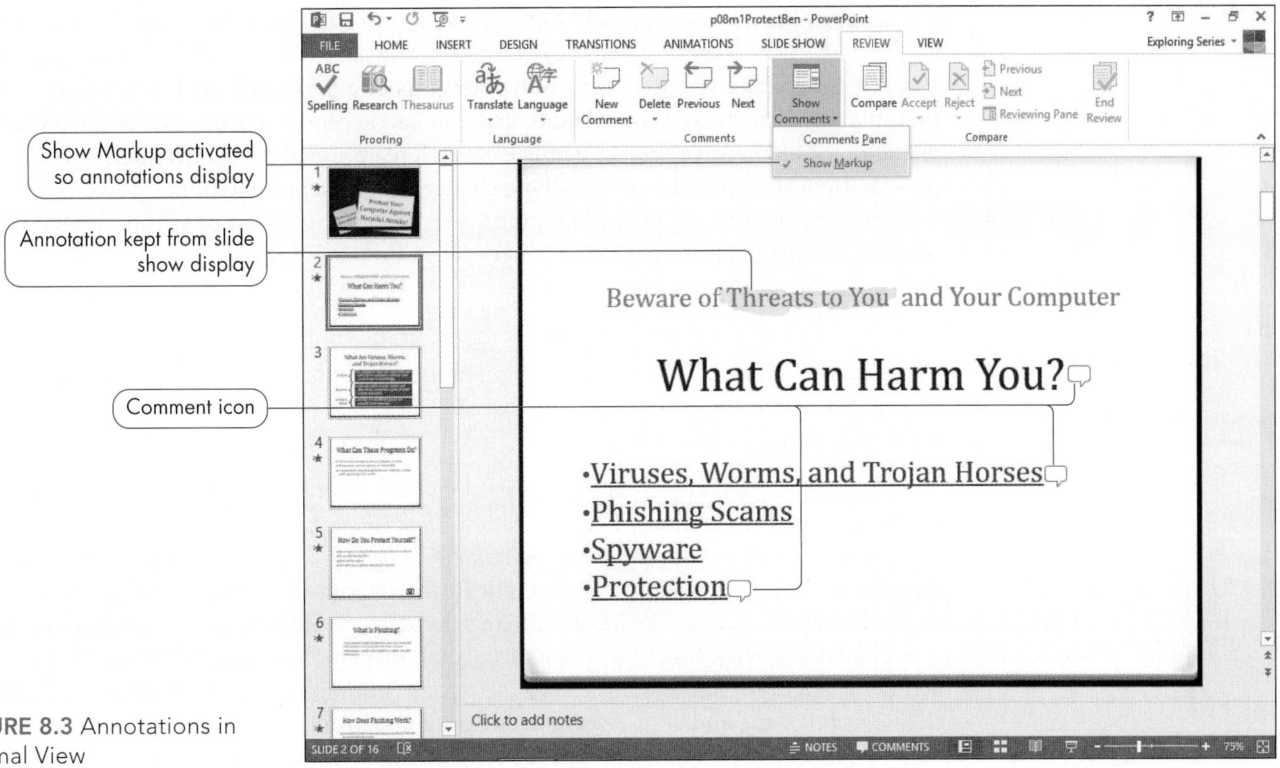
Show Markup activated so annotations display
Annotation kept from slide show display
Comment icon
p08m1ProtectBen - PowerPoint
FILE HOME INSERT DESIGN TRANSITIONS ANIMATIONS SLIDE SHOW REVIEW VIEW
Exploring Series
Spelling Research Thesaurus
Proofing
Translate Language
Language
New Comment Delete Previous Next
Comments
Show Comments
Comments Pane
Show Markup
Compare Accept Reject
Previous
Next
Reviewing Pane
End Review
Compare
Beware of Threats to You and Your Computer
What Can Harm You?
•Viruses, Worms, and Trojan Horses
•Phishing Scams
•Spyware
•Protection
Click to add notes
SLIDE 2 OF 16
NOTES COMMENTS
75%

FIGURE 8.3 Annotations in Normal View

Because it is sometimes easier to review comments and annotations in print format, you may choose to print the comments and annotations that have been stored on your slides. When you choose to print comments and annotations (markup), the comments print on a separate page from the slides that display the annotations. To print comments and ink markup, click the File tab and click Print. Select Full Page Slides (or whatever layout is desired) and if your slide show contains comments or annotations, the *Print Comments and Ink Markup* option is active. This option is grayed out if the presentation does not contain comments or annotations. Figure 8.4 displays the *Print Comments and Ink Markup* option.

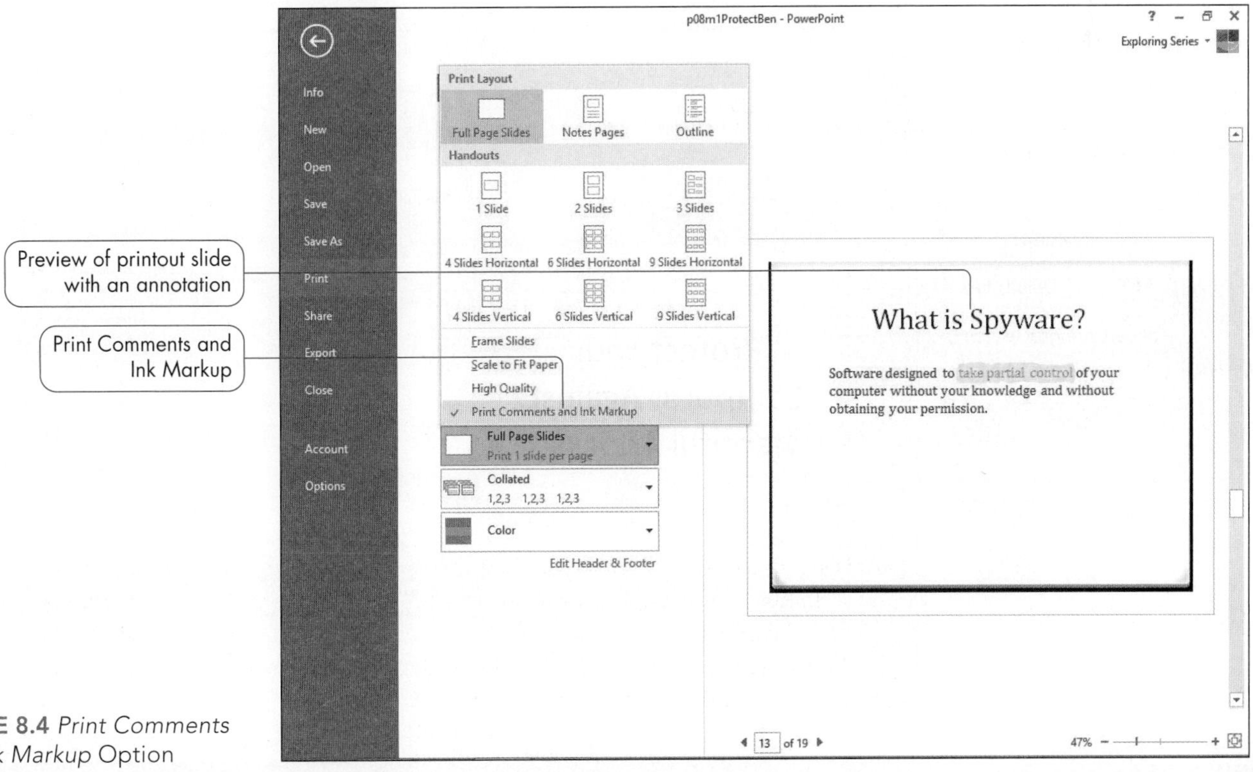
Preview of printout slide with an annotation
Print Comments and Ink Markup
p08m1ProtectBen - PowerPoint
Exploring Series
Info
New
Open
Save
Save As
Print
Share
Export
Close
Account
Options
Print Layout
Full Page Slides
Notes Pages
Outline
Handouts
1 Slide
2 Slides
3 Slides
4 Slides Horizontal
6 Slides Horizontal
9 Slides Horizontal
4 Slides Vertical
6 Slides Vertical
9 Slides Vertical
Frame Slides
Scale to Fit Paper
High Quality
Print Comments and Ink Markup
Full Page Slides
Print 1 slide per page
Collated
1,2,3 1,2,3 1,2,3
Color
Edit Header & Footer
What is Spyware?
Software designed to take partial control of your computer without your knowledge and without obtaining your permission.
13 of 19
47%

FIGURE 8.4 *Print Comments and Ink Markup Option*

Comparing and Merging Presentations

PowerPoint enables you to compare two versions of a presentation. The differences in the presentations are marked as revisions that you can accept or reject. This is extremely beneficial in a collaborative project because after all team members submit their version of the presentation, someone can merge all the changes into one presentation.

STEP 3 »

To compare and merge presentations, you need a minimum of two presentations: the original and the presentation with changes. Then do the following:

1. Open the original presentation.
2. Click the REVIEW tab and click Compare in the Compare group.
3. Locate and select the changed version of the presentation in the *Choose File to Merge with Current Presentation* dialog box.
4. Click Merge.

Once you have clicked Merge, the Revisions pane opens. The pane opens, by default, to a Details tab with two sections. The top section, *Slide Changes*, lists the changes to the slide currently selected. The bottom section, *Presentation Changes*, lists any slides that have been added or removed from the original presentation. The Revisions pane also includes a Slides tab that indicates whether the current slide has been changed and which slide contains the next set of changes.

The *Slide Changes* section of the Details tab displays icons and abbreviated text representing changes to objects on the slide. To accept an individual change, click the change in the Revisions pane and click Accept in the Compare group. You can also click the icon representing the object on the slide and select a check box in the Revisions checklist that opens. You can see the change that will result when you click a check box. To accept all changes on the current slide, click the Accept arrow in the Compare group on the Review tab and click *Accept All Changes to This Slide* or *Accept All Changes to the Presentation*.

If you accept a change and then decide you no longer want the change, click Reject in the Compare group. Any changes that you do not accept are discarded when you complete the review. To complete the review, click End Review in the Compare group. Figure 8.5 shows the Revisions pane with the Details tab selected. The *Slide Changes* section shows changes for slide properties on the current slide. The *Presentation Changes* section shows two changes in the presentation. All changes made in the slide are displayed in the Revisions check box on the slide. In this case, two slides were inserted.

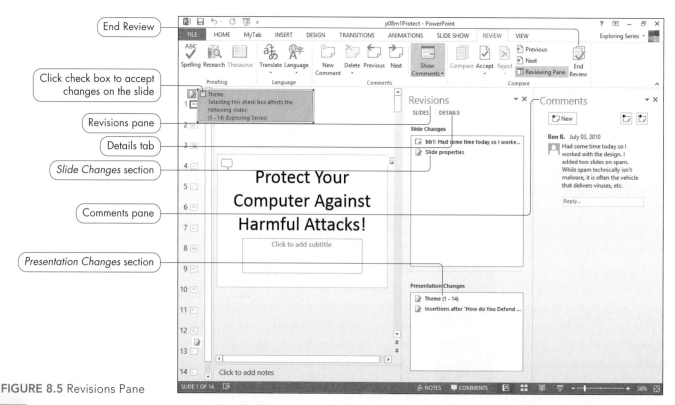

FIGURE 8.5 Revisions Pane

Viewing Presentation Properties

STEP 4 ▶

To view the original author(s) of a presentation and its creation date, or to see who last modified the presentation and when the modification took place, view the presentation properties. The presentation properties (*document properties* or *metadata*) are the attributes about a presentation that describe it or identify it. In addition to the author and modifier properties, you can view many details such as the title, file size, keywords, and statistics. Some of the properties are created and updated automatically, and some are created by the user. The presentation properties help you organize and search for your presentations.

To view presentation properties, click the File tab to display the Backstage Info view. The panel on the right side of the screen displays some properties. Click Show All Properties at the bottom of the panel to see all properties. You can change document properties not automatically set by PowerPoint by clicking the property box and typing the change. Figure 8.6 displays the properties for a presentation on protecting your computer.

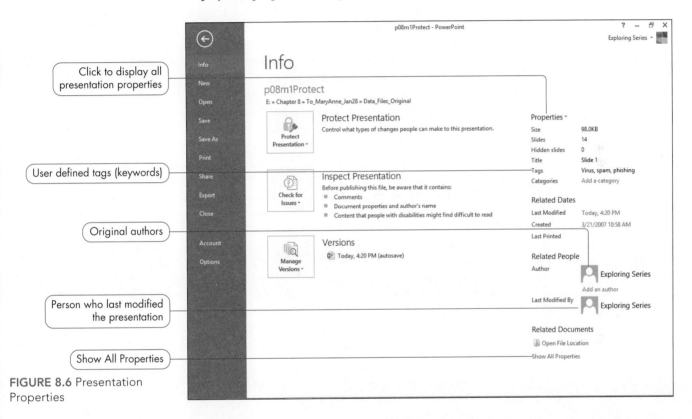

- Click to display all presentation properties
- User defined tags (keywords)
- Original authors
- Person who last modified the presentation
- Show All Properties

FIGURE 8.6 Presentation Properties

To set multiple document properties, click the Properties arrow in the right pane and click Show Document Panel. The Document Properties panel appears above the selected slide in Normal view. The Author and Title properties are entered automatically but can be changed. The words you type in the Keywords property box display as tags when you display the Properties panel in the Info view in the Backstage view. Figure 8.7 displays the Document Properties panel for a presentation on protecting your computer.

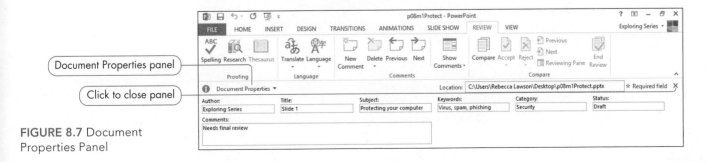

- Document Properties panel
- Click to close panel

FIGURE 8.7 Document Properties Panel

1. Explain how comments can be edited or deleted. *p. 475*

2. How can you print comments and ink markup? *p. 477*

3. Why is it beneficial to be able to compare two versions of a presentation? *p. 478*

Hands-On Exercises

1 Presentation Collaboration

You review the Harbor Business Center presentation and add comments and annotations. You print a copy of the presentation, comments, and ink markup for your records. When the presentation is returned to you by the reviewer, you compare and merge the presentations. Finally, you view and edit the presentation properties.

Skills covered: Insert Annotations and a Comment • Show, Hide, and Print Markup • Compare and Merge Presentations • View and Change Presentation Properties

STEP 1 ≫ INSERT ANNOTATIONS AND A COMMENT

You have completed the Harbor Business Center presentation, and you are ready to send it to Susil for her review. Before sending it to her, you review the presentation in Slide Show view. You have a question about the data as you watch the presentation, so you add annotations to mark the location that raised your question. Then you ask the questions as comments in the presentation. Refer to Figure 8.8 as you complete Step 1.

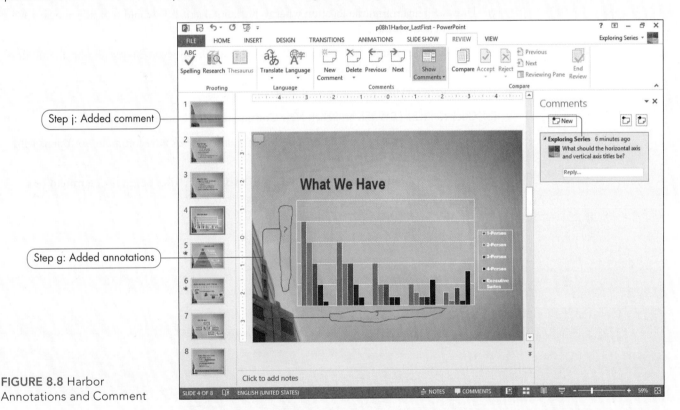

FIGURE 8.8 Harbor Annotations and Comment

a. Open the *p08h1Harbor* presentation and save it as **p08h1Harbor_LastFirst**.

The Harbor Business Center presentation opens. It has formatting problems that will be addressed in a later step.

> **TROUBLESHOOTING:** If you make any major mistakes in this exercise, you can close the file, open *p08h1Harbor* again, and then start this exercise over.

b. Create a handout header with your name and a handout footer with your instructor's name and your class. Include the current date.

c. Click the **FILE tab**, click **Options**, and then type your name in the **User name box** if necessary. Type your initials in the **Initials box** if necessary and click **OK**.

Figures in this chapter display the initials *ES* for "Exploring Series," and it is also used as the name.

> **TROUBLESHOOTING:** If your school lab has a software program installed to protect software and hardware settings from being changed, you will need to reset your user name and initials each time you log in.

d. Click the **SLIDE SHOW tab** and click **From Beginning** in the Start Slide Show group.

e. Click three times to advance to the fourth slide, titled *What We Have*. Note that no vertical or horizontal axis titles exist to describe what the columns in the chart represent.

> **TROUBLESHOOTING:** If you advance too far and display the next slide, right-click, and select See All Slides in the shortcut menu. Then select *4 What We Have*.

f. Right-click the slide, point to *Pointer Options*, and then select **Pen**.

g. Draw a circle around the location where a horizontal axis title would typically appear and draw a question mark within the circle.

h. Draw a circle around the location where a vertical axis title would typically appear and draw a question mark within the circle.

i. Press **Esc** and click **Keep** to save the ink annotations.

j. Click the **REVIEW tab** and click **New Comment** in the Comments group.

A comment icon appears in the top-left corner of Slide 4. A new comment box opens with your name in the Comments pane,

k. Type **What should the horizontal axis and vertical axis titles be?** in the **comment box**.

l. Save the presentation.

STEP 2 ≫ SHOW, HIDE, AND PRINT MARKUP

You view the slide with the markup showing, and then you hide the markup. You also preview the comment and the annotations printouts in Print Preview. Refer to Figure 8.9 as you complete Step 2.

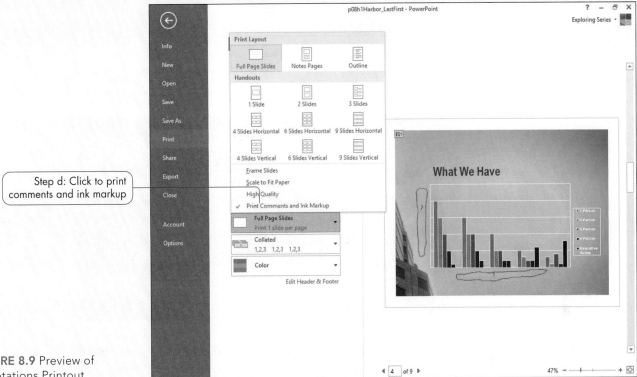

FIGURE 8.9 Preview of Annotations Printout

a. Click the **REVIEW tab** if necessary and click the **Show Comments arrow** in the Comments group. Click **Show Markup** to deselect it.

Clicking Show Markup toggles the feature off so the comment and the annotations no longer display.

b. Click **Show Comments** in the Comments group and click **Show Markup** so that it is now checked.

The comment and the annotations display again.

c. Click the **FILE tab** and click **Print**.

d. Click the **Full Page Slides arrow** and note that *Print Comments and Ink Markup* is checked. Click outside the dialog box to close it.

The annotations on Slide 4 display and will print if Slide 4 is printed. In the top-left corner of the slide, the initials of the person who made the comment is displayed.

> **TROUBLESHOOTING:** If *Print Comments and Ink Markup* is not selected, click the check box.

e. Click **Next Page** in the navigation control at the bottom center of the Backstage Print view to advance to page 5.

Page 5 displays the comment on Slide 4.

f. Save the presentation.

STEP 3 ≫ COMPARE AND MERGE PRESENTATIONS

Susil has returned her version of the Harbor Business Center presentation. You merge her presentation with your original, and then accept and reject changes. You remove all remaining comments, and then save the merged version of the presentation. Refer to Figure 8.10 as you complete Step 3. Although you will not access this particular view, it is used here to illustrate the final presentation.

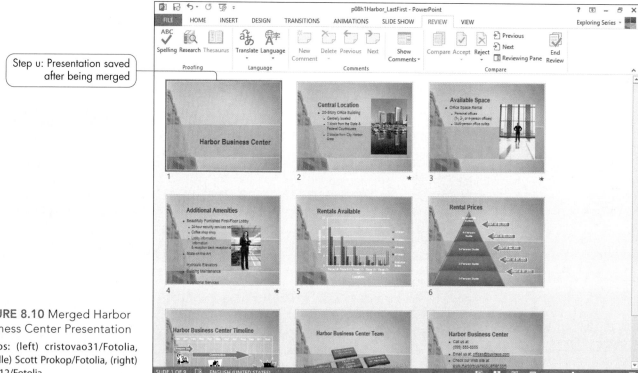

Step u: Presentation saved after being merged

FIGURE 8.10 Merged Harbor Business Center Presentation

Photos: (left) cristovao31/Fotolia, (middle) Scott Prokop/Fotolia, (right) bst2012/Fotolia

a. Click the **REVIEW tab** and click **Compare** in the Compare group.

The *Choose File to Merge with Current Presentation* dialog box opens.

b. Navigate to your student data files, select *p08h1HarborAkalushi*, and then click **Merge**.

The Revisions pane opens with the Details tab active. The first slide of the presentation displays in Normal view. The *Slide Changes* section displays one item, a comment from Susil. The *Presentation Changes* section shows two changes to the presentation: a theme change on Slides 1 through 8 and insertions after "Harbor Business Center." The Comments pane also opens. One comment from Susil exists.

c. Click the icon in the *Slide Changes* section, if necessary, and read the comment on the slide.

The comment box is open, and Susil's comment displays.

d. Click **Theme (1–8)** in the *Presentation Changes* section.

The Revisions box attached to the thumbnail of Slide 1 in the Slides tab opens and indicates the theme change made by Susil, which impacts Slides 1 through 8.

e. Click **Accept** in the Compare group.

A checked icon appears next to the Theme (1–8) item in the *Presentation Changes* section, indicating the change was accepted. A check mark also appears above the Slide 1 thumbnail in the Slides tab.

f. Select **Insertions after "Harbor Business Center"** in the *Presentation Changes* section.

A Revisions box displays between Slide 1 and Slide 2 that reads *Inserted "Central Location" (Susil Akalushi)*.

g. Click the **Inserted "Central Location" (Susil Akalushi) check box** above Slide 2 in the Slides pane.

A new Slide 2 is added to the presentation using the slide Susil created. A check mark also appears on the slide thumbnail in the Slides tab indicating a change was made. A check appears next to the Slide 2: Central Location item in the *Presentation Changes* section indicating the change was accepted.

h. Click the **Accept arrow** in the Compare group and select **Accept All Changes to the Presentation**.

All changes to the presentation by Susil are made.

i. Click the **SLIDE SHOW tab** and click **From Beginning** in the Start Slide Show group. Advance through the slides in the presentation. Press **Esc**.

j. Click **Slide 8** and click the **SLIDES tab** in the Revisions pane.

A thumbnail of Slide 8 displays in the Revisions pane.

k. Click the **Slide 8 thumbnail check box** in the Revisions pane to deselect it. Note that the organization chart is a SmartArt style that displays in 3D format.

l. Click the **Slide 8 thumbnail check box** again. Click the **REVIEW tab** and click the **Reject arrow** in the Compare group. Select **Reject All Changes to This Slide**.

All changes to Slide 8 are rejected.

m. Click the **DETAILS tab** in the Revisions pane and select **Rectangle 2: Who We Are**. Click **All changes to Rectangle 2**. Click the **Reject arrow** in the Compare group. Click **Reject All Changes to This Slide**.

The title changes from *Harbor Business Center Team* to *Who We Are* because you rejected Susil's changes.

n. On Slide 1, select the comment in the *Slide Changes* section of the DETAILS tab in the Revisions pane. Click **Delete** in the Comments group.

o. Click **Next** in the Comments group.

The *Slide Changes* section of the Details tab displays the two comments and three changes in Slide 5.

p. Read a comment and click **Next** in the Comments group. Read the next comment and click **Next** again in the Comments group.

The presentation advances to Slide 9.

q. Read the comment on Slide 9 regarding animating the content placeholders on Slides 2 through 4.

r. On Slide 2, select the **content placeholder**, click the **ANIMATIONS tab**, and then click **More** in the Animation group. Click **Wipe** in the Entrance category. Click **Effect Options** in the Animation group and click **From Left**. Click the **Start arrow** in the Timing group and select **After Previous**.

s. Deselect the **content placeholder** and select it again to enable the Animation Painter feature. Double-click **Animation Painter** in the Advanced Animation group and copy the content placeholder animation to the content placeholders on Slides 3 and 4. Deselect the **Animation Painter**.

t. Click the **REVIEW tab**, click the **Delete arrow** in the Comments group, and then click **Delete All Comments and Ink in This Presentation**. Click **Yes** and close the Revisions and Comments panes.

u. Save the presentation. If you get a message about ending the review, click **Save** again.

STEP 4 ›› VIEW AND CHANGE PRESENTATION PROPERTIES

To help you organize your presentation files and to help you and Susil locate the file through the Windows Search feature, you create document properties. Refer to Figure 8.11 as you complete Step 4.

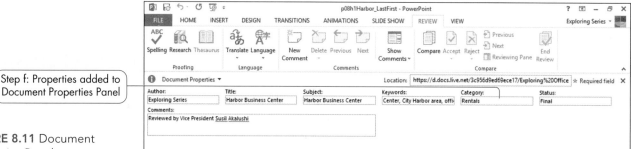

Step f: Properties added to Document Properties Panel

FIGURE 8.11 Document Properties Panel

a. Click the **FILE tab** and note the properties that are displayed on the right side of the Backstage Info view.

b. Click **Add a tag** next to the Tags property and type **Center**.

Center becomes a keyword that you can use to search for the presentation.

c. Click **Show All Properties** at the bottom of the Properties pane and note the additional properties that display.

d. Click **Properties** at the top of the Properties pane and click **Show Document Panel**.

The Document Properties Panel displays below the Ribbon and includes the following properties: Author, Title, and Keywords (Center).

e. Click in the **Subject box** and type **Harbor Business Center**.

f. Add the properties shown in the following table:

Type of Property	Property Information
Keywords	City Harbor area, office suites, space available
Category	Rentals
Status	Final
Comments	Reviewed by Vice President Susil Akalushi

> **TROUBLESHOOTING:** Be sure to keep the keyword *Center* from the merged presentation.

g. Click **Close the Document Information Panel** in the top-right corner of the panel.

h. Save the presentation. Keep the presentation open if you plan to continue with Hands-On Exercise 2. If not, close the presentation and exit PowerPoint.

Preparation for Sharing and Presentation Security

Once you complete a slide show, you can present it or distribute it to others to view. If you want to distribute the presentation to others, take advantage of PowerPoint's tools for preparing and securing a presentation for distribution. In addition to the ability to add and remove document properties that was covered in the previous section, these two collections of tools enable you to do the following:

- Check the content of the presentation for accessibility issues.
- Run a compatibility check to identify features that viewers using previous versions are not able to see.
- Mark the presentation as final and make it read only.
- Add a password.
- Allow people viewing rights but restrict their rights to edit, copy, and print.
- Attach a digital signature.

To access these features, click the File tab to display the Backstage Info view as shown in Figure 8.12.

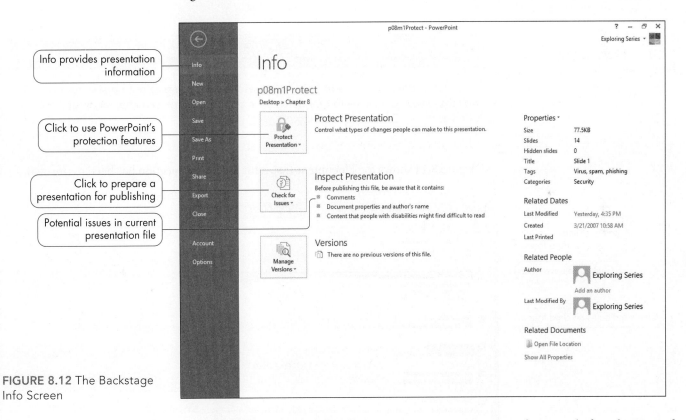

FIGURE 8.12 The Backstage Info Screen

In this section, you will learn how to inspect a presentation for issues before sharing and to secure a presentation for distribution.

Checking a Presentation for Issues

While adding details to the presentation properties helps you organize and locate your presentations, you may not wish other people to have access to that data. Your presentation may also contain content that someone with disabilities cannot view or someone using an earlier version of PowerPoint cannot view. The *Check for Issues* commands enable you to uncover issues that may cause difficulties for viewers.

Access Document Inspector

To check for hidden and personal data in the presentation or in its properties, use the *Document Inspector*. You can search the following content areas:

- Comments and Annotations
- Document Properties and Personal Information
- Custom XML Data
- Invisible On-Slide Content
- Off-Slide Content
- Presentation Notes

To use the Document Inspector, do the following:

1. Click the FILE tab to display the Backstage Info view.
2. Click Check for Issues.
3. Select Inspect Document.
4. Click the check box next to the content that you wish to inspect.
5. Click Inspect.
6. Review the results in the Document Inspector dialog box.
7. Click Remove All next to the types of content you want to remove from your presentation and click Close.

> ### TIP Be Cautious Using Document Inspector
>
> If you remove hidden content from your presentation, you may not be able to restore it with the Undo command. To be safe, make a copy of your presentation and use the copy when using the Document Inspector.

Figure 8.13 shows the Document Inspector after an inspection has been performed.

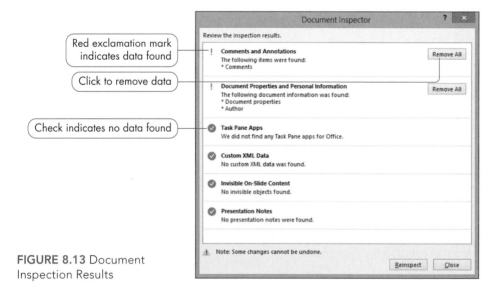

FIGURE 8.13 Document Inspection Results

Check Accessibility

Because you want your presentation to be accessible for users with varying challenges when you distribute it, you should use the Accessibility Checker before sharing it. The *Accessibility Checker* helps you identify and resolve problems with accessibility issues in your presentation. *Accessibility* in PowerPoint refers to the ease with which a person with physical challenges is able to access and understand a presentation. To fix some of the issues the Accessibility Checker identifies, you may have to change, reformat, or update your content.

The Accessibility Checker locates accessibility issues and assigns them to one of three categories:

- *Error*: Issues where content is unreadable. For example, no **alternative text (alt text)** means a text-based description of an image is not available.
- *Warning*: Issues where content is difficult to read. For example, a table is difficult to read because of complex formatting.
- *Tip*: Issues that may or may not make content difficult to read. For example, the order in which text should be read is unclear due to the order of objects on a slide.

To use the Accessibility Checker, do the following:

1. Click the FILE tab to access the Backstage Info view.
2. Click Check for Issues.
3. Select Check Accessibility.
4. Review and fix the issues in the Accessibility Checker pane that opens on the right side of the Normal view.

The Accessibility Checker pane enables you to find and fix the issues in the presentation. It is divided into two sections. The top section lists the inspection results and is divided into Errors, Warnings, and Tips. The bottom section describes why an issue should be fixed and provides a link to more information about making documents accessible. Figure 8.14 shows the Accessibility Checker pane with two errors displayed in the *Inspection Results* section along with a Warning and a Tip.

FIGURE 8.14 Accessibility Checker

Check Compatibility

Whenever you share your presentation with others, you need to consider what software they are using. If they are using an earlier version of PowerPoint, they may not be able to see or use some of the features available in PowerPoint 2013. You can check your presentation for features not supported by earlier versions of PowerPoint by activating the **Compatibility Checker**.

The Microsoft PowerPoint Compatibility Checker dialog box appears and warns you about features you used in your presentation that may be lost or degraded when you save the presentation to an earlier format for distribution.

STEP 2»

To use the Compatibility Checker, do the following:

1. Click the FILE tab to access the Backstage Info view.
2. Click Check for Issues.
3. Select Check Compatibility.
4. Read any messages that are generated and see what action to take.

Figure 8.15 displays the Microsoft PowerPoint Compatibility Checker dialog box with a warning about the compatibility of a SmartArt diagram with PowerPoint 97–2003 applications.

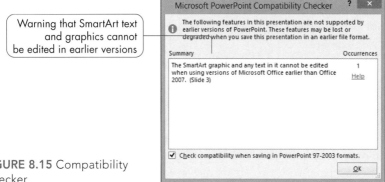

Warning that SmartArt text and graphics cannot be edited in earlier versions

FIGURE 8.15 Compatibility Checker

Protecting a Presentation

Anyone can open, copy, or change any part of a presentation unless you protect its integrity by using PowerPoint's Protect Presentation features. You can make a presentation read only; require a password; restrict the editing, copying, or printing; or add a digital signature. Figure 8.16 displays the Protect Presentation features available in PowerPoint.

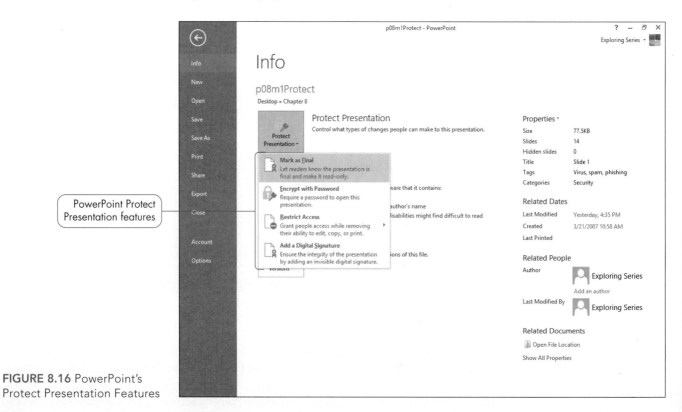

PowerPoint Protect Presentation features

FIGURE 8.16 PowerPoint's Protect Presentation Features

Mark as Final

After you prepare your presentation for distribution, you can mark it as a final version. This feature deactivates most PowerPoint tools and converts the presentation to read-only format. Doing this allows viewers to watch your presentation but not to edit it unless they turn off the *Mark as Final* feature—which is easy to remove if changes are needed. A *Mark as Final* designation lets your viewers know they are viewing a finished presentation.

STEP 4 ▶▶ To mark a presentation as final, do the following:

1. Click the FILE tab to access the Backstage Info view.
2. Click Protect Presentation.
3. Select *Mark as Final*.
4. Click OK in the warning message box that appears stating *This presentation will be marked as final and then saved*.
5. Click OK in the PowerPoint information message box (see Figure 8.17).

FIGURE 8.17 *Mark as Final* Information Box

A *Marked as Final* message bar appears below the Ribbon and a *Marked as Final* icon displays on the status bar. If you wish to make changes, however, you can click Edit Anyway on the warning bar. You can also turn off final status by clicking the File tab, clicking Protect Presentation, and then clicking *Mark as Final*. Figure 8.18 shows a presentation marked as final.

Most Ribbon features deactivated

Marked as Final message bar

Marked as Final icon

FIGURE 8.18 Presentation Marked as Final

Protect with a Password

Use *encryption* to protect the privacy of your presentation by converting the presentation into unreadable scrambled text that needs a password to be opened. Set a password on your presentation to prevent other people from opening or changing your presentation. Once you set a password, you can change it or remove it only if you know the original password.

STEP 3 »   To encrypt a presentation with a password, do the following:

1. Click the FILE tab to access the Backstage Info view.
2. Click Protect Presentation.
3. Select *Encrypt with Password*.
4. Type a password in the Encrypt Document dialog box.
5. Reenter the password in the Confirm Password dialog box and click OK.

You are prompted to reenter the password as a security measure to ensure you enter the password with no typographical errors. This is critical because if you type the password incorrectly or forget the password, you will not be able to open your presentation or change the password. Also be careful about what you type in capital letters and what you type lowercase. Passwords are intentionally case sensitive. Avoid creating passwords using dictionary words, words spelled backwards, common misspellings, and abbreviations. Do not use sequences or repeated characters such as 123456, 33333, or abcdef. Never use personal information such as your name, birthday, or driver's license number. See the reference table for Microsoft's recommendations for creating a strong password for online safety. These guidelines can help you set a pattern for all passwords you use.

REFERENCE | Password Tips

Tip	Background	Example
Think of a sentence or two about something meaningful to you. Use about 10 words.	Creating a sentence about something meaningful will help you remember the password.	King is an English Bulldog. He is my best friend. *10 words*
Turn your sentence into a row of letters.	Using the first letter of each word will help you remember the password.	kiaebhimbf *10 characters*
Add complexity.	Make some of the letters uppercase. For example, make only the letters in the first half or last half of the alphabet uppercase.	kiaebhiMbf *10 characters*
Add length with numbers.	Put two numbers that are meaningful to you between sentences.	kiaeb18hiMbf *12 characters*
Add length with punctuation.	Put a punctuation mark at the beginning of the password	!kiaeb18hiMbf *13 characters*
Add length with symbols.	Put a symbol at the end of the password.	!kiaeb18hiMbf& *14 characters*

Source: www.microsoft.com/security/online-privacy/passwords-create.aspx

Another method you can use to set a password for your presentation is to click the File tab, select Save As, select Browse, select Tools, and then select General Options. If you use this method to encrypt your document, you have more options. You can set one password to open the presentation and a different password to modify the presentation. You can also remove automatically generated personal information when you save. This does not, however, remove properties you have added. After setting it, a password takes effect the next time you open the presentation. When you attempt to open the presentation, the Password dialog box opens. Enter the password and click OK to open the presentation.

Restrict Access

Office 2013 uses an ***information rights management (IRM)*** feature to help businesses restrict the access of others to sensitive information such as financial records and employee data. In PowerPoint, IRM restricts presentations, templates, shows, and themes from being forwarded, edited, printed, or copied without authorization. It can also set an expiration date for a presentation so that it can no longer be viewed after a selected date. Using the IRM feature enables you to allow unrestricted access to your presentation or to specify the restrictions you want enabled, such as the permissions an individual user must possess to view the presentation.

IRM uses a server to authenticate the credentials of people who create or receive presentations with restricted permissions. Microsoft provides free access to the IRM service for users with a Microsoft account. To access the Restrict Permission feature, click the File tab, click Protect Presentation, point to Restrict Access, and then click *Connect Rights Management Servers and get templates*. The default is Unrestricted Access, but if you select either Restricted Access or Manage Credentials, a Service Sign-Up dialog box appears giving you information about IRM with a hyperlink you can click to learn more about information rights management. You can also click *Yes, I want to sign up for this free service from Microsoft* or *No, I do not want to use this service from Microsoft*.

 TIP **To Obtain a Microsoft Account**

Create your credentials for a Microsoft account, and you will have access to many more services than just IRM. Your Microsoft account, formerly referred to as a Windows Live ID, enables you to log in to such sites and services as OneDrive, MSN Messenger, MSN Hotmail, MSN Music, and other sites. To sign up for a Microsoft account, visit https://signup.live.com/signup.aspx.

Add a Digital Signature

A ***digital signature*** is an invisible, electronic signature stamp that is encrypted and attached to a certificate. The certificate is attached to the presentation. This is similar to signing a paper document. If you want those with whom you share your presentation to be able to verify the authenticity of your digital signature, you can obtain a digital ID from a Microsoft partner. You can also create your own digital ID; however, it will only enable you to verify that a presentation has not been changed on the computer on which you have saved the presentation.

To create your own digital signature, do the following:

1. Click the FILE tab to access the Backstage Info view.
2. Click Protect Presentation.
3. Select *Add a Digital Signature*, read the Microsoft PowerPoint Information dialog box, and then click Yes.
4. Choose among the Available Digital ID providers found on the Microsoft Office Web site. Each will have a different method to get the digital ID, so follow the onscreen steps to complete the process.

Adding a digital signature should be the last step you perform when preparing the document because, if you make any changes after the signature is added, your signature is invalidated.

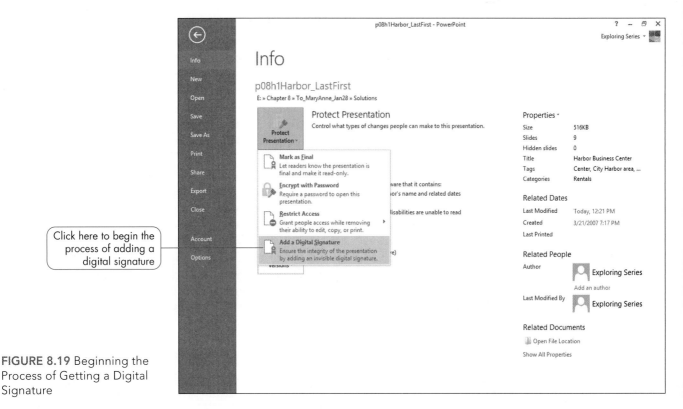

Click here to begin the process of adding a digital signature

FIGURE 8.19 Beginning the Process of Getting a Digital Signature

Quick **Concept** ✓

1. Which areas of content can be searched using the Document Inspector? *p. 488*

2. Explain why you should use the Accessibility Checker. *p. 488*

3. What does the Compatibility Checker do? *p. 489*

4. Describe two methods that can be used to set a password for your presentation. *p. 492*

Hands-On Exercises

Watch the Video for this Hands-On Exercise!

MyITLab®
HOE2 Training

2 Preparation for Sharing and Presentation Security

Now that you have incorporated Susil Akalushi's changes in the Harbor Business Center presentation, you prepare the presentation for sharing with other company employees. You check the presentation for issues and protect the presentation.

Skills covered: Inspect the Presentation • Check for Compatibility • Set and Remove a Password • Mark as Final

---

STEP 1 ≫ INSPECT THE PRESENTATION

Before you send the presentation out to other ACSL Development employees, you use the Document Inspector to check the document for information that you may not want others to view. Refer to Figure 8.20 as you complete Step 1.

Step d: Keep *Document Properties and Personal Information* and remove *Presentation Notes*

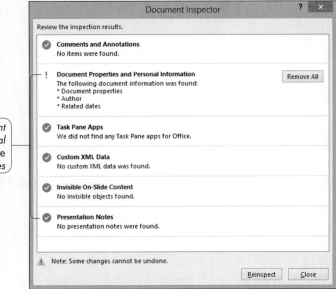

FIGURE 8.20 Document Inspector

a. Open *p08h1Harbor_LastFirst*, if necessary and save the presentation as **p08h2Harbor_LastFirst**, changing *h1* to *h2*.

b. Click the **FILE tab**, click **Check for Issues**, and then select **Inspect Document**.

   The Document Inspector dialog box opens and displays a list of items the inspector will search for.

c. Click **Inspect**.

   No comments or annotations were found because you removed them in Hands-On Exercise 1. Document properties and personal information were found, as well as presentation notes.

d. Keep the Document Properties and Personal Information and click **Remove All** in the *Presentation Notes* section.

   Because *p08h2Harbor_LastFirst* is a duplicate of *p08h1Harbor_LastFirst*, it is a convenient method to create a copy for distribution that has changes from the original document.

e. Click **Close**.

f. Save the presentation.

Some of the ACSL Development employees still use Office 2003 because the company has not updated software in all departments to the latest version of Office. You check the Harbor Business Center presentation's compatibility with the earlier versions of Office. Refer to Figure 8.21 as you complete Step 2.

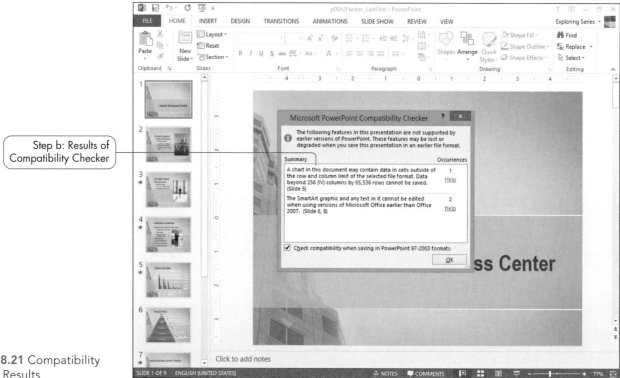

Step b: Results of Compatibility Checker

FIGURE 8.21 Compatibility Checker Results

a. Click the **FILE tab** and click **Check for Issues**.

b. Click **Check Compatibility** and read the summary of the features that cannot be supported in earlier versions of Microsoft Office.

Two issues are identified. The chart on Slide 5 contains data in cells outside of the row and column limit, and Slides 6 and 8 contain SmartArt graphics that cannot be edited when using versions of Microsoft Office earlier than Office 2007.

> **TROUBLESHOOTING:** A compatibility pack may download as part of this step.

c. Click **OK**.

Compatibility issues have been identified, but nothing has been changed.

d. Save the presentation.

STEP 3 ⟫ SET AND REMOVE A PASSWORD

To secure the Harbor Business Center presentation, you add a password to the file. Then, to make it easier for Susil to access the file, you use the Save As General Options to remove the password and set a new one. Refer to Figure 8.22 as you complete Step 3.

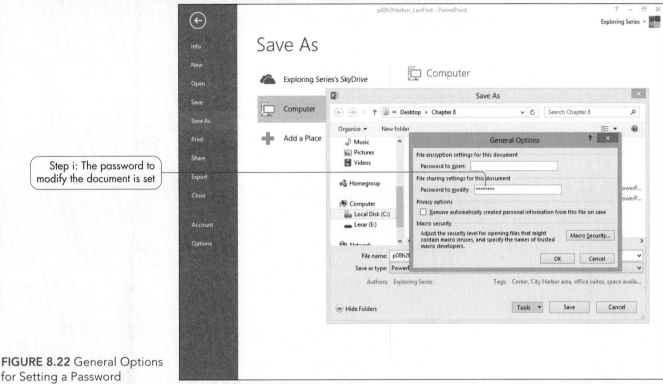

Step i: The password to modify the document is set

FIGURE 8.22 General Options for Setting a Password

a. Click the **FILE tab**, click **Protect Presentation**, and then click **Encrypt with Password**.

   The Encrypt Document dialog box opens.

b. Type **h@Rb0R!c3nT3R?** and click **OK**.

TROUBLESHOOTING: This is a secure password created from the name of the project, Harbor Center, and created using uppercase and lowercase letters and numbers and symbols from the top and bottom keyboards. It is 14 characters long.

---

c. Type **h@Rb0R!c3nT3R?** when you are prompted to reenter the password and click **OK**.

   The *Protect Presentation* section changes to a yellow color and reads *A password is required to open this presentation*.

TROUBLESHOOTING: If you typed the two passwords differently, you receive a warning that the passwords did not match and that the password was not created. Repeat the process until the passwords match. Never copy a password and paste it into the duplicate password box because if you copy and paste a typographical error, you will not be able to open the file or remove the password.

---

d. Save and close *p08h2Harbor_LastFirst* and reopen the presentation.

   The Password dialog box opens.

e. Type **h@Rb0R!c3nT3R?** in the **Password dialog box** and click **OK**.

   The Harbor Business Center presentation opens.

f. Click the **FILE tab** and click **Save As**. Click **Browse** to navigate to the location where you saved the presentation.

The Save As dialog box opens.

g. Click **Tools** just to the left of the Save button in the dialog box and click **General Options**.

The General Options dialog box opens and displays asterisks in the *Password to open* box.

h. Delete the password in the *Password to open* box.

The password to open is removed.

i. Type **password** in the **Password to modify box** and click **OK**.

> **TROUBLESHOOTING:** This is a very insecure password and would not be safe. It will, however, enable your instructor to open your file and verify that you have set a password.

j. Type **password** in the **Reenter password to modify box** and click **OK**.

k. Click **Save** and click **Yes** when prompted to overwrite.

STEP 4 ≫ MARK AS FINAL

You want the employees of ACSL Development to know that the presentation is finished, so you mark the presentation as final. Refer to Figure 8.23 as you complete Step 4.

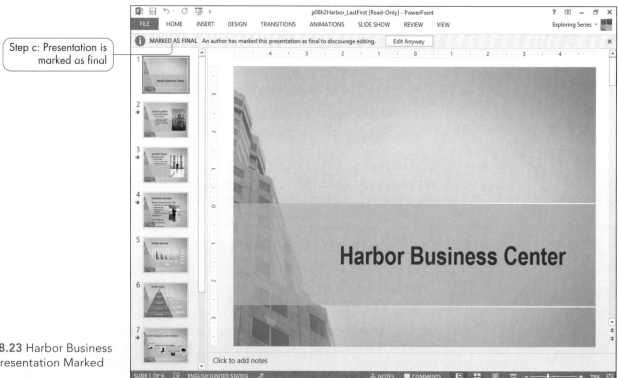

FIGURE 8.23 Harbor Business Center Presentation Marked as Final

a. Click the **FILE tab** and click **Protect Presentation**.

> **TROUBLESHOOTING:** If you closed the presentation after Step 3, the Password dialog box appears prompting you to enter the password to modify the presentation. If you do not enter the password, the presentation opens as a read-only version.

b. Select **Mark as Final** and click **OK** in the Microsoft PowerPoint Information dialog box that appears indicating that the presentation will be marked as final and then saved.

c. Click **OK** in the additional Microsoft PowerPoint Information dialog box indicating that the document has been marked final.

A *Marked as Final* message bar appears below the Ribbon and reads *An author has marked this presentation as final to discourage editing.*

d. Click the **HOME tab**.

The Ribbon appears over the message bar (*Marked as Final*). Most features have been greyed out, preventing the user from making changes.

e. Save and close the file, and submit based on your instructor's directions.

Presentation Sharing

You spent a great deal of time creating a professional presentation that delivers your message—now how will you deliver that message to your audience? Will you present it, or will you distribute it to your audience? If you are going to distribute it, what file format will you use? What distribution methods are available?

PowerPoint includes multiple distribution options using a variety of file formats. Among the variety of methods you can use to distribute your presentation are burning it to a CD or DVD, presenting it on the Web, delivering it on a network location, or printing the presentation in an image format. These methods may require different file formats. In this section, you will save your presentation using several file types and examine PowerPoint's distribution options.

Selecting a Presentation File Type

By default, PowerPoint saves a presentation in the .pptx file format, an open format that uses *eXtensible Markup Language (XML)*. XML is a set of encoding rules that creates a file format that is designed to provide maximum flexibility when storing and exchanging structured information. Microsoft Office moved to the use of XML file formats with Office 2007 and continues its use with Office 2013. Among the many benefits of XML are more compact files, improved damaged-file recovery, better privacy and control over personal information, better integration, and easier detection of documents that contain macros.

Change File Type

While you can change the file type of a PowerPoint presentation using the Save As feature, you may find it helpful to use Export to determine the file type you wish to use. Export includes a Change File Type option that provides a list of commonly used file types and a description of the file type to help you determine if it is appropriate for your needs. To change a file type using this method, do the following:

1. Click the FILE tab and click Export.
2. Click Change File Type (see Figure 8.24).
3. Select a file format from the *Presentation File Types*, *Image File Types*, or *Other File Types* sections.
4. Click Save As at the bottom of the list.
5. Navigate to the location where you want to store the file, type a file name in the *File name* box, and then click Save.

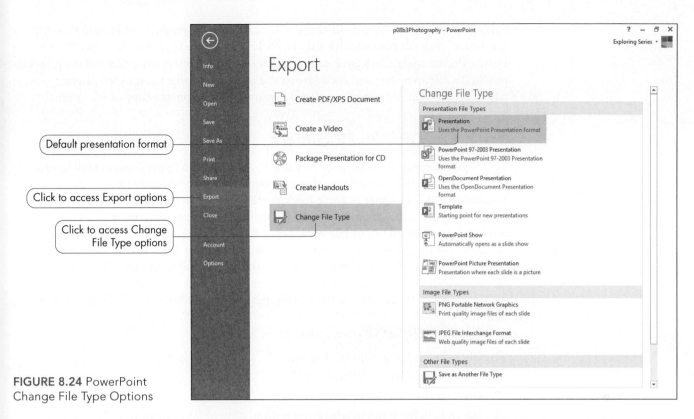

Default presentation format

Click to access Export options

Click to access Change File Type options

FIGURE 8.24 PowerPoint Change File Type Options

One option in the Change File Type list enables you to save a presentation as an *OpenDocument presentation (*.odp)*, a presentation that conforms to the OpenDocument standard for exchanging data between applications. This standard is an open XML-based format used in both free software and in proprietary software, such as Microsoft Office 2013, that seeks to make records and documents accessible across platforms and applications. Some PowerPoint 2013 features are fully supported when saved as an OpenDocument presentation, but others may be only partially or not at all supported. Be sure to save your presentation in a PowerPoint 2013 format before saving as an OpenDocument presentation to ensure that you have a backup of the original format if needed.

After creating a presentation, you may want to save the individual slide or slides as graphic images. You can save each slide or all slides in the presentation as PNG Portable Network Graphics (*.png) image(s) that use lossless compression and provide print-quality image files of each slide. You can also save each slide or all slides in the presentation as JPEG File Interchange Format (*.jpg) image(s) that use a lossy format, which makes the file size small and makes the files good for Web-quality images. To save a presentation slide(s) as an image file(s), do the following:

1. Click the FILE tab and click Export.
2. Click Change File Type.
3. Select PNG Portable Network Graphics (*.png) or JPEG File Interchange Format (*.jpg) from the Image File Types list.
4. Click Save As at the bottom of the list.
5. Navigate to the location where you want to store the file, type a file name in the *File name* box, and then click Save.

Create a PowerPoint Picture Presentation

STEP 1 »   PowerPoint 2013 has the PowerPoint Picture Presentation option. This option *flattens* (converts all objects on a slide to a single layer) the content of each slide and then saves the slides in the .pptx presentation format. By converting each slide into an image, the slides become harder for others to modify. In addition, the presentation file size is much smaller and it is easier to e-mail or download. To save a presentation in the PowerPoint Picture Presentation file format, click the File tab, click Export, click Change File Type, and then click PowerPoint Picture Presentation. Click Save As at the bottom of the list. Type the name of the presentation in the *File name* box and click Save. If you use the same file name as the original presentation, PowerPoint saves the PowerPoint Picture Presentation as a copy of the original.

Create a PDF/XPS Document

The ***PDF file format (PDF)*** (created by Adobe Systems) and ***XPS file format (XPS)*** (created by Microsoft) are excellent file formats to use when distributing files to others. This is because documents saved in either of these formats are fixed file formats—they retain their format regardless of the application used to create them. These formats enable the presentation to be viewed and printed by any platform. This is extremely helpful if you are sending your presentation out to viewers who do not have Microsoft Office 2013. Saving your presentation or document in a PDF or XPS file format makes it difficult to modify. When you distribute documents such as instructions, directions, legal forms, or reports, you probably want the document to be easy to read and print, but you do not want the document to be easily modified.

To create a PDF or XPS document, do the following:

1. Click the FILE tab and click Export.
2. Click Create PDF/XPS Document.
3. Click Create PDF/XPS.
4. Navigate to the location where you want to store the document when the *Publish as PDF or XPS* dialog box appears and type a file name in the *File name* box.
5. Select the *Optimize for Standard (publishing online and printing)* or *Minimize size (publishing online)* option.
6. Click Publish.

Create a Video

Take advantage of the excitement of video by converting your presentation into a dynamic video! PowerPoint 2013 includes an option for converting your presentation content into video that you can share with anyone. PowerPoint outputs your presentation as a Windows Media Video (WMV) video clip and includes all recorded timings and narrations, if used in the presentation; all slides that are not hidden; and all animations, transitions, and media.

Before creating a video, create your presentation and record any narration and timings you want as part of the video. You can use your mouse as a laser pointer to draw a viewer's attention to objects on your slides. Save the presentation. Then, to convert your presentation to a video, do the following:

1. Click the FILE tab and click Export.
2. Click *Create a Video*.
3. Click *Computer & HD Displays* to display video quality and size options and select the desired option.
4. Click *Don't Use Recorded Timings and Narrations* and click *Use Recorded Timings and Narration* if you wish to use any recorded timings and narration or laser pointer movements.
5. Click the *Seconds to spend on each slide* spin arrows to change the default time of 5 seconds if you are not using recorded timings and narrations.
6. Click Create Video.
7. Navigate to the location where you want to store the video when the Save As dialog box appears and type a file name in the *File name* box.
8. Click Save.

Before you determine the video quality and size for the presentation, you need to determine the output for the video. If you plan on the presentation video being displayed on a computer or high definition (HD) display, you need to create a high-quality video (960 × 720 pixels). This creates a large file size. If you plan to upload the video to the Internet or burn it to a DVD, you need to create a medium-quality video (640 × 480 pixels). This creates a moderate file size. If you plan on the video being played on a portable device, you need to create a low-quality video (340 × 240 pixels). This creates the smallest file size, but text would be difficult to read. Figure 8.25 displays the *Create a Video* options with the default setting for computer and HD displays.

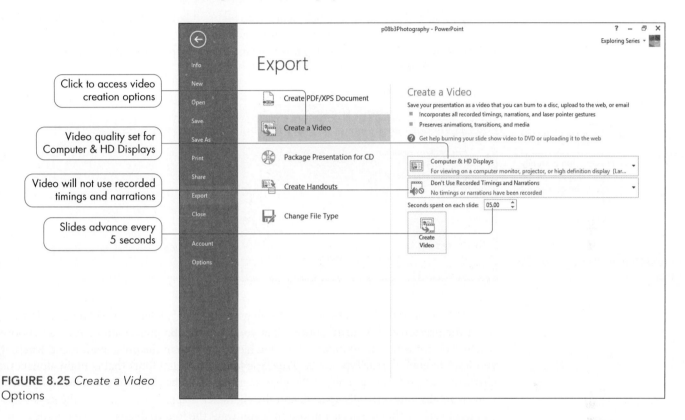

FIGURE 8.25 *Create a Video* Options

The length of time it takes to create a video depends on the content in the presentation and the length and quality of the video. The presentation will be recorded in real time, so it may take several hours to record. You can monitor the progress of the recording on the status bar. To play the video, locate and double-click the file.

Package Presentation for CD

STEP 2 ≫ ***Package Presentation for CD*** is a PowerPoint feature that enables you to copy your presentation to a CD or a storage location such as a hard drive, a network location, or a USB device. You can save the fonts you used, linked and embedded items, and a special PowerPoint Viewer. After you have packaged your presentation for CD, you can then distribute it to others, who do not even need to have PowerPoint installed on their computers to view it because the PowerPoint Viewer is part of the package. You may package your presentation on a CD for your personal use, too. If you are presenting at another location and are unsure of the system you will be using to present, you can package your presentation and carry the CD with you. At the new location, you simply play the presentation without worrying about whether the computer you are using to present has PowerPoint installed.

To package your presentation, do the following:

1. Save the presentation you want to package.
2. Insert a CD into the CD drive if you want to copy the presentation to a CD. Omit this step if you are copying the presentation to a folder on a USB device, a hard drive, or to a network location.
3. Click the FILE tab and click Export.
4. Click *Package Presentation for CD*.
5. Click *Package for CD* in the right pane.

The *Package for CD* dialog box opens (see Figure 8.26). Click in the *Name the CD* box and type a name for your CD. If you wish to include additional presentations or files on the CD, click Add. The Add Files dialog box appears. Select the presentation you want to include and click Add. Repeat this process until all files are added.

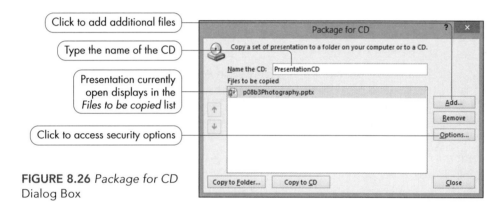

FIGURE 8.26 *Package for CD* Dialog Box

Click Options in the *Package for CD* dialog box to specify what files will be included and to set the privacy and security options that you want for the presentation. You can choose whether or not you want to include files you have linked to in the presentation and whether you want to embed TrueType fonts. **TrueType fonts** are digital fonts that contain alphabetic characters and information about the characters, such as the shape of the character, how it is horizontally and vertically spaced, and the character mapping that governs the keystrokes you use to access them. This is important if you want the font to display as the font designer created it and as you used it in the presentation. If you have used a nonstandard font in your presentation, you cannot be sure the computer on which you are going to display your presentation has the same font. If it does not have the same font, the computer substitutes another font, which can create havoc in your presentation design. If you embed the TrueType fonts you used in your presentation, you will have a larger file, but you can be sure that your presentation displays fonts accurately.

To ensure the security and privacy of your presentation, the *Package for CD* options also enable you to set a password for opening the presentation and a second password for modifying the presentation. You can also check the option to inspect the presentation for inappropriate or private information and remove it, a feature you explored earlier in this chapter. After setting the options you want, click OK. Figure 8.27 displays the Options dialog box.

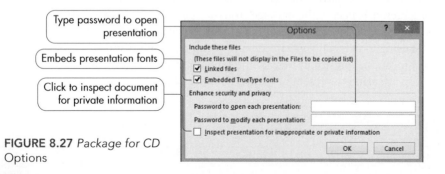

FIGURE 8.27 *Package for CD* Options

Once you have selected the options you want, click either *Copy to Folder* or *Copy to CD*. If you click *Copy to Folder*, you can copy the files to a new folder on your hard drive or a storage location such as a USB drive. You can create a name for the folder, browse to the location you wish to store the folder, and then copy the presentation to that location. If you click *Copy to CD*, for security purposes, you are asked if you want to include linked files. If you trust the linked files, click Yes. At that point, you see instructions for writing to your CD writer. These instructions vary depending on the device you use to burn CDs.

After you have packaged your presentation for CD and distributed it, the individual receiving the CD simply places the CD in his or her CD drive, and the CD loads and displays your presentation. If you included more than one presentation on the CD, the presentations load and display in the order in which you added them to the CD. This is the default setting for *Package for CD*. If the presentation was packaged to a folder, locate and open the folder and double-click the presentation name. This starts the Viewer, and a screen displays with a list of the presentations you packaged. Click the presentation you wish to display and click Open.

Create Handouts in Microsoft Word

In addition to the excellent handouts you can create in PowerPoint, you can prepare handouts in Word. When you create your audience handouts through Word, you can take advantage of all of Word's word-processing tools. In addition, you are given several helpful layouts not available in PowerPoint. For example, when you create notes page handouts in PowerPoint, the handouts consist of a thumbnail of the slide at the top of the page with its related notes beneath it—one slide per sheet of paper. If you have many slides, this can be an inefficient use of paper. By sending your presentation to Word, you can select a layout that puts thumbnails of the slides on the left side of the page and the related notes on the right side. Depending on the length of your notes, you may fit several slides per sheet of paper. This saves paper but can be time-consuming, as Word has to create a table and insert the slides and notes in the table cells. Figure 8.28 shows a notes page in PowerPoint, and Figure 8.29 shows its counterpart in Word.

FIGURE 8.28 PowerPoint Notes Page

Photo: Patryk Kosmider/Fotolia

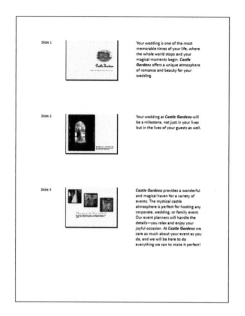

FIGURE 8.29 Word Notes Page

To create handouts in Word, do the following:

1. Click the FILE tab and click Export.
2. Select Create Handouts.
3. Click Create Handouts in the right pane.
4. Click the layout you want for your handouts in the *Send to Microsoft Word* dialog box (see Figure 8.30).
5. Click OK.

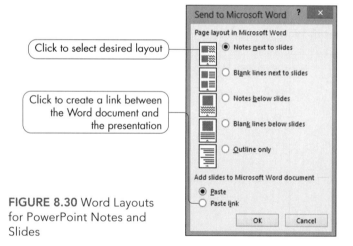

FIGURE 8.30 Word Layouts for PowerPoint Notes and Slides

The *Send to Microsoft Word* dialog box includes an option to paste a link between the Word document and the presentation so that changes you make in either one are reflected in the other. After you click OK in the dialog box, Microsoft Word opens and displays your presentation in the page layout you selected. When you are done making changes in Word and done printing the handout, click Close to quit Word.

Saving and Sharing a Presentation

A variety of methods exist for sharing a presentation to others, depending on your audience and how you want to connect with them. You can share the presentation by using e-mail, inviting people to OneDrive to view or collaborate on it, getting a Sharing Link, using the Present Online feature, or publishing the slides.

Send Using E-Mail

One easy-to-use method for distributing a presentation is to send it by e-mail. If your default e-mail client is Outlook, Windows Mail, or Outlook Express, you can send the presentation file directly from PowerPoint. Recipients receive the presentation as an attachment to the e-mail.

To e-mail a presentation from PowerPoint, do the following:

1. Click the FILE tab and click Share.
2. Click Email.
3. Click *Send as Attachment* or another send option (see Figure 8.31).
4. Type or select the e-mail addresses of the recipient(s) in the To box that opens in your default e-mail application.
5. Change the subject line from the name of the presentation if you want and add a message informing the recipient(s) of your purpose for sending the presentation.
6. Click Send.

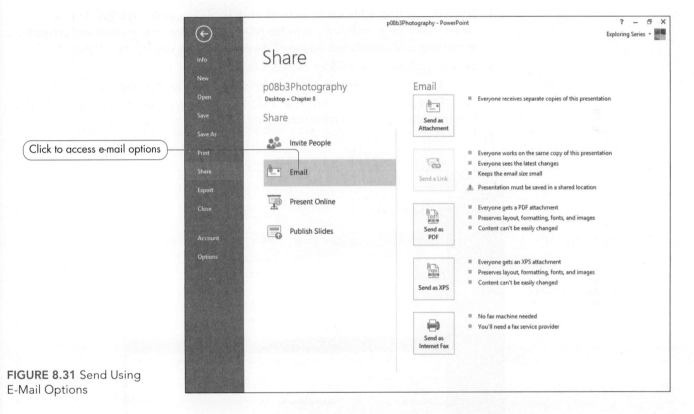

Click to access e-mail options

FIGURE 8.31 Send Using E-Mail Options

If you do not use Outlook, Windows Mail, or Outlook Express as your default e-mail client and want to send your presentation via e-mail, do the following:

1. Save the presentation in the file type that meets your needs and close the presentation.
2. Open your e-mail client.
3. Click Attach, locate the file, and then attach the file to the e-mail.
4. Type or select the e-mail addresses of the recipient(s) in the To box.
5. Change the subject line to the subject you want and add a message informing the recipient(s) of your purpose for sending the presentation.
6. Click Send.

Invite People to OneDrive

STEP 3 >> You can use PowerPoint to send your presentation to *OneDrive*, an app used to store, share, and access files and folders. OneDrive is part of Microsoft's *Windows Live* online services designed to help users communicate and collaborate, and it currently provides 7 GB of free online storage for photos and documents. OneDrive enables you to store, access, and share your files from anywhere with Internet access—no need to carry a USB or external drive with you! When you share a presentation stored in OneDrive, you can share a link to OneDrive with others rather than sending an attachment. This enables you to maintain a single version of the presentation and enables others to edit the presentation in their browsers. To log in to OneDrive, you will need a Microsoft account and password. If you use Hotmail, Messenger, or Xbox Live, you already have a Microsoft account.

To send a presentation to the Web using OneDrive, do the following:

1. Click the FILE tab and click Share.
2. Click Invite People. Click Save To Cloud.
3. Click *User name*'s OneDrive on the Save As pane. Then click Browse.
4. If you do not have a Microsoft account, click the Learn More hyperlink to go the sign-up Web page, and then follow the prompts to create your account and credentials. If you have a Microsoft account, the Save As dialog box displays (see Figure 8.32).
5. Double-click the Public folder and click Save.
6. Type the names or e-mail addresses of those you want to share the presentation with. You can include a personal message, and you can require users to sign in to OneDrive before accessing the document (see Figure 8.33).
7. Click Share.

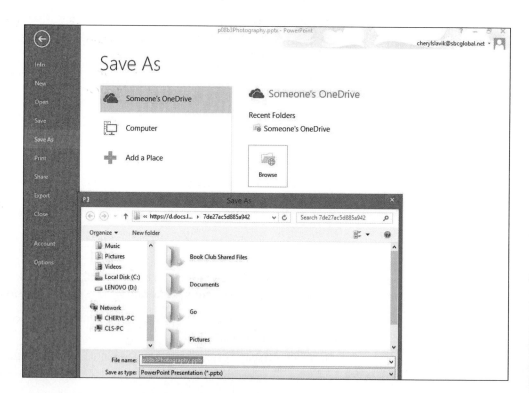

FIGURE 8.32 Saving to OneDrive

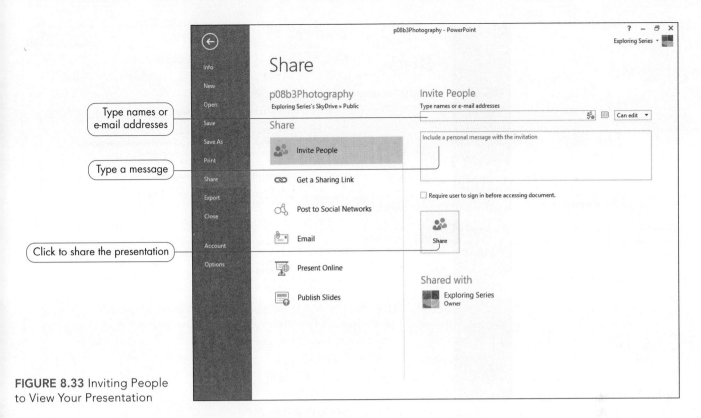

Type names or e-mail addresses

Type a message

Click to share the presentation

FIGURE 8.33 Inviting People to View Your Presentation

Present Online

It is possible for you to use **Present Online**, or transmit a presentation over the Internet to invited participants who are in different locations. To do this, you use a Microsoft account to log into the Office Presentation Service, a free service provided by Microsoft for PowerPoint users. To share the presentation, you send the URL for the presentation to your invited participants, and they watch your presentation on their Internet browser at the same time you deliver it.

To broadcast a presentation, do the following:

1. Click the FILE tab and click Share.
2. Click Present Online.
3. Click the Present Online button in the right pane (see Figure 8.34).
4. Sign in using your Microsoft account if prompted to do so.
5. Click Copy Link and share the link with participants via an instant messenger program or e-mail. Click *Send in Email* to send the link through Outlook, Windows Mail, or Outlook Express.
6. Click Start Presentation.
7. Advance through the slide show and exit the slide show when you have displayed all slides.
8. Click File and click Close to end the online presentation. When warned that everyone viewing the presentation will be disconnected if you continue, click End Online Presentation (see Figure 8.35).

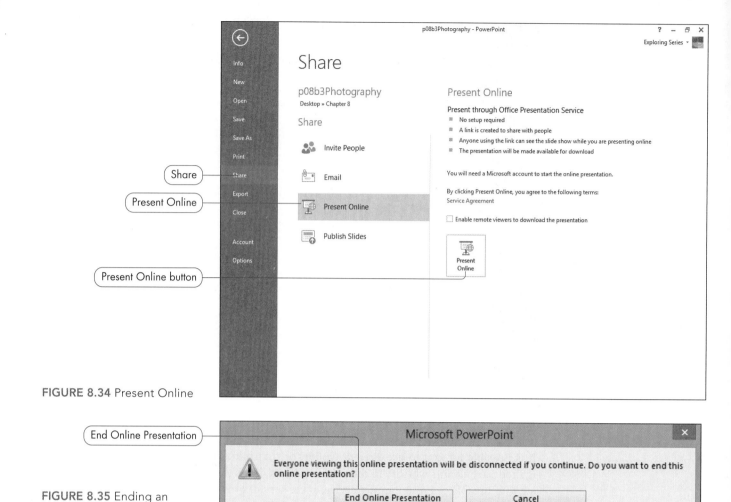

FIGURE 8.34 Present Online

FIGURE 8.35 Ending an Online Presentation

Publish Slides

You can share and reuse individual PowerPoint slides by storing them in a slide library on a server or at a SharePoint site.

In an office environment, you may have access to a Microsoft ***SharePoint library*** (a location on a SharePoint site where you can store and manage files you add to the library) or a ***SharePoint workspace*** (a copy of a SharePoint site for offline use). Access to a SharePoint site enables collaboration between team members on a project and provides additional services unavailable in PowerPoint. All SharePoint team members are able to save to and obtain files from a centralized browser-based location, depending on their permissions. A SharePoint site is generally found in a corporate environment, but check with your instructor or lab manager to see whether a SharePoint site is available for your use.

Using SharePoint for collaborating enables you to do the following:

- Store your presentations in a document workspace.

- Save and reuse presentations in a PowerPoint slide library so team members have access to each other's work.

- Have online discussions as presentations are being developed.

- Track the progress of a presentation using workflow.

SharePoint enables work teams to work together on a presentation, share files, and discuss presentations in progress. The workspace provides a set of icons to make sharing and updating documents easy. Slides can be saved directly to a slide library that has been created and published slides are available to team members for reuse in other presentations. The slides are available from the Reuse Slides pane. Finally, SharePoint sites provide for workflow management by monitoring the start, progress, and completion of a presentation review process.

You and your coworkers can access the slide library and do the following:

- Add slides to the slide library.
- Reuse slides in the slide library in a presentation.
- Track changes made to slides in the slide library.
- Locate the latest version of a slide in the slide library.
- Receive e-mail notifications when slides in the slide library are changed.

To publish slides from the current presentation to a slide library or a SharePoint site, do the following:

1. Click the FILE tab and click Share.
2. Click Publish Slides.
3. Select slides that you want to publish in the *Publish slides* dialog box. Click Browse to select a slide library where you want the presentation saved.
4. Click Select and click Publish.

Quick Concept

1. Explain when you might want to change file types for a presentation. Discuss two different file types you would use. **p. 501**

2. What are the benefits of saving a presentation using PowerPoint Picture Presentation? **p. 501**

3. What is the difference between sharing a presentation in OneDrive and sending the presentation as an attachment? **p. 508**

Hands-On Exercises

Watch the Video for this Hands-On Exercise!

MyITLab® HOE3 Training

3 Presentation Sharing

You want to share the Harbor Business Center presentation with an associate. You decide to save the presentation as a PowerPoint Picture Presentation to flatten the content to a single image per slide, and to invite your associate to view the presentation on OneDrive. You also package the presentation to a folder so that others can watch the presentation on most computers.

Skills covered: Create a PowerPoint Picture Presentation • Package a Presentation • Share by Inviting People

STEP 1 ≫ CREATE A POWERPOINT PICTURE PRESENTATION

You want to save the Harbor Business Center presentation as a PowerPoint Picture Presentation so each slide is flattened as an image, making it more difficult to modify. Refer to Figure 8.36 as you complete Step 1.

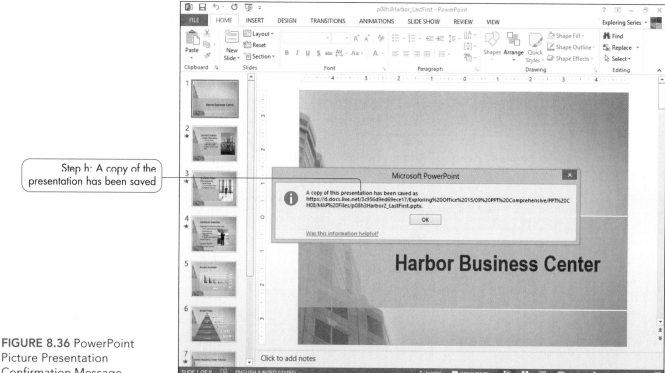

FIGURE 8.36 PowerPoint Picture Presentation Confirmation Message

a. Use File Explorer to make a copy of *p08h2Harbor_LastFirst*. Rename the copied presentation **p08h3Harbor_LastFirst**.

> **TROUBLESHOOTING:** If you open *p08h2Harbor_LastFirst* and try to save it as another file name, PowerPoint removes the digital signature and the *Marked as Final* designation. You need to preserve those settings so that your instructor can verify that you completed Hands-On Exercise 2.

b. Open *p08h3Harbor_LastFirst* and type **password** when prompted to enter the password to modify or open as read only. Click **OK**.

   You protected the presentation with a password in Hands-On Exercise 2.

c. Click **Edit Anyway** on the *Marked as Final* message bar.

The *Marked as Final* message bar is removed, and the status bar no longer contains the Digital Signature and *Marked as Final* icons.

d. Click the **FILE tab**, click **Export**, and then click **Change File Type**.

A list of file types display in the right pane, the Change File Type pane.

e. Click **PowerPoint Picture Presentation** and click **Save As** at the bottom of the pane.

A Save As dialog box displays.

f. Change the presentation to **p08h3HarborPicture_LastFirst**, adding *Picture* to the file name. Click **Save**.

A Microsoft PowerPoint dialog box displays indicating a copy of the presentation has been saved and giving the full path and file name of the copy.

g. Click **OK**.

The dialog box disappears and the *p08h3Harbor_LastFirst* presentation is onscreen.

h. Save *p08h3Harbor_LastFirst* and leave it open.

STEP 2 ≫ PACKAGE A PRESENTATION

You use the *Package a Presentation for CD* feature to package the Harbor Business Center presentation.

a. Open *p08h3Harbor_LastFirst*, if necessary.

TROUBLESHOOTING: If you closed *p08h3Harbor_LastFirst* while completing the previous step, you will need to type password in the Password dialog box and click OK.

---

b. Click the **FILE tab** and click **Export**.

The Export options display in the Backstage view.

c. Click **Package Presentation for CD** and click **Package for CD** in the right pane.

The *Package for CD* dialog box appears. The default name assigned by PowerPoint, *PresentationCD*, displays and the presentation file name is shown in the *Files to be copied* list.

d. Type **Harbor Business** in the **Name the CD box**.

e. Click **Copy to Folder**.

The *Copy to Folder* dialog box displays the name of the folder and the location in which it will be saved.

f. Click **Browse**, navigate to the location where you save your solution files, and then click **Select**.

g. Click **OK** and then click **Yes** to include linked files.

File Explorer opens and displays the PresentationPackage folder, an AUTORUN.INF file (the instruction file that starts the presentation when a CD is inserted), and the presentation file.

h. Close File Explorer and close the *Package for CD* dialog box.

i. Leave *p08h3Harbor_LastFirst* open for the next step.

STEP 3 » SHARE BY INVITING PEOPLE

You want to share the presentation by inviting your associate (your instructor) to see it at OneDrive. Refer to Figure 8.37 as you complete Step 2.

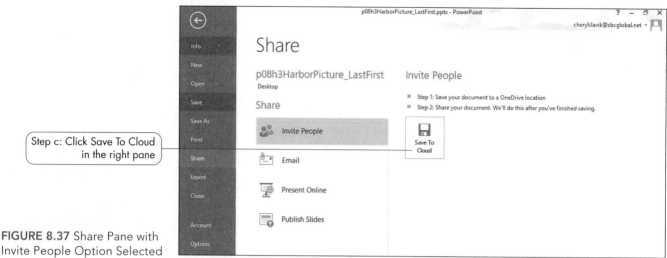

Step c: Click Save To Cloud in the right pane

FIGURE 8.37 Share Pane with Invite People Option Selected

TROUBLESHOOTING: You will not be able to do this step if you do not have a Microsoft account. To obtain a Microsoft account, refer to the Tip that appears just before the beginning of Hands-On Exercise 2.

---

a. Open *p08h3HarborPicture_LastFirst* if necessary.

b. Click the **FILE tab** and click **Share**.

c. Click **Invite People** and click **Save To Cloud** in the right pane.

The Save As pane opens where you can choose to save the presentation in OneDrive.

d. Click **User Name's OneDrive** on the Save As pane. Click **Browse**.

e. Double-click the **Public folders** and click **Save**.

f. Type the names or e-mail addresses of those you want to share the presentation with. Make sure the *Require user to sign in before accessing the document* check box is not checked.

g. Click **Share** as directed by your instructor.

h. Save and close the file, and submit based on your instructor's directions

Chapter Objectives Review

After reading this chapter, you have accomplished the following objectives:

1. **Work with comments and annotations.**
   - To facilitate the collaboration process, PowerPoint provides tools that team members can use to review a presentation.
   - The Review tab contains the Comments group, which has tools for adding a new comment on a slide, for editing or deleting existing comments, and for moving between comments.
   - While displaying a slide show, a team member can add ink annotations, such as highlighting or drawings, and save the annotations.

2. **Show, hide, and print markup.**
   - When the annotations are saved, they display on the slides in Normal view, or when comments have been added to a slide, the slide shows the markup.
   - The Show Markup button is located in the Comments group on the Review tab and can be toggled on or off to be hidden or displayed.
   - You can keep a record of markups made to a presentation by printing the comments and ink annotations. Comments will print on a separate page for each slide, whereas annotations print on the slide for which they were created.

3. **Compare and merge presentations.**
   - PowerPoint 2013 enables you to compare two versions of a presentation.
   - The differences in the presentations are marked as revisions that you can accept or reject.

4. **View presentation properties.**
   - PowerPoint automatically stores data about your documents as document properties.
   - It automatically stores the name of the author creating the presentation, as well as data such as the number of slides in the show and the number of words.
   - You can add additional properties such as a subject, keywords, status, and comments that can be used to search for and locate documents.

5. **Check a presentation for issues.**
   - Before distributing the slideshow, you can use the Inspect Document feature to find the document properties and strip out the properties you do not want others to see.
   - The Check Accessibility feature checks a presentation for issues that people with disabilities may find hard to read.
   - The Compatibility Checker inspects the presentation for features not supported by earlier versions of PowerPoint.

6. **Protect a presentation.**
   - To indicate that the presentation is completed, use the *Mark as Final* feature.
   - For security and privacy reasons, you may want to encrypt a presentation and set a password to open a document or modify a document.
   - IRM prevents presentations or other documents from being forwarded, edited, printed, or copied without your authorization.
   - Add a digital signature to your presentation if you want to authenticate it. To authenticate your presentation to others, you must sign up with a third-party signature service. You can create a personal digital signature for your use to authenticate that a presentation has not been modified since you last worked on it.

7. **Select a presentation file type.**
   - PowerPoint includes many options for saving a document based on your needs and the needs of your audience.
   - The file types are available in the Save As feature, but accessing the Change File Type option provides you with a list of commonly used file types and a description of the file type to help you determine if it is appropriate for your needs.

8. **Save and share a presentation.**
   - You have a variety of methods for sending a presentation to others. The method of distribution you select depends on your audience and how you want to connect with them.
   - You can send the presentation to your audience using e-mail, save the presentation to the Web or to a SharePoint location, transmit the presentation using the Present Online service, or publish the slides to a slide library.

Key Terms Matching

Match the key terms with their definitions. Write the key term letter by the appropriate numbered definition.

a. Accessibility
b. Accessibility Checker
c. Alternative text (alt text)
d. Comment
e. Compatibility Checker
f. Digital signature
g. Document Inspector
h. Document property
i. Encryption
j. eXtensible Markup Language (XML)

k. Markup
l. Metadata
m. OpenDocument presentation (.odp)
n. Present Online
o. Reviewer
p. SharePoint workspace
q. OneDrive
r. TrueType font
s. Windows Live
t. XPS file format (XPS)

1. _____ A Microsoft service that enables the transmission of a presentation in real time over the Internet to a remote audience. **p. 509**

2. _____ An app used to store, share, and access files and folders. **p. 508**

3. _____ A digital font that contain alphabetic characters and information about the characters, such as the shape, spacing, and character mapping of the font. **p. 504**

4. _____ A presentation that conforms to the OpenDocument standard for exchanging data between applications. **p. 501**

5. _____ Comments and ink annotations appearing in a presentation. **p. 474**

6. _____ Aids in identifying and resolving accessibility issues in a presentation. **p. 488**

7. _____ Checks for features in a presentation that are not supported by earlier versions of PowerPoint. **p. 489**

8. _____ Protects the contents of your presentation by converting it into unreadable scrambled text that needs a password to be opened. **p. 492**

9. _____ A set of encoding rules that create a file format that is designed to provide maximum flexibility when storing and exchanging structured information. **p. 500**

10. _____ Detects hidden and personal data in the presentation. **p. 488**

11. _____ In PowerPoint, refers to the ease with which a person with physical challenges is able to access and understand a presentation. **p. 488**

12. _____ An invisible, electronic signature stamp that is encrypted and attached to a certificate that can be added to a presentation. **p. 493**

13. _____ Data that describes other data. **p. 479**

14. _____ A copy of a SharePoint site that can be used while offline. **p. 510**

15. _____ A text-based description of an image. **p. 489**

16. _____ A text note attached to the slide. **p. 474**

17. _____ Someone who examines the presentation and provides feedback. **p. 474**

18. _____ An electronic file format created by Microsoft that preserves document formatting and is viewable and printable on any platform. **p. 502**

19. _____ A group of online services provided by Microsoft that are designed to help users communicate and collaborate. **p. 508**

20. _____ An attribute, such as an author's name or keyword, that describes a file. **p. 479**

Multiple Choice

1. The process whereby a team works together to accomplish a goal is referred to as which of the following?

   (a) Unification
   (b) Collusion
   (c) Collaboration
   (d) Deliberation

2. Which of the following is an Adobe electronic file format that preserves document formatting?

   (a) PDF
   (b) XPS
   (c) PDX
   (d) XML

3. Markup may consist of all of the following except:

   (a) Comments inserted by the presentation creator.
   (b) Annotations.
   (c) Comments inserted by a reviewer.
   (d) Passwords created for opening and modifying a presentation.

4. Which of the following statements regarding comments in a presentation is not true?

   (a) Comments are printed on a separate page than the slide.
   (b) Comments display as a small icon that may be clicked on to open so the comment text can be read.
   (c) Comments display in the bottom-right side of the presentation by default but may be dragged to any location.
   (d) Comments print when Show Markup on the REVIEW tab is selected.

5. Which of the following document properties is not created automatically by PowerPoint but can be added?

   (a) Number of slides in the presentation
   (b) Location of the presentation
   (c) Keywords
   (d) Date the presentation was created

6. Which of the following is not checked by the Document Inspector?

   (a) Comments and annotations
   (b) Version compatibility
   (c) Document properties and personal information
   (d) Presentation notes

7. Which of the following is a true statement regarding passwords?

   (a) One password may be set to open a document, and a second password may be set to modify a document.
   (b) Mary_Sept18_1990 is a more secure password than M@ryO9LB_L99O.
   (c) A password can only be set through the *Prepare for Sharing* feature.
   (d) If you forget a password you have created, contact www.microsoft.com for a tool that will restore your document without a password.

8. Which of the following may be packaged with your presentation when you use the *Package for CD* feature?

   (a) All TrueType fonts used in the presentation
   (b) Any files linked to the presentation
   (c) A PowerPoint Viewer
   (d) All of the above

9. All of the following statements about creating handouts in Microsoft Office Word are true except:

   (a) Create Handouts is available from the REVIEW tab.
   (b) Creating handouts in Microsoft Word enables you to use word-processing features to format the handouts.
   (c) Word provides layouts not available in PowerPoint.
   (d) A link can be pasted between PowerPoint and Word so changes can update in either document when made.

10. When merging presentations, the Reviewing pane does which of the following?

    (a) Displays a list of all comments and annotations created in the presentation
    (b) Lists features in the presentation that are not supported by earlier versions of PowerPoint
    (c) Lists changes to the slide currently selected and any slides that have been added or removed in the presentation
    (d) Enables you to add a digital signature to ensure the integrity of the presentation

Practice Exercises

1 Castle Gardens

Castle Gardens provides wedding packages that include the use of fabulous gardens or a castle great hall, a wedding planner, pewter tableware, old English décor, photography, and videography. You create a PowerPoint presentation advertising Castle Gardens and submit it to the owner, Ms. Grosscurth, for review. She reviewed the slides, added comments, and made changes. You merge the presentations and accept and reject changes. You view the presentation and highlight words and phrases you think create the emotional appeal of Castle Gardens and you keep the ink annotations when you exit Slide Show view. You print a copy of the comments and annotations to create a record of the changes you made and hide the markup. This exercise follows the same set of skills as used in Hands-On Exercise 1 in the chapter. Refer to Figure 8.38 as you complete this exercise.

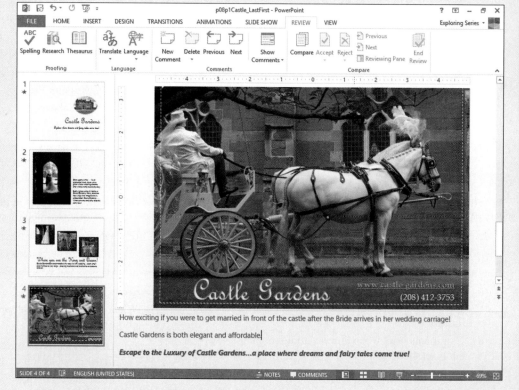

FIGURE 8.38 Castle Gardens Presentation

Photos: (Slide 2) Jon Turner/Fotolia, (Slide 3, left) gmg9130/Fotolia, (Slide 3, middle) ilfotokunst/Fotolia, (Slide 3, right) Mat Hayward/Fotolia, (Slide 4) Pefkos/Fotolia

a. Open *p08p1Castle* and save it as **p08p1Castle_LastFirst**. Click the **FILE tab**, click **Options**, and then change the user name to your name and the initials to your initials (if necessary). Click **OK**.

b. Create a handout header with your name and a handout footer with your instructor's name and your class. Include the current date.

c. On Slide 1, click the **REVIEW tab** and click **New Comment** in the Comments group. Type **Ms. Grosscurth, this is the beginning of the presentation we discussed. Please review it and make suggestions for changes. Thanks!**

d. Save the presentation and click **Compare** in the Compare group.

e. Navigate to your student data files, select *p08p1CastleGrosscurth*, and then click **Merge**.

f. On Slide 1, select and read the first comment in the *Slide Changes* section displayed in the DETAILS tab of the Revisions pane, the comment requesting that Ms. Grosscurth review the presentation.

g. Click **Delete** in the Comments group.

h. Click **Insertions at beginning of presentation** in the *Presentation Changes* section. Click **All slides inserted at this position** in the Slides pane. Select and read the next comment in the *Slide Changes* section, the comment requesting that you change the color tone of the castle picture.

i. Select the image of the castle and click the **FORMAT tab**. Click **Color** in the Adjust group. Click **Temperature: 4700 K** in the *Color Tone* section.

j. Click the **REVIEW tab**, click **Next** two times in the Comments group, and then read the comment on Slide 2. Click **Next** in the Comments group.

k. On Slide 3, read the comment, select the text *The castle*, and then type **Castle Gardens**.

l. Click **Next** two times in the Comments group and read the comment for Slide 4 at the top of the *Slide Changes* section.

m. Click the **Accept arrow** in the Compare group and click **Accept All Changes to the Presentation**. All of the changes are accepted, but the comments remain.

n. Close the Revisions pane. Close the Comments pane.

o. Click the **SLIDE SHOW tab** and click **From Beginning** in the Slide Show group.

p. On Slide 1, right-click anywhere on the slide, point to *Pointer Options*, and then select **Highlighter**. Highlight the following words in the presentation, selecting the highlighter on each slide:

Slide #	Words to Highlight
1	dreams, fairy tales
2	wishes came true
3	most lavish wedding

q. Exit the presentation and click **Keep** in the Microsoft PowerPoint dialog box asking if you want to keep your ink annotations.

r. Click the **FILE tab**, click **Print**, and then click **Full Page Slides**. Click **4 Slides Horizontal** in the *Handouts* section. Note the annotations display on the print preview.

s. Drag the vertical scroll bar down and note that comments from all four slides display.

t. Click the **REVIEW tab**, click the **Show Comments arrow**, and then click **Show Markup** to toggle the display of the markup off.

u. Save and close the file, and submit based on your instructor's directions.

2 Martin Luther King Jr. Commemoration Flyer

You are part of a student council committee working on the annual Martin Luther King Jr. Commemoration. You have created a one-page flyer that can be e-mailed to students and also printed and handed out in the Student Center. In this exercise, you change the presentation properties, check the presentation for issues, save the presentation as a PDF file to preserve the formatting and image when printing, and then create handouts in Microsoft Word. This exercise follows the same set of skills as used in Hands-On Exercises 2 and 3 in the chapter. Refer to Figure 8.39 as you complete this exercise.

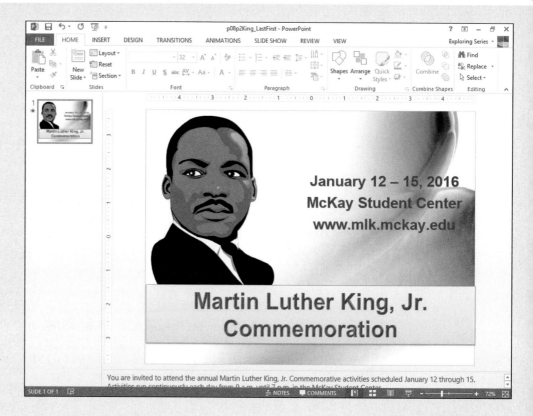

FIGURE 8.39 Accessibility Issues in Flyer

Photo: BasheeraDesigns/Fotolia

a. Open *p08p2King* and then save it as **p08p2King_LastFirst**.

b. Create a handout header with your name and a handout footer with your instructor's name and your class. Include the current date.

c. Click the **FILE tab**, click **Properties** in the right pane, and then click **Show Document Panel**. Make the following changes to the properties:

Property	Change
Title	Martin Luther King Jr. Commemoration
Subject	Annual MLK Commemoration Flyer
Keywords	Martin Luther King Jr., Commemoration, Flyer, MLK, Ad, civil rights
Category	Civil rights
Comments	Flyer to be mailed, and printed and distributed in the Student Center

d. Close the Document Properties panel.

e. Click the **FILE tab**, click **Check for Issues**, and then click **Check Accessibility**.

f. Note the Accessibility Checker shows two errors and one tip for making the document more accessible. Click **Picture 4 (Slide 1)** in the *Inspection Results* section of the Accessibility Checker and read why this error needs to be fixed and how to fix the error in the *Additional Information* section.

g. Click the picture of Martin Luther King Jr., if necessary, and click the **Format tab**. Click the **Size dialog box launcher**.

h. Click **Alt Text** in the Format Picture pane and type the following:

Alt Text	Text-Based Representation
Title	Martin Luther King Jr.
Description	This is an image of Martin Luther King Jr., an African American leader in the civil rights movement, an activist, and an American clergyman.

i. Click **Close** in the Format Picture Pane. Leave the Accessibility Checker open.

j. Click **Slide 1** in the *Errors* section of the *Inspection Results* section of the Accessibility Checker and read why this error needs to be fixed and how to fix the error in the *Additional Information* section.

k. Click in the **title placeholder** and type **Martin Luther King Jr. Commemoration**.

l. Click **Slide 1** displayed under *Tips* in the *Inspection Results* section of the Accessibility Checker and read the tip on why reordering the objects on the slide can benefit the comprehension of someone who cannot view the slide.

m. Click the **HOME tab**, click **Arrange** in the Drawing group, and then select **Selection Pane**. Ensure **Title 1** is selected and click the **Re-order up arrow** twice so that the title will be read first by a text reader. Select **Subtitle 2** and click the **Re-order up arrow** once so that the subtitle will be read next by a text reader. Close the Selection pane and the Accessibility Checker pane.

n. Click the **FILE tab**, click **Export**, and then click **Create PDF/XPS Document**, if necessary.

o. Click **Create PDF/XPS** in the right pane, navigate to the folder containing your files, and then click **Publish**.

p. Close Adobe Acrobat Reader or Adobe Acrobat.

q. Click the **FILE tab**, click **Export**, and then click **Create Handouts**.

r. Click **Create Handouts** in the right pane.

s. Click **Notes below slides**. Click **OK**.

t. Delete Slide 1 in the top-left corner when Word opens. Navigate to where you are saving your files and save the document as **p08p2KingHandout_LastFirst**. Close Word.

u. Save the presentation, and submit based on your instructor's directions.

Mid-Level Exercises

1 Protecting Your Computer Training Presentation

As an employee of your company's IT department, you sometimes prepare technology training materials. You are currently preparing a presentation on threats to computer security and computer safety tips. You ask Ben, a colleague in human resources, to review the presentation and insert comments with suggestions. Because the presentation is password protected, you share the password with him. When he returns the presentation, you merge and compare the presentations and decide which suggestions to incorporate. Then you prepare the presentation for distribution and select a presentation file type.

a. Open *p08m1Protect* and save it as **p08m1Protect_LastFirst**.

b. Create a handout header with your name and a handout footer with your instructor's name and your class. Include the current date.

c. Use Protect Presentation to encrypt the presentation with a password for opening. Use Th>3@t$ as the password.

d. On Slide 1, create a comment that reads **Ben, please review the presentation and make suggestions. Do I need to add anything? Thank you.**

e. Compare and merge *p08m1ProtectBen* with the open *p08m1Protect_LastFirst*.

f. Note that the Revisions pane lists two changes in the *Presentation Changes* section. Accept both of the presentation changes: *Theme (1-14)* and *Insertions after "How do You Defend Against Spyware."*

g. Starting with Slide 1, advance one by one through the comments on each slide using Next in the Comments group. Read each of the comments and make the following changes based on the comments:

Slide	Comment	Change
2	bb2	Link the *Viruses, Worms, and Trojan Horses* bullet to Slide 3.
2	bb3	Remove the *Protection* bullet.
2	bb4	Change slide titles to sentence case (the first letter of the sentence is capitalized, with the rest being lowercase unless requiring capitalization for a specific reason) on all slides except Slide 1. (Tip: Use Change Case in the Font group of the Home tab.)
5	bb5	Find and replace all occurrences of *E-mail* with *e-mail*. (Tip: Use Match Case)

h. Check the spelling in the presentation. Change all occurrences of *trojan* to **Trojan**. Ignore the suggestion for *OnGuard*.

i. View the presentation in Slide Show view. Annotate Slide 13, the *What is spam?* slide, by highlighting *spam* in the title to remind you to add a Spam hyperlink to the menu slide. Keep the ink annotations when you exit the slide show. On Slide 2, add **Spam** to the bulleted list and hyperlink it to Slide 13.

j. View the Print Preview for Handouts (4 slides Horizontal per page). Scroll through Print Preview and note the comments. Print as directed by your instructor.

k. Run the Compatibility Checker to check for features not supported by earlier versions of PowerPoint. Note that the SmartArt graphic on Slide 3 and any text in it cannot be edited when using versions of Microsoft Office earlier than Office 2007. Depending on the transition effect you selected, the transition effect may not be viewable using any earlier version of PowerPoint.

l. Change the file encryption settings for the presentation in General Options. Delete the password in the *Password to open* box.

m. Save the presentation and use the Export option Change File Type to save a version of the file to a PowerPoint Show so that it automatically opens as a slide show. Use the name **p08m1ProtectShow_LastFirst**.

n. Close the Revisions and Comments panes if necessary. Make the following changes to the properties:

Property	Change
Title	Protect Your Computer Against Harmful Attacks
Subject	Computer Safety
Keywords	Computer safety, viruses, worms, Trojan horses, spam
Category	Training
Comments	Presentation for Employee Education Program. Reviewed by Ben B.

o. Accept all changes and end the review. Close both of the presentations, and submit based on your instructor's directions.

2 Impressionist Artists

You have been refining a presentation on impressionist artists for your Nineteenth Century Art class. In this exercise, you prepare the presentation for distribution, create a handout in Microsoft Word, and then package the presentation. Finally, you present the presentation online to classmates who will be unable to be in class the day you present.

a. Open *p08m2Impressionism* and save it as **p08m2Impressionism_LastFirst**.

b. Create a handout header with your name and a handout footer with your instructor's name and your class in the presentation. Include the current date.

c. Inspect the presentation for hidden metadata or personal information. Check every type of information, including off-slide content.

d. Remove Document Properties and Personal Information. Do not remove presentation notes.

e. Run the Compatibility Checker to check for features not supported by earlier versions of PowerPoint. Note that earlier versions cannot change the shape and text in Slides 1 and 3.

f. Create handouts in Microsoft Word with notes next to the slides. Insert your name, instructor's name, and class in a header and print as directed by your instructor. Save the Word handout as **p08m2Handout_LastFirst**.

g. Use the *Package Presentation for CD* feature to copy the presentation and media links to the folder where you have saved your solution files. Name the CD **Impres_LastFirst**.

h. Create a Microsoft account so that you can access the Office Presentation Service.

 **i.** Use your Microsoft account to log into the Office Presentation Service.

j. Send an e-mail sharing the link for the online presentation with your instructor and start the slide show. After viewing the presentation, end the online presentation.

k. Save and close the file, and submit based on your instructor's directions.

3 Rescue Pets

You and your friends volunteer at the local animal shelter each week. You have been asked to put together a short presentation about some of the success stories for matching animals with loving families. The presentation will be used to solicit donations, to recruit more volunteers, and to attract more adoptive families. You and your friends can use OneDrive or pass the presentation among group members as an attachment using your Outlook accounts.

a. Open *p08m3Pets* and save it as **p08m3Pets_LastFirst**.

b. Add your name on the title slide. Create a handout header with your name and a handout footer with your instructor's name and your class in the presentation. Include the current date.

 c. Add one slide with a description and a photo of a pet.

d. Save the presentation and pass it to the next student so that he or she can perform the same tasks. Continue until all group members have created a slide in the presentation.

e. Inspect the presentation by inspecting the document and running the Accessibility Checker and the Compatibility Checker. Correct all errors.

f. Create and publish a PDF of the presentation. Name the PDF **p08m3PetsHandout_LastFirst**. Close Adobe Acrobat Reader or Adobe Acrobat.

g. Use the *Package Presentation for CD* feature to copy the presentation and media links to the folder where you have saved your solution files. Name the CD **PetsCD_LastFirst**.

h. Save and close the files, and submit based on your instructor's directions.

Flat Stanley Team Project

RESEARCH CASE

Jeff Brown created Flat Stanley, a completely flat boy, in a children's book in 1964. In 1995, Dale Hubert started the Flat Stanley Project to encourage international literacy and community building—a project that has had a phenomenal worldwide impact on collaboration in education. Research the project at www.flatstanley.com. Your goal is to participate in a collaborative project using Flat Stanley by joining with a team of two to three other students in your class.

Each team member must create a Flat Stanley, or download the Flat Stanley template from the Web site. Team members should journal Flat Stanley's activities for several days by recording them with a digital camera. Create a presentation using your images. Send the presentation to your teammates via e-mail so they can add comments, annotations, and their own Flat Stanley images. When they return the presentation to you, compare and merge the documents. Accept and reject changes as needed to create a cohesive presentation of Flat Stanley's activities. Insert a handout header with your name and a handout footer with your instructor's name and your class. Include the current date. Create presentation properties that could help you locate the presentation, if needed. Inspect the document and remove anything that appears except the properties. Check the compatibility of the presentation with earlier versions of PowerPoint. Save the presentation as a PowerPoint Show. Present the slide show online to your teammates, or package the presentation to a folder including all links. Save the presentation as **p08b2FlatStanley_LastFirst**. Submit to your instructor as directed.

Photography Class Project

DISASTER RECOVERY

As a project for your Art Appreciation class, you contacted a local photographer, Katherine Hulce, and asked her to share several of her digital images with you. The photographer gave you permission to use her images but retained the copyright. You created a presentation to introduce her work and e-mailed the presentation to her. She returned the presentation with some added images, annotations, comments, and changes.

Open *p08b3Photography* and save it as **p08b3Photography_LastFirst**. Compare and merge the presentation with *p08b3PhotographyHulce*. Accept all changes to the presentation and end the review. As you view each slide, you notice two other photographers are mentioned on Slide 2. Change the slide title to singular and delete their names, leaving only Katherine Hulce's information. Run the Document Inspector to ensure no other photographers' information is included. Remove all comments, annotations, document properties, and personal information. Create a handout header with your name and a handout footer with your instructor's name and your class. Include the current date. Add the photographer's name as key words in the presentation properties. Save the presentation and resave it as a PowerPoint Picture Presentation with the name **p08b3PhotographyShow_LastFirst**. Mark the presentation as final and submit as directed by your instructor.

E-Mail Etiquette

SOFT SKILLS CASE S

Create a brief presentation that explores proper e-mail etiquette. Include a comment asking for feedback and suggestions for improvement on the last slide. Add keywords to the presentation properties. Run the Accessibility Checker and fix issues as needed. Save the presentation as **p08b4Etiquette_LastFirst**.

Compare your presentation with a classmate's presentation. Make any modifications needed. Save this version of the presentation as a PowerPoint Show as **p08b4EtiquetteShow_LastFirst**. Submit both files to your instructor as directed.

Capstone Exercise

You just returned from your first visit to New York City. Your sister combined your digital images into a memories slide show and e-mailed it to you. She wants you to review the presentation and make suggestions. After you make suggestions, she incorporates the suggestions in her slides and then returns the presentation for you to compare and merge. After accepting the changes, you prepare the presentation for distribution.

Create Annotations and Comments, Hide Markup

You open the presentation your sister sent to you and add annotations on some slides and make a comment.

a. Open the *p08c1NewYork* presentation and save it as **p08c1NewYork_LastFirst**.

b. Create a handout header with your name and a handout footer with your instructor's name and your class. Include the current date.

c. Play the slide show from the beginning. On Slide 2, change your pointer options to **Pen** and circle the existing text by using the mouse. Continue advancing through the slide show, circling any existing text until you reach the end of the presentation.

d. When you reach the end of the presentation, keep the ink annotations as a reminder of changes you want to suggest.

e. On Slide 1, create a comment that reads **Hey Sis, Why don't you use this spot to identify where we were? That's a picture of Battery Park on the southern tip of Manhattan.** Drag the comment balloon so it is next to the vertical text placeholder.

f. Save the presentation.

Merge Presentations

You compare and merge your sister's presentation with the presentation you created. Your sister made the changes you suggested and removed all comments and annotations from her copy.

a. Compare and merge the onscreen *p08c1NewYork_LastFirst* presentation with *p08c1NewYorkMichelle*.

b. Accept all changes and end the review.

c. Close the Revisions and the Comments panes.

Inspect the Presentation and Check Compatibility

You inspect the presentation to ensure that only the metadata you want is retained. You run the Compatibility Checker to see which features you used that are not supported by earlier versions of PowerPoint.

a. Inspect the presentation for hidden metadata or personal information. The Document Inspector locates document properties and presentation notes. Do not remove these items. Close the Document Inspector.

b. Run the Compatibility Checker to see which features you used that are not supported by earlier versions of PowerPoint. Slides 11 and 12 have shapes with text that cannot be edited (WordArt) if you save the presentation in an earlier file format. You do not need to make changes for the earlier version as part of this exercise.

Package the Presentation

You are ready to package the presentation to a folder so that it can be uploaded to the family Web site.

a. Package the presentation for CD with **NY2016_LastFirst** as the name.

b. Copy the presentation to the folder where you store your files. Include the linked files in your package.

c. Close File Explorer and save the presentation.

Mark as Final

In addition to packaging your presentation and burning it to a CD, you plan to indicate that this presentation is complete. You mark the presentation as final.

a. Mark the presentation as **Final**.

b. Verify the presentation has been marked as final by checking the status bar for the *Marked as Final* icon.

c. Save and close the file. Submit all files as directed by your instructor.

PowerPoint Introductory Application Capstone Exercise

You are a student employee of your college's Student Success department. A previous employee created a presentation for students to view while they are waiting for their advisor. The goal of the presentation is to raise student awareness about available savings and discounts. You decide to modify the original slide show to add additional information and visual impact. You will insert and modify an image, a SmartArt graphic, and a reused slide containing a table.

Presentation Setup and Slide Creation

You need to open the original slide show, rename the file, and save it. You insert a new slide for additional information.

a. Start PowerPoint. Open *p00ac1Discounts* and save the file as **p00ac1Discounts_LastFirst**.

b. Create a *Notes and Handouts* header and footer with the date, your name in the header, and your instructor's name and your class in the footer.

c. Insert a new slide after Slide 4 with the *Title and Content* layout.

d. Move to the new Slide 5 if necessary and type **Travel Savings** in the **title placeholder**.

e. Type the following as Level 1 bullets for Slide 5: **Airfare discounts**, **Rail passes**, **Global phones**.

f. Apply the **Quotable Theme** and select the **lime green variant**. Change the color theme to **Green Yellow**.

Insert and Modify a Picture

You need to insert, resize, and position a picture. You also add a picture frame to the image.

a. On Slide 5, insert the picture file **p00ac1Rooftops.jpg**.

b. Change the width of the picture to **3"** and the height to **2"**. Deselect the **Lock aspect ratio option**, if necessary.

c. Move the picture to the bottom-right corner of the slide so that it aligns with the bottom and right edges of the slide.

d. Apply the Picture Style **Simple Frame, Black**.

Add a Shape

To draw attention to an instruction, you decide to add a shape to a slide and insert text. After adding the shape, you group it with another shape to form an attention-grabbing graphic.

a. Click **Slide 2** and insert the **Horizontal Scroll shape** (second row, sixth column in the *Stars and Banners* category).

b. Change the width of the shape to **2.5"** and the height to **1.75"**.

c. Position the shape horizontally at **4.5"** to the right of 0 and vertically at **1.5"** below 0.

d. Type **Use a search engine to find "Software Discounts"** in the shape.

e. Select both the **Explosion1 shape** and the **Horizontal Scroll shape** and align them by their middles. Group the shapes.

f. Make sure the shapes are still selected and apply the shape style **Light 1 Outline – Colored Fill – Blue Accent 6**.

Use WordArt, Format a Background, and Insert Audio

You decide to enhance the Title slide by changing text to WordArt, formatting the background to add an image, and then adding an audio clip.

a. Click **Slide 1**. Select the text in the title placeholder and apply the WordArt style **Fill - White, Text 1, Outline – Background 1, Hard Shadow – Background 1**.

b. Switch to the VIEW tab, select the **Outline View**, select the **subtitle placeholder** on Slide 1, and then delete it. Switch to Normal view.

c. Click the **DESIGN tab** and access the Format Background options so that you can select a picture fill.

d. Insert a picture from online by searching the term *Dollars* and inserting a picture of your choosing. Change the transparency to **20%**.

e. Insert online audio by searching for the term *Techno* and looking for Techno pop music. Apply a **02.00 Fade Out duration**.

f. Change the audio clip playback from *On Click* to **Play Across Slides** and to start automatically. Check the **Loop until Stopped audio option**.

g. Align the sound icon to the bottom left corner of the slide.

Add Content and Animation

You reuse a previously created slide to add content, and then you format the table on the reused slide. Next, you create a SmartArt graphic to include information about "free stuff" for students and animate the graphic.

a. Switch to the HOME tab and use the Reuse Slides feature to add the slide in *p00ac1Tips.pptx* to the end of the presentation.

b. Select the table on the new Slide 6 and set the height of all the rows to **1"**.

c. Center align the text in the table. Apply the **Medium Style 1 table style** to the table.

d. Move the table so that its top-left corner is at the 1" mark above the 0 on the vertical ruler. Center align the table on the slide.

e. Insert a new slide after Slide 6 using the *Title and Content* layout. Type **Free Stuff** in the **title placeholder**.

f. On the new Slide 7, insert a Vertical Box List SmartArt graphic. Type **Ringtones** in the top shape, **Online video games** in the middle shape, and **Magazines and samples** in the bottom shape.

g. Change the SmartArt layout to a **Horizontal Bullet List** and change the SmartArt style to **Inset** (3-D category).

h. Align the SmartArt graphic to the bottom of the slide and resize as necessary so that it fits on the slide.

i. Apply the **Fly In animation** (Entrance category) to the SmartArt. Change the sequence of the animation to the **One by One effect**.

Finalize the Presentation

To ensure the professionalism of the presentation, you review the presentation and make changes.

a. Spell-check the presentation and correct any misspelled words. Ignore the message that appears for *PacSun*.

b. Click **Slide 2**. Use the Thesaurus to replace the word generally with an appropriate synonym.

c. Apply the **Cube transition** to all slides.

d. Change the transition timing so that all slides advance automatically after 8 seconds.

e. View the presentation.

f. Save the presentation. Close the presentation and exit PowerPoint. Submit the presentation as directed by your instructor.

As a member the IPC International Photo Conference Committee, you have been asked to help create a presentation for the upcoming Conference & Expo at the Boston Bailey Expo Center. Some of the slides will be printed as posters and displayed at the conference. Charts will be used to highlight last year's worldwide workshops and total attendees, and a table will display the workshop schedule for the Boston conference. You will also apply some animations, insert hyperlinks, and work with the slide master.

Presentation Creation

   a. Start PowerPoint. Open *p00ac2IPC* and save the file as **p00ac2IPC_LastFirst**.
   b. Change Slide Size to **On-screen Show (16:10)** and **Ensure Fit**.

Design a Table and Change the Table Layout

   a. On Slide 2, insert a table with 3 columns and 5 rows. Add the following information to the table:

Left Column	Middle Column	Right Column
Capturing the Moment	9:00 AM	12:00 PM
Giving Your Images the Edge	10:30 AM	1:00 PM
From Stills to Motion	12:00 PM	3:30 PM
Social Media	2:00 PM	4:30 PM
Wedding Techniques	4:00 PM	7:00 PM

   b. Insert a new top row to the table. Add the following information to the new row:

Left Column	Middle Column	Right Column
WORKSHOP	START	END

   c. Add a new first column to the table. Merge all the cells in the first column and format the cell in the first column with a picture fill using the downloaded *p00ac2Snapshot.jpg* file.
   d. Center all of the text in the table vertically and horizontally. Apply the **Convex bevel effect** to all cells of the table except for the picture. Change the height of the table to **4.5"**.

Create and Insert a Chart, Change a Chart Type, and Change the Chart Layout

   a. On Slide 3, insert the chart found in the downloaded Excel file *p00ac2Workshops* as an object to the slide. Change the height of the object to **4.5"** and center it on the slide.
   b. On Slide 4, insert a Clustered Column chart. When Excel opens, resize the chart data range to A1:B6. Delete the contents of the cells in columns C and D. Replace the remaining content in the Excel worksheet with the following data:

   Cell A2: CTM
   Cell A3: GYITE
   Cell A4: FSTM
   Cell A5: SM
   Cell A6: WT
   Cell B1: Attendees
   Cell B2: 9,673
   Cell B3: 11,412
   Cell B4: 6,591
   Cell B5: 4,809
   Cell B6: 9,177

   Close Excel.
   c. On Slide 4, change the chart to a *Line with Markers* chart. Apply the **Layout 8 layout style** to the chart. Format the data labels to display to the right of the data points.

Insert and Use a Hyperlink and Add an Action Button

a. On Slide 6, insert a hyperlink from the text *IPCzone.org* to the Web page **http://www.ipczone.org**. Add the ScreenTip **Click for additional information** to the hyperlink.

b. Click at the end of the next line, *E-mail us at*, add a space, and then type **ipczone@domain.net**, followed by a space.

c. On the next line, insert a hyperlink from the text *Download Registration Materials* to the downloaded Word document *p00ac2Registration*.

d. On Slide 6, insert an Action Button: Beginning shape by clicking in the bottom-left corner of the slide. Set the action button to link to Slide 2 (Workshop Schedule) when clicked. Align the action button with the left and bottom borders of the slide.

Apply a Motion Path Animation and Specify Animation Settings and Timings

a. On Slide 5, apply a **Fly In entrance animation** to the text placeholder on the left. Set the effect options so that the text flies in from the top left. Set clicking the picture on the bottom left (Picture 3) as the trigger for the animation and set the Start to **After Previous**.

b. On the same slide, apply the **Fly In entrance animation** to the text placeholder on the right. Set the Effect Options so that the text flies in from the top right. Set clicking the picture on the bottom right (Picture 2) as the trigger for the animation and set the Start to **After Previous**.

c. On the same slide, add an action to each of the two pictures on the bottom so that when they are clicked, the Camera sound is played.

d. On Slide 6, apply the **Diagonal Down Right motion path** to the picture of the ink pen.

Customize the Ribbon

a. Create a custom tab to the right of the HOME tab. Name the tab **Shapes**. Name the group in the tab **Combine Shapes**. Include the following buttons from the *Commands Not in the Ribbon* list in the Combine Shapes group: Combine, Intersect, Subtract, and Union.

Use Combine Shape Commands

a. Switch to Slide Master view. There are three shapes in the top-left corner of the top-level Slide Master. Combine the three shapes. Remove the slide number placeholder from the slide.

Modify a Slide Master, Handout, and Notes Master

a. Apply the **Century Gothic-Palatino font theme** to the Slide Master. Apply the **Red Orange color theme** to the Slide Master. Beginning with the Comparison Layout, delete the remaining slide layouts.

b. Switch to Handout Master view. Change the page setup to **2 Slides** per page. Delete the Header placeholder.

c. Switch to Notes Master view. Type **Page** followed by a space before the number field in the **page number placeholder**. Close the Notes Master view.

Hide Slides and Create a Custom Slide Show

a. Hide Slides 3 and 4 in the presentation.

b. Create a new custom slide show named **Boston Show** using Slides 1, 2, 5, 7, and 6 (in that order). Start the custom show from the beginning.

Work with Comments and Annotations

a. On Slide 2, use the Highlight tool with the default color to highlight the words *Social Media* in the table. Disable the highlight tool and proceed through the presentation to the Registration slide.

b. On the Registration slide, change the ink color to **Blue** and use the Pen tool to draw a line connecting the pen tip next to the slide title to the bottom-right edge of the *n* in *Registration*. Exit the slide show and save the annotations that you've made.

c. Insert the comment **I'm not sure we need Slides 3 and 4** on Slide 3.

Check a Presentation for Issues and Protect a Presentation

a. Run the Compatibility Checker to see which features you used that are not supported by earlier versions of PowerPoint, but do not make any changes as a result.

b. Mark the presentation as final.

c. Save the presentation. Close the presentation and exit PowerPoint. Submit the presentation as directed.

Glossary

.potx The file extension assigned to a PowerPoint template.

.pptx The file extension assigned to a PowerPoint presentation.

Access Relational database management software that enables you to record and link data, query databases, and create forms and reports.

Accessibility Refers to the ease with which a person with physical challenges is able to access and understand a presentation.

Accessibility Checker Aids in identifying and resolving accessibility issues in a presentation.

Action button A ready-made button designed to serve as an icon that can initiate an action when clicked, pointed to, or moused over.

Adjustment handle A yellow diamond that enables you to modify a shape.

Align To arrange in a line to be parallel with other objects or in relation to the slide.

Alternative text (alt text) A text-based description of an image.

Animation An action used to draw interest to an object in a presentation; a movement that controls the entrance, emphasis, exit, and/or path of objects in a slide show.

Annotation A written note or drawing on a slide for additional commentary or explanation that is added while displaying a slide show presentation.

Area chart A chart type that emphasizes magnitude of changes over time by filling in space between lines with color.

Aspect ratio The ratio of an object's width to its height.

Background The portion of a picture that is deleted when removing the background of a picture.

Background Styles gallery Provides both solid color and background styles for application to a theme.

Backstage view A component of Office 2013 that provides a concise collection of commands related to common file activities and provides information on an open file.

Backup A copy of a file or folder on another drive.

Bar chart A type of chart used to show comparisons among items where the information is displayed horizontally.

Basic custom show A single presentation file from which you can create separate presentations.

Bitmap image An image created by bits or pixels placed on a grid to form a picture.

Brightness The lightness or darkness of a picture.

Bubble chart A chart type that shows relationships among three values by using bubbles to show a third dimension.

Callout A shape that includes a text box you can use to add notes.

CAPTCHA A scrambled code used with online forms to prevent mass sign-ups. It helps to ensure that an actual person is requesting the account.

Charms A toolbar for Windows 8.1.1 made up of five icons (Search, Share, Start, Devices, and Settings) that enables you to search for files and applications, share information with others within an application that is running, return to the Start screen, control devices that are connected to your computer, or modify various settings depending on which application is running when accessing the Setting icon.

Chart area The chart and all of its elements, bounded by the placeholder borders.

Clip art An electronic illustration that can be inserted into an Office project.

Clipboard An Office feature that temporarily holds selections that have been cut or copied and allows you to paste the selections.

Cloud storage A technology used to store files and to work with programs that are stored in a central location on the Internet.

Codec (coder/decoder) A digital video compression scheme used to compress a video and decompress for playback.

Collaboration A process by which two or more individuals work together to achieve an outcome or goal.

Collapsed outline Displays only the slide number, icon, and title of each slide in Outline view.

Color theme Consists of the color combinations for the text, lines, background, and graphics in a presentation.

Colors gallery Provides a set of colors for every available theme.

Column chart A type of chart used to show changes over time or comparisons among items where the information is displayed vertically.

Column header The text in the top row of the table that identifies the contents of the column.

Combine A Combine Shapes command that removes the overlapping area of two shapes.

Command A button or area within a group that you click to perform tasks.

Comment A text note attached to the slide.

Compatibility Checker Checks for features in a presentation that are not supported by earlier versions of PowerPoint.

Compression A method applied to data to reduce the amount of space required for file storage.

Connector A Lines shape that is attached to and moves with other shapes.

Contextual tab A Ribbon tab that displays when an object, such as a picture or table, is selected. A contextual tab contains groups and commands specific to the selected object.

Contrast The difference between the darkest and lightest areas of a picture.

Copy To duplicate an item from the original location and place the copy in the Office Clipboard.

Copyright The legal protection afforded to a written or artistic work.

Crop The process of reducing an image size by eliminating unwanted portions of an image or other graphical object.

Custom button An action button that can be set to trigger unique actions in a presentation.

Custom path An animation path that can be created freehand instead of following a preset path.

Custom show A grouped subset of the slides in a presentation.

Customize Ribbon tab A tab in the PowerPoint Options dialog box that enables you to create a personal tab on the Ribbon that includes features that are not available on the standard Ribbon.

Cut To remove an item from the original location and place it in the Office Clipboard.

Data series A chart element that contains the data points representing a set of related numbers.

Default Office settings that remain in effect unless you specify otherwise.

Destination application The application that created the document into which the object is being inserted.

Destination file The file that contains an inserted object, such as a PowerPoint presentation with an Excel worksheet embedded in it.

Dialog box A window that displays when a program requires interaction with you, such as inputting information, before completing a procedure. This window typically provides access to more precise, but less frequently used, commands.

Dialog Box Launcher An icon in a Ribbon group that you can click to open a related dialog box. It is not found in all groups.

Digital signature An invisible, electronic signature stamp that is encrypted and attached to a certificate that can be added to a presentation.

Distribute To divide or evenly spread selected shapes over a given area.

Document Inspector Detects hidden and personal data in the presentation.

Document property An attribute, such as an author's name or keyword, that describes a file.

Doughnut chart A chart type that shows proportions to a whole and can contain more than one data series.

Effects gallery Includes a range of effects for shapes used in the presentation.

Embed To store an object from an external source within a presentation.

Embedded object A part of the destination file that once inserted, no longer maintains a connection to the source file or source application in which the object was created.

Emphasis A PowerPoint animation type that draws attention to an object already on a slide.

Encryption Protects the contents of your presentation by converting it into unreadable scrambled text that needs a password to be opened.

End button An action button that moves to the last slide in the presentation.

Enhanced ScreenTip A feature that provides a brief summary of a command when you point to the command button.

Entrance A PowerPoint animation type that controls how an object moves onto or appears on a slide.

Excel A software application used to organize records, financial transactions, and business information in the form of worksheets.

Exit A PowerPoint animation type that controls how an object leaves or disappears from a slide.

Expanded outline Displays the slide number, icon, title, and content of each slide in Outline view.

eXtensible Markup Language (XML) A set of encoding rules that creates a file format that is designed to provide maximum flexibility when storing and exchanging structured information.

File Electronic data such as documents, databases, slide shows, worksheets, digital photographs, music, videos, and Web pages.

File Explorer A component of the Windows operating system that can be used to create and manage folders.

Fill The interior contents of a shape.

Find An Office feature that locates a word or phrase that you indicate in a document.

Flatten To convert all objects on a slide to a single layer.

Flip To reverse the direction an object faces.

Flow chart An illustration showing the sequence of a project or plan containing steps.

Folder A directory into which you place data files in order to organize them for easier retrieval.

Font A combination of typeface and type style.

Fonts gallery Contains font sets for title text and bulleted text.

Footer Information that generally displays at the bottom of a document page, worksheet, slide or database report.

Foreground The portion of the picture that is kept when removing the background of a picture.

Format Painter A command that copies the formatting of text from one location to another.

Freeform shape A shape that combines both curved and straight-line segments.

Gallery A set of selections that displays when you click a More button, or in some cases when you click a command, in a Ribbon group.

Gradient fill A fill that contains a blend of two or more colors or shades.

Grid A set of intersecting lines used to align objects.

Gridline A line that extends from the horizontal or vertical axes and that can be displayed to make the chart data easier to read and understand.

Group A subset of a tab that organizes similar tasks together; to combine two or more objects.

Guide A straight nonprinting horizontal or vertical line used to align objects.

Handout master Contains the design information for audience handout pages.

Header Information that generally displays at the top of a document page, worksheet, slide, or database report.

Help button An action button that can be set to open a document with instructions or help information.

Hierarchy Indicates levels of importance in a structure.

Home button An action button set to move to the first slide in the presentation by default.

Homegroup A Windows 8.1.1 feature that enables you to share resources on a home network.

HSL A color model in which the numeric system refers to the hue, saturation, and luminosity of a color.

Hyperlink A connection that branches to another location.

Hyperlinked custom show Begins with a main custom show and uses hyperlinks to link between other shows.

Infographic Information graphic that is a visual representation of data or knowledge.

Information rights management (IRM) Allows you or an administrator to specify access permissions to presentations.

Infringement of copyright Occurs when a right of the copyright owner is violated.

Interactivity The ability to branch or interact with a presentation based on decisions made by a viewer or audience.

Intersect A Combine Shapes command that removes any area that is not overlapped.

Kelvin The unit of measurement for absolute temperature.

Key Tip The letter or number for the associated keyboard shortcut that displays over features on the Ribbon or Quick Access Toolbar.

Kiosk An interactive computer terminal available for public use.

Label A chart element that identifies data in the chart.

Landscape An orientation for a displayed page or worksheet that is wider than it is tall.

Layout Determines the position of the objects or content on a slide.

Legend A chart element found in multiseries charts used to help identify the data series, assigns a format or color to each data series and then displays that information with the data series name.

Library A collection of files from different locations that is displayed as a single unit.

Line chart A type of chart used to display a large number of data points over time.

Line weight The width or thickness of a shape's outline.

Linear presentation A presentation where each slide is designed to move one right after another, starting with the first slide and advancing sequentially until the last slide is reached.

Link A connection from the presentation to another location such as a storage device or Web site.

Linked object A part of the destination file that is updated when the source file is updated because the information is stored in the source file but displayed as the object in the destination file.

Live Preview An Office feature that provides a preview of the results of a selection when you point to an option in a list or gallery. Using Live Preview, you can experiment with settings before making a final choice.

Lock Drawing Mode Enables the creation of multiple shapes of the same type.

Margin The area of blank space that displays to the left, right, top, and bottom of a document or worksheet.

Markup Comments and ink annotations appearing in a presentation.

Marquee A pane designed to help select objects from a listing of all objects on a slide.

Master Contains design information to control the layouts, background designs, and color combinations for handouts, notes pages, and slides, giving the presentation a consistent appearance.

Metadata Data that describes other data.

Microsoft Office A productivity software suite including four primary software components, each one specializing in a particular type of output.

Mini toolbar The feature that provides access to common formatting commands, displayed when text is selected.

Motion path A predetermined path an object follows as part of an animation.

Movie button An action button set to play a movie.

Multimedia Multiple forms of media used to entertain or inform an audience.

Multiseries data series A data series representing data for two or more sets of data.

Narration Spoken commentary that is added to a presentation.

Navigation Pane A section of the File Explorer interface that provides ready access to computer resources, folders, files, and networked peripherals.

Non-linear presentation A presentation that progresses according to choices made by the viewer or audience that determine which slide comes next.

Normal view The default view of a document, worksheet, or presentation.

Notes master Contains the design information for notes pages.

Notes Page view A view used for entering and editing large amounts of text to which the speaker can refer when presenting.

Object linking and embedding (OLE) A feature that enables you to insert an object created in one application into a document created in another application.

OneDrive An application used to store, access, and share files and folders.

Opaque A solid fill, one with no transparency.

OpenDocument presentation (*.odp) A presentation that conforms to the OpenDocument standard for exchanging data between applications.

Operating system Software that directs computer activities such as checking all components, managing system resources, and communicating with application software.

Outline A method of organizing text in a hierarchy to depict relationships.

Outline View Shows the presentation in an outline format displayed in levels according to the points and any subpoints on each slide.

Package Presentation for CD Copies a presentation, its fonts and embedded items, and a PowerPoint Viewer to a CD or folder for distribution.

Paste To place a cut or copied item in another location.

PDF file format (PDF) A more secure electronic file format created by Adobe Systems that preserves document formatting and is viewable and printable on any platform.

Photo Album A presentation containing multiple pictures organized into album pages.

Picture A graphic file that is retrieved from storage media or the Internet and placed in an Office project.

Picture fill Inserts an image from a file into a shape.

Pie chart A type of chart used to show proportions of a whole.

Placeholder A container that holds text, images, graphs, videos, or other objects to be used in the presentation.

Plain Text Format (.txt) A file format that retains only text but no formatting when you transfer documents between applications or platforms.

Plot area The region containing the graphical representation of the values in the data series.

Point The smallest unit of measurement in typography.

Portrait An orientation for a displayed page or worksheet that is taller than it is wide.

Poster frame The frame that displays on a slide when a video is not playing.

PowerPoint A software application used to create dynamic presentations to inform groups and persuade audiences.

PowerPoint Options A broad range of settings that enable you to customize the environment to meet your needs.

PowerPoint presentation A presentation that can be edited or displayed on a computer.

PowerPoint show An unchangeable electronic slide show format used for distribution.

Present Online A Microsoft service that enables the transmission of a presentation in real time over the Internet to a remote audience.

Presenter view A specialty view that delivers a presentation on two monitors simultaneously.

Public domain The rights to a literary work or property owned by the public at large.

Quick Access Toolbar A component of Office, located at the top-left corner of the Office window, that provides handy access to commonly executed tasks such as saving a file and undoing recent actions.

Quick Style A combination of formatting options that can be applied to a shape or graphic.

Radar chart A chart type that compares the aggregate values of three or more variables represented on axes starting from the same point.

Reading View A view that displays the slide show full screen, one slide at a time, complete with animations and transitions.

Recolor The process of changing picture colors to a duotone style.

Replace An Office feature that finds text and replaces it with a word or phrase that you indicate.

Reviewer Someone who examines the presentation and provides feedback.

RGB A numeric system for identifying the color resulting from the combination of red, green, and blue light.

Ribbon The long bar of tabs, groups, and commands located just beneath the Title bar.

Rotate To move an object around its axis.

Saturation The intensity of a color.

ScreenTip An object that the viewer can mouse over to obtain additional information about a hyperlink.

Section A division to presentation content that groups slides meaningfully.

Selection net A pane designed to help select objects from a listing of all objects on a slide.

Selection Pane A pane designed to help select objects.

Shape A geometric or non-geometric object, such as a rectangle or an arrow, used to create an illustration or highlight information.

SharePoint library A location on a SharePoint site where you can store and manage files you add to the library.

SharePoint workspace A copy of a SharePoint site that can be used while offline.

Sharpening Enhances the edges of the content in a picture to make the boundaries more prominent.

Shortcut menu Provides choices related to the selection or area at which you right-click.

Single-series data series A data series representing only one set of data.

Slide The most basic element of PowerPoint.

Slide master The top slide in a hierarchy of slides based on the master that contains design information for the slides.

Slide show A series of slides displayed onscreen for an audience.

Slide Show view A view used to deliver the completed presentation full screen to an audience, one slide at a time, as an electronic presentation.

Slide Sorter view A view that displays thumbnails of presentation slides, which allows you to view multiple slides simultaneously.

SmartArt A diagram that presents information visually to effectively communicate a message.

SmartGuide A dotted line that appears automatically to assist with lining up images or text.

Snip The output of using the Snipping Tool.

Snipping Tool A Windows 8.1.1 accessory program that provides users the ability to capture an image of all (or part of) their computer's screen.

Softening Blurs the edges of the content in a picture to make the boundaries less prominent.

Source application The application used to create the original object.

Source file The file that contains the original table or data that is used or copied to create a linked or embedded object, such as a Word document or an Excel worksheet.

Stacking order The order of objects placed on top of one another.

Start screen The display that you see after you turn on your computer and respond to any username and password prompts.

Status bar A horizontal bar found at the bottom of the program window that contains information relative to the open file.

Stock chart A chart type that shows fluctuations or the range of change between the high and low values of a subject over time.

Storyboard A visual plan of a presentation that displays the content of each slide in the slide show.

Stub column The first column of a table that typically contains the information that identifies the data in each row.

Subfolder A folder that is housed within another folder.

Subtract A Combine Shapes command that removes the shape of the second selected object from the area of the first object.

Surface chart A chart type that displays trends using two dimensions on a continuous curve.

Tab A component of the Ribbon that is designed to appear much like a tab on a file folder, with the active tab highlighted, that is used to organize groups by function.

Table An element that organizes information in a series of records (rows) with each record made up of a number of fields (columns).

Table style A combination of formatting choices for table components available to you that are based on a theme.

Template A predesigned file that incorporates formatting elements, such as theme and layouts, and may include content that can be modified.

Text box An object that provides space for text and graphics; it can be formatted with a border, shading, and other characteristics.

Text pane A pane for text entry used for a SmartArt diagram.

Text-based chart A chart that shows a relationship between words, numbers, and/or graphics that primarily arranges and organizes information by text.

Texture fill Inserts a texture such as canvas, denim, marble, or cork into a shape.

Theme A collection of design choices that includes colors, fonts, and special effects used to give a consistent look to a document, workbook, database form or report, or presentation.

Thumbnail A miniature view of a slide that appears in the Slides tab and Slide Sorter view.

Tile A colorful block on the Start screen that when clicked will launch a program, file, folder, or other Windows 8.1.1 app.

Title bar A component of Microsoft Office that identifies the current file name and the application in which you are working and includes control buttons that enable you to minimize, maximize, restore down, or close the application window.

Toggle The action of switching from one setting to another. Several Home tab tasks, such as Bold and Italic, are actually toggle commands.

Tone The temperature of a color.

Transition A specific animation that is applied as a previous slide is replaced by a new slide while displayed in Slide Show view or Reading view.

Transparency The visibility of fill.

Trigger An object that launches an animation that takes place when you click an associated object or a bookmarked location in a media object.

TrueType font A digital font that contain alphabetic characters and information about the characters, such as the shape, spacing, and character mapping of the font.

Ungroup To break a combined grouped object into individual objects.

Uniform resource locator(URL) The address used to locate a resource, or Web page, on the Web.

Union A Combine Shapes command that joins selected overlapping objects so they become one shape.

User interface The screen display through which you communicate with the software.

Variant A variation on a chosen design theme.

Vector graphic An object-oriented graphic that is math-based.

Vector image An image created by a mathematical statement; a form of clip art.

Vertex The point where a curve ends or the point where two line segments meet in a shape.

View The way a file appears onscreen.

Windows 8.1.1 A Microsoft operating system released in 2012 that can operate on touch-screen devices as well as laptops and desktops because it has been designed to accept multiple methods of input.

Windows 8.1.1 app An application specifically designed to run in the Start screen interface of Windows 8.1.1 that is either already installed and ready to use or can be downloaded from the Windows Store.

Windows Live A group of online services provided by Microsoft that are designed to help users communicate and collaborate.

Word A word processing software application used to produce all sorts of documents, including memos, newsletters, forms, tables, and brochures.

WordArt A feature that modifies text to include special effects, such as color, shadow, gradient, and 3-D appearance.

X-axis The horizontal axis and usually contains the category information, such as products, companies, or intervals of time.

XPS file format (XPS) An electronic file format created by Microsoft that preserves document formatting and is viewable and printable on any platform.

XY (scatter) chart A chart type that shows a relationship between two variables using their X and Y coordinates. One variable is plotted on the horizontal X-axis, and the other variable is plotted on the vertical Y-axis. Scatter charts are often used to represent data in educational, scientific, and medical experiments.

Y-axis The vertical axis and usually contains the values or amounts.

Z-axis The axis used to plot the depth of a chart.

Zoom slider A horizontal bar on the far right side of the status bar that enables you to increase or decrease the size of file contents onscreen.

Index

7 × 7 guideline, 98–99
17" × 22" poster, 316
.bmp/.dib (Windows Bitmap), 249
.emf/.wmf (Windows Enhanced
    Metafile), 249
.exportedUI, 426
.gif (Graphics Interchange Format), 249
.jpg/.jpeg (Joint Photographic Experts
    Group), 249
*.odp (OpenDocument presentation), 501
.pict/.pic/.pct (Macintosh PICT), 249
.png (Portable Network Graphics), 249, 501
.potx, 442
.pptx, 422
.rtf (rich text format), 156
.tif/.tiff (Tagged Image File Format), 249
.wmf (Microsoft Windows Metafile), 249

A

access, restrict, 493
Access 2013
    application characteristics, 22
    Help, 28–29
    interface components, 22–29
accessibility, 488–489
Accessibility Checker, 488–489
accounts, Microsoft, 2–3, 493
action buttons, 372, 376–379
Action Settings dialog box, 378, 379
active voice, presentations, 98
Add Chart Element, 349, 350
add commands, to Quick Access
    Toolbar, 24
add comments, 474–475
Add-Ins tab, 87
Address bar, 10, 11
add slide layouts, 438–439
add tabs, to Ribbon, 424–425
adjustment handle, 185
Adobe Flash Media, 271
Advanced Find feature, 53–54
Album Layout section, 291
albums, Photo Album feature, 289–291
Align feature, 226
aligning text, in cells/rows/columns,
    319–320
alignment of objects, 225–227
alternative text (alt text), 489
American Psychological Association (APA)
    style, 318
animating text, 396–397
animation(s). *See also* video
    advanced, 390–398
    audio sequence and, 283–284
    defined, 379
    in presentations, 106–109
    triggers, 379–380

Animation Dialog Box Launcher, 394, 395,
    396, 397
Animation Pane, 397–398
animation tags, 390, 391
annotating slide shows, 118–119
annotations, 474, 475–476
APA (American Psychological Association)
    style, 318
apps (non-Windows 8.1.1 apps). *See also*
    desktop; Office 2013
    closing, 39–40
apps (Windows 8.1.1 apps). *See also*
    Windows 8.1.1
    defined, 3
Apps for Office, 60
arranging objects, 224–227
area charts, 338
arrows
    back, 24
    commands and, 50
    artistic effects, pictures, 256–257
aspect ratio, 218
associations, color, 440–441
attaching actions, to objects, 378
attachments, presentations as, 507
audio, 281–285. *See also* presentations;
    slide(s)
    animate audio sequence, 283–284
    change settings, 283–285
    copyright protection, 262–263
    file formats, 281
    narration, 282–283
    sound over multiple slides, 284–285
AutoCorrect dialog box, 422
AutoFormat As You Type tab, 422
AutoRecover, 422

B

back arrow, 24
Back button, 377
File Explorer, 10, 11
background
    defined, 251
    picture, removing, 251–252
    pictures as, 260–261
background fill style, 327–328
Backstage Print view, 38–39
Backstage view, 420
    defined, 23
    tasks, 36–40
    using, 23–24
backups, defined, 16. *See also* OneDrive
Banded Columns, 326
Banded Rows, 326
banners, 314–317
bar charts, 338
basic custom shows, 453–454

Beginning button, 377
Bevel effect, 328, 329
bitmap images, 248–249
black, color associations, 440
blue, color associations, 440
blue underline, 63
Bold command, 48
bookmarks, video, 275–276
borders
    Draw Borders group, 317, 328, 330
    table, 328
brightness, picture, 253
brown, color associations, 440
bubble charts, 339
bullet text, animating, 396–397
buttons, 372, 376–379

C

callout, 185
captions, Photo Album feature, 290
CDs, Package Presentation for CD, 503–505
cell(s). *See also* columns; rows; tables;
    worksheets
    aligning text, 319–320
    background fill style, 327–328
    defined, 318
    Merge Cells, 318, 330
    pound signs, 341
Cell Bevel, 328
Change File Type option, 500–501
Charms, 2, 3–4
Charms bar, 3–4
chart(s) (statistical charts). *See also*
    text-based charts; worksheet(s)
    change type, 349
    creating, 340–342
    delete sample chart data, 341
    elements, 339–340
    flow, 187
    format chart elements, 350
    graphs versus, 337
    inserting, 340–342
    layout, 349–350
    modification, 349–350
    purpose, 337
    Shape Styles group, 350
    subtypes, 349
    types, 337–339
    worksheets and, 338–339
chart area, 339
Chart in Microsoft PowerPoint, 341
chart styles, 340, 341
chart template, 337
Check Accessibility feature, 488–489
check boxes for selecting items, 15
check hyperlinks, 376
checking presentations, for issues, 487–490

clip art, 327, 329, 391, 393, 394
  described, 26
  Office.com, 282
  recolored, 256
Clipboard, common features, 49–52
Clipboard Dialog Box Launcher, 51–52
Clipboard group commands, 49–52
Close (X) button, 23
closed shapes, 188
closing
  files, 39–40
  non-Windows 8.1.1 apps, 39–40
cloud storage, 2–3. See also OneDrive
clustered column charts, 340–341
codec, 271
collaboration, 474–479. See also
    presentation sharing
collapsed outline, 149–150
color(s)
  fonts, 48
  for objects, 223
  in pictures, 254–256
  recolored clip art, 256
  SmartArt theme colors, 207
color associations, 440–441
color themes, 439–442
color-coded animation effects, 397, 398
Colors dialog box, 191, 441–442
Colors gallery, 164
column(s)
  aligning text, 319–320
  Banded Columns, 326
  delete, 329–330
  Distribute Columns, 317
  First Column, 326
  insert, 329
  Last Column, 326
  multiplication table, 314–315
  rotate text, 319–320
  Rows & Columns group, 329
  stub, 318
  Table Column Height, 319
column charts, 338, 340
column headers, 318, 326
Combine Shapes commands, 426
command(s). See also specific commands
  added to Ribbon, 425–426
  arrows and, 50
  Clipboard group, 49–52
  Editing group, 52–54
  on Quick Access Toolbar, 24
  on Ribbon, 25
  toggle, 48
comments, 474–475, 477
comparing presentations, 478
compatibility, SmartArt, 490
compress pictures, 259
compression, 248
Computer area, 12
connectors, lines and, 186–188
constraining shapes, 186
Content pane, 10, 11
context menu, 49
contextual tabs, 27

contrast, picture, 253–254
control(s), slide shows, 117. See also specific
    controls
conversions, text to SmartArt, 209–210
copy (Ctrl+C), 27, 49, 51
copying
  files and folders, 16
  text, Clipboard group commands,
    50–51
copyright protection, 262–263
correcting pictures, 252–254
Create New Theme Colors dialog box,
    441, 442
cropping pictures, 258–259
Ctrl+C (copy), 27, 49, 51
Ctrl+End, 27
Ctrl+F (find), 53
Ctrl+Home, 27
Ctrl+K, 373
Ctrl+V (paste), 27, 49, 51
Ctrl+X (cut), 27, 49, 51
Ctrl+Z, 27
custom action buttons, 376–377
Customize Quick Access Toolbar, 24
Customize Ribbon tab, 423–426
customize shapes, 190–197
custom path, 392–394
custom slide shows, 453–457
Custom Tab, Colors dialog box, 442
cut (Ctrl+X), 27, 49, 51
Cycle, SmartArt diagram, 204

diagrams, SmartArt, 204–205. See also
    SmartArt
Dialog Box Launcher
  Clipboard, 51–52
  defined, 25
  Font, 48
  Format Shape, 194
  Page Setup, 66
  Shape Styles, 194
  Show, 225, 226
  Size, 218, 258
  Styles, 194
dialog boxes. See also specific dialog boxes
  Colors, 191
  described, 25–26
  Font, 48, 54
  Grid and Guides, 225
  Help button, 29
  Insert Picture, 61, 250
  Open, 36–37
  Page Setup, 66
  Paragraph, 54
digital signature, 493–494
disable Mini toolbar, 47
displaying hidden slides, 455–457
distribute table space, 317
distributing shapes, Align feature, 226
document(s). See also font(s); text
  link to, 375
  margins, 65–66
  orientation, 66
  shortcut text selection, 46
  source file, 330
  Zoom slider, 28
Document button, 377
document properties, 479
double-click, Format Painter, 50
doughnut charts, 338
Draw Borders group, 317, 328, 330
Drawing group, shapes and, 185
drawing tables, 317
Drawing Tools Format tab, 331

E

Edit Hyperlink dialog box, 376
Editing group commands, 52–54
editing text, Home tab, 45–48, 52–54
effects
  artistic, for pictures, 256–257
  shape, 196–197
Effects gallery, 164
e-mail
  address, link to, 375–376
  presentations in, 507–508
e-mail, Outlook Inbox, 3, 4. See also
    Microsoft account
embed video, 271
embedded HTML, 273
embedded object, 330–332
embedding
  fonts, 423
  worksheet, in slide, 330, 337
emphasis animation, 390